The Wiley Blackwell Handbook of Forensic Neuroscience

The Wiley Blackwell Handbook of Forensic Neuroscience

Volume 1

Edited by

Anthony R. Beech
Adam J. Carter
Ruth E. Mann
Pia Rotshtein

WILEY Blackwell

This edition first published 2018
© 2018 John Wiley & Sons Ltd

All rights reserved. No part of this publication may be reproduced, stored in a retrieval system, or transmitted, in any form or by any means, electronic, mechanical, photocopying, recording or otherwise, except as permitted by law. Advice on how to obtain permission to reuse material from this title is available at http://www.wiley.com/go/permissions.

The right of Anthony R. Beech, Adam J. Carter, Ruth E. Mann and Pia Rotshtein to be identified as the authors of the editorial material in this work has been asserted in accordance with law.

Registered Offices
John Wiley & Sons, Inc., 111 River Street, Hoboken, NJ 07030, USA
John Wiley & Sons Ltd, The Atrium, Southern Gate, Chichester, West Sussex, PO19 8SQ, UK

Editorial Office
111 River Street, Hoboken, NJ 07030, USA

For details of our global editorial offices, customer services, and more information about Wiley products visit us at www.wiley.com.

Wiley also publishes its books in a variety of electronic formats and by print-on-demand. Some content that appears in standard print versions of this book may not be available in other formats.

Limit of Liability/Disclaimer of Warranty
While the publisher and authors have used their best efforts in preparing this work, they make no representations or warranties with respect to the accuracy or completeness of the contents of this work and specifically disclaim all warranties, including without limitation any implied warranties of merchantability or fitness for a particular purpose. No warranty may be created or extended by sales representatives, written sales materials or promotional statements for this work. The fact that an organization, website, or product is referred to in this work as a citation and/or potential source of further information does not mean that the publisher and authors endorse the information or services the organization, website, or product may provide or recommendations it may make. This work is sold with the understanding that the publisher is not engaged in rendering professional services. The advice and strategies contained herein may not be suitable for your situation. You should consult with a specialist where appropriate. Further, readers should be aware that websites listed in this work may have changed or disappeared between when this work was written and when it is read. Neither the publisher nor authors shall be liable for any loss of profit or any other commercial damages, including but not limited to special, incidental, consequential, or other damages.

Library of Congress Cataloging-in-Publication Data

Names: Beech, Anthony R., editor. | Carter, Adam J., 1968– editor. | Mann, Ruth E., 1965– editor. | Rotshtein, Pia, editor.
Title: The Wiley Blackwell handbook of forensic neuroscience / edited by Anthony R. Beech, Adam J. Carter, Ruth E. Mann, Pia Rotshtein.
Description: First edition. | Hoboken, NJ : John Wiley & Sons, 2018. | Includes index. |
Identifiers: LCCN 2017034459 (print) | LCCN 2017044364 (ebook) | ISBN 9781118650905 (pdf) | ISBN 9781118650912 (epub) | ISBN 9781118650929 (cloth-set)
Subjects: LCSH: Forensic neuropsychology.
Classification: LCC RA1147.5 (ebook) | LCC RA1147.5 .W55 2018 (print) | DDC 614/.15–dc23
LC record available at https://lccn.loc.gov/2017034459

Cover image: © Sergey7777/Gettyimages
Cover design: Wiley

Set in 10/12pt GalliardStd by Aptara Inc., New Delhi, India

10 9 8 7 6 5 4 3 2 1

For Dawn who has had to put up with me through the long gestation of this volume – AB

For Anne and Leslie and the wonderful Ruby – AC

In memory of Ralph Mann 1927-2014 – RM

For my parents Alice and Gadi – PR

Contents

VOLUME 1

About the Editors   xi

List of Contributors   xiii

Part I   Introduction   1

1   Neuroscience in Forensic Settings: Origins and Recent Developments   3
Anthony R. Beech and Dawn Fisher

2   A Brief Introduction to Neuroscience   25
Pia Rotshtein and Ian J. Mitchell

Part II   General Neuroscience Research   59

3   The Neurobiology of Aggressive Behavior   61
Jens Foell and Christopher J. Patrick

4   The Neurobiology of Sexual Behavior and Sexual Attraction   83
Anders Ågmo

5   Reward Sensitivity and Behavioral Control: Neuroimaging Evidence for Brain Systems Underlying Risk-Taking Behavior   105
Renate L. E. P. Reniers, Ulrik R. Beierholm, and Stephen J. Wood

6   The Neurobiology of Emotion Regulation   125
Catherine L. Sebastian and Saz P. Ahmed

7   The Social Neuroscience of Empathy and its Relationship to Moral Behavior   145
Jean Decety and Jason M. Cowell

8   The Neuroscience of Deception   171
Jennifer M. C. Vendemia and James M. Nye

viii Contents

Part III	Neurobiology of Offending	189
9	The Neurobiological Underpinnings of Psychopathy *Stéphane A. De Brito and Ian J. Mitchell*	191
10	Antisocial Personality Disorder *Sheilagh Hodgins, Dave Checknita, Philip Lindner, Boris Schiffer, and Stéphane A. De Brito*	229
11	Offenders with Autism Spectrum Disorder *Björn Hofvander*	273
12	The Neuroscience of Violent Offending *Heather L. McLernon, Jeremy A. Feiger, Gianni G. Geraci, Gabriel Marmolejo, Alexander J. Roberts, and Robert A. Schug*	301
13	The Neuroscience of Sexual Offending *Andreas Mokros*	333
14	The Neuroscience of Acquisitive/Impulsive Offending *Claire Nee and Stephanos Ioannou*	359
15	Neurobiology of Brain Injury and its Link with Violence and Extreme Single and Multiple Homicides *Clare S. Allely*	385
16	The Neurobiology of Offending Behavior in Adolescence *Graeme Fairchild and Areti Smaragdi*	421
17	Alcohol-Related Aggression and Violence *Stefan Gutwinski, Adrienne J. Heinz, and Andreas Heinz*	455

VOLUME 2

About the Editors	xi
List of Contributors	xiii

Part IV	Neurobiological Bases to Risk Factors for Offending	481
18	Genetic Contributions to the Development of Psychopathic Traits and Antisocial Behavior in Youths *Nathalie M. G. Fontaine, Eamon J. McCrory, and Essi Viding*	483
19	Developmental Risk Factors *Anthony R. Beech, Ben Nordstrom, and Adrian Raine*	507
20	Mental Illness as a Putative Risk Factor for Violence and Aggression *Ahmad Abu-Akel and Sune Bo*	531
21	Modifying Risk Factors: Building Strengths *Corine de Ruiter*	553

Part V Rehabilitation — 575

22 Engaging with Forensic Populations: A Biologically Informed Approach — 577
Fiona Williams and Adam J. Carter

23 Brain Scanning and Therapeutics: How Do You Know Unless You Look? Neuroimaging Guided Treatment in Forensic Settings — 601
Daniel G. Amen and Kristen Willeumier

24 Therapy for Acquired Brain Injury — 631
Nick Alderman, Caroline Knight, Jennifer Brooks

25 The Impact of Physical Exercise on Antisocial Behavior: A Neurocognitive Perspective — 659
Dylan B. Jackson and Kevin M. Beaver

26 Treating Emotion Dysregulation in Antisocial Behavior: A Neuroscientific Perspective — 677
Steven M. Gillespie and Anthony R. Beech

27 The Pharmacological Treatment of Sex Offenders — 703
Don Grubin

28 Understanding and Using Compassion-Focused Therapy in Forensic Settings — 725
Russell Kolts and Paul Gilbert

29 The Neurobiology of Eye Movement Desensitization Reprocessing Therapy — 755
Derek Farrell

30 Adjusting the Lens: A Developmental Perspective for Treating Youth with Sexual Behavior Problems — 783
Kevin Creeden

Part VI Ethical, Legal, and Political Implications — 813

31 The Impact of Neglect, Trauma, and Maltreatment on Neurodevelopment: Implications for Juvenile Justice Practice, Programs, and Policy — 815
Bruce D. Perry, Gene Griffin, George Davis, Jay A. Perry, and Robert D. Perry

32 Forensic Neuropsychology and Violence: Neuroscientific and Legal Implications — 837
John Matthew Fabian

33 Forensic Neuropsychology in the Criminal Court: A Socio-legal Perspective — 889
Leon McRae

34 Forensic Neuropsychology: Social, Cultural, and Political Implications — 917
Jessica Pykett

Part VII Conclusions — 937

35 Explanation in Forensic Neuroscience — 939
Tony Ward and Carolyn E. Wilshire

36 Considerations for the Forensic Practitioner — 947
Adam J. Carter and Ruth E. Mann

Index — 959

About the Editors

Anthony R. Beech is an emeritus professor in criminological psychology at the University of Birmingham, UK and a fellow of the BPS. He has authored over 190 peer-reviewed articles, 50 book chapters and six books in the area of forensic science/criminal justice. In 2009 he received the Significant Achievement Award from the Association for the Treatment of Sexual Abusers in Dallas, and the Senior Award from the Division of Forensic Psychology, British Psychological Society. His particular areas of research interests are: risk assessment; the neurobiological bases of offending; reducing online exploitation of children; and increasing psychotherapeutic effectiveness of the treatment given to offenders. His recent research has examined: Internet offending; new approaches to treatment of offenders; and the neurobiological basis of offending.

Adam J. Carter is a chartered and registered forensic psychologist with over 20 years' experience working in National Offender Management Service (NOMS) and Her Majesty's Prison Service, predominantly in the assessment and treatment of sexual offending. Adam has a number of book chapters and journal articles published on the subject of the assessment and treatment of sexual offending, and is committed to improving practice in these areas. He received his Ph.D. from Leicester University in 2009 and is currently Head of Offence Specialism for Extremism Offending in Interventions Services, Her Majesty's Prison and Probation Service, UK.

Ruth E. Mann is employed by Her Majesty's Prison and Probation Service, England and Wales. As Head of Evidence-Based Practice, she monitors and translates research literature and oversees research projects designed to improve criminal justice processes. Previously Ruth managed the national strategy for the assessment and treatment of sexual offending in the prison and probation services. In 2010, Ruth received the BPS Division of Forensic Psychology Senior Award for her contribution to forensic psychology in the UK. Ruth has authored or co-authored over 70 scholarly publications on topics related to the treatment of sexual offending, program evaluations and large-scale studies of risk factors for crime.

Pia Rotshtein is a lecturer at the School of Psychology, University of Birmingham, UK. She has authored over 70 peer-reviewed publications. Her research interest focuses on understating the neuroscience of complex behaviors and cognition, like those involved in social cognition and emotional processing.

The editors would like to thank Francesca White and Fiona Screen for their hard work on the text, Jane Read for the index, and Baljinder Kaur at Aptara for the typesetting.

List of Contributors

Ahmad Abu-Akel is a research fellow at the Institute of Psychology, University of Lausanne, Switzerland. His research focuses on the neural bases of attentional and socio-cognitive abilities, and the relationship between autism and schizophrenia spectrum disorders using behavioral and neuroimaging paradigms.

Anders Ågmo is professor of psychobiology at the University of Tromsø, Norway. He has spent part of his career in France (Université Paris VI and Université de Tours) and Mexico (Universidad Anáhuac), and been a guest professor at the University of Düsseldorf, the Rockefeller University, the University of Nebraska at Omaha, and the University of Tsukuba, Japan. Professor Ågmo has published extensively on rodent sexual behavior and motivation, and on the potential usefulness of animal models for understanding human behavior.

Saz P. Ahmed recently completed her doctoral studies at the Department of Psychology, Royal Holloway, University of London, UK. Her research interests include cognitive and neural processes underpinning emotion regulation.

Nick Alderman is Director of Clinical Services & Consultant Clinical Neuropsychologist, Brain Injury Services, Partnerships in Care. He is acknowledged as one of the UK's foremost experts in the management of challenging behavior secondary to acquired brain injury and has over 30 years' experience working in and leading neurobehavioral rehabilitation services.

Clare S. Allely is a lecturer in psychology at the University of Salford in Manchester, UK, and is an affiliate member of the Gillberg Neuropsychiatry Centre at Gothenburg University, Sweden. Clare is also an Honorary Research Fellow in the College of Medical, Veterinary and Life Sciences affiliated to the Institute of Health and Wellbeing at the University of Glasgow. Dr. Allely holds a Ph.D. in psychology from the University of Manchester and has previously graduated with an M.A. (hons.) in Psychology from the University of Glasgow, an M.Res. in Psychological Research Methods from the University of Strathclyde, and an M.Sc. degree in Forensic Psychology from Glasgow Caledonian University. Between June 2011 and June 2014, Dr. Allely worked at the University of Glasgow as a postdoctoral researcher. Current research projects and interests include the path to intended violence in mass shooters; autism spectrum disorders in the criminal justice system (police, courts, prisons); the psychology of terrorism and research into brain injury or neurodevelopmental disorders in forensic populations.

Daniel G. Amen is the founder of Amen Clinics in Costa Mesa and San Francisco, CA, Bellevue, WA, Reston, VA, Atlanta, GA, and New York, NY. Amen Clinics have the world's largest database of functional brain scans relating to behavior, totaling more than 125,000 scans on patients from 111 countries. He is the lead researcher on the world's largest brain imaging and rehabilitation study on professional football players. He is the author or co-author of 70 professional articles, seven book chapters, and over 30 books, including the number one *New York Times* bestseller *The Daniel Plan* and *Change Your Brain, Change Your Life, Healing ADD*, and *The Brain Warrior's Way*. Dr. Amen's published scientific articles have appeared in a number of journal including: Molecular Psychiatry, PLOS One, and Nature's Translational Psychiatry, and his research teams' work was honored by *Discover* Magazine as one of the top 100 stories in science for 2015.

Kevin M. Beaver is a professor in the College of Criminology and Criminal Justice at Florida State University and a visiting distinguished professor in the Center of Social and Humanities Research at King Abdulaziz University. His research examines the development of antisocial behaviors from a biosocial perspective.

Anthony R. Beech is an emeritus professor in criminological psychology at the University of Birmingham, UK, and a fellow of the BPS. He has authored over 190 peer-reviewed articles, 50 book chapters, and six books in the area of forensic science/criminal justice. In 2009 he received the Significant Achievement Award from the Association for the Treatment of Sexual Abusers in Dallas, and the Senior Award from the Division of Forensic Psychology, British Psychological Society. His particular areas of research interests are: risk assessment; the neurobiological bases of offending; reducing online exploitation of children; and increasing psychotherapeutic effectiveness of the treatment given to offenders. His recent research has examined: Internet offending; new approaches to treatment of offenders; and the neurobiological basis of offending.

Ulrik R. Beierholm is assistant professor in psychology at the University of Durham, UK. He is a computational neuroscientist developing and testing theoretical models of information processing in the human brain, taking inspiration from economics and machine learning to explain human perception, learning, and decision making.

Sune Bo is a clinical psychologist at the Child and Adolescent Psychiatry and Psychiatric Research Unit, Region Zealand, Denmark. His research focuses on personality disorders, mentalizing, and psychotherapy treatment.

Jennifer Brooks is consultant clinical psychologist for Brain Injury Services, Partnerships in Care and has worked within neurobehavioral rehabilitation for ten years. She has delivered various conference papers on the assessment and treatment of challenging behavior after acquired brain injury and published clinical papers on risk assessment and rehabilitation approaches.

Adam J. Carter is a chartered and registered forensic psychologist with over 20 years' experience working in National Offender Management Service (NOMS) and Her

Majesty's Prison Service, predominantly in the assessment and treatment of sexual offending. Adam has a number of book chapters and journal articles published on the subject of the assessment and treatment of sexual offending, and is committed to improving practice in these areas. He received his Ph.D. from Leicester University in 2009 and is currently Head of Offence Specialism for Extremism Offending in Interventions Services, HMPPS UK.

Dave Checknita is a Ph.D. student in neuroscience at Uppsala University whose research examines how early life adversity associates with genetic and epigenetic factors to influence risk for mental disorders and antisocial behavior in adulthood.

Jason M. Cowell is a developmental psychologist (Ph.D. from the University of Minnesota). He is an associate professor of psychology at the University of Wisconsin at Green Bay, US. Dr. Cowell studies the development of moral cognition and behavior in young children across cultures.

Kevin Creeden, M.A., LMHC, is the Director of Assessment and Research at the Whitney Academy in East Freetown, MA. He has over 35 years of clinical experience treating children, adolescents, and their families, working extensively with sexually and physically aggressive youth. Over the past 25 years, his primary focus has been on issues of trauma and attachment difficulties, especially with regard to the neurological impact of trauma on behavior. He has authored articles and book chapters on the neuro-developmental impact of trauma on sexual behavior problems and sexual offending behavior. Mr. Creeden trains and consults nationally and internationally to youth service, community, mental health, and forensic service programs.

George Davis is a child and adolescent psychiatrist who currently serves as the Director of Psychiatry for the New Mexico Department of Children, Youth and Families. Dr. Davis previously served on faculty at the University of New Mexico School of Medicine as Residency Director, Division Director and Vice Chair of the Division of Child and Adolescent Psychiatry, and continues to teach and supervise there on a limited basis as adjunct faculty. In addition to the university and state service, Dr. Davis previously worked for five years at the Indian Health Service, providing care for several of the pueblos and tribal hospitals and clinics in New Mexico. He became a Fellow of the ChildTrauma Academy in 2011. His primary areas of interest are delinquency as an outcome of early neglect and abuse, extreme behavior disorders in young children, psychopharmacology, and systems of care for severely disabled and underserved populations.

Stéphane A. De Brito is a Birmingham Fellow in the School of Psychology at the University of Birmingham, UK. His research focuses on the social, cognitive, affective, and neurocognitive factors implicated in the development and persistence of antisocial and aggressive behavior. A second strand of his research examines those factors among youths who have experienced early adversity. A common goal across these two strands of research is to understand how environmental and individual factors interact throughout the lifespan to increase risks for poor outcomes or promote resilience.

Jean Decety is Irving B. Harris Distinguished Service Professor of Psychology and Psychiatry at the University of Chicago and the College. He is the director of the Child Neurosuite and the Social Cognitive Neuroscience Laboratory. He is a leading scholar on the social neuroscience of empathy, morality, and prosocial behavior. Dr. Decety is the co-founder of the *Society for Social Neuroscience*. He recently edited the *Oxford Handbook of Social Neuroscience* (2011), *Empathy from Bench to Bedside* (2012), *New Frontiers in Social Neuroscience* (2014), and *The Moral Brain – A Multidisciplinary Perspective* (2015).

Corine de Ruiter, Ph.D., is professor of Forensic Psychology at Maastricht University, the Netherlands. Her research interests include the relationship between mental disorders and violence, and the assessment and management of risk for future violence. She has authored more than 200 peer-reviewed publications and was one of the developers of the Structured Assessment of Protective Factors for violence risk (SAPROF). From 2009 to 2014, she served as Associate Editor of the *International Journal of Forensic Mental Health*. In 2015 she and Dr. Nancy Kaser-Boyd published *Forensic Psychological Assessment in Practice: Case Studies*. Her website is http://www.corinederuiter.eu.

John Matthew Fabian, PSY.D., J.D., ABPP, is a board-certified forensic and clinical psychologist and fellowship-trained clinical neuropsychologist. Dr. Fabian has a national practice specializing in criminal and civil forensic psychological and neuropsychological evaluations including competency to stand trial, insanity, death penalty litigation, sexually violent predator civil commitment, internet pornography/solicitation, and juvenile homicide, sentencing, and waiver cases. Dr. Fabian was formerly director of a state court psychiatric clinic, and he has worked and testified in adult and juvenile court psychiatric clinics, state forensic hospital, federal prison forensic psychiatric settings, and university medical school and VA Polytrauma center. In addition to teaching courses in forensic psychology, neuropsychology and the law, and violence risk assessment, he is published in law review, peer-reviewed, and bar journals. Dr. Fabian lectures at the University of Texas Dell Medical School Department of Psychiatry and the Department of Psychiatry at the University of Texas Health Sciences Center San Antonio.

Graeme Fairchild is senior lecturer in clinical psychology at the University of Southampton, UK. He did his Ph.D. in Neuroscience at the University of Newcastle and then moved to the University of Cambridge to carry out postdoctoral research on stress reactivity in adolescents with severe antisocial behavior. This led to a second project funded by the Wellcome Trust investigating brain structure and function in adolescents with conduct disorder using magnetic resonance imaging techniques. He was appointed as a lecturer in abnormal psychology at the University of Southampton in 2010 and became an associate professor in 2014. His research interests include the neurobiological basis of violence and antisocial behavior, sex differences in antisocial behavior, the impact of early adversity on brain development, and the cognitive neuroscience of emotion recognition and empathy.

Derek Farrell is a principal lecturer in psychology, and EMDR Therapy Europe accredited trainer and consultant, a chartered psychologist with the British Psychological Society, and an accredited psychotherapist with the British Association of Cognitive & Behavioural Psychotherapies (BABCP). He is currently president of the EMDR UK and Ireland Board, president of Trauma Aid Europe, co-vice president of EMDR Europe Board and chair of the EMDR Europe practice committee. He is involved in a number of humanitarian trauma capacity building projects in Pakistan, Turkey, India, Cambodia, Myanmar, Thailand, Indonesia, Lebanon, Poland, Palestine and Iraq. His

Ph.D. in psychology was researching survivor's experiences of sexual abuse perpetrated by clergy and consequently he has written several publications on this subject matter. In 2013, Derek was the recipient of the "David Servan Schreiber Award" for Outstanding Contribution to EMDR Therapy. In addition, Derek was also shortlisted for the prestigious *Times Higher Education Supplement* (TES) Awards (2017) for "International Impact" due to his humanitarian trauma capacity building work in Iraq with the Free Yezidi Foundation and the Jiyan Foundation for Torture and Human Rights.

Jeremy A. Feiger is a master of arts in psychological research candidate in the Department of Psychology at California State University, Long Beach, US. His research interests include investigating the neurocognitive factors – including brain injury – that contribute to aggressive and violent behaviors as well as mental illness.

Dawn Fisher is a chartered forensic and clinical psychologist and is head of psychology at St Andrews Healthcare Birmingham, UK. She has worked with offenders for over 30 years, and has written over 60 publications (book chapters, academic papers, and one book).

Jens Foell is a postdoctoral associate in Dr. Christopher Patrick's Clinical Neuroscience Laboratory at Florida State University. His expertise is in experimental clinical and cognitive neuroscience and his interests focus on brain processes and how they relate to personality traits and perception in differing modalities. He trained at Heidelberg University in Germany with eminent cognitive neuroscientist Dr. Herta Flor, where he collected data for his dissertation study – an award-winning fMRI investigation of the neural basis and amelioration of phantom limb pain in patients undergoing amputations. Topics of his publications include chronic pain treatment, psychopathy, externalizing, body perception, emotion processing, and borderline personality disorder, using a wide range of methods including neuroimaging, electrocortical measurements, virtual reality and augmented reality environments, fear conditioning, and body illusion experiments.

Nathalie M. G. Fontaine is an associate professor in the School of Criminology at the Université de Montréal. Her research focuses on the development and the prevention of antisocial behavior and related disorders using longitudinal and experimental designs.

Gianni G. Geraci graduated from California State University, Long Beach, US, with her master's degree in psychology. Presently, she conducts psychiatric and neurological evaluations of patients with severe mental illness who are participating in clinical trials. Her research interests aim to understand abnormal brain functioning in those with severe mental illness and that impact on subsequent aggression and/or criminal behavior.

Paul Gilbert, Ph.D., O.B.E., is the founder of Compassion-Focused Therapy and is world renowned for his work on depression, shame, and self-criticism. He is head of the mental health research unit at the University of Derby in the United Kingdom. Professor Gilbert is the author of *Mindful Compassion, The Compassionate Mind, Overcoming Depression*, and numerous other books and scholarly articles.

Steven M. Gillespie, Ph.D., is a lecturer in clinical psychology at the Institute of Psychology, Health and Society, University of Liverpool, UK. Before joining Liverpool in 2017 Steven worked as a lecturer in forensic psychology at Newcastle University and as a research fellow at the University of Birmingham. Steven has also worked as a research psychologist for the Lucy Faithfull Foundation, a UK-based charitable organization dedicated to preventing child sexual abuse. Steven uses laboratory-based methods, including eye tracking and tests of emotional face processing, to examine cognitive-affective functioning in psychopathic personality, and in men convicted of sexual and violent offenses. Steven's other research interests include female sexual offenders, Internet sexual offending, and the effectiveness of treatment given to sexual offenders.

Gene Griffin, J.D., Ph.D., is a clinical psychologist and attorney who works in the fields of child trauma, child welfare, children's mental health, and juvenile justice. He presently serves as the Director of Research for the ChildTrauma Academy. He retired in 2013 from Northwestern University's Feinberg School of Medicine in Chicago, where he was co-director of a project funded by the National Child Traumatic Stress Network. He was also the lead developer of the MacArthur Foundation Models for Change Action Network on Mental Health and Juvenile Justice's curriculum and was awarded the Network's 2012 Champion for Change award. Dr. Griffin has served as an expert witness and offered testimony to legislative bodies. As a clinician he was unit chief of adolescent, inpatient psychiatric units. He has also worked as an assistant public defender in Juvenile Court in Chicago.

Don Grubin is professor of forensic psychiatry at Newcastle University and (Hon) consultant forensic psychiatrist in the Northumberland, Tyne & Wear NHS Foundation Trust. He trained in psychiatry at the Institute of Psychiatry, and the Maudsley and Broadmoor Hospitals. He moved to Newcastle in 1994, and took up the Chair of Forensic Psychiatry in 1997. He has been psychiatric adviser to the English National Offender Management Service Sex Offender Treatment Programs and a member of the Ministry of Justice Correctional Services Accreditation Panel. He led the trials of sex offender polygraph testing that resulted in the introduction in England and Wales of mandatory testing for high-risk sex offenders on parole.

Stefan Gutwinski, M.D., Dr. med., is a consultant in the Department of Psychiatry and Psychotherapy, Charité Campus St. Hedwig Hospital, Berlin, Germany. He is head of the research group Psychotropic Substances. His main field of research is treatment and epidemiology of addiction.

Adrienne J. Heinz, Ph.D., is clinical research psychologist, Substance and Anxiety Intervention Laboratory, National Center for Posttraumatic Stress Disorder and Center for Innovation to Implementation, VA Palo Alto Health Care System. Dr. Heinz's research focuses on social and neurocognitive mechanisms that frustrate recovery from substance use disorders and post-traumatic stress and on improving existing evidence-based treatments for these conditions.

Andreas Heinz, M.D., Ph.D., is a full professor of psychiatry, Charité Universitätsmedizin Berlin, Germany. Director of the Department of Psychiatry and Psychotherapy, Charité Campus Mitte and Campus St. Hedwig Hospital, Berlin. His main field of research is transcultural psychiatry, etiology, treatment, and neurobiology of psychosis and addiction.

Sheilagh Hodgins, Ph.D., F.R.S.C., is currently professor at the Département de Psychiatrie, Université de Montréal and the Institut Universitaire de Santé Mentale de Montréal, Canada, and the Department of Clinical Neuroscience at the Karolinska Institutet, Sweden. Professor Hodgins has been studying antisocial behavior for many decades. She has published numerous studies focusing on the development and etiology of persons with antisocial personality disorder, conduct disorder, and psychopathy, and antisocial and violent behavior of individuals who develop severe mental illness. Presently, she is working on prospective, longitudinal studies, in Canada and in Sweden, that aim to unravel the complex interplay between genetic and environmental factors that impact the developing brain to promote antisocial and aggressive behavior.

Björn Hofvander, Ph.D., is a senior lecturer at Lund University, Sweden and clinical psychologist. His research focuses on the developmental aspects and longitudinal outcomes of aggressive and antisocial behavior.

Stephanos Ioannou is an assistant professor of physiology at Alfaisal University, Saudi Arabia. He holds a B.Sc. in psychology, an M.Sc. in functional neuroimaging, and a Ph.D. in neuroscience from the University of Parma, Italy. His interests lie in the domain of brain and behavior, currently he is investigating cognitive development through the peripheral nervous system while most of his recent work has focused on the psychophysiology of emotions.

Dylan B. Jackson is an assistant professor in the Department of Criminal Justice at the University of Texas at San Antonio. His research focuses on the developmental precursors to antisocial and criminal behaviors, including factors related to child neuropsychological functioning and health.

Caroline Knight is Lead Consultant Clinical Neuropsychologist for Brain Injury Services, Partnerships in Care. She has over 20 years' experience working with people with neurological conditions and challenging behavior. Her research has contributed to the development of bespoke assessment tools in challenging behavior and neuropsychological assessment and which are recognized nationally and internationally.

Russell Kolts, Ph.D., is a professor of psychology at Eastern Washington University and is a licensed clinical psychologist. He has authored or co-authored numerous books and scholarly articles, including CFT Made Simple and The Compassionate Mind Guide to Managing Your Anger. An international expert on CFT, Kolts developed the True Strength manualized group treatment of anger based on CFT principles, which has been run in a US prison for the past several years.

Philip Lindner is a clinical psychologist and clinical neuroscientist, currently working as a post-doctoral researcher at the Department of Psychology at Stockholm University. His research focus is using diffusion tensor imaging to investigate how abnormalities of the white matter tracts that connect different regions of the brain are associated with antisocial behavior, common psychiatric comorbidities, psychopathy, and personality traits, particularly in women.

Ruth E. Mann is employed by Her Majesty's Prison and Probation Service, England and Wales. As Head of Evidence-Based Practice, she monitors and translates research literature and oversees research projects designed to improve criminal justice processes.

Previously Ruth managed the national strategy for the assessment and treatment of sexual offending in the prison and probation services. In 2010, Ruth received the BPS Division of Forensic Psychology Senior Award for her contribution to forensic psychology in the UK. Ruth has authored or co-authored over 70 scholarly publications on topics related to the treatment of sexual offending, program evaluations and large-scale studies of risk factors for crime.

Gabriel Marmolejo graduated with his Master of Social Work degree from California State University, Los Angeles. He currently works as an emergency response social worker for Child Protection Services.

Eamon J. McCrory is a clinical psychologist and a professor of developmental neuroscience and psychopathology in the Division of Psychology and Language Sciences at University College London. His research focuses on the impact of early adversity on development and the mechanisms underlying childhood resilience.

Heather L. McLernon graduated with her masters in 2015 from California State University, Long Beach. She currently works as a survey manager for the US Census Bureau. Her interests continue to lie in research and statistics.

Leon McRae was most recently a lecturer in criminal law and mental health law (criminal context) at the Dickson Poon School of Law, King's College London. His research interests are in mental health law, criminal law, criminal justice, and aspects of health care law. He is especially interested in legal and medical responses to psychopathy, and the application of exculpatory defenses in criminal courts. Between 2007 and 2010, he was principal investigator on an Economic and Social Research Council (ESRC)-funded study looking into the therapeutic, legal and relational consequences of treating criminal psychopaths in secure hospital settings under the Mental Health Act 1983.

Ian J. Mitchell is a senior lecturer in psychology at the University of Birmingham, UK. His research focuses on how cortical, limbic and subcortical systems interact to affect social and antisocial behavior.

Andreas Mokros graduated with a Diploma degree (German Master's equivalent) in psychology, an M.Sc. in investigative psychology, and a Ph.D. in psychology, from the universities of Bochum, Germany, Liverpool, UK, and Wuppertal, Germany, respectively. In 2013 he was appointed adjunct professor ("Privatdozent") of psychology at the University of Regensburg, Germany. He is currently Chair of Personality Psychology, Assessment, and Consulting, Department of Psychology, University of Hagen. His main research topics are: experimental assessment of disorders of sexual preference using attentional methods; etiology and assessment of psychopathy; assessment of sexual sadism; forensic risk evaluation; and quantitative methods.

Claire Nee is a reader in forensic psychology and Director of the International Centre for Research in Forensic Psychology, University of Portsmouth, UK. She holds a B.A. and a Ph.D. in applied psychology from University College, Cork, Ireland. Her research interests lie in the development of criminality in children and in the offender's perspective of their cognition, emotion, and behavior leading up to, during, and after the criminal act. She has spent most of her academic career focusing on acquisitive offenders, particularly burglars.

Ben Nordstrom is a diplomate of the American Board of Psychiatry and Neurology and is board certified in both psychiatry and addiction psychiatry. He received his degree from Dartmouth Medical School and his Ph.D. in criminology from the University of Pennsylvania. He completed his training in psychiatry at the Columbia University Medical Center/New York State Psychiatric Institute where he was selected to be Chief Resident. Following his general training, Ben stayed at Columbia and completed a research and clinical fellowship in addiction psychiatry. He is currently an assistant professor of psychiatry at the Geisel School of Medicine at Dartmouth and the Director of Addiction Services and the Director of the Addiction Psychiatry Fellowship at Dartmouth-Hitchcock Medical Center.

James M. Nye is a doctoral candidate working under the mentorship of Jennifer M. C. Vendemia at the University of South Carolina, US. James's research on deception considers theories of cognitive psychology and language comprehension in order to examine the processes of planning and performing deceptive behavior.

Christopher J. Patrick is a professor of clinical psychology at Florida State University, US. His scholarly interests include psychopathy, antisocial behavior, substance abuse, personality, fear and fearlessness, psychophysiology, and affective and cognitive neuroscience. He is author of more than 220 articles and book chapters, and editor of the *Handbook of Psychopathy* (Guilford Press, 2006; 2nd ed. in press). He served in 2010 as a Workgroup Member for the National Institute of Mental Health's Research Diagnostic Criteria (RDoC) initiative, and from 2008 to 2013 as a scientific advisor to the DSM-5 Personality and Personality Disorders (PPD) Work Group. A recipient of Early Career awards from the American Psychological Association (APA; 1993) and the Society for Psychophysiological Research (SPR; 1995) and a Lifetime Career Contribution award from the Society for Scientific Study of Psychopathy (SSSP; 2013), Dr. Patrick is a past president of both SPR and SSSP, and a fellow of APA and the Association for Psychological Science.

Bruce D. Perry is the senior fellow of The ChildTrauma Academy, a not-for-profit organization based in Houston, TX and adjunct professor in the Department of Psychiatry and Behavioral Sciences at the Feinberg School of Medicine at Northwestern University in Chicago. Dr. Perry served as the Trammell Research Professor of Child Psychiatry at Baylor College of Medicine in Houston, Texas. During this time, Dr. Perry also was Chief of Psychiatry for Texas Children's Hospital and Vice-Chairman for Research within the Department of Psychiatry. Dr. Perry has conducted both basic neuroscience and clinical research. This work has examined the cognitive, behavioral, emotional, social, and physiological effects of neglect and trauma in children, adolescents and adults. This work has been instrumental in describing how childhood experiences, including neglect and traumatic stress, change the biology of the brain – and, thereby, the health of the child.

Jay A. Perry, J.D., is an attorney specializing in criminal defense. He is based in Chattanooga, Tennessee. He is a graduate of Sewanee (B.S) and the University of Colorado School of Law. Among his areas of interest and expertise are juvenile justice and child welfare law.

Robert D. Perry, B.S., is a graduate of the University of North Carolina-Chapel Hill (biology and psychology). He served as a Robin Fancourt Research Intern at The

ChildTrauma Academy in Houston, Texas where he is examined the role of relational health in buffering the adverse effects of traumatic experiences.

Jessica Pykett is a senior lecturer in human geography at the University of Birmingham. Her research interests are in social and political geography, including citizenship, governance, education, behavior change, welfare, and wellbeing. Her recent books on the role of the behavioral sciences, psychology and neurosciences in policy and practice include *Emotional States: Sites and Spaces of Affective Governance*, edited with Eleanor Jupp and Fiona Smith (2017, Routledge); *Brain Culture: Shaping Policy through Neuroscience* (2015, Policy Press); and *Changing Behaviors: On the Rise of the Psychological State*, with Rhys Jones and Mark Whitehead (2013, Edward Elgar Publishing).

Adrian Raine is visiting professor in the Department of Psychology at Nanyang Technological University, and the Richard Perry University Professor of Criminology, Psychiatry, and Psychology at the University of Pennsylvania. He gained his undergraduate degree in experimental psychology at the University of Oxford, and his Ph.D. in psychology from the University of York. His interdisciplinary research focuses on the etiology and prevention of antisocial, violent, and psychopathic behavior in children and adults. He has published 375 journal articles and book chapters, 7 books, and given 335 invited presentations in 26 countries. His latest book, *The Anatomy of Violence* (2013, Pantheon and Penguin), reviews the brain basis to violence and draws future implications for the punishment, prediction, and prevention of offending, as well as the neuroethical concerns surrounding this work. He is past-president of the Academy of Experimental Criminology, and received an honorary degree from the University of York (UK) in 2015.

Renate L. E. P. Reniers is a lecturer in Psychiatry at the University of Birmingham, UK. She is a research psychologist investigating the interplay between neurobiological, clinical, and behavioral aspects of adolescent development and youth mental health.

Pia Rotshtein is a lecturer at the School of Psychology, University of Birmingham, UK. She has authored over 70 peer-reviewed publications. Her research interest focuses on understanding the neuroscience of complex behaviors and cognition, such as those involved in social cognition and emotional processing.

Boris Schiffer, Ph.D., is currently professor of forensic psychiatry at LWL-University Hospital Bochum, Department of Psychiatry and Psychotherapy, University Bochum, Germany and Executive Clinical Director of the LWL-Hospital of Forensic Psychiatry, Herne, Germany. Professor Schiffer has been studying antisocial behavior for many years. He has published studies focusing on the neural correlates of pedophilia and child sexual abuse as well as antisocial and violent behavior in people with conduct disorder and antisocial personality disorder, substance use disorders and schizophrenia. Presently, he is working on cross sectional brain imaging studies, that aim to disentangle alterations in social brain functioning as well as the psychobiological stress regulation in men with antisocial personality disorder or substance use disorders.

Robert A. Schug is an associate professor of criminology, criminal justice, and forensic psychology. Dr. Schug's area of specialization is the biology and psychology of the criminal mind. His research interests are predominantly focused upon understanding the relationship between extreme forms of psychopathology and antisocial, criminal, and violent behavior from a bio-psycho-social perspective – with the application of advanced neuroscience techniques from areas such as neuropsychology, psycho-physiology, and brain imaging. He is particularly interested in the etiological mechanisms, risk factors, and developmental progression of antisocial behavior within major mental disorders such as psychopathy and schizophrenia, as well as the ability to predict antisocial behavioral outcomes within mentally ill individuals. It is his hope that a better understanding of the relationship between these disorders and antisociality will have important implications in research, treatment, and forensic arenas; and will help to reduce the negative stigma often associated with mentally ill individuals who are not criminal or violent, while contributing to more effective treatment and management strategies for those who are.

Catherine L. Sebastian is a reader in psychology at Royal Holloway University of London, UK. Her research focuses on the development of emotion processing and regulation in adolescence, using techniques from developmental psychology and cognitive neuroscience. Her particular interest is in mechanisms underpinning aggressive behaviour.

Areti Smaragdi is a Ph.D. student in developmental cognitive neuroscience at the University of Southampton, UK. She did her masters in cognitive neuroscience at the University of York, UK where she became familiar with several different neuroimaging methods. Her research interests include sex differences in antisocial behavior, the neurobiological basis of different types of aggression, and the relationship between antisocial behavior and psychopathy.

Jennifer M. C. Vendemia is an associate professor of psychology at the University of South Carolina and is Director of the Center for Advanced Technologies for Deception Detection, US. Her current research follows multiple threads which interweave deceptive behaviors, executive functions, memory, and emotional processes. Because deception represents a complex social behavior that recruits multiple regions of the brain, Dr. Vendemia's research examines how these distinct components are integrated together in order to bring about deceptive behavior.

Essi Viding is a professor of developmental psychopathology in the Division of Psychology and Language Sciences at University College London. Her research is combining cognitive experimental measures, twin model-fitting, brain imaging, and genotyping to study different developmental pathways to persistent antisocial behavior.

Tony Ward received his Ph.D. and trained as a clinical psychologist at Canterbury University, Christchurch, New Zealand. Tony was the former Director of the Kia Marama Sexual Offenders' Unit at Rolleston Prison in New Zealand and has taught clinical and forensic psychology at Victoria, Deakin, Canterbury, and Melbourne Universities. Tony is currently Professor of Clinical Psychology at Victoria University of Wellington, New Zealand. He is particularly interested in the critique and generation of theory within forensic and correctional psychology as well as the examination of ethical constructs in practice.

Kristen Willeumier, Ph.D., is the Director of Research at the Amen Clinics. She conducted her graduate research in neurophysiology at the University of California, Los Angeles and in Neurogenetics at Cedars-Sinai Medical Center using live cell imaging to investigate mechanisms of synaptic signaling in Parkinson's disease. She received

M.Sc. degrees in physiological science and neurobiology and a Ph.D. degree in neurobiology from the University of California, Los Angeles. She was a postdoctoral fellow in the Department of Neurology at Cedars-Sinai Medical Center where she continued her work in the field of neurodegenerative disease. She was the recipient of an NIH fellowship from the National Institute of Mental Health to study the molecular mechanisms underlying Parkinson's disease and has presented her work at national and international scientific meetings including the Society for Neuroscience, Gordon Conference and the World Brain Mapping Conference. Dr. Willeumier's published scientific articles have appeared in the Journal of Neuroscience, the Journal of Alzheimer's Disease, Brain Imaging and Behavior, Nature's Obesity, and the Archives of Clinical Psychiatry, among many others.

Fiona Williams is a chartered and registered forensic psychologist and is the Head of Interventions Services in HM Prison and Probation Service. She is responsible for the design, development, training, and quality assurance of offending behavior treatment programmes and services delivered across custody and in the community. Fiona has over 25 years' experience in the assessment and development of offending behavior programmes and has particular expertise in working with learning disabled offenders.

Carolyn E. Wilshire received her Ph.D. From the University of Cambridge in the area of neuropsychology. She is currently a senior lecturer in cognitive neuropsychology in the School of Psychology at Victoria University of Wellington, New Zealand. Carolyn's research primarily focuses on examining language in special populations, such as dyslexia and aphasia. She is also interested in the application of this understanding to the diagnosis and treatment of language disorders. Carolyn is currently working on a project examining the nature of explanation in psychopathology and neurology.

Professor Stephen J. Wood is associate director of research, and Head of Clinical Translational Neuroscience at Orygen, the National Centre of Excellence in Youth Mental Health; and at the Centre for Youth Mental Health, University of Melbourne, Australia. He explores the clinical, cognitive, and neurobiological predictors of severe mental illness in young people.

The unnumbered images in this book have been selected by the editors who take full responsibility for their content and also thank their students Safa Kaptan and Yang Pu who helped in selecting and organizing the images.

Part I
Introduction

1

Neuroscience in Forensic Settings: Origins and Recent Developments

Anthony R. Beech and Dawn Fisher

> **Key points**
> - The aim of the chapter is to give both an overview and history of the burgeoning field of neuroscience.
> - In the chapter, it is noted that the interest in understanding why individuals commit crime, from a neurobiological perspective, dates as far back as the early 19th century with Franz Joseph Gall's phrenology and the work of Italian criminologist Cesare Lombroso.
> - The heavy focus on the brain rather fell into abeyance in the early part of the 20th century, with there being more interest in sociological explanations of crime and only a relatively few researchers noticing the importance of the brain in understanding offending.
> - An understanding of the relationship between brain dysfunction and criminal behavior really started to pick-up again in the 1980s. Attention started to turn to why humans need such large brains, and the idea that this is needed for coalition formation and tactical deception, which interestingly are rarely seen in other species (the *social brain* hypothesis).
> - The most important area of the brain associated with social functioning is the *limbic system*. This area is a loosely defined collection of brain structures that play crucial roles in the control of emotions and motivation.
> - It is noted that a number of genetic and environmental problems (e.g., adverse developmental courses, early deprivation, and other suboptimal rearing conditions) can have an effect upon these areas.
> - The ensuing atypical morphological organization could result in social withdrawal, explosive and inappropriate emotionality, pathological shyness, and an inability to form normal emotional attachments (Joseph, 2003). It can also set the scene for later antisocial behaviors.

The Wiley Blackwell Handbook of Forensic Neuroscience, First Edition. Edited by Anthony R. Beech, Adam J. Carter, Ruth E. Mann and Pia Rotshtein.
© 2018 John Wiley & Sons Ltd. Published 2018 by John Wiley & Sons Ltd.

- Structural and functional evidence and neuropsychological and neurophysiological evidence of problems in offenders are then outlined, as well as techniques to examine these problems.
- The chapter also provides an outline of the structure of the book.

Terminology Explained

The **autonomic nervous system** is a control system that acts largely unconsciously and regulates the heart rate, digestion, respiratory rate, pupillary response, urination, and sexual arousal. This system is the primary mechanism in control of the fight-or-flight response.

Conduct disorder (CD) in childhood is a repetitive, and persistent, pattern of behavior in which the basic rights of others or social conventions are flouted. Many individuals with CD show little empathy and concern for others, and may frequently misinterpret the intentions of others as being more hostile and threatening than they actually are.

Cortisol is a steroid hormone, and is produced in humans by the adrenal cortex within the adrenal gland. It is released in response to stress and low blood glucose. High levels are associated with social withdrawal.

Epigenetics refers to heritable changes in gene expression (active to inactive genes or vice versa) that do not involve changes to the underlying DNA sequence (i.e., is a change in phenotype without a change in genotype). Epigenetic change can be influenced by a number of factors including: age, environment, lifestyle, and disease state. New and ongoing research is continuously uncovering the role of epigenetics in a variety of disorders.

The **limbic system** is a collection of structures that includes the hippocampus, amygdala, anterior thalamic nuclei, fornix, columns of fornix, mammillary body, septum pellucidum, habenular commissure, cingulate gyrus, parahippocampal gyrus, limbic cortex, and limbic midbrain areas. It supports a variety of functions including emotion, behavior, and motivation. Emotional life is largely housed in the limbic system, and it has a great deal to do with the formation of memories.

Monoamine oxidases (MAO) are enzymes that are involved in the breakdown of neurotransmitters such as serotonin, norepinephrine, and dopamine. They are capable of influencing the feelings, mood, and behavior of individuals. A deficiency in the MAO-A gene has been shown to be related to higher levels of aggression in males.

Neuroscience is defined as the study of the brain and nervous system. It is a discipline that collaborates with other fields such as chemistry, computer science, engineering, medicine (including neurology), genetics, philosophy, physics, and psychology.

Phrenology was a science of character divination, faculty psychology, theory of brain, and what the 19th-century phrenologists called "the only true science of mind."

The **thalamus** is the brain's "junction box," its main functions include relaying motor and sensory signals to the cerebral cortex. It is located just above the brain stem between the cerebral cortex and the midbrain.

White and grey matter White matter (consisting of myelinated[1] axons and glial cells[2]) actively affects how the brain learns and functions. While grey matter is primarily associated with processing and cognition, white matter modulates the distribution of action potentials, acting as a relay and coordinating communication between different brain regions

XYY syndrome is a genetic condition in which a human male has an extra male (Y) chromosome, giving a total of 47 chromosomes instead of the more usual 46. This produces a 47,XYY karyotype, which occurs every 1 in 1,000 male births. The syndrome has been associated with increased risk of learning disability and criminal behavior in some cases.

Introduction

There is a growing body of evidence that suggests that predisposition to offend can be associated with genetic, hormonal, or neurobiological factors. Nita Farahany, Professor of Law at Duke University, North Caroline, USA, and an advisor on President Obama's bioethics advisory panel, reported at the Society for Neuroscience in San Diego in 2013 on more than 1,500 judicial opinions in which a judge mentioned neurological or behavioral genetic evidence that had been used as part of a defense case in a criminal trial. Specifically, she noted that: "the biggest claim people are making is: 'Please decrease my punishment because I was more impulsive than the next person, I was more likely to be aggressive than the next person, I had less control than the next person'" (reported by Stix, 2013).

Of course, the rise of so-called "neurolaw" cases is becoming more pressing in that forensic practitioners are grappling with understanding the impact neuroscience is having upon the forensic field, both in terms of the court system, in a number of countries, and in producing effective treatments to reduce re-offending. As for the former, courts (particularly in the USA) are facing a huge increase in the numbers of legal councils mounting sophisticated defenses to indicate that individuals are not fully responsible for their crimes, due to their "dysfunctional" brains. As Farahany noted, the use of such brain science evidence is "challenging fundamental concepts of responsibility and punishment." As for the treatment question, Farahany added, "Should we hold people responsible for their actions … or do we need to rethink what we do and instead focus more on rehabilitation?" Stix (2013) observed, "whichever way things go, jurors and judges are going to be hearing a lot more about [the] amygdalae and orbitofrontal cortices." (see Box 1.1 for a description of these areas).

As for the etiology of offending behaviors, we are probably in a better position than ever before to understand how offending may come about, through the interaction between impact of genetic and environmental factors and their effect upon the brain, and how such an understanding can affect what we are able to do in treatment. We are clearly not currently in a position to tell a parole board, for example, to release someone based on a brain scan; but we may be nearer than we think in getting to this position. Hence, the aim of this book is to outline the importance of neuroscience to the understanding of the etiology of criminal behaviors, and to pull together the extant literature regarding forensic neuroscience.

Of course, this is an ongoing process, but what this volume attempts to do is to take stock of where we are in such an understanding of what neuroscience can tell us about offending. It goes without saying that any complete answer will encompass evolutionary, genetic, biochemical, neuropsychological, and cognitive factors as well as social factors (familial and societal), all of which will be described in some detail in this book. The genesis of the book came about through conversation between the editors regarding the understanding of sexual offending from a neuroscientific perspective. This seemed a tall order in. But once we started to mull over the idea we came up with an even bigger plan – that this should also include a wider consideration of the issues that forensic researchers, practitioners, and students in the field are currently grappling with, namely the profound leaps forward in knowledge that have been made in the last ten years in the understanding of the brain. It is self-evident that at the root of (anti)social behaviors are feelings, cognitions, and actions underpinned by the neurobiological actions in the brain. We will now give a brief history of the background and developments in neuroscience preceding the evidence base contained in the chapters of this book.

Forensic Neuroscience: Origins and Developments in 19th-Century Phrenology

Understanding why individuals commit crime from a neurobiological perspective probably dates back to Franz Joseph Gall in the 19th century and the pseudoscience of *phrenology* (although techniques such as *trepanning* – a surgical intervention in which a hole is drilled into the skull, to treat health problems related to intracranial diseases – predate these ideas by several millennia. Since Neolithic times, a person who was behaving in what was considered an abnormal way had holes drilled into them to let out "evil spirits"). Phrenology generally has had a bad press over the last 100 years, but Rafter (2005) noted that "Phenology [at its inception] produced one of the most radical reorientations in ideas about crime and punishment ever proposed in the Western world." (p. 65). She further noted that this approach was instrumental in: (1) developing a rehabilitation model (going against the 19th-century tide of retribution); (2) opposing capital punishment; and (3) proposing sentencing policy that was way ahead of its time. The system originally developed by Gall (1835) was based on the following propositions:

1 The brain is an organ of the mind.
2 The brain is as an aggregation of 52 different organs grouped around the following: ten *propensities* (from adhesiveness to secretiveness); four *lower sentiments* (cautiousness to truthfulness); nine *superior sentiments* (benevolence to wonder); 17 *intellectual faculties* (coloring to weight); and two *reflecting faculties* (causality and comparison).[3]

3 The relative size of the organs can be increased through exercise and discipline.
4 The more active the organ is the larger its size.
5 The relative size of the organ can be estimated by inspecting the contours of the skull.

Phrenology can therefore be seen as producing the first "comprehensive explanation of criminal behavior" (Rafter, 2005, p. 66), in that through this complete description of nearly all cognitions, emotions, behaviors, and phenomenological experience, every form of criminality can be explained. However, like many other 18–19th-century pseudosciences, it soon became little more than mere entertainment with the reading of personality from the bumps on an individual's head. Interestingly, though, some aspects of phrenology have influenced the concepts of deviance in the 20th century (Rafter, 2005), and the notion of brain modules continued to have a long history, for example, through Chomsky's language module (1980) and Fodor's (1983) modularity of mind. More recently, the concept of the brain as a series of subsystems with different structures and function has gained increasing support from structural and functional scanning techniques as outlined in Boxes 1.1 and 1.2, although sceptics of such scanning techniques have disparagingly likened the results of this work to little more than "colored" phrenology.[4]

The Case of Phineas Gage

As for problems in specific areas of the brain causing antisocial behaviors, probably the best-known case study is the 19th-century case of Phineas Gage. Gage was a foreman for the Rutland and Burlington Railroad in the USA who suffered a serious brain injury. Contemporary accounts indicate that he was a highly regarded "model citizen" prior to his accident. He was always on time for work, never swore, and abstained from tobacco and alcohol use (Beech, Nordstrom, & Raine, 2012). However, in September 1848, while supervising the blasting of rock to clear the way for more railway track to be laid, the tamping iron to compact the gunpowder that was used scraped the side of the hole generating a spark, which prematurely ignited the explosive. This caused the tamping iron to shoot out of the hole, enter Gage's head from under his chin, and pass straight through his skull. He was knocked unconscious but, despite serious injury, he surprised everyone by regaining consciousness almost immediately, talking, sitting up, and walking to the horse-drawn cart that took him to seek medical attention. Dr. John Harlow carried out extensive work on Gage including combating an infection that occurred sometime after the accident.

Most of the first-hand information about Gage before and after the accident comes from Harlow, who noted that Gage was a dramatically changed man after the accident – becoming impulsive, irascible, unreliable, and rude. Specifically, he summed up Gage's personality change by saying, "the equilibrium ... between his intellectual faculties and his animal propensities seems to have been destroyed." His friends simply said that Gage "was no longer Gage." As a result of the changes in his personality, the railroad refused to reinstate Gage as a foreman in their company. So he began traveling around New England instead, as an itinerant, displaying himself in travelling circuses. There is a slightly happier end to his story: Gage eventually found gainful employment driving a horse-drawn carriage.

As for the actual damage to Gage's brain, Damasio, Grabowski, Frank, Galaburda, and Damasio (1994) reconstructed his skull from previously taken measurements, and suggested that Gage had suffered damage to his left and right prefrontal cortices, specifically damaging the lower medial parts of the prefrontal cortex, an area known as the ventromedial prefrontal cortex (vmPFC), part of the orbital prefrontal cortex (OPFC) (see Box 1.4 for a description of the functions of this area of the brain). Damasio et al. suggested that such damage to the part of the brain that we now know is responsible for higher order executive functioning, and the modulation of emotional processing, led to the profound changes observed in Gage's personality and behavior. However, this conclusion may be not as clear cut as it seems. Two more recent studies (i.e., Ratiu & Talos, 2004; Van Horn et al., 2012) have questioned Damasio et al.'s conclusions as to the amount, and type, of brain damage that Gage actually suffered. For example, Van Horn et al. (2012) examined millions of possible trajectories for the iron rod, and ruled out all but a few, concluding that the rod could not have crossed over to the right hemisphere. They further speculate that it may be only 4% of Gage's grey matter that was actually destroyed, while more than 11% of his white matter suffered damage, including damage to the tracts that connect into both hemispheres. Van Horn et al. in fact compare this damage to that observed in neurodegenerative diseases such as Alzheimer's, in that Gage could have been displaying some of the symptoms of this disorder, such as an inability to complete tasks, poor judgment, and changes in mood and personality. Despite different interpretations, the tamping iron clearly destroyed a significant amount of brain tissue, and the flying bone "shrapnel," and subsequent infections would have produced further damage to Gage's brain. What this case does indicate is that damage to the brain has a clear effect upon an individual's behavior.

Other Early Genetic and Neurobiology Insights

In the 19th century the Italian criminologist Cesare Lombroso (1835–1909) attempted to explain criminality and took into account genetic and organic factors. He was the first to formally classify criminals in his influential criminological work *L'uomo delinquente* (1876), and also probably the first to think about understanding and treating offenders (see Box 1.1 for his typology of offenders).

Box 1.1   Lombroso's (1876) Typology

Derived from observations of 383 prisoners

Born criminals – degenerate, primitive offenders who were lower evolutionary reversions in terms of their physical appearance.

Criminaloids – those without specific characteristics but whose mental and emotional make-up predisposes them to criminal behavior under certain conditions.

Insane criminals – those suffering from mental/physical illnesses/deficiencies.

Lombroso's research methods were both clinical and descriptive,[5] with precise details of skull dimension and other measurements. His methods can be seen to be broadly influenced by Darwin's evolutionary theory, in that he believed that criminals represent a reversion to a more primitive state of being, and that such individuals will behave contrary to the rules and expectations of modern civilized society. As for the three types of criminal outlined in Box 1.1, he suggested that *born criminals* (or evolutionary "throwbacks") could be identified by the following:

- A sloping forehead
- Ears of unusual size
- Asymmetry of the face and the skull
- Excessive length of arms and other physical abnormalities
- Less sensibility to pain and touch

Less controversially Lombroso noted the following psychological characteristics of criminals:

- A lack of moral sense, including an absence of remorse
- Vanity
- Impulsiveness
- Vindictiveness
- Cruelty
- Excessive use of tattooing
- [But interestingly] acute insight

Lombroso notes that the psychological characteristics outlined above underpin a "moral insensibility." Individuals with these problems, but without the overt anatomical differences outlined above, were termed *criminaloids*. Today such individuals would probably be described as either having antisocial personality disorder (ASPD) (see Chapter 10) or *in extremis* psychopathy (Hare, 1991; 2003) (see Chapter 9). Lombroso also described *insane* criminals, who would nowadays be described as individuals with mental health problems (mental illness as a risk factor is described in Chapter 20).

Contrary to current popular opinion, Lombroso recognized the interaction between predisposing organic and genetic factors, and precipitating factors such as an individual's environment. But although he gave recognition to such psychological and sociological factors in the causes and background to crime, he remained convinced of criminal anthropometry (measurement of the human individual); and this, plus its association with eugenic ideas, meant that (quite rightly) such ideas fell into disrepute.

Lombroso's ideas regarding predisposing organic and genetic factors were most notably taken up by Kraepelin (1856–1926). In many ways his ideas formed the basis for later psychiatric classification[6] and for the proposition that different mental illnesses stem from discrete areas of the brain. Hence, Kraepelin is widely regarded as the founder of modern psychiatry, psychopharmacology, and psychiatric genetics. As for his ideas on criminality, in the various editions of his influential psychiatry textbook *Psychiatry: A Textbook for Students and Physicians* (Kraepelin, 1899) there is a section on **moral insanity** (i.e., a disorder of the emotions or moral sense without apparent delusions or hallucinations). This can probably best be described as a psychiatric redefinition of Lombroso's "born criminal," although Kraepelin noted that it was not yet possible to recognize such individuals by their physical characteristics.

This concept of moral insanity was in fact strongly influenced by the work of Philippe Pinel (1745–1826) (founder of the Pinel Institute) who noted that sufferers were "mentally ill" in just one area, while their intellectual faculties were unimpaired in other areas of functioning. The psychiatrist Julius Koch (1841–1908) sought to make the moral insanity concept more scientifically rigorous and suggested the phrase *psychopathic inferiority* (later *personality*) should be used instead. This referred to continual and rigid patterns of misconduct or dysfunction in the absence of apparent intellectual disability or illness. The diagnosis was meant to imply a congenital disorder, and to be made without moral judgment. Whitlock (1982) noted that the definition was later changed to *moral imbecility*, which is akin to what we now term *psychopathy*.

As for early notions of psychopathy, from 1904 onwards, versions of Kraepelin's textbook included a chapter on *psychopathic personalities*, where four types are outlined: (1) born criminals, (2) pathological liars, (3) querulous persons, and (4) *Triebmenschen* (persons driven by a basic compulsion, including vagabonds, spendthrifts, and dipsomaniacs [alcoholics]). However, an examination of Kraepelin's work would suggest that he had no evidence or explanation suggesting a congenital cause. For example, Kurt Schneider (1887–1967) criticized Kraepelin's categorical system (Schneider, reprinted in 1976) for appearing to be a list of behaviors that were considered undesirable, rather than specific medical conditions. Early versions of the *Diagnostic and Statistical Manual of Mental Disorders* (*DSM*) (e.g., American Psychiatric Association (APA), 1952), can be criticized for the same reason; homosexuality, for example, is described as a "sociopathic personality disturbance," and in fact homosexuality was not actually removed from the *DSM* until the seventh printing in 1974.

It would be remiss of us not to note that Kraepelin was a strong and influential proponent of eugenics and racial hygiene, and the appropriate backlash against these ideas, together with the growing influence of psychodynamic theory (Freud, 1904), with its emphasis on drives, and unconscious psychodynamic processes, broadly meant that any study of the genetic or biological underpinning of criminality was broadly frowned upon (even though Freud was, by background, a neurologist!) for the first half of the 20th century. For example, the first edition of the *DSM* (APA, 1952), was heavily influenced by Freudian ideas about neurosis, psychosis, and "character disturbances," without ascribing any neurobiological underpinnings to these disorders. In fact, the inclusion of a section on genetic, physiological, and prognostic risk factors, as related to ASPD, has only been fully described in the *DSM 5*. These observations may explain a relative dearth of research from anything other than psychodynamic, drive theory, and sociological perspectives in explaining and understanding crime until the second half of the 20th century.

Approaches to Explaining Crime from a Brain-based Perspective

A few psychologists and psychiatrists in the 1950s and 1960s can be seen as having bucked the trend for mainly sociological or criminological explanations of crime. Probably the foremost psychologist, in the UK, was the personality theorist Hans Eysenck who, in his book *Crime and Personality* (1964), noted that some individuals are predisposed to crime through having a particular personality type. Specifically, he argued that criminals would be highly extraverted (E) and highly neurotic (N). Eysenck was keen that any identified personality dimensions were orthogonal (i.e., had no relationship to each other – extraversion as being essentially unrelated to neuroticism). By the removal and addition of a number of items to tap different dimensions of personality, he later added a dimension of psychoticism (P). However, in order to produce such a third orthogonal scale, he ended up with a measure that is really more akin to psychopathy, in that individuals scoring highly on the P scale are described as aggressive, antisocial, cold, and egocentric.

Eysenck hypothesized that extraversion was associated with an under-arousal of the cortex due to low functioning of the ascending reticular activation system (the part of the brainstem that plays a central role in bodily and behavioral alertness). Therefore, extraverts are chronically under-aroused, constantly seek stimulation (to stay awake), and are difficult to condition (i.e., they have an inability to learn the associations between their behaviors and rewards/punishments). In contrast, introverts are over-aroused, hence they have a tendency to avoid arousing situations, and easily learn from experience. Neuroticism in Eysenck's system is associated with the lability of the autonomic nervous system. People with very labile autonomic nervous systems can be seen as being highly anxious. Eysenck did not really report any neurobiological underpinnings of P and the concept of impulsivity (one of the primary drivers of many types of violent and acquisitive offending) remained elusive in Eysenck's system. In early factor analyses impulsivity was seen as part of extraversion, but then it cropped up on the psychoticism dimension. In fact, it was only relatively later that Eysenck and Eysenck (1978) reported impulsivity as a personality construct in its own right, together with venturesomeness and empathy. More will be discussed about the neurobiological basis of these constructs in Part II of the book.

Eysenck suggested that people who are highly extraverted and neurotic do not condition easily, and therefore their behavior is developmentally immature, in that it is selfish and concerned with immediate gratification. As they do not learn easily, they respond to antisocial impulses with high levels of anxiety. The predictions from Eysenck's theory are that offenders will have higher E, N, and P scores. Rushton and Chrisjohn (1981) compared E, N, and P scores with self-reports of delinquency in adolescents, finding some support. However, Farrington, Biron, and LeBlanc (1982) looking at official studies of delinquency, found that such individuals have higher P scores (not unsurprising given that P is in part a measure of aggressive antisociality), and higher N scores, but not E. Importantly, impulsivity, as a crucial personality dimension, was found in this study (as it has in a number of other studies) to be a better predictor of subsequent offending. But like many theories of criminology since Lombroso, Eysenck's theory tells us little about why some people commit the crimes that they do. However, Eysenck's ideas do flag up the notion that underlying tendencies towards crime are identifiable in childhood, and hence that it may be possible to modify socialization experiences so that some individuals do not become criminals in adulthood. These ideas are more fully covered in Part V, where some potential interventions to reduce crime by addressing problematic brain function are outlined.

As for specific genetic explanations of crime, there was a great deal of excitement in the 1960s when a number of researchers (e.g., Jacobs, Brunton, Melville, Brittain, & McClemont, 1965; Price & Whatmore, 1967) reported that a specific genetic marker (an extra Y chromosome in men) was a physical indicator for criminal behavior. The condition occurs in 1 in 1,000 boys, individuals may be taller than average, and the condition can be associated with an increased risk of learning disabilities and delayed development of speech and language skills. A small percentage of males with 47,XYY syndrome are diagnosed with autistic spectrum disorders (see Chapter 11). However, in a recent study, Stochholm et al. (2012) found that the incidence of convictions was increased in those with the syndrome, compared to controls. However, adjusting for socioeconomic variables (education, fatherhood, retirement, and cohabitation) reduced offending levels to similar levels as the controls, although, some specific crime types (sexual abuse, arson, etc.) remained increased. This study's authors suggested that the increased risk of convictions may be somewhat explained by the poor socioeconomic conditions related to the chromosomal aberrations rather than the aberrations themselves.

In the 1980s attention started to turn to why humans need such large brains. The adult brain weighs about 2% of the individual's weight, but consumes about 20% of total energy take (Aiello & Wheeler, 1995). Dunbar (1998) commented that it is difficult to justify why we, and other primates, need larger brains than other species to perform in the same ecological niche. Hence, in the 1980s, a *social brain hypothesis* was put forward that suggests that our large brains, and those of other primates, reflect the computational demands that characterize our environments. Additionally, in some higher primates there is, from time-to-time, tactical deception (Whiten & Byrne, 1988) and coalition formation (Harcourt, 1988), which are rarely observed in other species. These noted manipulations led to the development of the Machiavellian intelligence hypothesis to explain the size of our brains (Byrne & Whiten, 1988). We will now examine some of the areas of the social brain.

The Social Brain

As a brief introduction, the most important area of the brain associated with social functioning is the *limbic system*, involving areas in the midbrain and the cerebral cortex. This area is a loosely defined collection of brain structures that play crucial roles in the control of emotions and motivation. The principal limbic structures involved are the *amygdala* and the *anterior cingulate cortex* along with the *orbital prefrontal cortex* and associated areas of the brain including the *insular*, as shown in Box 1.2.

Box 1.2   Important Areas Underpinning the Social Brain

The **orbitofrontal cortex (OFC)** is situated at the very front of the brain, is considered to be the apex of the neural networks of the social brain, and is critical to the adaptation of behavior in response to predicted changes in reinforcement. It bridges the cognitive analysis of complex social events taking place within the cerebral cortex, and emotional reactions mediated by the amygdala and the autonomic nervous system. The orbitofrontal cortex therefore acts as a "convergence zone" with its connections allowing it to integrate internal and external information. As this is part of the brain associated with reasoning, it would be expected to be under the most intense evolutionary pressure to improve the effectiveness of its functioning. The vmPFC is the medial part of the orbitofrontal cortex and is associated with morality and bodily awareness. It was also implicated as being abnormal in psychopathic individuals (Blair, 2007).

The **amygdala** is a set of almond shaped interconnected nuclei (large clusters of neurons) found deep within the temporal lobes, which are on the left and right sides of the brain. Amygdala functions are related to arousal, the control of autonomic responses associated with fear, emotional responses, and emotional memory, and are therefore centrally involved in attention, learning, and affect. The amygdala can be split into two major subdivisions: the *basolateral complex* and the *centromedial complex*. The **basolateral complex** can be roughly thought of as being the principal input region of the amygdala with afferents (incoming projections) arising principally from the OFC and the hippocampal regions (to do with memory), which exerts potent effects upon sexual behaviors. The basal nuclei, in conjunction with the lateral nuclei, also play a role in reinforcement more generally. The **centromedial complex** is involved in responding to fearful stimuli. The sensory inputs that drive these fear responses arise principally from cortical and thalamic projections to the lateral nuclei of the amygdala. These sensory inputs form synapses, which have a high degree of plasticity. This enables encoding of conditioned emotionally significant stimuli, and enables the amygdala to play a central role in aversive conditioning. The **medial nuclei** of the centromedial complex are also responsible for sexual and reproductive behaviors.

The **anterior cingulate cortex (ACC)**, situated below the cerebral cortices and wrapped around the corpus callosum, first appeared in animals demonstrating maternal behavior. This indicates that the ACC appears to provide the basic circuitry for communication, cooperation, and empathy. The ACC is involved in the simultaneous monitoring of personal, environmental information and allocation of attention to the most pertinent information in the environment and a particular moment in time. The ACC can be subdivided into affective and cognitive parts and therefore integrates emotional and attentional processing.

The **insular cortex** is a portion of the cerebral cortex folded deep within the lateral sulcus (the fissure separating the temporal lobe from the parietal) situated behind the frontal lobe and frontal lobes. It is a long-neglected brain region that has emerged as crucial to understanding what it feels like to be human. It is suggested that it is the source of social emotions like lust, disgust, pride and humiliation, guilt and shame. Together with the premotor cortex, it is part of the circuitry that allows us to vicariously share the actions and emotions of others. Hence, this area of the brain helps give rise to moral intuition, empathy and the capacity to respond emotionally.

The **basal ganglia** are a set of interconnected nuclei in the forebrain that are strongly interconnected with the cerebral cortex as well as several other brain areas. The basal ganglia are associated with a variety of functions including procedural learning, routine behaviors, cognitions, and emotions.

The **habenula** is a pair of small nuclei situated above the thalamus that receives information from the limbic system and basal ganglia. It sends information to areas of the midbrain that are involved in dopamine release. The habenula also has neurons that project to areas like the raphe nuclei, which are involved in serotonin release. Therefore, the habenula is one of the few known structures in the brain that can exert influence on the experience of reward (through dopamine release) and mood (serotonin release).

Mirror neurons can be seen as providing the infrastructure for empathy, in that they are a specific form of nerve cell that fire both when an individual acts and when the individual observes the same action performed by another. Thus, the neuron "mirrors" the behavior of the other. A number of experiments using functional fMRI, EEG, MEG (see Boxes 1.3 and 1.4 for a description of these imaging techniques) have shown that certain brain regions (in particular the anterior insula and ACC) are active when people experience an emotion (disgust, happiness, pain, etc.) *and* when they see another person experiencing an emotion.

Although a great deal is now being written about the neurobiology/neurochemistry of the "social brain," relatively less has been written about these in relationship to offending. But now a number of lines of evidence have pointed to impaired structure and function in areas of the social brain (i.e., the amygdala, the OFC, and the ACC, the insular), and in other associated areas. Problems here, it is argued, lead to increases in violence and instrumental aggression, and, in extremis, ASPD and psychopathic behaviors. These issues are further explored in Part III of this book.

Recent Approaches to Understanding Criminality from a Neurobiological Perspective

It is fair to say that Adrian Raine (1993) really set the scene for current thinking about the origins of crime in his book *The Psychopathology of Crime: Criminal Behavior as Clinical Disorder*. In the preface to this book he referred to "the rapidly growing and influential body of knowledge on the biological bases of criminal behavior," observing that "if we are to fully understand criminal behavior we need to fully are of all influences that bear on it" (p. xvii); that is to say biological as well as psychosocial and environmental factors. In Raine's seminal work he covers evolutionary, genetic, neurochemistry, brain imaging, psychophysiology, as well as what he called *other biological factors*, such as head injury, pregnancy, birth complications, diet, cognitive influences, and familial and non-familial influences.

Although Raine's ideas were deeply unpopular in some quarters at the time, this approach has certainly come of age, given what we now know about brain structure and functioning through some of the techniques outlined in Boxes 1.3 and 1.4. In fact, great strides have been made in the last 20 years in understanding how the brain actually works, and how it is wired up, as well as the functions of different parts of the brain and how they function together, using the developing technologies outlined in Boxes 1.3 and 1.4.

Box 1.3   Techniques Used to Examine the Structural Integrity of Different Areas of the Brain

Computerized axial tomography (CAT) scans are produced using a series of X-rays taken along the axis of the body. The X-rays pass unevenly through tissues of different densities, allowing for distinctions between fluid, bone, and brain tissue to be made. A computer then assembles these "slices" into a sequence of cross-sectional images.

Magnetic resonance imaging (MRI) scans are created by using powerful magnetic fields to orient all of the hydrogen atoms (primarily found in water molecules) in the brain in the same direction. A radio frequency electromagnetic field is introduced, which produces a signal that is detected by the MRI scanner's receiver. These signals are then assembled into high-resolution images that can distinguish the grey from the white matter of the brain. MRI scans do not use radiation and produce more detailed pictures than do CAT scans, but they also take much longer to obtain and are much more expensive. Both types of imaging produce images of brain structures that can then be measured and studied.

Diffusion tensor imaging (DTI) is a relatively new technique, allowing images to be taken of the structural integrity of the white matter tracts connecting various parts of the brain.

Box 1.4   Techniques Used to Examine the Functional Aspects of Different Areas of the Brain

In **electroencephalography (EEG)** the subject has electrodes placed in specific points over the scalp. These electrodes detect the brain's electrical impulses, which are then recorded and analyzed by a computer. The frequency and amplitude of the resultant signals can then be interpreted. Increasing frequency is associated with increasing arousal, and lower frequency is associated with lower arousal in particular areas of the brain.

Photon emission tomography (PET) is a technique that relies on injecting subjects with a radioactively labelled substance, such as glucose. Images of their brains can then be obtained, showing areas of higher radioactive signal due to glucose metabolism, which indicates level of neural activity.

The **single photon emission tomography (SPECT)** form of imaging also involves the injection of a radioactive tracer. The camera detects the amount of radiation coming from different parts of the brain. These differences are due to variations in *regional cerebral blood flow* (rCBF) and reflect different levels of activity in various parts of the brain.

Functional magnetic resonance imaging (fMRI) is an imaging technique that measures changes in blood oxygen in regions of interest in the brain before and after cognitive tasks are undertaken. These *blood oxygen level dependent*

> (BOLD) signals are used as a proxy for how active a region of the brain is. By comparing groups of interest with matched controls, the patterns of activation, or inactivation, in their brains can be studied to learn how the functioning of various brain regions relates to the condition in question.
>
> **Magnetoencephalography (MEG)** is a functional neuroimaging technique for mapping brain activity by recording magnetic fields produced by electrical currents occurring naturally in the brain, using very sensitive magnetometers. Arrays of superconducting quantum interference devices (cooled by liquid helium) are currently the most common magnetometer. This technique is used in clinical settings to find locations of abnormalities, as well as in experimental settings, to measure brain function.

Techniques like these allow us to examine the brains of criminals in order to give a better idea of the problems that many such individuals face. This is not to say we are at any level advocating genetic determinism to criminality, but, as outlined in Chapter 19, in many cases offenders have had to cope with a number of adverse risk factors (i.e., prenatal, perinatal, diet, traumatic head injury) and, as noted in that chapter, these can have a very big effect upon brain structure and function. Other studies (e.g., as outlined in Chapter 18 by Nathalie Fontaine and colleagues) suggest that recent twin and molecular genetic studies have the potential to inform a model of developmental vulnerability to offending more generally, and psychopathy in particular. Hence, in Part V of this book on rehabilitation, there are chapters describing interventions that we would suggest can ameliorate, to some extent, problems that either have a genetic basis or have arisen through adverse upbringings. We will now provide brief digression about the social brain, but of course the book itself will provide a lot more detail of these and other brain areas implicated in offending.

We will now very briefly outline some evidence of structural and functional problems that have been previously observed in offenders (until recently this has been mainly regarding psychopaths, ASPD, and CD individuals). These ideas will be broadened and deepened in subsequent chapters of this book.

Structural and Functional Evidence of Problems in Offenders

Raine, Lencz, Bihrle, LaCasse, and Colletti (2000) examined individuals with ASPD and compared them to a matched group of substance users, and non-offending controls. They found an 11% reduction in the grey matter of the OPFC of the ASPD group compared to the other two matched groups. Other researchers have found that, compared to non-offender controls, ASPD individuals had smaller temporal lobes (Dolan, Deakin, Roberts, & Anderson, 2002; Laakso et al., 2002), as well as reductions in their dorsolateral, medial frontal cortices, and the OPFC (Laakso et al., 2002). Laakso et al. (2000) found violent offenders with alcoholism and ASPD had smaller posterior hippocampi (an area that is associated with fear conditioning). Huebner et al. (2008) found smaller grey matter volumes in the OPFC and the temporal lobes of children with CD compared to normal controls. Sterzer, Stadler, Krebs, Kleinschmidt, and

Poustka (2005) found reduced grey matter volumes in the amygdala and the insular of adolescents with CD compared to normal controls. Kruesi, Casanova, Mannheim, and Johnson-Bilder (2004) reported that diminished right temporal lobe volume (which includes the amygdala) was associated with CD.

As for functional evidence of problems in offenders, Birbaumer et al. (2005) found that psychopaths show no significant activity in the limbic-prefrontal circuit (amygdala, OPFC, insula, and the ACC), using fMRI, during a task involving verbal and autonomic conditioning. This lack of recognition of fear in psychopaths, due to a measurable lack of amygdala and insular function, suggests that it is easier to offend, as a key component of committing interpersonal violence towards others is the requirement to not recognize, understand or empathize with the mental state of victims.

Raine et al. (1993) in a PET study, found that a sample of murderers demonstrated reduced glucose metabolism in the OPFC, the anterior medial and superior frontal cortices compared to a normal comparison group, after a continuous performance task. A follow-up study with a larger sample using a similar methodology found the same pattern of reduced glucose metabolism in the anterior frontal cortices, and in the amygdala and hippocampus as well (Raine, Buchsbaum, & LaCasse, 1997), suggesting reduced functions in these areas.

Sterzer et al. (2005) examined patterns of brain activation, using employed fMRI, in CD adolescent males compared to controls, as they looked at neutral pictures and pictures with a strong negative affective valence. It was found that when the CD youths viewed the distressing pictures they had significantly reduced activity to their left amygdalae compared to the controls. Marsh et al. (2008) using a similar methodology studied children and adolescents with callous-unemotional traits (CU) and controls. Those with CU traits demonstrated significantly reduced amygdala activation on viewing the fearful (but not the angry or neutral) faces. Further, on a functional connectivity analysis, the CU children showed reduced connectivity between the ventromedial prefrontal cortex and the amygdala. The degree of reduction in this connectivity was negatively correlated with the score on a scale that measured the degree of CU traits. Similar findings have been described in adult populations (Muller et al., 2003; Kiehl et al., 2004).

Neuropsychological and Neurophysiological Evidence of Problems in Offenders

Neuropsychological tests have provided another method for testing the functional level of various brain areas. One of the most consistent findings in the neuropsychological aspects of criminality is that antisocial populations have lower verbal IQs compared to non-antisocial groups even in adolescence (Brennan, Hall, Bor, Najman, & Williams, 2003; Déry, Toupin, Pauzé, Mercier, & Fortin, 1999). Additionally, researchers have found that verbal deficits on testing at age 13 predict delinquency at age 18 (Moffitt, Lynam, & Silva, 1994). However, it should be noted that such neuropsychological deficits show interactive effects with social risk factors (Aguilar, Sroufe, Egeland, & Carlson, 2000; Brennan et al., 2003). Other neuropsychological tests have focused on how antisocial populations respond to *affectively charged* stimuli. For example, Loney, Frick, Clements, Ellis, and Kerlin (2003) found that juveniles with CU traits showed slower reaction times after being presented with emotionally negative words, while those with impulsive traits showed faster reaction times to such stimuli.

A number of studies have also found biological correlates to be predictive of criminal behavior. Probably the longest term, and most important of these, is the Cambridge Study in Delinquent Development, headed by David Farrington, which is a prospective longitudinal survey of the development of offending and antisocial behavior in 411 males, all living in a deprived inner-city area of South London, first studied at age 8 in 1961. The findings of this study describe these individuals' criminal careers up to age 50, looking at both officially recorded convictions and self-reported offending. The most important risk factors were family criminality, risk taking (the neurobiology of which is described in Chapter 5), low school attainment, poverty, and adverse parenting. A series of analyses were also carried out to identify the most predictive risk factors for violence (Farrington, 1997). Only two risk factors were identified here – low resting heart rate and poor concentration – which were found, independently of all other potential risk factors, to predict violence.

Low resting heart rate is, in fact, the best-replicated biological correlate of antisocial behavior in juvenile samples, in that in longitudinal studies, low resting heart rate has been shown to accurately identify individuals who are at risk of later developing antisocial behavior (Ortiz & Raine, 2004). This finding has been replicated in many countries (Farrington, 1997; Mezzacappa et al., 1997; Moffitt & Caspi, 2001; Raine, Venables, & Mednick, 1997). However, it should also be noted that having a *high* resting heart rate is negatively correlated with later violent behavior (Raine, Venables, & Williams, 1995).

Raine (2013) notes that there are several different possible explanations for these findings. One is that a low resting heart rate is associated with a lack of fear, in that people whose heart rates are relatively low are relatively more fearless than the rest of the population. Raine notes that bomb disposal experts, for example, have low heart rates. Another explanation for these results is "sensation-seeking." Low heart rate has been linked with low physiological arousal (Ortiz & Raine, 2004), and hence some individuals may seek out stimulation to increase arousal. However, again, although low resting heart may be a bio-marker there is still an interaction between biology and the environment. Another area of interest to researchers attempting to understand from a biological level why some people commit antisocial acts is brain chemistry. Here work has looked at, for example, the relationship of testosterone and with aggressive behavior (e.g., Archer, 1991). Herbert (2015) noted that without testosterone none us would exist, as its main purpose is to drive reproductive function in men.[7] Testosterone is also central to sexual behavior in humans (Bancroft, 2009), in that sexual activity increases the level of testosterone, as does talking to an attractive other. However, there is an interaction between an array of neural and hormonal systems (including the neurotransmitters serotonin and dopamine) as well as sexual activity.

Clear evidence suggests that testosterone is one of the primary hormones underpinning aggression in non-human animals, such as rats, monkeys, hamsters, dogs, and deer (Rada, Kellner, & Winslow, 1976). Vom Saal (1983) proposed a model of testosterone and its relationship to aggression. According to this model, androgen prenatally influences the neural networks that mediate aggressive behavior. When these networks are again exposed to androgens (due to this hormone's release from the testes, where about 95% is located, with the other 5% in the adrenal glands) in males at puberty and beyond, the neural networks are again activated and aggression is released in relevant environmental stimuli, such as protection of territory, fighting over females, or position in a dominance hierarchy. Testosterone release in humans starts two weeks after birth and lasts until six months, where the child's testes are producing as much testosterone as an adult male, then recedes, and returns at high levels in puberty and adulthood.

However, adult human male testosterone levels vary in different circumstances, and are associated moderately with levels of aggression and violence. In a meta-analysis of 106 articles in the field reporting the relationship, Book, Starzyk, and Quinsey (2001) only found a weak correlation (r = .14) between levels of testosterone and aggression. As the square of the correlation gives the amount of variance accounted for from one variable to another in a correlation, then it can be that testosterone only accounts for around 2% of the variance in aggression across a number of studies.

It might be expected that those involved in warfare would have increased levels of testosterone, but in fact they often have levels similar to men who have been castrated. Here it is the stress hormone cortisol that significantly reduces the level of testosterone. For example, a study from the 1990s (Dabbs, Jurkovic, & Frady, 1991) examined testosterone and cortisol levels in male adolescent offenders. While they found that offenders with high levels of testosterone committed more crimes, there was a significant interaction between testosterone and cortisol, with the latter moderating the effect of testosterone.

Seo, Patrick and Kennealy (2008) have suggested that other neurochemical imbalances, specifically reduced levels of serotonin and higher levels of dopamine in the prefrontal cortex (the apex of the social brain, see Box 1.2), are also implicated in impulsive aggression. Serotonin hypofunction may represent a biochemical trait that predisposes individuals to impulsive aggression, while dopamine hyperfunction contributes in an additive fashion to the serotonergic problems.

Another example, of gene/environment interaction, is work that has found a connection between a version of the MAO-A gene (3R) (commonly known as the "warrior gene") and several types of antisocial behavior. Although overall MAO-A has been found to have no overall effect on antisocial behavior, low MAO-A activity in combination with abuse experienced during childhood results in an increased risk of aggressive behavior as an adult (Frazzetto et al., 2007). But high testosterone, maternal tobacco smoking during pregnancy, poor material living standards, dropping out of school, and low IQ can also trigger violent behavior in men with the low-activity alleles (which are overwhelmingly the 3R allele) (see, e.g., Fergusson, Boden, Horwood, Miller, & Kennedy, 2012). Another large study of gene–environment interaction identified people who carried a genotype that conferred a low expression MAO-A (Caspi et al., 2002). The researchers looked at the people with high versus low MAO-A activity, and also whether or not the individual had been abused as a child. They found evidence of a strong interaction between low MAO-A activity and childhood maltreatment in the likelihood of developing CD.

However, the evidence suggests that the impact of genetic or biological factors diminishes as young people are exposed to environmental factors that shape behavior. For example, genetic research focusing on studies of identical twins (some reared together, others reared apart) has found that heritability accounts for about 41% of childhood conduct disorder, but by adulthood accounts for only 28% of adult APD. The effect of biological factors is therefore highly likely to be mediated by other situational or environmental conditions. Therefore, increasingly influential in the coming years will be the science of epigenetics. The ability of the environment to switch genes on and off may be an important factor underpinning a number of risk factors for offending, which will be explored in Chapter 16 of this volume.

Conclusions and Structure of the Book

Genetic contributions, adverse developmental courses, early deprivation and other suboptimal rearing conditions, and substance abuse are often associated with severe problems in social and emotional functioning that potentially endure throughout life. It would be predicted that these early experiences would be reflected in long-term changes in the underlying neurobiology and the neurochemistry of the attachment/social brain systems as outlined in Box 1.3. The ensuing atypical morphological organization could result in social withdrawal, pathological shyness, explosive and inappropriate emotionality, and an inability to form normal emotional attachments (Joseph, 2003) and this sets the scene for later criminality. This broad thesis will be developed in subsequent chapters of the book, as outlined below.

The first volume contains three parts. In Part I we have begun by providing a background to the area in the current chapter. Chapter 2 provides an introduction to the principles of neuroscience. The aim of Part II of the book is to provide a more complete understanding of the principles of general neuroscience: aggression, sex, risk taking and decision making, emotional regulation, empathy and morality, and deception. Hence, Part II provides the necessary platform to understand the following sections of the book. Part III then explores what we know about the neuroscience of psychopathy, APD, and other personality disorders, offenders with autism, violent offending, sexual offending, homicide, adolescence, and alcohol.

The second volume contains four parts. Part IV contains what is currently known about the neurobiology of risk factors for offending, such as genetics, prenatal, developmental trauma, substance abuse problems, and mental illness, and how to modify such risk factors. Part V discusses current thinking about how the risk factors outlined in Part IV can be tackled in treatment. This part provides a broad sweep of approaches to treatments, with the first chapter (Chapter 22) describing engaging with offenders based on what we now know about biology and neurobiology. The rest of Part V considers a number of different treatment approaches as follows: the use of brain scanning to inform treatment; therapy for acquired brain injury developmental treatment models for adolescents; applications of mindfulness and controlled breathing techniques to improve self-regulation; compassion focused therapy; eye movement desensitization reprocessing therapy (EMDR); the impact of physical exercise; and drug treatments (specifically for sexual offenders). Part VI considers implications of neglect and trauma in understanding offending, as well as the ethical, legal, clinical, social, cultural, and political implications of forensic neuroscience and implications for forensic mental health programs and policy. Part VII provides some conclusions in terms of explanations in forensic neuroscience and considerations for the practitioner.

Notes

1 The fatty white substance that surrounds the axon of some nerve cells.
2 Glial cells surround neurons and provide support for and insulation between them. Glial cells are the most abundant cell types in the central nervous system.

3 See http://en.wikipedia.org/wiki/Phrenology for a complete list of phrenology modules from Coombe (1951).
4 For a discussion on this, see http://www.scientificamerican.com/article/a-new-phrenology/.
5 However, it is worth noting that he did not engage in such statistical comparisons with non-criminals.
6 Echoes can still be seen in the fifth edition of the *Diagnostic and Statistical Manual of Mental Disorders (DSM-5)* (American Psychiatric Association, 2013) and the World Health Organization's *International Classification of Diseases* psychiatric classifications systems (see http://www.who.int/classifications/icd/en/).
7 Although it should be noted that prior to the menopause women have five times more testosterone than oestrogen (Herbert, 2015).

Recommended reading

Berrios, G. E. (1996). *History of mental symptoms*. Cambridge: Cambridge University Press. *A fine review of the history of psychiatry.*

Hodgins, S., Viding, E., & Plodowski, A. (2009). *The neurobiological basis of violence: Science and rehabilitation*. Oxford: Oxford University Press. *Good overview of the neurobiology of violence, by leading researchers in the area.*

Keysers, C. (2011). *The empathic brain*. Amsterdam-Zuidoost, Netherlands: Social Brain Press. *A very readable account of how the discovery of mirror neurons has changed our understanding of empathy*

Longo, R. E., Prescott, D. S., Bergman, J., & Creeden, K. (2013) (Eds.) *Current perspectives and applications in neurobiology: Working with young persons who are victims and perpetrators of sexual abuse*. Holyoake, MA: Neeri Press. *A good overview of the applications of neuroscientific approaches to working with young people.*

Mitchell, I. (2014). *Broken brains*. Basingstoke, Hampshire: Palgrave Macmillan. *This is a good introduction to the brain, and what happens when things go wrong.*

Raine, A. (2013). *The anatomy of violence: The biological roots of crime*. London: Penguin. *An excellent overview of the link between biology and behavior by one of the foremost experts in the field.*

Spurzheim, J. G. (1815). The Physiognomical system of Drs. Gall and Spurzheim; founded on an anatomical and physiological examination of the nervous system in general, and of the brain in particular; and indicating the dispositions and manifestations of the mind. London: Baldwin, Cradock, and Joy. Retrieved from http://archive.org/stream/physiognomicalsy00spur/physiognomicalsy00spur_djvu.txt.

References

Aguilar, B., Sroufe, A., Egeland, B., & Carlson, E. (2000). Distinguishing the early-onset/persistent and adolescent-onset antisocial behavior types: From birth to six years. *Development and Psychopathology, 12*, 109–132.

Aiello, L. C., & Wheeler, P. (1995) The expensive tissue hypothesis. *Current Anthropology, 36*, 184–193.

American Psychiatric Association (1952). *Diagnostic and statistical manual of mental disorders*. Washington DC: American Psychiatric Association.

American Psychiatric Association (2013). *Diagnostic and statistical manual of mental disorders, fifth (DSM-5)*. Washington DC: American Psychiatric Association.

Archer, J. (1991). The influence of testosterone on human aggression. *British Journal of Psychology, 82*, 1–28.

Bancroft, J. (2009). *Human sexuality and its problems* (3rd ed.). Edinburgh: Churchill Livingtone/Elsevier.

Beech, A. R., Nordstrom, B., & Raine, A. (2012). Contributions of forensic neuroscience. In G. Davies & A. R. Beech (Eds.), *Forensic psychology* (2nd ed.). (BPS Textbooks in Psychology) (pp. 55–76). Chichester: John Wiley & Sons.

Birbaumer, N., Viet, R., Lotze M., Erb, M., Hermann, C., & Grodd, W. (2005). Deficient fear conditioning in psychopathy – A functional magnetic resonance imaging study. *Archives of General Psychiatry, 62,* 799–805.

Blair, R. J. R. (2007). The amygdala and ventromedial prefrontal cortex in morality and psychopathy. *Trends in Cognitive Sciences, 11,* 387–392, http://doi.org/10.1016/j.tics.2007.07.003.

Book, A. S., Starzyk, K. B., & Quinsey, V. L. (2001). The relationship between testosterone and aggression: A meta-analysis. *Aggression and Violent Behavior, 6,* 579–599.

Brennan, P. A., Hall, J., Bor, W., Najman, J. M., & Williams, G. (2003). Integrating biological and social processes in relation to early-onset persistent aggression in boys and girls. *Development and Psychopathology, 39,* 309–323.

Byrne, R., & Whiten, A. (Eds.). (1988). *Machiavellian intelligence.* Oxford: Oxford University Press.

Caspi, A., McClay, J., Moffitt, T. E., Mill, J., Martin, J., Craig, I. W., & Poulton, R. (2002). Role of genotype in the cycle of violence in maltreated children. *Science, 297,* 851–854.

Chomsky, N. (1980). *Rules and representations.* New York: Columbia University Press.

Dabbs, J. M., Jurkovic, G. J., & Frady, R. L. (1991). Salivary testosterone and cortisol among late adolescent offenders. *Journal of Abnormal Psychology, 19,* 469–478.

Damasio, H., Grabowski, T., Frank, R., Galaburda, A. M., & Damasio, A. R. (1994). The return of Phineas Gage: Clues about the brain from the skull of a famous patient. *Science, 264,* 1102–1105.

Dolan, M., Deakin, J. F. W., Roberts, N., & Anderson, I. M. (2002). Quantitative frontal and temporal structural MRI studies in personality-disordered offenders and control subjects. *Psychiatry Research Neuroimaging, 116,* 133–149.

Dunbar, R. I. M. (1998). The social brain hypothesis. *Evolutionary Anthropology, 6,* 178–190.

Eysenck, H. J. (1964). *Crime and personality.* London: Routledge & Kegan Paul.

Eysenck, S. B. G., & Eysenck, H. J. (1978). Impulsiveness and venturesomeness: Their position in a dimensional system of personality description. *Psychological Reports, 43,* 1247–1255.

Farrington, D. P. (1997). The relationship between low resting heart rate and violence. In A. Raine, P. Brennan, D. Farrington, & S. A. Mednick (Eds.), *Biosocial basis of violence* (pp. 89–106). New York: Plenum Press.

Farrington, D. P., Biron, L., & LeBlanc, M. (1982). Personality and delinquency in London and Montreal. In J. Gunn & D. P. Farrington (Eds.), *Abnormal offenders, delinquency, and the criminal justice system* (pp. 153–203). Chichester: John Wiley & Sons.

Fergusson, D. M., Boden, J. M., Horwood, L. J., Miller, A., & Kennedy, M. A. (2012). Moderating role of the MAOA genotype in antisocial behaviour. *British Journal of Psychiatry, 200,* 116–123.

Fodor, Jerry A. (1983). *Modularity of mind: An essay on faculty psychology.* Cambridge, MA: MIT Press.

Frazzetto, G., Di Lorenzo, G., Carola, V., Proietti, L., Sokolowska, E., Siracusano, A., & Troisi, A. (2007). Early trauma and increased risk for physical aggression during adulthood: The moderating role of MAOA genotype. *PloS One 2*(5), e486. doi:10.1371/journal.pone.0000486.

Freud, S. (1904). *The psychopathology of everyday life.* Seattle, WA: Pacific Publishing Studio.

Gall, F. G. (1835). *On the functions of the brain and each of its parts (6 volumes).* Boston, MA: Boston, Marsh, Capen and Lynn.

Harcourt, A. H. (1988). Alliances in contests and social intelligence. In R. Byrne & A. Whiten (Eds.), *Machiavellian Intelligence* (pp. 142–152). Oxford: Oxford University Press.

Hare, R. D. (1991). *The hare psychopathy checklist – Revised*. Toronto: Multi-Health Systems.
Hare, R. D. (2003). *The hare psychopathy checklist – Revised* (2nd ed.). Toronto: Multi-Health Systems.
Herbert, J. (2015). *Testosterone*. Oxford: Oxford University Press.
Huebner, T., Vloet, T. D., Marx, I., Konrad, K., Fink, G. R., Herpertz, S. C., & Herpertz-Dahlmann, B. (2008). Morphometric brain abnormalities in boys with conduct disorder. *Journal of the American Academy of Child and Adolescent Psychiatry, 47*, 540–547.
Jacobs, P., Brunton, M., Melville M., Brittain, R. P., & McClemont, W. F. (1965). Aggressive behavior, mental sub-normality and the XYY male. *Nature, 208*, 1351–1352.
Joseph, R. (2003). Environmental influences on neural plasticity, the limbic system, emotional development and attachment: A review. *Child Psychiatry and Human Development, 29*, 189–208.
Kiehl, K., Smith, A. M., Mendrek, A., Forster B. B., Hare, R. D., & Liddle, P. F. (2004). Temporal lobe abnormalities in semantic processing by criminal psychopaths as revealed by functional magnetic resonance imaging. *Psychiatry Research Neuroimaging, 130*, 27–42.
Kraepelin, E. (1899) *Psychiatrie: ein Lehrbuch für Studirende und Aertze* [Psychiatry: A Textbook for Students and Physicians] (6th ed.). Leipzig: Barth Verlag. Reprinted (1990). Canton, MA: Science History Publications.
Kruesi, M. J. P., Casanova, M. V., Mannheim, G., & Johnson-Bilder, A. (2004). Reduced temporal lobe volume in early-onset conduct disorder. *Psychiatry Research Neuroimaging, 132*, 1–11.
Laakso, M. P., Gunning-Dixon, F., Vaurio, O., Repo-Tiihonen, E., Soininen, H., & Tiihonen, J. (2002). Prefrontal volume in habitually violent subjects with antisocial personality disorder and Type 2 alcoholism. *Psychiatry Research Neuroimaging, 114*, 95–102.
Laakso, M. P., Vaurio, O., Savolainen, L., Repo, E., Soininen, H., Aronen, H. J., & Tiihonen, J. (2000). A volumetric MRI study of the hippocampus in Type 1 and 2 alcoholism. *Behavioral Brain Research, 109*, 117–186.
Lombroso, C. (1876). *L'uomo delinquente studiato in rapporto alla antropologia, alla medicina legale ed alle discipline carcerarie* [The criminal man studied in relationship to anthropology, forensic medicine and prison doctrines]. Milan: Ulrico Hoepli.
Loney, B. R., Frick, P. J., Clements, C. B., Ellis, M. L., & Kerlin, K. (2003). Callous-unemotional traits, impulsivity and emotional processing in adolescents with antisocial behavior problems. *Journal of Clinical Child and Adolescent Psychology, 32*, 66–80.
Marsh, A. A., Finger, E. C., Mitchell, D. G. V., Reid, M. E., Sims, C., Kosson, D. S., & Blair, R. J. (2008). Reduced amygdala response to fearful expressions in children and adolescents with callous-unemotional traits and disruptive behavior disorders. *American Journal of Psychiatry, 165*, 712–720.
Mezzacappa, E., Tremblay, R. E., Kindlon, D. J., Saul J. P., Arsenault, L., Seguin, J. R., & Earls, F. (1997). Anxiety, antisocial behavior and heart rate regulation in adolescent males. *Journal of Child Psychology and Psychiatry, 38*, 457–468.
Moffitt, T. E., & Caspi, A. (2001). Childhood predictors differentiate life-course persistent and adolescence-limited antisocial pathways among males and females. *Development and Psychopathology, 13*, 355–375.
Moffitt, T. E., Lynam, D. R., & Silva, P. A. (1994). Neuropsychological tests predicting persistent male delinquency. *Criminology, 32*, 277–300.
Muller, J. L., Sommer, M., Wagner, V., Lange, K., Taschler, H., Roöder, C. H., & Hajak, G. (2003). Abnormalities in emotion processing within cortical and subcortical regions in criminal psychopaths: Evidence from a functional magnetic imaging study using pictures with emotional content. *Psychiatry Research Neuroimaging, 54*, 152–162.
Ortiz, J., & Raine A. (2004). Heart rate level and antisocial behavior in children and adolescents: A meta-analysis. *Journal of American Academy of Child and Adolescent Psychiatry, 43*, 154–162.

Price, W., & Whatmore, P. (1967). Behaviour disorders and pattern of crime among XYY males identified at a maximum security hospital. *British Medical Journal, 1*, 533–536.

Rada, R. T., Kellner, R., & Winslow, W. W. (1976). Plasma testosterone and aggressive behavior. *Psychosomatics, 17*, 138–142.

Rafter, N. (2005). The murderous Dutch fiddler: Criminology, history and the problem of phrenology. *Theoretical Criminology, 9*, 65–96.

Raine, A. (1993). *The psychopathology of crime: Criminal behavior as a clinical disorder*. London: Academic Press.

Raine, A., Buchsbaum, M., & LaCasse, L. (1997). Brain abnormalities in murderers indicated by positron emission tomography. *Biological Psychiatry, 42*, 495–508.

Raine, A., Buchsbaum, M., Stanley, J., Lottenberg, S., Abel, L., & Stoddard, S. (1994). Selective reductions in prefrontal glucose metabolism in murderers. *Biological Psychiatry, 36*, 365–373.

Raine, A., Lencz, T., Bihrle, S., LaCasse, L., & Colletti, P. (2000). Reduced prefrontal gray matter volume and reduced autonomic activity in antisocial personality disorder. *Archives of General Psychiatry, 57*, 119–127.

Raine, A., Venables, P. H., & Mednick, S. A. (1997). Low resting heart rate age 3 years predisposes to aggression at age 11 years. Evidence from the Mauritius Child Health Project. *Journal of American Academy of Child and Adolescent Psychiatry, 36*, 1457–1464.

Raine, A., Venables, P. H., & Williams, N. (1995). High autonomic arousal and electrodermal orienting at age 15 years as protective factors against criminal behavior at age 29 years. *American Journal of Psychiatry, 152*, 1595–1600.

Ratiu, P., & Talos, I. F. (2004). The tale of Phineas Gage. Digitally remastered. *New England Journal of Medicine, 351*, e21–e21.

Rushton, J. P., & Chrisjohn, R. D. (1981). Extraversion, neuroticism, psychoticism and self-reported delinquency: Evidence from eight separate samples. *Personality and Individual Differences, 2*, 11–20.

Schneider K. (reprinted in 1976) Psychopath ische Persönlichkeiten. In *Klinische Psychopathologie. 11* (pp. 17–39). Stuttgart, Germany: Thieme Verlag.

Seo, D., Patrick, C. J., & Kennealy, P. J. (2008). Role of serotonin and dopamine system interactions in the neurobiology of impulsive aggression and its comorbidity with other clinical disorders. *Aggression and Violent Behavior, 13*, 383–395.

Sterzer, P., Stadler, C., Krebs, A., Kleinschmidt, A., & Poustka, F. (2005). Abnormal neural responses to emotional visual stimuli in adolescents with conduct disorder. *Biological Psychiatry, 57*, 7–15.

Stix, G. (2013). My brain made me pull the trigger. *Scientific American*, November, 2013. Retrieved from http://blogs.scientificamerican.com/talking-back/2013/11/20/my-brain-made-me-pull-the-trigger/.

Stochholm, K., Anders Bojesen, A., Skakkebæk Jensen, A., Juul, S., Højbjerg, & Gravholt, C. (2012). Criminality in men with Klinefelter's syndrome and XYY syndrome: A cohort study. *British Medical Journal Open, 2*:1 e000650.

Van Horn, J. D., Irimia, A., Torgerson, C. M., Chambers, M. C., Kikinis, R., & Toga, A. W. (2012). Mapping connectivity damage in the case of Phineas Gage. *PloS one, 7*, e37454.

Vom Saal, F. (1983). Models of early hormonal effects on intrasex aggression in mice. In B. Svare (Ed.), *Hormones and aggressive behavior* (pp. 197–222). New York: Plenum.

Whitlock, F. A. (1982). A note on moral insanity and psychopathic disorders. *Psychiatric Bulletin, 6*, 57-59.

Whiten, A., & Byrne, R. (1988) Tactical deception in primates. *Behavioural and Brain Sciences, 12*, 233–273.

2

A Brief Introduction to Neuroscience

Pia Rotshtein and Ian J. Mitchell

> **Key points**
> - This chapter gives an overview of neuroscience – the study of the brain – and of behavioral neuroscience – the study of the link between brain and behavior.
> - The chapter describes each of the key structures and functions of the brain in turn. The chapter also serves as a glossary in relation to the two types of cell in the human brain – neurons and glia – and the role of important neurotransmitters in the brain, such as glutamate, dopamine, serotonin, oxytocin, and vasopressin.
> - It is noted in the chapter that the main division in neuroscience is between the *central nervous system* – the brain and spinal cord – and the *peripheral nervous system* – the neurons that control bodily responses and provide feedback to the brain.
> - The brain is typically seen as dividing into three parts. The forebrain is the largest of the three parts in human beings and is the "thinking" part of the brain. The midbrain and hindbrain are smaller in humans and guide automatic and reflexive responses such as sleeping, freezing/fleeing, urinating, and defecating.
> - Neuropsychology (e.g., the study of lesions) and neuroimaging methods are used to establish links between the brain's structures and activity. Neuropsychology establishes causal connections and neuroimaging establishes correlational links.
> - Neuroimaging methods can be divided into those based on metabolic processes, measuring the concentration of certain molecules in the brain including: magnetic resonance imaging (MRI), functional near-infrared spectroscopy (fNIRS), positron emission tomography (PET), single positron emission computed tomography (SPECT), and those that measure signals

---

The Wiley Blackwell Handbook of Forensic Neuroscience, First Edition. Edited by Anthony R. Beech, Adam J. Carter, Ruth E. Mann and Pia Rotshtein.
© 2018 John Wiley & Sons Ltd. Published 2018 by John Wiley & Sons Ltd.

derived from the electrical current produced by neurons, that is, electroencephalography (EEG) and magnetoencephalography (MEG).
- Activity in the peripheral nervous system is measured by electromyography (e.g., eye-startle response), galvanic skin response, heart rate, and introspective awareness.
- It is of note that considerable progress has been made in understanding the human brain, despite the fact that further work still needs to be done that will enhance the health and wellbeing (addressed in later chapters in the book).

Terminology Explained

Blood-oxygen-level dependent contrast imaging, or BOLD-contrast imaging, is a method used in functional magnetic resonance imaging (fMRI) to observe different areas of the brain or other organs, which are found to be active at any given time.

Brodmann's areas. Brodmann (1909/2006) classified the whole of the cerebral cortex based on subtle differences in the cellular organization of these layers. These areas, defined in terms of this histological arrangements, map in large part to function, in a system that is still currently used. This means that any cortical area can be referred to in terms of a Brodmann number, for example, motor cortex is Brodmann's area 4 (BA4).

Electroencephalography (EEG) uses electrodes placed to measure electrical activity or voltage change. Changes in electrical activity can serve as a direct measure of neural responses.

Functional magnetic resonance imaging (fMRI) quantifies activity changes within circumscribed areas of the brain through registration of regional changes in blood oxygenation of neural tissue. Depending on the experimental paradigm, fMRI results support inferences about structures that are activated or deactivated in relation to the occurrence of certain stimuli, events, emotions, cognitions, or actions. fMRI can also inform on functional connections between regions.

In **genetics**, deoxyribonucleic acid (DNA) is a molecule that carries the genetic instructions used in the growth, development, functioning, and reproduction of all known living organisms – the **genotype**. Its overt manifestation is called the **phenotype**. A genotype can be viewed as a potential for showing a specific phenotype, but the relations are not deterministic. Two individuals with an identical gene may exhibit a very different phenotype, depending on the biological environment these genes have been exposed to. Epigenetics describes how specific gene expression depends on its immediate biological environment. Individuals' genotypes may vary based on only small change of the DNA, often referred to as mutation. These can have profound impact on individual phenotypes.

Haemodynamic response allows the rapid delivery of fresh blood to active neuronal tissues. Since higher processes in the brain occur almost constantly, cerebral blood flow is essential for the maintenance of neurons, astrocytes, and other cells of the brain.

Interoception refers to the perception of internal bodily sensations.

Magnetoencephalography (MEG) provides an alternative method to EEG for recording postsynaptic potentials of cortical neurons by measuring changes in the scalp magnetic field.

Systems neuroscience studies the function of neural circuits and systems. It is an umbrella term, encompassing a number of areas of study concerned with how nerve cells behave when connected together to form neural networks. At this level of analysis, neuroscientists study how different neural circuits analyze sensory information, form perceptions of the external world, make decisions, and execute movements.

Urbach–Wiethe disease is caused by a genetic mutation. Patients who carry that mutation typically have bilaterally symmetrical damage to the amygdalae.

White and grey matter. Grey matter is composed mainly of the cell bodies of neurons, dendrites, and synapses, and is primarily associated with processing and cognition. White matter consists of the myelinated (fat insulated) axons connecting between different neurons.

Introduction

Understanding the function of the brain has fascinated humans from the times of the Ancient Egyptians, while modern views of the brain have been largely shaped by academics in the 19th century (see Chapter 1 for an overview of this history). In the first half of the 20th century, psychology (especially experimental psychology) was dominated by behaviorism. Behaviorism assumes that all behavior, including emotions and thoughts, can be understood as part of stimulus–response associations (see Box 2.1 describing classical and operant conditioning). Behaviorists believed that environmental factors (including nurture) were the main driving forces in shaping an individual's behavior, in contrast to nature and genetic factors. A behaviorist treated the brain as a "black-box," avoiding research questions addressing internal mental processes. For example, radical behaviorism focused only on overt responses, rejecting introspection methods (such as those assessed through questionnaire and clinical interview).

Box 2.1 Conditioning

(Also known as associative learning)

Conditioning procedures play a key role in some forensic theories, models of substance abuse, and rehabilitation practices (e.g., behavior modification). Conditioning is one of the basic principles that govern learning in any organism. It enables learning from experience and facilitates responses to future events, enabling the organism to predict and prepare for upcoming emotive events. Conditioning is a form of learning that can be observed in many animals from reptiles to mammals, therefore it is unsurprising that it is mediated via evolutionary "old" structures (see Box 2.2 on brain development). There are two basic types of conditioning:

(1) *Classical conditioning* (also known as Pavlovian after Ivan Pavlov) is a learning process (originally noted in dogs) by which an initially neutral stimulus (e.g., sound of a bell) if repeatedly paired with a potent stimulus (such as food, which produces drooling) will eventually produce the conditioned response of drooling from the ringing of the bell.

(2) *Operant conditioning* (also known as instrumental conditioning) refers to the association of a *voluntary response* with a specific outcome. This procedure was first described by Skinner (1935). He showed that behavior can be shaped through positive (rewards) and negative (punishment) feedback (reinforcer), and is governed by the *law of effect*, which states that we are more likely to repeat a behavior that led to a desired positive outcome and not repeat a behavior that has led to a negative and undesired outcome. Hence, if an adolescent gains respect by committing antisocial behavior this may form a strong incentive to keep repeating this.

Behavior modification is one of the most common procedures used to change pattern of responses. It uses the principles of operant conditioning, where an individual is rewarded for desired behaviors and punished for undesired, also known as the carrot and stick approach. This method is used by parents, educators, peers, treatment facilities, and in many organizations. The *Teaching Family Model* is an example of a program utilizing behavior modification, which has been used successfully to deal with young people exhibiting behavioral problems (Fixsen, Blase, Timbers, & Wolf, 2007).

In the second half of the 20th century a cognitive science paradigm emerged. Cognitive scientists were inspired by computational information processing models, and used the computer as a metaphor of the human brain. Cognition describes all thought processes from perception to actions, including attention, executive functions, memory, planning, and decision making. Cognitive science asks questions about the underlining mechanisms that give rise to behaviors, and constructs information processing models using boxes and arrows to describe them. For example, an influential model of face processing (reported by Bruce & Young, 1986) suggests a hierarchical processing of faces, where there are independent processing streams for the expression, identity, lip movement, and gender of the face. This idea has been partially support by scanning studies of the brain (see Haxby, Hoffman, & Gobbini, 2002).

Technological advances in the second half of the 20th century, such as brain scans, have led to a dramatic increase in research and the allocation of resources directed toward neuroscience. This is a rapidly evolving and exciting research field spanning across multiple disciplines from physics, chemistry, biology, computing, and engineering sciences, through psychology, social sciences, archeology, and education. This chapter aims to provide a brief introduction to neuroscience. It gives a basic and simplified view of the current knowledge of the human brain. One can also use it as a glossary of terms, referring to it when clarification of methodological and background information is needed.

It is important to note that by the time this book reaches the shelves many further advances will have been made in understanding the structure and function of the healthy and unhealthy brain. As noted by Karl Popper (1959), good scientific work should consistently challenge and test the validity of existing knowledge. Hence it is difficult to predict which findings and theories would survive the testing and retesting procedures. We have attempted in this book to include primarily work that has been consistently replicated. However, we should be cautious when describing current knowledge, acknowledging the possibility that there is a lot more to know, or re-evaluate. We will now briefly outline the current situation regarding behavioral neuroscience.

Behavioral Neuroscience

Behavioral neuroscience is primarily concerned in linking biology and behavior. It is a branch of psychology also known as biological psychology, biopsychology, or psychobiology. Paradigm shifts in psychology affected the way we describe the function of the brain. Different from other psychology fields, a behavioral neuroscientist would attempt to present neurobiological roots to validate their behavioral observations and theories. For example, using cross-cultural research would be sufficient evidence for a psychologist to argue for the existence of six basic emotions that have evolutionary roots (Ekman & Friesen, 1972). A behavioral neuroscientist, arguing for basic emotion categories, examines neural-based evidence of dissociated neural structures of the basic emotions. The neuroscience-based evidence for the basic emotion hypothesis is still debated (Lindquist, Wager, Kober, Bliss-Moreau, & Barrett, 2012).

Neuroscientists use a large array of tools to measure overt behaviors. This ranges from relying on subjective reports and introspections common in observational studies and applied psychology, to more objective measures common in experimental psychology. Subjective, observational methods such as questionnaires and clinical interviews typically code behavior/trait/mood based on the responses given by the interviewee to a set of pre-specified questions. In some cases, a third party (e.g., parent, teacher) is asked to answer about the individual. Coding can be on a continuous scale (e.g., how much of a trait the individual exhibits) or categorical (using a cut off to determine whether an individual has or does not have a specific trait, or shows normal or abnormal (clinical) symptoms.

Objective measures are typically collected in the context of a laboratory experiment. The most commonly used method is the recording of response time and response accuracy for a stimulus. Participants are presented with a set of stimuli on a computer screen and are asked to make a response. The assumption is that the speed and accuracy of the response reflects underlying neural processes. Longer and less accurate responses are typically associated with more difficult and complex processing. Careful experimental manipulations can be used to identify the factors responsible for the increase in errors and response times. For example, the ability to recognize facial expression can be measured by presenting different expressions and asking participants to match the correct label to each expression; or asking them to indicate which of two faces show the same expression. This procedure can be used to identify dissociated patterns in recognizing different expressions. It is typically found that recognition of fearful expression is slower and susceptible to errors. In contrast, recognizing happy expression is very quick and easy (Wells, Gillespie, & Rotshtein, 2016).

Eye gaze patterns have also been used to study underlying neural processes. Eye tracking devices typically project infrared light onto the cornea. The wavelength of the returning light is affected by the angle of the surface and is used to infer the direction of the gaze. In the context of a laboratory experiment, one can measure how the gaze is affected by an experimental manipulation. The target of the first gaze, the timing to reach a specific area in the picture, and the dwell time on specific locations have all been used to describe the gaze pattern. In the context of expression processing, eyes are the target of the first gaze, and are associated with longer dwell times, especially if the face displays a fearful expression (Wells et al., 2016). However, this effect is attenuated in individuals with high primary psychopathic traits (Gillespie et al., 2015). We will describe what we know about human brain development.

Human Brain Development

Embryologists divide the human brain based on its developmental process. The brains of all vertebrates can be divided into the hindbrain, midbrain, and forebrain (see Box 2.2).

Box 2.2 Outline Morphology of Vertebrates' Brains

- The hindbrain includes the pons, medulla, and cerebellum.
- The midbrain includes the tectum (which consists mainly of the inferior and superior colliculi), periaquaductal grey, substantia nigra, and ventral tegmental area. It is a relatively small part of the human brain.
- The forebrain is divided into the cerebrum (cerebral cortex, amygdala, hippocampus, and basal ganglia), thalamus, and hypothalamus. The forebrain is the largest part of the human brain.

The relative size of each part varies dramatically between different species. It is important to note that all levels of brains are involved in functions related to the ongoing survival and maintenance of an organism and to its reproduction. However, the level of automaticity versus flexibility varies between brain parts. Ancient structures in the hindbrain and midbrain respond in a reflexive mode, while responses guided by the forebrain, especially the cortex, are more flexible and adaptive. These responses typically depend on complex integration of large amounts of information, consideration of both previous experiences and current short- and long-term goals. Human brain development is divided into two qualitatively different periods: prenatal and postnatal development as follows.

Prenatal development

The generation of the brain involves neurogenesis (cell proliferation), the organization of neurons (neural migration) to their final anatomical location, where they start the process of synaptogenesis (forming connections). The central nervous system of fish, birds, reptiles, and mammals is divided into four parts: the spinal cord, hindbrain, midbrain, and forebrain. In the human embryo, this division occurs at week four. The hindbrain develops to be part of the brain stem structures and the cerebellum. The midbrain develops into the tectum and cerebral peduncle – it is a relative small part in the adult brain. The substantia nigra and ventral tegmental area form part of the midbrain, are the main sources of dopamine in the brain, essential for learning, motivation, and motor functions. The forebrain divides into the cerebral cortex, thalamus, and hypothalamus structures. All brain parts contribute to the function of basic circuits required for survival, including energy supply (e.g., feeding, water, breathing), protection (defense), and reproduction. However, they differ in the level of flexibility in the response they produce, from a reflex-like involvement of the hindbrain, to a more complex and flexible processing of the forebrain.

The brain is constructed through processes of neurogenesis (creating of new neurons), differentiation, and migration. Neurons are created along the banks of the ventricles and then migrate to their final destination. The migration is guided by glia cells (see below). Once a neuron reaches its final destination, it starts forming connections with other neurons, by sending axons to them – through arborization (the fine branching structure at the end of a nerve fiber). During the 2–24 week period the development of the human brain follows a similar timeline to the evolution of brains across vertebrate species. This is assessed by the relative size of the three parts: hindbrain, midbrain, and forebrain. The development of the cerebral cortex starts with the primary sensory regions (e.g., somatosensory, auditory, and vision). Primary sensory regions form a large part of evolutionary "older" mammals' brains, for instance mice and squirrels. Associative sensory cortices develop next, making the brain more similar to those of monkeys and primates, with the final part to develop being the prefrontal cortex. This region is most developed in humans, relative to all other animals, hence our large forehead in comparison to other primates.

By weeks 26–29, the basic structure of the brain is complete, including the setting up of the framework and main pathways of the neurotransmitters. Thus, at this stage, the prenatal brain would respond to drugs and medication targeting the neuronal signals, though their impact on neural development is unclear. The number of neurons in the human brain peaks at week 28, with around half of the neurons dying off, through a process called *apoptosis*. Apoptosis is partly regulated by synaptic activity, with cells that make connections with the wrong locations being eliminated. The structural foundation of the brain, including the major connection pathways of neurons, is established before birth, with only around 5% of these pathways being insulated with myelin. Thus, most myelination processes occur after birth.

Postnatal development

Brain development is focused on establishing and fine-tuning connections between neurons to ensure maximum adaptability of an individual to their environment. Connections are developed through synaptogenesis (dendrite expansion and forming of new synapses and connections) and pruning (elimination) of unused synapses. Synaptic changes occur within the grey matter. Within white matter, myelination around axons develops, which facilitates rapid transmission of information across long distance axonal connections. At two weeks, the size of a newborn brain is about one-third of the adult brain. Any large deviation of brain size can indicate abnormal development. For example, malnutrition has been associated with relative small brain size, while autism has been associated with increased brain size.

Within the first two years the brain will double in size, and be more than three-quarters the size of an adult brain. This initial growth is primarily due to increase in grey matter connections (synaptogenesis) and the expansion of myelination. The peak density of synapses occurs within the first year of life, with infants having up to 150% more synapses than adults. As in prenatal development, postnatal development starts with primary sensory-motor regions located at the posterior part of the brain, and progresses forward to the frontal cortex. Synapse density in the prefrontal cortex (the most anterior part of the frontal cortex) peaks at the age of two to six. Following the peak density periods, the pruning process accelerates, with the trimming of synaptic connections, which results in a thinning of the cortical sheet. Sensory-motor areas are pruned first, progressing to the more associative cortex in anterior frontal regions. Brain volume development between two and five years of age is slowed, as the number of newly generated synapses is counteracted by elimination of synapses, through the pruning process. However, the amount of energy consumed by a child (four to ten years) brain is doubled compared to the adult brain. This potentially reflects the energy demands of the myelination, synapse shaping, and pruning. The pruning and thinning of the cortical sheet reflecting the fine-tuning of connections continues at a relative fast rate well into young adulthood. These neural developmental trajectories are mapped to functional changes where young children show adult-like abilities to sense the environment, followed by the development of attention and control processes, and ending with the development of emotion regulation and social skills.

The process of connection selection is heavily dependent on experience. Experience is gained through the interaction of the individual with their immediate internal and external environment. At the very basic level it depends on the sensory input they receive and the ability to explore and interact with the environment. Deprivation studies in animals have shown that eliminating sensory input (e.g., cutting input from one ear, restricting vision to one eye, restricting movement) have a profound impact on the way the functional brain is organized. For example, restricting auditory inputs lead to visual processing being carried out in cortical areas typically dedicated to audition. Sensory deprivation does not only lead to reorganization of brain functions but also to reduced tissue density in the brain. The concept of critical periods highlights the importance of timing in the interaction between the environment and development. Critical periods describe the stages in which different neural structures develop as dependent on input. Lack of input at these stages will alter development in an irreversible way. For example, the critical period for vision occurs between three to eight months of age; while for language the critical period is up to five years. Some level of the function can still be acquired after the critical period has passed, but at a much lower rate and proficiency levels never reaches that of a typically developed brain.

Abnormal development has been associated with both accelerated and decelerated cortical thickness and pruning. For example, relative to typically developed children, children with attentional deficit hyperactive disorder (ADHD) have a thinner cortical sheet in the frontal lobe. Before the age of ten years ADHD children show increases in cortical thickness, which then decreases at a slower rate than typically developed children. By the age of 17, cortical thicknesses and the pruning rate of the frontal cortex in ADHD individuals are roughly equivalent to those of typically developed children.

Understanding the Functions of the Brain and Peripheral Nervous Systems

At the system level, the main division is between the central and peripheral nervous system. The central nervous system includes the brain and the spinal cord, while the peripheral nervous system consists of neurons, which directly control the bodily responses and provide feedback to the brain on bodily states.

The central nervous system

The central nervous system "floats" in the cerebrospinal fluid (CSF), and is shielded by hard bone. The brain has three main components: grey matter, white matter, and CSF. The structural organization and its relation to the function of both grey and white matter is similar across most human brains, enabling group studies. There are also structural and functional similarities with other animals, which enable comparative studies across species. We will now briefly describe the anatomy and function of key brain structures, moving from the most ancient to the most recent evolutionary developments (see Figure 2.1 for the position of some of the structures outlined in this section).

The brainstem is continuous with the spinal cord. It includes the hindbrain (excluding the cerebellum) and other midbrain structures. In more primitive species (such as amphibians) it dominates the central nervous system. Thus, the forebrain is virtually absent from, for example, the frog brain. This means that many species' specific behaviors, including predatory, defensive and reproductive behaviors are encoded within the brainstem. The same is true, to some extent, in mammals. However, in the case of humans the organization and socially appropriate release of these behaviors is under

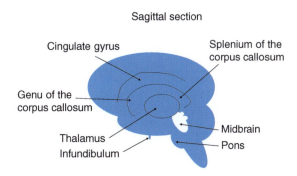

Figure 2.1 A cross (sagittal) section of human brain viewed to illustrate the relative positions of the corpus callosum, cingulate, thalamus, and brainstem.

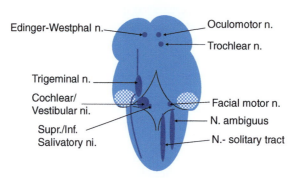

Figure 2.2 A dorsal (back) view of the brainstem following the removal of the cerebellum in order to show the relative positions of some of the cranial nerve nuclei.

the control of the massive forebrain. This organization is reflected in the clinical condition of "Locked-in syndrome" (which can result as a consequence of massive damage to the brain stem) where control over the body muscles is almost completely lost, although high-level cognitions are still maintained.

Cranial nerves Cranial nerves emerge directly from the brain, including the brainstem (see Figure 2.2 for the relative positions of some of these).

Cranial nerve nuclei are as the origin, or the target, of information conveyed by the cranial nerves. These enable rapid relay of information between the body and the central nervous system. Cranial nerves support communication between the brain (often via brainstem nuclei) and the head and neck, while spinal nerves relay information between the spinal cord and the rest of the body. Some of the cranial nerves are purely sensory; for example, cranial nerves one and two, the olfactory, and the optic nerves. Some cranial nerves are concerned with motor activity, such as the fourth, the trochlear, which helps control eye movements. Others have a mixed function and can include axons of the automatic nervous system neurons. The tenth cranial nerve (the vagus) provides the parasympathetic input to the heart as well as sensory and motor innervations of the parts of the mouth and throat. Circuits linking the cranial nerves with the cranial nerve nuclei form the basis of nerve reflexes. Examples of these include the pupillary light reflex, the corneal reflex, the coughing/gagging reflex, and the respiratory reflex. The latter involves the respiratory centers in the medulla. This emphasizes the vital role that the brainstem plays in maintaining basic vegetative functions.

The midbrain Species-specific behaviors are encoded in the midbrain (the top part of the brainstem). The neural structures involved are mainly grouped around the cerebral aqueduct. The cerebral aqueduct is part of the ventricular system, that is, a series of continuous CSF filled chambers that run through the brain. Stimulation of the tissue surrounding the aqueduct, the periaqueductal grey, can elicit specific behaviors such as freezing, fleeing, urination, defecation, and elements of copulatory behavior. The midbrain is involved in sleep–wake cycles, arousal, and temperature regulation and contributes to motor and sensory processing. Lying just above the periaqueductal grey, in the roof of the midbrain, is the tectum. The tectum is dominated by two pairs of small swellings: the inferior and the superior colliculi. The inferior colliculus is concerned with processing auditory information. It receives auditory information and projects to the medial geniculate nucleus of the thalamus, which in turn projects to the primary auditory cortex. One of the main functions of the superior colliculus, by contrast, is the processing of visual information.

The superior colliculus Much of the visual information is processed by the cerebral cortex via a circuit that runs from the retina via the thalamus to the primary visual cortex. However, a relatively small number of retinal ganglion cells project not to the thalamus but to the superior colliculus. In humans one of the main functions of the superior colliculus is to facilitate orienting responses. Suddenly appearing visual stimuli, especially moving stimuli in the peripheral visual field are rapidly processed by the colliculus. This can potentially trigger deeper layers of the colliculus to generate motor signals (e.g., by stimulating the oculomotor nuclei), which cause the eyes and/or head to orient to the object. This orientation places the object of interest in the center of the visual field (and attention) enabling the cortical visual systems to determine exactly what the stimulus is. This process happens very rapidly. There is considerable debate as to how much information the human colliculus can extract from a complex visual stimulus. It was originally thought that this was very limited and enabled only simple judgments. However, it is now thought that features such as the outline of a predator (snake) or emotional facial expressions can be extracted. This information is relayed in a direct manner to the amygdala. This means that the amygdala can make decisions about how to respond to potentially dangerous stimuli extremely rapidly, without cortical involvement and, consequently, without conscious awareness.

The amygdaloid complex At the rostral (anterior) pole of the temporal lobe of the brain lies the amygdaloid complex (the amygdala). It plays important roles in processing emotionally significant stimuli and organizing motivational responses. This is achieved via a complex series of other structures including the prefrontal cortex, the hypothalamus, and more primitive structures in the brainstem. It consists of a series of subnuclei, each of which has a specific set of neural connections and functions. It can be subdivided into two main parts: the centro-medial complex and the basolateral complex. At a very crude approximation the basolateral complex, which can be split into the basal nuclei and lateral nuclei, handles the main inputs to the amygdala; the centro-medial complex, which consists of the central nuclei and the medial nuclei, handles the outputs. See Figure 2.3 for a schematic representation of the major inputs and outputs of the amygdaloid complex.

The central amygdala nucleus The central amygdala nucleus is primarily concerned with organizing fear responses. The main output of this nucleus runs to the periaqueductal grey, which organizes species-specific behaviors including those involved in defense. It also connects with parts of the autonomic nervous system, which can prepare the body for flight and fight reactions, and projects to the monoamine systems, which contribute to arousal, and the parts of the hypothalamus that control the release of stress hormones. The sensory information relating to fear-inducing stimuli arrive in the amygdala via projections from cortical areas of different sensory modalities, which terminate in the lateral nuclei. In addition to these cortical inputs, sensory information is relayed to the lateral amygdala nuclei from subcortical sensory

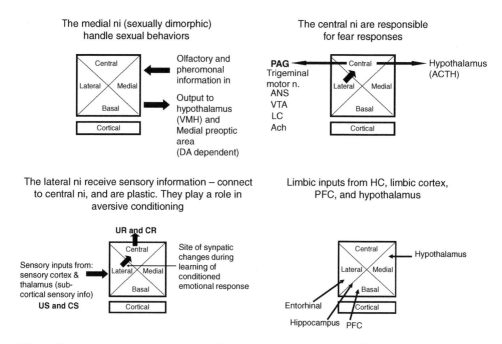

Figure 2.3 Schematic representation of the amygdaloid complex to illustrate the major input–output relations of the major amygdala nuclei.

structures such as the superior colliculus. This gives the amygdala potentially rapid access to fear-related information that can take place at a subconscious level. The **medial amygdala nucleus** (part of the centro-medial complex) is involved with reproductive behaviors. The nucleus accordingly receives olfactory and pheromonal information relating to sexual stimuli whereas their output is directed to parts of the hypothalamus that control sexual behaviors and endocrine responses related to reproduction. These areas include the ventromedial hypothalamus and the medial preoptic area.

Projections from the lateral nuclei to the central nuclei enable this fear related sensory information to drive fear responses. Synapses within this lateral amygdala nucleus are plastic, such that they can change their connectional strength. This plasticity underlies the role that the amygdala plays in aversive conditioning. The amygdala also plays a role in the establishment of conditioned reinforcers and in encoding the salience of emotionally significant stimuli. These functions are handled by the basal and lateral nuclei via connections with the brain's reward systems, which are focused on the dopamine neurons in the ventral tegmental area (VTA) and the nucleus accumbens. The basolateral amygdala complex also receives inputs from the prefrontal cortex and the limbic cortex.

The hippocampus Behind the amygdala lies the hippocampus, which has an important role in memory. Damage to the hippocampus is associated with amnesia and hippocampal neurons become active when "remembered" places are revisited. The main inputs to the hippocampus come from the entorhinal cortex and the cingulate cortex. Some of the axons that contribute to the cingulate input run in a big arching bundle of fibers called the fornix. One of the main outputs of the hippocampus is to the anterior thalamic nuclei that then project back onto the cingulate cortex. The hippocampus is typically considered to be a complex, which is made up of three main substructures: the dentate gyrus, the CA-3 subfield, and the CA-1 subfield. It has an important role in associative learning, navigation, and the formation of new episodic memories.

The cingulate   The cingulate includes the *cingulate gyrus* and the *sulcus* and represents a relatively simple form of cerebral cortex. It forms an arch-like structure, which lies on the medial surface of each cerebral hemisphere and follows the "C" shape of the corpus callosum, the massive bundle of axons that connects the two hemispheres to each other. The cingulate is often subdivided into an anterior (front) part and a posterior (back) part. The anterior cingulate cortex is further divided into a dorsal, – the more cognitive part – and the ventral – the more emotive part.

The cerebellum   Tucked under the occipital lobe, attached to the brainstem via three pairs of cerebellar peduncles, lies the cerebellum. The structure is a major component of the motor control systems though it is now appreciated that it plays a role in many cognitive processes, including emotions as well as controlling movement. The lateral parts of the cerebellum are the last to develop. These handle the most complex aspects of movement control whereas the medial parts handle more simplistic motor functions. For example, the medial parts, which constitute the flocculonodular lobe, connect with the vestibular system of the inner ear via the eighth cranial nerve and this system is important for controlling eye and head movements. It is hypothesized that this part is involved in conditioning based on the eye-startle reflex. Similarly, some of the medial parts, which form the vermis, connect with the motor neurons of the spinal cord. These are needed for maintaining balance and the righting reflex.

The forebrain   The forebrain is the most developed part in the mammalian brain. It primarily consists of the basal ganglia, the thalamus, hypothalamus, and the cortex. In humans, the cerebral cortex, especially that in the frontal lobe, is substantially larger than that seen in all other species. This potentially enables the great leap of flexibility and adaptability of human behavior, in comparison to all other animals.

The basal ganglia   The basal ganglia is mainly composed of the striatum, globus pallidus, and the subthalamic nucleus. The striatum consists of three dissociable parts, the caudate nucleus and the putamen, which form the dorsal striatum, and the nucleus accumbens, which is often referred to as the ventral striatum. The accumbens is sometimes considered to be a part of the limbic system and plays a role in reinforcement and reward. One popular theory of reward argues that any event that is reinforcing causes the release of dopamine in the nucleus accumbens. By contrast, the putamen is implicated in the control of movement and dysfunction of this structure is associated with a range of movement disorders including Parkinson's disease and Huntington's chorea.

The hypothalamus   The hypothalamus is a collection of nuclei and its main function is to control the endocrine system, via the pituitary gland. It has bi-directional connections with many parts of the brain including the brainstem, amygdala, thalamus, and cortex. Several nuclei of the hypothalamus differ in structure and function between males and females. The hypothalamus plays an important role in most survival circuits, including regulating body temperature, sleep, feeding, defense, and reproduction. It is the source for oxytocin and vasopressin, which have been linked to parental and pro-social behaviors.

The thalamus Consisting of around 40 subnuclei the thalamus lies at the junction of the cerebral hemisphere and the midbrain. All of the major cortical areas receive an input from this area. It is divided into three major nuclear masses: the anterior nuclei, which are associated with the limbic system (see Box 2.3); the dorsomedial nuclei, which are connected with the prefrontal cortex; and the ventral nuclei, which process and relay sensory information relating to a specific modality or motor information. In general, all sensory information reaching the cerebral cortex is relayed to it via the thalamic nuclei. A noticeable exception is olfactory information, which is sent in a more direct manner to the olfactory cortex.

Box 2.3 The Limbic System

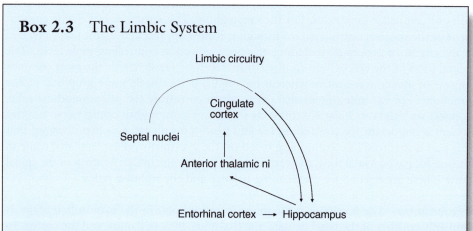

Figure 2.4 A schematic diagram illustrating the interconnections of major limbic structures.

The limbic system refers to a collection of neuronal structures, which play pivotal roles in emotional and motivated behaviors and in the formation of memories. The function and structure of components of this system are thought to be abnormal in offending populations, and in mental health conditions. The limbic system was originally seen as comprising of structures that lie around the medial rim of the cerebral hemisphere. However, the term limbic has now been broadened to encompass other structures, especially those that can be found in the temporal lobe. Precise definitions of the limbic system are difficult to make. Historically, the limbic system has been viewed as being relatively primitive (evolutionary old) and its sensory information dominated by olfaction. In keeping with the idea that the limbic system is a primitive "system" some parts of the cerebral cortex associated with it are relatively simple. For example, instead of being made up of the six separable layers of cells they are composed of only three layers. This type of cerebral cortex is referred to as allocortex rather than neocortex. Most of the allocortex is found in the temporal lobe.

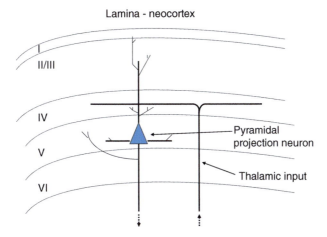

Figure 2.5 Sketch of the different cellular layers (lamina) of the cerebral cortex – where separate layers can be discerned with layer 5 being dominated by pyramidal projection neurons.

The cerebral cortex The grey matter of this area is referred to as the cortical sheet. In humans, the thickness of the cortical sheet is around 3mm, and it has up to six layers (lamina) (see Figure 2.5 for a description of these layers).

Each lamina is dominated by a specific cellular feature. The fourth layer represents the main input layer, the afferents arising mainly from the thalamus. The fifth layer is dominated by neurons with large cell bodies (or soma). The relative size of each layer varies across the cortical sheet. Most noticeable is the difference between the output motor cortex and the input-primary sensory cortex. The primary motor cortex is dominated by a thick fifth layer, which contains pyramidal neurons (see Box 2.4) with particularly soma used to project motor output; whereas the sensory cortex, like the primary visual cortex, has a highly developed input fourth layer.

> **Box 2.4 Pyramidal neurons (cells)**
>
> These play a key role in cognition and motor control. They receive their name from the pyramidal shape of their soma (the cell body). They can be found in the cerebral cortex, hippocampus, and the amygdala (see above). They receive input from around 6,000 terminals, meaning they can integrate huge amounts of information. They are most numerous in the fifth layer of the cortical sheet. It is hypothesized that their activation is the source of EEG and MEG signals. It is also assumed that their large dendritic trees use lots of energy and hence they also drive hemodynamic signals (the basis of fMRI).

To increase surface area, the human cortex is folded, forming the curved texture of the human brain. The curved structure is carved by sulci (depressions on the surface) and the gyri (gyrus in singular, ridge-like features). The two cerebral hemispheres roughly mirror each other. The sulci and gyri structure is roughly equivalent across human brains, and their labels are used when describing brain anatomy. The mapping of function to the anatomical structures is roughly similar across human brains, which can be used as landmarks when "normalizing" brain images to a common stereotactic space, enabling group studies.

The two cerebral hemispheres are separated by the median longitudinal fissure. This is a very deep fissure, which means that each cerebral hemisphere has a medial or inner surface and a lateral or outer surface. The cortical hemispheres are connected via the corpus callosum, massive bundles of axons or white matter, located just above the lateral ventricles (ventricles are cavities in the brain containing CSF). There is a tight functional coupling between homologous brain regions, those on similar anatomical location but at opposite hemispheres, though the precise function of each hemisphere is different. At the sensory-motor level, each hemisphere processes information from the opposite side of the body. For example, the left hemisphere controls the right hand and right leg. At higher levels, the left hemisphere (in right handed) supports language processing, while the right hemisphere supports visual-spatial processing. The potential of laterality of other cognitive functions, including emotions, is still debated. Each of the two cerebral hemispheres can be subdivided into four lobes based on the location of gross anatomical land marks (e.g., deep fissures and sulci) namely the occipital, temporal, parietal, and frontal lobes. Figure 2.6 shows the relative positions of these lobes and the position of the major sulci (fissures).

The **occipital lobe** can be found at the back of the head, on top of the cerebellum and just above the neck. It is specialized in vision. The **temporal lobe** is located behind the ear and the cheek, in front of (anterior to) the occipital cortex. The temporal lobe is further located beneath (inferior to) the frontal cortex, separated from it by the lateral fissure. Its top-posterior part is dedicated to auditory processing; its bottom-posterior part is concerned with advanced visual processing; and its anterior (front) part stores semantic knowledge. The amygdala and hippocampus are also part of the temporal lobe. Both structures are located at the inner part of the lobe, the medial temporal lobe. The **parietal lobe** is located above/anterior to the occipital lobe. It is separated from the occipital lobe by the parieto-occipital fissure. It plays specialized roles in spatial perception, eye-hand coordination, and allocation of attention. Its most anterior part is the post-central gyrus, which is involved in tactile and

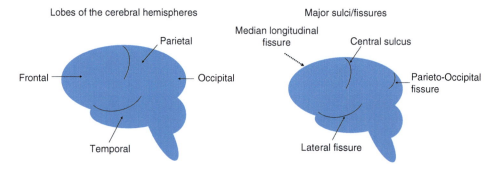

Figure 2.6 Cross section of the cerebral hemispheres showing the positions of the four lobes of the cerebral hemispheres and the major sulci/fissures.

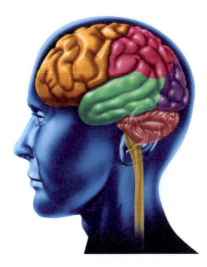

The human brain *This is a schematic view of the central nervous system. It depicts a side view of the human brain, its outside layer of the brain known as the cortex, the cortical sheet and the cerebrum. The cortex is divided to four lobes: frontal (yellow), parietal (magenta), occipital (purple) and temporal (green). The structure at the bottom is the cerebellum (orange), the bundle of fibres living the brain is the spinal cord.*

Source: © lightwise. Used under licencse from 123RF.

somatosensory perception. The central sulcus is the posterior part of the **frontal lobe**. Little sensory information is relayed directly to the cortex of the frontal lobe. Instead, a strip lying just in the central sulcus (BA4) controls voluntary movements of various body parts, while narrow regions just anterior to it are responsible for planning movements. Regions in the frontal cortex that are not directly linked to the control or planning of movement are called the prefrontal cortex. These extensive regions extend all the way to the front of the brain. These are high-level associative regions that are involved in regulation of behavior, including decision making, emotion regulation, and goal achievements.

The prefrontal cortex This is the area that dominates the frontal lobe, and can be thought of as being responsible for some of the most advanced functions that the brain performs. Damage to the prefrontal cortex can result in personality change and an increased tendency for an individual to react aggressively. The structure is said to be responsible for executive functions including planning, organizing, and self-monitoring as well as inhibiting pre-potent responses and working memory. Disruption of the prefrontal cortex can lead to an impaired ability to assess risk. The prefrontal cortex undergoes major organization and morphological changes during adolescence, as noted previously. This includes changes to the dendritic trees of its neurons and the pruning of axonal collaterals. The prefrontal cortex is also the last area of the brain to undergo myelination. The densities of receptors for some neurotransmitters (including dopamine and noradrenalin) also change during development. The release of these transmitters in some brain circuits, including those terminating in the prefrontal cortex, increase during arousal. This then means that the prefrontal cortex of adolescents, and young adults, may function in an idiosyncratic manner during arousal and stress.

The prefrontal cortex is divided into two major anatomical subdivisions, dorsolateral and ventromedial. The dorsomedial prefrontal cortex (dmPFC) is involved in abstract reasoning whereas the ventromedial is concerned with social cognition and response inhibition. These social roles reflect the interconnections between the ventromedial prefrontal cortex (vmPFC) and the amygdala, the brain structure most strongly associated with emotions. To some extent, the activity of the amygdala can be thought of as being held in check by the prefrontal cortex. Consequently, disruption of the prefrontal cortex function can release the amygdala from the inhibitory control and enable the release of emotive responses.

The insula   Situated beneath the frontal and temporal lobes is the insula, which processes taste information. The insula also receives signals on the state of the body (e.g., body arousal levels, heartbeat) and, as a consequence, it is suggested that it is involved in interoception awareness. The insula is also implicated in addiction. Taken together, the occipital, temporal, and parietal lobes and the insula are responsible for processing sensory inputs to the brain while the frontal cortex is responsible for producing appropriate outputs, in response to these inputs.

The peripheral nervous system

The peripheral nervous system refers to all the neurons that branch out from the central nervous system to the body. It can be divided into somatic and autonomic components.

The somatosensory system   The somatosensory system contains neurons that connect to muscles and external organs. It relays motor and sensory information between the body and the central nervous system. It controls voluntary movements, relayed through the central sulcus in the cortex and the thalamus, and reflex movements that bypass cortical processing.

The autonomic nervous system   The autonomic nervous system regulates the activity of the internal bodily organs and is relatively unaffected by voluntary actions. The hypothalamus represents the brain structures that are most commonly implicated in the functioning of the ANS. Via these autonomic connections the hypothalamus can play pivotal roles in many bodily functions ranging from feeding behavior and aggressive responses to sexual arousal. The autonomic system is composed of the parasympathetic and the sympathetic divisions.

The **sympathetic** system is activated during stressful situations when there is a survival danger. It has been termed the "fight or flight" system. It prepares the body to immediately react: through increasing heart rate, channeling blood to skeletal muscle, and inhibiting costly energy consumption (involved, for example, in digestion). The **parasympathetic** system is activated at the opposite state, ensuring the body fulfills its long-term needs. It suppresses the sympathetic system and activates the digestion and reproduction systems. It has been termed the "feed and breed" system. The sympathetic and the parasympathetic systems typically work in an oppositional manner to achieve homeostasis and so enable the organism to flexibly adjust and adapt to its ever-changing needs and environment. We will now examine the cellular neuroscience of the brain.

Cellular Neuroscience

The cells in the human brain are divided into two types: neurons and glial cells (glia). Neurons are the critical information processing cells, while glia provide the essential support. The majority of neurons are created before birth in a process known as neurogenesis.

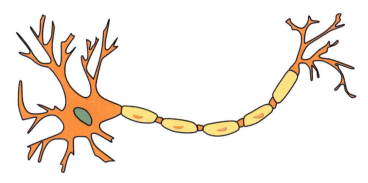

A neuron *This is a schematic description of a neuron. The human brain has approximately 100 billion neurons of different shape, size, and purpose. The vast majority of neurons are created (neurogenesis) before birth. A neuron has a prominent cell body (on the left), which gives rise to the filamentous structure (the axon toward the right). It also gives rise to the branch-like structures (the dendrites – toward the left), which are specialized for receiving inputs from other neurons. The neuron's axon is typically less than 1mm in length, although many may be considerably longer. The axon usually has several branches at its end. The tips of the branches are called terminals. The terminal of one neuron frequently lies in the vicinity of the dendrite of a target neuron.*

Source: © Clker-Free-Vector-Images. Used under license from Pixabay.

Neurons

The idea that the neurons are individual units forming the building blocks of the nervous system was first proposed by Santiago Ramon y Cajal in the 19th century. This is called the neuron doctrine, and is still the dominant view today. The neuron has a prominent cell body, which gives rise to the filamentous structure (the axon). It also causes the branch-like structures (the dendrites), which are specialized for receiving inputs from other neurons. The neuron's axon is typically less than 1mm in length, although many may be considerably longer. The axon usually has several branches at its end. The tips of the branches are called terminals. The terminal of one neuron frequently lies in the vicinity of the dendrite of a target neuron. The physical gap between them is a specialized junction called the synaptic gap (see Figure 2.7 for an illustration of the synapse).

Within a neuron the information is transmitted as an electrical current. Information is transmitted between neurons by means of chemical signaling, which involves the

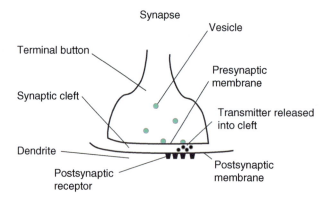

Figure 2.7 Illustration of the synapse.

release of neurotransmitters. Thus, while the most obvious indicator of neuronal activity is electromagnetic change, communication between neurons happens at a chemical level. At rest, when the neuron is not generating an action potential (i.e., when the electrical membrane potential of the cell rapidly rises and falls), there is a difference in the concentration of certain ions (charged atoms or molecules) between the inside (intracellular) and the outside (extracellular) of the neuronal membrane. This creates a chemical and electrical imbalance. This imbalance at rest is achieved through the activation of energy costly ion pumps, which transport ions across the neuron membrane in the opposite direction to this concentration gradient and to the direction of their electrical charge. When the ion channels are opened, these imbalances lead to a passive but rapid flow of ions across the cell membrane. This flow affects the potential of the membrane. At rest the neural membrane is negatively charged (polarized), but when the ion channels are open the membrane potential is depolarized.

A given neuron may receive inputs from several thousands of synapses each of which can lead to local change in the membrane potential. If the sum depolarization of these inputs passes a specific threshold (large enough depolarization) voltage-gated ion channels (as opposed to ligand-gated ion channels) are opened. This generates the action potential (an electrical current), which is propagated through the axon by opening and closing voltage-gated ion channels. When the action potential arrives at the terminals (tip of the axon) a neurotransmitter is released. Neurons operate in an all-or-none fashion. This means that a neuron will transmit a fixed intensity signal to the next neuron ("fire," "be active") only if its membrane potential passes a specific threshold. The intensity of activation is typically encoded by the frequency of the firing rate (i.e., how many action potentials the neuron generated per second). It is important to note that neurons would have a spontaneous firing rate at rest. Activation or deactivation of specific neurons would be reflected as change from the spontaneous firing rate.

Neurons vary in their structure, the neurotransmitter that they release, their location in the central nervous system and their connection pattern. Different neurons are associated with different functions, for example, pyramidal cells that play a key role in cognition and motor control. They receive their name from the pyramidal shape of their soma, cell body. They can be found in the cerebral cortex, hippocampus, and amygdala. Pyramidal cells receive input from around 6,000 terminals, meaning they can integrate a huge volume of information. They are most numerous in the fifth layer of the cortical sheet. It is hypothesized that their activation is the source of the electrical signals of the brain that can be picked up by EEG and MEG(see below). It is also assumed that their large dendritic trees use lots of energy and hence they also drive hemodynamic signals (blood flow), as picked up by imaging techniques.

Glia

Glia (glial cells, from the Greek for glue; also called neuroglia) are the backbone of the nervous system. There are multiple types of glia and their functions range from providing physical support to controlling the internal environment. There are four main functions of glia:

1. Providing the scaffold structure holding the neurons in place and guiding them to their place during development
2. Coordinating energy delivery to neurons (oxygen and food) – therefore, they play an important role in the coupling of neural activity and hemodynamic responses
3. Creating an insulation of tissue (fat) around each neuron to facilitate the conductance of the electrical signal (though this role is played by Schwann cells in the peripheral nervous system)
4. Cleaning the nervous systems, in that they monitor neuronal health, and can repair or destroy non-healthy/dead neurons

Neurotransmitters

Neurotransmitters are endogenous chemicals of the brain that are ejected from neuronal axons, following the passage of an action potential, and are received by postsynaptic receptors. The transmitter diffuses randomly within the synaptic gap and will bind to any membrane bound receptor with a suitable shape that it happens to meet. These receptors are typically expressed on the postsynaptic membrane, the recipient neuron, whereas the release of the transmitter is from the presynaptic neuron. Neurotransmitters can act to excite or inhibit postsynaptic neurons, or induce other changes to their metabolism. Specifically, neurotransmitters are released by the axon's terminal. The binding of a neurotransmitter to a receptor causes a nearby ion channel to open. This causes an influx or efflux of a specific type of ion (charged particle), which in turn causes the electrical properties of the nearby neuronal membrane to change. Receptors are typically located on dendrites.

There are two types of receptors: *ionotropic* and *metabotropic*. When a neurotransmitter binds to an ionotropic receptor, it opens a specific ion channel. When a neurotransmitter binds to metabotropic receptor, it triggers a series of complex process in the neuron, which affect intracellular signaling and can ultimately lead to the opening of an ion channel. Ion channels that change their state in response to binding of a neurotransmitter are called ligand-gated (ligand being a collective term for any chemical that binds with specificity to the binding site of a receptor). The binding of a neurotransmitter causes an opening of an ion channel leading to depolarization of the membrane potential and has an excitatory effect. The binding of a transmitter that causes the opening of an ion channel that leads to hyperpolarization of the membrane is said to have an inhibitory effect.

This process of signaling by synaptic transmission must be terminated once the signal has been received to avoid continuous activation of the recipient neuron. The neurotransmitter acetylcholine (ACh) is broken down in the synapse by the enzyme acetylcholine esterase (AChE). All the other neurotransmitters are inactivated by reuptake processes. This involves the neurotransmitter attaching to a specialized transporter molecule, which is then incorporated into the presynaptic neuron. Drugs that block the actions of these transporters cause the levels of a transmitter to build up in the synapse and so potentiate the effects mediated by the transmitter. Once a neurotransmitter has been taken back up into the axon, it is packaged into vesicles and shunted towards the axon terminals ready to be released again.

The monoamines: dopamine, noradrenalin, and 5-hydroxytryptamine (5-HT) (serotonin) are three common neurotransmitters found in the brain. These neurotransmitters play striking roles in many aspects of emotional and motivated behaviors. Most of the monoaminergic neurons have cell bodies that are found in relatively small nuclei within the brainstem. The cell bodies of the 5-HT neurons lie in the dorsal raphe nucleus whereas those of the noradrenalin neurons lie in the locus coeruleus. Both sets of neurons give rise to axons that run through the base of the forebrain before branching to produce an enormous number of collaterals, which then terminate in most areas of the cerebral cortex and much of the limbic system. The cell bodies of the dopaminergic neurons lie in the substantia nigra and nearby VTA. The dopamine neurons in the substantia nigra, or more accurately the substantia nigra pars compacta, give rise to axons that run through the base of the forebrain as part of the medial forebrain bundle to terminate in the dorsal striatum. It is these neurons that degenerate in Parkinson's disease. The dopamine neurons whose cell bodies lie in the VTA have axons that also run in the medial forebrain bundle. These neurons, however, innervate the ventral portion of the striatum, known as the nucleus accumbens, the hippocampus, the amygdala, the prefrontal cortex, and the cingulate cortex.

Monoamine neurons have some additional regulatory mechanisms which control how efficiently this recycling process works. When the levels of monoamines rise, the excess is broken down within the terminal by a group of enzymes called monoamine oxidases (MAO). A class of antidepressants, which block the actions of MAO are referred to as MAOIs or monoamine oxidase inhibitors. An additional enzyme, Catechol-O-methyltransferase (COMT), breaks down Levodopa (L-dopa), the precursor of dopamine, when levels are high. COMT inhibitors are used in the treatment of Parkinson's disease. Genes that are involved in the production of MAO and COMPT enzymes have been suggested to increase susceptibility to mental health conditions, while the MAO-A (a variant of MAO) has been implicated in antisocial behavior (see Box 2.5).

Box 2.5 MAO-A – The Warrior Gene

The levels of monoamine neurotransmission are regulated in part by enzymes that breakdown an excess of the transmitter within the presynaptic neuron. MAO enzymes are involved in this breakdown process. Inhibiting the action of these enzymes with MAO inhibitors has formed the basis of one pharmacological approach to the treatment of depression. MAOs exist in two types,

A and B, with the former exerting an action on dopamine, noradrenalin, and serotonin whereas the latter only acts on dopamine. The production of MAOs is governed by MAO genes. The MAO-A gene occurs in several forms or polymorphisms, each of which results in slightly different biochemical properties. Consequently, inheriting a particular MAO-A polymorphism can have a marked impact upon cerebral MAO functioning, and this can manifest itself in terms of unusual patterns of social behavior. Via such mechanisms, the MAO-A gene has been associated with aggressive, antisocial behavior and with CD. These relationships are, however, complex and influenced by epigenetic factors including stress, smoking, and alcohol (see Chapters 17, 18, 19, and 20).

A given neurotransmitter will bind with great specificity to receptors associated with that transmitter. However, most neurotransmitters are associated with different subtypes of receptor. For example, over 30 different subtypes of 5-hydroxytryptamine (5-HT, serotonin) receptor have been identified, each with its own set of binding properties (different affinities for different ligands) and own anatomical distribution. Similarly, there are said to be two families of dopamine receptors subtypes: D-1 and D-2. The configuration of the receptor dictates whether the neurotransmitter acts as an inhibitory transmitter, or an excitatory one. Dopamine typically acts as an inhibitory neurotransmitter but, rather confusingly, can act as an excitatory one at some D-1 receptors. We will now briefly examine these different types of neurotransmitters.

Glutamate   The most common excitatory transmitter in the human brain is glutamate. It is used in all cortical projection neurons and in all the sensory systems. It is thought that every neuron in the brain has a glutamate synapse on it. Glutamate plays a key role in memory formation and learning. Some drugs that block the activation of glutamate are used as recreational drugs, like ketamine. Ketamine causes dissociation experiences, similar to psychosis. It should be noted, however, that ketamine has a complex pharmacological profile and binds with high affinity to several receptor systems including those for opiates and monoamines. Recent trials have tested the potential use of drugs that modify glutamate function in the treatment of various psychiatric and neurological conditions. Glutamate typically leads to depolarization of the membrane after binding to a variety of ionotropic glutamate receptors and hence is considered to be an excitatory transmitter. Conversely, gamma-aminobutyric acid (GABA) is said to be an inhibitory transmitter. Glutamate and GABA are the two most ubiquitous neurotransmitters in the human brain and it is argued that all neurons within the mammalian central nervous system will express receptors for both transmitters.

GABA (gamma-aminobutyric acid)   This is the most common inhibitory neurotransmitter in the mammalian nervous system. GABA can act at GABA-A receptors. These are exceptionally complex receptors in which a central chloride ion channel is surrounded by several binding sites, one of which is for GABA itself. The other binding sites are for ligands, which include alcohol and barbiturates, some steroids, and benzodiazepines. The binding of ligands to these sites exerts a synergistic action on GABA.

Benzondiazepines are accordingly said to be indirect GABA agonists. Boosting GABA mediated neurotransmission with drugs, such as valium (a frequently prescribed benzodiazepine) or alcohol, in limbic structures can induce anti-anxiety effects.

Dopamine Released in response to reward stimuli and believed to be a generic signal for reward in the brain. Dopamine involves initiating an approach behavior to obtain a desired (rewarding) stimulus, and is involved in the hedonic and pleasure feeling obtained from rewarding stimuli. Although, the desire for stimulus, and the pleasure gained from it, are assumed to be mediated by different systems. Stimulants, such as cocaine, amphetamines, and Methylphenidate (Ritalin), increase the levels of dopamine in the brain by blocking the dopamine transporter, leading to increased synaptic concentrations of the transmitter. It is assumed that at the addiction stage these drugs affect the desire to obtain a drug more than the pleasure obtained from it.

It is hypothesized that the positive symptoms (hallucinations and delusions) of schizophrenia result from over-activation of subtypes of the family of D-2 dopamine receptors. This conclusion has been derived from the observations of the effects of dopaminergic drugs and from postmortem studies, which have sometimes revealed an increase in the number of D-2 receptors in the striatum of some patients who had suffered from schizophrenia. Alterations in dopamine transmission are also assumed to underlie some of the critical aspects of addictive behaviors. Here the critical population of dopamine neurons involved are thought to lie in the VTA and project to the nucleus accumbens. The dopamine system also innervates areas of the prefrontal cortex, the cingulate cortex and the amygdala, and the hippocampus. Disordered dopamine transmission in these systems has been speculatively linked with ADHD. It is hypothesized that dopamine is involved in decision making through action selection.

Serotonin This is produced by neurons whose cell bodies lie in the dorsal raphe nucleus, which lies in the brainstem (hindbrain). These neurons send projections to diverse targets including much of the forebrain. Serotonin plays a pivotal role in a vast number of behaviors and physiological functions, perhaps reflecting the complexity and variety of its receptor subtypes. It plays marked roles in the control of appetite and in organizing social behaviors. For example, social rank in dominance hierarchies in primates is reflected in serotonin levels. In humans, serotonin levels are assumed to be related to aggressive tendencies and to mood. Although different types of antidepressant medication can vary considerably in their pharmacological mode of action most nonetheless boost the cerebral levels of 5-HT. Some 5-HT agonists are used as recreational drugs. These include lysergic acid diethylamide (LSD) and methylenedioxymethamphetamine (ecstasy).

The neuropeptides: oxytocin and vasopressin Other types of neurotransmitter include the neuropeptides. These compounds can also function as hormones. As such they are released into the systemic blood supply and can act by binding to receptors expressed by a variety of distant target organs. The same chemicals can also be released by neurons within the brain where they act as neurotransmitters. Two neuropeptides that may be of specific interest, in a forensic context, are oxytocin and vasopressin. These neuropeptides are believed to be involved in social bonding and parenting behavior. Oxytocin and vasopressin are normally thought of as being released from neurons in the posterior pituitary. These peptides, which have very similar chemical structures, are made in the hypothalamic neurons, the axons of which run down to the pituitary where they are released into the blood stream from specialized nerve endings. Oxytocin plays a role in breast-feeding and uterine contractions (as a hormone) while vasopressin is concerned with water and salt regulation. Both peptides can also be released from dendrites directly into the brain. They are implicated in facilitating specific acts of social behavior including the promotion of social bonding, the formation of social attachments, particularly with in-group members, maternal aggression, and mate guarding. Oxytocin has been referred to in the popular media as the "love" hormone.

Methods to Examine the Brain's Structure and Activity

The function of brain systems has been studied using neuropsychological and neuroimaging methods. Neuropsychology can be used to infer a causal relation between a brain area and a function, thus providing a definitive answer that the normal function of a given region is necessary for carrying out the process in question and produces a specific behavior. Neuroimaging techniques, on the other hand, are based on correlation analysis. Hence, they can only conclude that region has been activated during a task while the question of whether its function is necessary for the completion of the task cannot be answered. In the following subsections, we will briefly look at research that has examined the functions of the brain systems described in this section.

Examining the effects of lesions on an individual's neuropsychology

Neuropsychology assesses the impact of brain lesion on behavior. Brain lesions refer to damage to the structure of the brain and are typically identified using neuroimaging methods. The underlying assumption is that change of behavior following damage to a specific brain region is evidence that this brain region supports this behavior. Damage can be developmental, acquired (stroke, tumor, accident), degenerative, or virtual (experimentally induced). We will now examine each of these.

Developmental lesions   Also known as congenital brain lesions, developmental lesions are present at birth. They can be caused by a genetic condition, or abnormal conditions during pregnancy. One particular case, with relevance to the forensic field, is SM (reported by Adolphs, Tranel, Damásio, & Damásio, 1994). SM suffered from the genetic condition Urbach–Wiethe disease and, among other pathological problems, SM's bilateral amygdalae structures never developed. Many ideas and hypotheses regarding the function of the human amygdala have emerged following the work with SM, including, for example, linking amygdala function to fear perception and experience. Alcohol fetal spectrum disorder (related to impaired cognitive control following consumption of alcohol by the mother during pregnancy), and autism are examples of developmental disorder, though in these cases the lesion to the structure of the brain is typically not obvious to the naked eye.

Acquired lesion   An acquired lesion is a condition in which damage occurs in the brain region after birth. It usually has a clear onset and is marked by a distinct change in behavior. The damage, often associated with neural death, can be caused by stroke, tumor, or accident. In animal research, lesions are experimentally induced. A famous neuropsychological case in the context of forensic psychology is that of Phineas Gage. In brief, as a product of a workplace accident (see Chapter 1 for more detail here), Gage acquired a lesion to the ventral medial prefrontal cortex (vmPFC). Following this lesion, he started displaying impulsive, aggressive and antisocial behaviors. This case is used to infer the importance of the vmPFC to the regulation of behaviors.

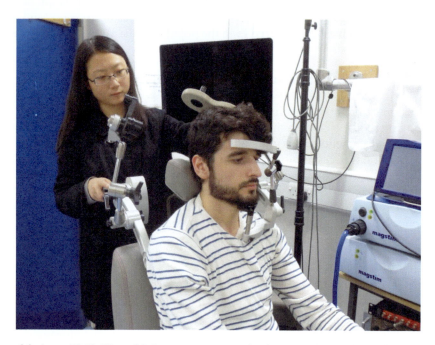

Virtual lesions: TMS *Virtual lesions are an approach where experimental procedures induce a temporary change in the functioning of a brain region of healthy humans. In a transcranial magnetic stimulation (TMS) procedure a strong magnetic pulse is transmitted to the brain, through a figure of eight shaped coil that is placed above the area of interest. This magnetic pulse causes the neurons to be fired. This artificially induced activation prevents the region from participating in any other processing. The timing of the TMS effect on the region function depends on the duration and frequency of the delivery of the magnetic pulses. TMS is also used in medical context, for example, to treat depression.*
Source: Scanner Source @ BUIC UoB.

Degenerative brain damage Associated with various types of dementia, degenerative brain damage reflects an ongoing deterioration of brain cells. While dementia is most often associated with memory loss following Alzheimer's disease to the hippocampus, other types of dementia, such as temporal-frontal dementia, can result in personality changes, including changes to the way emotions are regulated and triggered.

Virtual lesions An approach where experimental procedures induce a temporary change in the functioning of a brain region of healthy humans. Two methods are commonly used: transcranial magnetic stimulation (TMS), and transcranial direct current stimulation (tDCS). Both methods typically affect the function of cortical regions close to the surface and skull of the brain. In a TMS procedure a strong magnetic pulse is transmitted to the brain, through a figure of eight shaped coil that is placed above the area of interest. This magnetic pulse causes the neurons to be fired. This artificially induced activation prevents the region from participating in any other processing. The timing of the TMS effect on the region function depends on the duration and frequency of the delivery of the magnetic pulses. TMS is also used in medical context, for example, to treat depression. In a tDCS procedure a mild electrical current (1–2 mA) is delivered to the brain. It is transmitted using two electrodes that are placed on the scalp. The placement of these affects the way the current will flow through the brain. The amplitude of the current used in these procedures is too weak to cause the neurons to be active; but it changes the electrical field around the neuron, making it likely to become active. It is assumed that the negative charged electrode (cathodal) can facilitate task-related neural activity, while the positive charged electrode (anodal) inhibits it.

Temporary interference with neural activity has also been achieved using intracranial electrical stimulation, in both animals and humans. These procedures are invasive, as they require the electrodes to be in direct contact with the neurons and hence the removal of parts of the skull. The neurons are directly activated using an electrical current and the impact on behavior is recorded. In humans, this procedure can be done as part of medical treatment. For example, intracranial stimulation can be performed during a brain operation to remove a tumor, and following the permanent implantation of a deep brain stimulator when treating conditions such as Parkinson's disease.

Neuroimaging

Impressive technological advantages in the past decades have enabled us to apply imaging methods to measure the function of the brain. Neuroimaging methods do not alter the function of the brain, but simply measure it under different conditions. Neuroimaging methods can be divided into those based on metabolic processes, measuring the concentration of certain molecules in the brain (magnetic resonance imaging functional near-infrared spectroscopy, positron emission tomography, single positron emission computed tomography) and those that measure signals related to the electrical current produced by the neurons (electroencephalography and magnetoencephalography). We will now briefly examine these techniques.

Magnetic resonance imaging (MRI) This is a non-invasive method that utilizes the natural magnetic property of molecules. One crucial component of MRI is that the initial strength of the magnetic field is known. The tube of the scanner generates the magnetic field. In most human scanners participants lie on their back and are placed in the middle of the tube. MRI is mostly used to measure the responses of water molecules to changes in the magnetic field. The response of the molecules to these changes depends on their immediate surrounding and chemical environment. For example, molecules will react differently if they are within dense tissue or within fluid. Molecules would also react differently in the presence of oxygenated and deoxygenated blood. The strengths of the responses are typically coded with brighter colors indicating a stronger signal. It is important to note that an MRI provides a relative signal, meaning the absolute value of signal strength is meaningless as this depends on many technical, physical, and biological factors related to each scan. Most often the brain images are normalized (digitally transformed to a common standard space – e.g., to have the same shape, size, and orientation) to enable group comparisons. MRI can be set up to measure different properties of the underlying tissue and can be used to measure structural (the hardware) of the brain function (the brain's software).

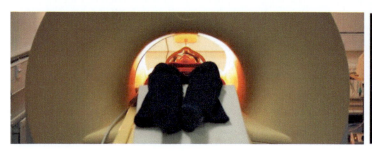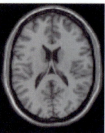

MRI scanner *Magnetic Resonance Imaging (MRI) is a non-invasive method that utilizes the natural magnetic property of molecules. MRI scanner can be used to image the structural properties of the brain (e.g. hardware) and the functional properties of the brain (software). The image on the right is an example of a structural MR image from a healthy participant, a T1-weighted image. T1-weighted image provide a relative good contrast between grey and white matter. From the outside, the bright surface is the signal arising from the fat tissue around the head. Underneath it in black is the skull (MRI typically image tissues that contain water, hence bones cannot be imaged using MRI). The thin dark grey folded line around the brain is the grey matter, the cortical sheet. Underneath it is the white matter, the fibers and axons that connect between different grey matter regions. In the middle the black chamber like structure are the ventricles filled with cerebral blood fluid (CSF). To achieve optimal protection, the brain floats in the CSF and is protected by the skull.*

Source: Scanner Source @ BUIC UoB; T1 image source @ canonical single subject template SPM fil.ucl.ac.uk.

Structural MRI There are multiple structural measures that can be obtained with MRI, the most commonly used one being T1-weighted images. In this sequence, grey matter appears darker than white matter and CSF is darker then grey matter. Thus, in T1-weighted image, water in CSF transmits a weaker signal than that in grey matter, with the strongest signal being transmitted by water in white matter. Hence, it is often used to assess the volume of the grey matter and its thickness. One common analysis is called voxel-based morphometry (VBM) where the grey matter integrity at each location in the brain is compared between groups of participants to identify structural differences.

Diffusion tensor imaging (DTI) This is a method for measuring the property of white matter integrity. DTI measures the diffusion pattern of water. In white matter, the myelinated fatty tissue restricts the diffusion direction. As every axon in white matter is surrounded by myelinated tissue, DTI provides a measure of underlying structural connectivity, or the development of structural connectivity. DTI has been used to study differences between groups in their structural connectivity architecture.

Functional MRI (fMRI) Primarily, fMRI measures the responses within grey matter regions. Hence, it is used to measure function related activation and functional connections between regions. Functional mapping of activation is typically inferred based on an experimental manipulation. Participants are asked to perform a task (or are presented with different stimuli) while being scanned. A comparison between conditions highlights changes in signal amplitude in relation to the task. For example, when participants view emotionally negative (relative to neutral) pictures, the amygdala shows an increase in signal amplitude. Pseudo coloring (e.g., a red–yellow gradient) is used to indicate reliability of the signal change in specific comparisons. The most common method here is called echo planner imaging (EPI), which is a relatively fast acquisition method that images the whole brain in two to three seconds. This enables the acquisition of multiple images of the brain, which adds a time dimension to the measurement. The EPI signal is sensitive to the level of oxygen in the blood as deoxygenated blood has different magnetic properties from that of oxygenated blood. EPI measures the BOLD (blood oxygenated level dependent) contrast – the hemodynamic response. As neural activity is tightly linked to the level of oxygen in the blood, this can be used as a proxy for neural activity (Logothetis, 2003). The time resolution of fMRI is assumed to be in the order of seconds, while the spatial resolution is in the order of millimeters.

Connectivity analysis Recent thinking suggests understanding the function of the brain at the "network level" rather than as a collection of anatomical localized distinct functions. This research applies functional connectivity analysis to the data. Connectivity analysis can be measured in the context of spontaneous activation or during a task. In this case, participants are not given any task and are asked to rest and not to think of anything specifically. This enables the measurement of spontaneous changes in activation. The analysis focuses on correlations between regions during these spontaneous activations. It is assumed that correlations of the time course between regions reflect intrinsic connection, since spontaneous increase/decrease activation of one region is coupled with increase/decrease activation in another. The most famous network is called the default mode network. The default mode network includes the anterior and posterior midline structures and the bilateral temporal-parietal junction. This network is also typically active in resting periods between tasks and has been linked to processing of information related to the self. In the context of a task, researchers are interested to test whether the connection pattern between regions changes as a function of task requirement, a phenomenon known as effective connectivity. For example, when participants are required to regulate their emotions, the connectivity pattern between the prefrontal cortex and the amygdala changes.

Functional near-infrared spectroscopy (fNIRS) This measures light absorption. In the context of neuroscience, it measures the redness of the blood. The blood color is affected by the amount of oxygen in it. Hence, fNIRS relies on similar assumptions to the fMRI that link changes in blood to changes in neural activation. It requires an LED that emits light and light detectors, to measure the reflection of the light spectrum from the surface. Its advantages are that it is relatively cheap; participants can be mobile while data is recorded; and it has slightly better temporal resolution, relative to fMRI, although it has a poor spatial resolution, and has limited brain coverage.

Positron emission tomography (PET) Gamma rays emitted from a radioactive tracer are measured by PET. Participants are injected with a radioactive tracer. The distribution and concentration of these tracer molecules are measured. It is assumed that high concentrations of the tracer in each area are linked to an activation of the region from the time of injection until the time of measurement (which is usually a couple of minutes). The most common tracers used in PET are linked to glucose (FDG-PET) and oxygen (Oxygen-15), although recent developments include tracers that are specific to individual neurotransmitters, including dopamine and serotonin. In contrast to MRI, PET has a clear biological meaning. Therefore, PET can be used to measure baseline responses, as well as experimental induced responses. PET has a time resolution in the order of minutes, and spatial resolution in the order of millimeters, although it is poorer than MRI.

Single positron emission computed tomography (SPECT) This is a lot less costly than PET. Like PET, SPECT measures the emission of gamma rays from a tracer that is injected into the blood. While the tracers used by PET are observed in the tissue, a SPECT tracer typically stays in the blood. Hence, SPECT provides a measure of blood flow. Like fMRI, the interpretation of brain function by fNIRS and PET relies on the link between blood flow and neural activity. SPECT's tracer has a half-life of around six hours, meaning it captures blood flow changes in the past six hours. This is lower time resolution than PET imaging, which typically produces radioactive tracers in the order of minutes.

Electroencephalography (EEG) With EEG, electrodes are placed on the surface of the scalp (or sometimes on the surface of the cortex in intracranial-EEG) to measure electrical activity or voltage change. Changes in electrical activity can serve as a direct measure of neural responses. EEG readings reflect the sum of voltage changes in a large population of neurons. Like the metabolic imaging methods, EEG is assumed to primarily reflect activity of the grey matter, and even more specifically the activity within the dendrites of pyramidal neurons. As the electrical signal relies on the conductivity of the tissue, it primarily measures signals that are close to the surface. Though given the complex structure of the cortical sheet, the localization of the source of any scalp recorded EEG signal is computationally challenging. EEG, therefore has an excellent temporal resolution, in the order of milliseconds (ms), but poor spatial resolution in the order of centimeters.

The EEG signal is typically analyzed in two ways: as an event-related potential (ERP) or at the frequency domain, oscillation analysis. ERPs reflect the amplitude change of electrical voltage relative to a stimulus onset. The data look like a wave, with positive and negative peaks. The polarity of the peaks depends on the spatial relations between the electrode and the activated neurons. The wave peaks are labeled based on their properties. For example, the N170, is a negative wave that peaks at around 170ms after a stimulus onset. It is typically recorded in electrodes that are placed above the temporal cortex (behind the ear). The N170 is larger when participants are presented with facial stimuli, relative to non-facial stimuli (Bentin, Allison, Puce, Perez, & McCarthy, 1996). It is suggested that it primarily responds to the eyes or the face. The P300 is a wide positive wave that occurs between 250–500ms. It is assumed to reflect the classification and evaluation of the input and other high order cognitive processes. It has been found to be weaker in individuals who exhibit antisocial behaviors (Gao & Raine, 2009). Oscillation analysis identifies repeated rhythms of voltage changes in the EEG signal. Neural activity oscillates in different frequencies. These frequencies have been associated with different brain states (e.g., alert, awake, asleep). There is a growing interest in understanding the cognitive function and impact of brain oscillation. For

Electroencephalography (EEG) uses electrodes placed on the surface of the scalp to measure electrical activity or voltage change. Changes in electrical activity can serve as a direct measure of neural responses. EEG readings reflect the sum of voltage changes in a large population of neurons. EEG is assumed to primarily reflect activity of the grey matter, and even more specifically the activity within the dendrites of pyramidal neurons. Recording can be made in parallel to participants engaging in a task.

Source: Scanner Source © BUIC UoB.

example, alpha frequencies are 10Hz oscillations, meaning that a network of neurons would exhibit ten peaks of activation per second. Alpha is typically observed when participants are awake but at rest. Frontal alpha asymmetry, the difference in alpha amplitude over the left and right frontal cortex, is used as a marker for mood and approach-avoidance related processing (Harmon-Jones, Gable, & Peterson, 2010).

Magnetoencephalography (MEG) An expensive variant of EEG is MEG. It measures changes in magnetic field, which are coupled to changes in the electrical field as any electrical current produces a magnetic field. In contrast to EEG, magnetic fields are not dependent upon the conductivity of the tissue, which makes the localization of the signal source slightly easier. Like EEG, MEG signal is assumed to reflect the activity of the pyramidal neurons in the cortical sheet. The MEG signal is analyzed in the same way as an EEG signal, as an event-related analysis focuses on amplitude changes along time, or analysis of signal oscillations. It has an equivalent time resolution to EEG (which is in the order of milliseconds), and better spatial resolution then EEG.

Methods to examine activity in the peripheral nervous system

Given the complexity of the peripheral nervous system there are many ways its function can be measured. Here we provide only a partial list that have been used that have relevance to the forensic field.

Electromyography (MEP) Activation within the somatosensory system is measured using electromyography. Like EEG, electromyography is measured using electrodes that are placed on the skin surface. Changes in the electrical field can be detected following the transmission of electrical current by peripheral neurons to activate the muscles. Like EEG, electromyography is often analyzed in relation to a specific trigger, where it is referred to as a motor evoked potential (MEP). The eye-startle response is an example of an MEP that measures the response of the muscles involved in blinking. Startle is a reflexive defensive response to a sudden unexpected stimulus that is potentially threatening (like a puff of air or loud noise). Despite the reflex nature of the startle response, it is shown to be modulated by the emotional state of the observer (potentially through signals sent from the amygdala to the brainstem). Stronger and faster startle responses are recorded when the observer is in a negative emotional state.

Electrodermal/galvanic skin response (GSR) This process measures the electrodermal activity (skin conductance) of the skin. Perspiration initiated by the sympathetic component of the autonomic nervous system (fight or flight responses) increases this conductivity. It is measured using a small current that is passed between two electrodes placed on the skin surface, typically on the fingers or the arms. GSR measures the arousal levels of the body. In contrast to the eye-startle measure, it is not dependent on the emotional valence.

Heart rate The function of the heart is also tightly linked to the activation of the sympathetic and parasympathetic divisions of the autonomic nervous system. The sympathetic system increases the heart rate while the parasympathetic reduces it through dissociable mechanisms. Hence, increases in heart rate reflect increases in arousal levels. There are many ways of analyzing data from heart rate. Heart rate variability (HRV) has become a popular way of analyzing the function of the vagus nerve, a cranial nerve associated with the function of the parasympathetic system. It measures the variability of time between two heartbeats (beat-to-beat variability). Low HRV is a marker for poor physical and mental health. Introspective awareness is another frequently used task. This is often combined with measurement of heart rate. In this task participants' conscious awareness of their heart rate is compared with objective measures of this. Participants with a high level of anxiety tend to be more aware to their own heart rate.

Conclusions

The current chapter has presented a top–down view of neural functioning and the current approach in neuroscience research. We have attempted to highlight relevant aspects of neuroscience to forensic and offending behavior. More detailed discussion is provided in the following chapters of this book. Despite being active neuroscientist researchers ourselves, we have learned a lot in the process of writing the chapter. The amount of knowledge and progress gained in understanding the brain is very impressive. This reflects the work of many people across the globe who dedicate the most powerful and efficient computing system invented (i.e., their brains) to try and decipher its mysteries. While we have progressed a long way, there are still many questions and unknowns that need to be resolved. We hope that by gaining a better understanding of the human brain, we can find ways of improving the wellbeing and health of all humans. These issues will be discussed in other chapters in this book (in particular Part V).

Recommended Reading

A Clockwork Orange (directed by Stanley Kubrick). *This is a classic 1970s movie which shows an example of the implementation of classical conditioning to "cure" the protagonist – Alex. Alex exhibits extreme sadistic and psychopathic behavior. Alex is made to watch scenes of violence in movies while being inflicted with a burning sensation to the eyes (by preventing him to blink). In other words, he is being classically conditioned to associate an aversive experience with violent acts.*

Damásio, A. (1994). *Descartes' error: Emotion, reason, and the human brain.* London: Random House Books. *This book is in part a critique of Descartes' mind–body dualism question. Damásio argues that Descartes' "error" was the dualist separation of mind and body (i.e., rationality versus emotion).*

Kandel, E. R., Schwartz, J. H., Jessell, T. M., Siegelbaum, A. A., & Hudspeth, A. J. (2012). *Principles of neural science* (5th ed.). New York: McGraw-Hills Companies. *An excellent primer of the area.*

Martin, P., & Bateson, P. (2007). *Measuring behavior: An introductory guide* (3rd ed.). Cambridge: Cambridge University Press. *This book acts as a guide to the principles and methods of quantitative studies of behavior, with an emphasis on techniques of observation, recording and analysis.*

Mitchell, I. (2014). *Broken brains.* Basingstoke, UK: Palgrave Macmillan.

This is a good introduction to the brain, and what happens when things go wrong.

Pinker, S. (2003) *The blank slate: The modern denial of human nature.* London: Penguin Books. *A powerful description and defence of human nature.*

Plomin, R., DeFries, J. C., Knopik, V. S., & Neuderhiser, J. M. (2013). *Behavioral genetics, sixth edition.* New York: Worth Publishers. *This book introduces the field's underlying principles, recent advances and ongoing controversies.*

WiKiBooks, Cognitive psychology and cognitive neuroscience/behavioural and neuroscience methods. https://en.wikibooks.org/wiki/Cognitive_Psychology_and_Cognitive_Neuroscience/Behavioural_and_Neuroscience_Methods. *It does what is says in the title.*

References

Adolphs, R., Tranel, D., Damásio, H., & Damásio, A. (1994) Impaired recognition of emotion in facial expressions following bilateral damage to the human amygdala. *Nature, 372,* 669–672. doi:10.1038/372669a0.

Bentin, S., Allison, T., Puce, A., Perez, E., & McCarthy, G. (1996). Electrophysiological studies of face perception in humans. *Journal of Cognitive Neuroscience, 8,* 551–565. doi: 10.1162/jocn.1996.8.6.551.

Brodmann, K. (2006) *Brodmann's localization in the cerebral cortex: The principles of comparative localisation in the cerebral cortex based on cytoarchitectonics* (Garey, I. J. Trans.). The 3rd ed. of this work is published by permission of World Scientific Publishing Co Pte Ltd, Singapore. Retrieved from http://www.wordsscibooks.com/meds/sci/p151.html. The original English-language edition was published in the United Kingdom by Smith-Gordon Company Limited (London: 1994). (Original paper published in 1909).

Bruce, V., & Young, A. (1986). Understanding face recognition. *British Journal of Psychology, 77,* 305–327. 0.1111/j.2044-8295.1986.tb02199.x

Ekman, P., & Friesen, W. V. (1972). Hand movements. *Journal of Communication, 22*, 353–374.

Fixsen, D. L., Blase, K. A., Timbers, G. D., & Wolf, M. M. (2007). In search of program implementation: 792 replications of the teaching-family model. *The Behavior Analyst Today, 8*, 96–110. Available from: http://files.eric.ed.gov/fulltext/EJ800975.pdf

Gao, Y., & Raine, A. (2009). P3 event-related potentail impairments in antisocial and psychopathic individuals: A meta-analysis. *Biological Psychology, 82*, 199–210. doi:10.1016/j.biopsycho.2009.06.006.

Gillespie S. M., Rotshtein P., Wells, L. J., Beech, A. R., & Mitchell, I. J. (2015). Psychopathic traits are associated with reduced attention to the eyes of emotional faces among adult male non-offenders, 552. doi: 10.3389/fnhum.2015.00552. eCollection 2015.

Harmon-Jones, E., Gable, P. A., & Peterson, C. K. (2010). The role of asymmetric frontal cortical activity in emotion-related phenomena: A review and update. *Biological Psychology, 84*, 451–462. doi:10.1016/j.biopsycho.2009.08.010.

Haxby, J. V, Hoffman, E. A., & Gobbini, M. I. (2002). Human neural system for face recognition and social communication. *Biological Psychiatry, 51*, 59–67. doi: http://dx.doi.org/10.1016/S1364-6613(00)01482-0.

Lindquist, K. A., Wager, T. D., Kober, H., Bliss-Moreau, E., & Barrett, L. F. (2012). The brain basis of emotion: a meta-analytic review. *Behavioral and Brain Sciences, 35*, 121–143. doi: 10.1017/S0140525X11000446.

Logothetis, N. K. (2003). The underpinnings of the BOLD functional magnetic resonance imaging signal. *Journal of Neuroscience, 2*, 3963–3971. Retrieved from http://www.jneurosci.org/content/jneuro/23/10/3963.full.pdf

Pavlov, I. P. (1927/2010). Conditioned reflexes: An investigation of the physiological activity of the cerebral cortex. (Anrep, A. V. Trans). *Annals of Neurosciences, 17*(3), 136–141. Lecture series. Retrieved from http://doi.org/10.5214/ans.0972-7531.1017309.

Popper (1934/1959). *The logic of scientific discovery.* London: Hutchinson & Co.

Skinner, B. F. (1935). Two types of conditioned reflex and a pseudo type. *Journal of General Psychology, 12*, 66–77. Retrieved from http://doi.org/52, 281–302.

Wells, L. J., Gillespie, S. M., & Rotshtein, P. (2016). Identification of emotional facial expressions: Effects of expression, intensity, and sex on eye gaze. *PLoS One, 11*(12), e0168307. doi: 10.1371/journal.pone.0168307. eCollection 2016.

Part II
General Neuroscience Research

3
The Neurobiology of Aggressive Behavior

Jens Foell and Christopher J. Patrick

> **Key points**
> - Three types of questions are asked in aggression behavior research:
>   1. What is the etiology or origin of the behavior (e.g., genetic, environmental, or a combination of the two)?
>   2. Are there biomarkers that reliably predict aggressive behavior?
>   3. What underlying neurocognitive mechanisms are associated with aggressive and violent behavior?
> - Both twin and molecular genetic studies have been used to investigate the role of environmental and genetic influences on aggressive tendencies. These studies show a largely heritable common factor underlying a variety of aggression-related issues.
> - Aggression and violence committed by psychopathic individuals are associated with different biomarkers and processes than those committed by non-psychopathic individuals.
> - Non-psychopathic aggression is associated with hypo-arousal at rest, but overreactivity coupled with inability to downregulate it in response to stressful events. This suggests an abnormality in functioning of the sympathetic and parasympathetic nervous systems.
> - Non-psychopathic aggression is associated with failure to regulate emotions and behavioral responses.
> - Non-psychopathic aggression or impulsive aggression is linked with impaired inhibitory control, which is associated with aberrant electroencephalogram (EEG) response to target stimuli in a performance task.
> - Violent behavior is associated with abnormal function, structure, and connections of the medial temporal (amygdala) and frontal cortex network.
> - The triarchic model of psychopathy hypothesizes three core components to this psychiatric condition: disinhibition, meanness, and boldness. This model can be used as a general framework for describing psychopathic and antisocial behavior, including aggressive tendencies.

- Empirical findings presented are based on group averages and statistical analyses. Hence any inferences to the individual level should be made with caution, especially with regards to biomarkers for violence.

Terminology Explained

The **autonomic nervous system (ANS)**, also known as the involuntary nervous system, controls visceral functions (such as heart rate, digestion, respiration, salivation, and sexual arousal) below the level of conscious awareness. It can be parsed into the subdivisions of parasympathetic and sympathetic nervous systems and its functioning has been connected to a variety of medical and psychological symptoms.

Cyberball is a virtual ball-tossing game, ostensibly for several players simultaneously, which is programmed to exclude the player, inducing feelings of ostracism, social exclusion, and rejection. Its application in the context of physiological or neuroimaging studies combines methods from social psychology and psychophysiology.

Diffusion tensor imaging (DTI) uses a magnetic resonance imaging (MRI) magnet to quantify the movement of water molecules inside the brain within a specified time interval. Since molecular diffusion is restricted by the density of surrounding tissue, information about the preferred direction of diffusion provides for reconstruction of a three-dimensional image of the neural architecture, which in turn can be used to gauge the level of interconnectivity between specific brain areas.

Electroencephalography (EEG) entails recording of electrical activity from electrodes positioned over the scalp that transmit signals reflecting summated activity from populations of similarly-oriented neurons within the brain. This allows for real-time assessment of cortical activity at rest or during performance of tasks for purposes of scientific hypothesis testing or applied clinical assessment.

An **event-related potential (ERP)** is an average EEG signal time-locked to the occurrence of a discrete event, such as a presented stimulus or an emitted response, across multiple trials. The high temporal resolution of ERP response variables provides for the precise tracking of perceptual and cognitive processes in relation to psychologically significant events.

Externalizing is the prominently heritable factor reflecting variance in common among tendencies toward antisocial-aggressive, substance-related problems, and impulsive personality traits. Also termed disinhibition, this common factor has reliable neural (ERP) correlates and can be viewed as a brain-based dispositional liability to impulse-related problems including angry/reactive aggression (Krueger et al., 2002; Yancey, Venables, Hicks, & Patrick, 2013).

Functional magnetic resonance imaging (fMRI) quantifies activity changes within circumscribed areas of the brain through registration of regional changes in blood oxygenation of neural tissue. Depending on the experimental paradigm and the specific brain areas of interest, fMRI results can provide for precise inferences about structures that are activated or de-activated in relation to the occurrence of certain stimuli, events, emotions, cognitions, or actions.

Magnetoencephalography (MEG) provides an alternative method to EEG for recording postsynaptic potentials of cortical neurons. While both methods yield fine-grained temporal information about neuroelectrical activity, the signal associated with EEG is presumed to arise mainly from extracellular ionic currents (caused by dendritic electrical activation), whereas MEG signals reflect intracellular ionic currents. The two methods complement one another and can be combined to produce maximally informative data.

Magnetic resonance imaging (MRI) utilizes the basic physical properties of atomic nuclei in the brain or body to distinguish tissue of differing types, thereby producing high-resolution images of discriminable structures in a completely non-invasive manner. A structural MRI scan can provide information about the thickness, density, and interconnections of differing brain areas.

Neuroimaging is a collective term encompassing various existing methods for imaging the structure, function, or pharmacology of the brain – including techniques of MRI/fMRI, EEG, MEG, and positron emission tomography (PET) highlighted in the current chapter. Other available methods produce brain images using X-rays (computed axial tomography (CT)), infrared light (diffuse optical imaging (DOI)), or radioactive tracer substances (single-photon emission computed tomography (SPECT)).

Neurotransmitters are endogenous chemicals of the brain that are ejected from neuronal axons and received by postsynaptic receptors. Neurotransmitters can act to excite or inhibit postsynaptic neurons, or induce other changes to their metabolism. Thus, while the most obvious indicant of neuronal activity is electromagnetic change, communication between neurons happens on a chemical level as well.

Oddball task is an experimental procedure in which the participant is asked to respond (e.g., push a button) upon the occurrence of a target stimulus. The target stimuli appear as rare events among an ongoing sequence of frequently occurring non-target stimuli that require no response. The oddball task has been used extensively to investigate effects of stimulus meaningfulness/salience and novelty on information processing.

P300 is an ERP waveform component that has been connected to information processing and decision making. Variants of the P300 response have been shown to be related to attention, orienting, cognitive workload, and stimulus novelty.

Positron emission tomography (PET) provides a three-dimensional image of functional processes in the brain, or other parts of the body. It is produced by detecting gamma ray (positron) emissions from an injected radioisotope. In brain PET imaging, it is assumed that more active regions demand higher blood flow, thereby attracting more tracer molecules and producing a stronger gamma ray signal.

Introduction

Aggressive behavior, in the sense of behavior that is hostile and/or involves some type of physical attack, has been widely observed in both humans and animals. In the context of the role of competition in the evolution of humans and animals, aggression can be understood to be an important form of social interaction within and across species, alongside other social phenomena such as predation, parasitism, and mutualism (Grether et al., 2013). The ubiquity of aggressive behavior in the animal kingdom and its evolutionary relevance suggest strong biological and physiological foundations to such behavior in humans that warrant systematic investigation.

Recent decades have witnessed an explosion of research applying neuroimaging, psychophysiology, genetics, and other biological methods to the study of aggression in humans. Insights gained from work of this kind, in turn, have led to new and refined conceptions of psychological dispositions contributing to aggressive tendencies and behavior disorders marked by persistent aggression. The current chapter reviews experimental findings in the context of prominent theoretical models in order to provide a perspective on how aggressive behavior can be understood in neurobiological terms. In addition to reviewing relevant data and theories, we also provide some discussion of the practical and ethical implications of biologically-oriented research on aggression.

Alternative Approaches to Neurobiological Investigation of Aggressive Behavior

Diverse methods, ranging from self-report and clinical interviewing to behavioral observation to psychophysiology, neuroimaging, and behavioral/molecular genetics, have been used to investigate aggressive behavior. These various methods can be categorized according to the types of questions that each is best suited to addressing. Some methods are particularly useful for clarifying sources of **etiological** influence, others for establishing predictive indicators (*markers*), and some for specifying **processes** of relevance to aggressive behavior.

Etiological approaches seek to clarify causal determinants, in terms of genetic and environmental influences contributing to the occurrence of aggressive behavior. One such approach entails investigating the degree of resemblance (concordance) for aggression and aggression-related dispositions in twins. By comparing concordances for a behavioral tendency (phenotype) in identical versus fraternal (i.e., monozygotic versus dizygotic) twins, or for twins raised in the same versus different families, it is possible to estimate the relative contributions of genetic and environmental influences to the phenotype. In standard twin concordance analyses, an additive genetic (A) term is computed that is presumed to reflect the aggregate influence of multiple relevant genes, along with C and E terms reflecting, respectively, shared environmental influences (i.e., experiences common to offspring within a family, such as parental rearing style, quality of nutrition, etc.) and nonshared environmental influences (i.e., experiences unique to individuals, such as injury or illness, random trauma, etc., along with unsystematic variance attributable to measurement error). Beyond this, advanced twin modeling techniques can be used to quantify more complex interactions between genetic and environmental influences in determining phenotypic outcomes. For example, environmental stressors of certain types have been shown to exert an epigenetic influence on behavior, effectively activating genes for a phenotypic outcome that would otherwise remain unexpressed (e.g., Caspi et al., 2002; Hunter & McEwen, 2013). Documented effects of this kind blur the line between genetic and environmental influences, complicating the task of specifying the etiological bases of target behavioral phenotypes (Kan, Ploeger, Raijmakers, Dolan, & van der Maas, 2010). However, the use of twin modeling approaches that accommodate the presence of linear or nonlinear moderator variables can provide important insights into gene–environment interactions that account for important aspects of behavioral outcomes (Purcell, 2002).

As an alternative to twin studies, the role of constitutional factors in behavioral outcomes can also be examined through molecular genetic studies. In this case, specific genes or gene sequences (or their interactions with environmental variables) identified via molecular quantification methods are evaluated in terms of their impact on behavioral dispositions or outcomes. While the genomes of any two humans differ in many millions of nucleotides (the building blocks of the genetic code), the advent of genome-wide association studies in recent years has led to a large number of findings relating to single- and multiple-gene influences on aggressive behavior (cf. Craig & Halton, 2009). Findings from studies of this type serve to highlight the complex interplay that can occur between genes, gene expression, and environmental influences, and have led to new and valuable insights into how genes can influence the function and structure of the brain as well as the observed behavior of individuals (Craig & Halton, 2009).

While the foregoing approaches mainly seek to specify average effects of genetic and environmental influences on aggressive tendencies (i.e., among people in general), **marker** studies seek to identify characteristics of individuals that predict greater versus lesser engagement in aggressive acts. Markers can be established at a variety of levels. The level most closely related to the genetic analyses described above is that of **neurotransmitters** – messenger molecules in the brain that transmit information between nerve cells. The level and degree of activity of these transmitters, as well as the frequency and distribution of specific neurotransmitter receptors, directly influence neuronal activation. The observation of the **firing behavior** of single neurons or neuron groups is the next higher level of investigation. The activation of neurons in specific areas of the brain has been related to many different behaviors, perceptions, and cognitions, and the fact that the firing patterns of individual neurons can alter the activity and even the structure of neighboring neurons (a process known as *neuroplasticity*; Buonomano & Merzenich, 1998) makes investigation at this level critically important, albeit complex. Single- and multi-cell recording provides one method for investigation at this level. The activation and structure of nerve clusters in the brain can also be investigated using neuroimaging methods of differing types.

Still another level of investigation is provided by **psychophysiological** or electrophysiological measures such as autonomic activity, muscle flexion, or scalp-recorded brain response. Established physiological markers of aggression include low resting heart rate level (Scarpa, Haden, & Tanaka, 2010) and reduced amplitude of event-related brain responses (Patrick et al., 2006; Venables, Patrick, Hall, & Bernat, 2011). Marker studies are of particular value because they provide empirical yardsticks for quantifying aggression proneness on an individual level. The precision of such yardsticks can be enhanced by aggregating physiological indicators of differing types to form composite markers of dispositional tendencies (Nelson, Patrick, & Bernat, 2011;

Patrick et al., 2013). Composite physiological markers could potentially serve as a basis for early identification of individuals at risk for becoming violent offenders, or for estimating the likelihood of continuing violent behavior in offenders being evaluated for treatment or release. Of course, as will be discussed, approaches like this pose important ethical issues.

In contrast with etiological and marker studies, process studies focus on how aggressive individuals differ from non-aggressive individuals in psychological processes associated with registration of stimulus events and performance of behavioral tasks. The aim is to understand deviations in cognitive and emotional processing of events and situations that contribute to aggressive modes of responding. Studies of this type entail online observation of behavior or real-time recording of physiological or metabolic changes in the context of laboratory procedures. Techniques for indexing online neural processing include neuroimaging methods such as magnetoencephalography (MEG), positron emission tomography (PET), and functional magnetic resonance imaging (fMRI), and brain electrophysiological methods of electroencephalography (EEG) and event-related potential (ERP) measurement. Each of these methods possesses certain advantages and disadvantages relative to others. A well-known example is the high spatial resolution of fMRI (able to determine the location of activation inside the brain at a resolution of millimeters) at the cost of low temporal resolution (due to reliance on a metabolic signal with a time course of several seconds), in direct contrast to EEG/ERP, which has sharp temporal resolution but poor spatial resolution. While strategies have been developed to compensate for these weaknesses (e.g., deconvolution analyses for fMRI, source modeling for EEG), combined use of the two methods – i.e., integration of localization information provided by fMRI with time course data provided by EEG – provides a particularly powerful approach to delineating brain activity relevant to psychological processes of interest.

Experimental Findings

Autonomic activity and reactivity

Low resting heart rate has been identified as one stable biological correlate of antisocial behavior, particularly in children and adolescents (Ortiz & Raine, 2004). This effect holds even after controlling for potential confounding variables such as gender, age, method of recording, recruitment source, and concurrent versus prospective nature of testing. Further, some studies have reported evidence for a prospective relationship between resting heart rate earlier in life and subsequent criminal offending (Nordstrom et al., 2011). However, findings for autonomic *reactivity* (i.e., responsiveness to phasic stimuli) have been mixed. A systematic meta-analysis of 95 studies suggests that, at least in children, conduct disorder (CD) problems may in fact be associated with *higher* heart rate reactivity to noxious or threatening stimuli (Lorber, 2004).

These contrasting results for tonic autonomic activity as compared to phasic reactivity suggest differing roles for sympathetic and parasympathetic nervous systems in antisocial behavior. Relevant to this, evidence has been reported for weaker parasympathetic regulation of heart rate activity by the vagus nerve in aggressive children and adolescents (Mezzacappa et al., 1997; Beauchaine, Katkin, Strassberg, & Snarr, 2001). The implication is that deficient top–down-regulation results in augmented autonomic reactivity to stressors or challenges. In conjunction with general under-arousal, as indicated by low resting heart rate, this enhanced responsivity to immediate stressors would be expected to lower the threshold for impulsive aggressive behavior (Beauchaine et al., 2001). Along related lines, Davidson, Putnam, & Larson (2000) hypothesized that violent behavior results from dysfunction of core affective-regulatory circuitry in frontal regions of the brain.

More broadly, weak vagal regulation has been implicated in anxious depressive conditions as well as impulsive aggressive behavior (El-Sheikh, Harger, & Whitson, 2001), with distinct branches of the vagus thought to be involved in differing regulatory deficits, leading to a polyvagal theory of psychopathology (Beauchaine, Gatzke-Kopp, & Mead, 2007). This theory acknowledges protective environmental factors (e.g., parents/guardians who are able to de-escalate arousal and apply consistent consequences for aggressive acts) and individual differences in sympathetic nervous system function as variables that can influence parasympathetic regulation of autonomic reactivity during development (see Box 3.1).

Box 3.1 Autonomic activity and relational aggression

Murray-Close (2011) tested 131 healthy women between the ages of 18 and 22 in a social exclusion experiment – the so-called cyberball paradigm (Williams, Cheung, & Choi, 2000) – in which participants are led to believe they are engaging with other players in an online virtual ball-throwing game; in actuality, the game is pre-programmed to exclude the participant from the game after a short period of time. This procedure has been shown to induce feelings of social rejection and physiological changes associated with the experience of rejection (Cacioppo et al., 2013; Seidel et al., 2013). Self-report and interview measures were also administered in the experiment to assess for levels of relational aggression and relational victimization in the context of current or recent romantic relationships, and hostile attributional biases for romantic provocations. During the experiment, skin conductance reactivity, resting heart rate, phasic heart rate response, and respiration were assessed. Results showed that physiological arousal measures were indeed associated with romantic relational aggression. However, the nature of this association was determined by the participant's level of relational victimization at the hands of romantic partners, as well as by the participant's hostile attributional biases. The findings indicate that exaggerated responsiveness of the autonomic nervous system (ANS) to social exclusion can contribute to aggressive behavior – but mainly in individuals exhibiting hostile attributional bias, perhaps arising in part from experiences of victimization.

Studies examining autonomic reactivity to stressors in adults with or without a history of violent behavior toward relationship partners have also yielded inconsistent results. Gottman et al. (1995) sought to account for this inconsistency by positing two distinct subtypes of male perpetrators of intimate partner violence. Type 1 batterers according to these authors score higher in antisocial traits and display higher levels of hostility and contemptuousness both toward relationship partners and people in general, whereas Type 2 batterers score higher in interpersonal dependency. As a function of the differing characteristics, Type 1 batterers are expected to show lower heart rate reactivity in the context of adversarial marital interactions, whereas Type 2 perpetrators are expected to show enhanced heart rate reactivity (see Box 3.2). While this subtype conception has been subjected to serious criticism (e.g., Babcock, Green, Webb, & Graham, 2004), it has served to connect a psychophysiological research perspective on aggression to the applied clinical domain, where heterogeneity among perpetrators of intimate partner violence has also been postulated (e.g., Walsh et al., 2010). For example, there is evidence that women engage in perpetration of some but not all types of intimate partner violence at rates similar to men (Langhinrichsen-Rohling, 2010).

With respect to the classification of studies described above, most existing research on the relationship between autonomic responsivity and aggression belongs to the class of *marker* studies, insofar as such studies focus on differences between aggressive and non-aggressive participants in discrete response indicators. While some findings from studies of this type have served as referents for process-oriented explanations (e.g., lack of vagal regulation leading to exaggerated phasic reactivity), the processes in question have typically been inferred offline rather than measured online.

A further point that warrants mention is that the finding of enhanced reactivity to stressful events does not appear to apply to a particular subgroup of violent perpetrators – namely, those diagnosable as psychopathic. Psychopathy, a condition marked by persistent behavioral deviance in conjunction with distinct affective-interpersonal features (Patrick, Fowles, & Krueger, 2009), is reliably predictive of violence and violent recidivism in criminal offender samples (Porter & Woodworth, 2006). However, in contrast with findings for aggressive individuals in general, it has consistently been shown that psychopathic individuals display *reduced* rather than augmented autonomic reactivity to aversive stimuli and signals of impending stressful events (Hare, 1978; Arnett, 1997; Lorber, 2004). An explanation for this disparity appears to lie in the affective-interpersonal features that are distinctive to psychopathy (Hare, 2003; Patrick et al., 2009). While many psychopathic offenders exhibit tendencies toward impulsivity, recklessness, and aggression that are conducive to acts of violence, the full diagnosis also requires specific tendencies toward deficient empathy, absence of remorse, shallow affectivity, glibness, grandiosity, and manipulativeness (Hare, 2003) that are theorized to reflect a general impairment in emotional responsiveness (Blair, 2006; Cleckley, 1976) or a more specific deficit in fear or punishment sensitivity (Fowles, 1980; Lykken, 1995). From this perspective, aggressive behavior associated with the presence of psychopathic personality is distinct from aggressive behavior more broadly – a position supported by research demonstrating that violent acts perpetrated by psychopaths are more proactive or instrumental in nature than those perpetrated by low-psychopathic individuals, or those high in antisocial deviance features of psychopathy only (Porter & Woodworth, 2006). In view of such evidence, it is important to consider psychopathic expressions of aggression separately from aggressive behavior of other types.

> **Box 3.2** *Partner-directed aggression*
>
> Research into husband-to-wife domestic violence demonstrates the importance of psychophysiological investigations into the mechanisms behind aggressive behavior. One key study by Gottman et al. (1995) examined heart rate (HR) reactivity in male spousal assaulters during conflictual marital interactions. They found that some of these men responded with a decelerating HR whereas others responded with HR acceleration, and they named these groups Type 1 and Type 2 responders, respectively. Importantly, Type 1 and Type 2 responding men differed in other types of aggressive behavior; for example, Type 1 men were also violent towards friends or strangers, while Type 2 men were not. Efforts to replicate these findings have led to an important modification in this typology: In place of a dichotomous approach to categorization, Babcock et al. (2004) proposed a dimensional approach. Like Gottman et al. (1995), these authors found a subgroup of about 20% of partner-aggressive men who exhibited HR deceleration. However, they failed to find significant differences between Type 1 and Type 2 groups in regard to antisocial behavior. Still, these authors found continuous-score associations between degree of HR reactivity and physical as well as psychological spousal abuse, supporting the importance of HR as an indicator of proneness to domestic violence.

Electrocortical activation and reactivity

In analogy to the distinction between baseline autonomic activation and autonomic responses to stimuli, investigations using electrocortical measures have focused on both resting EEG activity and the EEG-derived measure of ERP. In an EEG investigation, changes in electrical activity within the brain are recorded continuously using electrodes positioned over the scalp. Analysis of these signals focuses on the frequency and scalp location of the assessed signals. In normal resting conditions in healthy participants, EEG activation is generally characterized by slow to moderate oscillations, typically in the delta (less than four cycles per second [Hz]), theta (4–8 Hz), and alpha frequency bands (8–12 Hz). An ERP is an average EEG signal time-locked to the occurrence of a distinct event, such as a presented stimulus or an emitted response, across multiple trials. The averaging of the time-locked EEG signal across trials results in accentuation of the systematic event-related brain activity relative to random EEG activity, or signal "noise." ERP measures provide an index of real-time changes in brain activity in relation to events of psychological interest – such as novel or emotionally-evocative stimuli, or errors in instructed performance. Parameters of response that are typically examined include timing/latency, morphology/amplitude, location on the scalp surface, and (in the case of dense-electrode recording, which provides for estimation of sources of underlying signal activity) locations within the brain.

The assumption behind the use of EEG/ERP measures to investigate aggressive behavior is that individuals with the tendency to act violently display cortical immaturity that impairs inhibitory control (Volavka, 1990) and/or cortical under-arousal that predisposes them to seek stimulation as a compensatory response (Raine, Venables, &

Williams, 1990). This perspective is supported by replicable findings of increased slow-wave (delta) activity in resting EEG data collected from violent psychiatric inpatients (cf. Volavka, 1990; Convit, Czobor, & Volavka, 1991). Further, this enhanced slow-wave activity in adolescence predicts the occurrence of general antisocial behavior later in life (Raine et al., 1990; Scarpa & Raine, 1997). Another line of EEG research has produced evidence relating angry mood states, and trait differences in anger proneness, to asymmetry in left versus right frontal EEG activation at rest (Harmon-Jones, 2003). Interestingly, this anger-related asymmetry pattern appears susceptible to affective and cognitive manipulations, such as inducement of a belief that the angering situation cannot be changed, or encouragement of empathy toward the aggressor.

Different brain ERP components have been related to aggressiveness and impulsive antisocial tendencies more broadly. One well-established brain indicator of such tendencies is reduced amplitude of the P300 response, a positive-polarity component that occurs following task-relevant or otherwise salient stimuli in a sequence. The P300 has been studied most extensively in the context of so-called oddball paradigms, in which participants are instructed to respond motorically or verbally to infrequent target stimuli occurring among more frequent non-target stimuli (Comerchero & Polich, 1999). Reduced amplitude of the P300 response has been reported reliably in individuals prone to violent behavior, especially of the impulsive type (Branchey, Buydens-Branchey, & Lieber, 1988; Barratt, Stanford, Kent, & Felthous, 1997; Gerstle, Mathias, & Stanford, 1998). This reduced response has been interpreted as a sign of diminished cognitive function in aggressive individuals.

However, while robust across studies, this effect it is not specific to aggressive behavior: reduced P300 response has also been found in relation to other disinhibitory conditions including antisocial personality disorder (Bauer, O'Connor, & Hesselbrock, 1994), child CD, attention deficit disorder, and dependence on alcohol and other drugs – ranging from nicotine to cocaine (Polich et al., 1994; Iacono et al., 2002). Other work demonstrating a largely heritable common factor underlying this array of problems (Krueger et al., 2002; Young, Stallings, Corley, Krauter & Hewitt, 2000) has suggested the possibility that P300 response acts as a neurophysiological marker of this dispositional liability. Converging lines of evidence, including direct demonstrations of a phenotypic association between scores on this liability factor and reduced P300 response (Patrick et al., 2006; Nelson et al., 2011) and studies demonstrating a genetic basis to this association (Hicks et al., 2007; Yancey et al., 2013), provide strong support for this notion.

Consistent with evidence for its status as a marker of disinhibitory liability, reduced P300 amplitude appears to be associated specifically with impulsive aggression. Studies comparing P300 response in psychiatric patients or delinquents characterized by a history of premeditated, instrumental violence with P300 in healthy controls have consistently yielded null results (Barratt et al., 1997; Stanford, Houston, Villemarette-Pittman, & Greve, 2003; Zukov et al., 2009). This suggests different neuronal mechanisms underlying impulsive and instrumental violence, with P300 response indicative of dispositional deficits in inhibitory control associated exclusively with the former.

Findings from studies of P300 in psychopathic offenders have also been notably mixed. The inconsistency in findings led Gao & Raine (2009) to undertake a meta-analysis comparing findings for psychopathy with those for antisocial personality disorder. Whereas antisocial personality was found to be consistently associated with reduced amplitude and longer latency of P300 response, psychopathy showed more limited evidence of an association with diminished P300 response – mainly in standard oddball tasks. Paralleling aforementioned findings for autonomic reactivity (Drislane, Vaidyanathan, & Patrick, 2003), these results indicate that psychopathy is a distinct condition entailing a different mechanism for violent behavior – namely deficits in affective sensitivity and social connectedness that give rise to a more proactive, predatory aggressive style.

In summary, reduced amplitude of P300 response to salient stimuli in oddball and other experimental tasks has been shown to operate as a marker for impulsive aggression and other disinhibitory problems, but not instrumental aggression. Although the neurocognitive basis of this response impairment remains unclear, further systematic research utilizing variants of the oddball P300 task, alone or in combination with tasks that yield other measures of brain response with clearer functional meaning (e.g., Hall, Bernat, & Patrick, 2007; Nelson et al., 2011), should contribute to improved understanding of the specific neuronal mechanisms underlying this phenomenon.

Neuroimaging

The predecessor to neuroimaging, which aims to relate variations in brain morphology and activation to psychological processes in people as a whole and across individuals, is often seen in the pseudoscience of phrenology, which sought to predict behavior by evaluating dips and bumps in the bones of the skull. A notable target for this crude first attempt at relating brain areas to individual difference factors was evil behavior, as illustrated in Figure 3.1; this depiction of the devil examining the heads of young boys was used as the frontispiece of a phrenology manual in the mid-19th century. Recent decades have seen the emergence of a number of more credible neuroimaging techniques, which provide for objective delineation of aspects of the structure or function of clusters or networks of neurons involved in perception, cognition, or emotion. Each of these techniques has been used, to some extent at least, to investigate processes related to aggressive behavior.

Early neuroimaging investigations of aggression and violent behavior focused on the structure of specific brain regions and found evidence of atrophy in temporal or frontal regions in the brains of violent offenders (Langevin, Ben-Aron, Wright, Marchese, & Handy, 1988; Chesterman, Taylor, Cox, & Hill, 1994; Blake, Pincus, & Buckner, 1995). Subsequent to this, more precise measurement methods revealed decreases in grey matter volume in prefrontal regions for individuals diagnosed with antisocial personality disorder (Raine, Lencz, Bihrle, LaCasse, & Colletti, 2000) and psychopathic participants characterized as unsuccessful (i.e., adjudicated criminal offenders scoring high on psychopathy; Yang et al., 2005). Further studies have reported significantly diminished volumes of prefrontal and temporal structures in children diagnosed with CD (Huebner et al., 2008) and criminal psychopaths (Müller et al., 2008). Findings relating to these brain areas are particularly notable since prefrontal regions have been reliably related to executive functioning (Teffer & Semendeferi, 2012), higher cognition (Wood & Grafman, 2003), and voluntary action (Haggard, 2008). The temporal lobe, on the other hand, contains structures such as the amygdala and hippocampus, known to be associated, among other things, with fear conditioning (Pare & Duvarci, 2012; Pohlack et al., 2012) and other learning processes (Rugg et al., 2012). Other evidence for brain anomalies in aggressive-antisocial individuals has been obtained using diffusion tensor imaging (DTI), a structural imaging technique that quantifies the extent of neural white matter connectivity between differing brain regions. Studies using this method have found neural tract abnormalities in fronto-temporal brain areas

Figure 3.1 The devil examining the head of a boy; three other boys lurk under the devil's wings.

Source: Steel engraving by Jean Denis Nargeot, 1847, after Hippolyte Bruyères. Credit: Wellcome Library, London; Copyrighted work available under Creative Commons.

among adolescents with disruptive behavior problems (Li, Mathews, Wang, Dunn, & Kronenberger, 2005) and abnormal structural connectivity between the amygdala and orbitofrontal cortex in adolescents with CD (Passamonti et al., 2012).

This evidence for structural brain differences associated with aggressive behavior is complemented by evidence from studies employing functional neuroimaging techniques of differing types. Studies of this kind have revealed abnormal activity in the amygdala and regions of frontal cortex in particular (Coccaro, Sripada, Yanowitch, & Phan, 2011). Variations in amygdala activity have been related to readiness for the initiation of "fight-flight" responses to threats (Davis & Whalen, 2001) and to aggressive impulses (Davidson et al., 2000), suggesting an important role for this subcortical structure in the initiation of aggression acts. By contrasts, frontal and prefrontal brain areas including the dorsolateral, ventrolateral, and ventromedial prefrontal cortices and the anterior cingulate cortex are active during instructed down-regulation of emotion that results in reduced amygdala activation, suggesting a role for these structures in the control of aggression impulses (Ochsner, Bunge, Gross, & Gabrieli, 2002; Seo, Olman, Haut, Sinha, Macdonald, & Patrick, 2014). Additionally, other frontal regions (orbitomedial prefrontal cortex, in particular) known to be involved in decision making (Fellows, 2004) and social fairness judgment (Mehta & Beer, 2010; see Box 3.3) exhibit atypical co-activation with the amygdala in aggressive depressed patients (Dougherty et al., 2004).

Taken together, these findings point to a coordinated system for the initiation, regulation, and expression of aggressive impulses in subcortical (e.g., amygdala) and fronto-cortical regions of the brain. Dysfunctions in this circuitry, such as overreactivity of the amygdala, hypoactivation in frontal regulatory regions, or impaired connectivity between the amygdala and frontal regions or among frontal regions, have the potential to shift social behavior and decision making from non-aggressive to more aggressive modes. Importantly, this perspective on aggressive behavior is supported not only by structural and functional neuroimaging findings, but also by results from research on the effects of brain lesions (e.g., Grafman et al., 1996), implanted-electrode stimulation (e.g., Halgren, Walter, Cherlow, Crandall, 1978), and transcranial magnetic stimulation (e.g., Van Honk et al., 2002) on behavioral responding.

Box 3.3 Testosterone, the orbitofrontal cortex, and aggression

Mehta and Beer (2010) investigated whether higher testosterone levels would increase aggressive behavior in a social game paradigm and, if so, whether this effect might have functional correlates in the brain. These investigators had 32 participants play a real-money game in which fair or unfair offers were presented that could either be accepted or rejected. The rejection of a lucrative offer after being treated unfairly was considered to be an aggressive response, since participants sacrificed funds of their own in order to "punish" the other player. Brain activity during the game was recorded using fMRI. The study revealed that the occurrence of aggressive acts of this type was indeed connected to high testosterone levels as indexed by saliva assay, and that activation in the medial orbitofrontal cortex was decreased in individuals exhibiting more such aggressive acts. It was inferred that testosterone down-regulates activation in the orbitofrontal cortex, an area that is involved in affect regulation and impulse control. While further work is needed to corroborate this perspective, this innovative combination of behavioral endocrinology and cognitive neuroscience represents an important step toward understanding processes underlying aggressive responding under conditions of social provocation.

In summary, converging lines of evidence from neuroimaging research point to a likely role for abnormalities in fronto-limbic circuitry in aggressive behavior – in particular, impulsive or angry-reactive aggression (Davidson et al., 2000). Alternative mechanisms appear necessary to invoke to account for proactive-predatory aggressive behavior associated with psychopathy (Blair & Lee, 2013; but see also Wahlund & Kristiansson, 2009).

An Integrative Conceptual Framework for Understanding Aggression Proneness

As described already, multiple lines of evidence indicate that there are distinct subtypes of aggressive individuals, with differing processes likely contributing to impulsive/reactive aggression as compared to premeditated/instrumental aggression. Specifically, available data indicate that impulsive aggression relates to hyperreactivity of the amygdala in combination with hyporeactivity of the prefrontal cortex (e.g., Davidson et al., 2000). The implication is that antisocial individuals prone to impulsive aggression respond more strongly to emotional events and are less able to control their reactions through internal regulatory mechanisms. Differing processes appear to be at work in instrumental aggressive behavior (i.e., characteristic of psychopaths), despite its phenotypic resemblance to reactive aggression. Individuals exhibiting instrumental aggression are distinguished by an intact responsiveness of the prefrontal cortex (Raine et al., 1998) in combination with a decreased (as opposed to increased) responsivity of the amygdala (e.g., Marsh et al. 2008).

This evidence for differing etiologies underlying distinct subtypes of aggression creates challenges for integrating findings across studies of violent individuals. A recent model that provides a helpful point of reference for integration is the triarchic model of psychopathy (Patrick et al., 2009). Although the model was formulated in particular to reconcile differing conceptions of psychopathy, the distinctions it makes among psychopathy-relevant dispositions are also useful to consider in relation to aggressive behavior.

The triarchic model characterizes psychopathy in terms of three dispositional tendencies: disinhibition, meanness (callousness), and boldness. **Disinhibition**, which is closely related to the concept of externalizing proneness (Venables & Patrick, 2012), entails impairments in the ability to regulate emotions and behavior, and is expressed in the form of impulsivity, boredom, irresponsibility, mistrust, and rule-breaking. **Meanness** entails deficient empathy, low social connectedness, and disregard for and exploitation of others (Venables & Patrick, 2012), and is related to constructs of callousness, unemotionality, coldheartedness, and antagonism, **boldness** encompasses features of social confidence and efficacy, resiliency to stressors, and tolerance for uncertainty and danger. High boldness is associated with tendencies toward interpersonal dominance, narcissism, and sensation-seeking (Benning et al., 2005) and low levels of anxious-depressive (internalizing) problems. From the standpoint of this model, distinguishable variants of psychopathy (Poythress & Skeem, 2006) reflect differing blends of these three dispositional tendencies.

The distinction between disinhibition and meanness in the triarchic model, which is of direct relevance to subtypes of aggression, is based on research on the structure of disinhibitory problems and traits in adults (Krueger et al., 2002; Krueger, Markon, Patrick, Benning, & Kramer, 2007) along with research on the expression of psychopathy early in life (Frick & Marsee, 2006). These lines of research converge in demonstrating that impulsive-disinhibitory tendencies and callous disregard for others, although correlated, are dissociable from one another and show contrasting external correlates. For example, disinhibition relates distinctively to stress reactivity, substance-related problems, and impulsive-irresponsible features of psychopathy, whereas callousness (meanness) relates distinctively to Machiavellianism, lack of empathic concern, and core affective symptoms of psychopathy (Sellbom & Phillips, 2013;

Venables & Patrick, 2012). Additionally, disinhibition relates more to impulsive-angry aggression whereas callousness relates more to instrumental expressions of aggression (Frick & Marsee, 2006; Krueger et al., 2007).

Although characterized as observable tendencies (phenotypes) in the triarchic model, disinhibition, meanness, and boldness are hypothesized to differ in terms of their etiological underpinnings – with disinhibitory tendencies presumed to reflect dysfunction in fronto-cortical regulatory systems (implicated also in impulsive aggression; Davidson et al., 2000), meanness deficits in emotional sensitivity and affiliative capacity, and boldness hyporeactivity of the brain's defensive (fear) system. Systematic research across multiple levels of analysis – from genetic through neural to behavioral and social levels (Patrick, Durbin, & Moser, 2012; Patrick et al., 2013) – will be needed to clarify the contributions of biological systems to these distinct phenotypes, and in turn, the role these systems play in documented variants of psychopathy. Given the clear points of intersection between antisociality/psychopathy and aggressive behavior, work along these lines will also contribute to improved understanding of contrasting variants of human aggression and their bases in neurobiological systems.

Violence in men *Men are more likely to show physical violent behavior than women. This may relate to the finding that high levels of testosterone increase aggressive behavior in the context of social games (Mehta & Beer, 2010). The hormone testosterone, the chemical structure of which is presented in the figure, is much more prevalent in men.*

Source: © Vladimir Fedorchuk. Used under license from 123RF.

Practical and Ethical Implications

The research findings reviewed in this chapter have important implications for identification and management of individuals who are prone to aggressive behavior. In particular, as knowledge accumulates regarding the role of neurobiological systems and processes in aggression and violence, and effective models are established for integrating neurobiological findings with observations at more macro levels of analysis (e.g., cognitive-affective, behavioral, social), the coming years are sure to provide unprecedented insights into factors that initiate and perpetuate or inhibit aggressive acts. Some particularly noteworthy implications of research on the neurobiology of aggression are as follows.

Identification of aggressive individuals

The neurobiological markers discussed in this chapter could conceivably be used, either individually (Hall et al., 2007; Yancey et al., 2013) or perhaps more effectively in combination (Nelson et al., 2011; Patrick et al., 2013), as a basis for identifying individuals with high dispositional proneness to violent behavior, or to assess for risk of future violence in individuals with a prior history of such behavior. Process-oriented accounts of observed relations between indicators of these types and aggressive behavior, focusing on neural circuits and their known psychological functions, have the potential to improve the reliability and validity of neurobiologically-based assessments. However, most existing research provides only for probabilistic statements on a group level, and applying findings from empirical studies to characterization of individuals – and the technical, legal, and ethical consequences of group-to-individual level inference – are important topics of ongoing discussion (Faigman, Monahan, & Slobogin, 2013).

Legal categorization

As discussed when describing integrative frameworks, another important question is when and how existing conceptions of psychopathology and normal psychological functioning should be refined on the basis of new empirical evidence. From a scientific and applied-practice standpoint, this challenge can be addressed by constantly updating ideas regarding the nature of mental disorders and procedures for diagnosing them. From a legal standpoint, however, characterizing the influence of physiological state and trait factors on individual behavior has become increasingly important and complex. Neuroimaging results are increasingly being used in the courtroom to support diminished-capacity defense arguments (Haque & Guyer, 2010), and debate exists regarding whether diminished-capacity standards should be applied to individuals diagnosed as psychopathic (Nair & Weinstock, 2007). Apart from the direct ethico-legal implications of these developments, basic questions exist regarding the accuracy with which probabilistic statements can be rendered on an individual level based on aggregate research results.

Refinement of violence interventions

A recent comprehensive review of research on the prevention and treatment of violent behavior indicates a lack of reliable data on the effectiveness of intervention programs, with only small-to-moderate effects evident for non-pharmaceutical approaches in general (Hockenhull et al., 2012). Understanding the neural bases of aggressive behavior in process terms will undoubtedly contribute to improvements in both pharmaceutical and psychological approaches to the prevention and treatment of violence, similar to how neurobiological findings have contributed to improved interventions for other clinical conditions (Gabbard, 2000).

Conclusions

Aggressive behavior is a complex phenomenon without simple monocausal explanations. However, research using psychophysiological and neuroimaging approaches has demonstrated reliable neurobiological correlates of aggression and provided insights into brain circuits and processes underlying violent behavior and affiliated disinhibitory tendencies. Further systematic research directed at elucidating the origins and consequences of core biological processes in aggression is essentially improving approaches to the diagnosis and treatment of violent offenders.

Recommended Reading

Davis, M., & Whalen, P. J. (2001). The amygdala: vigilance and emotion. *Molecular Psychiatry*, 6, 13–34. *This classic and extensive review paper presents an overview of the diverse roles of the amygdala, including learning, reaction to stimuli, relationship to physiological responses, and connection to psychopathological disorders.*

Krueger, R. F., Markon, K. E., Patrick, C. J., Benning, S. D., & Kramer, M. D. (2007). Linking antisocial behavior, substance use, and personality: An integrative quantitative model of the adult externalizing spectrum. *This paper presents the externalizing spectrum model, an integrative model encompassing antisocial behavior in children and adults, alcohol and drug problems, and more. It conceives of traits and problem behaviors as arising from a broad underlying vulnerability (predominantly genetic in origin) along with other specific etiologic influences that determine its distinctive expression. It also offers novel research strategies for studying causal factors and processes underlying these disorders: rather than studying each as a separate entity, one can study the broad dispositional factor these disorders have in common, as well as studying the unique variance associated with each individual disorder.*

Raine, A., Meloy, J. R., Bihrle, S., Stoddard, J., LaCasse, L., & Buchsbaum, M. S. (1998). Reduced prefrontal and increased subcortical brain functioning assessed using positron emission tomography in predatory and affective murderers. *Behavioral Sciences and the Law*, 16, 319–332. *This study is the first of many neuroimaging approaches to show a combination of reduction of activation in regulatory areas and increase of activation in limbic regions. What is demonstrated here by using glucose metabolism as a marker has later been replicated using other imaging methods, and the effects shown here in impulsive vs. instrumental murderers have been extended to include criminal and non-criminal people with different levels of trait impulsivity.*

Yancey, J. R., Venables, N. C., Hicks, B. M., Patrick, C. J. (2013). Evidence for a Heritable Brain Basis to Deviance-Promoting Deficits in Self-Control. *Journal of Criminal Justice* 41(5). doi: 10.1016/j.jcrimjus.2013.06.002. *This study used twin modeling analyses to demonstrate that trait disinhibition, i.e. an individual predisposition toward a lack of inhibition regarding one's own behavior, as well as symptoms of antisocial disorders, reflect a common genetic liability. Furthermore, it supports the notion of using certain ERPs as psychophysiological markers for disinhibition.*

References

Arnett, P. A. (1997). Autonomic responsivity in psychopaths: A critical review and theoretical proposal. *Clinical Psychological Review*, 17, 903–936.

Babcock, J. C., Green, C. E., Webb, S. A., & Graham, K. H. (2004). A second failure to replicate the Gottman et al. (1995) typology of men who abuse intimate partners ... and possible reasons why. *Journal of Family Psychology*, 18(2), 396–400.

Barratt, E. S., Stanford, M. S., Kent, T. A., & Felthous, A. R. (1997). Neuropsychological and cognitive psychophysiological substrates of impulsive aggression. *Biological Psychiatry*, 41, 1045–1061.

Bauer, L. O., O'Connor, S., & Hesselbrock, V. M. (1994). Frontal P300 decrements in antisocial personality disorder. Alcoholism: *Clinical and Experimental Research*, 18, 1300–1305.

Beauchaine, T. P., Gatzke-Kopp, L., & Mead, H. K. (2007). Polyvagal theory and developmental psychopathology: Emotion dysregulation and conduct problems from preschool to adolescence. *Biological Psychology*, 74(2), 174–184.

Beauchaine, T. P., Katkin, E. S., Strassberg, Z., & Snarr, J. (2001). Disinhibitory psychopathology in male adolescents: Discriminating conduct disorder from attention-deficit/

hyperactivity disorder through concurrent assessment of multiple autonomic states. *Journal of Abnormal Psychology, 110*, 610–624.

Benning, S. D., Patrick, C. J., Blonigen, D. M., Hicks, B. M., & Iacono, W. G. (2005). Estimating facets of psychopathy from normal personality traits: A step toward community-epidemiological investigations. *Assessment, 12*, 3–18.

Blair, R. J. R. (2006). Subcortical brain systems in psychopathy: The amygdala and associated structures. In C. J. Patrick (Ed.), *Handbook of psychopathy* (pp. 296–312). New York, NY: Guilford Press.

Blair, R. J. R., & Lee, T. M. C. (2013). The social cognitive neuroscience of aggression, violence, and psychopathy. *Social Neuroscience, 8*(2), 108–111.

Blake, P. Y., Pincus, J. H., & Buckner, C. (1995). Neurologic abnormalities in murderers. *Neurology 45*, 1641–1647.

Branchey, M. H., Buydens-Branchey, L., & Lieber, C. S. (1988). P3 in alcoholics with disordered regulation of aggression. *Psychiatry Research, 25*, 49–58.

Buonomano, D. V., & Merzenich, M. M. (1998). Cortical plasticity: From synapses to maps. *Annual Review of Neuroscience, 21*, 149–186.

Cacioppo, S., Frum, C., Asp, E., Weiss, R. M., Lewis, J. W., & Cacioppo, J. T. (2013). A quantitative meta-analysis of functional imaging studies of social rejection. *Scientific Reports 3*(2027).

Caspi, A., McClay, J., Moffitt, T. E., Mill, J., Martin, J., Craig, I. W., ... Poulton, R. (2002). Role of genotype in the cycle of violence in maltreated children. *Science, 297*(5582), 851–854.

Chesterman, L. P., Taylor, P. J., Cox, T., & Hill, M. (1994). Multiple measures of cerebral state in dangerous mentally disordered inpatients. *Criminal Behavior and Mental Health, 4*, 228–239.

Cleckley, H. (1976). *The mask of sanity, 5th ed.* St. Louis, MO: Mosby. (Original ed. published in 1941; 3rd ed. 1955).

Coccaro, E. F., Sripada, C. S., Yanowitch, R. N., & Phan, K. L. (2011). Corticolimbic Function in Impulsive Aggressive Behavior. *Biological Psychiatry, 69*(12), 1153–1159.

Comerchero, M. D., & Polich, J. (1999). P3a and P3b from typical auditory and visual stimuli. *Clinical Neurophysiology, 110*(1), 24–30.

Convit, A., Czobor, P., & Volavka, P. (1991). Lateralized abnormality in the EEG of persistently violent psychiatric inpatients. *Biological Psychiatry, 30*(4), 363–370.

Craig, I. W., & Halton, K. E. (2009). Genetics of human aggressive behavior. *Human Genetics, 126*, 101–113.

Davidson, R. J., Putnam, K. M., & Larson, C. L. (2000). Dysfunction in the neural circuitry of emotion regulation – a possible prelude to violence. *Science, 289*, 591–594.

Davis, M., & Whalen, P. J. (2001). The amygdala: Vigilance and emotion. *Molecular Psychiatry, 6*, 13–34.

Dougherty, D. D., Rauch, S. L., Deckersbach, T., Marci, C., Loh, R., Shin, L. M., ... Fava, M. (2004). Ventromedial prefrontal cortex and amygdala dysfunction during an anger induction positron emission tomography study in patients with major depressive disorder with anger attacks. *Archives of General Psychiatry, 61*(8), 795–804.

Drislane, L. E., Vaidyanathan, U., & Patrick, C. J. (2013). Reduced cortical call to arms differentiates psychopathy from antisocial personality disorder. *Psychological Medicine 43*, 825–835.

El-Sheikh, M., Harger, J., & Whitson, S. M. (2001). Exposure to interparental conflict and children's adjustment and physical health: The moderating role of vagal tone. *Child Development, 72*, 1617–1636.

Faigman, D. L., Monahan, J., & Slobogin, C. (2013). Group to individual (G2i) inference in scientific expert testimony. *University of Chicago Law Review, 81*(2), 2014; Virginia Public Law and Legal Theory Research Paper No. 2013-2034.

Fellows, L. K. (2004). The cognitive neuroscience of human decision making: A review and conceptual framework. *Behavioral and Cognitive Neuroscience Reviews 3*, 159–172.

Fowles, D. C. (1980). The three arousal model: Implications of Gray's two-factor learning theory for heart rate, electrodermal activity, and psychopathy. *Psychophysiology, 17*(2), 87–104.

Frick, P. J., & Marsee, M. A. (2006). Psychopathy and developmental pathways to antisocial behavior in youth. In C. J. Patrick (Ed.), *Handbook of psychopathy* (pp. 353—74). New York, NY: Guilford Press.

Gabbard, G. O. (2000). A neurobiologically informed perspective on psychotherapy. *British Journal of Psychiatry, 177*, 117–122.

Gao, Y., Raine, A. (2009). P3 event-related potential impairments in antisocial and psychopathic individuals: A meta-analysis. *Biological Psychology, 82*(3), 199–210.

Gerstle, J. E., Mathias, C. W., & Stanford, M. S. (1998). Auditory P300 and self-reported impulsive aggression. Prog. Neuropsychopharmacol. *Biological Psychiatry, 22*, 575–583.

Gottmann, J. M., Jacobson, N. S., Rushe, R. H., Shortt, J. W., Babcock, J., LaTaillade, J. J., & Waltz, J. (1995). The relationship between heart rate reactivity, emotionally aggressive behavior, and general violence in batterers. *Journal of Family Psychology, 9*, 227–248.

Grafman, J., Schwab, K., Warden, D., Pridgen, A., Brown, H. R., & Salazar, A. M. (1996). Frontal lobe injuries, violence, and aggression: A report of the Vietnam Head Injury Study. *Neurology, 46*, 1231–1238.

Grether, G. F., Anderson, C. N., Drury, J. P., Kirschel, A. N., Losin, N., Okamoto, K., & Peiman, K. S. (2013). The evolutionary consequences of interspecific aggression. *Annals of the New York Academy of Sciences, 1289*, 48–68.

Haggard, P. (2008). Human volition: Towards a neuroscience of will. *Nature Reviews Neuroscience, 9*(12), 934–946.

Halgren, E., Walter, R. D., Cherlow, D. G., & Crandall, P. H. (1978). Mental phenomena evoked by electrical stimulation of the human hippocampal formation and amygdala. *Brain, 101*(1), 83–117.

Hall, J. R., Bernat, E. M., & Patrick, C. J. (2007). Externalizing psychopathology and the error-related negativity. *Psychological Science, 18*, 326–333.

Haque, S., & Guyer, M. (2010). Neuroimaging studies in diminished-capacity defense. *Journal of the American Academy of Psychiatry and the Law, 38*(4), 605–607.

Hare, R. D. (1978). Electrodermal and cardiovascular correlates of psychopathy. In R. D. Hare & D. Schalling (Eds.), *Psychopathic behavior: Approaches to research* (pp. 107–143). Chichester: John Wiley & Sons.

Hare, R. D. (2003). *Manual for the Hare Psychopathy Checklist-Revised* (2nd ed.). Toronto, ON: Multi-Health Systems.

Harmon-Jones, E. (2003). Clarifying the emotive functions of asymmetrical frontal cortical activity. *Psychophysiology, 40*, 838–848.

Hicks, B. M., Bernat, E. M., Malone, S. M., Iacono, W. G., Patrick, C. J., Krueger R. F., & Mcgue M. (2007). Genes mediate the association between P300 amplitude and externalizing disorders. *Psychophysiology, 44*, 9—105.

Hockenhull, J. C., Whittington, R., Leitner, M., Barr, W., McGuire, J., Cherry, M. G., ... Dickson, R. (2012). A systematic review of prevention and intervention strategies for populations at high risk of engaging in violent behavior update 2002-8. *Health Technology Assessment, 16*(3); doi: 10.3310/hta16030.

Huebner, T., Vloet, T. D., Marx, I., Konrad, K., Fink, G. R., Herpertz, S. C., & Herpertz-Dahlmann, B. (2008). Morphometric brain abnormalities in boys with conduct disorder. *Journal of the American Academy of Child and Adolescent Psychiatry, 47*, 540–547.

Hunter, R. G., & McEwen, B. S. (2013). Stress and anxiety across the lifespan: Structural plasticity and epigenetic regulation. *Epigenomics, 5*(2), 177–194.

Iacono, W. G., Carlson, S. R., Malone, S. M., & McGue, M. (2002). P3 event-related potential amplitude and risk for disinhibitory disorders in adolescent boys. *Archives of General Psychiatry, 59*, 750–757.

Kan, K. J., Ploeger, A., Raijmakers, M. E., Dolan, C. V., & van der Maas, H. L. (2010). Nonlinear epigenetic variance: Review and simulations. *Developmental Science, 13*(1), 11–27.

Krueger, R. F., Hicks, B. M., Patrick, C. J., Carlson, S., Iacono, W. G., & McGue, M. (2002). Etiological connections among substance dependence, antisocial behavior, and personality: Modeling the externalizing spectrum. *Journal of Abnormal Psychology, 111*, 411–424.

Krueger, R. F., Markon, K. E., Patrick, C. J., Benning, S. D., & Kramer, M. D. (2007). Linking antisocial behavior, substance use, and personality: An integrative quantitative model of the adult externalizing spectrum. *Journal of Abnormal Psychology, 116*, 645–666.

Langevin, R., Ben-Aron, M. H., Wright, P., Marchese, V., & Handy, L. (1988). The sex killer. *Annals of Sex Research, 1*, 263–301.

Langhinrichsen-Rohling, J. (2010). Controversies involving gender and intimate partner violence in the United States. *Sex Roles, 62*, 179–193.

Li, T.Q., Mathews, V. P., Wang, Y., Dunn, D., & Kronenberger, W. (2005). Adolescents with disruptive behavior disorder investigated using an optimized MR diffusion tensor imaging protocol. *Annals of the New York Academy of Sciences, 1064*, 184–192.

Lorber, M. F. (2004). Psychophysiology of aggression, psychopathy, and conduct problems: A meta-analysis. *Psychological Bulletin, 130*, 531–552.

Lykken, D. T. (1995). *The antisocial personalities.* Hillsdale, NJ: Erlbaum.

Marsh, A. A., Finger, E. C., Mitchell, D. G., Reid, M. E., Sims, C., Kosson, D. S., ... Blair, R. J. R. (2008). Reduced amygdala response to fearful expressions in children and adolescents with callous-unemotional traits and disruptive behavior disorders. *The American Journal of Psychiatry, 165*, 712–720.

Mehta, P. H., & Beer, J. (2010). Neural mechanisms of the testosterone-aggression relation: The role of orbitofrontal cortex. *Journal of Cognitive Neuroscience, 22*(10), 2357–2368.

Mezzacappa, E., Tremblay, R. E., Kindlon, D., Saul, J. P., Arseneault, L., Seguin, J., ... Earls, F. (1997). Anxiety, antisocial behavior, and heart rate regulation in adolescent males. *Journal of Child Psychology and Psychiatry, 38*, 457–469.

Müller, J. L., Gänssbauer, S., Sommer, M., Döhnel, K., Weber, T., Schmidt-Wilcke, T., & Hajak, G. (2008). Gray matter changes in right superior temporal gyrus in criminal psychopaths. Evidence from voxel-based morphometry. *Psychiatry Research, 163*, 213–222.

Murray-Close, D. (2011). Autonomic reactivity and romantic relational aggression among female emerging adults: Moderating roles of social and cognitive risk. *International Journal of Psychophysiology, 80*, 28–35.

Nair, M. S., & Weinstock, R. (2007). Psychopathy, diminished capacity and responsibility. In A.R. Felthous & H. Sass (Eds.) *The international handbook of psychopathic disorders and the law.* Chichester: John Wiley & Sons.

Nelson, L. D., Patrick, C. J., & Bernat, E. M. (2011). Operationalizing proneness to externalizing psychopathology as a multivariate psychophysiological phenotype. *Psychophysiology, 48*(1), 64–72.

Nordstrom, B. R., Gao, Y., Glenn, A. L., Peskin, M., Rudo-Hutt, A. S., ... Raine, A. (2011). Neurocriminology. *Advances in Genetics, 75*, 255–283.

Ochsner, K. N., Bunge, S. A., Gross, J. J., & Gabrieli, J. D. (2002). Rethinking feelings: An fMRI study of the cognitive regulation of emotion. *Journal of Cognitive Neuroscience, 14*, 1215–1229.

Ortiz, J., & Raine, A. (2004). Heart rate level and antisocial behavior in children and adolescents: A meta-analysis. *Journal of the American Academy of Child and Adolescent Psychiatry, 43*, 154–162.

Pare, D., Duvarci, S. (2012). Amygdala microcircuits mediating fear expression and extinction. *Current Opinion in Neurobiology, 22*(4), 717–723.

Passamonti, L., Fairchild, G., Fornito, A., Goodyer, I. M., Nimmo-Smith, I., Hagan, C. C., & Calder, A. J. (2012). Abnormal anatomical connectivity between the amygdala and orbitofrontal cortex in conduct disorder. *PLoS One*, *7*(11), e48789.

Patrick, C. J., Bernat, E. M., Malone, S. M., Iacono, W. G., Krueger, R. F., & McGue, M. (2006). P300 amplitude as an indicator of externalizing in adolescent males. *Psychophysiology*, *43*, 84–92.

Patrick, C. J., Durbin, C. E., & Moser, J. S. (2012). Conceptualizing proneness to antisocial deviance in neurobehavioral terms. *Development and Psychopathology*, *24*, 1047–1071.

Patrick, C. J., Fowles, D. C., & Krueger, R. F. (2009). Triarchic conceptualization of psychopathy: Developmental origins of disinhibition, boldness, and meanness. *Developmental Psychopathology*, *21*(3), 913–938.

Patrick, C. J., Venables, N. C., Yancey, J. R., Hicks, B. M., Nelson, L. D., & Kramer, M. D. (2013). A construct-network approach to bridging diagnostic and physiological domains: Application to assessment of externalizing psychopathology. *Journal of Abnormal Psychology*, *122*(3), 902–916.

Pohlack, S. T., Nees, F., Liebscher, C., Cacciaglia, R., Diener, S. J., Ridder, S., ... Flor, H. (2012). Hippocampal but not amygdalar volume affects contextual fear conditioning in humans. *Human Brain Mapping*, *33*(2), 478–488.

Polich, J., Pollock, V. E., & Bloom, F. E. (1994). Meta-analysis of P300 amplitude from males at risk for alcoholism. *Psychological Bulletin*, *115*, 55–73.

Porter, S., & Woodworth, M. (2006). Psychopathy and aggression. In C. J. Patrick (Ed.), *Handbook of psychopathy* (pp. 481–494). New York, NY: Guilford Press.

Poythress, N. G., & Skeem, J. L. (2006). Disaggregating psychopathy: When and how to look for variants. In C. J. Patrick (Ed.), *Handbook of psychopathy* (pp. 172–192). New York, NY: Guilford Press.

Purcell, S. (2002). Variance components models for gene-environment interaction in twin analysis. *Twin Research*, *5*(6), 554–571.

Raine, A., Lencz, T., Bihrle, S., LaCasse, L., & Colletti, P. (2000). Reduced prefrontal gray matter volume and reduced autonomic activity in antisocial personality disorder. *Archives of General Psychiatry*, *57*(2), 199–127.

Raine, A., Meloy, J. R., Bihrle, S., Stoddard, J., LaCasse, L., & Buchsbaum, M. S. (1998). Reduced prefrontal and increased subcortical brain functioning assessed using positron emission tomography in predatory and affective murderers. *Behavioral Sciences and the Law*, *16*, 319–332.

Raine, A., Venables, P. H., & Williams, M. (1990). Relationships between N1, P300 and CNV recorded at age 15 and criminal behavior at age 24. *Psychophysiology*, *27*, 567–575.

Rugg, M. D., Vilberg, K. L., Mattson, J. T., Yu, S. S., Johnson, J. D., & Suzuki, M. (2012). Item memory, context memory and the hippocampus: fMRI evidence. *Neuropsychologia*, *50*(13), 3070–3079.

Scarpa, A., Haden, S. C., & Tanaka, A. (2010). Being hot-tempered: Autonomic, emotional, and behavioral distinctions between childhood reactive and proactive aggression. *Biological Psychology*, *84*(3), 488–496.

Scarpa, A., & Raine, A. (1997). Psychophysiology of anger and violent behavior. *The Psychiatric Clinics of North America*, *20*(2), 375–394.

Seidel, E. M., Silani, G., Metzler, H., Thaler, H., Lamm, C., Gur, R. C., ... Derntl, B. (2013). The impact of social exclusion vs. inclusion on subjective and hormonal reactions in females and males. *Psychoneuroendocrinology*, *38*(12), 2925–2932.

Sellbom, M., & Phillips, T. R. (2013). An examination of the triarchic conceptualization of psychopathy in incarcerated and nonincarcerated samples. *Journal of Abnormal Psychology*, *122*(1), 208–214.

Seo, D., Olman, C. A., Haut, K. M., Sinha, R., Macdonald, A. W. 3rd, & Patrick, C. J. (2014). Neural correlates of preparatory and regulatory control over positive and negative emotion. *Social Cognitive and Affective Neuroscience, 9*(4), 494–504.

Stanford, M. S., Houston, R. J., Villemarette-Pittman, N. R., & Greve, K. W. (2003). Premeditated aggression: Clinical assessment and cognitive psychophysiology. *Personality and Individual Differences, 34*, 773–781.

Teffer, K., & Semendeferi, K. (2012). Human prefrontal cortex: Evolution, development, and pathology. *Progress in Brain Research, 195*, 191–218.

Van Honk, J., Hermans, E. J., d'Alfonso, A. A., Schutter, D. J., van Doornen, L., & de Haan, E. H. (2002). A left-prefrontal lateralized, sympathetic mechanism directs attention towards social threat in humans: Evidence from repetitive transcranial magnetic stimulation. *Neuroscience Letters, 319*(2), 99–102.

Venables, N. C., & Patrick, C. J. (2012). Validity of the externalizing spectrum inventory in a criminal offender sample: Relations with disinhibitory psychopathology, personality, and psychopathic features. *Psychological Assessment, 24*(1), 88–100.

Venables, N. C., Patrick, C. J., Hall, J. R., & Bernat, E. M. (2011). Clarifying relations between dispositional aggression and brain potential response: Overlapping and distinct contributions of impulsivity and stress reactivity. *Biological Psychology, 86*(3), 279–288.

Volavka, J. (1990). Aggression, electroencephalography, and evoked potentials: A critical review. Neuropsychiatry, *Neuropsychology and Behavioral Neurology, 3*, 249–259.

Wahlund, K., & Kristiansson, M. (2009). Aggression, psychopathy and brain imaging – Review and future recommendations. *International Journal of Law and Psychiatry, 32*(4), 266–271.

Walsh, Z., Swogger, M. T., O'Connor, B. P., Chatav Schonbrun, Y., Shea, M. T., & Stuart, G. L. (2010). Subtypes of partner violence perpetrators among male and female psychiatric patients. *Journal of Abnormal Psychology, 119*(3), 563–574.

Williams, K. D., Cheung, C. K. T., & Choi, W. (2000). Cyberostracism: Effects of being ignored over the Internet. *Journal of Personality and Social Psychology, 79*, 748–762.

Wood, J. N., & Grafman, J. (2003). Human prefrontal cortex: Processing and representational perspectives. *Nature Reviews Neuroscience, 4*, 139–147.

Yancey, J. R., Venables, N. C., Hicks, B. M., & Patrick, C. J. (2013). Evidence for a heritable brain basis to deviance-promoting deficits in self-control. *Journal of Criminal Justice, 41*(5), doi: 10.1016/j.jcrimjus.2013.06.002.

Yang, Y., Raine, A., Lencz, T., Bihrle, S., LaCasse, L., & Colletti, P. (2005). Volume reduction in prefrontal gray matter in unsuccessful criminal psychopaths. *Biological Psychiatry, 57*(10), 1103–1108.

Young, S. E., Stallings, M. C., Corley, R. P., Krauter, K. S., & Hewitt, J. K. (2000). Genetic and environmental influences on behavioral disinhibition. *American Journal of Medical Genetics (Neuropsychiatric Genetics), 96*, 684–695.

Zukov, I., Ptacek, R., Kozelek, P., Fischer, S., Domluvilova, D., Raboch, J., … Susta, M. (2009). Brain wave P300: A comparative study of various forms of criminal activity. *Medical Science Monitor, 15*(7), 349–354.

4
The Neurobiology of Sexual Behavior and Sexual Attraction

Anders Ågmo

Key points

- Sexual behavior involves stimulation of a sexual organ and leads to positive affect.
- Sexual behaviors are triggered by a wide range of stimuli and involve a wide range of responses, which are specific to a particular species or a group of species.
- Activation of a sexual response requires both an appropriate central motive state and appropriate external stimuli. In humans, it is believed this can be replaced by mental representation.
- In rodents, sexual response to external stimuli (i.e., odor) does not depend on learning. It is unclear whether this is the case for humans or other primates.
- There is some evidence that naked flesh as well as suggestive movements act as sexual incentives in men.
- Research has shown that conditioning can turn neutral stimuli into sexual incentives and that the learning processes for sexually unacceptable stimuli are no different from socially acceptable counter parts.
- The search for a biological basis for social entities such as pedophilia is unlikely to lead to fruition.
- Increased testosterone levels may increase sexual arousal via androgens in women.
- Testosterone is vital for sexual behavior in men as well.
- Different parts of the hypothalamus (nucleus in the brain) control sexual behavior in men and women.
- Sexual behavior involving the same sex is a common phenomenon across different species. Preference for same-sex sexual behavior is rarer.
- Paraphilias have been argued to be linked to unusually high sexual motivation.

- Drugs that potentially impact testosterone can reduce sexual behavior by decreasing the sexual motivation.
- While all aspects of sexual behavior in principle can be modified by drugs, drugs have rarely been shown to greatly impact upon sexuality in humans.
- An ethical and moral consideration should account for the fact that treatment that efficiently reduces socially unacceptable behavior also reduces socially acceptable behavior.

Terminology Explained

Aromatization describes a process that is carried out by an enzyme called aromatase. This process is involved in the transformation of androgens (e.g,. testosterone) to estrogen (e.g., estradiol).

Testosterone is **aromatized to estradiol**. A number of research studies have found that testosterone is converted (aromatized) to estradiol (a form of estrogen) in the hypothalamus and limbic system.

Central motive states activate specific behaviors. They describe a condition in which an internal drive (e.g., drop in sugar level, hunger, change in hormonal state) is matched by an external stimulus (e.g., smell of food, sounds of desired object). The central motive state typically triggers a set of bodily responses preparing the animal (human) to act upon the incentive, the object.

Classical conditioning (also known as **Pavlovian conditioning** after Ivan Pavlov) is a learning process (originally noted in dogs) by which an initially neutral stimulus such as the sound of a bell, if repeatedly paired with a potent stimulus such as food, which produces drooling, will eventually produce the conditioned response of drooling from the ringing of the bell.

Dihydrotestosterone (DHT, or 5α-DHT) is both a sex steroid and an androgen hormone. It is a relative of testosterone that plays an important role in the development of male sexual organs and in other male characteristic (including body and facial hair).

Hormones (sex steroids) include estradiol, progesterone, and testosterone, see below for definitions of all of these.

Endogenous hormones are naturally produced by our bodies as part of normal healthy activity.

Estradiol is both a steroid and estrogen sex hormone, and is the primary female sex hormone.

Gonadal hormones are steroids produced by the **gonads** (testes or ovaries). They stimulate reproduction and secondary sex characteristics (in both males and females).

Lordosis is a posture assumed by some female mammals during reproduction, where the back is arched downward.

Medial preoptic area controls male sexual behaviour. A part of it, the median preoptic nucleus, is larger in males than in females.

Ovariectomized means the surgical removal of the ovaries.

The term **paraphilia** is a biomedical term used to describe sexual arousal to objects, situations, or non-consenting individuals, which are outside the range of "normal" sexual interests.

A **photoplethysmogram(PPG)** is an optical measurement of an organ.

Progesterone is an endogenous sex hormone involved in the menstrual cycle, pregnancy, and embryogenesis of female humans and other species. In the male body it gets converted into testosterone.

Sexual incentive motivation theory is a theoretical framework for understanding sexual motivation, arousal, and behavior, as such it combines the principles of incentive motivation theory as well as the hierarchical control of behavior.

Testosterone's main function is to drive reproductive function in men in that sexual activity may increase the level of testosterone.

The **ventromedial hypothalamus (VMH)** is a distinct morphological part of the brain located at the bottom of the hypothalamus. It regulates feeding, fear, thermoregulation, and sexual activity.

Introduction

Most research concerning the neurobiological mechanisms involved in sexual behavior has been performed on non-human animals. An old, still unresolved, issue is whether findings in such animals can be generalized to the human (for an informed discussion see Blaustein, 2008). Without pretending to provide a definite answer to this question of generalizability, it might be maintained that the theoretical framework necessary for understanding the intricacies of sexual behavior applies equally to humans and non-human animals. Likewise, there are many reasons to believe that the neurobiological underpinnings of sexual behavior are similar in all mammals, perhaps even in all vertebrates.

In this chapter, the incentive motivational framework used for the analysis of sexual behavior will be outlined, and the endocrine and neural bases of this behavior will be summarized. The importance of gonadal hormones in males and females, including humans will also be described. The principal brains sites involved in the control of sexual behavior as well as a short discussion of drug actions will also be included, and the relevance of neurobiological data for understanding socially unacceptable sexual behaviors will be discussed. The explanatory force of the incentive motivational system is finally illustrated in two examples, bi- and homosexuality and the display of sexual behavior in response to socially unacceptable stimuli. Before looking at these areas, it is important to define what is considered sexual behavior.

What is Sexual Behavior?

Most people would maintain that they have a clear intuitive knowledge of what is understood by the term "sexual behavior." However, if we would ask for a definition, the answer would probably be meager, and whichever answer we get could probably be subjected to dispute. Therefore, for the purposes of clarity, we will provide a usable definition at the outset: "Sexual behavior; any action leading to sexual reward. Sexual reward is a state of positive affect activated by physical stimulation of the genitalia or mental representations of such stimulation" (Ågmo, 2007, p. 3). This definition accounts for the fact that the motor patterns potentially involved in precopulatory, paracopulatory, and copulatory behaviors are extremely variable, precluding any definition based on these patterns. Human sexual interactions may, for example, involve different body orifices, and different objects may be inserted into one or several of these orifices. Even though the penis is the most common of the inserted objects, there are an almost infinite number of other things that can serve as alternatives. Some of the more unusual objects and a creative use of an unexpected orifice can be found in a recent case report (Naidu, Chung, & Mulcahy, 2013). A man inserted a 10 cm long, steel dining fork deep into the urethra for obtaining autoerotic pleasure. Because he was unable to remove it, he had to present himself at a hospital. This peculiar case illustrates the enormous variety of human sexual behaviors, and the usefulness of the definition provided above. The action, fork insertion, involved the genitals and it led to positive affect, thereby satisfying the criteria established in this definition.

Unlike the human, non-human animals almost always show highly stereotyped motor patterns when copulating. The favorite subjects among neurobiologists, rodents, simply display a series of somatic reflexes. In males, the basic somatic reflex is the mount, which may or may not lead to penile insertion and eventually ejaculation. In female rodents, the basic motor pattern is another somatic reflex termed *lordosis*.

Sexual behavior *involves stimulation of a sexual organ and leads to positive affect.*
Source: © Michal Bednarek. Used under license from 123RF.

Because of the stereotyped nature of rodent sexual behavior, it would be perfectly possible to define that behavior in terms of specific motor patterns. However, whereas the definition of sexual behavior provided above is applicable to all species, definitions based on species-specific motor patterns would be limited to a particular species or a group of closely related species. This would mean that we needed to operate with many definitions of sexual behavior, making generalizations from one species to another very difficult or impossible.

From this brief discussion of what sexual behavior may be, we can now turn to an analysis of the basic behavioral, endocrine, and nervous mechanisms underlying the expression of that behavior. Much more extensive accounts of specific aspects of these mechanisms can be found elsewhere (Ågmo, 2007; Blaustein, 2008).

Sexual Motivation

The probability that an individual will display sexual behavior in response to a constant stimulus varies from zero to one. The female rodent is a good example of this. During most of the adult life, she will not respond with lordosis to a male's mounts. Usually she does not even allow the male to mount her. However, for a few hours every fourth or fifth day the female will allow herself to be mounted and she will respond with lordosis to every mount received. The construct used to explain such variations in the likelihood of response to a particular stimulus is called motivation. If we refer to the likelihood that a sexually relevant stimulus will activate sexual behavior we talk about sexual motivation. If we instead refer to the likelihood that an alimentary stimulus, like a cheeseburger, will activate the response of eating, we talk about motivation for food, or, in vernacular language, hunger.

The intensity of motivation is determined by external stimuli as well as by internal states. Since the exact nature of relevant internal states is often poorly known, it is helpful to consider these states as theoretical constructs, often called the central motive state (Bindra, 1978). In the case of the sexual central motive state, the construct can be filled with empirical content, since at least some of the neurobiological events underlying it are known. Obviously, there are still many unknown elements, but it is important to point out that the sexual central motive state can be partly anchored in rather well described neurobiological processes.

Activation of sexual responses requires both an appropriate central motive state and appropriate external stimuli. Efficient stimuli are called incentives, and are characterized by their capacity to provoke approach behaviors, among other things. In the human, there is much evidence showing that the external incentive stimuli can be replaced by mental representations of sexually relevant stimuli. Thus, no external stimulus is necessary. In non-human animals, an external stimulus is necessary for the activation of sexual responses. This important difference depends most likely on the fact that the human, at difference to other animals, possesses the capacity of symbolic language, allowing us to create mental representations of events in the past, in the future, or that never have and never will occur (fantasies). The fact that humans may create mental representations of stimuli that are not present sometimes has led to the misunderstanding that humans do not need a stimulus to be sexually motivated. This mistake fitted into the old notion that the sexual impulse or drive is of purely internal origin. In its most extreme form the internal drive hypothesis maintained that some mysterious "sexual energy" accumulates and eventually will require outlet (e.g., Moll, 1897). Fortunately, it appears that the incentive motivational approach is replacing the outdated idea of an irresistible and uncontrollable internal drive in analyses of human sexual behavior (e.g., Janssen, 2011).

Sexual motivation does not only determine the likelihood for the display of sexual behavior but also the intensity of approach to a potential mate and the magnitude of certain visceral responses. Paramount among the visceral responses to a sexual incentive stimulus in the human is enhanced genital blood flow, manifested as erection in men and vaginal lubrication in women. These responses are called sexual arousal (Ågmo, 2008).

> **Box 4.1   Organization of sexual behavior**
>
> The basic organization of sexual behavior (see Figure 4.1) is as follows: distant sexual incentive stimuli, emitted by a potential mate, activate approach behaviors. If successful, the approach behaviors will lead to the establishment of physical contact with the potential mate. Eventually copulatory motor patterns may be activated. These motor patterns will bring the male genitals in contact with the female genitals and normally continue until the deposit of sperm in the female reproductive tract has been accomplished. Sensory stimulation from the genital area causes a state of positive affect. In the human, copulation leads frequently to orgasm, a state of intense positive affect.

The Sexual Incentive Stimuli

A schematic illustration of the sequence of events associated with the display of sexual behavior is shown in Figure 4.1 (also see Box 4.1).

Most sexual behaviors require that two or more individuals are in close proximity. The exception is solitary sexual activities, that is, masturbation. Nevertheless, it can be maintained that the most common of the sexual behaviors, copulation, is always preceded by approach behavior of some kind. This applies equally to humans and non-human animals. In rodents and humans, these approach behaviors are highly variable. A rat may walk, run, jump, swim, or dig to get close to another rat, while a human may

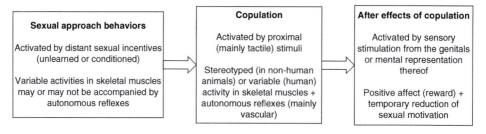

Figure 4.1   The basic organization of sexual behavior.

do all these in addition to jump into a car or onto a plane before taking the prospective partner out for dinner, to a bar, to the theater, or whatever, before engaging in sexual activities. In some mammals, birds and other vertebrates and many invertebrates, the approach behaviors include, but are not limited to, stereotyped courtship behaviors. However, since none of these behaviors involve the genitals, they cannot be considered sexual. Furthermore, the approach behaviors do not necessarily lead to copulation, and identical motor patterns are displayed in many non-sexual contexts. The variable, context-dependent approach behaviors preceding sexual interactions are fundamentally different from the stereotyped copulatory behaviors in non-human animals, and also from the capricious human sexual activities. Whereas copulation, be it human or not, is heavily dependent on proximate stimuli, mostly tactile, approach behaviors are activated by distant stimuli.

The stimuli inducing rodents of opposite sex to approach each other have been carefully studied. The role of the different sensory modalities – that is, sight, hearing, and smell – has been evaluated. It is quite clear that olfactory stimuli are necessary and sufficient for activating approach behaviors, whereas visual and auditory stimuli are not (for a review, see Hernández-González, Guevara, & Ågmo, 2008). The sexual incentive properties of olfactory stimuli are not dependent on learning. Rats of both sexes without any sexual experience at all readily approach odors from individuals of the opposite sex. This means that the capacity to react to these stimuli is built into the rats' nervous system. In fact, in rats' approach is an unconditioned (unlearned) response to an unconditioned stimulus (the opposite-sex odor). However, any stimulus can acquire sexual incentive properties through learning. A neutral odor, like fish or garlic oil, or a light, not causing any response at all in an untrained rat, can become a sexual incentive for male rats through classical conditioning (e.g., Chu & Ågmo, 2012).

In non-human primates, little is known about distant sexual incentives. Nonetheless, there is a series of most elegant studies in the chacma baboon showing that visual stimuli emitted by the female have sexual incentive properties for males, whereas odors and sounds from females have not. Female chacma baboons have a sexual skin, the size of which is estrogen dependent. Females with large sexual skins, because of estrogen treatment, made males masturbate far more than untreated, ovariectomized females did. In fact, the males did not masturbate at all when exposed to these latter females. When the males were separated from the females with an opaque screen, even a large sexual skin failed to stimulate masturbation (Bielert, 1982; Bielert & van der Walt, 1982). The screen efficiently prevented the males from viewing the females, but it did not block sounds and odors. Thus, it can be concluded that, in chacma baboons, visual stimuli are necessary and sufficient for activating the male sexual behavior of masturbation, whereas sounds and odors are not. It is not known whether the sexual skin has acquired incentive properties because of learning or if these properties are unconditioned. Nevertheless, it appears that visual stimuli are crucial in non-human primates, unlike in rodents.

In humans there is a considerable literature concerning the relative attractiveness of bodily forms (e.g., Singh, 1993), but judging one picture more attractive than another does not say anything at all about its sexual incentive value. However, there is one informative study of incentive stimuli causing sexual approach behavior in humans (Hendrie, Mannion, & Godfrey, 2009). Hidden observers determined approaches to individuals of the opposite sex in the dance area of a nightclub. Eighty per cent of all approaches were initiated by a male. The number of male approaches to women exposing more than 40% of flesh was far superior to approaches to women exposing less than 20%. Likewise, males approached women exposing more than 75% of their breasts much more than women exposing less than 25%. Men also spent more time dancing with women moving in a sexually suggestive manner than with women that just gently swayed. That the approaches were of a sexual nature is suggested by the observation that 80% of the night club attendees entered without a partner while 50% were leaving with a partner. The results of this most ingenious study suggest that female naked flesh and breasts as well as suggestive movements function as sexual incentives for men.

Sexual incentive *Evidence suggests that naked flesh as well as suggestive movements act as sexual incentives in men.*
Source: © Concord. Used under license from Pixabay.

Contrary to sexual approach behaviors, the stimulus control of sexual arousal has been much studied in human. A very important advantage of the arousal response is that it can be objectively measured, and solid knowledge can consequently be obtained. Auditory stimuli in the form of texts with sexual content, still pictures of nude individuals either alone or engaging in sexual activities, and moving pictures of individuals having sex are all efficient for enhancing genital blood flow. It is believed that moving pictures with sound are superior to all other stimuli (e.g., Golde, Strassberg, & Turner, 2000), but even purely mental representations of sexual activities are enough to cause arousal.

It is not known whether there are any human unconditioned sexual incentive stimuli or not. It has been suggested that there are none (Hardy, 1964). If this suggestion is correct, then all sexual incentives are the result of learning. The intrinsically rewarding properties of genital stimulation can transform any stimulus into a sexual incentive by simple, accidental contiguity, not fundamentally different from the experimental contiguities arranged in studies of classical conditioning of sexual responses in rats. It is also likely that many stimuli acquire sexual incentive properties through social learning (Ågmo, 2007; Gagnon & Simon, 2002). There are no experimental studies of social learning of sexual incentives in the human, but there are many studies showing that conditioning can turn neutral stimuli into sexual incentives. The most elegant of those studies employ an undoubtedly unconditioned stimulus, mechanical stimulation of the clitoris, and the ensuing unconditioned response, enhanced vaginal blood flow (e.g., Both, Brauer, & Laan, 2011). A neutral stimulus that by itself had no effect on that blood flow strongly enhanced it after a few pairings, that is, the stimulus had acquired sexual incentive properties through classical conditioning. This and many other studies show that any stimulus may acquire sexual incentive properties. Different forms of associative learning can explain the enormous variety of stimuli causing sexual excitement in the human.

When humans learn to respond sexually to socially unacceptable stimuli – children or inanimate objects like underwear or boots, for example – they often receive the diagnosis of paraphilia, with the subcategories of pedophilia and fetishism, respectively. Nevertheless, it is extremely important to note that the learning processes involved are indistinguishable from those operating in learning to respond sexually to socially acceptable stimuli.

The Sexual Central Motive State: Hormones

Female rodents

In female rats and mice, sexual behavior coincides with the sharp increase in serum concentration of estrogens and progesterone occurring around ovulation. In females lacking endogenous hormone production, sexual behavior can be activated by the administration of estradiol followed by progesterone or by estradiol alone. Estradiol actions at the estrogen receptor α are essential (Ogawa et al., 1998), whereas the estrogen receptor β is believed to be of little or no importance for this behavior.

Activation of the androgen receptor does not stimulate sexual behavior in female rodents (see Figure 4.2). Ovariectomized females treated with the androgen agonist dihydrotestosterone do not display lordosis (van de Poll, van Zanten, & de Jonge, 1986) and they are not attracted to sexually active males (McDonald & Meyerson, 1973). There is even data showing that androgen receptor agonists inhibit estrogen-induced lordosis in female rats (e.g., Dohanich & Clemens, 1983). In sum, female rodent sexual behavior is strictly dependent on estrogens, mainly acting at the estrogen receptor α. Activation of the progesterone receptor enhances the actions of estrogens, but is not indispensable. The androgen receptor has no stimulatory effect, but it may be inhibitory under some circumstances.

Female, non-human primates

The importance of ovarian hormones for sexual behavior in female primates has been a matter of debate for decades, and the issue is not yet resolved. Contrary to rodents, females of many primate species continuously display sexual behavior. Thus, a strict dependence on ovarian hormones is unlikely. Nevertheless, even if primate sexual behavior was not absolutely dependent on ovarian hormones as it is in rodents, these hormones could modulate the intensity of that behavior. One approach to this issue has consisted of searching for changes in sexual behavior during the menstrual cycle. Since the serum concentration of ovarian hormones greatly varies between phases, concurrent variation in the intensity of sex would constitute evidence for a role of

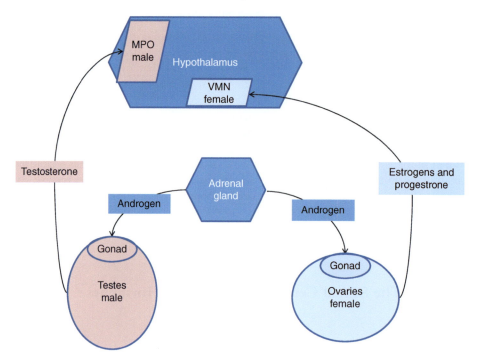

Figure 4.2 Different parts of the hypothalamus (nucleus in the brain) control sexual behavior in men and women.

Sexual motivation *In a night club, men tend to approach women, especially those who expose more of their breasts. One third of those coming on their own leave the club with a partner, suggesting sexual motivation partly drives nightclub participation (Hendrie, Mannion, & Godfrey, 2009).*

Source: © Geralt. Used under license from 123RF.

these hormones. In an extensive review of primate studies of the menstrual cycle published before 1930, it was concluded that "Monkeys that copulate in captivity do so at all times, but copulation occurs most frequently during the period of maximum sexual skin activity" (Zuckerman, 1930, p. 749). The size and color of the sexual skin is estrogen dependent, suggesting that maximal sexual behavior coincides with the estrogen peak preceding ovulation. Results from a large number of more recent studies of nonhuman primates support the association between serum estrogen concentration and the intensity of sexual behavior (see Michael & Zumpe, 1993, for a review). However, there are also data showing that primate female sexual behavior does not vary significantly during the estrous cycle (e.g., Slob, Wiegand, Goy, & Robinson, 1978), and if it does there may be explanations unrelated to that cycle (e.g., Fürtbauer, Mundry, Heistermann, Schülke, & Ostner, 2011).

Instead of analyzing relations between serum hormone concentrations and sexual behavior during the menstrual cycle it is perfectly possible to remove the ovaries, thereby causing a drastic reduction in the serum concentration of estrogens and progesterone. This approach has been employed in a number of studies. Generally, ovariectomy leads to a reduction of female sexual behavior, but not to a complete absence of such behavior as is seen in rodents. The most reasonable conclusion that can be drawn from these studies is that estrogens are not absolutely necessary for female sexual behavior, but they enhance female sexual motivation as well as female attractiveness. In short, studies of ovariectomized animals with or without hormone replacement lead to the same conclusion as the studies of the menstrual cycle: estrogens seem to have a facilitatory effect but do not seem to be indispensable.

While ovariectomy reduces, but does not eliminate, sexual behavior in female rhesus monkeys, adrenalectomy does (e.g., Everitt, Herbert, & Hamer, 1972). Estrogen treatment does not ameliorate behavior, but treatment with testosterone does. The rather obvious conclusion is that testosterone, mostly from the adrenals, is necessary for sexual behavior in the female rhesus monkey. This conclusion was challenged by the results of a study in which an androgen receptor antagonist was administered to intact, cycling females. No reduction in sexual behavior was observed, suggesting that the androgen receptor is not needed for that behavior (Johnson & Phoenix, 1978). Almost 30 years would pass before the effects of testosterone were evaluated in additional studies. It turns out that intranasal administration of this androgen stimulates sexual motivation in a new world monkey, the *Cebus paella* (Topic, Tavares, Tomaz, & Mattern, 2007). In spite of this exciting observation, no further studies seem to have been performed concerning androgens and non-human primates. At present, it is difficult to express any clear opinion about their actual importance.

Women

Many scientists have focused their attention on the menstrual cycle when searching for evidence for a role of ovarian hormones in the sexual behavior of women. Some studies have indeed reported maximal sexual activity and/or motivation around ovulation, coinciding with the peak in serum estrogen concentration (e.g., Udry & Morris, 1968), or just after menstruation, that is, early in the follicular phase when estrogen concentrations begin to rise (e.g., Dobbins, 1980). Others have found a maximum shortly before menstruation (e.g., Greenblatt, Mortara, & Torpin, 1942) when estrogen concentration is low and progesterone concentration high. There are also many studies that have failed to detect systematic variations in sexual behavior during the menstrual cycle (e.g., Morotti et al., 2013). All these studies are based on self-reports of some kind (often questionnaires or diaries). Since self-reports of behavior, particularly of intimate behaviors like sex (e.g., Fisher, 2013) are extremely unreliable and basically reflect dominant social norms or prejudices, they are of limited value. Rather than discussing data with unknown relationships to reality, it can be useful to focus on objective studies of sexual behavior in women.

Even though it is not customary to install surveillance cameras in peoples' bedrooms, which would be necessary for obtaining real life data, it is possible to create conditions in which women can display sexual responses under controlled conditions. A pioneering study (Schreiner-Engel, Schiavi, Smith, & White, 1981) employing an audiotape with explicit sexual content or self-generated sexual fantasies as stimuli revealed that the vaginal response, as determined by photoplethysmography, was at a minimum around ovulation. Another study, also employing an erotic audiotape or fantasies as stimuli and photoplethysmography to quantify the vaginal response, found no effect of the menstrual cycle phase (Hoon, Bruce, & Kinchloe, 1982). Similar results have been obtained when a pornographic movie segment is used as sexual stimulus (e.g., Meuwissen & Over, 1992). Other objective measures of sexual motivation have also failed to detect variations during the menstrual cycle (Abler et al., 2013; Slob, Ernste, & van der Werff ten Bosc, 1991).

In addition to changes in ovarian hormones during the menstrual cycle, women experience drastic changes in hormone production during the life span. Sooner or later menstrual cycles start to become irregular (the climacteric) and eventually menopause sets in. There is a dramatic reduction in ovarian hormone production, and the cyclicity is lost. If ovarian hormones were important for sexual behavior, a drastic reduction would be observed in menopause. This hypothesis has been evaluated in a large number of studies based on self-reports of different kinds. As always occurs with this type of study, results are contradictory. Some find no effect of menopause (e.g., Kinsey, Pomeroy, Martin, & Gebhard, 1953) while others do (e.g., Dennerstein, Randolph, Taffe, Dudley, & Burger, 2002). Fortunately, there are several comparisons between premenopausal and menopausal women with regard to sexual functions using objective data. The results of the many studies performed over the last 25 years coincide in showing that the vaginal response to sexually relevant stimuli is of equal magnitude in premenopausal and menopausal (because of age or ovariectomy) women (e.g., Suh et al., 2004). There is not one single study showing otherwise. This most unusual concordance clearly shows that a drastic reduction in serum concentrations of ovarian hormones does not reduce sexual motivation in the human female.

Ever since it was reported that adrenalectomy has much more profound effects on sexuality in women than removal of the ovaries (Waxenberg, Drellich, & Sutherland, 1959), there has been a widespread belief that androgens are important for sexual behavior. A somewhat more recent self-report study of women with much reduced serum androgen concentration confirmed that sexual behavior was seriously affected (Kaplan & Owett, 1993). When the vaginal response to sexually relevant stimuli – that is, sexual arousal – is evaluated, a relationship between serum testosterone concentration and response magnitude has been reported (Heiman et al., 2011). There are even data showing that acute treatment with testosterone enhances sexual arousal in healthy, young women (Tuiten et al., 2000) as well as in women in menopause (Heard-Davison, Heiman, & Kuffel, 2007). It seems, then, that as soon as an objective measure of sexual arousal is employed, androgens turn out to be important for sexual motivation in women.

Male rodents

Castration of rats and mice leads to reduce and eventually absent sexual behavior, showing that some products from the testicles are needed. Long ago that product was found to be testosterone. This hormone is easily aromatized to estradiol and reduced to 5α-dihydrotestosterone. The enzymes responsible for these conversions, aromatase and 5α-reductase are widely distributed in the organism and present in the brain structures important for sexual behavior. Consequently, there is simultaneous activation of estrogen and androgen receptors in intact males (as well as castrated testosterone-treated animals) exposed to both estradiol and dihydrotestosterone. There is also abundant evidence showing that activation of both these receptors is required for sexual behavior in rodents (Baum, 2003). In female rodents, the estrogen receptor α rather than the β is involved (Ogawa, Lubahn, Korach, & Pfaff, 1997).

Male non-human primates

Castration of primates has consequences very similar to those of castration of rodents. Dihydrotestosterone alone has been found to activate male sexual behavior in castrated rhesus monkeys (e.g., Phoenix, 1974), suggesting that only androgen receptors are needed for that behavior. However, dihydrotestosterone failed to activate sexual behavior in *Macaca fascicularis*, whereas testosterone was efficient (Michael, Zumpe, & Bonsall, 1986). It would seem, then, that some primate species may need stimulation of both androgen and estrogen receptors while others do not.

The human male

Sexual behavior in men is as dependent on testicular hormones as it is in rats and non-human primates. Reduction of serum testosterone concentration, be it because of castration or because of drugs altering gonadotrophin production or action, leads to strongly diminished sexual behavior, even in healthy, young men (e.g., Bagatell, Heiman, Rivier, & Bremner, 1994). There is no evidence that aromatization to estradiol is necessary, showing that only the androgen receptor is needed for sexual behavior in men.

The Sexual Central Motive State: Brain Sites

Females

Even though the estrogen receptor α is widely distributed in the brain, it is a small hypothalamic structure, the ventromedial nucleus, that controls female sexual behavior. Lesions of this nucleus strongly reduce sexual behavior in females treated with estradiol and progesterone, whereas electrical stimulation of it facilitates sex. Local implants of estradiol into the ventromedial nucleus activate sexual behavior in ovariectomized females, and local infusion of an estrogen receptor antagonist blocks the stimulatory action of systemically administered estradiol. There is, in fact, an overwhelming amount of evidence firmly establishing a role for the ventromedial nucleus in the control of female sexual behavior in rodents and other mammals (see Pfaff, 1999, for a review). There is no reason to believe that the human should be an exception to this principle, but unequivocal data are still lacking.

Many other brain structures have been implicated in the central nervous control of female sexual behavior. Sensory information must be processed, and motor systems must be activated for the display of the behavior. Consequently, sensory as well as motor areas participate, but none of them is essential in the same way as the ventromedial nucleus.

Males

Data from fish, reptiles, amphibians, birds, and mammals show that the medial preoptic area is essential for sexual behavior. Medial preoptic lesion strongly reduces or eliminates all aspects of this behavior, from sexual approach to execution of the copulatory reflexes. Implantation of testosterone into this area in castrated animals restores sexual behaviors. Sensory structures conveying information to the preoptic area as well as output to motor structures controlling the muscles involved in sexual activities are also important, but, exactly as was the case in females, they are not essential (see Paredes, 2003, for a review).

Bisexuality and Homosexuality

Many animals are perfectly able to display behaviors typical of the other sex. Male rats easily display lordosis, whereas female rats often mount other females or males. They can also display the behavior patterns of intromission (vaginal penetration) and ejaculation even though no intromission and no seminal emission actually occur. Detailed studies have revealed that male and female mounts are indistinguishable. Interestingly, preoptic lesion in female rats eliminates mounting, but it facilitates lordosis in some conditions. Similarly, lesion of the ventromedial nucleus in male rats reduces lordosis, while mounting is facilitated. It seems that there is a reciprocal inhibition between the area controlling male-typical sexual behavior and the area controlling female-typical behavior. In males, the preoptic area dominates over the ventromedial nucleus, whereas the opposite is true for females. It can be proposed that there is no qualitative difference between male and female. It is only more likely that a male will display male-typical behaviors than female-typical, whereas the inverse is true for females.

The capacity to show motor patterns typical of the opposite sex has nothing to do with homosexuality. A male rat mounting another (lordosis displaying male), does not allow us to call any of these males homosexual. Neither could we call a female mounting another female, or the female being mounted by another female, homosexual. It is usually considered that the notion of homosexuality refers to a preference for having sex with the own sex, even when a choice is available (Vasey, 2002). Using that definition, homosexuality is completely unknown in non-manipulated rats and in most other mammals. There are, however, examples of non-human animal species in which preference for the own sex has been repeatedly found. Some male rams choose to copulate with other males even when females are available (Zenchak, Anderson, & Schein, 1981), and some female Japanese snow monkeys choose to copulate and form lasting relationships with other females (Vasey, 1996). There is no systematic difference in serum hormone concentrations or in brain structures between homosexual and heterosexual rams and monkeys. This coincides with data from humans, in which no reliable difference in brain and hormones between same-sex and opposite-sex preferring individuals has been found (e.g., Mbugua, 2003).

Male rats can be trained to show preference for members of the same sex. Repeated exposure to same-sex individuals associated with an injection of a rewarding drug makes the male prefer to interact with another male at a later test, when a sexually receptive female is also available (Cibrian-Llanderal et al., 2012). These studies are the first demonstration of how a conditioning procedure can change a rat's preference from heterosexual to homosexual. If confirmed, these observations lends support to the notion that same-sex preferences may be learned in the human as well, something that has been suggested several times already (e.g., Ågmo, 2007; Kinsey, 1941).

Drugs and Sexual Motivation

Every part of the sequence of sexual behavior illustrated in Figure 4.1 may be modified by drugs. The reactivity to sexual incentives may be enhanced or reduced, having as consequence increased or decreased likelihood for the display of sexual approach behaviors. The copulatory motor patterns themselves are rarely affected by drug treatment, but their frequency or intensity may be affected. Finally, the hedonic consequences of sexual activity may be enhanced or reduced by drugs.

Although a large number of drugs have been found to inhibit or stimulate sexual behavior in non-human animals, very few have established effects on human sexuality. Curiously enough, this is entirely different from the large number of anecdotes about the dramatic consequences some drugs may have upon individuals. Unfortunately, all anecdotes about aphrodisiacs (compounds enhancing sexual activity or sexual pleasure) remain unsubstantiated, whereas controlled clinical studies have shown that some drugs indeed reduce sexual activity. Opiates have long been known to be inhibitory, probably because of their action on the endocrine system. Gonadotrophin release is strongly reduced by opiates, leading to a profound decrease in serum testosterone concentrations, which in turn leads to reduced sexual activity. A different group of drugs, the specific serotonin reuptake inhibitors, used for the treatment of depression, inhibits all aspects of sexual behavior because of an action within the central nervous system (Rosen, Lane, & Menza, 1999). The deleterious effect on sexual functions is actually the main side effect of these kinds of drugs. It may be interesting to note that these drugs also are inhibitory in rodents.

Whereas the gonadotrophin inhibition caused by opiates is a side effect of these drugs, there are several compounds specifically designed to suppress the release of gonadotrophins from the pituitary. There are also compounds blocking the androgen receptor. Regardless of the mechanism of action, all these drugs cause a substantial reduction in sexual motivation and behavior in men. It could be reasoned that if a dramatic decrease in testosterone availability reduces sexual behavior, then a dramatic increase would enhance that behavior. This, however, is not the case. Data from intact rats and healthy men clearly show that testosterone treatment does not enhance sexual motivation and behavior. In hypogonadal men and rats, supplementary testosterone restores sexual behavior to a normal level, but even massive doses fail to increase behavior beyond that level (e.g., Anderson, Bancroft, & Wu, 1992). This fact also applies to the group of compounds labeled anabolic steroids. Even when consumed in large quantities they do not affect sexual motivation in the slightest.

Sexual dismophism *Different parts of the brain (different nucleus of the hypothalamus) control sexual behavior in men and women. It is their relative activation that may partially contribute to gender differences (sexual dismophsim).*
Source: © Metsi. Used under license from 123RF.

Conclusions: Is There Any Neurobiological Basis for Socially Unacceptable Sexual Behaviors?

First of all, it must be pointed out that the acceptability of any behavior pattern is a social construction completely independent of any possible biological bases for that behavior. A simple example can be micturition. In some places, execution of this basic behavior pattern in a public space is considered completely unacceptable, and it may even be legally punished. In other places, this same behavior is routine, and it does not produce the slightest reaction from other people or from law enforcement agencies. In both cases the biological bases for micturition are identical. This means that a behavior pattern may be socially acceptable in one place while it is unacceptable in another. For example, the definition of pedophilia varies from one place to another and from one time to another, and the concept may be entirely absent in cultures where sexual relations with children is the norm (Green, 2002). Nevertheless, there is no reason to believe that the biological basis, if any, of pedophilia varies from one place to another. The search for the biological basis of socially constructed entities is probably a futile enterprise.

Having said this, it should also be observed that it is possible to find clear differences between people responding sexually to children versus those not doing so. Pedophilic men will respond with erection to pictures of nude children, whereas non-pedophilic men will respond less (e.g., Grossman, Cavanaugh, & Haywood, 1992). Nevertheless,

25% of the men in a community sample responded equally to children and adults (Hall, Hirschman, & Oliver, 1995). However, none of them had reportedly engaged in sexual activities with children, showing that there is not necessarily an association between being sexually aroused and the execution of socially unacceptable acts.

It is quite obvious that individuals with absent or low activity in the central motive state will not respond to any sexual incentive at all, or respond weakly to such incentives. To the contrary, individuals with a very active central motive state may emit strong responses even to weak sexual incentives. There are some observations suggesting that the paraphilias may be associated with unusually high sexual motivation (Kafka, 2003), but solid empirical evidence is still lacking. However, the fact that drugs reducing sexual motivation are quite efficient for treating the paraphilias (Garcia, Delavenne, Assumpcao, & Thibaut, 2013) might render indirect support to heightened sexual motivation as a potential cause. It has also been proposed that rapists suffer from unusually high levels of sexual motivation. Unfortunately, there are no conclusive empirical data on this issue, but at least it appears that heightened motivation is not a major cause of rape. It has even been proposed that rape is a crime of violence essentially unrelated to sexuality (see Bryden & Grier, 2011, for an excellent discussion of this issue). Observations showing that treatments that lower serum testosterone concentration and consequently reduce sexual motivation are efficient for diminishing recidivism among rapists does not constitute unequivocal evidence for a role of motivation in rape. Reduced testosterone concentration is associated with diminished aggression as much as with lowered sexual motivation. If rape were a crime of violence it should be reduced by anti-aggressive treatments, exactly as is the case.

A rather unfortunate problem with the treatments that efficiently reduce socially unacceptable sexual behaviors is that they reduce the acceptable behaviors just as much. This holds for all available pharmacological treatments, regardless of whether they are based on lowering serum testosterone concentration in one way or another or on enhancing central serotonergic activity. Philosophers and lawmakers must decide whether the social benefits of these treatments outweigh the cost to the individual. Independently of this problem, it must be recognized that the neurobiological knowledge about sexual behavior allows us to purposefully alter the intensity of that behavior, at least in a downward direction.

Recommended Reading

Ågmo, A. (2007). *Functional and dysfunctional sexual behavior. A synthesis of neuroscience and comparative psychology*. San Diego, CA: Academic Press. *An extensive analysis of the neurobiological bases of mammalian (including human) sexual behavior and a detailed account of the incentive motivational framework. Its application to some sexual dysfunctions is also described.*

Gagnon, J. H., & Simon, W. (2002). *Sexual conduct: The social sources of human sexuality* (2nd ed.). New Brunswick, NJ: AldineTransaction. *The social determinants of human sexuality are brilliantly discussed in this legendary book.*

Kim, S. W., Schenck, C. H., Grant, J. E., Yoon, G., Dosa, P. I., Odlaug, B. L., ... Pfaus, J. G. (2013). Neurobiology of sexual desire. *Neuroquantology 11*, 332–359. *This paper presents a charming proposal concerning the central circuits and transmitters involved in the activation of sexual motivation, and some data from trials of drugs potentially useful for the treatment of hypoactive sexual desire disorders.*

Kinsey, A. C., Pomeroy, W. B., & Martin, C. E. (1948). *Sexual behavior in the human male*. Philadelphia, PA: Saunders; and Kinsey, A. C., Pomeroy, W. B., Martin, C. E., & Gebhard, P. H. (1953). *Sexual behavior in the human female*. Philadelphia, PA: Saunders. *For a general overview of human sexual behavior these classic books by Kinsey and collaborators are still unsurpassed.*

References

Ågmo, A. (2007). *Functional and dysfunctional sexual behavior. A synthesis of neuroscience and comparative psychology*. San Diego, CA: Academic Press.

Ågmo, A. (2008). On the concept of sexual arousal: A simpler alternative. *Hormones and Behavior, 53*, 312–314.

Abler, B., Kumpfmuller, D., Grön, G., Walter, M., Stingl, J., & Seeringer, A. (2013). Neural correlates of erotic stimulation under different levels of female sexual hormones. *Plos One, 8*, e5447.

Anderson, R. A., Bancroft, J., & Wu, F. C. W. (1992). The effects of exogenous testosterone on sexuality and mood of normal men. *Journal of Clinical Endocrinology and Metabolism, 75*, 1503–1507.

Bagatell, C. J., Heiman, J. R., Rivier, J. E., & Bremner, W. J. (1994). Effects of endogenous testosterone and estradiol on sexual behavior in normal young men. *Journal of Clinical Endocrinology and Metabolism, 78*, 711–716.

Baum, M. J. (2003). Activational and organizational effects of estradiol on male behavioral neuroendocrine function. *Scandinavian Journal of Psychology, 44*, 213–220.

Bielert, C. (1982). Experimental examinations of baboon (*Papio ursinus*) sex stimuli. In C. T. Snowdon, C. H. Brown, & M. R. Petersen (Eds.), *Primate communication* (pp. 373–395). Cambridge, UK: Cambridge University Press.

Bielert, C., & van der Walt, L. A. (1982). Male Chacma baboon (*Papio ursinus*) sexual arousal: Mediation by visual cues from female conspecifics. *Psychoneuroendocrinology, 7*, 31–48.

Bindra, D. (1978). How adaptive behavior is produced: A perceptual-motivational alternative to response reinforcement. *Behavioral and Brain Sciences, 1*, 41–52.

Blaustein, J. D. (2008). Neuroendocrine regulation of feminine sexual behavior: Lessons from rodent models and thoughts about humans. *Annual Review of Psychology, 59*, 93–118.

Both, S., Brauer, M., & Laan, E. (2011). Classical conditioning of sexual response in women: A replication study. *Journal of Sexual Medicine, 8*, 3116–3131.

Bryden, D. P., & Grier, M. M. (2011). The search for rapists' "real" motives. *Journal of Criminal Law & Criminology, 101*, 171–278.

Chu, X., & Agmo, A. (2012). Pavlovian conditioning with sexually relevant UCS: Which is the necessary UCR? *Journal of Experimental Psychology-Animal Behavior Processes, 38*, 346–358.

Cibrian-Llanderal, T., Rosas-Aguilar, V., Triana-Del Rio, R., Perez, C. A., Manzo, J., Garcia, L. I., & Coria-Avila, G. A. (2012). Enhaced D2-type receptor activity facilitates the development of conditioned same-sex partner preference in male rats. *Pharmacology Biochemistry and Behavior, 102*, 177–183.

Dennerstein, L., Randolph, J., Taffe, J., Dudley, E., & Burger, M. D. (2002). Hormones, mood, sexuality, and the menopausal transition. *Fertility and Sterility, 77*, Suppl. 4, S42–S48.

Dobbins, J. G. (1980). Implications of a time-dependent model of sexual intercourse within the menstrual cycle. *Journal of Biosocial Science, 12*, 133–140.

Dohanich, G. P., & Clemens, L. G. (1983). Inhibition of estrogen-activated sexual behavior by androgens. *Hormones and Behavior, 17*, 366–373.

Everitt, B. J., Herbert, J., & Hamer, J. D. (1972). Sexual receptivity of bilaterally adrenalectomized female rhesus monkeys. *Physiology and Behavior, 8*, 409–415.

Fisher, T. D. (2013). Gender roles and pressure to be truthful: The bogus pipeline modifies gender differences in sexual but not non-sexual behavior. *Sex Roles, 68*, 401–414.

Fürtbauer, I., Mundry, R., Heistermann, M., Schülke, O., & Ostner, J. (2011). You mate, I mate: Macaque females synchronize sex not cycles. *Plos One, 6*, e26144.

Gagnon, J. H., & Simon, W. (2002). *Sexual conduct: The social sources of human sexuality* (2nd ed.) New Brunswick, NJ: AldineTransaction.

Garcia, F. D., Delavenne, H. G., Assumpcao, A. D. A., & Thibaut, F. (2013). Pharmacologic treatment of sex offenders with paraphilic disorder. *Current Psychiatry Reports, 15*(5), 356. doi: 10.1007/s11920-013-0356-5.

Golde, J. A., Strassberg, D. S., & Turner, C. M. (2000). Psychophysiologic assessment of erectile response and its suppression as a function of stimulus media and previous experience with plethysmography. *Journal of Sex Research, 37*, 53–59.

Green, R. (2002). Is pedophilia a mental disorder? *Archives of Sexual Behavior, 31*, 467–471.

Greenblatt, R. B., Mortara, F., & Torpin, R. (1942). Sexual libido in the female. *American Journal of Obstetrics and Gynecology, 44*, 658–663.

Grossman, L. S., Cavanaugh, J. L., & Haywood, T. W. (1992). Deviant sexual responsiveness on penile plethysmography using visual stimuli: Alleged child molesters vs. normal control subjects. *Journal of Nervous and Mental Disease, 180*, 207–208.

Hall, G. C. N., Hirschman, R., & Oliver, L. L. (1995). Sexual arousal and arousability to pedophilic stimuli in a community sample of normal men. *Behavior Therapy, 26*, 681–694.

Hardy, K. R. (1964). An appetitional theory of sexual motivation. *Psychological Review, 71*, 1–18.

Heard-Davison, A., Heiman, J. R., & Kuffel, S. (2007). Genital and subjective measurement of the time course effects of an acute dose of testosterone vs. placebo in postmenopausal women. *Journal of Sexual Medicine, 4*, 209–217.

Heiman, J. R., Rupp, H., Janssen, E., Newhouse, S. K., Brauer, M., & Laan, E. (2011). Sexual desire, sexual arousal and hormonal differences in premenopausal US and Dutch women with and without low sexual desire. *Hormones and Behavior, 59*, 772–779.

Hendrie, C. A., Mannion, H. D., & Godfrey, G. K. (2009). Evidence to suggest that nightclubs function as human sexual display grounds. *Behavior, 146*, 1331–1348.

Hernández-González, M., Guevara, M. A., & Ågmo, A. (2008). Motivational influences on the degree and direction of sexual attraction. *Annals of the New York Academy of Sciences, 1129*, 61–87.

Hoon, P. W., Bruce, K. E., & Kinchloe, B. (1982). Does the menstrual cycle play a role in sexual arousal? *Psychophysiology, 19*, 21–27.

Janssen, E. (2011). Sexual arousal in men: A review and conceptual analysis. *Hormones and Behavior, 59*, 708–716.

Johnson, D. F., & Phoenix, C. H. (1978). Sexual behavior amd hormone levels during the menstrual cycles of rhesus monkeys. *Hormones and Behavior, 11*, 160–174.

Kafka, M. P. (2003). Sex offending and sexual appetite: The clinical and theoretical relevance of hypersexual desire. *International Journal of Offender Therapy and Comparative Criminology, 47*, 439–451.

Kaplan, H. S., & Owett, T. (1993). The female androgen deficiency syndrome. *Journal of Sex and Marital Therapy, 19*, 3–24.

Kinsey, A. C. (1941). Criteria for a hormonal explanation of the homosexual. *Journal of Clinical Endocrinology, 1*, 424–428.

Kinsey, A. C., Pomeroy, W. B., Martin, C. E., & Gebhard, P. H. (1953). *Sexual behavior in the human female*. Philadelphia: Saunders.

Mbugua, K. (2003). Sexual orientation and brain structures: A critical review of recent research. *Current Science, 84*, 173–178.

McDonald, P. G., & Meyerson, B. J. (1973). The effect of oestradiol, testosterone and dihydrotestosterone on sexual motivation in the ovariectomized female rat. *Physiology and Behavior, 11*, 515–520.

Meuwissen, I., & Over, R. (1992). Sexual arousal across phases of the human menstrual cycle. *Archives of Sexual Behavior, 21*, 101–119.

Michael, R. P., & Zumpe, D. (1993). A review of hormonal factors influencing the sexual and aggressive behavior of Macaques. *American Journal of Primatology, 30*, 213–241.

Michael, R. P., Zumpe, D., & Bonsall, R. W. (1986). Comparison of the effects of testosterone and dihydrotestosterone on the behavior of male cynomolgus monkeys (*Macaca fascicularis*). *Physiology and Behavior, 36*, 349–355.

Moll, A. (1897). *Untersuchungen über die Libido sexualis*. Berlin: Buchhandlung H. Kornfeld.

Morotti, E., Battaglia, B., Persico, N., Zampieri, M., Busacchi, P., Venturoli, S., & Battaglia, C. (2013). Clitoral changes, sexuality, and body image during the menstrual cycle: A pilot study. *Journal of Sexual Medicine, 10*, 1320–1327.

Naidu, K., Chung, A., & Mulcahy, M. (2013). An unusual urethral foreign body. *International Journal of Surgery Case Reports, 4*(11), 1052–1054. doi: 10.1016/j.ijscr.2013.07.017.

Ogawa, S., Eng, V., Taylor, J., Lubahn, D. B., Korach, K. S., & Pfaff, D. W. (1998). Roles of estrogen receptor-α gene expression in reproduction-related behaviors in female mice. *Endocrinology, 139*, 5070–5081.

Ogawa, S., Lubahn, D. B., Korach, K. S., & Pfaff, D. W. (1997). Behavioral effects of estrogen receptor gene disruption in male mice. *Proceedings of the National Academy of Sciences of the United States of America, 94*, 1476–1481.

Paredes, R. G. (2003). Medial preoptic area/anterior hypothalamus and sexual motivation. *Scandinavian Journal of Psychology, 44*, 203–212.

Pfaff, D. W. (1999). *Drive. Neurobiological and molecular mechanisms of sexual motivation*. Cambridge, MA: MIT Press.

Phoenix, C. H. (1974). Effects of dihydrotestosterone on sexual behavior of castrated male rhesus monkeys. *Physiology and Behavior, 12*, 1045–1055.

Rosen, R. C., Lane, R. M., & Menza, M. (1999). Effects of SSRIs on sexual function: A critical review. *Journal of Clinical Psychopharmacology, 19*, 67–85.

Schreiner-Engel, P., Schiavi, R. C., Smith, H., & White, D. (1981). Sexual arousability and the menstrual cycle. *Psychosomatic Medicine, 43*, 199–214.

Singh, D. (1993). Body shape and women's attractiveness. The critical role of waist-to-hip ratio. *Human Nature, 4*, 297–321.

Slob, A. K., Ernste, M., & van der Werff ten Bosch, J. J. (1991). Menstrual cycle phase and sexual arousability in women. *Archives of Sexual Behavior, 20*, 567–577.

Slob, A. K., Wiegand, S. J., Goy, R. W., & Robinson, J. A. (1978). Heterosexual interactions in laboratory-housed stumptail macaques (*Macaca arctoides*): Observations during the menstrual cycle and after ovariectomy. *Hormones and Behavior, 10*, 193–211.

Suh, D. D., Yang, C. C., Cao, Y., Heiman, J. R., Garland, P. A., & Maravilla, K. R. (2004). MRI of female genital arousal and pelvic organs during sexual arousal. *Journal of Psychosomatic Obstetrics and Gynecology, 25*, 153–162.

Topic, B., Tavares, M. C., Tomaz, C., & Mattern, C. (2007). Prolonged effects of intra-nasally administered testosterone on proceptive behavior in female capuchin monkeys (*Cebus apella*). *Behavioral Brain Research, 179*, 60–68.

Tuiten, A., van Honk, J., Koppeschaar, H., Bernaards, C., Thijssen, J., & Verbaten, R. (2000). Time course of effects of testosterone administration on sexual arousal in women. *Archives of General Psychiatry, 57*, 149–153.

Udry, J. R., & Morris, N. M. (1968). The distribution of coitus in the menstrual cycle. *Nature, 220*, 593–596.

van de Poll, N. E., van Zanten, S., & de Jonge, F. H. (1986). Effects of testosterone, estrogen, and dihydrotestosterone upon aggressive and sexual behavior of female rats. *Hormones and Behavior, 20,* 418–431.

Vasey, P. L. (1996). Interventions and alliance formation between female Japanese macaques, *Macaca fuscata,* during homosexual consortships. *Animal Behavior, 52,* 539–551.

Vasey, P. L. (2002). Same-sex sexual partner preference in hormonally and neurologically unmanipulated animals. *Annual Review of Sex Research, 13,* 141–179.

Waxenberg, S. E., Drellich, M. G., & Sutherland, A. M. (1959). Role of hormones in human behavior. I. Changes in female sexuality after adrenalectomy. *Journal of Clinical Endocrinology and Metabolism, 19,* 193–202.

Zenchak, J. J., Anderson, G. C., & Schein, M. W. (1981). Sexual partner preference of adult rams (*Ovis aries*) as affected by social experiences during rearing. *Applied Animal Ethology, 7,* 157–167.

Zuckerman, S. (1930). The menstrual cycle of the primates. Part 1. General nature and homology. *Proceedings of the Zoological Society of London, 1930,* 691–754.

5

Reward Sensitivity and Behavioral Control

Neuroimaging Evidence for Brain Systems Underlying Risk-Taking Behavior

Renate L. E. P. Reniers, Ulrik R. Beierholm, and Stephen J. Wood

> **Key points**
> - Risk taking is characterized by engagement in behaviors that concurrently involve the chance of a beneficial outcome but also possible negative or harmful consequences.
> - The interplay between reward sensitivity and behavioral control is central to risk-taking behavior on both the conceptual and neural level.
> - Variation in risk taking is linked to altered brain functioning and development, individual differences, and, less clearly, differences between genders.
> - It is the interaction between these trait and state factors that determines whether this vulnerability is translated into actual risk-taking behavior.
> - Neuroimaging evidence that these patterns of functioning and development impact "real-world" behavior is still limited and warrants further research.
> - Forensic practice and policy should look at cases in their specific context to identify relationships with behavior, but also developmental processes, individual characteristics, and gender related differences need to be considered.

> **Terminology Explained**
>
> **Sensation seeking** is the inclination to take part in new/exciting activities despite the risks associated with such behaviors.

> **Delay discounting** is the process by which the perceived value of a reward is reduced as the time to receive that reward is increased.
>
> The **nucleus accumbens** plays a central role in reward. Its operation is underpinned by dopamine (which underpins motivation); and serotonin (which acts as a mood stabilizer).
>
> The **ventral striatum** is the front part of the striatum, and functions as part of the reward system. It consists of the nucleus accumbens and the olfactory tubercle (a processing center in the olfactory cortex).

Introduction

Risk taking is characterized by engagement in behaviors that concurrently involve the chance of a beneficial outcome but also possible negative or harmful consequences (Boyer, 2006; Ernst, Pine, & Hardin, 2006). As such, it is part of a decision-making process during which an action is selected from a set of alternatives that have an uncertain outcome (Paulus, Rogalsky, Simmons, Feinstein, & Stein, 2003). Risk-taking behavior constitutes a part of normal behavior but where this behavior becomes too frequent or too severe it has been deemed one of the major causes of morbidity and mortality (Steinberg, 2008). Substance use, unprotected sexual activity, dangerous driving and sports (see Figure 5.1), gambling, violence, and aggression are clear examples of excessive risk-taking behavior and have been implicated in debates around criminal responsibility (see, e.g., Brain Waves Model, The Royal Society, 2011; The Teen Mental Health log, 2009.)

Even though taking risks can be harmful, the behavior is presumably engaged in because of the promise of positive and desirable results from successful completion of the action or because the risk-taking behavior in itself is rewarding. The interaction between one's sensitivity to a reward and the ability to control one's behavior is key in the process of deciding whether or not to take a risk. One needs to consider magnitude and value of the reward, but this decision-making process can be biased

Figure 5.1 An example of risk-taking behavior.

by (social) context, for example, pressure incurred by peers, and reduced behavioral control, demonstrated in an inability to delay the receipt of a reward, or personality characteristics such as a propensity for novelty and excitement. In this chapter, we will discuss neuroimaging evidence behind these processes and the developmental changes that result in behavior with fewer propensities for risky choices.

Brain Systems Underlying Risk-Taking Behavior in Adolescence and Young Adulthood

Risk-taking behavior occurs throughout the lifespan, but its extent varies with age. The peak period for enhanced risk-taking behavior is adolescence and young adulthood (Arnett, 2000; Gardner & Steinberg, 2005). Adolescence is described as a formative period of development characterized by heightened reactivity to emotions coupled with a reduced or still immature ability to self-regulate (Steinberg, 2008). It is furthermore characterized by increased interest in and sensitivity towards peer relationships, and an enhanced capacity to engage in behavior directed towards long-term goals (Carr-Gregg, Enderby, & Grover, 2003; Ernst et al., 2006; Pfeifer et al., 2011; Steinberg et al., 2008). These behavioral changes are accompanied by major changes in brain structure and functioning (Paus, 2005; Yurgelun-Todd, 2007). As a consequence of different rates of development of these behavioral changes in relation to maturing biological processes, adolescence is considered a period of high vulnerability that offers both opportunities and risks (Steinberg, 2005). It is therefore not surprising that adolescents are more likely to engage in risky behavior than children or adults (Steinberg, 2008) and that this period of development holds a central position in neurobiological models explaining risk-taking behavior (see Box 5.1 for a discussion of the most influential models).

Box 5.1 Neurobiological Models Explaining Risk-Taking Behavior

The dual systems model, or maturational imbalance theory, argues that brain regions involved in reward sensitivity and behavioral control develop at different rates. Development of the reward regions peaks in adolescence while regions involved in behavioral control develop more linearly through to adulthood (Blakemore & Robbins, 2012; Casey, Jones, & Somerville, 2011; Van Leijenhorst, Gunther Moor et al., 2010). This developmental "gap" between reward and behavioral control systems may be an important contributor to increased risk-taking behavior (Casey et al., 2011; Steinberg, 2008; Van Leijenhorst, Gunther Moor et al., 2010) (see Figure 5.1). Steinberg (2008) argues that risk taking takes place when either the brain's socioemotional network is relatively more activated, or when processes mediated by the brain's cognitive control network are disrupted. Activity of the socioemotional network results in increased reward-seeking behavior, while the cognitive control network is responsible for self-regulation.

> The latter network also holds a central position in the self-regulation model (SRM) (Byrnes, 1998; Byrnes, Miller, & Reynolds, 1999), which states that risk taking is initiated because of a failure to self-regulate resulting in the bypassing of rational decision-making processes, such as attention to incoming information, analysis of probability and outcome variables, and consolidation of these outcome variables for future use. Nelson, Leibenluft, McClure, and Pine (2005) share this point of view and propose that developmental changes in the brain's social information processing network (SIPN) are translated into behavioral changes such as risk-taking behavior. Changes in the SIPN are caused, on one hand, by a surge of gonadal steroids resulting in changes within the limbic system that affect emotional attributions to social stimuli and, on the other hand, by a gradual maturation of the prefrontal cortex that facilitates complex and controlled responses to social information. This is also in agreement with the triadic model (Ernst, 2013; Ernst & Fudge, 2009; Ernst et al., 2006) that links developmental processes to key structures in the brain: a reward-driven approach system associated with positively valenced emotions and mediated by the ventral striatum and nucleus accumbens in particular, a harm-avoidant system associated with negatively valenced emotions and mediated by the amygdala, and finally a regulatory or supervisory system mediated by the medial/ventral prefrontal cortex. Together, these models propose the imbalance of a stronger reward system and a weaker harm-avoidant system or poor regulatory control to result in risk-taking behavior.

In hypothetical situations, adolescents can reason about risky situations and estimate their vulnerability to risk at a similar level to adults (Reyna & Farley, 2006; Steinberg, 2008). However, when adolescents actually find themselves in these situations they struggle to make the safer decision (Millstein & Halpern-Felsher, 2002; Steinberg, 2008). It may be that the lack of coordination of emotion and cognition, demonstrated by a wider distributed activation in cognitive control areas, rather than emotion dominating cognition, characterizes risk-taking behavior in adolescence (Steinberg, 2008). However, more than in adults, adolescents' risk-taking behavior is sensitive to the immediate consequences of decisions (Mitchell, Schoel, & Stevens, 2008) and demonstrates a shift in focus towards the anticipation of positive outcomes (Galvan, Hare, Voss, Glover, & Casey, 2007). This increased sensitivity to reward is accompanied by increased activation of the ventral striatum and in particular the nucleus accumbens, ventromedial prefrontal cortex, and amygdala (see Figure 5.2) (Ernst et al., 2005; Galvan et al., 2007; Galvan et al., 2006; Pfeifer & Allen, 2012; Van Leijenhorst, GuntherMoor et al., 2010).

The circuitry that is composed of these regions has been suggested to underlie the propensity to take risks (Blum et al., 2000; Galvan et al., 2007; O'Doherty, 2004). Many studies have shown that two regions within this circuitry, the ventral striatum and the nucleus accumbens in particular, respond to the anticipation of reward (see Knutson, Adams, Fong, & Hommer (2001), Diekhof Kaps, Falkai, and Gruber (2012), and Volman et al. (2013) for further reading). In the context of risk taking,

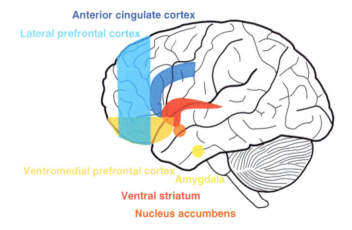

Figure 5.2 Approximate location of the main brain regions associated with sensitivity to reward.

Note: Approximate location of the main brain regions associated with sensitivity to reward (warm colors: ventral striatum, nucleus accumbens, ventromedial prefrontal cortex, and amygdala) and those associated with cognitive abilities to control the reward system (cold colors: lateral prefrontal and anterior cingulate cortex).

these regions have shown involvement in risky choices (Kuhnen & Knutson, 2005) but also responsiveness to the delivery of reward (Van Leijenhorst, Gunther Moor et al., 2010; Van Leijenhorst, Zanolie et al., 2010). Reward related activation in ventral striatum peaks in middle adolescence (Galvan et al., 2006; Geier, Terwilliger, Teslovich, Velanova, & Luna, 2010; Van Leijenhorst, Zanolie et al., 2010), is more pronounced during the outcome phase than the decision phase of the decision-making process (Ernst et al., 2005; Eshel, Nelson, Blair, Pine, & Ernst, 2007; Hare, O'Doherty, Camerer, Schultz, & Rangel, 2008; Van Leijenhorst, Zanolie et al., 2010), and is, in comparison to adults, more strongly influenced by feedback (J. R. Cohen et al., 2010; Ernst et al., 2006).

Alongside the ventral striatum, a complex network of brain areas has been implicated in the process of making risky decisions involving reward, including orbitofrontal and ventromedial prefrontal cortex, parietal cortex, and the insula. For example, the orbitofrontal cortex has been associated with the tracking of losses, while the parietal cortex has been associated with tracking risk (Wright et al., 2012). The insula, on the other hand, is responsive to anticipation of both gain and loss (Knutson & Greer, 2008). More specifically, activation of the anterior insula precedes riskless choices and decisions to not take a risk when it would have been more advantageous to do so (Kuhnen & Knutson, 2005). Its activation possibly reflects response of the autonomic nervous system to risk or uncertainty associated with a decision (Singer, Critchley, & Preuschoff, 2009; Van Leijenhorst, Zanolie et al., 2010), perhaps in particular association with risk aversion (Kuhnen & Knutson, 2005; Paulus et al., 2003). The orbitofrontal cortex has furthermore been associated with the evaluation of rewards (Elliott, Agnew, & Deakin, 2008; O'Doherty, 2007; O'Doherty, Critchley, Deichmann, & Dolan, 2003; Wallis, 2007), and the rapid learning of associations between visual stimuli and rewarding or punishing outcomes (Kertzman, Grinspan, Birger, & Kotler, 2006).

Influences on Risk-Taking Behavior in Adolescence and Young Adulthood

Compared to other age groups, adolescents are more susceptible to the influence of social factors such as the presence of peers, possibly because they spend more time with them and identify themselves with each other's behavior (Boyer, 2006; Steinberg, 2008). Consequently, their risk-taking behavior is far more likely to take place in groups (Steinberg, 2008). When together with their peers adolescents focus more on the benefit than the cost of the risk than do children or adults (Gardner & Steinberg, 2005) and the intense peer relationships that are formed during adolescence have been suggested to heighten sensitivity to the potential reward value of risky decisions and subsequently modulate them (Chein, Albert, O'Brien, Uckert, & Steinberg, 2010; Steinberg, 2008). Testing this hypothesis in adolescents relative to young adults and adults, Chein et al. (2010) compared brain activity during performance of a simulated driving task in the presence of peers to performance of the task when alone (see Box 5.2 for a more detailed description of this experimental design).

Box 5.2   The Stoplight Driving Game

In this simulated driving task, participants drive a vehicle on a straight track with 20 intersections. It is the participant's task to drive the vehicle from start to finish as quickly as possible. Risk taking is encouraged by monetary incentives offered for completion of the course in a timely fashion. At each intersection, participants need to decide whether or not to brake in response to a changing traffic signal. If the participant travels through the intersection successfully without braking, time is saved, whereas braking and waiting for the traffic signal to turn green results in a short time delay. Importantly, if the participant does not brake and crashes the vehicle at the intersection, a relatively long time delay is incurred. To manipulate social context, the task is completed alone and under the observation of two peers.

In a functional magnetic resonance imaging (fMRI) study, Chein et al. (2010) aimed to explore the neurobiological correlates of age differences in the impact of social context on risky decision making. Participants were adolescents (14–18 years old), young adults (19–22 years old), and adults (24–29 years old). Data were analyzed using an event-related design in which the event was indexed by the moment the traffic signal at each intersection changed from green to yellow. A single general linear model was created in which social context (alone and peer) were condition regressors. Using group random effects analysis regions exhibiting main and interactive effects for age (between-subjects factor) and social context (within-subjects factor) were identified. Compared to the alone condition, risk taking under the observation of peers was shown to result in increased activity in reward related regions, such as the ventral striatum and orbitofrontal cortex. Activity in these regions predicted subsequent risk-taking behavior. Activation in areas associated with cognitive control was less strong in adolescents than adults during risk taking. The sensitivity of the ventral striatum to the presence of peers was found to correspond to lower levels of self-reported resistance to peer influence while, in contrast, activation associated with cognitive control seemed unaffected by the presence of peers.

In addition to an increased sensitivity to reward, adolescence is also associated with increased sensation and novelty seeking behavior. This has, like reward processing, been linked to increased activation of the ventral striatum, but it has also been associated with immature cognitive abilities to control the reward system, related to slow maturation of lateral prefrontal and anterior cingulate cortex (see Figure 5.2) (Chambers, Taylor, & Potenza, 2003; Ernst et al., 2006; Eshel et al., 2007; Pfeifer & Allen, 2012; Romer, 2010; Steinberg, 2004; Van Leijenhorst, Gunther Moor et al., 2010). It is this interplay between reward and behavioral control systems that is key to risk-taking behavior; one seeks reward but with an immature or insufficient ability to control one's behavior (see Figure 5.3).

Indeed, sensation seeking has been associated with strong approach and weak avoidance behaviors (Collins et al., 2012; Joseph, Liu, Jiang, Lynam, & Kelly, 2009) and

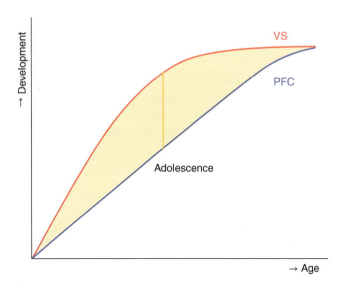

Figure 5.3 Development into adulthood of two systems associated with risk-taking behavior.

Note: A simplified representation of the development into adulthood of two systems associated with risk-taking behavior: reward sensitivity (red line) and behavioral control (blue line). On one hand, there is an increased sensitivity to reward, coupled with a rapid development of reward related regions such as the ventral striatum, while, on the other hand, there is a steadier development of one's ability to control behavior in association with maturation of the prefrontal regions. The imbalance caused by the different developmental patterns of these systems results in a period of high vulnerability (yellow area between the lines) that may contribute to increased risk-taking behavior. Risk-taking behavior occurs across all ages but peaks in adolescence. VS = ventral striatum; PFC = prefrontal cortex.

increased ventral striatal response during anticipation and receipt of reward (Bjork, Knutson, & Hommer, 2008). Indexed by differential response in insula and prefrontal cortex, high sensation seekers are insensitive to the absence of reward making them more vulnerable to maladaptive choices and putting them at higher risk for negative outcomes (Cservenka, Herting, Seghete, Hudson, & Nagel, 2013). In addition, they show increased responsiveness to high-arousal stimuli (Joseph et al., 2009) and delayed or negligible inhibitory control, which suggests that low level engagement of inhibitory control areas may underlie some of the risk-taking behaviors observed in high-sensation seekers (Collins et al., 2012).

The ability to inhibit behavior is critical for response selection processes and does not simply stop an action but is an active process that can suppress an action that is already prepared (Kertzman et al., 2006). This behavioral inhibition is thought to involve a frontoparietal network, including the dorsolateral, ventrolateral, orbitofrontal, premotor, and inferior parietal cortices (Garavan, Ross, Murphy, Roche, & Stein, 2002; Liddle, Kiehl, & Smith, 2001; Nakata et al., 2008; Rubia et al., 2001; Simmonds, Pekar, & Mostofsky, 2008). Moreover, the anterior cingulate has been implicated in monitoring response conflict and error detection (Garavan, Hester, Murphy, Fassbender, & Kelly, 2006; Hester, Fassbender, & Garavan, 2004; Jaffard et al., 2008; Nakata et al., 2008) and relates to lateral prefrontal activation to enable awareness of an error (Hester, Foxe, Molholm, Shpaner, & Garavan, 2005; Hester, Madeley, Murphy, & Mattingley, 2009). The ability to inhibit behavior plays an important role in the delay discounting process by which the subjective value of reward is reduced as the time to receive that reward becomes delayed (see McClure, Laibson, Loewenstein, & Cohen (2004), Ballard & Knutson (2009), and Kable & Gimchler (2007) for further reading).

Continuous strengthening of connections between prefrontal regions and the limbic system allows better coordination of emotion and cognition throughout adolescence (Steinberg, 2008). Compared to adults, adolescents show greater behavioral and striatal sensitivity to not only appetitive stimuli but also aversive stimuli with stronger effects seen for the latter in correspondence with reduced activation in the insula (Galvan & McGlennen, 2013). Seeing that potential losses may have a greater impact on risky decisions than potential gains (Barkley-Levenson, Van Leijenhorst, & Galvan, 2013; Tversky & Kahneman, 1981), this has clear implications for adolescent behavior. Whereas adults may view behavior as too risky, adolescents may be more likely to see the possible positive outcome of the behavior and seem more able to deal with or even enjoy the unpredictability of a situation (Boyer, 2006; Leather, 2009; Moore & Gullone, 1996; Tymula et al., 2012). This is important in that adolescent risk-taking behavior cannot be attributed to feelings of invulnerability or an inability to estimate the probability of negative outcomes (Boyer, 2006). Indeed, adolescents show increased activation in anterior cingulate in response to uncertain outcomes and increased lateral orbitofrontal activation in response to omitted rewards in comparison to young adults (see Box 5.3 for a more detailed description of this experimental design) (Van Leijenhorst, Zanolie et al., 2010). Furthermore, while adolescents and adults recruit a similar neural network while taking a gamble, increased activation of the frontostriatal circuit, in particular the caudate and frontal pole, has been observed in adolescents compared to adults when choosing to reject a gamble. Adolescents thus have the ability to refrain from taking risks but may require increased inhibitory control to do so (Barkley-Levenson et al., 2013).

Box 5.3   The Slot Machine Task

In this fMRI task, participants are presented with three empty slot machines. After 500 milliseconds (ms), a cue in the form of a coin is presented for the duration of 1000ms. The participant is then to start the machines by pressing a prespecified button. Following this 1000ms response window, three fruit pictures (kiwi, pear, or a pair of cherries) are presented consecutively, from left to right in the slot machines, with the next picture appearing every 1500ms. There are three experimental conditions representing three possible outcomes: three different fruits, two identical and one different fruit, and three identical fruits. The order of presentation of the outcomes is randomised. Participants receive €0.05 each time three identical fruits are presented while no money is offered for the other conditions. Failure to respond within the 1000ms response window results in a €0.10 loss. Total winnings on the task are €1.50. In their study, Van Leijenhorst, Zanolie et al. (2010) aimed to dissociate effects of the anticipation, receipt, and omission of reward and show the developmental trajectories of the associated brain regions in participants aged 10–12, 14–15, and 18–23 years old. To achieve this, analysis was done using an event-related design using zero-duration events around the onset times of the second and third fruit pictures. Anticipation of reward was modelled by the comparison of brain activation associated with trials where participants first saw two identical pictures versus two different pictures. Processing of outcome was modelled by the comparison of three identical pictures versus two identical and one different picture.

Offending across the lifespan *According to a UK government report in 2016 (Allen and Dempsey) the distribution of age across incarcerated offenders is negatively skewed, with over 38% being younger than 30 years old. This may be linked to a reduced and immature ability to self-regulate typical to youth.*

Source: Pixabay. https://pixabay.com/en/smoking-young-people-youth-be-cool-737057/.

Taking Risks across the Lifespan

Risk-taking behavior is not just limited to adolescence and young adulthood, but is also commonly observed in adults. All age groups make decisions under clearly deliberated conditions but are also tempted and influenced by emotions and impulses (Willoughby, Good, Adachi, Hamza, & Tavernier, 2013). Some of these factors may be more tempting or rewarding for one age group compared to the other and may therefore require more willpower (Willoughby, Tavernier, Hamza, Adachi, & Good, 2013). The factors most influential for the decision-making process vary by age group and may be more or less associated with developmental processes in the brain (Lee, Leung, Fox, Gao, & Chan, 2008; Willoughby, Good et al., 2013). Older adults have, for example, been shown to focus more on positive emotions and to weigh certainty more heavily than younger adults when considering risky options (Mather et al., 2012). This may be reflected in stronger activation of the right insula during risky decision making with activation in this region being associated with a tendency to avoid risky situations, as well as the anticipation of a greater negative impact when a risky choice is selected (see Box 5.4 for a more detailed description of this experimental design) (Lee, Leung, et al., 2008).

> **Box 5.4 The Risky-Gains Task**
>
> In this task (original by Paulus et al., 2003), participants are presented with the numbers 20, 40, and 80 in a fixed order and each appearing on a screen for 1000ms. Participants are instructed to win points and if they press a button when the number 20 is on the screen, 20 points are gained. For both numbers 40 and 80, this can be either −40 and −80, representing a loss of points, or +40 and +80, representing a gain of points. Participants have to decide whether to wait for +40 after gaining 20 points or +80 after gaining 40 points, with the risk of losing points, or to avoid risk completely and take the 20 points. Points are accumulated on a trial by trial basis and feedback is received immediately after a choice is made. The probability of the appearance of −40 and −80 is set in such a way that the participant's final score would be identical were 20, 40, or 80 chosen consistently, thereby leaving no advantage to only making risky (40 or 80) or safe (20) choices. The total of 96 trials is divided into 54 non-punishing trials (20, +40, and +80), 24 −40 punishing trials and 18 −80 punishing trials, presented in random order. Before performing the task, participants complete a set of practice trials to familiarize themselves with the task requirements.
>
> In their fMRI study, Lee, Chan et al. (2008) aimed to identify the neural correlates of risky versus safe choices in young adults (23–36 years old) compared with older adults (61–69 years old). The rate of selecting 20, 40, and 80 points was calculated as an index of task performance. As both the choices of 40 and 80 points involved risk-taking behavior, selection of either number was grouped together as risky response, while selection of 20 points represented the safe response. Response regressors (risky response and safe response) were identified from the start of the trial to the time when the choice was made. Areas of significant activation associated with risky versus safe choices were identified and compared between the two groups of adults.

Individual Differences and Risk-Taking Behavior: The Effect of Personality Traits

Besides age, other factors such as personality characteristics have an impact on risk-taking behavior. Personality traits are commonly assessed using self-report questionnaires but state related factors can also be assessed using behavioral tasks (see Box 5.4 for a detailed description of the risky gains task that provides an index of risk aversion). Risk averse individuals display stronger responses in ventral striatum and anterior insula in anticipation of high-risk gambles when compared to individuals with a higher tendency to take risks (Rudorf, Preuschoff, & Weber, 2012). In addition, increased risk averse activity in the insula has been shown to correlate with higher levels of self-reported harm avoidance and neuroticism (Paulus et al., 2003). Harm avoidance has also been positively related to nucleus accumbens activation in association with the deliberation process prior to making a risky decision (Matthews, Simmons, Lane, & Paulus, 2004).

Risk-taking behavior *Risk-taking behavior is more common in youth and males. This is hypothesized to be related to brain development stages (Arnett, 2000; Gardner & Steinberg, 2005) and physiological differences in hormonal makeup (Coates and Herbert, 2008, PNAS).*
Source: © Vitalii Nesterchuk. Used under license from 123RF.

Sensitivity to reward and punishment, as well as impulsivity and sensation seeking, have commonly been linked to risk-taking behavior (see, e.g., Boyer, 2006; Chein et al., 2010; Deckman & DeWall, 2011; Lejuez et al., 2002; Robbins & Bryan, 2004; Scott-Parker, Watson, King, & Hyde, 2012). Apart from sensitivity to punishment, these relationships with risk-taking behavior have mainly been positive, however, with varying strengths of the correlations depending on sample composition and type of risk taking assessed. Differences between the left and right side of the brain in prefrontal electroencephalogram (EEG) activation at rest have been shown to have stronger predictive power for risk-taking behavior in those with high scores on sensitivity to punishment compared to those with lower scores (Studer, Pedroni, & Rieskamp, 2013), while higher levels of self-reported extraversion have been linked to reward related increases in orbitofrontal cortex and nucleus accumbens activation (Cohen, Young, Baek, Kessler, & Ranganath, 2005). Reduced medial prefrontal activation to negative feedback has furthermore been related to higher levels of self-reported personality traits characterizing excitement, reward, and sensation seeking (Segalowitz et al., 2012). Those scoring high on measures of impulsivity have been shown to rely more heavily on recruitment of the insula–orbitofrontal–parietal network than those who score low on impulsiveness when making risky decisions (Lee, Chan, et al., 2008).

Gender Differences in Risk-Taking Behavior

Reports regarding gender differences in the neural mechanisms underlying risk-taking behavior are sparse, with the sample sizes reported in fMRI studies being too small to allow meaningful group comparisons. The few studies available show contrasting results. Galvan et al. (2007) showed that there were no gender differences in brain activation during a delayed response task. However, using different tasks, both Lee, Chan, Leung, Fox, and Gao (2009) and van den Bos, Homberg, and de Visser (2013) demonstrated differences between genders. Lee et al. (2009) found stronger activation in right insula and bilateral orbitofrontal cortex in females compared to males during performance on a risky decision-making task. The strength of neural activity in the insula correlated with the rate of risky behaviors for females but not males. Likewise, the percent signal change in the right orbitofrontal cortex correlated negatively with the rate of selecting risky options for females but not males. The increased neural activation observed in females compared to males may index gender differences regarding the update and valuation of uncertainty associated with risky decisions (Lee et al., 2009). This uncertainty may induce stress, which has been shown to increase risk-taking behavior in men but results in risk-avoidant behavior in women (Lighthall, Mather, & Gorlick, 2009). Differential activation of orbitofrontal cortex (lateral activation in men compared to more medial activation in women) has also been observed during performance of a gambling task and may relate to gender differences in information processing: women may be more sensitive to losses and focus on both frequency of wins and losses and long-term pay-off, while men focus merely on the long-term pay-off (van den Bos et al., 2013).

Right dorsolateral prefrontal cortex activation has been associated with achieving optimal performance on a gambling task in men, but in women, who needed more trials in order to achieve the same optimal performance, this area was not recruited (van den Bos et al., 2013). In contrast, active losses on a risk-taking task were associated with strong dorsolateral prefrontal activation in females compared to little activation in this area in males (Cazzell, Li, Lin, Patel, & Liu, 2012). The females in this study tried to avoid losses, demonstrating a risk averse approach as associated with increased inhibitory control mediated by lateral prefrontal regions. This is consistent with work by Knoch et al. (2006) who demonstrated reduced inhibitory control and increased risk-taking behavior after suppression of right dorsolateral prefrontal cortex activity using low-frequency repetitive transcranial magnetic stimulation (rTMS). Differences between genders have thus been observed but are subtle and warrant further research, particularly in relation to personality characteristics and the different rates and patterns of development associated with males and females.

Conclusions

Risky decision making is a common occurrence in healthy individuals. However, excessive risk taking is linked to vulnerabilities in brain functioning and development (Steinberg, 2008; Van Leijenhorst, Gunther Moor et al., 2010), individual differences (Galvan et al., 2007; Van Leijenhorst, Gunther Moor et al., 2010), and tentative differences between genders (Gardner & Steinberg, 2005; Harris, Jenkins, & Glaser, 2006). It is the interaction between these trait and state factors that determines whether this vulnerability is translated into actual risk-taking behavior (Willoughby, Good et al., 2013). Risks are taken with the prospect of gain but with the probability of negative consequences making the interplay between reward sensitivity and behavioral control central to risk-taking behavior on both the conceptual and neural level (see Figure 5.4). It needs a word of caution that although there are substantial behavioral and an increasing amount of neuroimaging data showing that the reward and behavioral control systems function and mature differently (Strang, Chein, & Steinberg, 2013), the neuroimaging evidence that these patterns of functioning and development impact "real-world" behavior is still limited (Pfeifer & Allen, 2012). Risk taking is multifactorial and the neural mechanisms underlying this behavior should be considered as such. Ideally, this should be done from a whole brain network perspective using a longitudinal approach across the lifespan (Pfeifer & Allen, 2012; Willoughby, Good et al., 2013; Willoughby, Tavernier et al., 2013) that includes an analytic approach for exploring correlations with real-world behavior. Multi-modal imaging techniques should be employed alongside carefully chosen behavioral and self-report assessments. Together this will give a comprehensive picture of the neural mechanisms associated with risk-taking behavior in a research context that will make a valid translation to risk taking in the real world.

Figure 5.4 The interplay between reward sensitivity and behavioral control.

Note: The interplay between reward sensitivity and behavioral control is central to risk-taking behavior on both the conceptual and neural level.

An increased understanding of the structure and functioning of the brain in the risk-taking process has clear, but limited, implications for forensic practice and policy. Cases need to be looked at in their specific context to identify relationships with behavior, but developmental processes, individual characteristics, and gender related differences also need to be considered. Firstly, can we hold someone whose brain has not yet fully matured accountable for their decisions, no matter how risky they are? (for a more detailed discussion of this question on adolescents' criminal culpability see Steinberg, 2013.) Secondly, how much consideration should be given to someone's susceptibility to peer pressure, personality, or gender when risky behavior is displayed? Importantly, the observed relationships between these factors consist of correlations and are by no means to be assumed linear or causal. Nevertheless, they make an important contribution to our understanding of the structure and functioning of the brain in relationship to mental processes and behavior, may they be risky or not.

Recommended Reading

Blakemore, S. J., & Robbins, T. W. (2012). Decision-making in the adolescent brain. *Nature Neuroscience*, *15*(9), 1184–1191. *This is a review of decision making in adolescence.*

Boyer, T. W. (2006). The development of risk-taking: A multi-perspective review. *Developmental Review*, *26*, 291–345. *This is a review on the development of risk taking.*

Chein, J., Albert, D., O'Brien, L., Uckert, K., & Steinberg, L. (2010). Peers increase adolescent risk taking by enhancing activity in the brain's reward circuitry. *Developmental Science*, *14*, 1–10. *An fMRI study investigating the influence of peer presence on risk taking.*

Pfeifer, J. H., & Allen, N. B. (2012). Arrested development? Reconsidering dual-systems models of brain function in adolescence and disorders. *Trends in Cognitive Sciences*, *16*(6), 322–329. *This paper contains critical consideration of the dual systems model.*

Steinberg, L. (2008). A social neuroscience perspective on adolescent risk-taking. *Developmental Review*, *28*(1), 78–106. *Describes risk taking in the context of developmental neuroscience.*

Van Leijenhorst, L., Gunther Moor, B., Op de Macks, Z. A., Rombouts, S. A., Westenberg, P. M., & Crone, E. A. (2010). Adolescent risky decision-making: Neurocognitive development of reward and control regions. *NeuroImage*, *51*(1), 345–355. *This fMRI study provides evidence for the hypothesis that adolescent risk taking is associated with an imbalance caused by different developmental trajectories of brain areas associated with reward and behavioral control.*

References

Arnett, J. J. (2000). Emerging adulthood. A theory of development from the late teens through the twenties. *American Psychologist*, *55*(5), 469–480.

Ballard, K., & Knutson, B. (2009). Dissociable neural representations of future reward magnitude and delay during temporal discounting. *NeuroImage*, *45*(1), 143–150.

Barkley-Levenson, E. E., Van Leijenhorst, L., & Galvan, A. (2013). Behavioral and neural correlates of loss aversion and risk avoidance in adolescents and adults. *Developmental Cognitive Neuroscience*, *3*, 72–83. doi: S1878-9293(12)00082-5 [pii] 10.1016/j.dcn.2012.09.007 [doi].

Bjork, J. M., Knutson, B., & Hommer, D. W. (2008). Incentive-elicited striatal activation in adolescent children of alcoholics. *Addiction*, *103*(8), 1308–1319. doi: ADD2250 [pii] 10.1111/j.1360-0443.2008.02250.x.

Blakemore, S. J., & Robbins, T. W. (2012). Decision-making in the adolescent brain. *Nature Neuroscience*, *15*(9), 1184–1191.

Blum, K., Braverman, E. R., Holder, J. M., Lubar, J. F., Monastra, V. J., Miller, D., ... Comings, D. E. (2000). Reward deficiency syndrome: A biogenetic model for the diagnosis and treatment of impulsive, addictive, and compulsive behaviors. *Journal of Psychoactive Drugs*, 32 Suppl, i–iv, 1–112.

Boyer, T. W. (2006). The development of risk-taking: A multi-perspective review. *Developmental Review*, 26, 291–345.

Byrnes, J. P. (1998). *The nature and development of decision making: A self-regulation model*. Mahwah, NJ: Lawrence Erlbaum.

Byrnes, J. P., Miller, D. C., & Reynolds, M. (1999). Learning to make good decisions: A self-regulation perspective. *Child Development*, 70, 1121–1140.

Carr-Gregg, M. R., Enderby, K. C., & Grover, S. R. (2003). Risk-taking behavior of young women in Australia: Screening for health-risk behaviors. *Medical Journal of Australia*, 178(12), 601–604. doi: car10800_fm [pii].

Casey, B., Jones, R. M., & Somerville, L. H. (2011). Braking and accelerating of the adolescent brain. *Journal of Research on Adolescence*, 21(1), 21–33. doi: 10.1111/j.1532-7795.2010.00712.x.

Cazzell, M., Li, L., Lin, Z. J., Patel, S. J., & Liu, H. (2012). Comparison of neural correlates of risk decision making between genders: An exploratory fNIRS study of the Balloon Analogue Risk Task (BART). *NeuroImage*, 62(3), 1896–1911. doi: S1053-8119(12)00518-6 [pii]10.1016/j.neuroimage.2012.05.030.

Chambers, R. A., Taylor, J. R., & Potenza, M. N. (2003). Developmental neurocircuitry of motivation in adolescence: A critical period of addiction vulnerability. *American Journal of Psychiatry*, 160(6), 1041–1052.

Chein, J., Albert, D., O'Brien, L., Uckert, K., & Steinberg, L. (2010). Peers increase adolescent risk taking by enhancing activity in the brain's reward circuitry. *Developmental Science*, 14, 1–10.

Cohen, J. R., Asarnow, R. F., Sabb, F. W., Bilder, R. M., Bookheimer, S. Y., Knowlton, B. J., & Poldrack, R. A. (2010). A unique adolescent response to reward prediction errors. *Nature Neuroscience*, 13(6), 669–671. doi: 10.1038/nn.2558.

Cohen, M. X., Young, J., Baek, J. M., Kessler, C., & Ranganath, C. (2005). Individual differences in extraversion and dopamine genetics predict neural reward responses. *Brain Research. Cognitive Brain Research*, 25(3), 851–861. doi: S0926-6410(05)00288-0 [pii]10.1016/j.cogbrainres.2005.09.018.

Collins, H. R., Corbly, C. R., Liu, X., Kelly, T. H., Lynam, D., & Joseph, J. E. (2012). Too little, too late or too much, too early? Differential hemodynamics of response inhibition in high and low sensation seekers. *Brain Research*, 1481, 1–12. doi: S0006-8993(12)01295-4 [pii]10.1016/j.brainres.2012.08.004.

Cservenka, A., Herting, M. M., Seghete, K. L., Hudson, K. A., & Nagel, B. J. (2013). High and low sensation seeking adolescents show distinct patterns of brain activity during reward processing. *NeuroImage*, 66C, 184–193. doi: S1053-8119(12)01098-1 [pii]10.1016/j.neuroimage.2012.11.003

Deckman, T., & DeWall, C. N. (2011). Negative urgency and risky sexual behaviors: A clarification of the relationship between impulsivity and risky sexual behavior. *Personality and Individual Differences*, 51, 674–678.

Diekhof, E. K., Kaps, L., Falkai, P., & Gruber, O. (2012). The role of the human ventral striatum and the medial orbitofrontal cortex in the representation of reward magnitude – an activation likelihood estimation meta-analysis of neuroimaging studies of passive reward expectancy and outcome processing. *Neuropsychologia*, 50(7), 1252–1266. S0028-3932(12)00077-2 [pii] doi: 10.1016/j.neuropsychologia.2012.02.007.

Elliott, R., Agnew, Z., & Deakin, J. F. (2008). Medial orbitofrontal cortex codes relative rather than absolute value of financial rewards in humans. *The European Journal of Neuroscience*, 27(9), 2213–2218.

Ernst, M. (2013). The triadic model perspective for the study of adolescent motivated behavior. *Brain and Cognition, 89*, 104–111.

Ernst, M., & Fudge, J. L. (2009). A developmental neurobiological model of motivated behavior: Anatomy, connectivity and ontogeny of the triadic nodes. *Neuroscience and Biobehavioral Reviews, 33*(3), 367–382. doi: S0149-7634(08)00186-3 [pii]10.1016/j.neubiorev.2008.10.009.

Ernst, M., Nelson, E. E., Jazbec, S., McClure, E. B., Monk, C. S., Leibenluft, E., … Pine, D. S. (2005). Amygdala and nucleus accumbens in responses to receipt and omission of gains in adults and adolescents. *NeuroImage, 25*(4), 1279–1291. doi: S1053-8119(04)00777-3 [pii]10.1016/j.neuroimage.2004.12.038 [doi].

Ernst, M., Pine, D. S., & Hardin, M. (2006). Triadic model of the neurobiology of motivated behavior in adolescence. *Psychological Medicine, 36*(3), 299–312. doi: S0033291705005891 [pii]10.1017/S0033291705005891 [doi].

Eshel, N., Nelson, E. E., Blair, R. J., Pine, D. S., & Ernst, M. (2007). Neural substrates of choice selection in adults and adolescents: Development of the ventrolateral prefrontal and anterior cingulate cortices. *Neuropsychologia, 45*(6), 1270–1279. doi: S0028-3932(06)00398-8 [pii]10.1016/j.neuropsychologia.2006.10.004 [doi].

Galvan, A., Hare, T. A., Parra, C. E., Penn, J., Voss, H., Glover, G., & Casey, B. J. (2006). Earlier development of the accumbens relative to orbitofrontal cortex might underlie risk-taking behavior in adolescents. *Journal of Neuroscience, 26*(25), 6885–6892. doi: 26/25/6885 [pii]10.1523/JNEUROSCI.1062-06.2006 [doi].

Galvan, A., Hare, T., Voss, H., Glover, G., & Casey, B. J. (2007). Risk-taking and the adolescent brain: Who is at risk? *Developmental Science, 10*(2), F8–F14. doi: DESC579 [pii]10.1111/j.1467-7687.2006.00579.x [doi].

Galvan, A., & McGlennen, K. M. (2013). Enhanced striatal sensitivity to aversive reinforcement in adolescents versus adults. *Journal of Cognitive Neuroscience, 25*(2), 284–296. doi: 10.1162/jocn_a_00326 [doi].

Garavan, H., Hester, R., Murphy, K., Fassbender, C., & Kelly, C. (2006). Individual differences in the functional neuroanatomy of inhibitory control. *Brain Research, 1105*(1), 130–142.

Garavan, H., Ross, T. J., Murphy, K., Roche, R. A., & Stein, E. A. (2002). Dissociable executive functions in the dynamic control of behavior: Inhibition, error detection, and correction. *NeuroImage, 17*(4), 1820–1829.

Gardner, M., & Steinberg, L. (2005). Peer influence on risk taking, risk preference, and risky decision making in adolescence and adulthood: An experimental study. *Developmental Psychology, 41*(4), 625–635. doi: 2005-08221-004 [pii]10.1037/0012-1649.41.4.625 [doi].

Geier, C. F., Terwilliger, R., Teslovich, T., Velanova, K., & Luna, B. (2010). Immaturities in reward processing and its influence on inhibitory control in adolescence. *Cerebral Cortex, 20*(7), 1613–1629. doi: bhp225 [pii]10.1093/cercor/bhp225 [doi].

Hare, T. A., O'Doherty, J., Camerer, C. F., Schultz, W., & Rangel, A. (2008). Dissociating the role of the orbitofrontal cortex and the striatum in the computation of goal values and prediction errors. *Journal of Neuroscience, 28*(22), 5623–5630. doi: 10.1523/jneurosci.1309-08.2008.

Harris, C., Jenkins, M., & Glaser, D. (2006). Gender differences in risk assessment: Why do women take fewer risks than men? *Judgment and Decision Making, 1*, 48–63.

Hester, R., Fassbender, C., & Garavan, H. (2004). Individual differences in error processing: A review and reanalysis of three event-related fMRI studies using the GO/NOGO task. *Cerebral Cortex, 14*(9), 986–994.

Hester, R., Foxe, J. J., Molholm, S., Shpaner, M., & Garavan, H. (2005). Neural mechanisms involved in error processing: A comparison of errors made with and without awareness. *NeuroImage, 27*(3), 602–608.

Hester, R., Madeley, J., Murphy, K., & Mattingley, J. B. (2009). Learning from errors: Error-related neural activity predicts improvements in future inhibitory control performance. *The*

Journal of Neuroscience: The official journal of the Society for Neuroscience, 29(22), 7158–7165.

Jaffard, M., Longcamp, M., Velay, J. L., Anton, J. L., Roth, M., Nazarian, B., & Boulinguez, P. (2008). Proactive inhibitory control of movement assessed by event-related fMRI. *NeuroImage, 42*(3), 1196–1206.

Joseph, J. E., Liu, X., Jiang, Y., Lynam, D., & Kelly, T. H. (2009). Neural correlates of emotional reactivity in sensation seeking. *Psychological Science, 20*(2), 215–223. doi: PSCI2283 [pii]10.1111/j.1467-9280.2009.02283.x [doi].

Kable, J. W., & Glimcher, P. W. (2007). The neural correlates of subjective value during intertemporal choice. *Nature Neuroscience, 10*(12), 1625–1633.

Kertzman, S., Grinspan, H., Birger, M., & Kotler, M. (2006). Computerized neuropsychological examination of impulsiveness: A selective review. *The Israel Journal of Psychiatry and Related Sciences, 43*(2), 74–80.

Knoch, D., Gianotti, L. R., Pascual-Leone, A., Treyer, V., Regard, M., Hohmann, M., & Brugger, P. (2006). Disruption of right prefrontal cortex by low-frequency repetitive transcranial magnetic stimulation induces risk-taking behavior. *Journal of Neuroscience, 26*(24), 6469–6472. doi: 26/24/6469 [pii]10.1523/JNEUROSCI.0804-06.2006 [doi].

Knutson, B., Adams, C. M., Fong, G. W., & Hommer, D. (2001). Anticipation of increasing monetary reward selectively recruits nucleus accumbens. *Journal of Neuroscience, 21*(16), RC159. doi: 20015472 [pii].

Knutson, B., & Greer, S. M. (2008). Anticipatory affect: Neural correlates and consequences for choice. *Philosophical Transactions of the Royal Society of London. Series B: Biological Sciences, 363*(1511), 3771–3786. doi: 406873695606G704 [pii]10.1098/rstb.2008.0155 [doi].

Kuhnen, C. M., & Knutson, B. (2005). The neural basis of financial risk taking. *Neuron, 47*(5), 763–770. doi: S0896-6273(05)00657-4 [pii]10.1016/j.neuron.2005.08.008 [doi].

Leather, N. C. (2009). Risk-taking behavior in adolescence: A literature review. *Journal of Child Health Care, 13*(3), 295–304. doi: 13/3/295 [pii]10.1177/1367493509337443 [doi].

Lee, T. M., Chan, C. C., Han, S. H., Leung, A. W., Fox, P. T., & Gao, J. H. (2008). An event-related fMRI study on risk taking by healthy individuals of high or low impulsiveness. *Neuroscience Letters, 438*(2), 138–141. doi: S0304-3940(08)00540-5 [pii]10.1016/j.neulet.2008.04.061 [doi].

Lee, T. M., Chan, C. C., Leung, A. W., Fox, P. T., & Gao, J. H. (2009). Sex-related differences in neural activity during risk taking: an fMRI study. *Cerebral Cortex, 19*(6), 1303–1312. doi: bhn172 [pii]10.1093/cercor/bhn172 [doi].

Lee, T. M., Leung, A. W., Fox, P. T., Gao, J. H., & Chan, C. C. (2008). Age-related differences in neural activities during risk taking as revealed by functional MRI. *Social Cognitive and Affective Neuroscience, 3*(1), 7–15. doi: nsm033 [pii]10.1093/scan/nsm033 [doi].

Lejuez, C. W., Read, J. P., Kahler, C. W., Richards, J. B., Ramsey, S. E., Stuart, G. L., ... Brown, R. A. (2002). Evaluation of a behavioral measure of risk taking: The Balloon Analogue Risk Task (BART). *Journal of Experimental Psychology. Applied, 8*(2), 75–84.

Liddle, P. F., Kiehl, K. A., & Smith, A. M. (2001). Event-related fMRI study of response inhibition. *Human Brain Mapping, 12*(2), 100–109.

Lighthall, N. R., Mather, M., & Gorlick, M. A. (2009). Acute stress increases sex differences in risk seeking in the balloon analogue risk task. *PLoS One, 4*(7), e6002. doi: 10.1371/journal.pone.0006002 [doi].

Mather, M., Mazar, N., Gorlick, M. A., Lighthall, N. R., Burgeno, J., Schoeke, A., & Ariely, D. (2012). Risk preferences and aging: The "certainty effect" in older adults' decision making. *Psychology and Aging, 27*(4), 801–816. doi: 2012-27541-001 [pii]10.1037/a0030174 [doi].

Matthews, S. C., Simmons, A. N., Lane, S. D., & Paulus, M. P. (2004). Selective activation of the nucleus accumbens during risk-taking decision making. *Neuroreport, 15*(13), 2123–2127. doi: 00001756-200409150-00025 [pii].

McClure, S. M., Laibson, D. I., Loewenstein, G., & Cohen, J. D. (2004). Separate neural systems value immediate and delayed monetary rewards. *Science, 306*(5695), 503–507.

Millstein, S. G., & Halpern-Felsher, B. L. (2002). Perceptions of risk and vulnerability. *Journal of Adolescent Health, 31*(1 Suppl), 10–27. doi: S1054139X02004123 [pii]

Mitchell, S. H., Schoel, C., & Stevens, A. A. (2008). Mechanisms underlying heightened risk taking in adolescents as compared with adults. *Psychonomic Bulletin and Review, 15*(2), 272–277.

Moore, S. M., & Gullone, E. (1996). Predicting adolescence risk behavior using a personalised cost–benefit analysis. *Journal of Youth and Adolescence, 25*(3), 343–359.

Nakata, H., Sakamoto, K., Ferretti, A., Gianni Perrucci, M., Del Gratta, C., Kakigi, R., & Luca Romani, G. (2008). Somato-motor inhibitory processing in humans: An event-related functional MRI study. *NeuroImage, 39*(4), 1858–1866.

Nelson, E. E., Leibenluft, E., McClure, E. B., & Pine, D. S. (2005). The social re-orientation of adolescence: A neuroscience perspective on the process and its relation to psychopathology. *Psychological Medicine, 35*(2), 163–174.

O'Doherty, J. (2004). Reward representations and reward-related learning in the human brain: Insights from neuroimaging. *Current Opinion in Neurobiology, 14*(6), 769–776.

O'Doherty, J. (2007). Lights, camembert, action! The role of human orbitofrontal cortex in encoding stimuli, rewards, and choices. *Annals of the New York Academy of Sciences, 1121*, 254–272. doi: annals.1401.036 [pii]10.1196/annals.1401.036 [doi].

O'Doherty, J., Critchley, H., Deichmann, R., & Dolan, R. J. (2003). Dissociating valence of outcome from behavioral control in human orbital and ventral prefrontal cortices. *The Journal of Neuroscience: The official journal of the Society for Neuroscience, 23*(21), 7931–7939.

Paulus, M. P., Rogalsky, C., Simmons, A., Feinstein, J. S., & Stein, M. B. (2003). Increased activation in the right insula during risk-taking decision making is related to harm avoidance and neuroticism. *NeuroImage, 19*(4), 1439–1448. doi: S1053811903002519 [pii].

Paus, T. (2005). Mapping brain maturation and cognitive development during adolescence. *Trends in Cognitive Sciences, 9*(2), 60–68. doi: S1364-6613(04)00320-1 [pii] 10.1016/j.tics.2004.12.008 [doi].

Pfeifer, J. H., Masten, C. L., Moore, W. E., 3rd, Oswald, T. M., Mazziotta, J. C., Iacoboni, M., & Dapretto, M. (2011). Entering adolescence: Resistance to peer influence, risky behavior, and neural changes in emotion reactivity. *Neuron, 69*(5), 1029–1036. doi: S0896-6273(11)00117-6 [pii]10.1016/j.neuron.2011.02.019 [doi].

Reyna, V. F., & Farley, F. (2006). Risk and rationality in adolescent decision-making: Implications for theory, practice, and public policy. *Psychological Science in the Public Interest, 7*, 1–44.

Robbins, R. N., & Bryan, A. (2004). Relationships between future orientation, impulsive sensation seeking, and risk behavior among adjudicated adolescents. *Journal of Adolescent Research, 19*(4), 428–445. doi: 10.1177/0743558403258860 [doi].

Romer, D. (2010). Adolescent risk taking, impulsivity, and brain development: Implications for prevention. *Developmental Psychobiology, 52*(3), 263–276. doi: 10.1002/dev.20442 [doi].

Royal Society (2011). *Brain Waves Module 4: Neuroscience and the law*. Retrieved from https://royalsociety.org/~/media/Royal_Society_Content/policy/projects/brain-waves/Brain. Waves-4.pdf.

Rubia, K., Russell, T., Overmeyer, S., Brammer, M. J., Bullmore, E. T., Sharma, T., ... Taylor, E. (2001). Mapping motor inhibition: Conjunctive brain activations across different versions of go/no-go and stop tasks. *NeuroImage, 13*(2), 250–261.

Rudorf, S., Preuschoff, K., & Weber, B. (2012). Neural correlates of anticipation risk reflect risk preferences. *Journal of Neuroscience, 32*(47), 16683–16692. doi: 32/47/16683 [pii]10.1523/JNEUROSCI.4235-11.2012 [doi].

Scott-Parker, B., Watson, B., King, M. J., & Hyde, M. K. (2012). The influence of sensitivity to reward and punishment, propensity for sensation seeking, depression, and anxiety on the risky behavior of novice drivers: A path model. *British Journal of Psychology, 103*(2), 248–267. doi: 10.1111/j.2044-8295.2011.02069.x [doi].

Segalowitz, S. J., Santesso, D. L., Willoughby, T., Reker, D. L., Campbell, K., Chalmers, H., & Rose-Krasnor, L. (2012). Adolescent peer interaction and trait surgency weaken medial prefrontal cortex responses to failure. *Social Cognitive and Affective Neuroscience, 7*(1), 115–124. doi: nsq090 [pii]10.1093/scan/nsq090 [doi].

Simmonds, D. J., Pekar, J. J., & Mostofsky, S. H. (2008). Meta-analysis of Go/No-go tasks demonstrating that fMRI activation associated with response inhibition is task-dependent. *Neuropsychologia, 46*(1), 224–232.

Singer, T., Critchley, H. D., & Preuschoff, K. (2009). A common role of insula in feelings, empathy and uncertainty. *Trends in Cognitive Sciences, 13*(8), 334–340. doi: 10.1016/j.tics.2009.05.001.

Steinberg, L. (2004). Risk taking in adolescence: What changes, and why? *Annals of the New York Academy of Sciences, 1021*, 51–58. doi: 10.1196/annals.1308.005 [doi] 1021/1/51[pii].

Steinberg, L. (2005). Cognitive and affective development in adolescence. *Trends in Cognitive Sciences, 9*(2), 69–74. doi: S1364-6613(04)00317-1 [pii]10.1016/j.tics.2004.12.005 [doi].

Steinberg, L. (2008). A social neuroscience perspective on adolescent risk-taking. *Developmental Review, 28*(1), 78–106.

Steinberg, L. (2013). The influence of neuroscience on US Supreme Court decisions about adolescents' criminal culpability. *Nature Reviews Neuroscience, 14*(7), 513–518. doi: nrn3509 [pii]10.1038/nrn3509 [doi].

Steinberg, L., Albert, D., Cauffman, E., Banich, M., Graham, S., & Woolard, J. (2008). Age differences in sensation seeking and impulsivity as indexed by behavior and self-report: Evidence for a dual systems model. *Developmental Psychology, 44*(6), 1764–1778. doi: 2008-16008-019 [pii]10.1037/a0012955 [doi].

Strang, N. M., Chein, J. M., & Steinberg, L. (2013). The value of the dual systems model of adolescent risk-taking. *Frontiers in Human Neuroscience, 7*, 223. doi: 10.3389/fnhum.2013.00223 [doi].

Studer, B., Pedroni, A., & Rieskamp, J. (2013). Predicting risk-taking behavior from prefrontal resting-state activity and personality. *PLoS One, 8*(10), e76861. doi: 10.1371/journal.pone.0076861. [doi]PONE-D-13-19865 [pii].

Teen Mental health (2009). Risk-taking Behaviour in Adolescence. Retrieved from http://tmentalhealth.blogspot.co.uk/2009/02/risk-taking-behaviour-in-adolescence.html.

Tversky, A., & Kahneman, D. (1981). The framing of decisions and the psychology of choice. *Science, 211*(4481), 453–458.

Tymula, A., Rosenberg Belmaker, L. A., Roy, A. K., Ruderman, L., Manson, K., Glimcher, P. W., & Levy, I. (2012). Adolescents' risk-taking behavior is driven by tolerance to ambiguity. *Proceedings of the National Academy of Sciences of the United States of America, 109*(42), 17135–17140. doi: 1207144109 [pii]10.1073/pnas.1207144109 [doi].

van den Bos, R., Homberg, J., & de Visser, L. (2013). A critical review of sex differences in decision-making tasks: Focus on the Iowa Gambling Task. *Behavioral Brain Research, 238*, 95–108. doi: S0166-4328(12)00641-9 [pii]10.1016/j.bbr.2012.10.002 [doi].

Van Leijenhorst, L., Gunther Moor, B., Op de Macks, Z. A., Rombouts, S. A., Westenberg, P. M., & Crone, E. A. (2010). Adolescent risky decision-making: Neurocognitive development of reward and control regions. *NeuroImage, 51*(1), 345–355.

Van Leijenhorst, L., Zanolie, K., Van Meel, C. S., Westenberg, P. M., Rombouts, S. A., & Crone, E. A. (2010). What motivates the adolescent? Brain regions mediating reward sensitivity across adolescence. *Cerebral Cortex, 20*(1), 61–69. doi: bhp078 [pii] 10.1093/cercor/bhp078 [doi].

Volman, S. F., Lammel, S., Margolis, E. B., Kim, Y., Richard, J. M., Roitman, M. F., & Lobo, M. K. (2013). New insights into the specificity and plasticity of reward and aversion encoding in the mesolimbic system. *Journal of Neuroscience, 33*(45), 17569–17576. doi: 33/45/17569 [pii]10.1523/JNEUROSCI.3250-13.2013 [doi].

Wallis, J. D. (2007). Orbitofrontal cortex and its contribution to decision-making. *Annual Review of Neuroscience, 30*, 31–56. doi: 10.1146/annurev.neuro.30.051606.094334[doi].

Willoughby, T., Good, M., Adachi, P. J., Hamza, C., & Tavernier, R. (2013). Examining the link between adolescent brain development and risk taking from a social-developmental perspective. *Brain and Cognition, 83*(3), 315–323. doi: S0278-2626(13)00143-7 [pii]10.1016/j.bandc.2013.09.008 [doi].

Willoughby, T., Tavernier, R., Hamza, C., Adachi, P. J., & Good, M. (2013). The triadic systems model perspective and adolescent risk taking. *Brain and Cognition*. doi: S0278-2626(13)00164-4 [pii]10.1016/j.bandc.2013.11.001 [doi].

Wright, N. D., Symmonds, M., Hodgson, K., Fitzgerald, T. H., Crawford, B., & Dolan, R. J. (2012). Approach-avoidance processes contribute to dissociable impacts of risk and loss on choice. *Journal of Neuroscience, 32*(20), 7009–7020. doi: 32/20/7009 [pii] 10.1523/JNEUROSCI.0049-12.2012 [doi].

Yurgelun-Todd, D. (2007). Emotional and cognitive changes during adolescence. *Current Opinion in Neurobiology, 17*(2), 251–257. doi: S0959-4388(07)00041-4 [pii]10.1016/j.conb.2007.03.009 [doi].

6
The Neurobiology of Emotion Regulation

Catherine L. Sebastian and Saz P. Ahmed

Key points
- Emotion regulation (ER) is crucial in order for us to control our behavior effectively. It comprises multiple components, and includes both implicit or automatic processes, as well as explicit use of conscious strategies to down-regulate emotions.
- A wide network of brain regions is involved in the detection, expression and regulation of emotion.
- Regions such as amygdala and ventral striatum have typically been characterized as generating emotional states such as fear and reward, with dorsolateral, ventromedial, and ventrolateral prefrontal cortex providing top-down inhibitory control.
- However, recent models of the neurobiology of ER suggest a more nuanced picture, with bidirectional connections between contributing brain regions.
- As such, it is difficult to isolate regulatory processes from those involved in generating emotional responses.
- This chapter will discuss the neurobiology of ER in the typically functioning human brain.
- It will briefly look at the development of these processes, as well as implications for forensic psychopathology.
- Key words include: emotion, regulation, neurobiology, affective neuroscience, development, amygdala, and prefrontal cortex.

Terminology Explained

Cognitive reappraisal is the process of cognitively changing the interpretation of an emotion-eliciting situation to alter its emotional impact.

The Wiley Blackwell Handbook of Forensic Neuroscience, First Edition. Edited by Anthony R. Beech, Adam J. Carter, Ruth E. Mann and Pia Rotshtein.
© 2018 John Wiley & Sons Ltd. Published 2018 by John Wiley & Sons Ltd.

> **Emotional go/no-go task** is commonly used to assess inhibitory control; participants are asked to either respond (go trials) or withhold response (no-go trials) to different affective stimuli. Because go trials are more common, the task is able to measure one's ability to inhibit a prepotent response under different emotional conditions.
>
> **Emotional Stroop task** is commonly used to assess attentional bias in which participants are required to name the color of ink in which an emotional item is printed, while attempting to ignore the item itself.
>
> **Explicit ER** requires conscious effort during initiation, and some level of monitoring during implementation in order to change an emotional response. A common explicit strategy is cognitive reappraisal (see below for definition).
>
> **Expressive suppression** involves reducing the outward display of an emotional reaction.
>
> **Implicit ER** operates without the need for conscious supervision or explicit intentions, and automatically modifies the quality, intensity, or duration of an emotional response, for example, ignoring a negatively valenced word during the emotional Stroop task.

Introduction

Emotions exert a powerful influence over our lives and serve a wide range of functions, from alerting us to a threat to helping us build relationships. Emotions serve an adaptive role by motivating us to take action to maximize our chances for success. However, emotions can become dysfunctional when they are exaggerated in intensity, last for long periods of time, occur unpredictably, or are evoked out of context. In these cases, emotions must be regulated to control our behavior effectively. Emotion regulation (ER) is not a single process, and has been defined broadly as the monitoring, evaluation, and modifying of emotional reactions in order to accomplish goals (Thompson, 1994). This can include both implicit ER – that is, processes which occur automatically and largely outside conscious awareness – and explicit ER, which involves using conscious strategies to down-regulate emotional responses. This chapter will first review evidence suggesting that a wide network of brain regions is involved in the detection, expression, and regulation of emotion. We will then discuss recent models of ER, largely based on human behavioral and functional magnetic resonance imaging (fMRI) data, which seek to link cognitive and neural levels of explanation. We will also provide a short overview of research into the neurodevelopment of these processes in childhood and adolescence, since emotional dysregulation associated with forensic psychopathology so often has its roots in development (see Chapter 16 of this volume and Part IV of Volume 2.). We end with practical and policy implications of affective neuroscience research for forensic populations.

Key Brain Regions to Consider in ER

ER research has benefited from the use of functional neuroimaging techniques. Numerous studies in healthy participants have helped delineate the neurobiology of ER. This section will give an overview of the key regions involved in the detection, expression, and regulation of emotion.

Subcortical regions

The amygdala The amygdala is an almond-shaped collection of nuclei located within the temporal lobes of the brain, which has vast connectivity with several regulatory regions. Ventral and dorsal pathways connect the amygdala to prefrontal brain regions such as the medial and lateral orbitofrontal cortices, as well as the anterior cingulate cortex and dorsolateral prefrontal cortex (Bracht et al., 2009; Johansen-Berg et al., 2008). Unsurprisingly, the amygdala has a key role in ER, being functionally linked to both learning and expressing the fear response (LeDoux, 2000). fMRI studies have found increased amygdala activation to threat-relevant stimuli such as angry faces and pictures of threatening situations (Whalen et al., 1998). Moreover, **lesion studies** (see Box 6.1) in non-human primates have supported the critical role of the amygdala in fear response. For instance, monkeys with amygdala lesions showed less caution when approaching predators such as snakes, which they ordinarily have an innate fear response to (Machado, Kazama, & Bachevalier, 2009).

The amygdala has also been implicated in reward processing, in part through critical interactions with the ventral striatum for stimulus–reward associations (Baxter & Murray, 2002). fMRI studies have also reported amygdala activation in the context of potential reward (McClure, York, & Montague, 2004). However, when controlling for arousal, direct comparison of amygdala responses to rewarding versus punishing stimuli often reveals no significant differences, leading researchers to infer that the amygdala signal in fMRI responds more to stimulus salience than valence (Small et al., 2003).

The bed nucleus of the stria terminalis The bed nucleus of the stria terminalis (BNST) is a limbic forebrain structure that consists of a heterogeneous group of nuclei that receive projections from the amygdala (Walker & Davis, 2008). While the amygdala mediates responses to briefly presented emotional stimuli, the BNST is thought to be involved in more sustained anxiety processing (Walker & Davis, 2008). An fMRI study by Yassa, Hazlett, Stark, and Hoehn-Saric (2012) found that, under conditions of high and sustained anxiety, individuals with generalized anxiety disorder (GAD) showed decreased activity in the amygdala and increased activity in the BNST, relative to healthy controls. The authors suggested that GAD patients disengage the amygdala and its response to acute stress earlier than non-anxious controls, making way for the BNST to maintain a more sustained anxious response.

The habenula The habenula comprises a pair of small nuclei located above the thalamus, near the stalk of the pineal gland. Neuroimaging findings have closely linked the lateral habenula with the encoding of negative feedback and depression. For example, the habenula responded when participants received negative feedback during a motion prediction task (Ullsperger & von Cramon, 2003). Both the medial and lateral habenula showed reduced volume in those with depression compared to healthy controls as well as a reduction in neuronal cell number in depressive patients for the right side compared to controls (Ranft, Dobrowolny, Krell, Bielau, Bogerts, & Bernstein, 2010).

The striatum The striatum is part of the basal ganglia and comprises the caudate nucleus, the putamen, and the **nucleus accumbens** (see Box 6.1). It receives direct input from many regions of the cerebral cortex and **limbic system** (see Box 6.1), including the amygdala and hippocampus. Typically, most studies differentiate between the dorsal and ventral striatum, with dorsal striatum more associated with sensorimotor information processing, and the ventral striatum with emotional and motivational aspects of behavior (Voorn, Vanderschuren, Groenewegen, Robbins, & Pennartz, 2004). The ventral striatum is particularly involved in the processing and anticipation of rewards, via dopaminergic **prediction errors** (see Box 6.1). Dopaminergic reward learning is associated with increased activation of midbrain dopamine neurons, which stimulate synaptic dopamine release in the striatum and throughout the brain (Schultz, 2006). The dopamine system, and the ventral striatum in particular, play a central role in impulsive and reckless behavior such as pathological gambling. For example, Linnet, Møller, Peterson, Gjedde, and Doudet (2011) found that pathological gamblers, who continue gambling despite losses, had significantly increased dopamine release in the left ventral striatum when they lost money, compared with controls. Findings regarding the role of this region in ER have been mixed. Some studies show that activity in the striatum, specifically the nucleus accumbens, is reduced during the regulation of emotional responses to aversive stimuli (e.g., Phan et al., 2005), while others show increased activity in the dorsal striatum (e.g., van Reekum et al., 2007); however, this disparity may be due to methodological differences.

Box 6.1 Definitions

In **lesion studies** an area of the brain is surgically or chemically lesioned (animal studies) or is accidentally damaged (human studies). Behavior of the subject is then assessed to determine the functions of the lesioned structure.

The **nucleus accumbens** is located at the base of the forebrain and plays a central role in the brain's reward circuitry.

The **limbic system** is a set of subcortical and cortical brain structures broadly involved in emotion and memory processes.

Prediction error signals code the difference between a reward and its prior prediction, such that an unpredicted reward elicits a positive prediction error, a fully predicted reward elicits no response, and the omission of a predicted reward induces a negative prediction error.

Cortical regions

The prefrontal cortex   The prefrontal cortex is located at the front of the brain and supports executive functions such as inhibitory control, planning, and working memory. Therefore, prefrontal structures are thought to be central to generating and maintaining ER strategies. Subdivisions of the prefrontal cortex implicated in emotion processing and regulation include the dorsolateral (dlPFC), ventrolateral (vlPFC), and ventromedial regions (vmPFC).

dlPFC   The dlPFC is situated in the middle frontal gyrus and is usually attributed anatomically to Brodmann areas (BA) 9 and 46 (Cieslik et al., 2013). The dlPFC is consistently associated with cognitive control processes, that is, coordinating thoughts and actions in accordance with overarching internally represented goals. These processes are implicated in emotional control, particularly the down-regulation of negative emotion (Davidson, Putnam, & Larson, 2000).

vlPFC The vlPFC is located in the inferior frontal gyrus and comprises BA 47 and BA 44/45, which constitute the anterior, posterior, and mid subregions of the vlPFC, respectively (Levy & Wagner, 2011). The vlPFC is activated by both positive and negative stimuli, and activity in this region is evident when reducing subjective negative affect during effortful regulation. These functions may result from interactions with dissociable neural regions, particularly amygdala, and ventral striatum (Mitchell, 2011). The vlPFC is also thought to play a critical role in inhibitory control for both emotional and non-emotional stimuli. Neuroimaging studies requiring participants to respond on "go" trials but inhibit responding on "no-go" or "stop" trials typically reveal activation in right vlPFC (Elliott & Deakin, 2005, Rubia, Smith, Brammer, & Taylor, 2003). Evidence of causal involvement comes from lesion studies showing that inhibitory control deficits correlate with vlPFC lesion size (Aron, Fletcher, Bullmore, Sahakian, & Robbins, 2003).

vmPFC The vmPFC is located in the ventral portion of the frontal lobe and encompasses ventral BA 10 and parts of medial orbitofrontal cortex (BA 11). vmPFC activation is associated with successful suppression of emotional responses to negative stimuli, and is also important for encoding outcome expectations. For example, patients with vmPFC lesions exhibit poorly regulated anger and frustration following the omission of an expected reward (Mitchell, 2011).

Anterior cingulate cortex The anterior cingulate cortex (ACC) describes a strip of cortex that follows the curve of the corpus callosum and has extensive bidirectional connections with dorsolateral, orbitofrontal, and insular regions of the cerebral cortex. Neuroimaging studies have found increased activation of the ACC in both emotional and cognitive executive functions, suggesting it is a neural relay structure where these influences impact response behavior (Gasquoine, 2013).

The subgenual ACC (sgACC), which has connections with the orbitofrontal cortex (OFC), nucleus accumbens, amygdala, hippocampus, and hypothalamus (Johansen-Berg et al., 2008), is particularly associated with emotion dysregulation, and is implicated in depression. Several fMRI studies have shown that the sgACC is dysfunctional in depressed adults. For example, compared with non-depressed controls, depressed participants exhibited increased activation in the sgACC to both sad and happy (relative to neutral) facial expressions (Gotlib et al., 2005). Given these functions, the ACC is thought to be a key structure underlying adaptive and maladaptive ER, and is an intermediary between higher order cognition and emotional arousal (Paus, 2001).

Models of ER

Given that there are numerous strategies for regulating emotional responses, attempts have been made to organize regulatory processes based on their behavioral and physiological correlates. We will briefly review key models of ER, before discussing the neurobiology underpinning different ER strategies outlined by these models.

Modal and process models

One of the most influential approaches has been to focus on the time point at which regulatory processes are brought to bear on emotion-evoking situations. The "modal

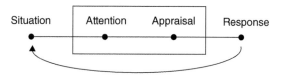

Figure 6.1 Modal model of emotion regulation.
Source: Redrawn from Gross and Thompson (2007), with permission from James Gross.

model" of emotion posits that the emotion generation process occurs in a particular sequence over time (Gross, 1998a). As shown in Figure 6.1, the sequence starts with a situation that is emotionally significant, thus causing attention to be directed towards the emotional situation. This emotional situation is then appraised and evaluated giving rise to behavioral, physiological, and neural responses. Since emotional responses can modify the situation that gave rise to the response in the first place, the modal model contains a feedback loop, implying that the emotion generation process can occur recursively, is ongoing, and dynamic (Gross & Thompson, 2007).

The modal model was then extended into the "process model" (Gross, 1998b; see Figure 6.2), which contended that each of the four points in the emotion generation process could be subjected to regulation. Gross (1998b) described five families of ER strategies comprising the process model. The first two forms of ER – *situation selection* and *situation modification* – both help to shape the situation to which an individual will be exposed. The individual actively selects which situation they will place themselves in and modifies its emotional impact. Situation selection is commonly seen in psychopathology, for example, where an individual with social anxiety disorder avoids social situations to regulate their emotions (Wells & Papageorgiou, 1998). Similarly, in forensic psychopathology, individuals with aggressive tendencies may avoid situations that could provoke them to behave aggressively (Anderson & Bushman, 2002). A third strategy is to use attentional deployment to focus attention away from aspects of the situation that provoke undesired emotions. The fourth family of strategies, referred to as *cognitive change*, involves changing how one evaluates a situation so as to alter its emotional impact. One form of cognitive change that has received particular attention is reappraisal, which will be discussed in more detail below. The final point in the process model is *response modulation*, which refers to direct attempts to influence physiological, experiential, or behavioral emotional responses once they already have

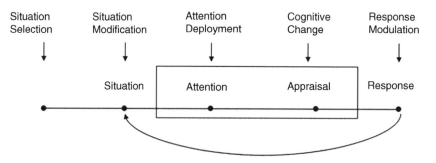

Figure 6.2 Process model of emotion regulation.
Source: Redrawn from Gross and Thompson (2007), with permission from James Gross.

been elicited. For example, exercise and relaxation techniques may be used to decrease physiological and experiential effect of negative emotions (Oaten & Cheng, 2006). One of the most researched forms of response modulation is expressive suppression, which entails inhibiting emotional expressions (Gross, 2002) (see below).

The process model further divides these ER strategies into antecedent-focused and response-focused subtypes. Antecedent-focused strategies (i.e., situation selection, situation modification, attentional deployment, and cognitive change) occur before an emotional response is fully generated and has had a chance to change behavior and physiological responding. Response-focused strategies (response modulation processes such as expressive suppression) refer to things we do once an emotional response is already underway (Gross, 1998a).

Although the process model has enabled us to think about ER more systematically, it does not always capture the complexity of the processes involved in regulating emotions. For example, ER is a continuous process, and different processes in the model can occur in parallel. When monitoring our emotional response, we can choose a preferable strategy to regulate emotions (consciously or unconsciously), and can switch between strategies. It is also worth noting that the process model was not originally developed as a neurobiological model. However, the framework it has provided has been an important starting point for neuroscience research in this area.

Methods for regulating emotion *ER is crucial in order for us to control our behavior effectively. It comprises multiple components, and includes both implicit or automatic processes as well as explicit use of conscious strategies to down-regulate or manage emotions (like meditation).*
Source: © ID218217. Used under license from 699pic.

Dual-process framework

A variant of the above models, the dual process model (Gyurak, Gross, & Etkin, 2011), distinguishes between effortful, conscious, and explicit; and automatic unconscious and implicit forms of ER. A central tenet of this framework is that behavior is determined by the interplay of automatic and controlled processing. Furthermore, the dual process framework distinguishes between **top-down** and **bottom-up** processing (see Box 6.2), with the former determined by the current goals of the observer (e.g., searching for friend in a crowd) and the latter determined by the physical characteristics of the scene in question (e.g., a loud and sudden noise) (Awh, Belopolsky, & Theeuwes, 2012). ER strategies comprise both bottom-up and top-down processes.

Although explicit and implicit forms of ER are framed as opposites, evidence is suggesting that such a distinction may be too simplistic (Pfeifer & Allen, 2012). Some researchers believe that the boundaries between explicit and implicit are porous. Gyurak et al. (2011) suggested that implicit emotional regulation might sometimes stem from the habitual use of specific explicit strategies. For example, explicitly reminding oneself that an angry colleague had a bad day may over time lead to the same reappraisal process occurring implicitly, without awareness. This habitual use of reappraisal to down-regulate emotions has been showed to be beneficial behaviorally and in terms of physiological responding. For instance, when participants were made angry in a laboratory setting, those that reappraised more often reported less anger, less negative emotion, and demonstrated more adaptive cardiovascular responses in comparison to low reappraisers (Mauss, Cook, Cheng, & Gross, 2007).

Box 6.2   Bottom-Up and Top-Down Processing

Bottom-up processing is processing driven by factors *external* to the observer, such as stimulus salience (e.g., stimuli that contrast strongly with surrounding items, sudden flashes of light, or loud noises in an otherwise quiet environment).

Top-down processing is processing driven by factors *internal* to the observer, such as specific goals.

Neural Bases of ER

We will now review literature on the neural bases of the regulatory processes discussed above. For convenience, we divide processes into explicit and implicit domains, although, as discussed above, this distinction is likely an oversimplification.

Explicit ER

Explicit ER strategies require conscious effort during initiation, and some level of monitoring during implementation (Gyurak et al., 2011). The process model (Gross, 1998b) predicts that instigating regulation relatively early on in the emotion-generative process should be more effective in modifying the course of the response.

The process of this type, which has received the most empirical attention is **cognitive reappraisal**. In contrast, **expressive suppression** is a response-focused explicit regulatory process that occurs once an emotional response has been generated, and which prevents emotional responses from being overtly expressed (Gross & Thompson, 2007). The following section compares and contrasts the neurobiological underpinnings of these distinct explicit strategies.

Reappraisal

Reappraisal involves an attempt to change the interpretation of an emotional stimulus or situation. For example, an image of a woman crying can be reappraised by thinking that she is crying tears of joy (Etkin, Egner, & Kalisch 2011). In the first study to investigate the neural bases of reappraisal, Ochsner, Bunge, Gross, and Gabrieli (2002) instructed participants to reappraise negative emotion-eliciting photos to modify their emotional response. It was found that, relative to simply attending to the negative photos, reappraisal successfully diminished subjective negative affect. Effective reappraisal was also associated with increased activation in lateral and medial prefrontal cortex, and decreased activation in amygdala and medial OFC (mOFC). Furthermore, the magnitude of vlPFC activation during reappraisal was inversely correlated with activation in the amygdala and mOFC. Taken together, these findings suggest that engagement of cognitive control-related areas dampens neural activity associated with emotional reactivity.

A related study by Kim and Hamann (2007) looked at whether the same neural circuitry used to reappraise negative pictures would be engaged in reappraising positive ones. They also asked participants to either increase (up-regulate) or decrease (down-regulate) the intensity of their positive and negative emotional responses. Although there were small differences, the overall pattern of results revealed generally shared activations in prefrontal regions (dorsomedial prefrontal cortex, left lateral prefrontal cortex, left OFC, ACC) when participants engaged in both up- and down-regulation for both negative and positive pictures. These findings support the notion that reappraisal engages the same processes regardless of emotional valence or regulatory goal.

The studies discussed above all used instructed reappraisal in an experimental setting. However, one study looked at the link between reappraisal use in everyday life and neural responses to facial expressions during an incidental face-matching task (Drabant, McRae, Manuck, Hariri, & Gross, 2009). Participants who reported using reappraisal as an ER strategy in everyday life showed decreased amygdala activation and greater activity in prefrontal and parietal regions in response to viewing negative facial expressions. Thus, the findings suggest a link between explicit ER strategy use and basic emotional responses to affective stimuli in the absence of explicit instructions to regulate these (see Box 6.3).

Box 6.3 Pathways Mediating ER

An influential study by Wager, Davidson, Hughes, Lindquist, and Ochsner. (2008) investigated whether subcortical regions mediate the relationship between key PFC regions and reappraisal success. Using pathway-mapping analysis, the authors identified two separable pathways linking prefrontal activation

> with reductions in self-reported negative emotion during reappraisal. One path was through the nucleus accumbens, which predicted greater reappraisal success (i.e., less negative emotion), and the other was through the amygdala, which predicted reduced reappraisal success. These results show that the vlPFC is involved in both the generation and regulation of emotion through different subcortical pathways, suggesting a general role for this region in appraisal processes.

Suppression

Suppression involves inhibiting emotional expressions (e.g., facial expressions, verbal utterances, gestures) and usually takes place after emotional responses have been generated. Unlike reappraisal, suppression does not reliably reduce subjective negative emotion (Gross, 1998b) and can even lead to increases in sympathetic activation of the cardiovascular system (Gross, 2002). Compared to reappraisal, the neural bases of suppression have been studied less extensively. A recent study assessed the neural correlates of suppression by instructing participants to suppress their emotions while viewing negative and neutral film clips (Shimamura, Marian, & Haskins, 2012). Arousal inducing, non-valenced films (e.g., car chase) were also included to control for potential confounding effects of arousal. Suppression during the negative clips activated a broad frontoparietal network; including lateral, medial (anterior cingulate gyrus), and orbital regions in the prefrontal cortex. There was also increased activation of the insula. Suppression during the arousal clips also activated prefrontal regions, though not to the same extent as during the negative clips. Findings were similar to a previous study in which regions in the superior prefrontal gyrus and anterior cingulate gyrus mediated emotional suppression while viewing erotic film clips (Beauregard, Lévesque, & Bourgouin, 2001).

Few fMRI studies have compared reappraisal and suppression in typical adult participants. Goldin et al. (2008) directly compared the two strategies by instructing participants to either reappraise or suppress their ongoing emotion-expressive behavior in the scanner during 15-second neutral and disgusting (e.g., animal slaughter) films. Findings indicated that, relative to suppression, reappraisal increased activity in medial, dorsolateral, and ventrolateral prefrontal cortex regions within 4.5 seconds of the film starting, and decreased amygdala and insula responses. In contrast, relative to reappraisal, suppression led to increased activation in the amygdala, insula, and several prefrontal regions including right vlPFC, which has previously been implicated in inhibitory control (Aron et al., 2003; Elliott & Deakin, 2005; Rubia et al., 2003). However, as the process model predicts, these activations were apparent late in the responding period (10.5–15 seconds). This delay may reflect amygdala and insula activity "breaking through" increasingly strained efforts of cognitive control. Behaviorally, both strategies reduced subjective negative emotions and extent of disgust expressions as coded by two raters. However, reappraisal was more effective in reducing negative affect, while suppression was better for reducing negative facial expressions. Thus, although both strategies engage the prefrontal cortex, suppression seems less effective than reappraisal at reducing activation of the limbic system. This is consistent with autonomic nervous system activation studies measuring skin conductance, heart rate, and blinking, showing that suppression has an effect on visible displays of emotion but does not alter emotional reactivity (Gross & Levenson, 1993).

Implicit ER

Neuroimaging has also provided insights into the mechanisms underpinning more automatic forms of ER. Implicit ER is generally defined as "any process that operates without the need for conscious supervision or explicit intentions, and aims at modifying the quality, intensity, or duration of an emotional response" (Koole & Rothermund, 2011, p. 1). As discussed above, explicit ER is usually measured by comparing emotional responses elicited in one condition in which participants are instructed to adopt a certain ER strategy with another condition in which participants are not given such instructions. This is more difficult for implicit ER because there is no obvious baseline against which the automatic occurrence of implicit ER processes should be compared. Below, we provide a few examples of studies addressing interactions between cognitive control and emotion in the absence of explicit instructions to regulate emotion. An exhaustive discussion of cognition–emotion interactions is beyond the scope of this chapter, but see Pessoa (2008), and Cromheeke and Mueller (2013), for reviews.

To investigate cognitive conflict caused by emotional stimuli, Etkin, Egner, Peraza, Kandel, and Hirsch (2006) developed an emotional face version of the Stroop task (Stroop, 1935). In this task participants were shown photographs of happy or fearful facial expressions with either the word "happy" or "fearful" superimposed. Participants were asked to identify the emotional expression of the faces while ignoring the printed words, which were either of the same emotion (congruent) or of a different emotion (incongruent) as the facial expression. Incongruent stimuli were therefore associated with response conflict arising from an emotional mismatch between task-relevant and task-irrelevant stimulus dimensions (e.g., a fearful expression with the word "happy"). Consistent with this, reaction times to incongruent trials were longer than to congruent trials. fMRI data additionally revealed brain regions which reflected the degree of emotional conflict. High-conflict trials were defined as those in which an incongruent trial was preceded by a congruent trial, meaning regulatory resources were required to be brought online specifically at the onset of that trial. On these trials (relative to low-conflict trials) activity in the amygdala, dorsomedial prefrontal cortex, and bilateral dlPFC was also predictive of rostral ACC (rACC) activity on the subsequent trial. In contrast, high control trials were defined as those in which an incongruent trial is preceded by another incongruent trial. On these trials, activation of the rACC was associated with a reduction in amygdala activity and enhanced task performance. Etkin et al. (2006) concluded that amygdala activity is increased when two conflicting emotional states are represented in the same trial and that the rACC is involved in resolving this conflict through top-down inhibition of amygdala activity.

In a follow-up study, Egner, Etkin, Gale, and Hirsch (2008) had participants perform the same emotional Stroop task as well as a non-emotional variation of the task, where participants were asked to judge the gender of emotional faces while ignoring the word "male" or "female" written over them. The authors found that while dACC was activated during high-conflict trials in both tasks, the rACC was activated only during conflict resolution (high control) trials in the emotional version. Connectivity analyses showed that rACC activity was associated with decreased amygdala activity only in the emotional Stroop task. Although this study did not support Etkin et al.'s (2006) findings that the amygdala detects conflicts arising from emotional stimuli, both studies did suggest that the rACC is involved in cognitive control during emotional Stroop tasks through inhibition of amygdala activity.

In sum, it appears that the brain both implicitly processes emotion and down regulates neural responses to it, even when we are not consciously aware of doing so. The neural circuitry involved in implicit regulation of emotion seems to overlap quite considerably with that involved in explicit regulation, with studies even demonstrating this overlap within the same study (e.g., Drabant et al., 2009).

Neurodevelopment of ER

So far, we have focused on mechanisms of ER in the typical human brain. Dysfunction of emotion processing and regulatory mechanisms in forensic psychopathology will be the focus of several subsequent chapters, and so will not be discussed here. However, complete understanding of an adult psychological process and how it may develop atypically relies on understanding its developmental trajectory in typical individuals (Karmiloff-Smith, 1998). In Box 6.4, we briefly review evidence on the development of ER and its underlying neurobiology. The development of ER is relatively protracted over the lifespan. While it might be predicted that ER would develop linearly, neuroimaging research suggests some processes follow a non-linear developmental trajectory, particularly over the course of adolescence.

Box 6.4 Increasing Connectivity across Development

In one developmental fMRI study, participants engaged in a go/no-go task in which they gained and lost points towards a desired prize (Perlman & Pelphrey, 2011). Children aged 5-11 and adults displayed distinct patterns of ACC and amygdala activation when ER was required. The task was designed such that participants lost all of the points they had previously won, in order to induce negative emotions of frustration. Connectivity analyses showed that as frustration (and thus ER demands) increased, effective connectivity between the ACC and amygdala also increased. Importantly, this connectivity increased with age, suggestive of ongoing neural maturation underlying this process between late childhood and early adolescence.

The neurodevelopment of ER across the lifespan is a growing area of research, and to date few studies have investigated the neural correlates of ER in children. Before a child is able to self-regulate, caregivers effectively act as regulators for their child by soothing and rocking them to reduce distress or by distracting their attention away from the cause of distress. This helps to scaffold the development of the child's own regulatory abilities (Fonagy, Gergely, & Jurist, 2003). Self-regulation of emotion is evident from an early age, and includes self-soothing behaviors such as sucking and self-distraction. For example, in a study of 6-, 12-, and 18-month-old infants (Buss & Goldsmith, 1998), the use of infant self-distraction and approach behaviors (attempts to retrieve the toy that was taken away from them) reduced the expression of anger during emotional challenges, although these activities were less effective in reducing fear.

With continuing neural development and increasing cognitive abilities, ER strategies shift from being externally driven by the caregiver and behaviorally focused, to being more cognitive and internally focused in older children (Kopp, 1989). For example, internally-generated reappraisal processes have been demonstrated in children as young as eight years old. Lévesque et al. (2004) examined neural responses to sad films in 8–10-year-old girls when instructed to either watch passively or use reappraisal to reduce negative affect. Reappraisal was associated with activations of several prefrontal loci including the lateral, ventrolateral, orbital and medial prefrontal cortex as well as in the right ACC. In an identical previous study involving adult women (Lévesque et al., 2003), fewer prefrontal loci were active. The authors suggested that the greater number of prefrontal cortex regions activated in the children may reflect inefficiency and immaturity of prefrontal regulatory circuitry (although children and adults were not directly compared).

One prominent set of theories argues that during adolescence the development of prefrontal regions lags behind that of the limbic structures such as the amygdala and ventral striatum (e.g., Nelson, Leibenluft, McClure, & Pine, 2005). At the same time, connectivity between brain regions involved in ER are still developing, thus ER abilities are potentially poorer in adolescence than in earlier childhood. Hare et al. (2008) investigated this using an emotional go/no-go task and found that adolescents and children were relatively slower than adults when responding to fearful target faces implying that they were less efficient at overriding affective interference compared to adults. Moreover, adolescents showed exaggerated amygdala activity relative to children and adults, a difference that decreased with repeated exposure to the stimuli. Furthermore, functional connectivity analysis showed a negative correlation between activity in the amygdala and ventral prefrontal cortex. This exaggerated activation from limbic structures relative to ventral prefrontal cortex may play a role in the increased emotional reactivity, poor decision making and increased risk for affective disorders associated with adolescence.

Studies by Sebastian and colleagues investigating developmental differences in the neural processing of social rejection further suggest that prefrontal cortex regions involved in regulating emotional distress undergo protracted development in adolescence. In a rejection-themed emotional Stroop task, adolescents aged 14–16 showed attenuated right vlPFC responses relative to adults during the processing of rejection-related words compared with neutral and acceptance words (Sebastian et al., 2010). Another study (Sebastian et al., 2011) found the same pattern of attenuated right vlPFC response in adolescents relative to adults during social rejection in the cyberball game; a virtual ball-tossing game in which participants can be systematically included and excluded over the course of the experiment (Williams, Cheung, & Choi, 2000). These findings suggest potential overlaps in the circuitry used to regulate emotion during both implicit (Stroop) and explicit (cyberball) social rejection paradigms, and highlight potential functional immaturity of this region in adolescence.

The neuroscience literature highlights several important developmental issues related to ER. Although ER tends to improve over childhood, such development is unlikely to be linear due to uneven maturation of the neural circuitry and neurobiology underlying motivational and regulatory processes and their interplay during childhood and adolescence.

Emotion regulation across the lifespan *The development of emotion regulation improves throughout the lifespan, with adults demonstrating a better ability to regulate their emotions than children and adolescents, and the elderly further showing enhanced emotion regulation abilities compared to young adults.*

Source: © Franck Boston. Used under license from 123RF.

Implications for Forensic Applications

The neuroscience of emotion and ER is changing how we think about criminal and antisocial behavior. As we will see in future chapters, researchers have begun to elucidate the neural mechanisms underpinning antisocial behavior, most of which are also implicated in emotion dysregulation.

At the same time, brain scans are already being admitted as evidence in court (see Glenn & Raine, 2014; Steinberg, 2013), suggesting that neuroscientific findings will have increasingly important implications for forensic populations and settings. For example, a recent ruling by the US Supreme Court prohibited states from mandating life without parole for crimes committed by minors (Miller v. Alabama, 2012). Drawing on scientific studies of the adolescent brain, the Court concluded that due to their inherent psychological and neurobiological immaturity, adolescents are not as responsible for their behavior as adults (Steinberg, 2013). The application of neuroscience to the law has led to a growing interest in whether neurobiological data can improve the prediction of future behavior at the individual level, either with respect to reoffending or responses to intervention. However, while there may be an important role for neuroscience to play in informing decisions that affect particular groups (such as minors), we need to be cautious about applying such findings to individuals: neuroimaging data based on groups of participants may not be applicable to individual cases. Psychologists and neuroscientists need to be vigilant about how such research is applied in forensic and legal settings (Steinberg, 2013).

We can also learn a lot from understanding the typical and atypical development and function of neural circuitry underpinning emotion processing, generation, and regulation. Neural data is helping to refine models of ER, and to develop and test further predictions about how the brain works. This will then likely feed into our understanding of psychopathology and its prevention and treatment, including within a forensic context.

Conclusions

ER is a crucial, adaptive set of skills, and refers to the heterogeneous set of processes by which emotions are controlled. Neuroscience research has revealed a broad and integrated neural network of regions involved in ER. This has further elucidated the neurobiology underlying the explicit and implicit strategies used to regulate our emotions, as well as the generative process of the effortful explicit strategies as demonstrated by models of ER. Given the complexity of the ER process, further research is needed to develop accurate and applicable models. The protracted development of ER has also been investigated, with findings suggesting that these processes develop non-linearly, particularly over the adolescent period. As the volume and scope of affective neuroscience research increases, so too do the practical and policy implications for forensic populations.

Recommended Reading

Goldin, P. R., McRae, K., Ramel, W., & Gross, J. J. (2008). The neural bases of ER: Reappraisal and suppression of negative emotion. *Biological Psychiatry, 63*(6), 577–86. doi:10.1016/j.biopsych.2007.05.031. *This paper directly compares the neural underpinnings of reappraisal and suppression using fMRI.*

Gross, J. J. (1998b). The emerging field of ER: An integrative review. *Review of General Psychology.* doi:10.1037/1089-2680.2.3.271. *Gross describes the process model in detail.*

Gyurak, A., Gross, J. J., & Etkin, A. (2011). Explicit and implicit ER: A dual process framework. *Cognition and Emotion, 25*(3), 400–412. doi:10.1080/02699931.2010.544160. *This paper discusses the dual-process framework and well as reviewing neuroscience research investigating explicit and implicit ER.*

Steinberg, L. (2013). The influence of neuroscience on US Supreme Court decisions about adolescents' criminal culpability. *Nature Reviews. Neuroscience, 14,* 513–58. doi:10.1038/nrn3509. *This paper looks at the forensic implications of neuroscience research on ER.*

References

Anderson, C. A., & Bushman, B. J. (2002). Human aggression. *Annual Review of Psychology, 53,* 27–51. doi:10.1016/0191-8869(94)90294-1.

Aron, A. R., Fletcher, P. C., Bullmore, E. T., Sahakian, B. J., & Robbins, T. W. (2003). Stop-signal inhibition disrupted by damage to right inferior frontal gyrus in humans. *Nature Neuroscience, 6,* 115–116. doi:10.1038/nn1003.

Awh, E., Belopolsky, A. V., & Theeuwes, J. (2012). Top-down versus bottom-up attentional control: A failed theoretical dichotomy. *Trends in Cognitive Sciences, 16*(8), 437–443. doi:10.1016/j.tics.2012.06.010.

Baxter, M. G., & Murray, E. A. (2002). The amygdala and reward. *Nature Reviews Neuroscience, 3*(7), 563–573.

Beauregard, M., Lévesque, J., & Bourgouin, P. (2001). Neural correlates of conscious self-regulation of emotion. *The Journal of Neuroscience: The Official Journal of the Society for Neuroscience, 21*(18), RC165. doi:20015619.

Bracht, T., Tüscher, O., Schnell, S., Kreher, B., Rüsch, N., Glauche, V., ... Saur, D. (2009). Extraction of prefronto-amygdalar pathways by combining probability maps. *Psychiatry Research, 174*, 217–222. doi:10.1016/j.pscychresns.2009.05.001.

Buss, K. A., & Goldsmith, H. H. (1998). Fear and anger regulation in infancy: Effects on the temporal dynamics of affective expression. *Child Development, 69*, 359–374. doi:10.1111/j.1467-8624.1998.tb06195.x.

Cieslik, E. C., Zilles, K., Caspers, S., Roski, C., Kellermann, T. S., Jakobs, O., ... Eickhoff, S. B. (2013). Is there "one" dlPFC in cognitive action control? Evidence for heterogeneity from co-activation-based parcellation. *Cerebral Cortex, 23*, 2677–2689. doi:10.1093/cercor/bhs256.

Cromheeke, S., & Mueller, S. C. (2013). Probing emotional influences on cognitive control: An ALE meta-analysis of cognition emotion interactions. *Brain Structure & Function, 219*(3), 995–1008. doi:10.1007/s00429-013-0549-z.

Davidson, R. J., Putnam, K. M., & Larson, C. L. (2000). Dysfunction in the neural circuitry of ER – A possible prelude to violence. *Science, 289*, 591–594. doi:10.1126/science.289.5479.591.

Dehaene, S., Posner, M. I., & Tucker, D. M. (1994). Localization of a neural system for error detection and compensation. *Psychological Science, 5*(5), 303–305. doi:10.1111/j.1467-9280.1994.tb00630.x.

Drabant, E. M., McRae, K., Manuck, S. B., Hariri, A. R., & Gross, J. J. (2009). Individual differences in typical reappraisal use predict amygdala and prefrontal responses. *Biological Psychiatry, 65*(5), 367–373. doi:10.1016/j.biopsych.2008.09.007.

Egner, T., Etkin, A., Gale, S., & Hirsch, J. (2008). Dissociable neural systems resolve conflict from emotional versus nonemotional distracters. *Cerebral Cortex, 18*, 1475–1484. doi:10.1093/cercor/bhm179.

Elliott, R., & Deakin, B. (2005). Role of the orbitofrontal cortex in reinforcement processing and inhibitory control: Evidence from functional magnetic resonance imaging studies in healthy human subjects. *International Review of Neurobiology, 65*, 89–116. doi:10.1016/S0074-7742(04)65004-5.

Etkin, A., Egner, T., & Kalisch, R. (2011). Emotional processing in anterior cingulate and medial prefrontal cortex. *Trends in Cognitive Sciences, 15*(2), 85–93. doi:10.1016/j.tics.2010.11.004.

Etkin, A., Egner, T., Peraza, D. M., Kandel, E. R., & Hirsch, J. (2006). Resolving emotional conflict: A role for the rostral anterior cingulate cortex in modulating activity in the amygdala.' *Neuron, 51*, 871–882. doi:10.1016/j.neuron.2006.12.003.

Fonagy, P., Gergely, G., & Jurist, E. L. (Eds.). (2003). *Affect regulation, mentalization and the development of the self*. London: Karnac Books.

Gasquoine, P. G. (2013). Localization of function in anterior cingulate cortex: From psychosurgery to functional neuroimaging. *Neuroscience and Biobehavioral Reviews, 37*, 340–348. doi:10.1016/j.neubiorev.2013.01.002.

Glenn, A. L., & Raine, A. (2014). Neurocriminology: Implications for the punishment, prediction and prevention of criminal behaviour. *Nature Reviews Neuroscience, 15*, 54–63. doi:10.1038/nrn3640.

Gotlib, I. H., Sivers, H., Gabrieli, J. D. E., Whitfield-Gabrieli, S., Goldin, P., Minor, K. L., & Canli, T. (2005). Subgenual anterior cingulate activation to valenced emotional stimuli in major depression. *Neuroreport, 16*, 1731–1734. doi:10.1097/01.wnr.0000183901.70030.82.

Gross, J. J. (1998a). Antecedent- and response-focused ER: Divergent consequences for experience, expression, and physiology. *Journal of Personality and Social Psychology, 74*(1), 224–237. Retrieved from http://www.ncbi.nlm.nih.gov/pubmed/9457784.

Gross, J. J. (1998b). The emerging field of ER: An integrative review. *Review of General Psychology, 2*(3), 271–299. doi:10.1037/1089-2680.2.3.271.

Gross, J. J. (2002). ER: Affective, cognitive, and social consequences. *Psychophysiology, 39*, 281–291. doi:10.1017.S0048577201393198.

Gross, J. J., & Levenson, R. W. (1993). Emotional suppression: Physiology, self-report, and expressive behavior. *Journal of Personality and Social Psychology, 64*, 970–986. doi:10.1037/0022-3514.64.6.970.

Gross, J. J., & Thompson, R. A. (2007). ER: Conceptual foundations. In J. Gross (Ed.) *Handbook of ER* (pp. 3–24). New York, NY: Guilford Press.

Hare, T. A., Tottenham, N., Galvan, A., Voss, H. U., Glover, G. H., & Casey, B. J. (2008). Biological substrates of emotional reactivity and regulation in adolescence during an emotional go-nogo task. *Biological Psychiatry, 63*, 927–934. doi:10.1016/j.biopsych.2008.03.015.

Johansen-Berg, H., Gutman, D. A., Behrens, T. E. J., Matthews, P. M., Rushworth, M. F. S., Katz, E., ... Mayberg, H. S. (2008). Anatomical connectivity of the subgenual cingulate region targeted with deep brain stimulation for treatment-resistant depression. *Cerebral Cortex, 18*, 1374–1383. doi:10.1093/cercor/bhm167.

Karmiloff-Smith, A. (1998). Development itself is the key to understanding developmental disorders. *Trends in Cognitive Sciences, 2*, 389–398. doi:10.1016/S1364-6613(98)01230-3.

Kim, S. H., & Hamann, S. (2007). Neural correlates of positive and negative ER. *Journal of Cognitive Neuroscience, 19*, 776–798. doi:10.1162/jocn.2007.19.5.776.

Koole, S. L., & Rothermund, K. (2011). "I feel better but I don't know why": The psychology of implicit ER. *Cognition & Emotion, 25*(3), 389–399. doi:10.1080/02699931.2010.550505.

Kopp, C. B. (1989). Regulation of distress and negative emotions: A developmental view. *Developmental Psychology, 25*(3), 343–354. doi:10.1037/0012-1649.25.3.343.

LeDoux, J. E. (2000). Emotion circuits in the brain. *Annual Review of Neuroscience, 23*, 155–184. doi:10.1146/annurev.neuro.23.1.155.

Lévesque, J., Eugène, F., Joanette, Y., Paquette, V., Mensour, B., Beaudoin, G., ... Beauregard, M. (2003). Neural circuitry underlying voluntary suppression of sadness. *Biological Psychiatry, 53*, 502–510. doi:10.1016/S0006-3223(02)01817-6.

Lévesque, J., Joanette, Y., Mensour, B., Beaudoin, G., Leroux, J-M., Bourgouin, P., & Beauregard, M. (2004). Neural basis of emotional self-regulation in childhood.' *Neuroscience, 129*(2), 361–369. doi:10.1016/j.neuroscience.2004.07.032.

Levy, B. J., & Wagner, A. D. (2011). Cognitive control and right ventrolateral prefrontal cortex: Reflexive reorienting, motor inhibition, and action updating.' *Annals of the New York Academy of Sciences, 1224*, 40–62. doi:10.1111/j.1749-6632.2011.05958.x.

Linnet, J., Møller, A., Peterson, E., Gjedde, A., & Doudet, D. (2011). Dopamine release in ventral striatum during Iowa gambling task performance is associated with increased excitement levels in pathological gambling. *Addiction, 106*, 383–390. doi:10.1111/j.1360-0443.2010.03126.x.

Machado, C. J., Kazama, A. M., & Bachevalier, J. (2009). Impact of amygdala, orbital frontal, or hippocampal lesions on threat avoidance and emotional reactivity in nonhuman primates. *Emotion, 9*, 147–163. doi:10.1037/a0014539.

Mauss, I. B., Cook, C. L., Cheng, J. Y. J., & Gross, J. J. (2007). Individual differences in cognitive reappraisal: Experiential and physiological responses to an anger provocation. *International Journal of Psychophysiology: Official Journal of the International Organization of Psychophysiology, 66*, 116–124. doi:10.1016/j.ijpsycho.2007.03.017.

McClure, S. M., York, M. K., & Montague, P. R. (2004). The neural substrates of reward processing in humans: The modern role of fMRI. *The Neuroscientist: A Review Journal Bringing Neurobiology, Neurology and Psychiatry, 10*, 260–268. doi:10.1177/1073858404263526.

Miller v. Alabama, 567 U.S. No. 10-9646 (2012).

Mitchell, D. G. V. (2011). The nexus between decision making and ER: A review of convergent neurocognitive substrates. *Behavioural Brain Research, 217*, 215–231. doi:10.1016/j.bbr.2010.10.030.

Nelson, E. E., Leibenluft, E., McClure, E. B., & Pine, D. S. (2005). The social re-orientation of adolescence: A neuroscience perspective on the process and its relation to psychopathology. *Psychological Medicine, 35*, 163–174. doi:10.1017/S0033291704003915.

Oaten, M., & Cheng, K. (2006). Longitudinal gains in self-regulation from regular physical exercise. *British Journal of Health Psychology, 11*, 717–733. doi:10.1348/135910706X96481.

Ochsner, K. N., Bunge, S. A., Gross, J. J., & Gabrieli, J. D. E. (2002). Rethinking feelings: An fMRI study of the cognitive regulation of emotion. *Journal of Cognitive Neuroscience, 14*, 1215–1229. doi:10.1162/089892902760807212.

Paus, T. (2001). Primate anterior cingulate cortex: Where motor control, drive and cognition interface. *Nature Reviews Neuroscience, 2*, 417–424. doi:10.1038/35077500.

Perlman, S. B., & Pelphrey, K. A. (2011). Developing connections for affective regulation: Age-related changes in emotional brain connectivity. *Journal of Experimental Child Psychology, 108*, 607–620. doi:10.1016/j.jecp.2010.08.006.

Pessoa, L. (2008). On the relationship between emotion and cognition. *Nature Reviews Neuroscience, 9*, 148–158. doi: 10.1038/nrn2317.

Pfeifer, J. H., & Allen, N. B. (2012). Arrested development? Reconsidering dual-systems models of brain function in adolescence and disorders. *Trends in Cognitive Sciences, 16*, 322–329. doi: 10.1016/j.tics.2012.04.011.

Phan, K. L., Fitzgerald, D. A., Nathan, P. J., Moore, G. J., Uhde, T. W., & Tancer, M. E. (2005). Neural substrates for voluntary suppression of negative affect: A functional magnetic resonance imaging study. *Biological Psychiatry, 57*, 210–219. doi:10.1016/j.biopsych.2004.10.030.

Phelps, E. A., Delgado, M. R., Nearing, K. I., & LeDoux, J. E. (2004). Extinction learning in humans: Role of the amygdala and vmPFC. *Neuron, 43*, 897–905. doi:10.1016/j.neuron.2004.08.042.

Ranft, K., Dobrowolny, H., Krell, D., Bielau, H., Bogerts, B., & Bernstein, H-G. (2010). Evidence for structural abnormalities of the human habenular complex in affective disorders but not in schizophrenia. *Psychological Medicine, 40*, 557–567. doi:10.1017/S0033291709990821.

Rubia, K., Smith, A. B., Brammer, M. J., & Taylor, E. (2003). Right inferior prefrontal cortex mediates response inhibition while mesial prefrontal cortex is responsible for error Detection. *NeuroImage, 20*(1), 351–358. doi:10.1016/S1053-8119(03)00275-1.

Scherer, K. R., Schorr, A. E., & Johnstone, T. E. (2001). *Appraisal processes in emotion: Theory, methods, research*. Oxford: Oxford University Press.

Schultz, W. (2006). Behavioral theories and the neurophysiology of reward. *Annual Review of Psychology, 57*, 87–115. doi:10.1146/annurev.psych.56.091103.070229.

Sebastian, C. L., Roiser, J. P., Tan, G. C. Y., Viding, E., Wood, N. W., & Blakemore, S-J. (2010). Effects of age and MAOA genotype on the neural processing of social rejection. *Genes, Brain, and Behavior, 9*, 628–637. doi:10.1111/j.1601-183X.2010.00596.x.

Sebastian, C. L., Tan, G. C. Y., Roiser, J. P., Viding, E., Dumontheil, I., & Blakemore, S-J. (2011). Developmental influences on the neural bases of responses to social rejection: Implications of social neuroscience for education. *NeuroImage, 57*, 686–694. doi:10.1016/j.neuroimage.2010.09.063.

Shimamura, A. P., Marian, D. E., & Haskins, A. L. (2012). Neural correlates of emotional regulation while viewing films. *Brain Imaging and Behavior, 7*(1), 77–84. doi:10.1007/s11682-012-9195-y.

Small, D. M., Gregory, M. D., Mak, Y. E., Gitelman, D., Mesulam, M. M., & Parrish, T. (2003). Dissociation of neural representation of intensity and affective valuation in human gustation. *Neuron, 39,* 701–711. doi:10.1016/S0896-6273(03)00467-7.

Stroop, J. R. (1935). Studies of interference in serial verbal reactions. *Journal of Experimental Psychology, 18,* 643–662. doi:10.1037/h0054651.

Thompson, R A. (1994). ER: A theme in search of definition. *Monographs of the Society for Research in Child Development, 59,* 25–52. doi:10.1111/j.1540-5834.1994.tb01276.x.

Ullsperger, M., & von Cramon, D. Y. (2003). Error monitoring using external feedback: Specific roles of the habenular complex, the reward system, and the cingulate motor area revealed by functional magnetic resonance imaging. *The Journal of Neuroscience: The Official Journal of the Society for Neuroscience, 23,* 4308–4314. doi:23/10/4308 [pii].

Van Reekum, C. M., Johnstone, T., Urry, H. L., Thurow, M. E., Schaefer, H. S., Alexander, A. L., & Davidson, R. J. (2007). Gaze fixations predict brain activation during the voluntary regulation of picture-induced negative affect. *NeuroImage, 36,* 1041–1055. doi:10.1016/j.neuroimage.2007.03.052.

Voorn, P., Vanderschuren, L. J. M. J., Groenewegen, H. J., Robbins, T. W., & Pennartz, C. M. A. (2004). Putting a spin on the dorsal-ventral divide of the striatum. *Trends in Neurosciences, 27,* 468–474. doi:10.1016/j.tins.2004.06.006.

Wager, T. D., Davidson, M. L., Hughes, B. L., Lindquist, M. A., & Ochsner, K. N. (2008). Prefrontal-subcortical pathways mediating successful ER. *Neuron, 59*(6), 1037–1050. doi:10.1016/j.neuron.2008.09.006.

Walker, D. L., & Davis, M. (2008). Role of the extended amygdala in short-duration versus sustained fear: A tribute to Dr. Lennart Heimer. *Brain Structure & Function, 213,* 29–42. doi:10.1007/s00429-008-0183-3.

Wells, A., & Papageorgiou, C. (1998). Social phobia: Effects of external attention on anxiety, negative beliefs, and perspective taking. *Behavior Therapy, 29*(3), 357–370. doi:10.1016/S0005-7894(98)80037-3.

Whalen, P. J., Rauch, S. L., Etcoff, N. L., McInerney, S. C., Lee, M. B., & Jenike, M. A. (1998). Masked presentations of emotional facial expressions modulate amygdala activity without explicit knowledge. *The Journal of Neuroscience: The Official Journal of the Society for Neuroscience, 18,* 411–418. doi: 9412517.

Williams K. D., Cheung, C. K., & Choi, W. (2000). Cyberostracism: Effects of being ignored over the Internet. *Journal of Personality and Social Psychology, 79,* 748–762.

Yassa, M. A., Hazlett, R. L., Stark, C. E. L., & Hoehn-Saric, R. (2012). Functional MRI of the amygdala and bed nucleus of the stria terminalis during conditions of uncertainty in generalized anxiety disorder. *Journal of Psychiatric Research, 46,* 1045–1052. doi:10.1016/j.jpsychires.2012.04.013.

7

The Social Neuroscience of Empathy and its Relationship to Moral Behavior[1]

Jean Decety and Jason M. Cowell

> **Key points**
> - In evolutionary terms, the benefits of empathy are evident in the role it plays in the care for offspring as well as facilitation in group living.
> - In humans, rudimentary signs of empathy and caring for others can be observed during the first year of life.
> - Empathy is a multidimensional construct, encompassing affective, cognitive and motivational dimensions.
> - The affective, cognitive and motivational facets involve brain areas associated with pain, reward, and emotional processing. These areas include: the amygdala, hypothalamus, insula, anterior cingulate, and the orbital frontal cortex.
> - Morality is a fundamental aspect of all human societies that has evolved to regulate social interactions in large social groups.
> - Empathy can lead to partiality by favoring one individual over a group, and produce myopia. Thus, it is important not to confuse empathy and morality.

> **Terminology Explained**
> **Autonomic nervous system**, also known as the involuntary nervous system, controls visceral functions (such as heart rate, digestion, respiration, salivation, and sexual arousal) below the level of conscious awareness. It can be parsed into the subdivisions of parasympathetic and sympathetic nervous systems and

its functioning has been connected to a variety of medical and psychological symptoms.

The **economic trust game** is a game of two players where each player is given the same amount of money at the beginning. The first person in the game decides whether they want to pass any of their money to the second person where this amount is tripled by the experimenter; the second person then decides whether they want to return any part of the amount received. The trust game incorporates motives of trust in positive reciprocity.

An **emotion** is both a feeling and physiological response elicited by an interaction between a person and the environment.

Empathy is an other-oriented emotional response congruent with the perceived welfare of another person.

Morality is centrally concerned with how individuals ought to interact and get along with others.

Neuropeptides are small protein-like molecules (peptides) used by neurons to communicate with each other. They influence the activity of the brain in very specific ways.

Introduction

Empathy – the natural capacity to share and understand others' feelings and thoughts – is a fundamental component of emotional experience and plays a vital role in social interaction. Beginning in infancy, humans are affected by others' signs of distress and show concern and comforting behavior. Empathy-related processes motivate prosocial behavior and caring for others, inhibit aggression, and provide the foundation for care-based morality. One corollary of this neuroevolutionary model is that caregiving and empathy produce preferences that can conflict with moral judgment, fairness and justice. Kin selection, reciprocal altruism, and group selection can be viewed as consequences of the caring inclination. There is behavioral and neuroscientific evidence demonstrating that group-level processes critically moderate the conditions in which empathic understanding and empathic concern are expressed. While empathy plays a fundamental role in the development of morality, moral development cannot be reduced to only empathy and emotion sensitivity.

Empathy, the social-emotional response that is induced by the perception of another person's affective state, is a fundamental component of emotional experience, and plays a vital role in social interaction. Empathy can provide the motivation to help others in distress, plays an essential role in inhibiting aggression, and facilitates cooperation between members of a similar species. Despite its complex nature, the construct of empathy involves cognitive, emotional, and motivational facets, none of these are specific to humans. Emergent in infancy, empathy is deeply rooted in the proclivity for feeling and reacting to the emotions of others (Decety & Svetlova, 2012).

Humans, like other mammals, rely on parental care for survival in early life, and possess an attachment system to regulate close relationships. The social attachment system was gradually built up from more primitive regulation systems such as those involved in thermoregulation and physical pain (Panksepp, 1998). Recent evidence from pharmacological and social neuroscience converges to suggest that social pain and physical pain operate via common neurophysiological mechanisms. Inclusion in social groups has been essential for survival as a highly social species. Consequently, threats to social connectivity are processed by individuals as severe threats to personal safety and bodily integrity (MacDonald & Leary, 2005). From an evolutionary perspective, physical and social pain were both necessary for the promotion of survival and to motivate defensive and protective behaviors. Moreover, sensitivity to emotions of others likely played a crucial role in the development of care-based morality in humans.

Taking a social neuroscience and evolutionary perspective on the development of empathy and morality, we will clarify the interactions between the affective processes involved in the experience and perception of physical and social pain and their relationship to moral behavior. We begin by exploring animal studies of empathy-like behavior, particularly the sensitivity to signs of suffering in the parent–offspring context. Following this evolutionary and translational discussion, we examine the neurobiological and neurodevelopmental mechanisms supporting empathy and morality. We discuss the literature regarding the early signs of the ability to perceive sensitivity and fairness and exhibit concern for others, abilities posited to be precursors of a more mature understanding of morality. The chapter also addresses a number of emotion-processing dysfunctions in individuals with psychopathy to further illustrate how the lack of sensitivity to others' suffering can contribute to a callous disregard for the welfare of others and amoral conduct. Finally, in the last section of the chapter, and perhaps surprising to the reader, we introduce the idea that empathy can conflict with morality. Knowledge from multiple levels of analysis (which characterized social neuroscience) is critical for a better understanding of the relationship between empathy and morality.

The Evolutionary Roots of Empathy

Humans are, by nature, highly social mammals and social behaviors, particularly positive ones such as caregiving, are essential for survival of young as well as for reproductive success. The ability to model the emotions of others, and react appropriately when interacting within a social group, probably confers a number of evolutionarily advantageous skills (e.g., increased ability to communicate and detect distress in group members and use this information to protect them). Much of our knowledge of the evolutionary roots of empathy arises from animal models of social behavior and social distress. For instance, rats that had learned to press a lever to obtain food stop doing so if their action is paired with the delivery of an electrical shock to a visible neighboring rat (Church, 1959). Rats will press a bar to lower another rat suspended in mid-air, interpreted as relieving the suspended animal's distress (Rice & Gainer, 1962). Recently a series of studies have documented that rats will intentionally free a cage mate locked in a restrainer even when social reward is prohibited (Ben-Ami Bartal, Decety, & Mason, 2011). Additionally, this latter study found that when the act of liberating a cage mate was pitted against the release of a highly palatable food (chocolate chips) contained within a second restrainer, rats opened both restrainers and exhibited rudimentary pro-social behavior, typically sharing the chocolate.

Furthermore, studies have also demonstrated that rodents show social modulation of emotional responses and learning. In one study, pain sensitivity was modulated in mice by the presence of other mice displaying pain behaviors (Langford et al., 2006). Interestingly, this relationship is conditional upon the identity of the target mouse such that observing pain behaviors in conspecifics (same species) only influences pain behavior when the target mouse is their cage mate. Female mice increased freezing behavior when exposed to the pain of a close relative compared to when exposed to the pain of a more distant relative, suggesting that it serves an adaptive function (Jeon et al., 2010). A further investigation found that female mice approaching a dyad member in physical pain led to less writhing from the mouse in pain. Importantly, these beneficial effects of social approach were seen only when the mouse was a cage mate of the mouse in pain rather than a stranger (Langford et al., 2010). These results replicate a previous study that reported reduced pain sensitivity in mice when interacting with siblings, but no such analgesic effect when the mice interacted with a stranger (D'Amato & Pavone, 1993). Moreover, socially isolated mice display significantly higher levels of mechanical pain sensitivity as well as depressive-like responses following peripheral nerve injury as compared to their pair housed counterparts, potentially through a mechanism involving the neuropeptide oxytocin (Norman et al., 2010) and endogenous opioids. Importantly, it is not necessarily genetic affiliation that solely facilitates assistive behaviors. Rats fostered from birth with another strain have been shown to help strangers of the fostering strain but not rats of their own strain (Ben-Ami Bartal, Rodgers, Bernardez Sarria, Decety, & Mason, 2014). Thus, strain familiarity, even to one's own strain, seems to be required for the expression of pro-social behavior in rodents.

In humans too, the presence of an individual who provides support reduces experimental pain (Brown, Sheffield, Leary, & Robinson, 2003) and attenuates activation in the neural systems supporting emotional and behavioral threat responses (Coan, Schaefer, & Davidson., 2006). Similarly, the presence of others and perceived empathy (defined as participants' knowledge of the extent to which observers felt they understood and shared their pain) modulates subjective and autonomic responses to physical pain, and these influences can be explained by individual variations in pain coping strategies and social attachment (Sambo, Howard, Kopelman, Williams, & Fotopoulou, 2010).

Nearly a half-century ago, experiments with primates demonstrated that rhesus monkeys refrained from operating a device to obtain food if it resulted in another monkey receiving an electric shock (Wechkin, Masserman, & Terris, 1964). In other research, a stronger response was observed if the macaque was familiar with the shocked conspecific or if the observer had the experience of being shocked (Masserman, Wechkin, & Terris, 1964). More recently, an experiment in which peripheral skin temperature was measured in chimpanzees while they viewed an emotionally-laden video demonstrated a decrease of skin temperature, indicative of sympathetic arousal, when they viewed videos of conspecifics injected with needles or videos of the needles themselves, whereas these changes were not observed when the chimpanzees viewed videos of a conspecific chasing the veterinarian (Parr, 2001). Indeed, chimpanzees show physiological changes quite similar to humans when they perceive a conspecific exposed to potentially painful stimuli.

Chimpanzees are known to spontaneously provide contact comfort to recent victims of aggression, a behavior termed consolation. This consolation behavior reduces the recipient's state of arousal, likely so as to alleviate distress (Romero, Castellanos, & de Waal, 2010). Research examining post-conflict interactions showed that bonobos across age and sex classes spontaneously offered consolation to distressed parties (Clay & de Waal, 2013). Moreover, bystanders were significantly more likely to console relatives or closely bonded partners, and the consolation was more likely to be offered by younger bystanders compared to adults. Additionally, mother-reared individuals were significantly more involved in post-conflict interactions than orphans. This latter finding highlights the role of early attachment in emotional development.

Taken together, continuity in empathy and empathetic concern across mammalian species is evident. Human social behavior can be uniquely informed by approaching the study of social behaviors in this translational, evolutionary manner. Indeed, rudimentary characteristics of empathy and empathetic concern seen in non-human primates and other species act as models for the study of early empathy in infants and children, and also adults. Most mammals, including humans, are immature in motor function at birth, and caregiving is necessary to compensate for the infant's undeveloped motor and autonomic nervous systems (Porges & Carter, 2012). Many of the same neurophysiological and endocrine systems that permit birth, lactation, and parental behavior have been implicated in the giving and receiving of positive experiences (Carter, 1998). Importantly, these processes are not limited to mother–infant interactions.

Biological unrelated individuals may express and experience concern for others and engage in caregiving (Hrdy, 2008). This suggests that the motivational system, which originally developed to promote care for offspring, was co-opted to facilitate positive relationships between biologically unrelated group members. For example, in humans, relationships with spouses, friends, and co-workers are highly valued despite requiring vast amounts of psychological resources to maintain. In fact, perceiving such relationships as threatened engenders profound emotional and physiological stress responses (Norman, Hawkley, Cole, Berntson, & Cacioppo, 2012). Conversely, feeling appropriately connected to, and supported by, friends and family provides a strong behavioral and psychological buffer that can actually diminish stress responses and result in improved health (Uchino, Cacioppo, & Kiecolt-Glaser, 1996). These findings provide strong support for the notion of repurposing motivational components of pro-social behaviors such as empathetic concern, which was originally developed to motivate parental care, as invaluable tools for the formation and maintenance of strong social bonds between unrelated individuals.

Ingroup empathy in animals *Empathetic behavior is higher toward ingroup members. For example, rats fostered from birth with another strain have been shown to help strangers of the fostering strain but not rats of their own strain, meaning that strain familiarity seems to be required for the expression of pro-social behavior in rodents (Langford et al., 2010).*

Source: © Ewastudio. Used under license from 123RF.

The Development of Empathy

Infants are sensitive to social stimuli (particularly faces) early in development, potentially from birth. They readily attend to and engage in social interactions. For instance, newborns look significantly longer at a happy facial expression than a fearful one, indicating that this preference reflects experience acquired over the first few days of life (Farroni, Menon, Rigato, & Johnson, 2007). Moreover, when an infant looks at her mother, she instinctively engages in some forms of prototypical conversations, which facilitates the sharing of basic emotional expressions and affective states (Nadel, 2002). Because of the importance of perceiving other conspecifics in distress to survival and its adaptive value, human infants are biologically predisposed to be sensitive to others' emotional expressions, especially when the expressions are vocalized. Neonates appear to possess a neural mechanism for discriminating vocalizations associated with emotions. They exhibit a mismatched electroencephalographic response over the right hemisphere in response to emotionally laden syllables (happy or fearful versus neutral) within the first few days of life (Cheng, Lee, Chen, Wang, & Decety, 2012). In infants aged three to seven days old, another person's sad vocalizations are associated with a selective increase of neural activity in brain regions involved in processing affective stimuli, such as the orbitofrontal cortex and insula (Blasi et al., 2011). These results suggest remarkably early functional specialization for processing negative emotions expressed in the human voice.

Neonates contagiously cry in response to the distress of conspecifics in their proximity (Martin et al., 1982), a reaction which is heightened when another child's crying is heard compared to the child's own crying (Dondi, Simion, & Caltran, 1999). The specificity of contagious crying and characteristics of affect sharing have prompted the hypothesis that contagious crying is one of the earliest forms of empathetic arousal. Importantly, newborns discriminate between their own (previously recorded) cries and those of another infant. Thus, neonates' contagious crying cannot be explained by lack of differentiation between the distress of self and other. Subcortical pathways connecting the brainstem, superior colliculus, hypothalamus, pulvinar, and amygdala, all of which develop very early in fetal brain development, mediate this affect sharing in neonates (Decety, 2010a).

Beyond rudimentary forms of empathy and affect sharing expressed early in postnatal development, more complex characterizations of empathy emerge later in early toddlerhood and the preschool years. Empathetic concern typically arises during the first year of life and develops in the context of social interactions. While the cognitive components of empathy (emotion interpretation and perspective taking) gradually increase during the first three to five years of life, the affective components are in place very early. Infants begin to show signs of concern for others when they are in distress and are already responding in socially appropriate ways when viewing others in distress or pain (Zahn-Waxler, Radke-Yarrow, Wagner, & Chapman, 1992). This basic emotional motivation requires not only an affective reaction elicited by someone else's emotional state, but also a basic attribution of mental states. These early signs of empathy require only minimal mindreading and perspective-taking capacities; instead they necessitate the capacity for emotional contagion and the capacity to attribute distress to another. Not only do very young children make pain attributions, but studies on comforting behavior demonstrate that they also respond to a variety of distress cues, and they direct their comforting behavior in ways that are appropriate to the target's distress. For example, in experimental studies of one-year olds, crying, coughing, and gagging elicited comforting behaviors, (Roth-Hanania, Davidov, & Zahn-Waxler, 2011). Furthermore, in these studies, young children often comfort a target in appropriate ways, make a pain attribution in conjunction with their comforting behavior, and recognize what the target is distressed about.

In early childhood, pro-social behavior also becomes more selective, directed towards friends and relations (rather than all conspecifics), and increasingly governed by display rules and social norms (Hay & Cook, 2007). Heritable individual differences in empathy and pro-social behavior soon emerge (Knafo & Plomin, 2006). Thus, the very high rates of helpfulness observed in nearly all toddlers are likely to decline in favor of more selective displays of helpfulness by particular children to particular people, under particular conditions (Hay, 2009).

The key to infants' social development is their increasing ability to evaluate and differentiate agents based on their social actions towards each other. Already at three months of age, infants preferentially attend to a character who has previously acted in a pro-social (versus antisocial) manner (Hamlin et al., 2010), suggesting a partiality towards those that "do good things." By six months of age, this visual preference has expanded to behaviors, with participants not only selectively attending to pro-social agents (when paired with antisocial or neutral characters) but also selectively approaching them (Hamlin, Wynn, & Bloom, 2007). At around ten months of age, infants distinguish between a victim and an attacker in an aggressive social interaction and prefer the victim, while actively avoiding the aggressor (Kanakogi, Okumura, Inoue, Kitazaki, & Itakura, 2013). Further, by 15 months of age, some infants are able to evaluate the fairness of an agent in a third-party situation.

Additionally, children around two years of age are sensitive to the truthfulness of informants and curb their future actions based on whom they trust (Cowell, Casey, Hetherington, Stephens, & Koenig, 2014). Preschoolers also differentiate between those who have previously helped or harmed another individual (successfully or unsuccessfully) and spontaneously assist the previously helping individual, but not the harming individual (Vaish, Carpenter, & Tomasello 2010). A study examining the relationship between a visual violation of expectation task and infants' sharing behaviors, found that infants who shared a toy they preferred (over a non-preferred toy or no toy at all) also attended significantly longer to a third-party interaction in which the allocation of resources among conspecifics was unequal (Schmidt & Sommerville, 2011). This suggests that those infants who behaved altruistically or morally also expanded their pro-social expectations to the interactions of others.

In the second year of life, signs of helping behavior are reported, with 14–18-month-olds fetching objects of desire that appear out of reach for an experimenter (Warneken & Tomasello, 2006) and helping to complete household chores (Rheingold, 1982). Early other-oriented empathetic responding to the distress of another was observed from the age of 8–16 months and continued to increase gradually into the second year (Roth-Hanania et al., 2011). Children in between the first and second year of life actively recognize and comfort individuals in distress (Zahn-Waxler et al., 1992). Similarly aged children have even donated their own favorite objects to a distressed individual in an empathetic gesture (Svetlova, Nichols, & Brownell, 2010). Individual differences in empathetic responsiveness also manifest in the second year of life, characterized by indiscriminate empathetic responses to peers or parents in those with more advanced social understanding (Nichols, Svetlova, & Brownell, 2009).

Furthermore, toddlers have been found to exhibit more concern towards the victim of a moral transgression than the transgressor, even if the victim did not show any behavioral markers of distress (Vaish, Carpenter, & Tomasello, 2009). This suggests that 18–25-month-olds are not simply reacting to emotional displays but to the intentions and desires of others. Taken together, children under the age of two clearly respond in socially appropriate ways while viewing others in distress or pain, and are able to make social evaluations based on observed behavior.

While the influence of emotion and empathy in the development of moral cognition has long been acknowledged (Blair, 1995), few studies have characterized the neurodevelopment of moral sensitivity in typically developing children. One recent developmental study combined neurophysiological measures, including functional magnetic resonance imaging, eye-tracking, and pupillary response with behavioral measures to examine affective and moral judgments across age (Decety et al., 2012). Participants between 4 and 37 years old viewed scenarios depicting intentional versus accidental actions that caused harm/damage to people and objects. Morally salient scenarios evoked stronger empathetic sadness in young participants and were associated with enhanced activity in the amygdala, insula, and temporal poles. While intentional harm was evaluated as equally wrong across all participants, ratings of deserved punishments and malevolent intent gradually differentiated with age. As age increased, participants punished an agent who damaged an object less severely than an agent who harmed a person. Furthermore, age-related increases in activity were detected in the ventromedial prefrontal cortex (vmPFC) in response to intentional harm to people, as well as increased functional connectivity between this region and the amygdala. In all participants, irrespective of their age, perceived intentional harm to people (as opposed to accidental harm) was associated with increased activation in brain regions sensitive to the perception, prediction, and interpretation of others' intentions such as the right posterior superior temporal sulcus (Blakemore et al., 2003), as well as regions processing the affective consequences of these actions, namely the temporal poles, insula, vmPFC, and amygdala. The more participants reported being upset about harmful actions, the higher the activity in the amygdala. The younger the participants were, the greater their empathetic sadness for the victim of harm.

Ratings of sadness for the victim correlated with activity in the insula, thalamus, and subgenual prefrontal cortex. This latter region has extensive connections with circuits implicated in emotional behavior and autonomic/neuroendocrine response to stressors, including the amygdala, lateral hypothalamus, and brainstem serotonergic, noradrenergic, and dopaminergic nuclei (Drevets et al., 1997). Damage to this region, especially if it occurs during early childhood, is associated with abnormal autonomic responses to emotional experiences and impaired comprehension of the adverse consequences of pernicious social behaviors (Bechara, Tranel, Damasio, & Damasio, 1996). In addition, functional connectivity analyses showed that in early childhood, the brainstem shows greater functional connectivity with vmPFC, while in young adults the vmPFC increases its connectivity with the amygdala and posterior superior temporal sulcus. These connectivity data highlight the critical role of regions involved in emotion processing in moral sensitivity in young children.

In another study, adolescents were scanned while they observed another adolescent their age being ostensibly rejected in order to examine neural responses during observed exclusion (Masten, Eisenberger, Pfeifer, & Dapretto, 2010). Participants self-reported their trait levels of empathy so that the relation between neural responses to observed peer rejection and individual differences in empathy could be explored. In addition, adolescents wrote emails to the "victim" of the exclusion following the scan, which were later rated for pro-social behavior (i.e., efforts to be comforting/supportive toward the victim), so that neural responses during observed peer rejection could be related to actual pro-social actions following the rejection episode. Adolescents exhibited a heightened neural response in regions involved in mentalizing (such as the medial prefrontal cortex) when observing a peer's rejection, and this was particularly true among adolescents who reported high levels of trait empathy (Masten et al., 2010). Of interest, however, adolescents displaying more affect-related neural activity (i.e., in the anterior insula) during observed rejection were the ones who subsequently wrote more pro-social emails to the excluded victims.

One possibility for why heightened pain responses, rather than empathy responses, might drive subsequent pro-social behaviors is that adolescents may observe peer rejection on a daily basis and consider it commonplace – they may even feel that their own peer status would be jeopardized if they were to interfere. As a result, adolescents' empathetic ability might have little bearing on their actions in these situations, and instead greater feelings of distress (e.g., as evidenced by greater activation in pain/affective regions) might drive their pro-social actions. Similarly, adults who watch the social rejection of a friend (a ball-playing game where a friend is excluded), recruit neural areas usually associated with both their own experience of social rejection and those associated primarily with physical pain, such as the right anterior cingulate cortex, anterior insula, and prefrontal cortex (Beeney, Franklin, Levy, & Adams, 2011). Overall, studies of the neurodevelopment of morality suggest that the pattern of developmental change in response to the perception of harm and suffering is indicative of a gradual shift from a strong affective and somatovisceral response in young children to a more cognitive evaluative response associated with executive control of higher-order emotion and moral judgment in older participants.

Neurobiological Mechanisms Underpinning Empathy

Animal models have demonstrated that the ability to be affected by others' emotional states, an ability integral to maintaining the social relationships important for survival, is organized by basic neural, autonomic, and endocrine systems subserving attachment-related processes. These areas include the brainstem, the preoptic area of the thalamus, and paralimbic areas, as well as the autonomic nervous system (Panksepp, 1998). These systems underlying attachment appear to exploit the strong, established physical pain system, borrowing aversive signals associated with pain to indicate when relationships are threatened (Eisenberger et al., 2011). Moreover, higher-level cortical structures have been proposed to reflect a system involved in detecting, processing, and reacting to the occurrence of salient events regardless of the sensory modality through which these stimuli are conveyed. Therefore, just as the physical pain system alerts organisms to the presence of a noxious environmental stimuli so too does the social pain system: the experience of social pain alerts an individual to potential threats in their social environment and can induce various coping strategies to attempt to mitigate the threat (e.g., increase motivation to strengthen relationships) (MacDonald & Leary 2005).

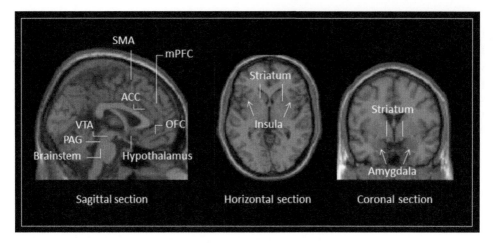

Figure 7.1 Neural network involved in empathy and caring for others.

Note: Empathic arousal (the first component to develop) is mediated by the coupling of perceptual processing and emotion-related neural circuits. Strong bidirectional connections between the brainstem, amygdala, and sensory cortices, as well as connections with the hypothalamus, insula, and somatosensory cortex, are the essential neural components of affective arousal. The cognitive aspects of empathy such as emotion understanding and emotion regulation are closely related to processes involved in perspective taking, self-regulation, and executive attention subserved by the medial prefrontal cortex, dorsolateral prefrontal cortex, and temporoparietal junction (not shown). Finally, the ability to feel concern and care for others has deep evolutionary roots that evolved in the context of parental care, and its neural underpinnings are found in subcortical neural systems similar to those known to regulate parental behavior, especially the hypothalamus and OFC.

Converging evidence from animal behavior (Insel & Young 2001), neuroimaging studies in healthy individuals (Lamm, Decety, & Tania Singer, 2011), and lesion studies in neurological patients (Leigh et al., 2013; Shamay-Tsoory, Aharon-Peretz, & Perry, 2009) indicates that the processes of empathy and caring for others employ a large array of systems and neural mechanisms extending beyond the cortex, including the amygdala, hypothalamus, insula, anterior cingulate cortex, and orbitofrontal cortex. This complex array also involves the autonomic nervous system, hypothalamic-pituitary-adrenal axis (HPA), and endocrine and hormonal systems that regulate bodily states, emotion, and reactivity. See Figure 7.1 for a neuroanatomical map of relevant regions.

A number of neuropeptides in the regulation of sociality, emotion, and the autonomic nervous system have been implicated in the neurobiology of empathy and social interaction. In particular, oxytocin, both a hormone and a neuromodulator, is causally related to caring behavior and stress regulation and has receptors throughout the maternal caregiving circuit (Carter, 1998). Increasing evidence for the role of oxytocin in human social cognition, empathy, and pro-social behavior is amassing. Oxytocin administration via nasal spray decreases neurophysiological responses to social stress (Heinrichs, Baumgartner, Kirschbaum, & Ehlert, 2003). Intranasal administration of oxytocin, compared to placebo, reduces amygdala activation and modulates its coupling with brainstem regions that are involved in automatic fear reactivity (Kirsch et al., 2005).

In a double-blind placebo-controlled study a single dose of oxytocin or placebo was randomly given to male participants 50 minutes before playing the standard behavioral economic trust game (Kosfeld, Heinrichs, Zak, Fischbacher, & Fehr, 2005). The results showed that investors receiving oxytocin displayed more maximum sharing behavior and had a significantly higher median and higher average transfers of monetary units. The oxytocin group did not significantly differ from the control group on measures of risk taking, accounting for the possibility that oxytocin did not simply increase risk-taking behaviors (instead of interpersonal trust) in the risk game. Additionally, a single dose of intranasally administered oxytocin is sufficient to cause a substantial increase in an individual's ability to accurately identify affective states on a test relying on the detection of subtle affective facial expressions (Domes et al., 2007). A more nuanced role of oxytocin in social behavior was documented in a study which found that normal variance in baseline social-cognitive competence moderates the effects of oxytocin. In that study, oxytocin administration improved empathetic accuracy only for individuals with lower social-cognitive competence (Bartz et al., 2010).

In a structural neuroimaging study, variability in the grey matter volume of several regions was observed based off of individual differences in affective empathy and cognitive empathy (Banissy, Kanai, Walsh, & Rees, 2012). Adults with greater other-oriented affective empathy had smaller grey matter volumes in the precuneus, inferior frontal gyrus, and anterior cingulate cortex. Individuals with greater self-oriented affective empathy showed greater volumes in the insula, but smaller grey matter volumes in somatosensory cortex than those with less self-oriented affective empathy. Finally, participants with increased cognitive perspective-taking abilities displayed larger grey matter volumes in the anterior cingulate. These findings underscore the fundamental morphological changes related to individual differences in empathetic ability.

Pain is a particularly salient signal that facilitates evolved protective social functions, not only warning the sufferer that something is amiss, but also providing the understanding that another conspecific is at risk and inducing expressive behaviors that attract the attention of others and motivate pro-social behavior. In support of this, when exposed to their infants' cries (compared to neutral sounds), first time mothers who were breast-feeding reported higher ratings of sadness and desire to help upon hearing their infants' cries versus control sounds (Lorberbaum et al., 2002).

Neuroimaging studies have shown that, when individuals are presented with stimuli conveying another person's distress and physical pain, reliable activation is detected in a neural network involved in the first-hand experience of pain, including the anterior midcingulate cortex (aMCC), anterior insular cortex (AIC), supplementary motor area (SMA), and periaqueductal gray area (PAG). Activation in this network has been reported in response to facial expressions of pain, injury of body parts, imagining the pain of others, being socially excluded, or simply observing a signal indicating that someone will receive painful stimulation (Lamm et al., 2011).

Activation of the neural circuitry involved in the first-hand experience of pain, the viewing of others in pain, or being in social pain is not specific to the sensory qualities of pain, nor to nociception. Instead, this response seems to be associated with more general survival mechanisms such as aversion and withdrawal when exposed to danger and threat (Decety, 2010b). In the context of social pain, this response acts as a signal that promotes social bonding. The same network of regions is also involved in grief or extreme sadness (Meerwijk, Ford, & Weiss, 2013). For example, bereaved participants scanned while viewing pictures of their deceased relatives, compared with pictures of strangers, showed greater activity in the anterior cingulate cortex and anterior insula (O'Connor et al., 2008). Activation in these regions does not appear to be specific to processing distress in other humans; in fact, recent studies suggest that these regions are also recruited when processing the distress of domesticated animals (i.e., dogs). In one study, participants were shown pictures of either humans or dogs in some state of suffering (e.g., starvation, physical pain) and were instructed to simply pay attention (Franklin et al., 2013).

The same network of regions, especially the dorsal anterior cingulate cortex and anterior insula, is also involved in the experience of social exclusion. Many of the functional magnetic resonance imaging (MRI) studies that examined the neural response to social exclusion have used the cyberball paradigm. Participants in the scanner are led to believe that they are playing a game (tossing a ball between three individuals) with two other people (in fact it is a computer game). Then they play one round of the ball-tossing game in which they are included and a second round in which they are excluded partway through the game (Eisenberger, 2011). When participants are excluded from the game, increased hemodynamic activity is detected in the anterior cingulate cortex and anterior insula. The more participants subjectively feel rejected, the greater the activity in the anterior cingulate cortex.

Pharmacological studies with non-human animals and humans also support the idea that physical and social pain rely on shared neurochemistry by demonstrating that certain drugs have similar effects on both types of pain. For example, opiate drugs, such as morphine and heroin, known primarily for their pain-relieving qualities, have also been shown to reduce behaviors indicative of social pain in animals (Carden et al., 1991; Warnick, McCurdy, & Sufka, 2005). In humans, it was shown that acetaminophen, a medication commonly used to reduce physical pain, also lessens

Development of empathy *Empathetic behavior is observed in newborns. Infants will often show contagious emotional response: such as crying and laughter.*

Source: © Oksana Kuzmina. Used under license from 123RF.

the pain of social rejection, at both neural (significantly less hemodynamic response in the anterior cingulate cortex, anterior insula, and amygdala to social exclusion) and behavioral levels (deWall et al., 2010). Thus, various types of unpleasant and socially painful experiences, not just the perception of physical pain, activate the same neural network that first evolved to support the processing of nociceptive information and the control of homeostasis (i.e., the visceral regulation of internal states, such as temperature, thirst, hunger, and pain, required for the life of an organism).

Social Factors Impact the Neural Response to the Distress of Others

The neural network associated with the perception of others' distress and caring for others is modulated by various social, contextual, and interpersonal factors. For instance, one functional MRI (fMRI) study demonstrated that empathetic arousal is moderated early during information processing by a priori attitudes toward other people (Decety et al., 2010). In that study, participants were significantly more sensitive to the pain of individuals who had contracted HIV/AIDS as the result of a blood transfusion – evidenced by significantly higher pain and empathy ratings and significantly greater hemodynamic activity in areas associated with pain processing when they viewed videos of facial expression of pain – and much less to the pain of individuals who had contracted HIV/AIDS as the result of an illicit drug addiction (sharing needles). Another fMRI study found evidence for the modulation of empathetic neural responses by racial group membership (Xu, Zuo, Wang, & Han, 2010). The neural response in the anterior cingulate cortex to perception of others in pain decreased remarkably when participants viewed faces of racial out-group members being pricked by a needle relative to racial in-group members. Furthermore, activity in the pain network was enhanced when people viewed their loved ones in physical pain compared to strangers (Cheng, Chen, Lin, Chou, & Decety, 2010) and reduced if the person in pain had been unfair in a prior interaction (Singer et al., 2006).

From recent literature, one would predict that if affective arousal promotes empathetic concern and helping behavior, then individuals would display reduced concern for out-group members. Research provides support for this hypothesis. Soccer fans in one study observed either another fan of their favored team (in-group) or a fan of their rival team (out-group) experiencing painful shocks (Hein, Silani, Preuschoff, Batson, & Singer, 2010). Participants showed increased empathy for in-group over out-group targets, reporting higher pain ratings and showing greater activation in the anterior insula for in-group targets. Participants also reported feeling more empathetic concern for in-group targets, and they were more likely to volunteer to help by sharing the pain of in-group than out-group targets. Moreover, the difference in anterior insula activation when viewing in-group versus out-group members in pain predicted group differences in helping behavior. Another neuroimaging study demonstrated that the failures of an in-group member are perceived as painful, whereas those of a rival out-group member give pleasure to the participant – a feeling that may motivate harming rivals (Cikara, Botvinick, & Fiske, 2011).

The personal context and accumulated experiences of an individual influence the degree to which affective arousal is experienced when viewing others in pain. Two functional neuroimaging studies have shown that physicians do not react to the pain of others in the same way as non-physicians do. One study compared the neurohemodynamic response in a group of physicians and a group of matched control participants while they viewed short video clips depicting hands and feet being pricked by a needle (painful situations) or being touched by a cotton bud (non-painful situations). The results demonstrated activation of the pain matrix in controls when they attended to the painful situations relative to the non-painful ones. However, when physicians watched painful procedures, a different pattern of activation with cortical regions underpinning executive function and self-regulation (dlPFC and mPFC) and executive attention (precentral, superior parietal, and pSTS/TPJ) being activated (Cheng et al., 2007). Unlike in the control group, no signal increase was detected in the pain matrix in the physicians. A second study recorded event-related potentials (ERPs) from physicians and matched controls while they were presented with the same visual stimuli (Decety et al., 2010). The results showed early signal change 110 milliseconds (ms) after stimulus presentation, which differentiated between pain and no pain over the frontal cortex, reflecting negative arousal, as well as late P3 over the centro-parietal regions in control participants. In contrast, no such early ERP response was detected in physicians, indicating that affect regulation has very early effects, inhibiting the bottom-up processing of negative arousal from the perception of painful stimuli. Consequently, viewing another in some form of distress or pain induces a visceral psychophysiological arousal in humans.

As will be discussed in more depth later in this chapter, evolutionary theory predicts that our relationships and attachment with others and other contextual and interpersonal factors modulate the degree of psychophysiological arousal experienced in response to the distress of another. Critically, we propose that empathy may in fact be a limited resource and extending it to members of the out-group or people who are not like us is possible but effortful. Empathizing with someone's affective experience that is distinct from our own requires the integration of cognitive control with processes of self–other distinction and perspective taking (Lamm, Meltzoff & Decety, 2010).

The Lack of Empathy Contributes to Callous Disregard of the Welfare of Others

Empathy is such a necessary component of healthy co-existence that its absence leads to serious social-cognitive dysfunctions. Among the various psychopathologies marked by such deficits, the impact of the lack of empathy is most central to psychopathy. Psychopathy (see Chapter 9 for a discussion of the neurobiology of this disorder), a neurodevelopmental personality disorder believed to affect approximately 1% of the general population, epitomizes the process through which a lack of sensitivity to another's distress or suffering contributes to callous disregard to others (Hare, 1999). Individuals with psychopathy demonstrate stunted emotional development and a general lack of empathy exhibited through specific individual traits. Psychopathy has been associated with uncommitted mating behaviors, increased sexual coercion, lack of parental investment, and increased sexual promiscuity. Psychopaths are often callous, shallow, and superficial, and have no attachment to others. They do not fear punishment, and do not experience insight into or empathy for the effect of their behaviors on others.

There is solid evidence that empathy deficits and a lack of regard for others may play a role in aspects of moral judgment, particularly those associated with care-based morality. Adult psychopaths fail to experience distress cues as aversive regardless of whether that observer is the aggressor or a bystander (Blair, 1995), evidenced by work indicating that offenders with high levels of psychopathy show reduced autonomic arousal while viewing a confederate receiving electric shocks (Aniskiewicz, 1979). The ability to experience distress as aversive is critical for the development of moral emotions (e.g., guilt and remorse) as distress cues are assumed to activate tendencies to withdraw in any observer who processes them.

These abnormal responses to moral transgressions or the distress of others are evident as early as childhood. For example, children with psychopathic tendencies exhibit reduced electrodermal responses to distress cues (e.g., a crying face) and threatening stimuli (e.g., a pointed gun) relative to controls (Blair, 1999). A study using electroencephalography examined this phenomenon by assessing how callous-unemotional traits in juvenile psychopaths are related to empathetic arousal deficits (Cheng, Hung, & Decety, 2012). In this study, juvenile offenders with high callous-unemotional traits, juvenile offenders with low callous-unemotional traits, and age-matched typically developing adolescents were shown images of people in pain while EEG/ERPs were recorded. Results demonstrated that youth with high callous-unemotional traits exhibit atypical neural dynamics of pain empathy processing in the early stages of affective arousal. This abnormality was exemplified by a lack of the early EPR response (120ms), thought to reflect an automatic aversive reaction to negative stimuli, and was coupled with relative insensitivity to actual pain (as measured with the pressure pain threshold). Nevertheless, their capacity to understand intentionality was not impaired, nor was their sensorimotor resonance. This uncoupling between affective arousal and emotional understanding likely contributes to psychopaths' callous disregard for the rights and feelings of others.

Functional MRI studies have reported that adolescents with disruptive psychopathic traits show reduced activity to increasing perceived pain intensity within structures typically implicated in affective responses to others' pain, including the rostral anterior cingulate cortex, insula, and amygdala (Marsh et al., 2013). Another study also found reduced neural response to others' physical pain in children with conduct problems in the insula and anterior cingulate cortex (Lockwood et al., 2013). Youths with psychopathic traits exhibit reduced amygdala responses to fearful facial expressions (Marsh et al., 2008) and during affective theory of mind tasks (Lockwood et al., 2013).

Perspective taking is important for engaging in intentional moral conduct and for facilitating social functioning. A substantial body of behavioral studies has documented that affective perspective taking is a powerful way to elicit empathy and concern for others (Batson, 2012). For instance, Oswald (1996) found that affective perspective taking is more effective than cognitive perspective taking in evoking empathy and altruistic helping. Additionally, children with conduct disorder and low callous-unemotional traits have deficits in both cognitive and affective perspective taking (Anastassiou-Hadjicharalambous & Warden, 2008). A recent neuroimaging study examined affective perspective taking in incarcerated psychopaths by showing them visual scenarios of physical pain, such as a finger caught between a door, or a toe caught under a heavy object (Decety et al., 2013). The participants were asked to imagine that this accident happened to themselves, or somebody else. When participants high in psychopathy imagined themselves in pain, they showed a typical neural response within the brain regions involved in empathy for pain, including the anterior insula, the anterior midcingulate cortex, somatosensory cortex, the right amygdala, and vmPFC. But when they imagined others in pain, these regions failed to become active. Moreover, psychopaths showed an increased response in the ventral striatum, an area known to be involved in pleasure, when imagining others in pain. This atypical activation suggests that individuals with high scores on psychopathy actually enjoyed imagining pain inflicted on others and did not care for them. The vmPFC is a region that plays a critical role in empathetic decision making, such as caring for the wellbeing of others.

Further research that demonstrates abnormalities in moral reasoning in individuals with psychopathy indicates that individuals who score high on psychopathy evaluations understand moral norms but generally disregard them. For instance, a study that evaluated incarcerated offenders found no evidence that offenders high in psychopathy – as measured by total psychopathy score – were any worse at distinguishing moral from conventional transgressions than were low-psychopathy offenders (Aharoni et al., 2012). These results are consistent with an fMRI study examining psychopathic responses to pictures depicting morally wrong social actions, unpleasant but not immoral social scenes, and neutral social scenes (Harenski, Harenski, Shane, & Kiehl, 2010). In this research, psychopathic and non-psychopathic criminal offenders rated the severity of the moral violation depicted in each type of stimuli. Both groups rated moral violations significantly higher in moral severity than unpleasant but not immoral scenes, and no differences were observed between groups within any of the image conditions, suggesting equally accurate abilities to distinguish moral violations. Interestingly, brain activation recorded during the evaluation of moral violation pictures did detect differences in processing between psychopaths versus

Empathy and social relations *Empathy, a natural ability, observed in early childhood. It is the ability to share and understand others' feelings and thoughts. Empathy is a fundamental component of emotional experience and plays a vital role in social interaction.*

Source: © Szefei. Used under license from 123RF.

non-psychopaths. Atypical brain activity was detected in several regions involved in moral decision making, including reduced moral/non-moral picture distinctions in the vmPFC, amygdala, and anterior temporal cortex in psychopaths relative to non-psychopaths. These results indicate that psychopaths use different brain regions when making moral decisions than do non-psychopaths. Importantly, psychopaths have a dysfunction in the vmPFC – a critical region that supports the integration of emotional responses with moral decision making, which contributes to moral insensitivity and lack of empathetic responses. Youths with psychopathic traits showed reduced amygdala responsiveness to legal actions relative to healthy youths, and reduced amygdala–orbitofrontal cortex connectivity relative to healthy youths during task performance (Marsh et al., 2011).

Overall, neuroscience research with juvenile and adult psychopaths points out a dysfunction in the response and in the functional connectivity between the amygdala and vmPFC, a circuit integral in forming associations between environmental cues and affective states. This lends support to the notion that emotion reactivity plays a central role in empathetic concern, moral decision making, and care-based morality.

Empathy can Conflict with Morality

One corollary of the evolutionary origins of empathy is that caregiving produces social preferences and biases. Kin selection, reciprocal altruism, and group selection can be viewed as consequences of the caring motivation, rather than the causes. As was previously discussed, behavioral and neuroscience studies indicate that group membership moderates the conditions in which empathetic understanding and empathetic concern are expressed (Echols & Correll, 2012). For instance, the mere act of categorizing people in distinct social groups is sufficient to elicit an in-group bias in empathy for pain (Montalan, Lelard, Godefroy, & Mouras, 2012). Empathy can even conflict with moral judgment. Too often, our concern for specific individuals means neglecting crises that will harm countless people in the future. A series of studies conducted by Kogut and Ritov (2005) demonstrated that a single identified victim elicited higher monetary contributions than a non-identified individual or a group of individuals, and showed that empathic distress (and not empathic concern) predicted participants' willingness to contribute. A single identified victim evoked more distress and elicited more contributions than the group of identified victims. Moral judgment entails more than putting oneself in another's shoes or being moved by another's distress.

Thus, while empathy plays a fundamental role in the development of care-based morality, by no means is morality reducible to empathy and emotion sensitivity. Contextualizing empathy and morality, particularly the inclusion of group membership and social preference, challenges the previously held commonsense notion that those with greater empathetic abilities will naturally engage in more moral decision making. However, as was previously hypothesized, empathy can be a powerful source of immoral behavior (e.g., Batson, Klein, Highberger, & Shaw, 1995). It is the contention herein that the social preferences derived from evolution, particularly preferences for in-group or familial conspecifics, can bias our moral decision making and moral behavior. Such biases emerge early in development. For example, children will readily engage in and advocate for pro-social behaviors such as sharing resources or spontaneously helping (e.g., Vaish et al., 2009). Yet, when children see group membership and loyalty as obligatory, they do not advocate for punishing a tribe member who does harmful actions to another tribe (Rhodes & Chalik, 2013). In this study, children were told a story about two different tribes where individuals from one tribe were described as either harming a member of their own tribe or harming a member of another tribe. Without explicit directions, children only viewed harm to tribe members as moral violations, not harm to other tribe members. Moreover, in another study exploring the consequences of group membership, children expected group membership to constrain pro-social and antisocial behaviors, dictating who it was appropriate to help and who it was ok to hinder (Rhodes & Brickman, 2011). Group preference has been shown to be relatively fast-forming in children and quite pervasive in influence (Sherif, Harvey, White, Hood, & Sherif, 1961), see Box 7.1 for a description of the well-known "Robbers" cave experiment.

Box 7.1 The Robbers Cave Experiment

In the famous Robbers Cave[2] experiment (Sherif et al., 1961), groups of young boys were grouped and allowed to interact in relative solitude (separate camps, no knowledge of the existence of the other group). For the first week, the young boys in each camp developed strong group preferences through shared experiences, hardships, and interactions. In the second week, the experimenters left clues that another group may exist and that the other group was using a proprietary resource (the fire pit). Children expressed anger and hostility toward the potential out-group members and solidarity with in-group members. Finally, groups were brought together and extensive conflict was observed. In short, group membership and subsequent social preference modulated the decision-making processes involved in intergroup interactions. This study is a historical and powerful example of the way that social preferences, which have been evolutionarily adaptive, form swiftly, particularly when shared experiences occur, fundamentally alter the nature of the emotional arousal one experiences to the distress of another (in-group versus out-group), and ultimately shifts one's judgments and behavior in morally laden situations, likely leading to moral behavior in in-group situations, but amoral behavior towards the out-group.

In sum, while oftentimes more empathetic individuals will, on the whole, engage in greater pro-social behaviors and make more moral decisions, empathy is influenced by interpersonal relationships and group membership, which produce preferences and favoritism that can conflict with moral principles and justice (Decety & Cowell, 2014).

Conclusions

Evolution has tailored the mammalian brain to be sensitive and responsive to the emotional states of others, especially one's offspring, kin, and members of one's social group. These empathy-based behaviors have co-opted primitive homeostatic processes involved in reward and pain systems in order to facilitate various social attachment processes. Encephalization of pain evaluation transitions the pain experience from being purely a physical phenomenon, in which the body and brain react to physical nociceptive stimuli, to a psychophysiological phenomenon, in which the loss of social contact produces psychological pain (Tucker, Luu, & Derryberry, 2005). The social bonds supported by this nociceptive mechanism, in its most important form, facilitate parental behaviors that ensure the survival of the young. Empathy clearly increases fitness and has a value for survival, insofar as it serves as a mode of attachment and communication between members of a social group.

Developmentally, pro-social behavior emerges early in life, and is expressed by signs of concern for the other. Such a concern requires only a minimal capacity for mindreading and self-awareness. Social neuroscience research clearly indicates that emotional reactivity and empathetic arousal are necessary (but not sufficient) in the development of moral decision making and care-based morality. Children with psychopathic tendencies lack empathetic arousal. They may cognitively understand the emotional state of others without being moved by their distress. The sharing of vicarious negative arousal provides a strong signal that can promote empathetic concern and caring for others. To be motivated to help another, one needs to be affectively and empathetically aroused and anticipate the cessation of the mutually experienced personal distress. Without input from the affective system and processing of that input by the orbitofrontal cortex, moral behavior is understandably difficult to develop. However, one corollary of this evolutionary perspective is that empathy produces preferences and biases that can conflict with moral judgment and justice.

Once we become aware that empathy at times may override moral motivation and produce partiality, we can think of using them in concert. After all, humans possess high-level domain general cognitive abilities such as executive functions, language, and theory of mind, largely implemented in the prefrontal cortex, that are layered on phylogenetically older social and emotional capacities. These evolutionarily newer aspects of information processing, like the capacity to generalize, expand the range of cognitions and behaviors that can be motivated by empathy beyond kin and kith such as caring for and helping out-group members and even members of a different species (Decety, 2011). Our natural empathy can be accessed in reflexive awareness, and over the course of history, humans have enlarged the range of beings whose interests they value as their own. This contributed to the production of meta-level symbolic social structures, like upholding moral principles to all humanity (e.g., human rights, International Criminal Court) that are clear examples of how empathy can be and has been seen to extend beyond the tribe.

Notes

1 The writing of this chapter was supported by two grants from the John Templeton Foundation (Wisdom Research and Science of Philanthropy Initiative) to Jean Decety.
2 Boys were transported to a 200-acre Boy Scouts of America camp in the Robbers Cave State Park in Oklahoma, US.

Recommended Reading

Ben-Ami Bartal, I., Rodgers, D. A., Bernardez Sarria, M. S., Decety, J., & Mason, P. (2014). Pro-social behavior in rats is modulated by social experience. *eLife, 3*: e1385. *How early social experience, rather than genetics, shapes pro-social motivation in rodents.*

Brown, J. L., Sheffield, D., Leary, M. R., & Robinson, M. E. (2003). Social support and experimental pain. *Psychosomatic Medicine, 65*(2), 276–283. *Empirical data suggesting that the presence of an individual who provides passive or active support reduces experimental pain.*

Decety, J., & Cowell, J. M. (2014). The complex relation between morality and empathy. *Trends in Cognitive Sciences, 18*, 337–339. *A concise analysis, based on developmental psychology, evolutionary theory, and social neuroscience, explains why at times empathy guides moral judgment, yet at other times it can interfere with it.*

Decety, J., Echols, S., & Correll, J. (2010) The blame game: The effect of responsibility and social stigma on empathy for pain. *Journal of Cognitive Neuroscience, 22*, 985–997. *Evidence from a functional neuroimaging study demonstrating that emotional sharing, a basic component of empathy is dramatically modulated by implicit attitudes and prejudice.*

References

Aharoni, E., Sinnott-Armstrong, W., & Kiehl, K. A. (2012). Can psychopathic offenders discern moral wrongs? A new look at the moral/conventional distinction. *Journal of Abnormal Psychology, 121*, 484–497.

Anastassiou-Hadjicharalambous, X., & Warden, D. (2008). Cognitive and affective perspective-taking in conduct-disordered children high and low on callous-unemotional traits. *Child and Adolescent Psychiatry and Mental Health, 11*, 1–11.

Aniskiewicz, A. S. (1979). Autonomic components of vicarious conditioning. *Journal of Clinical Psychology, 35*, 60–68.

Banissy, M. J., Kanai, R., Walsh, V., & Rees, G. (2012). Inter-individual differences in empathy are reflected in human brain structure. *NeuroImage, 62*(3), 2034–2039.

Bartz, J. A., Zaki, J., Bolger, N., Hollander, E., Ludwig, N. N., Kolevzon, A., & Ochsner, K. N. (2010). Oxytocin selectively improves empathic accuracy. *Psychological Science, 21*(10), 1426–1428.

Batson, C. D. (2012). The empathy-altruism hypothesis: Issues and implications. In J. Decety (Ed.), *Empathy: From bench to bedside* (pp. 41–54). Cambridge, MA: MIT Press.

Batson, C. D., Klein, T. R., Highberger, L., & Shaw, L. L. (1995). Immorality from empathy-induced altruism: When compassion and justice conflict. *Journal of Personality and Social Psychology, 68*(6), 1042–1054.

Bechara, A., Tranel, D., Damasio, H., & Damasio, A. R. (1996). Failure to respond autonomically to anticipated future outcomes following damage to prefrontal cortex. *Cerebral Cortex, 6*(2), 215–225.

Beeney, J. E., Franklin, R. G., Levy, K. N., & Adams, R. B. (2011). I feel your pain: Emotional Closeness modulates neural responses to empathically experienced rejection. *Social Neuroscience, 6*(4), 369–376.

Ben-Ami Bartal, I., Decety, J., & Mason, P. (2011) Empathy and pro-social behavior in rats. *Science, 334*(6061), 1427–1430.

Ben-Ami Bartal, I., Rodgers, D. A., Bernardez Sarria, M. S., Decety, J., & Mason, P. (2014) Prosocial behavior in rats is modulated by social experience. *eLife, 3*, e1385.

Blair, R. J. (1995) A cognitive developmental approach to morality: Investigating the Psychopath. *Cognition, 57*(1), 1–29.

Blair, R. J. (1999). Responsiveness to distress cues in the child with psychopathic tendencies. *Personality and Individual Differences, 27*, 135–145.

Blakemore, S-J., Boyer, P., Pachot-Clouard, M., Meltzoff, A., Segebarth, C., & Decety, J. (2003). The detection of contingency and animacy from simple animations in the human brain. *Cerebral Cortex, 13*(8), 837–844.

Blasi, A., Mercure, E., Lloyd-Fox, S., Thomson, A., Brammer, M., Sauter, D., Deeley, Q., ... Murphy, D. J. (2011). Early specialization for voice and emotion processing in the infant brain. *Current Biology, 21*(14), 1220–1224.

Brown, J. L., Sheffield, D., Leary, M. R., & Robinson, M. (2003). Social support and experimental pain. *Psychosomatic Medicine, 65*(2), 276–283.

Carden, S. E., Barr, G. A., & Hofer, M. A. (1991). Differential effects of specific opioid receptor agonists on rat pup isolation calls. *Developmental Brain Research, 62*(1), 17–22.

Carter, C. S. (1998). Neuroendocrine perspectives on social attachment and love. *Psychoneuroendocrinology, 23*(8), 779–818.

Cheng, Y., Chen, C., Lin, C-P., Chou, K-H., & Decety, J. (2010). Love hurts: An fMRI study. *Neuroimage, 51*(2), 923–929.

Cheng, Y., Hung, A-Y., & Decety, J. (2012). Dissociation between affective sharing and emotion understanding in juvenile psychopaths. *Development and Psychopathology, 24*(2), 623–636.

Cheng, Y., Lee, S-L., Chen, H-Y., Wang, P-Y., & Decety, J. (2012). Voice and emotion processing in the human neonatal brain. *Journal of Cognitive Neuroscience, 24*(6), 1411–1419.

Cheng, Y., Lin, C-P., Liu, H-L., Hsu, Y-Y., Lim, K-E., Hung, D., & Decety, J. (2007). Expertise modulates the perception of pain in others. *Current Biology, 17*(19), 1708–1713.

Church, R. M. (1959). Emotional reactions of rats to the pain of others. *Journal of Comparative and Physiological Psychology, 52*(2), 132–134.

Cikara, M., Botvinick, M. M., & Fiske, S. T. (2011). Us versus them: Social identity shapes neural responses to intergroup competition and harm. *Psychological Science, 22*(3), 306–313.

Clay, Z., & de Waal, F. B. M. (2013). Bonobos respond to distress in others: Consolation across the age spectrum. *PloS One, 8*(1), e55206.

Coan, J. A., Schaefer, H. S., & Davidson, R. J. (2006). Lending a hand: Social regulation of the neural response to threat. *Psychological Science, 17*(12), 1032–1039.

Cowell, J. M., Casey, E. C., Hetherington, C., Stephens, E. C., & Koenig, M. (2014). Children's selective trust in others: Practices, problems, and challenges. In O. Saracho (Ed.), *Handbook of research methods in early childhood education: Review of research methodologies Vol 2*. Charlotte: Information Age Processing.

D'Amato, F. R., & Pavone, F. (1993). Endogenous opioids: A proximate reward mechanism for kin selection? *Behavioral and Neural Biology, 60*(1), 79–83.

Decety, J. (2010a). The neurodevelopment of empathy in humans. *Developmental Neuroscience, 32*(4), 257–267.

Decety, J. (2010b). To what extent is the experience of empathy mediated by shared neural circuits? *Emotion Review, 2*(3), 204–207.

Decety, J. (2011). The neuroevolution of empathy. *Annals of the New York Academy of Sciences, 1231*, 35–45.

Decety, Jean, Chen, C., Harenski, C., & Kiehl, K. A. (2013). An fMRI study of affective perspective taking in individuals with psychopathy: Imagining another in pain does not evoke empathy. *Frontiers in Human Neuroscience, 7*, 1–12.

Decety, J., & Cowell, J. M. (2014). The complex relation between morality and empathy. *Trends in Cognitive Sciences, 18*, 337–339.

Decety, J., Echols, S., & Correll, J. (2010). The blame game: The effect of responsibility and social stigma on empathy for pain. *Journal of Cognitive Neuroscience, 22*, 985–997.

Decety, J., Michalska, K. J., Akitsuki, Y., & Lahey, B. (2009). Atypical empathic responses in adolescents with aggressice conduct disorder: A functional MRI investigation. *Biological Psychology, 80*(2), 203–211.

Decety, J., Michalska, K. J., & Kinzler, K. D. (2012). The contribution of emotion and cognition to moral sensitivity: A neurodevelopmental study. *Cerebral Cortex, 22*, 209–220.

Decety, J., & Svetlova, M. (2012). Putting together phylogenetic and ontogenetic perspectives on empathy. *Developmental Cognitive Neuroscience, 2*(1), 1–24.

Decety, J., Yang, C-Y., & Cheng, Y. (2010). Physicians down-regulate their pain empathy response: An event-related brain potential study. *NeuroImage, 50*(4), 1676–1682.

DeWall, C. N., Macdonald, G., Webster, G. D., Masten, C. L., Baumeister, R. F., Powell, C., Combs, D., ... Eisenberger, N. I. (2010). Acetaminophenreduces social pain: Behavioral and neural evidence. *Psychological Science, 21*(7), 931–937.

Domes, G., Heinrichs, M., Gläscher, J., Büchel, C., Braus, D. F., & Herpertz, S. C. (2007). Oxytocin attenuates amygdala responses to emotional faces regardless of valence. *Biological Psychiatry, 62*(10), 1187–1190.

Dondi, M., Simion, F., & Caltran, G. (1991). Can newborns discriminate between their own cry and the cry of another newborn infant? *Developmental Psychology, 35*(2), 418–426.

Drevets, W. C., Price, J. L., Simpson, J. R., Todd, R. D., Relch, T., Vannier, M., & Raichle, M. E. (1997). Subgenual prefrontal cortex abnormalities in mood disorders. *Nature, 386*, 824–827.

Echols, S., & Correll, J. (2012). It's more than skin deep: Empathy and helping behavior across social groups. In J. Decety (Ed.), *Empathy: From bench to bedside* (pp. 55–71). Cambridge, MA: MIT Press.

Eisenberger, N. I., Master, S. L., Inagaki, T. K., Taylor, S. E., Shirinyan, D., Lieberman, M. D., & Naliboff, B. D. (2011). Attachment figures activate a safety signal-related neural region and reduce pain experience. *Proceedings of the National Academy of Sciences, 108*(28), 11721–11726.

Farroni, T., Menon, E., Rigato, S., & Johnson, M. H. (2007). The perception of facial expressions in newborns. *The European Journal of Developmental Psychology, 4*(1), 2–13.

Franklin, R. G., Nelson, A. J., Baker, M., Beeney, J. E., Vescio, T. K., Lenz-Watson, A., & Adams, R. B. (2013). Neural responses to perceiving suffering in humans and animals. *Social Neuroscience, 8*(3), 217–227.

Hamlin, J. K., Wynn, K., & Bloom, P. (2007). Social evaluation by preverbal infants. *Nature, 450*(7169), 557–559.

Hamlin, J. K., Wynn, K., & Bloom, P. (2010). 3-month-olds show a negativity bias in their social evaluations. *Developmental Science, 13*(6), 923–929.

Hare, R. D. (1999) *Without conscience: The disturbing world of the psychopaths among us.* New York, NY: Guilford Press.

Harenski, C. L., Harenski, K. A., Shane, M. S., & Kiehl, K. A. (2010). Aberrant neural processing of moral violations in criminal psychopaths. *Journal of Abnormal Psychology, 119*(4), 863–874.

Hay, Dale F. (2009) The Roots and Branches of Human Altruism. *British Journal of Psychology 100*, 473–9.

Hay, D. F., & Cook, K. V. (2007). The transformation of pro-social behavior from infancy to childhood. In C. A. Brownell & C. B. Kopp (Eds.), *Socioemotional development in the toddler years: Transitions and transformations* (pp. 100–131). New York, NY: Guilford Press.

Hein, G., Silani, G., Preuschoff, K., Batson, C. D., & Singer, T. (2010). Neural responses to ingroup and outgroup members' suffering predict individual differences in costly helping. *Neuron, 68*(1), 149–160.

Heinrichs, M., Baumgartner, T., Kirschbaum, C., & Ehlert, U. (2003). Social support and oxytocin interact to suppress cortisol and subjective responses to psychosocial stress. *Biological Psychiatry, 54*(12), 1389–1398.

Hrdy, S. B. (2008). *Mothers and others: Evolutionary origins of mutual understanding.* Cambridge, MA: Belknap Press.

Insel, T. R., & Young, L. J. (2001). The neurobiology of attachment. *Nature Reviews Neuroscience, 2*(2), 129–136.

Jeon, D., Kim, S., Chetana, M., Jo, D., Ruley, H. E., Rabah, D., ... Shin, H-S. (2010). Observational fear learning involves affective pain system and Ca1.2 CA channels in ACC. *Nature Neuroscience, 13*(4), 482–488.

Kanakogi, Y., Okumura, Y., Inoue, Y., Kitazaki, M., & Itakura, S. (2013). Rudimentary sympathy in preverbal infants: Preference for others in distress. *PloS One 8*(6), e65292.

Kirsch, P., Esslinger, C., Chen, Q., Mier, D., Lis, S., Siddhanti, S., ... Meyer-Lindenberg, A. (2005). Oxytocin modulates neural circuitry for social cognition and fear in humans. *Journal of Neuroscience, 25*(49), 11489–11493.

Knafo, A., & Plomin, R. (2006). Pro-social behavior from early to middle childhood: Genetic and environmental influences on stability and change. *Developmental Psychology, 42*(5), 771–786.

Kogut, T., & Ritov, I. (2005). The 'identified victim' effect: An identified group, or just a single individual? *Journal of Behavioral Decision Making, 18*(3), 157–167.

Kosfeld, M., Heinrichs, M., Zak, P. J., Fischbacher, U., & Fehr, E. (2005). Oxytocin increases trust in humans. *Nature, 435*(7042), 673–676.

Lamm, C., Decety, J., & Singer, T. (2011). Meta-analytic evidence for common and distinct neural networks associated with directly experienced pain and empathy for pain. *NeuroImage, 54*(3), 2492–2502.

Lamm, C., Meltzoff, A. M., & Decety, J. (2010) How do we empathize with someone who is not like us? A functional magnetic resonance imaging study. *Journal of Cognitive Neuroscience, 22*, 362–376.

Langford, D. J., Crager, S. E., Shehzad, Z., Smith, S. B., Sotocinal, S. G., Levenstadt, J. S., ... Mogil, J. S. (2006). Social modulation of pain as evidence for empathy in mice. *Science, 312*(5782), 1967–1970.

Langford, D. J., Tuttle, A. H., Brown, K., Deschenes, S., Fischer, D. B., Mutso, A., ... Sternberg, W. F. (2010) Social approach to pain in laboratory mice. *Social Neuroscience, 5*(2), 163–170.

Leigh, R., Oishi, K., Hsu, J., Lindquist, M., Gottesman, R. F., Jarso, S., ... Hillis, A. E. (2013). Acute lesions that impair affective empathy. *Brain: A Journal of Neurology, 136*(8), 2539–2549.

Lockwood, P. L., Sebastian, C. L., McCrory, E. J., Hyde, Z. H., Gu, X., De Brito, S. A., & Viding, E. (2013). Association of callous traits with reduced neural response to others' pain in children with conduct problems. *Current Biology, 23*(10), 901–905.

Lorberbaum, J. P., Newman, J. D., Horwitz, A. R., Dubno, J. R., Lydiard, R. B., ... George, M. S. (2002). A potential role for thalamocingulate circuitry in human maternal behavior. *Biological Psychiatry, 51*, 431–445.

Macdonald, G., & Leary, M. R. (2005). Why does social exclusion hurt? The relationship between social and physical pain. *Psychological Bulletin, 131*(2), 202–223.

Marsh, A. A., Finger, E. C., Fowler, K. A., Adalio, C. J., Jurkowitz, I. T. N., Schechter, J. C., ... Blair, R. J. (2013). Empathic responsiveness in amygdala and anterior cingulate cortex in youths with psychopathic traits. *Journal of Child Psychology and Psychiatry, 54*(8), 900–910.

Marsh, A. A., Finger, E. C., Fowler, K. A., Jurkowitz, I. T. N., Schechter, J. C., Yu, H. H., ... Blair, R. J. (2011). Reduced amygdala-orbitofrontal connectivity during moral judgments in youths with disruptive behavior disorders and psychopathic traits. *Psychiatry Research, 194*(3), 279–286.

Marsh, A. A., Finger, E. C., Mitchell, D. G. V., Reid, M. E., Sims, C., Kosson, D. S., ... Blair, R. J. (2008). Reduced amygdala response to fearful expressions in children and adolescents with callous-unemotional traits and disruptive behavior disorders. *The American Journal of Psychiatry, 165*(6), 712–720.

Martin, G. B., Clark, R. D., Hicks, N., Martin, H. R., Masterton, R. B., Rashotte, M., ... Whitney, G. (1982). Distress crying in neonates: Species and peer specificity. *Developmental Psychology, 18*(1), 3–9.

Masserman, J. H., Wechkin, S., & Terris, W. (1964). 'Altruistic' behavior in rhesus monkeys. *The American Journal of Psychiatry, 121*(6), 584–585.

Masten, C. L., Eisenberger, N. I., Pfeifer, J. H., & Dapretto, M. (2010). Witnessing peer rejection during early adolescence: Neural correlates of empathy for experiences of social exclusion. *Social Neuroscience, 5*(5–6), 496–507.

Meerwijk, E. L., Ford, J. M., & Weiss, S. J. (2013). Brain regions associated with psychological pain: Implications for a neural network and its relationship to physical pain. *Brain Imaging and Behavior, 7*(1), 1–14.

Montalan, B., Lelard, T., Godefroy, O., & Mouras, H. (2012). Behavioral investigation of the influence of social categorization on empathy for pain: A minimal group paradigm study. *Frontiers in Psychology, 3*, 1–4.

Nadel, J. Imitation and imitation recognition: Functional use in preverbal infants and nonverbal children with autism. In A. N. Meltzoff & W. Prinz (Eds.), *The imitative mind: Development, evolution, and brain bases* (pp. 42–62). Cambridge: Cambridge University Press.

Nichols, S. R., Svetlova, M., & Brownell, C. A. (2009). The role of social understanding and empathic disposition in young children's responsiveness to distress in parents and peers. *Cognition and Brain Behavior, 13*(4), 449–478.

Norman, G. J., Hawkley, L. C., Cole, S. W., Berntson, G. G., & Cacioppo, J. T. (2012). Social neuroscience: The social brain, oxytocin, and health. *Social Neuroscience, 7*(1), 18–29.

Norman, G. J., Karelina, K., Morris, J. S., Zhang, N., Cochran, M., & DeVries, A. C. (2010). Social interaction prevents the development of depressive-like behavior post nerve injury in mice: A potential role for oxytocin. *Psychosomatic Medicine, 72*(6), 519–526.

O'Connor, M-F., Wellisch, D. K., Stanton, A. L., Eisenberger, N. I., Irwin, M. R., & Lieberman, M. D. (2008). Craving love? Enduring grief activates brain's reward center. *Neuroimage, 42*(2), 969–972.

Oswald, P. A. (1996). The effects of cognitive and affective perspective taking on empathic concern and altruistic helping. *The Journal of Social Psychology, 136*(5), 613–623.

Panksepp, J. (1998). *Affective neuroscience: The foundations of human and animal emotions.* London: Oxford University Press.

Parr, L. A. (2001). Cognitive and physiological markers of emotional awareness in chimpanzees (pan troglodytes). *Animal Cognition, 4*(3–4), 223–229.

Porges, S., & Carter, C. S. (2012). Mechanisms, mediators, and adaptive consequences of caregiving. In S. L. Brown, R. M. Brown, & L. A. Penner (Eds.), *Moving beyond self-interest: Perspectives from evolutionary biology, neuroscience, and the social sciences* (pp. 53–71). New York: Oxford University Press.

Rheingold, H. L. (2013). Little children's participation in the work of adults: A nascent prosocial behavior. *Child Development, 53*(1), 114–125.

Rhodes, M., & Brickman, D. (2011). The influence of competition on children's social categories. *Journal of Cognition and Development, 12*(2), 194–221.

Rhodes, M., & Chalik, L. (2013). Social categories as markers of intrinsic interpersonal obligations. *Psychological Science, 24*(6), 999–1006.

Rice, G. E., & Gainer, P. (1962). "Altruism" in the albino rat. *Journal of Comparative and Physiological Psychology, 55*(1), 123–125.

Romero, T., Castellanos, M. A., & de Waal, F. B. M. (2010). Consolation as possible expression of sympathetic concern among chimpanzees. *Proceedings of the National Academy of Sciences of the United States of America, 107*(27), 12110–12115.

Roth-Hanania, R., Davidov, M., & Zahn-Waxler, C. (2011). Empathy development from 8 to 16 months: Early signs of concern for others. *Infant Behavior & Development, 34*(3), 447–458.

Sambo, C. F., Howard, M., Kopelman, M., Williams, A., & Fotopoulou, A. (2010). Knowing you care: Effects of perceived empathy and attachment style on pain perception. *Pain, 151*(3), 687–693.

Schmidt, M. F. H., & Sommerville, J. A. (2011). Fairness expectations and altruistic sharing in 15-month-old human infants. *PloS One 6*(10), e23223.

Shamay-Tsoory, S. G., Aharon-Peretz, J., & Perry, D. (2009). Two systems for empathy: A double dissociation between emotional and cognitive empathy in inferior frontal gyrus versus ventromedial prefrontal lesions. *Brain, 132*(3), 617–627.

Sherif, M., Harvey, O. J., White, B. J., Hood, W. R., & Sherif, C. W. (1961). *The robbers cave experiment: Intergroup conflict and cooperation.* Norman, OK: University Book Exchange.

Singer, T., Seymour, B., O'Doherty, J. P., Stephan, K. E., Dolan, R. J., & Frith, C. D. (2006). Empathic neural responses are modulated by the perceived fairness of others. *Nature, 439*(7075), 466–469.

Svetlova, M., Nichols, S. R., & Brownell, C. A. (2010). Toddlers' pro-social behavior: From instrumental to empathic to altruistic helping. *Child Development, 81*(6), 1814–1827.

Tucker, D. M., Luu, P., & Derryberry, D. (2005). Love hurts: The evolution of empathic concern through the encephalization of nociceptive capacity. *Development and Psychopathology, 17*, 699–713.

Uchino, B. N., Cacioppo, J. T., & Kiecolt-Glaser, J. K. (1996). The relationship between social support and physiological processes: A review with emphasis on underlying mechanisms and implications for health. *Psychological Bulletin, 119*(3), 488–531.

Vaish, A., Carpenter, M., & Tomasello, M. (2009). Sympathy through affective perspective taking and its relation to pro-social behavior in toddlers. *Developmental Psychology, 45*(2), 534–543.

Vaish, A., Carpenter, M., & Tomasello, M. (2010). Young children selectively avoid helping people with harmful intentions. *Child Development, 81*(6), 1661–1669.

Warneken, F., & Tomasello, M. (2009). The roots of human altruism. *British Journal of Psychology, 100*(3), 455–471.

Warnick, J. E., McCurdy, C. R., & Sufka, K. J. (2005). Opioid receptor function in social attachment in young domestic fowl. *Behavioural Brain Research, 160*(2), 277–285.

Wechkin, S., Masserman, J. H., & Terris, W. Jr. (1964). Shock to a conspecific as an aversive stimulus. *Psychonomic Science, 1*(2), 47–48.

Xu, X., Zuo, X., Wang, X., & Han, S. (2009). Do you feel my pain? Racial group membership modulates empathic neural responses. *Journal of Neuroscience, 29*(26), 8525–8529.

Zahn-Waxler, C., Radke-Yarrow, M., Wagner, E., & Chapman, M. (1992). Development of concern for others. *Developmental Psychology, 28*(1), 126–136.

8
The Neuroscience of Deception
Jennifer M. C. Vendemia and James M. Nye

Key points
- The act of deception utilizes multiple cognitive systems: including attention, memory, motivation, and emotions.
- Three core cognitive processes support deception: working memory, inhibition, and task switching.
- Working memory represents true and false information simultaneously; inhibition is needed to suppress the truth as this is often more salient and vivid in memory, while task switching is recruited to switch between the description of true and false details.
- There are many different types of lies: spontaneous lie, calculated lie, long-term lie, polite lie, and so on – each lie varies in the type of cognitive process required to create and realize it.
- Regions in the front of the brain (anterior frontal) are involved in deceptive behavior.
- Polygraph measures the responses of the autonomic nervous system.
- Neurophysiological biomarkers for infrequent stimulus are used to test untruthful information; as the later are assumed to represent rare events.
- Deception ability appears first around the age of three years and develops in parallel with mentalizing ability, the understanding that others have minds.
- There are large individual differences in the ability to deceive.
- Autism is characterized with poor ability to deceive. This potentially is associated with impaired mentalizing ability.
- Aggressive behavior in children is positively associated with deceptive behavior.
- Individuals showing Machiavellianism, narcissism, psychopathy, and antisocial personality traits tend to be confident in their ability to deceive others.
- Trust boosts honesty, while punishment and threat have little effect on deceitful behavior.
- Parkinson's disease and schizophrenia alter the ability to engage in deceitful acts.

Terminology Explained

Autonomic nervous system, also known as the involuntary nervous system, controls visceral functions (such as heart rate, digestion, respiration, salivation, and sexual arousal) below the level of conscious awareness. It can be parsed into the subdivisions of parasympathetic and sympathetic nervous systems and its functioning has been connected to a variety of medical and psychological symptoms.

Electrodermal/galvanic skin response relates to a change in the electrical properties of the skin in response to stress or anxiety (due to perspiration). It can be measured by recording the electrical resistance of the skin or the weak currents in the body.

Electroencephalography (EEG) entails recording of electrical activity from electrodes positioned over the scalp that transmit signals reflecting summated activity from populations of similarly oriented neurons within the brain. This allows for real-time assessment of cortical activity at rest or during performance of tasks for purposes of scientific hypothesis testing or applied clinical assessment.

An **event-related potential (ERP)** is an average EEG signal time locked to the occurrence of a discrete event, such as a presented stimulus or an emitted response, across multiple trials. The high temporal resolution of ERP response variables provides for the precise tracking of perceptual and cognitive processes in relation to psychologically significant events.

Functional magnetic resonance imaging (fMRI) measures changes in the level of oxygen in the blood in regions of interest in the brain before and after tasks are undertaken. These blood oxygen levels dependent (BOLD) signals are said to indicate how active a specific region of the brain actually is.

P300 is an ERP waveform component that has been connected to information processing and decision making. Variants of the P300 response have been shown to be related to attention, orienting, cognitive workload, and stimulus novelty.

Polygraphy measures physiological responses that are considered to be the product of dissembling, such as changes in autonomic responding (e.g., heart rate, respiration, and skin response). Hence, the polygraph does not detect lies, but physiological changes in response to carefully crafted questions. The most commonly used techniques include the relevant/irrelevant technique, the control or comparisons question test, the directed lie test, and the guilty knowledge test.

Pupillometry is the measurement of pupil dilation. Greater pupil dilation is associated with increased processing in the brain.

Working memory is the system in the brain said to be responsible for the transient holding, and processing of new and stored information, and hence is an important process for reasoning, comprehension, learning, and memory.

Introduction

Our understanding of how humans behave deceptively advanced enormously over the last several decades due to the development imaging techniques that can measure distinct patterns of brain activity (e.g., blood flow, brain cell activity). The availability of such techniques allows researchers to precisely examine how the brain processes information.

Over the past two decades, we have learned that deception is a higher-order cognitive process. Multiple cognitive subprocesses, also known as systems, operate in conjunction during deceptive acts (e.g., deception requires the inhibition of physical signs of nervousness during the communication of a coherent narrative). By learning more about the subprocesses involved in deception, researchers can clarify the complexity of a deceptive act, and this clarity can be used to help inform real-world scenarios. For example, recent studies of patients with Parkinson's disease suggest that portions of the motor system are involved during deception. The key role of the motor system in deception was not discovered by laboratory research, but by naturalistic observation of patients by trained therapists. New neuroscientific models of deception are more accurate now that the role of motor systems is considered.

Deception requires many cognitive systems (e.g., attention, memory, motivation, emotion), but those systems are not exclusive to deception nor are they universally employed across all deceptive acts. We used to think that attentional orienting was necessary during deception and, therefore, researchers exaggerated the pre-eminence of measures of attentional orienting while neglecting measures associated with other systems. Attentional orienting varies across deceptive acts (well-practiced lies are different than spontaneous lies). Orienting also varies based on a number of factors that have little to do with deception. Relying on a single component to identify deception can result in an unbalanced understanding of the process of deception.

The Neuroscience of Deception

Three papers have extensively reviewed the data from fMRI studies of deception (Bhatt, et al., 2009; Christ, Van Essen, Watson, Brubaker, & McDermott, 2009; Vendemia, Schillaci, Buzan, Green, & Meek, 2009). But before discussing these studies, a quick note about anatomical names. The field is currently in a period of rapid growth as previously unknown information is uncovered. This has resulted in different fields of neuroscience having different preferences for naming cortical anatomy. Naming conventions will continue to change as the breadth of our knowledge expands and our ability to map the brain improves. Some researchers prefer reporting Brodmann's areas, which represent numbered regions of the brain, organized by the type of neurons in the region and their interconnections. Other researchers prefer a strictly anatomical name that is based solely on the physical structures of the brain. The third group has developed a merging of these naming systems to best represent what we know of the function of the underlying cortex. The structures outlined in Figure 8.1 are most often described in the literature.

The test formats designed to examine brain regions, outlined in Figure 8.1, include modified versions of the guilty knowledge task, lying about recently acquired knowledge, prepared or spontaneous lies about past experiences, and lies about recent actions. Christ et al., (2009) identified regional brain activity common across these studies in a meta-analysis, and then compared them to areas of the brain associated with three cognitive processes: 1) working memory, 2) inhibitory control, and 3) task switching. These processes are the most consistently reported throughout the deception literature, and are supported by measures of reaction

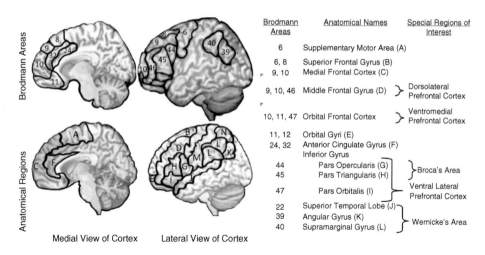

Figure 8.1 An overview of brain regions associated with deception and the different names that are reported in the literature of deception neuroscience.

time, pupillometry, electrodermal skin response, and brain wave recordings obtained through event-related potentials (ERP).

In studies of deception, researchers associate activations in the cingulate cortex, which is related to error detection, attention shifting, and performance monitoring among other processes (Ganis, Kosslyn, Stose, Thompson, & Yurgelun-Todd, 2003; Kozel et al., 2004b; Lee, et al., 2002; Mohamed, et al., 2006), fusiform/parahippocampal area, which is associated with image recognition (Ganis et al., 2003; Kozel, Padgett, & George, 2004a), ventrolateral prefrontal cortex, which is related to inhibition (Mohamed, et al., 2006; Spence, et al., 2001), medial prefrontal cortex, which is related to various components of decision making (Ganis et al., 2003; Langleben, et al., 2002; Spence, et al., 2001), left inferior parietal, which is related to associating multiple information streams including language (Langleben, et al., 2002; Lee, et al., 2002; Spence, et al., 2001), and temporal regions, which are involved in both memory processing and language (Kozel et al., 2004a; Lee, et al., 2002; Mohamed, et al., 2006; Stelmack, Houlihan, Doucet, & Belisle, 1994) with the act of deception. In later sections, we will go into more detail regarding the involvement of these regions in particular facets of deceptive behavior when the information about their functioning, development, or involvement is pertinent to the neuroscience of deception. Table 8.1 lists fMRI studies in which participants engaged in deceptive behavior or observed deceptive behavior, and the specifics of each paradigm.

Parts of the Brain Associated with Deception

We will now briefly examine the parts of the brain associated with deception.

The prefrontal cortex

John Gabrieli and other fMRI researchers argue that the anterior prefrontal cortex, or Brodmann's area 10, is involved in the act of deception (Gabrieli, 2005). Ramnani and Owen (2004) argue that this area is activated when an individual must use the

Table 8.1 A comparison of paradigms investigating deception

	Paradigm Description	Lie Type
Bhatt et al., 2009	Participants responded to grayscale images of faces presented in lineups	Facial recognition
Ganis et al., 2003	Recorded work/vacation scenarios, after 1-week delay generated alternate scenarios and memorized them	Memorized and Spontaneous
German et al., 2004	Observers indicated whether real or acted clips revealed completed acts	Observation only
Grezes et al., 2004	Observers indicated whether actors actually lifted heavy boxes or pretended to lift heavy boxes	Observation only
Kozel et al., 2004a	For a reward, participants lied and told the truth regarding objects under which $50 was hidden	Concealed information
Kozel et al., 2004b	For a reward, participants, lied and told the truth regarding an object under which $50 was hidden	Concealed information
Kozel et al., 2005	For a reward, participants, lied and told the truth regarding an object under which $50 was hidden	Concealed information
Langleben et al., 2002	Deception to cards in a concealed information test	Concealed information
Langleben et al., 2005	For a reward participants were instructed to (lie) deny possession of one playing card and (truth) acknowledge the possession of a different playing card	Directed lie about objects in possession
Lee et al., 2002	For a reward, participants lied in a card playing scenario	Concealed information
Lee et al., 2002	For an imaginary reward, participants faked amnesia to digits and autobiographical information	Simulated amnesia digits and autobiographic memory
Mohamed et al., 2006	Participants responded to previously recorded questions in a concealed information test	Concealed information
Nunez et al., 2005	Subjects instructed to give truthful or "false" answers (blocked) to a series of yes/no questions that also varied in autobiographical content	Autobiographical Memory
Phan et al., 2005	For a reward, participants lied in a card playing scenario	Concealed information
Spence et al., 2005	Participants were told to lie and tell the truth to events that happened earlier in the day	Directed lie to episodic memory
Spence et al., 2001	Participants were told to lie and tell the truth to events that happened earlier in the day	Directed lie to episodic memory

result of one decision to inform subsequent decisions. When an individual deceives, these contingent decisions are informed by situational context, goal-driven behavior, divergence of the deceptive information from truthful information, and a variety of internal states. Given the generalist nature of these "simultaneous considerations," it is no surprise that several researchers identified activation in the anterior prefrontal cortex during the act of deception (Bhatt, et al., 2009; Ganis et al.; Lee, et al., 2002; Mohamed, et al., 2006; Vendemia & Buzan, 2004a).

The anterior cingulate cortex

The most widely reported region of activation during deception is the anterior cingulate (Spence, et al., 2001; Vendemia & Buzan, 2004b). This activation is broken down into two main areas, the ventral anterior cingulate and the dorsal anterior cingulate. Some researchers believe that this area is involved in conflict resolution, while others believe that it is involved in attention shifting and resource allocation processes. It is possible that the more ventral regions are involved in conflict resolution, while the more dorsal area is involved in attention shifting. Given the complex nature of deception, it is theoretically probable that the act of deception involves both processes. Most of the fMRI research on deception is designed to examine patterns that generalize across individuals as opposed to identifying specific patterns within a single individual. Bhatt et al.'s (2009) review of the brain regions involved in deceptions revealed stable differences between truthful responding and deceptive responding at the group level. Vendemia et al. (2009) evaluated the intersubject variability between the studies, finding that the difference in brain activity between individual participants was greater than that between truthful and deceptive responding. At first the variability seems overwhelming, but this variability is exactly what research with the fMRI is designed to identify.

Measuring Deception

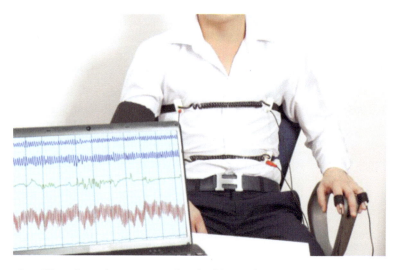

Lie detection *The polygraph measures galvanic skin conductance response. Two electrodes are placed on the skin and the electricity conducted between these electrode is measured. When aroused, we tend to sweat and flex our muscles, which increases the conductivity. Hence the polygraph (GSR) measures changes in arousal levels. Polygraphs rely on the assumption that, when an individual attempts to conceal information or lie, there will an increase in their arousal levels in comparison to when they tell the truth.*

Source: © Burmakin Andrey. Used under license from 123RF.

The polygraph is a reliable and robust measure of autonomic nervous system responses. A variety of test formats elicit similar patterns of activity from the autonomic nervous system, even though the test formats measure different aspects of cognition, attention, and emotion. The reason that the tests are robust is that the autonomic nervous system responds reliably even under different conditions. For example, the guilty knowledge ("concealed information") test depends on the presentation of the infrequent "relevant" item among high frequency irrelevant items. Extensive research using the infrequent/frequent paradigm, also known as the "oddball" paradigm, suggests that "the expectation of the infrequent stimulus" drives the autonomic system activity.

Particular cognitive functions are associated with the identification of the infrequent stimulus including attention resource allocation (Comerchero & Polich, 1999), and the consequential updating of information held in working memory (Donchin & Coles, 1988; Ruchkin, Johnson, Canoune, Ritter, & Hammer, 1990). When the anticipated infrequent stimulus is encountered and subsequently recognized, a particular brainwave, the oddball ERP P300, occurs (Allen & Iacono, 1997; Allen, Iacono, & Danielson, 1992; Farwell & Donchin, 1991; Rosenfeld, et al., 1999). Thus, this brainwave is a reliable indicator that a subject had been anticipating specific information and, upon encountering the information, they mentally considered it differently than if they had not been anticipating it.

This process of inhibition is a cortical network distributed across anterior and posterior regions including bilateral dorsolateral and ventrolateral prefrontal cortex, the right inferior parietal lobe, and the medial aspect of the anterior cingulate cortex (Asahi, Okamoto, Okada, Yamawaki, & Yokota, 2004; Braver, Barch, Gray, Molfese, & Snyder, 2001; Bunge, Ochsner, Desmond, Glover, & Gabrieli, 2001; Garavan, Ross, & Stein, 1999; Konishe, et al., 1999; Rubia, 2001). The medial aspect of the anterior cingulate is more involved in formation of appropriate responses than inhibition of inappropriate responses (Asahi et al., 2004; Little, Kiehl, & Smith, 2001) while the ventrolateral prefrontal cortex (vlPFC) has been associated with the ability to override a salient response in the case of deceptive behavior overriding a truthful response. There is evidence in the ERP and fMRI literature that inhibition occurs during the act of deception. Spence et al. (2001) argue that inhibition during deception is related to an inhibition of a pre-potent truthful response. However, Vendemia, Buzan, and Simon-Dack (2005) argue that, although the truthful response is pre-potent, both responses are temporarily held in working memory during situationally appropriate contexts and inhibition occurs in both truthful and deceptive responses.

Two separate lines of evidence support the supposition that truthful responses are pre-potent, although neither of them are particularly compelling. From open-ended inventories administered online, our lab identified a small number of respondents who reported, "accidentally telling a lie" or "telling a lie that I knew wouldn't work" (instead of an effective lie). These types of errors could be viewed as cognitive failures, that is, suggesting a failure in selecting the appropriate response when a secondary response was more salient (Broadbent, Cooper, Fitzgerald, & Parkes, 1982). In a directed lie two-stimulus task, individuals who reported higher levels of cognitive failures made more errors and had longer reaction times (RTs) for truthful and deceptive responses (Meek, Phillips, Boswell, & Vendemia, 2013).

Using fMRI, along with other technologies and techniques, we can begin to parcel the specific cortical activity that occurs during the act of deception. The task is far from simple, and the studies conducted thus far are rife with errors in test construction. They repeat errors that occurred in the early 1990s with the first studies of brain wave measures of deception, which repeated errors in the first designs of polygraph tests. In order to better understand deception within the laboratory, and construct better methods to examine deception, we can use knowledge regarding the development of deceptive behaviors, the effects of neurological disease processes, and the impact of certain psychological disorders to inform our neuroscientific models.

The Development of Deceptive Behavior

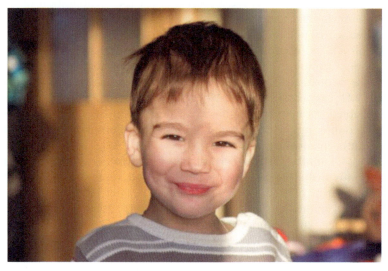

Development of deception *Deception is one of the early landmarks in cognitive development. The capacity for children to tell a lie requires meta cognition, the understanding that reality and mental processes are distinct. This ability typically develops between the age of three and four years.*
Source: © Sergey Sergeev. Used under license from 123RF.

A convincing deception requires that the deceiver understand how the person who is being told the lie thinks and acts with respect to the social situation. The development of behaviors relating to the comprehension, interpretation, and telling of lies coincides with the developmental landmarks associated with the theory of mind (McCann, 1998). As children develop reasoning related to other's perceptions, the development of theory of mind, they also develop reasoning related to deception. Between the ages of 18 and 24 months, children develop the awareness that another person's perceptions and thoughts about the world are separate from their own. Detection and interpretation of pretense is one of the earliest landmarks in cognitive development and it coincides with the period in which theory of mind develops (e.g., Leslie, 1994). Given that deception involves intentionally misleading another person, one's understanding that other people possess a mind and intentions distinct from one's own is crucial to the ability to deceive. Theory of mind enables one to consider the extent of another person's knowledge as well as their goals and desires, all of which are useful in crafting a plausible lie.

As was previously discussed, inhibition is an important cognitive ability to successfully deceive another person. First, producing a lie requires the ability to inhibit a particular response (i.e., the truth) and instead, choose to conduct a different response (i.e., "the lie"). Additionally, liars must also work to inhibit behavioral signs of nervousness, guilt, or discomfort in order to conceal their deceptive intents. The capacity for children to inhibit a response develops rapidly between the ages of three and four years, particularly with regards to inhibiting muscle activity. In a deception study with three- to four-year olds, the age groups did not differ in their ability to deceive using a physical symbol (e.g., using an arrow to point towards a direction), but when the children were required to respond by physically pointing, four-year olds outperformed three-year olds in their ability to deceive (Carlson, Moses, & Hix, 1998), revealing that muscular control is an important component of a deceptive act.

By age five, normally developing children knowingly exhibit deceptive behavior, but these behaviors are rarely verbally complex (Newton, Reddy, & Bull, 2000). At this age, deception generally consists of one-word responses (Bussey, 1992), omitting information (Peskin, 1992), or a single meaningful gesture, such as pointing towards the wrong direction (Russell, Mauthner, Sharpe, & Tidswell, 1991). As children age, their general cognitive abilities (language, memory, etc.) become more complex, and the detail of their deceptive behaviors become more sophisticated. The ability to compose a detailed lie is at least partially dependent on these cognitive abilities and therefore the sophistication of a lie will always be somewhat constrained by the developmental limits of the distinct cognitive systems involved in the deception.

A problem with detecting deception within children is that differentiating between true and false accounts becomes increasingly difficult as the child becomes more familiar with the situation. Children who lack the sophistication to understand the ramifications of a lie can still be sophisticated enough to provide surprisingly detailed information based on indirect sources (e.g., media content, see Pezdek, et al., 2004). Normally developing children are able to engage in pretend play with no intent to deceive by the age of three years and six months (Ahern, Lyon, & Quas, 2011). Therefore, appreciating the difference between truth telling, deceiving, and pretending is important in judging the veracity of a child's report.

Developmental Disorders Associated with Deception

Autism

Autism spectrum disorder (ASD) is a neurodevelopmental disorder associated with deficits in motor functioning (repetitive behaviors) and communication abilities (inability to infer another person's intentions). One of these communication deficits is the inability to lie, which is potentially related to difficulties pertaining to theory of mind (Leekam & Perner, 1991). Autistic patients have much more difficulty lying than mental-age matched controls (Sodian & Frith, 1992). When directed, autistic patients are competent at deception, but they have difficulty maintaining the lie; they tend to leak the truth in later statements, thus resulting in their being caught after the fact (Li, Kelley, Evans, & Lee, 2011; Talwar, et al., 2012). In addition, those with autism are impaired at detecting deception and are less likely to tell lies. When children with ASD are bullied at school, bullies often tell lies that are not plausible but are effective because the child with ASD does not discriminate this implausibility (Ranick, Persicke, Tarbox, & Kornack, 2013). This complex disorder has only begun to be studied recently, but it is believed that the lack of deceptive behaviors is the result of the overall failure to initiate or respond to social interactions.

Oppositional defiant disorder

In preschool aged children (approximately three to five years old) general aggression and social threats towards friends and classmates were positively associated with deceptive behavior suggesting a link between the inability to inhibit anger and deceptive behavior (Ostrov, Ries, Stauffacher, Godleski, & Mullins, 2008). The inhibition of anger is associated with activity in the right orbitofrontal cortex, and damage to this region results in uncontrolled aggressive behavior. The correlation of aggression and deception, particularly deceptions told with the intent to harm another, are related to the role of the orbital frontal cortex (brain region in the prefrontal cortex roughly corresponding to Brodmann's Area 10) because this region is highly involved in moderating anger. Given that the prefrontal cortex is the last area of the brain to develop and is not fully developed until the age of 25, the development of this region is particularly susceptible to environmental factors that occur throughout the lifespan. Similarly to how damage to this region results in inhibitory deficits, underdevelopment or maladaptive development leads to impulsive aggression and deception. In an fMRI study of psychopathy in which the participants either lied or told the truth, lower relative activation in the right orbital frontal cortex was associated with less concern for consequences and this relationship covaried with age (Fullam, McKie, & Dolan, 2009), further implicating that age-related development of the right orbital frontal cortex influences deceptive behaviors.

When children experience the social ramifications of lying (personally or through the observation of others' deceptions), they are less likely to rely on deception for self-serving purposes. When receiving socialization about the importance of honesty, which emphasizes the positive outcomes associated with honest behavior, children are also less likely to deceive (Talwar & Crossman, 2011). In the next section, we will continue to address the role of environment in the development of antisocial personality disorders.

Neurological and Personality Disorders and Deceptive Behavior

Antisocial personality disorder and malevolent use of deception

Antisocial personality disorder (APD) is highly relevant to deception detection because APD individuals are more confident in their ability to deceive. Perceived ability to deceive positively correlates with the following personality qualities associated with APD: Machiavellianism (cynical, unprincipled, and manipulative), narcissism (grandiosity, entitlement, dominance, and superiority), and psychopathy (impulsivity, emotional detachment, and low empathy). The personality characteristics of agreeableness and conscientiousness, on the other hand, are related to the lack of confidence in deceptive ability (Giammarco, Atkinson, Baughman, Veselka, &

Vernon, 2013). The fact that certain personality traits, particularly those relating to APD, influence self-beliefs about deceptive skill suggests that identifying how these personality traits influence deceptive behaviors will help deception detection.

An interesting finding across studies of psychopathologies is that they occur equally among boys and girls, but are more prevalent among adult men than adult women (Loeber, Burke, & Pardini, 2009), suggesting a strong influence of the environment in shaping antisocial behaviors. Although children become more honest after learning about the positive outcomes that result from truth-telling (Lee, et al., 2014), it appears this capacity to reinforce honest behavior is contingent on perceived trustworthiness, meaning that someone is only more likely to be swayed towards honesty if they trust the other person; threats and punishment do little to instill honest behaviors (Wang, Galinsky, & Murnighan, 2009). Psychopathic behaviors can manifest themselves as a result of genetic predispositions, but the dynamic nature of the parent–child relationship across development is a significant contributor to the formation of these personality disorders (Tuvblad, Bezdjian, Raine, & Baker, 2013). This relationship is important to the development of psychopathic tendencies because it implicates the role of reward and punishment networks in the formation of prefrontal cortical networks that moderate deceptive behavior.

Using ERP methods in a concealed information test, the P300 ERP brainwave can be used to measure a person's neural response to a highly infrequent stimulus only 300 milliseconds (ms) after the stimulus has appeared, thus allowing researchers to measure a fairly immediate response to a stimulus. This method has been shown to differentiate deception in psychopaths just as well as in non-psychopaths (Miller & Rosenfeld, 2004). Although minimal differences between psychopaths and non-psychopaths were observed in the P300 waveform, these researchers observed that a later waveform (500ms after the stimulus appeared) was weaker for the psychopaths only during the deceptive act, suggesting that the psychopaths were less affected by lying than the non-psychopaths. These findings suggest that ERP methods are able to detect deception in psychopaths and non-psychopaths, as well as differentiate psychopaths from non-psychopaths.

Furthermore, deception detection using neuroimaging methods has revealed certain patterns of brain activity when those with APDs are being deceptive. The activation of specific brain regions during deception changes as a function of certain traits of APD (Fullam et al., 2009) as well as the patient's rate of lying (Jiang et al., 2013). Those who score highly on psychopathic traits and lie frequently in the real world show a reduction in brain activity associated with deception. Identifying the deception patterns that are subject to change (e.g., brain activity in the right orbitofrontal cortex) and those that are more stable (e.g. P300 waveforms associated with decision making) improves our ability to determine the behavioral indicators of deception.

Parkinson's disease and the inability to produce a lie

Parkinson's disease is a neurogenerative disorder that is most associated with a wide number of deficits in the ability to coordinate motor function, including resting tremor, rigidity, bradykinesia or slowness, gait disturbance, and postural instability (Olanow & Tatton, 1999). Additionally, a unique cluster of personality traits and behaviors are found in those who later develop Parkinson's disease. This premorbid personality consists of traits such as industriousness, punctuality, inflexibility, cautiousness, and lack of novelty seeking, and persists after the onset of the motor illness (Menza, 2000).

Patients with Parkinson's disease have difficulty integrating multiple cognitive processes, such as modifying past knowledge after encountering new information. Abe et al. (2009) compared Parkinson's patients to normal controls in a deceptive task while monitoring brain activity in a PET machine, which measures regional cerebral glucose metabolism. The anterior prefrontal cortex is the region most highly associated with integration, and it is also associated with deceptive behavior. Abe et al. reported this region to be hypometabolized (under activated) while patients with Parkinson's were attempting to be deceptive. The left dorsolateral prefrontal cortex (dlPFC) was hypometabolized as well. This region is associated with the selection of a single response from competing responses, especially when the selected response is not necessarily the most predictable response. Given that deception requires one to inhibit a truthful response while deploying a deceptive response, the relationship between under activation in the left dlPFC and difficulties in deceptive responding is not surprising.

Schizophrenia and disorganized planning

Schizophrenia is a heterogeneous psychological disorder that is associated with a wide variety of potential cognitive deficits, which can include disorganized thinking, delusional beliefs, auditory hallucinations, and a variety of depression-like psychomotor deficits which inhibit a patient's ability to interact with the world (e.g., lack of motivation, reduced feelings of pleasure, flat vocal affect, poverty of speech). Additionally, schizophrenia is associated with the inability to intentionally mislead. Individuals with schizophrenia perform poorly on tasks that require strategic social thinking, such as predicting others' reactions (Mazza, De Risio, Tozzini, Roncone, & Casacchia, 2003; Sullivan & Allen, 1999). These patients simply do not understand situations involving interpersonal deception (Mazza et al., 2003). Schizophrenics are unable to recognize when a deceptive strategy is viable, and thusly they are unable to plan the deception.

Research regarding deception in schizophrenia is important for two reasons beyond greater understanding of the process of human deception. First, those with schizophrenia are significantly more violent than the normal population, resulting in law enforcement officials being more likely to intervene (Wallace, Mullen, & Burgess, 2004). Therefore, knowledge regarding deceptive behavior in schizophrenics can be a valuable tool for law enforcement officials. Second, schizophrenia is a neurogenerative disorder with a wide variety of symptoms, some of which include auditory hallucinations (e.g., hearing voices that they don't self-identify with) and delusions. Schizophrenics maintain beliefs that are not based in reality, suggesting that their deceptive behaviors may differ in "intentionality" from that of the normal population. The normal population is well versed in differentiating between facts that are based in reality and facts that are false, but a deluded schizophrenic will truthfully believe a fact that is not true. Differentiating between a delusional belief and an intentional deception is integral to selecting the best course of action if someone needs to extract information from a schizophrenic.

One study examined individuals with schizophrenia in an fMRI while they performed a classic directed lie task (Kaylor-Hughes et al., 2011). Although the findings suggested that schizophrenics' cortical activations do not differ significantly from the normal population, the analysis of that data is unusual. In addition, the behavioral data show that schizophrenics made more errors while trying to respond, and had longer RTs than those reported in studies of normal populations, which suggested that they do respond differently from the normal population.

One intriguing finding was that the severity of certain symptoms (e.g., bizarre behavior, delusions, and hallucinations) was associated with a reduction in brain activity in the left BA 47, a region involved in selecting a single option when several different options exist, suggesting that the severity of a patient's delusions altered their brain's ability to construct a deceptive response. Schizophrenics who exhibit auditory hallucinations attribute their hallucinations to external sources (i.e., they hallucinate speech and misattribute the source), making it difficult for a schizophrenic to organize a coherent reality. These hallucinations render theory of mind difficult because the schizophrenic is less able to differentiate between auditory content that exists in reality and auditory content that the schizophrenic is misattributing to reality. The fact that symptoms such as hallucinations reduced activity in BA 47 suggests that the hallucinations of schizophrenics impair their ability to consider each option in isolation and select the one that is most appropriate for a situation.

Conclusions

Three cognitive processes: 1) working memory, 2) inhibitory control, and 3) task switching are the most consistently reported in studies of deception. Experimental investigations of deception correlated activity in the lateral prefrontal cortex with working memory, activity in the vlPFC with inhibitory control, and activity in the cingulate cortex with task switching. However, the neurocortical systems involved in deception are far richer than the reported activations in these three regions would suggest – in that the systems develop and change throughout the lifespan.

Neurological disorders that affect deceptive behavior can disrupt portions of the system involved in understanding the social context which merit deception, such as the temporal parietal junction, or systems involved in encoding the consequence of deceptive acts, such as the right orbital frontal cortex. Certain disorders impair the ability to deploy deceptions due to hypometabolism of regions involved in selecting a single response from several competing responses including the dlPFC, while other disorders impair the ability to plan a deceptive strategy due to an inability to maintain coherent narrative of real-world events resulting from decreased activation in the left ventral lateral region.

The fact that unique neurological disorders are linked to specific deficits in deceptive functioning supports the multi-systemic view of deceptive processing. But using an understanding of the developmental time course of deceptive behavior and exploring the links between neurological disorders and deception we can formulate hypotheses based on our understanding of these deficits. Like most systems grounded in neuroscience, we can use developmental landmarks and deficits unique to particular disorders to identify the distinct role of each system during a deceptive act. The next step is experimentally manipulating the systems in the laboratory in order to develop paradigms for exploring them in the real world.

Recommended Reading

Abe, N., Fujii, T., Hirayama, K., Takeda, A., Hosokai, Y., Ishioka, T., … Fukuda, H. (2009). Do Parkinsonian patients have trouble telling lies? The neurobiological basis of deceptive behaviour. *Brain, 132*(5), 1386–1395. *Clinicians who work with Parkinson's patients have long reported that they tend to be incredibly honest individuals. The authors wanted to test if their honesty was a personality characteristic or if the neurological deficits involved in Parkinson's disease impaired their capacity to deceive. The results supported the latter, revealing that deception deficits in the Parkinson's patients were specifically to hypometabolism in prefrontal cortices, even after controlling for age, sex, disease severity, and medication. More specifically, the affected regions are involved when one must use the result of one decision to inform subsequent decisions, especially when those subsequent decisions require suppressing a pre-potent response. These results suggest that an inability to suppress pre-potent responses on the basis of an earlier decision will undermine one's capacity to deceive (e.g., inadvertently blurting out the truth after being interrogated for an hour). Because Parkinson's disease disrupts specific pathways in the brain related to motoric control and motoric learning, deception researchers are beginning to investigate the role of the motor system in deceptive behavior.*

Carlson, S. M., Moses, L. J., & Hix, H. R. (1998). The role of inhibitory processes in young children's difficulties with deception and false belief. *Child Development, 69*(3), 672–691. *The ability to deceive is subject to developmental constraints such that three-year olds are less effective liars than four-year olds. However, the simultaneous development of multiple systems (e.g., physical, emotional, cognitive, etc.) makes it difficult to identify the source of this difference. These authors tested if the development of deceptive skill between the ages of three and four was related to cognitive development or motoric development. They reported that both age groups were equally competent at deceiving when the deceptive task was motorically simple (i.e., pointing by moving a physical arrow), but when the deceptive task was motorically difficult (i.e., physically pointing with their fingers), the four-year olds outperformed the three-year olds. This paper reveals that cognitive competence is not sufficient for deceptive behavior. Although cognitive systems are vital in coordinating the distinct systems in order to effectively deceive, the integrity of these subsystems is just as vital to effective deception as is the integrity of the prefrontal cortex.*

Christ, S. E., Van Essen, D. C., Watson, J. M., Brubaker, L. E., & McDermott, K. B. (2009). The contributions of prefrontal cortex and executive control to deception: Evidence from activation likelihood estimate meta-analyses. *Cerebral Cortex, 19*(7), 1557–1566. *The authors conducted a meta-analysis to identify deception-related activity that was consistently observed in fMRI studies, and compared these patterns to meta-analyses of executive function, specifically related to working memory, inhibition, and task switching. The researchers observed 13 deception-related brain regions that overlapped with executive function regions. Ten of these regions were active for working memory, inhibition, and task switching, reaffirming the argument that deception requires the coordination of multiple subsystems. The other three deception-related regions were solely related to working memory, with no overlap between deception-related regions and those related to either task switching or inhibition. The authors also reported that non-executive function regions related to selective attention of salient environment stimuli are involved in deception. They argue that deception could require an alerting mechanism that operates to signal the liar when the social interaction requires a deceptive response. The authors conclude that deception is a higher order cognitive process, where executive control, specific involvement of working memory, and selective-attention are coordinated in order to bring about deceptive behavior.*

Langleben, D. D., Schroeder, L., Maldjian, J. A., Gur, R. C., McDonald, S., Ragland, J. D., … Childress, A. R. (2002). Brain activity during simulated deception: An event-related functional magnetic resonance study. *NeuroImage, 15*(3), 727–732. *This experiment was the first major fMRI research study on deception. Previous deception researchers used methods that* relied on temporal precision (e.g., ERP, polygraph, response time), meaning that this study represented the first attempt to spatially localize neural correlates of deceptive behavior. Participants performed the guilty knowledge test (GKT), which is designed to detect if someone is concealing information. Because detection of concealed information was commonly examined in ERP studies, those results could inform interpretations. The authors observed activation patterns that suggested deception involved the suppression of pre-potent responses and subsequent selection of less salient responses, and that truth did not elicit greater activation than deception in any regions. Although they do consider the possibility that some effects were artificially induced by the experiment, and offer suggestions to improve future methodologies. The authors conclude that deception is more cognitively demanding than truth telling, and that truth telling may be a baseline cognitive state. These conclusions have been generally replicated through the years.

Spence, S. A., Hunter, M. D., Farrow, T. F., Green, R. D., Leung, D. H., Hughes, C. J., & Ganesan, V. (2004). A cognitive neurobiological account of deception: Evidence from functional neuroimaging. *Philosophical Transactions of the Royal Society of London B: Biological Sciences, 359*(1451), 1755–1762. The authors describe the close relationship between the prefrontal cortex and tactical deception from the perspective of evolution, human development, and cognitive neuroscience. First, they discuss the prevalence of deception in non-human animals, revealing that the amount of deception in a species is predicted by the size of that species' neocortex. Then, they discuss deception across the lifespan, revealing that deceptive abilities are constrained by cognitive development (e.g., inhibition of truthful responses is constrained by the development of inhibitory control). They provide a cognitive framework for deceptive behavior, which is then used to interpret findings from several major neuroimaging studies, enabling the authors to connect neural correlates of deceptive behavior with specific cognitive mechanisms. Finally, they advise deception researchers to expand their methods and examine deception in different contexts. Preliminary data from a study is reported that supports their suggestion. They finish the paper by considering the legal implications of deception research as well as providing suggestions for improving future research.

References

Abe, N., Fujii, T., Hirayama, K., Takeda, A., Hosokai, Y., Ishioka, T., … Mori, E. (2009). Do Parkinsonian patients have trouble telling lies? The neurobiological basis of deceptive behaviour. *Brain, 132*(5), 1386–1395.

Ahern, E. C., Lyon, T. D., & Quas, J. A. (2011). Young children's emerging ability to make false statements. *Developmental Psychology, 47*(1), 61–66.

Allen, J. J., & Iacono, W. G. (1997). A comparison of methods for the analysis of event-related potentials in deception detection. *Psychophysiology, 34*(2), 234–240.

Allen, J. J., Iacono, W. G., & Danielson, K. D. (1992). The identification of concealed memories using the event-related potential and implicit behavioral measures: A methodology for prediction in the face of individual differences. *Psychophysiology, 29*, 504–522.

Asahi, S., Okamoto, Y., Okada, G., Yamawaki, S., & Yokota, N. (2004). Negative correlation between right prefrontal activity during response. *European Archives of Psychiatry and Clinical Neuroscience, 254*, 245–251.

Bhatt, S., Mbwana, J., Adeyemo, A., Sawyer, A., Hailu, A., & Vanmeter, J. (2009). Lying about facial recognition: An fMRI study. *Brain and Cognition, 69*(2), 382–390.

Braver, T. S., Barch, D. M., Gray, J. R., Molfese, D. L., & Snyder, A. (2001). Anterior cingulate cortex and response conflict: Effects of frequency, inhibition, and errors. *Cerebral Cortex, 11*, 825–836.

Broadbent, D. E., Cooper, P. F., Fitzgerald, P., & Parkes, K. R. (1982). The Cognitive Failures Questionnaire (CFQ) and its correlates. *British Journal of Clinical Psychology, 21*, 1–16.

Bunge, S. A., Ochsner, K. N., Desmond, J. E., Glover, G. H., & Gabrieli, J. D. (2001). Prefrontal regions involved in keeping information in and out of mind. *Brain, 124,* 2074–2086.

Bussey, K. (1992). Children's Lying and Truthfulness: Implications. In S. J. Ceci, M. D. Leichtman, & M. Putnick, *Cognitive and social factors in early deception* (pp. 89–110). Hillsdale, NJ: Erlbaum.

Carlson, S. M., Moses, L. J., & Hix, H. R. (1998). The role of inhibitory processes in young children's difficulties with deception and false belief. *Child Development, 69*(3), 672–691.

Christ, S. E., Van Essen, D. C., Watson, J. M., Brubaker, L. E., & McDermott, K. B. (2009). The contribution of prefrontal cortex and executive control to deception: Evidence from activatin likelihood estimate meta analyses. *Cerebral Cortex, 19*(7), 1557–1566.

Comerchero, M. D., & Polich, J. (1999). P3a and P3b from typical auditory and visual stimuli. *Clinical Neurophysiology, 110*(1), 24–30.

Donchin, E., & Coles, M. G. (1988). Is the P300 component a manifestation of context updating? *Behavioral and Brain Sciences, 11,* 357–427.

Farwell, L. A., & Donchin, E. (1991). The truth will out: Interrogative polygraphy ("lie detection") with event-related brain potentials. *Psychophysiology, 28*(5), 531–547.

Fullam, R. S., McKie, S., & Dolan, M. C. (2009). Psychopathic traits and deception: Functional magnetic resonance imaging study. *The British Journal of Psychiatry, 194*(3), 229–235.

Gabrieli, J. (2005). Personal communication (July).

Ganis, G., Kosslyn, S. M., Stose, S., Thompson, W. L., & Yurgelun-Todd, D. A. (2003). Neural correlates of different types of deception: An fMRI investigation. *Cerebral Cortex, 13*(8), 830–836.

Garavan, H., Ross, T. J., & Stein, E. A. (1999). Right hemispheric dominance of inhibitory control: An event-related functional mri study. *Proceedings of the National Academy of Sciences, 96,* 8301–8306.

Giammarco, E., Atkinson, B., Baughman, H. M., Veselka, L., & Vernon, P. A. (2013). The relation between antisocial personality and the perceived ability to deceive. *Personality and Individual Differences, 54*(2), 246–250.

Jiang, W., Liu, H., Liao, J., Ma, X., Rong, P., Tang, Y., & Wang, W. (2013). A functional MRI study of deception among offenders with antisocial personality disorders. *Neuroscience, 244,* 90–98.

Kaylor-Hughes, C. J., Lankappa, S. T., Fung, R., Hope-Urwin, A. E., Wilkinson, I. D., & Spence, S. A. (2011). The functional anatomical distinction between truth telling and deception is preserved among people with schizophrenia. *Criminal Behaviour and Mental Health, 21*(1), 8–20.

Konishe, S., Nakajima, K., Uchida, I., Kikyo, H., Kameyama, M., & Miyashita, Y. (1999). Common inhibitory mechanism in human inferior prefrontal cortex revealed by event-related functional mri. *Brain, 122,* 981–991.

Kozel, F. A., Padgett, T. M., & George, M. S. (2004a). A replication study of the neural correlates of deception. *Behavioral Neuroscience, 118*(4), 852–856.

Kozel, F. A., Revell, L. J., Lorberbaum, J. P., Shastri, A., Elhai, J. D., & Horner, M. D. (2004b). A pilot study of functional magnetic resonance imaging brain correlates of deception in healthy young men. *16,* 295–305.

Langleben, D. D., Schroeder, L., Maldjian, J. A., Gur, R. C., McDonald, S., Ragland, J. D., ... Childress, A. R. (2002). Brain activity during simulated deception: An event-related functional magnetic resonance study. *NeuroImage, 15*(3), 727–732.

Lee, K., Talwar, V., McCarthy, A., Ross, I., Evans, A., & Arruda, C. (2014). Can classic moral stories promote honesty in children? *Psychological Science, 25*(8), 1630–1636.

Lee, T. M., ling Liu, H., hai Tan, L., Chan, C. C., Mahankali, S., mei Feng, C., ... Hong Gao, J. (2002). Lie detection by functional magnetic resonance imaging. *Human Brain Mapping, 164*(3), 157–164.

Leekam, S. R., & Perner, J. (1991). Does the autistic child have a metarepresentational deficit? *Cognition, 40*(3), 203-218.

Leslie, A. M. (1994). Pretending and believing: Issues in the theory of ToMM. *Cognition, 50*(1), 211–238.

Li, A. S., Kelley, E. A., Evans, A. D., & Lee, K. (2011). Exploring the ability to deceive in children with autism spectrum disorders. *Journal of Autism and Developmental Disorders, 41*(2), 185–195.

Little, P. F., Kiehl, K. A., & Smith, A. M. (2001). Event-related fMRI study of response inhibition. *Human Brain Mapping, 10*, 120–131.

Loeber, R., Burke, J., & Pardini, D. (2009). Perspectives on oppositional defiant disorder, conduct disorder, and psychopathic features. *Journal of Child Psychology and Psychiatry, 50*(1–2), 133–142.

Mazza, M., De Risio, A., Tozzini, C., Roncone, R., & Casacchia, M. (2003). Machiavellianism an theory of mind in people affected by schizophrenia. *Brain and Cognition, 51*(3), 262–269.

McCann, J. T. (1998). *Malingering and deception in adolescents: Assessing credibility in clinical and forensic settings.* American Psychological Association.

Meek, S. W., Phillips, M. C., Boswell, C. P., & Vendemia, J. M. (2013). Deception and the misinformation effect: An Event-Related Potential study. *International Journal of Psychophysiology, 87*(1), 81–87.

Menza, M. (2000). The personality associated with Parkinson's disease. *Current Psychiatry Reports, 2*(5), 421–426.

Miller, A. R., & Rosenfeld, J. P. (2004). Response-specific scalp distributions in deception detection and ERP correlates of psychopathic personality traits. *Journal of Psychophysiology, 18*(1), 13–26.

Mohamed, F., Faro, S., Gordon, N., Platek, S., Ahmad, H., & Williams, J. (2006). Brain mapping of deception and truth telling about an ecologically valid situation: Functional MR imaging and polygraph invstigation—initial experience. *Radiology, 238*, 679–688.

Newton, P., Reddy, V., & Bull, R. (2000). Children's everyday deception and performance on false-belief tasks. *British Journal of Developmental Psychology, 18*(2), 297–317.

Olanow, C. W., & Tatton, W. G. (1999). Etiology and pathogenesis of Parkinson's disease. *Annual Review of Neuroscience, 22*(1), 123–144.

Ostrov, J. M., Ries, E. E., Stauffacher, K., Godleski, S. A., & Mullins, A. D. (2008). Relational aggression, physical aggression and deception during early childhood: A multimethod, multi-informant short-term longitudinal study. *Journal of Clinical Child & Adolescent Psychology*, 664–675.

Peskin, J. (1992). Ruse and representations: On children's ability to conceal information. *Developmental Psychology, 28*(1), 84–89.

Pezdek, K., Morrow, A., Blandon-Gitlin, I., Goodman, G. S., Quas, J. A., Saywitz, K. J., ... Brodie, L. (2004). Detecting deception in children: Event familiarity affects criterion-based content analysis ratings. *Journal of Applied Psychology, 89*(1), 119–126.

Ramnani, N., & Owen, A. M. (2004). The anterior prefrontal cortex: What can functional imaging tell us about function? *Nature Reviews: Neuroscience, 5*, 184–194.

Ranick, J., Persicke, A., Tarbox, J., & Kornack, J. A. (2013). Teaching children with autism to detect and respond to deceptive statements. *Research in Autism Spectrum Disorders, 7*(4), 503–508.

Rosenfeld, J. P., Ellwanger, J. W., Nolan, K., Wu, S., Bermann, R. G., & Sweet, J. (1999). P300 scalp amplitude distribution as an index of deception in a simulated cognitive deficit model. *International Journal of Psychophysiology, 33*, 3–19.

Rubia, K. R. (2001). Mapping motor inhibition: Conjunction brain activations across different versions of go/no-go and stop tasks. *NeuroImage, 13*, 250-261.

Ruchkin, D. S., Johnson, R., Canoune, H. L., Ritter, W., & Hammer, M. (1990). Multiple sources of the p3b associated with different types of information. *Psychophysiology, 27,* 157–176.

Russell, J., Mauthner, N., Sharpe, S., & Tidswell, T. (1991). The "windows task" as a measure of strategic deception in preschoolers and autistic subjects. *British Journal of Developmental Psychology, 9*(2), 331–349.

Sodian, B., & Frith, U. (1992). Deception and sabotage in autistic, retarded and normal children. *Journal of Child Psychology and Psychiatry, 33*(3), 591–605.

Spence, S. A., Farrow, T. F., Herford, A. E., Wilkinson, I. D., Zheng, Y., & Woodruff, P. W. (2001). Behavioural and functional anatomical correlates of deception in humans. *Neuroreport, 12*(13), 2849–2853.

Stelmack, R. M., Houlihan, M., Doucet, C., & Belisle, M. (1994). Event-related potentials and the detection of deception: A two-stimulus paradigm. *Psychophysiology, 7,* s94.

Sullivan, R., & Allen, J. (1999). Social deficits associated with schizophrenia defined in terms of interpersonal Machiavellianism. *Acta Psichiatrica Scandinavica, 99*(2), 148–154.

Talwar, V., & Crossman, A. (2011). From little white lies to filthy liars: The evolution of honesty and deception in young children. *Advances in Child Development and Behaviour, 40,* 139–179.

Talwar, V., Zwaigenbaum, L., Goulden, K. J., Manji, S., Loomes, C., & Rasmussen, C. (2012). Lie-telling behavior in children with autism and its relation to false-belief understanding. *Focus on Autism and Other Developmental Disabilities, 27*(2), 122–129.

Tuvblad, C., Bezdjian, S., Raine, A., & Baker, L. A. (2013). Psychopathic personality and negative parent-to-child affect: A longitudinal cross-lag twin study. *Journal of Criminal Justice, 41*(5), 331–341.

Vendemia, J. M., & Buzan, R. F. (2004a). HD-ERP correlates of workload during deception in two mock crime paradigms. *Poster presented at the 11th annual Cognitive Neuroscience Society (CNS) meeting.* San Francisco, CA.

Vendemia, J. M., & Buzan, R. F. (2004b). Mapping the brain during deception: Extended studies of deception using hd-ERP and fMRI. *Paper presented at the Annual Meeting of the American Polygraph Association.* Orlando, FL.

Vendemia, J. M., Buzan, R. F., & Simon-Dack, S. L. (2005). Reaction time of motor responses in two-stimulus paradigms involving deception and congruity with varying levels of difficulty. *Behavioural Neurology, 16*(1), 25–36.

Vendemia, J. M., Schillaci, M. J., Buzan, R. F., Green, E. P., & Meek, S. W. (2009). Alternate technologies for the Detection of Deception. In D. Wilcox (Ed.), *The use of the polygraph in assessing, treating and supervising sex offenders: A practitioner's guide* (pp. 267–296). Chichester, UK: John Wiley & Sons.

Wallace, W., Mullen, P., & Burgess, P. (2004). Criminal offending in schizophrenia over a 25-year period marked by deinstitutionalisation and increasing prevalence of co-morbid substance use disorders. *The American Journal of Psychiatry, 161,* 716–727.

Wang, C. S., Galinsky, A. D., & Murnighan, J. K. (2009). Bad drives psychological reactions, but good propels behavior responses to honesty and deception. *Psychological Science, 20*(5), 634–644.

Part III
Neurobiology of Offending

9

The Neurobiological Underpinnings of Psychopathy

Stéphane A. De Brito[1] and Ian J. Mitchell

> **Key points**
> - This chapter provides an overview of recent neuroscience research that has examined the neurobiological underpinnings of adult psychopathy and psychopathic tendencies in antisocial youths.
> - First, the syndrome of psychopathy, its assessment, common misconceptions, and two prominent subtyping approaches to psychopathy will be described.
> - This will be followed by a section on the downward extension of this construct to antisocial youths as operationalized by the construct of callous-unemotional traits (see also Chapter 18).
> - Next, evidence from studies that have examined the neurobiological correlates of adult psychopathy and callous-unemotional traits in antisocial youths, including autonomic, neuroendocrine, neuropsychological, structural and functional brain imaging, will be reviewed and the extent to which they have shed light the underpinnings and development of and the core features of the syndrome will be discussed.
> - Finally, methodological consideration of this research will be highlighted and future directions will be identified.
> - In the chapter, it is also noted that:
>   - psychopathy is not synonymous with antisocial personality disorder;
>   - variants of psychopaths have been identified, with the most common ones being primary versus secondary psychopaths and successful versus unsuccessful psychopaths;
>   - not all psychopaths are criminal offenders, but those who are commit violent crimes and have higher recidivism rate;
>   - psychopathy is associated with diminished bodily responses to emotional stimuli.

The Wiley Blackwell Handbook of Forensic Neuroscience, First Edition. Edited by Anthony R. Beech, Adam J. Carter, Ruth E. Mann and Pia Rotshtein.
© 2018 John Wiley & Sons Ltd. Published 2018 by John Wiley & Sons Ltd.

Terminology Explained

Affective decision making involves considering a number of possible options, estimating the likelihood of getting reward or punishment for each, and then choosing the most beneficial option. Poor decision makers may show a bias towards receiving reward and attach less significance to the likelihood of punishment. Often tested by gambling tasks such as the Iowa gambling task (see below).

The **autonomic nervous system** is the part of the nervous system responsible for control of unconsciously controlled or involuntary bodily functions, such as breathing, the heartbeat, and digestive processes, as well as reflex reactions. It contains the sympathetic nervous system, often termed the "fight or flight" system.

Diffusion tensor imaging (DTI) (a type of diffusion MRI) is a neuroimaging technique that uses water diffusion to map out white matter tracts in the brain.

Electrodermal activity (EDA), historically known as galvanic skin response (GSR) as well as various other terms, is an indication of stress (arousal of the sympathetic nervous system) in the body by appearing as continuous variation in the electrical characteristics of the skin.

Extinction tasks require the participant to stop responding to an initially rewarded stimulus when rewards cease.

The **fusiform gyrus** is a ridge in the lower part of the temporal lobe. Its functions are linked with various neural pathways related to recognition and visual processing. That is, it is involved in processes such as recognizing faces and facial expressions, and in categorizing objects, as well as tasks such as recognizing numbers, words, and colors. In relation to psychopathy, the fusiform gyrus has particularly been of interest in establishing weaker responses for recognition of facial expression.

The **Iowa gambling task** is an experimental task to assess decision making and how participants weigh up reward versus penalty. Participants are presented with four virtual decks of cards and told that they can win money from choosing certain cards but that others incur a penalty. Of the four decks, two lead to wins over time and two lead to losses over time. Over time, most participants learn which deck of cards bring rewards, and get better at choosing them routinely. However, some participants continue to choose "bad" decks, showing an apparent desire for reward that overcomes a sensitivity to punishment. The task is used to measure affective decision making (see above).

Oxytocin is a neurohormone. It is released directly into the blood system where it can act as a hormone as well as being released into the brain where it can act as a neurotransmitter. It is popularly known as the "love hormone" because it is released during orgasm, childbirth, and breastfeeding, and is involved in social connection, bonding, trust, empathy, and altruism.

Response reversal tasks require the participant to learn that, during the presentation of a pair of stimuli, one stimulus is rewarded and the other is not. They then must adapt to reversed response-reinforcement contingencies, in which the previously unrewarded stimulus is now rewarded, and vice versa (Baxter & Browning, 2007).

Triiodothyronine (T3) is a thyroid hormone. It affects almost every physiological process in the body, including growth and development, metabolism, body temperature, and heart rate.

The **ventromedial prefrontal cortex (vmPFC)** is a part of the prefrontal cortex in the brain. It is located in the frontal lobe at the bottom of the cerebral hemispheres and is implicated in the processing of risk and fear. It also plays a role in the inhibition of emotional responses, and in the process of decision making.

Introduction

Any handbook of forensic neuroscience without a chapter on psychopathy would be incomplete. Indeed, psychopathy has been defined as the "single most important clinical construct in the criminal justice system" (Hare, 1998, p. 189) and by others as the most important forensic concept of the 21st century (Monahan, 2006). This is because psychopathy has been found to provide high predictive validity when it comes to risk assessment for violence and recidivism, institutional adjustment, and assessment of treatment suitability (Douglas, Vincent, & Edens, 2006; Harris & Rice, 2006).

There is indeed a considerable amount of evidence showing that a diagnosis of psychopathy is linked to a heightened propensity for violent behavior and that the psychopathy severity is also positively associated with violent crimes and physically aggressive behavior (Hare, Clark, Grann, & Thornton, 2000; Porter & Woodworth, 2006). This association has been shown in different populations (i.e., prisoners and forensic patients), contexts (community and institution), and using different measures of physical aggression (criminal convictions and self-report).

Offenders with psychopathy, as compared to those without, have more often been convicted of at least one violent crime (Hare & McPherson, 1984), have a higher number of convictions or charges for violent offences overall (Hare & McPherson, 1984; Kosson, Lorenz, & Newman, 2006; Kosson, Smith, & Newman, 1990; Porter, Birt, & Boer, 2001; Serin, 1991), and have more charges and more convictions for violent crimes per year spent in the community (Hare & Jutai, 1983; Hare & McPherson, 1984). In terms of recidivism, a review of the literature found that within one year of release psychopaths were approximately three times more likely to reoffend and four times more likely to violently reoffend than non-psychopaths (Hemphill, Hare, & Wong, 1998). As a result, psychopathy has been described as a "socially devastating disorder" (Hare, 1998, p. 188).

Before discussing the neuroscientific evidence on psychopathy, we will describe the scope of the studies that were reviewed for this chapter. Here, we will mostly focus on studies where the authors investigated either antisocial adults with psychopathy or high psychopathic traits using the Psychopathy Checklist-Revised (PCL-R; (Hare, 2003), and its derivatives (e.g., the Psychopathy Checklist: Screening Version; Hart, Cox, & Hare, 1995) or antisocial youths with callous-unemotional traits. As a result, recent neuroscientific evidence on antisocial traits (e.g., violence, aggression, or impulsivity) or antisocial populations (antisocial personality disorder (ASPD) and conduct disorder (CD))[2] often including, but not specific to, psychopathy is not reviewed. As noted by Koenigs, Kruepke, and Newman (2010), while these constructs may overlap with that of psychopathy, they are not unique to psychopathy and thus may not provide unique information about the neurobiological correlates of psychopathy. Indeed, it has been argued that violent and antisocial youths and adults are heterogeneous, with many presenting with comorbid mood and anxiety disorders (see De Brito & Hodgins, 2009a), and therefore a specific focus on the more homogenous subgroup with psychopathy might bring us closer to unravelling the neurobiology of the disorder (Blair, 2013).

Psychopathy: From Definition Through Assessment to Misconceptions

Psychopathy is a syndrome characterized by a constellation of affective, interpersonal, and behavioral features (Cleckley, 1941; Hare, 2003). The clinical description of this personality disorder can be summarized as follows: interpersonally, psychopaths are arrogant, superficial, grandiose, and manipulative; affectively, they lack empathy, guilt, or remorse and have shallow affect; behaviorally, they are irresponsible, impulsive, and thrill seekers (Hare, 1998). The conceptualization that has dominated contemporary research, forensic and clinical practice is the construct assessed by the PCL-R (Hare, 2003). This instrument was developed based on the clinical description of psychopathy provided by the American psychiatrist Hervey Cleckley (1941) in his seminal book the *Mask of Sanity*. The PCL-R is a clinical rating scale consisting of 20 items used to make a diagnosis of psychopathy.

Originally the PCL-R was developed to assess a putatively unitary construct, but early factor analytic work has yielded a two-factor structure indicating that psychopathy, as defined by this rating scale, is underpinned by two correlated dimensions (Hare, 1991). **Factor 1** includes items indexing the interpersonal and affective features of psychopathy (charm, grandiosity, and deceitfulness/conning; absence of remorse, empathy, and emotional depth; and blame externalization), while **Factor 2** includes items assessing a chronic antisocial lifestyle (early behavior problems and juvenile delinquency, impulsivity, irresponsibility, and lack of long-term goals). More recently, Hare (2003) proposed a four-facet model in which the original Factors 1 and 2 are each parsed into two separate facets: Factor 1 into an arrogant and deceitful interpersonal style (**Facet 1**) and deficient affective experience (**Facet 2**); and Factor 2 into impulsive, irresponsible, parasitic lifestyle (**Facet 3**), and antisocial manifestations (**Facet 4**). Each item is scored on a three-point rating scale based on information collected from prison files and a semi-structured interview conducted by a trained person. When an interview is not possible, however, ratings can be completed based on file information alone. Scores on the PCL-R range from 0 to 40. In North America, the cutoff for the diagnosis of psychopathy is 30 or higher, whereas in Europe it is 25 (Cooke & Michie, 1997).

We shall see below that for those studies that have taken a group approach (i.e., psychopaths versus non-psychopaths), a number have relied on different cutoff scores to define their psychopathy group, which has implications for the interpretation of the results and possibly partly explains some of the inconsistent findings across studies. The question of whether psychopathy identifies a distinct category or taxon (qualitatively different from the healthy individual) or exists along a continuum (quantitatively different) is an ongoing question, but as Skeem, Polaschek, Patrick, and Lilienfeld (2011) have noted, there is now a good deal of evidence that "psychopathy is a dimensional trait or configuration of traits rather than a discrete category (or taxon)" (p. 101). That is, "despite the routine use of PCL-R cutoff scores for diagnosing psychopathy, available data indicate that psychopathic individuals differ from other people in degree rather than in kind" (Skeem et al., 2011, p. 102). Thus, we will see that the neuroscientific literature on psychopathy includes studies that have considered psychopathy as a category and, accordingly, used the group comparison approach, while others have relied on the dimensional approach where psychopathy scores are related to neuroscientific measures through correlation or regression analyses.

At this stage, three common misconceptions regarding the phenotypic characteristics of psychopathy need to be briefly discussed (Skeem et al., 2011). First, although the most widely used measure of psychopathy in forensic settings – the PCL-R – includes several items that are associated with an increased risk of violence and antisocial behavior, these are not defining features of the disorder and indeed there is evidence that many psychopathic individuals, often referred to as "successful psychopaths," do not have a history of criminal convictions or of violence (Hall & Benning, 2006).

Second, often lay people think that psychopaths are completely irrational and out of touch with reality, probably because the words psychopath and psychotic are so similar (Skeem et al., 2011). However, while there is evidence that psychosis and psychopathy are highly comorbid, especially in forensic settings (Bo et al., 2013), the characteristics of individuals with psychopathy alone and those with only psychosis are different. In contrast to psychotic individuals, psychopaths are rational, not delusional, and they appreciate the distinction between right and wrong, but they just do not care about the consequence of their immoral behavior (Cima, Tonnaer, & Hauser, 2010).

Third, often the diagnosis of ASPD and that of psychopathy are considered synonymous and many articles and chapters purporting to focus on ASPD in fact review findings about offenders with psychopathy (De Brito & Hodgins, 2009a; see also Chapter 10). While both psychopathy and ASPD include a life-long pattern of antisocial behavior that begins in childhood, those offenders who are designated as psychopaths also have an emotional impairment evidenced by a lack of empathy, callousness, shallow affect and a failure to take responsibility for their actions, and an interpersonal style involving grandiosity, glibness, superficial charm, and the manipulation of others (Hart & Hare, 1996). Consequently, the relationship between psychopathy and ASPD is asymmetric in that about 90% of offenders with a diagnosis of psychopathy would meet criteria for a diagnosis of ASPD, while only about 25% of individuals with a diagnosis of ASPD meet criteria for psychopathy (Hare, 2003).

Despite the fact that Cleckley (1941) conceptualized psychopathy as a single syndrome and the fact that in his book *The Mask of Sanity* he devoted little attention to the possibility of distinct subtypes of psychopaths, the cases he described clearly suggest that subtypes of psychopaths exist (Patrick, 2007). There is now a growing body of evidence, which indeed suggests that individuals with psychopathy can be divided into variants (Poythress & Skeem, 2006; Skeem, Johansson, Andershed, Kerr, & Louden, 2007). In Box 9.1 we briefly describe two of the most prominent ones to have been investigated in recent neuroscientific investigations: primary versus secondary psychopathy and successful versus unsuccessful psychopaths.

> **Box 9.1** Variants of psychopathy
>
> *Primary versus secondary psychopathy* With his seminal distinction between primary and secondary psychopathy, Karpman (1941) was among the first to suggest that there are variants of psychopathy. According to this author, these two variants are phenotypically similar. However, primary psychopath's affective deficit is constitutional (heritable) in nature, whereas the affective disturbance of the secondary psychopath is the result of early – environmentally acquired – psychosocial adversity such as parental abuse or rejection. Furthermore, Karpman considered the secondary psychopath to be more anxious and emotionally volatile than the primary psychopath who in contrast presents with poverty of emotional expression and low levels of anxiety. Not surprisingly, the two variants were also considered to differ in their patterns of aggression, with the primary psychopath characterized by instrumental/proactive aggression while secondary psychopaths' aggressive behavior was considered to be more reactive and motivated by hate and revenge (Poythress & Skeem, 2006). In the last decade, a corpus of studies that have used various designs, variables, and data analytic strategies have supported this distinction by identifying groups of psychopaths exhibiting affective and behavioral characteristics consistent with these two variants (see Skeem et al., 2011).
>
> *Successful versus unsuccessful psychopaths* This distinction was first coined by Adrian Raine's lab, who compared autonomic stress reactivity and executive functions of successful psychopaths (those without a history of criminal convictions) and unsuccessful psychopaths (those with a conviction record) (Ishikawa, Raine, Lencz, Bihrle, & LaCasse, 2001). As we will see, a limited amount of research conducted over the last decade has compared the two groups and suggests that successful psychopaths are characterized by intact or enhanced neurobiological functioning, which might act as a protective factor, enabling them to avoid the most risky and overt criminal activities and thus avoid arrest, conviction, and incarceration (Gao & Raine, 2010).

Conduct Problems and Callous-Unemotional Traits: Psychopathy in Youth

The fact that most offenders with psychopathy have a long history of antisocial behavior dating back to childhood (e.g., Marshall & Cooke, 1999) is consistent with the view that personality disorders exhibit their first manifestations in childhood or late adolescence to continue into adulthood (American Psychiatric Association, 2013; World Health Organization, 1992; see also Chapter 18 for a further discussion of these issues). Coinciding with the publication year of the *Diagnostic and Statistical Manual of Mental Disorder* fourth edition (*DSM-IV*) over 20 years ago (American Psychiatric Association, 1994), in 1994 Paul Frick and colleagues published the first paper extending to youths the construct of psychopathy as defined by the PCL-R, thereby marking the beginning of a new approach to subtyping youths with severe conduct problems (Frick, O'Brien, Wootton, & McBurnett, 1994). This approach differentiates between youths with conduct problems with high levels of callous-unemotional traits (CP/HCU) and those with low levels of these traits (CP/LCU) (Frick & Marsee, 2006). This distinction in youths mirrors the distinction made within samples of antisocial adults between those who only meet diagnostic criteria for ASPD and those who, in addition to meeting diagnostic criteria for ASPD, also meet diagnostic criteria for psychopathy (Hare, 1998; Patrick, 2006). Indeed, callous-unemotional traits include a lack of guilt, lack of empathy, and shallow affect, which constitute the core characteristics in most conceptualizations of adult psychopathy (Cleckley, 1941; Hare, 1998). Historically and conceptually, this subtyping approach has sought to establish a downward extension of the construct of psychopathy and stems from research on adult psychopathy (Frick & Marsee, 2006).

As discussed already, the construct of psychopathy in adult samples has gained impressive face validity due primarily to its ability to designate a particular severe and violent group of offenders (Porter & Woodworth, 2006). Similarly, there is substantial evidence from research conducted among prison, clinic-referred, and community samples that callous-unemotional traits also designate an important subgroup of antisocial youths characterized by more severe conduct problems, aggressive and violent behavior, and delinquency (Frick, Ray, Thornton, & Kahn, 2014). While the majority of these studies have been cross-sectional, there is also evidence that callous-unemotional traits predict later delinquency and antisocial and aggressive behaviors (Frick et al., 2014). Finally, research has shown that youths with CP/HCU traits display higher levels of both reactive and instrumental aggression than youths with CP/LCU traits whose aggressive behavior tends to be reactive (Frick et al., 2014). This ever-growing evidence base regarding the incremental validity of callous-unemotional traits in identifying a distinct subgroup among antisocial youths has culminated in their inclusion in the *DSM-5* (American Psychiatric Association, 2013) under the form of the specifier "With Limited Pro-social Emotions" for the diagnosis of CD.

As we shall see, in addition to presenting behavioral and temperamental characteristics consistent with the syndrome of adult psychopathy, youths with CP/HCU traits also show autonomic, neuroendocrine, and neurocognitive features consistent with the disorder. Thus, since psychopathy is considered by some to be a neurodevelopmental disorder (Blair, Peschardt, Budhani, Mitchell, & Pine, 2006; Raine, Lee, Yang, & Colletti, 2010), it is thought that youths with CP/HCU traits constitute a group at possible risk of developing the full-blown adult syndrome of psychopathy (Blair et al., 2006; Frick et al., 2014).

Autonomic Abnormalities in Psychopathy

There is an assumed close relationship between the experiencing of emotions and the autonomic nervous system and the endocrine system. This reflects the assumption that emotions represent cognitive interpretations of physiological changes made in response to arousing stimuli. The non-emotionality of psychopaths, and in particular, their lack of fear in anticipation of aversive stimuli, would be predicted to reflect poor autonomic nervous system functioning. Considerable evidence has demonstrated that this is indeed the case (Lorber, 2004). Most studies exploring these issues have focused on heart rate, electrodermal responses, and startle responses. We will now examine these in more detail.

Heart rate

Low resting heart rate has long been associated with a propensity to aggressive, antisocial behavior (see Armstrong, Keller, Franklin, & Macmillan, 2009). Such abnormalities are particularly apparent in convicted psychopaths (Armstrong et al., 2009; Arnett, Howland, Smith, & Newman, 1993; Patrick, 2008; Pham, Philippot, & Rime, 2000). Psychopaths also show reduced cardiovascular reactivity to emotionally salient stimuli such as stressors and punishments (Arnett et al., 1993; Ishikawa et al., 2001; Patrick, 2008; Pham et al., 2000). For example, Pham et al. (2000) demonstrated that psychopaths show lower blood pressure before and during emotional stimulation while Arnett et al. (1993) found that psychopaths have lower heart rate following punishment feedback than controls. The cardiovascular abnormalities seen in psychopaths are generally assumed to be linked to Factor 1 of the PCL-R and are assumed be related to a fearlessness and sensation-seeking temperament (Dindo & Fowles, 2011).

The abnormalities may reflect interactions between the autonomic nervous system and the functioning of brain circuits that exert high-level influence on visceral functioning. Such circuits include structures such as the prefrontal cortex, anterior cingulate, and hypothalamus, some of which are also implicated in psychopathy. This postulated relationship is supported by the work of Gao, Raine, and Schug (2012) who showed that high PCL-R scores were associated with individuals' weak ability to identify and recognize their own bodily states following the application of a social stressor. However, it has also been suggested that poor cardiovascular reactivity is not a characteristic feature of psychopaths per se, but rather it is a marker of unsuccessful psychopaths (Ishikawa et al., 2001). As psychopathy is considered to be a developmental disorder, similar idiosyncratic patterns of cardiovascular output would be expected to be found in youths with CP/HCU traits. There is evidence to support the position. Youths with antisocial, aggressive tendencies and an early tendency toward externalizing behavior problems have low resting heart rates (Gao, Baker, Raine, Wu, & Bezdjian, 2009; Patrick, 2008).

The relationship between cardiovascular reactivity and Factor 2 of the PCL-R is less clear-cut. Autonomic abnormalities have been observed in offenders who scored highly on Factor 2 (chronic antisocial lifestyle) of the PCL-R (Patrick, Cuthbert, & Lang, 1994). However, several studies have also shown that reactive and impulsive aggression is related to cardiovascular hyper-reactivity (Lorber, 2004). This effect may reflect a tendency for aggressive behaviors to be elicited from individuals with emotional instability and poor vagal control whereby the parasympathetic division of the autonomic nervous system is not sufficiently potent to return the heart to its normal resting level (Patrick, 2008).

Electrodermal activity

The sweat glands, activity of which underlies variations in electrodermal activity, are under similar autonomic control to the cardiovascular system. It would be predicted, therefore, that psychopaths would also show abnormalities in electrodermal responsivity. Considerable support for this position has been found. For example, the meta-analysis of Lorber (2004) concluded that low resting levels of electrodermal activity are shown by psychopaths, sociopaths, and youths with conduct problems. Similarly, psychopaths show poor electrodermal responsivity when anticipating punishments and in aversive conditioning tasks (Arnett, 1997; Patrick, 2008; Rothemund et al., 2012) and psychopathic prone youths show weak anticipatory response to aversive white noise (Fung et al., 2005). This inability to initiate appropriate autonomic responses to the anticipation of aversive stimuli leaves psychopaths unresponsive to threats of punishment (Arnett, 1997). Some evidence suggests that hypo-electrodermal activity is related to Factor 1 (interpersonal and affective features) of the PCL-R (Dindo & Fowles, 2011; Fowles, 2000; Lorber, 2004) whereas high scores on Factor 2 are predictive of hyper-electrodermal activity (Dindo & Fowles, 2011; Lorber, 2004).

Startle response

The hyporeactive autonomic responses of psychopaths are reflected in reduced startle responses in response to exposure to emotionally significant stimuli. For example, psychopaths fail to display the normal exaggerated blink potentiation when viewing unpleasant images (Pastor, Molto, Vila, & Lang, 2003; Patrick, Bradley, & Lang, 1993). These abnormalities appear to be related to the affective features of psychopathy rather than the antisocial aspects of the condition. Similar observations have been made in non-offenders with psychopathic traits (Anderson, Wan, Young, & Stanford, 2011; Benning, Patrick, & Iacono, 2005; Newman, Curtin, Bertsch, & Baskin-Sommers, 2010) and in youths with CP/HCU traits (Syngelaki, Fairchild, Moore, Savage, & van Goozen, 2013).

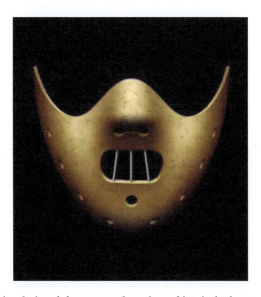

Hannibal *Hannibal is a fictional character, a forensic psychiatrist by day profession, who epitomizes the ultimate psychopathic personality. He was first described in a book called The Red Dragon by Thomas Harris in 1981 and has since been adopted by multiple films and TV series.*

Source: © Alhovik. Used under license from 123RF.

Endocrine Abnormalities in Psychopathy

Abnormalities in endocrine activity in relation to psychopathy have been reported. Such abnormalities might be predicted as some endocrine responses are influenced by similar high-level control processes to those that regulate autonomic responses. The hormonal systems most strongly implicated in psychopathy are the corticosteroid and thyroid systems.

Cortisol abnormalities

Cortisol is the major corticosteroid in humans. Under normal circumstances cortisol is released on a strong daily rhythm such that blood levels surge just before waking, and again in the early evening. The release of cortisol is ultimately controlled by the hypothalamus. The hypothalamus releases a hormone (CRF), which acts on the pituitary causing it to release another hormone (ACTH), which acts on the adrenal cortex to release cortisol. Strong stressors also cause the levels of cortisol to surge. Indeed, cortisol acts on the amygdala to potentiate fear responses (Reidy, Shelley-Tremblay, & Lilienfeld, 2011). Many patients with clinical depression show continuously elevated levels of cortisol or abnormalities with the daily pattern of release. The lack of arousal shown by psychopaths in situations, which would normally be considered threatening might be expected to be associated with lower levels of cortisol. Evidence to support this association has indeed been reported. For example, Van Honk, Schutter, Hermans, and Putman (2003) showed that low levels of cortisol are related to psychopathy, and argues that this may predispose the individual to being relatively insensitive to punishments. Similarly, Cima, Smeets, and Jelicic (2008) showed that incarcerated psychopaths exhibit low diurnal cortisol concentrations.

Some equivalent relationships, in terms of low diurnal cortisol concentrations, have been seen in non-offenders with psychopathic traits (Reidy et al., 2011); but the relationship between cortisol levels and offending behavior in non-psychopaths is less clear-cut. Reidy et al. (2011) cite evidence to show that low cortisol levels are associated with CD rather than general antisocial behavior. Cima et al. (2008) produced some evidence to show that cortisol levels are actually raised in such individuals. Similarly, Decker (2000) showed that higher cortisol levels in Dominican villagers were related to various aspects of antisocial behavior. Conversely, Susman (2006) reported that cortisol levels are lower in aggressive and antisocial adult males and incarcerated males who were habitual violent offenders. Glenn, Raine, Schug, Gao, and Granger (2011) studied the potential relationships between cortisol and testosterone. They showed that psychopathy is associated with a high ratio of testosterone to cortisol. Testosterone is thought to inhibit the action of the hypothalamic-pituitary-adrenal system and autonomic nervous system, which could lead to a reduced sensitivity to punishments.

Thyroid dysfunction

A limited number of studies have revealed abnormalities in thyroid function in psychopaths. The major hormone secreted by the thyroid gland is the thyroxine (T4). This, however, is relatively inactive and is converted into the far more potent hormone triiodothyronine (T3). Two studies of convicted psychopaths showed that they had elevated levels of T3 relative to T4 (Soderstrom & Forsman, 2004; Stalenheim, von Knorring, & Wide, 1998). Similarly, Alm et al. (1996) showed that elevated levels of T3 are associated with psychopathy. These findings imply that increased peripheral deiodination, that is, the process by which the inactive thyroxine (T4) gets converted into the active hormone T3, may act as a biological marker of psychopathy.

Oxytocin levels

Boosting cerebral oxytocin levels is associated with enhancing several pro-social behaviors and emotions including trust (Kosfeld, Heinrichs, Zak, Fischbacher, & Fehr, 2005), empathy (Hurlemann et al., 2010), and altruism (Barraza, McCullough, Ahmadi, & Zak, 2011). Similarly, Dadds, Jambrak, Pasalich, Hawes, and Brennan (2011) have shown that deficits in the ability of youths with CD to recognize facial emotional expressions can be ameliorated by intranasal oxytocin. Accordingly, it would be strongly predicted that psychopaths would show low levels of cerebral oxytocin. To date, only one published studied has explored this issue. Mitchell et al. (2013) assayed the levels of urinary oxytocin, which can act as an index of cerebral levels, in a group of serious offenders. Surprisingly, the offending sample show dramatically raised oxytocin levels relative to non-offender controls. Furthermore, the oxytocin levels correlated very strongly with Factor 2 scores on the PCL-R.

The effects of oxytocin are mediated via interactions of the ligand with the oxytocin receptor. Only one form of the receptor is thought to exist though there are several different polymorphisms of the oxytocin receptor gene. These subtle genetic variations could result in differential responses from the oxytocin systems. The rs35576A variant has been associated with decreased levels of sociality and abnormalities in the structure and function of the amygdala (Tost et al., 2010). Equally, Malik, Zai, Abu, Nowrouzi, and Beitchman (2012) showed that other polymorphisms, rs6770632 and rs1042778, may be associated with extreme and pervasive aggressive behaviors in females and males, respectively. However, these polymorphisms do not appear to be related to callous-unemotional traits.

Neuropsychological Evidence

The neuropsychological literature on psychopathy is extensive and a detailed review is beyond the scope of this chapter (for reviews, see Blair et al., 2006; De Brito & Hodgins, 2009b; Rogers, 2006). Consequently, we will focus on the body of evidence pertaining to the role of the ventromedial prefrontal cortex (vmPFC) and the amygdala, two brain regions that are central to a host of processes that neuropsychological research has shown to be disrupted in adults with psychopathy and youths with CP/HCU traits. Later, we shall see that structural and functional neuroimaging investigations in individuals with psychopathy have provided additional support for abnormalities and dysfunctions within those regions, among others.

Since the case of Phineas Gage (see Chapter 1), observations on neurological damage have abounded in the literature demonstrating that the changes in personality and affect often manifest in aggressive behavior and poor decision making (Blair & Cipolotti, 2000; Grafman et al., 1996; Meyers, Berman, Scheibel, & Hayman, 1992).

For example, Meyers et al. (1992) described the case of a 33-year old man who received the diagnosis of "acquired antisocial personality disorder" (American Psychiatric Association, 1987) based on his personality changes (i.e., increased irresponsibility, impulsivity, poor decision making, and disinhibition) following unilateral left orbitofrontal lobe damage.

More recently, Blair and Cipolotti (2000) reported a case study of a 56-year old man who, following bilateral trauma to his orbitofrontal lobes and left amygdala, failed to conform to social norms and to accept responsibility for his actions, became notably irritable, impulsively aggressive, reckless, and showed lack of empathy. Based on these studies, along with clinical observations, researchers have coined terms such as "acquired sociopathy" or "pseudopsychopathy" to describe behavioral and personality characteristics that resemble those presented by individuals with psychopathy (Blumer & Benson, 1975; Damasio, 1994). One brain region that seems to be particularly implicated is the vmPFC; we will now briefly review putative problems in this area.

Evidence of vmPFC dysfunction

The vmPFC plays a crucial role in a wide range of processes including, but not limited to, affective decision making, response reversal, extinction, response inhibition, facial emotion recognition, and moral judgment (Heberlein, Padon, Gillihan, Farah, & Fellows, 2008; Koenigs et al., 2007; Wallis, 2007). Both adults with psychopathy and youths with CP/HCU traits have been shown to be impaired on tasks assessing affective decision making (Blair, Colledge, & Mitchell, 2001; De Brito, Viding, Kumari, Blackwood, & Hodgins, 2013; Molto, Poy, Segarra, Pastor, & Montanañé, 2007), response reversal (Budhani & Blair, 2005; Budhani, Richell, & Blair, 2006), extinction (Fisher & Blair, 1998; Newman, Patterson, & Kosson, 1987), facial emotion recognition (Dawel, O'Kearney, McKone, & Palermo, 2012), and moral judgment (R. J. R. Blair, 1997; Young, Koenigs, Kruepke, & Newman, 2012).

In term of affective decision making, a number of studies have used the Iowa gambling task and demonstrated that, while controls learn to avoid the high-risk decks, adults with psychopathy and youths with CP/HCU traits have a tendency for risky decision making such that they draw more cards from the high-risk deck in comparison to controls (Blair et al., 2001; Molto et al., 2007). In one of the few studies directly comparing patients with vmPFC lesions to psychopaths (Mitchell, Avny, & Blair, 2006) it was shown that offenders with psychopathy and the patients with vmPFC lesions displayed similar patterns of risky decision making on the Iowa gambling task. However, some of our recent work using the Cambridge gamble task, where all the information for optimal decision making is presented up front (i.e., it does not involve a learning component), suggests that psychopaths might not exhibit risky decision making under such conditions (De Brito et al., 2013).

Another form of decision making that has been widely investigated in psychopaths is their (in)ability to make moral judgments (i.e., ability to decide between right and wrong). This avenue of research may bear important implications in the legal domain where, in some jurisdictions, a compromised ability in moral reasoning could be used as an excuse for diminished responsibility on the basis of insanity (Aharoni, Sinnott-Armstrong, & Kiehl, 2012). While earlier studies on adult psychopaths and youths with CP/HCU traits (Blair, 1995, 1997) had observed a consistent deficit in making the "moral–conventional distinction" (i.e., one's ability to distinguish violations of other's welfare (e.g., hitting a classmate) from violations of social convention (e.g., not talking during class)), more recent studies exploring psychopaths' responses to moral dilemmas (e.g., the permissibility of harming one to save many also referred to as "utilitarian" moral judgment) or to the "moral-conventional distinction" have failed to observe consistent deficits (Aharoni et al., 2012; Cima et al., 2010; Koenigs, Baskin-Sommers, Zeier, & Newman, 2011).

For example, Cima et al. (2010) observed that the pattern of judgments on different moral dilemmas was the same across offenders with and without psychopathy and healthy controls and concluded that psychopaths know what is right and wrong, but they do not care. In view of those results, Koenigs et al. (2011) suggested that the heterogeneity among psychopaths might explain the conflicting results and compared primary and secondary psychopaths to non-psychopath offenders on the same task. In line with their hypothesis, they observed that only the primary psychopaths were significantly more likely to endorse the action for the personal dilemmas (involving direct physical harms), a pattern similar to what they had previously reported in vmPFC patients (Koenigs et al., 2007).

These studies suggest that vmPFC dysfunction might underpin some aspects of psychopathic symptomatology (e.g., impulsivity, risky behavior, and lack of concerns for others), but individuals with vmPFC lesion and those with psychopathy present important differences, particularly regarding the kind of aggression that they display (Blair, 2006). While patients with vmPFC lesion are characterized by a tendency towards aggression that is sporadic, reactive (i.e., impulsive and frustration or threat related), and directed towards objects, individuals with psychopathy are at increased risk of displaying both reactive and premeditated/instrumental (i.e., goal-directed) aggression against other individuals (Blair, 2006). It has been suggested that the reactive aggression seen in individuals with psychopathy is frustration based rather than threat related and may be related to an inability of the vmPFC to compute changes in reinforcement contingencies in the environment, while their instrumental aggression reflects impairments in emotional learning and the processing of distress cues, processes central to early socialization, which are posited to be mediated by amygdala dysfunctions (Blair, 2007).

Evidence of amygdala dysfunction

Because of its dense reciprocal connections with subcortical and cortical areas (Freese, 2009) the amygdala is involved in a host of different processes including, but not limited to, classical aversive conditioning, stimulus-reinforcement learning (i.e., learning by trial and errors to respond to stimuli that give rise to reward and to avoid responding to stimuli that give rise to punishment), face processing (particularly sad and fearful facial expressions), and memory for emotional event, and response to threat (Whalen & Phelps, 2009).

Neuropsychological evidence suggesting amygdala dysfunctions in adults with psychopathy and youths with CP/HCU traits has mostly come from investigations focusing on their emotional response to threatening stimuli, their ability to learn from reward and punishment, and their processing of others' emotional facial expressions (Blair, 2013).

In terms of response to threatening stimuli, a number of studies have shown that adults with psychopathy, like patients with amygdala lesions (Angrilli et al., 1996;

Bechara et al., 1995), exhibit impairments in classical aversive conditioning and fear-potentiated startle reflex (e.g., Hare & Quinn, 1971; Patrick, 1994). Several studies have now shown that the aberrant fear-potentiated startle reflex response seen in psychopathy is related to the core affective-interpersonal (Factor 1) component of the disorder rather than its behavioral features (Factor 2) (Patrick, 2007).

With regards to the fear conditioning, it is interesting to note that, while offenders with psychopathy have a normal response to unconditioned aversive stimuli (Birbaumer et al., 2005; Flor, Birbaumer, Hermann, Ziegler, & Patrick, 2002), several studies have reported that psychopaths showed a decreased electrodermal response to the neutral stimuli previously associated with the electric shock (Birbaumer et al., 2005; Rothemund et al., 2012). Crucially, psychopaths and controls did not differ in terms of contingency ratings (i.e., the awareness that a neutral stimulus is paired with an electric shock in the acquisition phase). Together, these findings suggest that, while their fear response is not impaired, their ability to respond to stimuli that predict aversive outcome is impaired. The contingency ratings results support the view that psychopathy is associated with cold emotional processing in the absence of true emotional involvement (Hare, 1993).

A number of studies involving patients with bilateral amygdala lesions have demonstrated that the amygdala is necessary to recognize both fearful and sad facial expressions (Adolphs & Tranel, 2004; Adolphs et al., 1999; Calder et al., 1996). Numerous studies among adults with psychopathy (e.g., Blair et al., 2004; Dolan & Fullam, 2006) and youths with CP/HCU traits (e.g., Dadds et al., 2006; Fairchild, Van Goozen, Calder, Stollery, & Goodyer, 2009) have reported impaired recognition of fearful and/or sad facial expressions in these groups, supporting amygdala dysfunction accounts of psychopathy (Blair, 2013; Moul, Killcross, & Dadds, 2012; Patrick, 1994).

It has been suggested that the impairments in processing fearful facial expressions might be due to the central role the amygdala plays in focalizing attention on the most important part of the face to process fear, the eye region (Adolphs et al., 2005). In a series of studies combining eye tracking technologies and experimental manipulations, Dadds and colleagues have indeed shown that the fear blindness observed in youths with CP/HCU traits is related to the fact that, in comparison to controls, they fixate and spend less than time on the eye regions of the face when processing fearful facial expressions (Dadds, El Masry, Wimalaweera, & Guastella, 2008), but when instructed to focus on the eyes regions, they process fearful faces as well as controls (Dadds et al., 2006).

A recent study examining child–parent interactions also reported that boys with CP/HCU traits show impairments in eye contact with their parents, which was associated with measures of fear recognition and general empathy (Dadds et al., 2011). Interestingly, in contrast to a previous meta-analysis (i.e., Marsh & Blair, 2008), which only found impairments in fearful and sad face recognition among antisocial populations, including those with psychopathy, a more recent meta-analysis reported that adults with psychopathy and youths with CP/HCU traits show impairments for positive and negative emotions, across both facial and vocal modalities (Dawel et al., 2012). This finding is in line with other neuropsychological and neuroimaging evidence supporting a wider role for the amygdala in processing salient social information (Adolphs et al., 1999; Santos, Mier, Kirsch, & Meyer-Lindenberg, 2011).

The mask of sanity *One of the paradoxes of psychopathic individuals is their deceiving normality, as described in Cleckley's seminal work The Mask of Sanity (1941).*
Source: © Geralt. Used under license from 699pic.

Neuroimaging Research in Psychopathy

In the last decade, there has been an explosion of neuroimaging research on psychopathy (for reviews, see Anderson & Kiehl, 2012; Glenn & Yang, 2012; Koenigs et al., 2010; Seara-Cardoso & Viding, 2015; Y. Yang & Raine, 2009). The aim of part of the chapter is to critically examine the most recent functional (fMRI) and structural (sMRI) magnetic resonance imaging studies that have focused on the adult syndrome of psychopathy as well as the smaller body of evidence that has focused on youths with CP/HCU traits, as it might provide some information about the possible neurodevelopmental precursors of the adult syndrome.

Functional neuroimaging

Following the clinical and experimental evidence accumulated during the second half of the 20th century, the extent fMRI work of the last 15 years has sought to understand the brain functional correlates of key processes known to be impaired in psychopathy such as their response to negative emotional stimuli, processing of emotional facial expressions, empathy and morality, and affective decision making. We will now look at these processes in turn.

Response to negative emotional stimuli In the first fMRI study on psychopathy, Kiehl et al. (2001) compared prisoners with and without psychopathy and community controls while performing an affective recognition memory task requiring the identification of previously presented negative or neutral words. Compared to the non-psychopaths and the community controls, psychopaths exhibited reduced neural activity to the negative words (as compared to that for the neutral words) in the amygdala/hippocampal formation, parahippocampal gyrus, ventral striatum, and the anterior and posterior cingulate gyri, but increased activity in the bilateral frontotemporal cortex.

In contrast, Müller et al. (2003) found that when passively viewing IAPS[3] pictures psychopaths, as compared to controls, exhibited *increased* response in the right amygdala, anterior cingulate cortex (ACC), and right prefrontal areas. Extending the results of Birbaumer et al. (2005), Veit et al. (2002) examined skin conductance neural response during the acquisition, habituation, and extinction phases of a classical aversive conditioning paradigm (unconditioned stimulus = pain; conditioned stimulus = neutral faces) and showed that during the acquisition phase psychopaths, as compared to controls, showed a lack of skin conductance response and reduced activation in the left amygdala, bilateral insula, right ventromedial orbitofrontal cortex, the ACC, and the right secondary somatosensory cortex. These findings of impaired emotional learning suggest that the aversive stimulus was not salient for the psychopaths who also failed to anticipate the punishment (however, a study by Schneider et al. (2000) found *superior* aversive conditioning and *increased* amygdala activity to the conditioned stimulus in psychopaths compared to controls).

Emotional facial expressions There is a wealth of evidence indicating that psychopaths are impaired at processing others' emotional facial expressions, particularly sad and fearful expressions, an impairment that might in turn contribute to their lack of empathy and instrumental aggression (Blair, 2013). Several fMRI studies have now shown aberrant neural response to emotional facial expression in psychopathy. Using an implicit face processing task, where participants have to indicate the gender of the face, Deeley et al. (2006) found that, in comparison to controls, psychopaths had reduced activity in the fusiform gyrus and extrastriate cortex for both happy and fearful expressions. No group differences were observed in the amygdala, possibly due to the acquisition parameters combined with a small sample size (six psychopaths versus nine controls).

More recently, Contreras-Rodriguez et al. (2014) used an emotional face-matching task (Hariri, Bookheimer, & Mazziotta, 2000) with fearful and happy faces to compare brain activation and task-induced functional connectivity between the amygdala and the face network in 22 psychopaths and 22 controls. In line with other studies (e.g., Glenn, Raine, & Schug, 2009; Kiehl et al., 2001), as compared to the controls, psychopaths had greater activation in neocortical areas such as visual and prefrontal cortices, but in addition they showed decrease in functional connectivity between those regions and the amygdala, which was only activated in the controls. Furthermore, interpersonal and affective features of psychopathy were positively correlated with higher activation seen in the medial prefrontal cortex of the psychopaths. Given the absence of behavioral group difference, the authors concluded that psychopaths are characterized by a disruption in the processing of emotional faces as indicated by weaker limbic involvement, but that compensatory neocortical resources important for visuo-perceptual abilities allowed them to perform the task as well as the controls. These results lend further support to the view that psychopaths process emotional information in the absence of true emotional involvement.

Decety, Skelly, Yoder, and Kiehl (2014) extended the above studies in three ways: 1) by comparing neural processing of several facial expressions including fear, sadness, happiness, and pain; 2) by presenting short dynamic clips to prisoners; and 3) by dividing prisoners into high, medium, and low psychopathy scorers. Results indicated that, as compared to the low and medium groups, the high psychopathy group showed lower neural response to all type of emotions in the face-processing network (inferior occipital gyrus, fusiform gyrus, superior temporal sulcus) and the extended face processing network (inferior frontal gyrus, orbitofrontal cortex, and vmPFC). This work is in line with Dawel et al.'s (2012) recent meta-analysis of behavioral evidence indicating that psychopathy is characterized by a pervasive deficit across emotion. Surprisingly, however, as compared to the two other groups, in response to negative expressions the high psychopathy group exhibited increased activity in the dorsal anterior insula, which is functionally connected to a group regions part of a cognitive control network.

Mier et al. (2014) (and see Sommer et al., 2010, for similar results) examined in psychopaths and healthy controls brain activation to a task indexing face processing, emotion recognition, and affective theory of mind (i.e., understanding emotions in others). In terms of face processing, in line with Deeley et al. (2006), there was fusiform, but not amygdala, hypoactivation in the psychopaths compared to controls. For affective theory of mind, psychopaths had hypoactivation in amygdala, inferior prefrontal gyrus and superior temporal sulcus and showed reduced connectivity between the amygdala and superior temporal sulcus, an area central to all forms of empathy. In line with Contreras-Rodriguez et al. (2014), the groups did not differ in terms of their ability to identify emotions and mental states, which, according to Mier et al. (2014) together with the fMRI results, reflects the fact that psychopaths are good at manipulating people without showing any empathy (see Sebastian et al., 2012 below for a similar interpretation in youths with CP/HCU traits).

The results of the studies on youths with CP/HCU traits have been more consistent, particularly in terms of atypical amygdala response to fearful faces. Indeed, these studies have consistently found that youths with CP/HCU show amygdala hyporeactivity when processing supraliminal (Jones, Laurens, Herba, Barker, & Viding, 2009; Marsh et al., 2008) and subliminal facial expressions (Viding et al., 2012). More recently, White et al. (2012) showed that in this population lower amygdala response to consciously processed fearful faces does not result from an attentional deficit, but instead is specifically related to the callous-unemotional traits. Finally, an influential model of psychopathy posits that amygdala hyporeactivity could partly account for the high levels of proactive aggression seen in psychopathy (Blair, 2013). Consistent with this model, a recent study reported that reduced amygdala response to fearful faces in youths with conduct problems mediated the association between callous-unemotional traits and proactive aggression (Lozier, Cardinale, Van Meter, & Marsh, 2014).

Empathy and morality Surprisingly, it is only recently that the neural correlates of empathy in psychopathy have been investigated. These studies have generally used stimuli depicting others in painful and non-painful situations, stimuli that are known to consistently activate in healthy individuals a network of regions including, among others, the inferior frontal gyrus, dorsal ACC, and anterior insula (Lamm, Decety, & Singer, 2011). Decety, Skelly, and Kiehl (2013) compared prisoners with psychopathy to prisoners with medium and low levels of psychopathy when they were observing body parts in painful situations or people showing facial expressions of pain. When observing the facial expressions, psychopaths, as compared to controls, showed reduced activity in the inferior frontal gyrus and dorsal ACC, but increased activity in the anterior insula. By contrast, for the body parts, psychopaths, as compared to controls, showed reduced activity in the vmPFC, lateral orbitofrontal cortex, and periaqueductal grey, but surprisingly *increased* activation in the inferior frontal gyrus, dorsal ACC, and anterior insula. As noted by Seara-Cardoso and Viding (2015), this latter finding might reflect that the psychopaths imagined themselves as experiencing the pain rather than others. This is supported by the results of Decety, Chen, Harenski, and Kiehl (2013) who observed increased activity in psychopaths in those regions when they were instructed to imagine themselves in those pictures showing body parts in painful situations. However, when psychopaths were instructed to imagine others in the pictures, they exhibited reduced activity and connectivity of the anterior insula and amygdala with the orbitofrontal cortex and vmPFC. Neural response in the amygdala and insula was negatively correlated with affective/interpersonal components of psychopathy. These results, together with those of Meffert, Gazzola, den Boer, Bartels, and Keysers (2013) who showed that when they are explicitly instructed to empathize with others, psychopaths' spontaneous reduced response in the above regions is dramatically reduced, indicate that psychopaths' brain response to empathic-eliciting stimuli is context dependent and can be increased. While it remains to be established whether these results mean that psychopaths did actually feel more empathy following the instructions, they at least provide evidence that empathy-eliciting stimuli can generate neural response in this network in psychopaths. The challenge for therapeutic interventions, however, is to make this neural response more automatic (Meffert et al., 2013) and to establish whether it is in turn accompanied by altered empathic experience akin to that of healthy individuals (Seara-Cardoso & Viding, 2015).

It has been suggested that immoral judgment seen in psychopathy results from impairments in emotional empathy and affective decision making, which reflect dysfunctions within the amygdala and the vmPFC, respectively (Blair, 2013). Recent studies have indeed shown abnormal response within those regions and others in psychopathic individuals. In a community sample with varying degrees of psychopathy (PCL-R range: 7.4–32), Glenn et al. (2009) showed that, although high psychopathic individuals did not differ from low psychopathic individuals in their moral judgments, total PCL-R scores (and each of the four facets of psychopathy) were negatively correlated with response in the amygdala when contrasting extreme moral personal dilemmas (e.g., killing a baby to save yourself and others) to less emotional impersonal dilemmas (e.g., keeping the money you found in a lost wallet). Scores on the interpersonal facets of psychopathy indexing manipulation, conning, superficiality, and deceitfulness were also negatively correlated with response within the medial prefrontal and posterior cingulate cortices, and angular gyrus (see Pujol et al., 2012, for similar results in prisoners). Interestingly, scores for the lifestyle and antisocial facets were positively correlated with activity within the orbital prefrontal cortex prefrontal cortex (DLPFC) (Glenn et al., 2009), a region implicated in cognitive control and abstract reasoning during moral judgments (Greene, Nystrom, Engell, Darley, & Cohen, 2004).

Taken together, these results suggest that, while individuals with high psychopathy scores show less input from emotion-related (e.g., amygdala) and perspective-taking regions than low scorers, they might recruit other regions such as DLPFC to use alternative, more cognitive, and abstract strategies to solve moral dilemmas (Glenn et al., 2009; see also the result of Harenski, Harenski, Shane, & Kiehl, 2010, in prisoners supporting this hypothesis). These results further shed light on the putative neural correlates underlying the disconnection seen in psychopathy between the cognitive *knowledge* of the moral rules and their subsequent immoral behavior, possibly because the *feeling* of what is right and wrong is absent.

Lockwood et al. (2013) reported that in youths with conduct problems hypoactivation in the ACC and anterior insula to pictures depicting others' pain was negatively correlated with unique variance associate with callous traits. Similarly, in comparison to controls, Marsh et al. (2013) found that youths with CP/HCU traits showed reduced response in the ACC and ventral striatum to increases in perceived pain in others. Crucially, these youths also showed reduced response in the amygdala and insula when rating increases in others' pain, but not their own pain. The affective and interpersonal features of psychopathy were negatively correlated with amygdala and ACC response to others' pain.

Using a more complex affective-processing task including cartoon vignettes, Sebastian et al. (2012) extended the above findings by showing that in response to cartoons requiring understanding of others' distress in social situations, amygdala and anterior insula activity in youths with conduct problems was negatively correlated with the unique variance associated with callous-unemotional traits (for similar findings among adults, see Mier et al., 2014). Using the same task, this group also observed that during cartoons requiring the understanding of others' intentions, the brain response of youths with CP/HCU traits did not differ from that of controls (O'Nions et al., 2014). The results are consistent with those of the adult studies above and dovetail with experimental and behavioral data indicating that youths with CP/HCU traits "know" about others' mental states and know how to manipulate them for their own benefit, but they do not "care" about hurting others' feelings (Jones, Happé, Gilbert, Burnett, & Viding, 2010).

Immoral judgment seen in youths with CP/HCU traits might be a consequence of their lack of empathy and affective decision making, which have been posited to reflect dysfunctions within the amygdala-vmPFC circuitry and striatum (Blair, 2013). Consistent with this view and the neuropsychological evidence reviewed above, Marsh et al. (2011) reported that, compared to controls, youths with CP/HCU traits had reduced amygdala response and reduced amygdala-orbitofrontal cortex connectivity during moral judgments about legal actions.

Decision making and reward Given the strong experimental evidence that psychopathy is associated with impaired affective decision making (see De Brito & Hodgins, 2009b), most likely because of abnormalities in the processing of reward and punishment information (Blair, 2013), it is surprising that only two fMRI studies have examined these aspects in relation to PCL-R psychopathy. The first study by Prehn et al. (2013) compared the neural response offender with ASPD and high total and Factor 1 PCL-R scores to offenders with ASPD and borderline personality disorder and to controls while they performed a financial decision-making task involving choosing between low-risk and high-risk options. While the groups did not differ in terms of task performance, the psychopathic group, as compared to the controls, showed lower response in the ACC and in the inferior frontal gyrus in response to trials with high uncertainty and before choosing the low-risk option under high uncertainty, respectively. In the inferior frontal gyrus, psychopaths showed increased response when choosing the high-risk option. According to the authors, these findings provide evidence that psychopaths show lower arousal when anticipating possible punishment and have a decreased ability to represent uncertainty and to regulate their behavior in those circumstances.

In the second study, Pujara, Motzkin, Newman, Kiehl, and Koenigs (2013) compared psychopathic offenders with non-psychopathic offenders while they performed a task involving the passive gain or loss of money. They observed no group difference in neural response in the ventral striatum, a key region of the brain's reward circuitry (Haber, 2011). However, they did find a positive correlation between psychopathy scores and neural response in and volume of the ventral striatum within the psychopathy group only.

As discussed above, youths with CP/HCU traits show similar impairments in affective decision making to those observed in adult psychopathy (Blair, 2013), but it is only recently that their neural correlates have been examined. Studies using standard learning (i.e., passive avoidance learning) and reversal learning paradigms have shown that, compared to typically developing youths (Finger et al., 2011; Finger, Mitchell, Jones, & Blair, 2008) and youths with ADHD (Finger et al., 2008), youths with CP/HCU traits exhibit atypical response to reward and punishment within the orbitofrontal cortex/vmPFC and caudate. White, Pope et al. (2013) recently showed that these results reflect atypical representation of reinforcement expectancies (i.e., the expected value associated with a stimulus or action) within the vmPFC and aberrant prediction error signaling (i.e., the signal representing the difference between the level of reward or punishment received and the level expected, which enables reinforcement expectancies to be updated) within the caudate.

Structural magnetic resonance imaging (sMRI)

It is likely that atypical brain function in psychopaths and youths with CP/HCU traits might be underpinned by abnormalities in brain structure and/or connectivity. In this section, we review sMRI studies using manual tracing or semi-automated region-of-interest guided measurement of brain structures and more recent studies that have relied on automated, whole-brain approaches. We then discuss the smaller body of studies that have examined white matter tracts in adults and youths.

Manual tracing A number of studies have relied on manual tracing or semi-automated region-of-interest guided measurement of brain structures to focus on regions of interest or particular lobes identified *a priori*. For example, Laakso et al. (2001) examined the association between PCL-R scores and hippocampal volume in habitually violent offenders with alcoholism and high psychopathy scores (mean = 31.2). Volume of the posterior half of the hippocampus bilaterally, which explained up to 62% of the variance in the total psychopathy scores in the sample, was negatively correlated ($r = -0.79$) with psychopathy scores. Given the central role of this region in classical fear conditioning, the authors concluded that their findings could partly explain earlier observations of impaired classical fear conditioning in psychopathy (Lykken, 1995).

A subsequent study, which compared unsuccessful psychopaths, successful psychopaths, and controls, found an exaggerated structural asymmetry (right > left) in the anterior hippocampus in unsuccessful psychopaths relative to both successful psychopaths and controls (Raine et al., 2004). This result was not explained by environmental or diagnostic confounds and, according to the authors, might reflect neurodevelopmental abnormalities in unsuccessful psychopaths, which lead to emotion dysregulation, impaired classical fear conditioning, and insensitivity to signals predicting punishment. Two more recent studies have reported abnormal shape of the amygdala and hippocampus reflecting a combination of local increases and decreases in nuclei and subregions of those structures in violent offenders with psychopathy compared with controls (Boccardi et al., 2011; Boccardi et al., 2010). Another study found significant bilateral reduction in amygdala volume in psychopathic individuals in comparison to controls, with lower amygdala volumes being associated with the affective and interpersonal facets of psychopathy (Yang, Raine, Narr, Colletti, & Toga, 2009).

Two recent studies have examined the volumes of the dorsal (i.e., caudate and lenticular nuclei – putamen and globus pallidus) and the ventral striatum (nucleus accumbens) given their role in reinforcement learning, and their connections with the amygdala and the vmPFC. Glenn, Yang, Raine, and Colletti (2010) reported a 9.6% increase in the volume of the striatum in individuals from the community with high psychopathy scores (≥ 23) as compared to control subjects. Correlation analyses showed that the volume of the caudate body was primarily associated with the interpersonal and affective features of psychopathy, while the volume of the caudate head was primarily associated with the impulsive, stimulation-seeking features. Volumes of the lenticular nuclei were positively correlated with both factors of psychopathy. More recently, Boccardi et al. (2013) extended those results in a sample of violent offenders who, in comparison to controls, exhibited a 13% volume reduction of the ventral striatum (i.e., nucleus accumbens). The caudate and putamen had normal global volume, but different morphology, which was negatively correlated with the lifestyle factor of the PCL-R. The findings of abnormal volume of the striatum fit well with the neuropsychological and fMRI evidence discussed above, indicating abnormal processing of reward and punishment information in psychopaths and youths with CP/HCU traits.

In another study, Glenn, Yang, Raine, and Colletti (2010) reported an absence of group difference in the volume of the ACC and its subdivisions. This result is somewhat surprising given: 1) previous fMRI studies which had observed reduced activity in psychopaths in its dorsal-cognitive and ventral-affective subdivisions; and 2) its key role in self-regulation, decision making, and empathy – processes that have been shown to be compromised in psychopathy (Blair, 2013). According to Glenn et al. (2010), the discrepancy between their sMRI finding and previous fMRI data might reflect that the ACC shares dense connections with the amygdala and the vmPFC and thus reduced ACC activity in previous fMRI study might have been the result of reduced input from these regions. It must also be noted that Glenn et al.'s finding is in line with neuropsychological evidence indicating that psychopaths do not present with a neuropsychological profile as seen in patient with ACC lesion (Blair, 2007).

Finally, a recent study that examined whether individuals with a large cavum septum pellucidum (CSP), a marker of abnormal limbic brain development, would have higher levels of psychopathy and ASPD has lent further support to the view that psychopathy might be a neurodevelopmental disorder (Raine et al., 2010). Supporting the authors' hypothesis, individuals with large CSP had significantly higher levels of psychopathy, ASPD, arrests, and convictions compared with controls (however, for a failure to replicate those findings, see Toivonen et al., 2013). A study examining the same marker in youths replicated, but also qualified, those findings, by showing that, while a large CSP was associated with aggression, conduct problems, and callous-unemotional traits when youths with conduct problems and healthy controls were compared, youths with conduct problems with and without a large CSP did not differ on those variables (White, Brislin, et al., 2013). These results suggest that, while large CSP may increase the risk for antisocial behavior, it is not a neurodevelopmental marker for psychopathy.

The above studies have furthered our understanding of the structural neural correlates of psychopathy, but the manual tracing approach has three major limitations: 1) high intra- and inter-raters variability in the manual tracing of specific regions within and between laboratories can introduce a bias and thus render difficult subsequent replications; 2) manual tracing is time consuming and might not be feasible in the context of large samples focusing on multiple a *priori* regions; and 3) by focusing on *a priori* regions of interest, it is possible that abnormalities in other regions implicated in the pathophysiology of the disorder might go unnoticed (Eckert et al., 2005; see also Chapter 10 this volume).

Automated whole-brain approaches In contrast to manual approaches, automated morphometry approaches allow, in a single analysis and across large groups of subjects, an objective examination of the shape, size, and position of brain structures throughout the brain (Ashburner & Friston, 2000). One such technique that is increasingly being used in psychopathy research is voxel-based morphometry (VBM), which uses statistics to conduct voxel-wise comparisons of grey and white matter volume between two or more experimental groups to identify local differences irrespective of large scale differences in anatomy (Mechelli, Price, Friston, & Ashburner, 2005). Tiihonen et al. (2008) observed focal, symmetrical, bilateral atrophy in the postcentral gyri, frontopolar cortex, and orbitofrontal cortex, and reduced volume in right insula in violent offenders with psychopathy scores as compared to healthy men. The violent offenders, as compared to the healthy men, presented *larger* white matter volumes, bilaterally, in the occipital and parietal lobes and in the left cerebellum, and *larger* grey matter in the right cerebellum.

However, these analyses did not control for cognitive abilities. De Oliveira-Souza et al. (2008) reported decreased grey matter in the frontopolar, orbital and anterior temporal cortices, superior temporal sulcus region, and insula among psychiatric outpatients with high psychopathy scores as compared to healthy individuals. Among the patients, grey matter was significantly and inversely correlated with scores for the interpersonal/affective factor of psychopathy. The analyses, however, did not control for substance misuse. Similarly, Müller et al. (2008) found grey matter reduction in the left prefrontal cortex, right – middle – cingulate gyrus, and bilaterally in the superior temporal gyrus of offenders with psychopathy, as compared to healthy men. Importantly, however, these group differences disappeared after controlling for group difference in drug use.

More recent studies have controlled for history of substance use and cognitive abilities in their analyses. In the only study to directly compare violent offenders with APSD with and without psychopathy to healthy non-offenders, those with ASPD and psychopathy exhibited reduced grey matter bilaterally in the rostral prefrontal cortex and temporal poles as compared to the violent offenders with ASPD without psychopathy and the healthy non-offenders (Gregory et al., 2012). Interestingly, in another study on a community sample of substance abusers, psychopathic traits were found to be negatively correlated with grey matter volumes in the right insula and right hippocampus, but positively correlated with volumes of the left superior/middle frontal gyrus, caudate head and right ACC (Cope et al., 2012). Finally, in a large sample of prisoners (n = 254), psychopathy was associated with reduced grey matter volume bilaterally in the parahippocampal cortex, amygdala, hippocampus, bilateral temporal pole, posterior cingulate, and orbitofrontal cortices (Ermer, Cope, Nyalakanti, Calhoun, & Kiehl, 2012).

Grey matter volume in VBM is thought to reflect several structural parameters of the cortex, including its thickness, surface area, and gyrification (i.e., folding of the cerebral cortex). Recent evidence has shown that these parameters are under distinct genetic influences (Panizzon et al., 2009) and follow divergent developmental trajectories (Raznahan et al., 2011). Recent sMRI studies have employed surface-based morphometry to investigate cortical thickness in psychopathy. Using a community sample, Yang, Raine, Colletti, Toga, and Narr (2009) found reduced cortical thickness in the right temporal and prefrontal lobes in psychopathic individuals, as compared to non-psychopathic controls. These deficits were correlated with the affective facet scores of the PCL-R.

Reduced cortical thickness in the orbitofrontal cortex and anterior temporal lobes has also been associated with increased response perseveration in psychopaths (Yang, Raine, Colletti, Toga, & Narr, 2011). Yang et al. also reported that, in comparison to controls, unsuccessful psychopaths, but not successful psychopaths, exhibited reduced cortical thickness in the middle frontal and orbitofrontal cortices (Yang et al., 2009). More recently, Ly et al. (2012) reported that, as compared to controls, prisoners with psychopathy exhibited reduced cortical thickness in the inferior frontal gyrus, insula, dorsal anterior cingulate cortex, bilaterally in the precentral gyrus and anterior temporal cortices.

Few sMRI studies have been conducted on youths with CP/HCU traits or investigated the association between callous-unemotional traits and grey matter in antisocial youths. In the first published study, we showed that, in comparison to controls, community boys aged 10–13.5 years with CP/HCU traits exhibited increased grey matter concentration in several regions, including the medial orbitofrontal and anterior cingulate cortices, as well as increased grey matter volume and concentration in the temporal lobes bilaterally (De Brito, Mechelli, et al., 2009). Follow-up VBM analyses of the white matter on this sample identified increases in white matter concentration in the boys with CP/HCU traits, as compared to controls (De Brito et al., 2011). Given evidence of decrease in grey matter and increase in white matter in this age range in typically developing boys (Lenroot et al., 2007), taken together, these results may reflect a delay in cortical maturation in boys with CP/HCU traits.

In line with the results of De Brito, Mechelli, et al. (2009), a recent VBM study on a community sample of females with CD and controls observed a positive correlation across groups between self-reported callous-unemotional traits and grey matter volume in the orbitofrontal cortex bilaterally (Fairchild et al., 2013). Consistent with the adult finding of Glenn, Raine, Yaralian, and Yang (2010), self-report callous-unemotional traits in males with CD were positively correlated with the volumes of the dorsal and ventral striatum (Fairchild et al., 2011). Finally, similar to some of the adult VBM studies reviewed above, a study on a large sample of incarcerated youths (n = 191) that controlled for substance use found psychopathy scores to be negatively associated with grey matter volume in paralimbic regions such as the orbitofrontal cortex, temporal poles, parahippocampal region, and posterior cingulate cortex, but positively associated with grey matter volume in the medial prefrontal cortex (Ermer, Cope, Nyalakanti, Calhoun, & Kiehl, 2013).

Imaging white matter tracts Raine et al. (2003) reported that psychopathic individuals from the community had increased corpus callosum white matter volume and increased callosal length, but reduced callosal thickness compared to controls, results which might account for fMRI (Raine et al., 2003) and neurophysiological evidence (Hoppenbrouwers et al., 2014) of abnormal interhemispheric connectivity in psychopaths. More recent studies investigating white matter tracts in psychopathy have used diffusion tensor imaging. Two studies reported reduced fractional anisotropy (FA) in psychopaths as compared to controls only in the right uncinate fasciculus, a white matter tract connecting the vmPFC and the anterior temporal lobe including the amygdala (Craig et al., 2009; Motzkin, Newman, Kiehl, & Koenigs, 2011). In particular, Motzkin et al.'s findings were driven by a group difference between the primary psychopaths and the low anxious controls, while the FA reduction observed by Craig et al. was negatively correlated with the factor 2 of the PCL-R.

The results of the two other studies, however, revealed reduced FA not only in the uncinate fasciculus, but also in a striato-thalamo-frontal network connecting the nucleus accumbens, thalamus, and prefrontal cortex of psychopathic offenders (Hoppenbrouwers et al., 2014) and reduced FA, but increase mean diffusivity in the corpus callosum, internal capsule, anterior corona radiata, and inferior fronto-occipital fasciculus among men with ASPD and high psychopathy scores (Sundram et al., 2012). To date, two DTI studies have examined the white matter correlates of callous-unemotional traits in antisocial youths (Finger et al., 2012; Sarkar et al., 2013). While Finger et al. did not observe any abnormalities, Sarkar et al. found that, as compared to controls, youths with CD exhibited a decreased perpendicular diffusivity (Dperp), but increased FA in the left uncinate fasciculus, with the latter being positively correlated ($r = .27$; $p = .09$) with psychopathic tendencies (Sarkar et al., 2013).

Methodological Considerations in Neuroimaging Studies

The results of the above literature and some of the inconsistent results, particularly for the neuroimaging investigations in adults (Koenigs et al., 2010), need to be considered in light of several methodological considerations, which influence the interpretation of the results and their generalizability (for more detailed discussions, see Anderson & Kiehl, 2012; Hodgins, De Brito, Simonoff, Vloet, & Viding, 2009; Koenigs et al., 2010; Seara-Cardoso & Viding, 2015). These include, among others, sample size, the PCL-R cutoff used to identify the psychopathic group, the nature of the control group, demographical and clinical variables (e.g., sex, IQ, associated comorbidities), and the cross-sectional design of the studies.

Most neuroimaging studies include very small samples resulting in low statistical power, which, in turn, decreases the chance of detecting a true effect, but also decreases the chance that a statistically significant result reflects a true effect (Button et al., 2013). Consequently, reproducibility across studies is low. Somewhat related, Koenigs et al. (2010) noted the huge variability among neuroimaging studies in the total PCL-R cutoff score used to define the psychopathic group (range across studies:

15–31). While such practice increases statistical power through a higher number of individuals in the clinical group, it might also partly explain the substantial differences in results observed across studies examining the same process, especially if they are underpowered.

In terms of comparison group, while some studies compared psychopathic prisoners with prisoners with low psychopathy score, others have relied on healthy controls as a comparison group. These approaches lead to two problems (Seara-Cardoso & Viding, 2015). In the first case, for both groups, the absence of a healthy comparison group precludes a comparison to a typical baseline whether any observed group difference represent departure from healthy functioning. In the second case, it is difficult to know whether any significant group differences are due to psychopathy per se or confounded by other variables (e.g., length of incarceration, substance misuse) associated with incarceration.

Demographical variables such as age, sex, and IQ are all associated with brain development and anatomy (Giedd & Rapoport, 2010; Hackman, Farah, & Meaney, 2010) and the same holds for psychiatric comorbidities typically associated with psychopathy such as substance misuse and ADHD (Shaw et al., 2007). The distribution of those demographic and clinical variables varies greatly across studies and within the same study whereby groups are sometimes poorly matched on those variables whose influence is not systematically investigated (De Brito, Hodgins, et al., 2009).

Finally, psychopathy is hypothesized to be a neurodevelopmental disorder (Blair et al., 2006; Raine et al., 2010), but this still remains to be established given that all but one (Pardini, Erickson, Loeber, & Raine, 2013) studies examining neurobiological correlates of psychopathy are cross-sectional or correlational, designs which preclude any valid inference to be made regarding developmental processes (Kraemer, Yesavage, Taylor, & Kupfer, 2000).

Conclusions

Despite the methodological challenges, neuroscience research on psychopathy is rapidly growing and keeping pace with the wave of new developments in methods. We see many exciting future avenues for this research, some of which are briefly described here. Recent advances in the way neuroimaging data are analyzed such as pattern recognition and graph theory methods will further our understanding of the various brain networks disturbances implicated in psychopathy. Indeed, these multivariate approaches do take into account the fact that the brain is a complex patchwork of interconnected brain regions, which influence each other, both structurally and functionally (Menon, 2011).

These approaches have recently been applied in two sMRI studies of psychopathy. One study used methods from graph theory and showed altered frontal information flow and connectivity in psychopaths (Yang et al., 2012), while the other used pattern recognition methods and found that psychopaths could be distinguished from controls based on grey matter MRI features (Sato et al., 2011). Future research should seek to integrate genetics and neuroimaging approaches to try to identify potential structural and functional endophenotype of callous-unemotional traits and psychopathy in youths and adults (see Chapter 18 in this volume). One study on twins revealed that increased grey matter concentration in the ACC and posterior cingulate cortex in boys with CP/HCU traits (De Brito, Mechelli, et al., 2009) might represent potential endophenotypes for the development of psychopathy (Rijsdijsk et al., 2010). Investigations examining how genetic variants known to modulate affective and cognitive processes interact with environmental factors to either increase or decrease the risk of developing psychopathy are also urgently needed. Further, future research should seek to identify diagnostic biomarker of psychopathy as well as biomarkers contributing to the prediction of long-term prognosis and treatment efficacy (Blair, 2013). While it is unlikely that those biomarkers will be part of clinical assessment in the near future, it has been proposed that such biomarkers could help differentiate subgroups of individuals with a distinct neurobiological profile among diagnostic categories (Insel et al., 2010).

Implications for Practice

There is a need for prospective validation studies to be performed to examine whether neurobiological measures can help differentiate which at risk youth will develop the most severe outcomes (Moffitt et al., 2008; Sterzer, 2010). Two recent prospective neuroimaging studies among adult violent males have shown that lower error-related neural activity in the ACC predicted subsequent re-arrest four years later (Aharoni et al., 2013) and that reduced amygdala volume was negatively correlated with aggression, violence, and psychopathic traits at a three-year follow-up (Pardini et al., 2013). However, no such studies exist among at risk youths. This type of research is an essential step to further our understanding of the pathophysiological processes implicated in the development of psychopathy, and to ultimately design targeted prevention and interventions efforts and assess their mode of action and their efficacy (Blair, 2013; Viding & McCrory, 2012).

Notes

1. Stéphane De Brito was supported by a research fellowship from the Swiss National Science Foundation (FNS PA00P1_139586) during the writing of this chapter.
2. See Chapter 11 in this volume by Hodgins, Checknita, Lindner, Schiffer, and De Brito
3. The International Affective Picture System (IAPS) is a database of pictures designed to provide a standardized set of pictures for studying emotion and attention.

Recommended Reading

Blair, R. J. R. (2013). The neurobiology of psychopathic traits in youths. *Nature Reviews Neuroscience, 14*(11), 786–799. *This review discusses the most recent neuroscientific evidence on psychopathic traits in youths and also introduces one of the most clearly articulated neurocognitive models of psychopathy.*

Cleckley, H. (1941). *The mask of sanity.* St-Louis, MO: Mosby. *In this seminal book, the American psychiatrist relied on patients from his own clinical practice to describe the hallmark features of what eventually became the modern conceptualization of psychopathy on which most existing measures are based.*

Frick, P. J., Ray, J. V., Thornton, L. C., & Kahn, R. E. (2014). Can callous-unemotional traits enhance the understanding, diagnosis, and treatment of serious conduct problems in children and adolescents? A comprehensive review. *Psychological Bulletin, 140*(1), 1–57. *This* is a thorough and in-depth review of the most recent evidence base focusing on the use of the callous-unemotional traits construct and how it can advance the understanding, diagnosis, and treatment of youths with conduct problems.

Hare, R. D. (1999). *Without conscience: The disturbing world of the psychopaths among us*. New York, NY: Guilford Press. *This is "a must read" from the author of the Psychopathy Checklist – Revised (PCL-R), where the author uses real-life cases to describe the hallmark features of psychopathy.*

Patrick, C. J. (Ed.). (2007). *Handbook of psychopathy*. New York, NY: Guilford Press. *Here Christopher Patrick presents an excellent collection of edited chapters covering definition, assessment, clinical and applied issues, and etiological mechanisms, including genetics, family factors, brain function, and neurochemistry*. The 2nd edition is in press, and will be published in 2018.

References

Adolphs, R., Gosselin, F., Buchanan, T. W., Tranel, D., Schyns, P., & Damasio, A. R. (2005). A mechanism for impaired fear recognition after amygdala damage. *Nature*, *433*(7021), 68–72.

Adolphs, R., & Tranel, D. (2004). Impaired judgments of sadness but not happiness following bilateral amygdala damage. *Journal of Cognitive Neuroscience*, *16*(3), 453–462.

Adolphs, R., Tranel, D., Hamann, S., Young, A. W., Calder, A. J., Phelps, E. A., ... Damasio, A. R. (1999). Recognition of facial emotion in nine individuals with bilateral amygdala damage. *Neuropsychologia*, *37*(10), 1111–1117.

Aharoni, E., Sinnott-Armstrong, W., & Kiehl, K. A. (2012). Can psychopathic offenders discern moral wrongs? A new look at the moral/conventional distinction. *Journal of Abnormal Psychology*, *121*(2), 484–497.

Aharoni, E., Vincent, G. M., Harenski, C. L., Calhoun, V. D., Sinnott-Armstrong, W., Gazzaniga, M. S., & Kiehl, K. A. (2013). Neuroprediction of future rearrest. *Proceedings of the National Academy of Sciences of the United States of America*, *110*(15), 6223–6228.

Alm, P. O., af Klinteberg, B., Humble, K., Leppert, J., Sorensen, S., Tegelman, R., ... Lidberg, L. (1996). Criminality and psychopathy as related to thyroid activity in former juvenile delinquents. *Acta Psychiatrica Scandinavica*, *94*(2), 112–117.

American Psychiatric Association. (1987). *Diagnostic and statistical manual of mental disorders* (3rd ed., revised ed.). Washington DC: American Psychiatric Association.

Anderson, N. E., & Kiehl, K. A. (2012). The psychopath magnetized: Insights from brain imaging. *Trends in Cognitive Sciences*, *16*(1), 52–60.

Anderson, N. E., Wan, L., Young, K. A., & Stanford, M. S. (2011). Psychopathic traits predict startle habituation but not modulation in an emotional faces task. *Personality and Individual Differences*, *50*(5), 712–716.

Angrilli, A., Mauri, A., Palomba, D., Flor, H., Birbaumer, N., Sartori, G., & Di Paola, F. (1996). Startle reflex and emotion modulation impairment after a right amygdala lesion. *Brain*, *119*(6), 1991–2004.

Armstrong, T. A., Keller, S., Franklin, T. W., & Macmillan, S. N. (2009). Low resting heart rate and antisocial behavior. A brief review of evidence and preliminary results from a new test. *Criminal Justice and Behavior*, *36*(11), 1125–1140.

Arnett, P. A. (1997). Autonomic responsivity in psychopaths: A critical review and theoretical proposal. *Clinical Psychology Review*, *17*(8), 903–936.

Arnett, P. A., Howland, E. W., Smith, S. S., & Newman, J. P. (1993). Autonomic responsivity during passive avoidance in incarcerated psychopaths. *Personality and Individual Differences*, *14*(1), 173–184.

Ashburner, J., & Friston, K. J. (2000). Voxel-based morphometry – the methods. *NeuroImage*, *11*(6 Pt 1), 805–821.

Barraza, J. A., McCullough, M. E., Ahmadi, S., & Zak, P. J. (2011). Oxytocin infusion increases charitable donations regardless of monetary resources. *Hormones and Behavior, 60*(2), 148–151.

Baxter, M. G., & Browning, P. G. F. (2007). Two wrongs make a right: Deficits in reversal learning after orbitofrontal damage are improved by amygdala ablation. *Neuron, 54*(1), 1–3.

Bechara, A., Tranel, D., Damasio, H., Adolphs, R., Rockland, C., & Damasio, A. R. (1995). Double dissociation of conditioning and declarative knowledge relative to the amygdala and hippocampus in humans. *Science, 269*(5227), 1115–1118.

Benning, S. D., Patrick, C. J., & Iacono, W. G. (2005). Psychopathy, startle blink modulation, and electrodermal reactivity in twin men. *Psychophysiology, 42*(6), 753–762.

Birbaumer, N., Veit, R., Lotze, M., Erb, M., Hermann, C., Grodd, W., & Flor, H. (2005). Deficient fear conditioning in psychopathy: A functional magnetic resonance imaging study. *Archives of General Psychiatry, 62*(7), 799–805.

Blair, R. J. R. (1995). A cognitive developmental approach to mortality: Investigating the psychopath. *Cognition, 57*(1), 1–29.

Blair, R. J. R. (1997). Moral reasoning in the child with psychopathic tendencies. *Personality and Individual Differences, 22,* 731–739.

Blair, R. J. R. (2006). The emergence of psychopathy: Implications for the neuropsychological approach to developmental disorders. *Cognition, 101*(2), 414–442.

Blair, R. J. R. (2007). The amygdala and ventromedial prefrontal cortex in morality and psychopathy. *Trends in Cognitive Sciences, 11*(9), 387–392.

Blair, R. J. R. (2013). The neurobiology of psychopathic traits in youths. *Nature Reviews Neuroscience, 14*(11), 786–799.

Blair, R. J. R., & Cipolotti, L. (2000). Impaired social response reversal. A case of "acquired sociopathy". *Brain, 123*(6), 1122–1141.

Blair, R. J. R., Colledge, E., & Mitchell, D. G. V. (2001). Somatic markers and response reversal: Is there orbitofrontal cortex dysfunction in boys with psychopathic tendencies? *Journal of Abnormal Child Psychology, 29*(6), 499–511.

Blair, R. J. R., Mitchell, D. G. V., Peschardt, K., Colledge, E., Leonard, R., Shine, J., … Perrett, D. (2004). Reduced sensitivity to others' fearful expressions in psychopathic individuals. *Personality and Individual Differences, 37*(6), 1111–1122.

Blair, R. J. R., Peschardt, K. S., Budhani, S., Mitchell, D. G. V., & Pine, D. S. (2006). The development of psychopathy. *Journal of Child Psychology and Psychiatry, 47*(3–4), 262–276.

Blumer, D., & Benson, D. (1975). Personality changes with frontal and temporal lesions. In D. Blumer & D. Benson (Eds.), *Psychiatric Aspects of Neurologic Disease.* New York: Grune & Stratton.

Bo, S., Forth, A., Kongerslev, M., Haahr, U. H., Pedersen, L., & Simonsen, E. (2013). Subtypes of aggression in patients with schizophrenia: The role of psychopathy. *The Journal of Forensic Psychiatry & Psychology, 24*(4), 496–513.

Boccardi, M., Bocchetta, M., Aronen, H. J., Repo-Tiihonen, E., Vaurio, O., Thompson, P. M., … Frisoni, G. B. (2013). Atypical nucleus accumbens morphology in psychopathy: Another limbic piece in the puzzle. *International Journal of Law and Psychiatry, 36*(2), 157–167.

Boccardi, M., Frisoni, G. B., Hare, R. D., Cavedo, E., Najt, P., Pievani, M., … Tiihonen, J. (2011). Cortex and amygdala morphology in psychopathy. *Psychiatry Research-Neuroimaging, 193*(2), 85–92.

Boccardi, M., Ganzola, R., Rossi, R., Sabattoli, F., Laakso, M. P., Repo-Tiihonen, E., … Tiihonen, J. (2010). Abnormal hippocampal shape in offenders with psychopathy. *Human Brain Mapping, 31*(3), 438–447.

Budhani, S., & Blair, R. J. R. (2005). Response reversal and children with psychopathic tendencies: Success is a function of salience of contingency change. *Journal of Child Psychology and Psychiatry, 46*(9), 972–981.

Budhani, S., Richell, R. A., & Blair, R. J. R. (2006). Impaired reversal but intact acquisition: Probabilistic response reversal deficits in adult individuals with psychopathy. *Journal of Abnormal Psychology, 115*(3), 552–558.

Button, K. S., Ioannidis, J. P. A., Mokrysz, C., Nosek, B. A., Flint, J., Robinson, E. S. J., & Munafò, M. R. (2013). Power failure: Why small sample size undermines the reliability of neuroscience. *Nature Reviews Neuroscience, 14*(5), 365–376.

Calder, A. J., Young, A. W., Rowland, D., Perrett, D. I., Hodges, J. R., & Etcoff, N. L. (1996). Facial emotion recognition after bilateral amygdala damage: Differentially severe impairment of fear. *Cognitive Neuropsychology, 13*(5), 699–745.

Cima, M., Smeets, T., & Jelicic, M. (2008). Self-reported trauma, cortisol levels, and aggression in psychopathic and non-psychopathic prison inmates. *Biological Psychology, 78*(1), 75–86.

Cima, M., Tonnaer, F., & Hauser, M. D. (2010). Psychopaths know right from wrong but don't care. *Social Cognitive and Affective Neuroscience, 5*(1), 59–67.

Cleckley, H. (1941). *The mask of sanity*. St-Louis, MO: Mosby.

Contreras-Rodriguez, O., Pujol, J., Batalla, I., Harrison, B. J., Bosque, J., Ibern-Regas, I., ... Cardoner, N. (2014). Disrupted neural processing of emotional faces in psychopathy. *Social Cognitive and Affective Neuroscience, 9*(4), 505–512.

Cooke, D. J., & Michie, C. (1997). An item response theory analysis of the hare psychopathy checklist – revised. *Psychological Assessment, 9*(1), 3–14.

Cope, L. M., Shane, M. S., Segall, J. M., Nyalakanti, P. K., Stevens, M. C., Pearlson, G. D., ... Kiehl, K. A. (2012). Examining the effect of psychopathic traits on gray matter volume in a community substance abuse sample. *Psychiatry Research – Neuroimaging, 204*(2–3), 91–100.

Craig, M. C., Catani, M., Deeley, Q., Latham, R., Daly, E., Kanaan, R., ... Murphy, D. G. M. (2009). Altered connections on the road to psychopathy. *Molecular Psychiatry, 14*(10), 946–953.

Dadds, M. R., El Masry, Y., Wimalaweera, S., & Guastella, A. J. (2008). Reduced eye gaze explains "Fear Blindness" in childhood psychopathic traits. *Journal of the American Academy of Child and Adolescent Psychiatry, 47*(4), 455–463.

Dadds, M. R., Jambrak, J., Pasalich, D., Hawes, D. J., & Brennan, J. (2011). Impaired attention to the eyes of attachment figures and the developmental origins of psychopathy. *Journal of Child Psychology and Psychiatry, 52*(3), 238–245.

Dadds, M. R., Perry, Y., Hawes, D. J., Merz, S., Riddell, A. C., Haines, D. J., ... Abeygunawardane, A. (2006). Attention to the eyes reverses fear-recognition deficits in child psychopathy. *British Journal of Psychiatry, 189*(3), 280–281.

Damasio, A. R. (1994). *Descartes's error: Emotion, rationality and the human brain*. New York: Putnam.

Dawel, A., O'Kearney, R., McKone, E., & Palermo, R. (2012). Not just fear and sadness: Meta-analytic evidence of pervasive emotion recognition deficits for facial and vocal expressions in psychopathy. *Neuroscience and Biobehavioral Reviews, 36*(10), 2288–2304.

De Brito, S. A., & Hodgins, S. (2009a). Antisocial personality disorder. In M. McMurran & R. Howard (Eds.), *Personality, personality disorder, and risk of violence: An evidence based approach* (pp. 133–154). Chichester: John Wiley & Sons.

De Brito, S. A., & Hodgins, S. (2009b). Executive functions of persistent violent offenders: A critical review of the literature. In S. Hodgins, E. Viding & A. Plodowski (Eds.), *Persistent violent offenders: Neurobiology and rehabilitation* (pp. 167–199). Oxford: Oxford University Press.

De Brito, S. A., Hodgins, S., McCrory, E. J. P., Mechelli, A., Wilke, M., Jones, A. P., & Viding, E. (2009). Structural neuroimaging and the antisocial brain. *Criminal Justice and Behavior*, *36*(11), 1173–1186.

De Brito, S. A., McCrory, E. J., Mechelli, A., Wilke, M., Jones, A. P., Hodgins, S., & Viding, E. (2011). Small, but not perfectly formed: Decreased white matter concentration in boys with psychopathic tendencies. *Molecular Psychiatry*, *16*(5), 476–477.

De Brito, S. A., Mechelli, A., Wilke, M., Laurens, K. R., Jones, A. P., Barker, G. J., … Viding, E. (2009). Size matters: Increased grey matter in boys with conduct problems and callous-unemotional traits. *Brain*, *132*(4), 843–852.

De Brito, S. A., Viding, E., Kumari, V., Blackwood, N., & Hodgins, S. (2013). Cool and hot executive function impairments in violent offenders with antisocial personality disorder with and without psychopathy. *PLoS ONE*, *8*(6).

de Oliveira-Souza, R., Hare, R. D., Bramati, I. E., Garrido, G. J., Azevedo Ignacio, F., Tovar-Moll, F., & Moll, J. (2008). Psychopathy as a disorder of the moral brain: Fronto-temporo-limbic grey matter reductions demonstrated by voxel-based morphometry. *NeuroImage*, *40*(3), 1202–1213.

Decety, J., Chen, C., Harenski, C., & Kiehl, K. A. (2013). An fMRI study of affective perspective taking in individuals with psychopathy: Imagining another in pain does not evoke empathy. *Frontiers in Human Neuroscience*, *7*, 489.

Decety, J., Skelly, L. R., & Kiehl, K. A. (2013). Brain response to empathy-eliciting scenarios involving pain in incarcerated individuals with psychopathy. *JAMA Psychiatry*, *70*(6), 638–645.

Decety, J., Skelly, L., Yoder, K. J., & Kiehl, K. A. (2014). Neural processing of dynamic emotional facial expressions in psychopaths. *Social Neuroscience*, *9*(1), 36–49.

Decker, S. A. (2000). Salivary cortisol and social status among Dominican men. *Hormones and Behavior*, *38*(1), 29–38.

Deeley, Q., Daly, E., Surguladze, S., Tunstall, N., Mezey, G., Beer, D., … Murphy, D. G. (2006). Facial emotion processing in criminal psychopathy: Preliminary functional magnetic resonance imaging study. *British Journal of Psychiatry*, *189*(6), 533–539.

Dindo, L., & Fowles, D. (2011). Dual temperamental risk factors for psychopathic personality: Evidence from self-report and skin conductance. *Journal of Personality and Social Psychology*, *100*(3), 557–566.

Dolan, M., & Fullam, R. (2006). Face affect recognition deficits in personality-disordered offenders: Association with psychopathy. *Psychological Medicine*, *36*(11), 1563–1569.

Douglas, K. S., Vincent, G. M., & Edens, J. F. (2006). Risk for criminal recidivism: The role of psychopathy. In C. J. Patrick (Ed.), *Handbook of psychopathy* (pp. 533–554). New York, NY: Guilford Press.

Eckert, M. A., Leonard, C. M., Wilke, M., Eckert, M., Richards, T., Richards, A., & Berninger, V. (2005). Anatomical signatures of dyslexia in children: Unique information from manual and voxel based morphometry brain measures. *Cortex*, *41*(3), 304–315.

Ermer, E., Cope, L. M., Nyalakanti, P. K., Calhoun, V. D., & Kiehl, K. A. (2012). Aberrant Paralimbic gray matter in criminal Psychopathy. *Journal of Abnormal Psychology*, *121*(3), 649–658.

Ermer, E., Cope, L. M., Nyalakanti, P. K., Calhoun, V. D., & Kiehl, K. A. (2013). Aberrant paralimbic gray matter in incarcerated male adolescents with psychopathic traits. *Journal of the American Academy of Child and Adolescent Psychiatry*, *52*(1), 94–103.

Fairchild, G., Hagan, C. C., Walsh, N. D., Passamonti, L., Calder, A. J., & Goodyer, I. M. (2013). Brain structure abnormalities in adolescent girls with conduct disorder. *Journal of Child Psychology and Psychiatry and Allied Disciplines*, *54*(1), 86–95.

Fairchild, G., Passamonti, L., Hurford, G., Hagan, C. C., Von Dem Hagen, E. A. H., van Goozen, S. H. M., … Calder, A. J. (2011). Brain structure abnormalities in early-onset and adolescent-onset conduct disorder. *American Journal of Psychiatry*, *168*(6), 624–633.

Fairchild, G., van Goozen, S. H. M., Calder, A. J., Stollery, S. J., & Goodyer, I. M. (2009). Deficits in facial expression recognition in male adolescents with early-onset or adolescence-onset conduct disorder. *Journal of Child Psychology and Psychiatry and Allied Disciplines*, *50*(5), 627–636.

Finger, E. C., Marsh, A., Blair, K. S., Majestic, C., Evangelou, I., Gupta, K., ... Blair, R. J. R. (2012). Impaired functional but preserved structural connectivity in limbic white matter tracts in youth with conduct disorder or oppositional defiant disorder plus psychopathic traits. *Psychiatry Research – Neuroimaging*, *202*(3), 239–244.

Finger, E. C., Marsh, A. A., Blair, K. S., Reid, M. E., Sims, C., Ng, P., ... Blair, R. J. R. (2011). Disrupted reinforcement signaling in the orbitofrontal cortex and caudate in youths with conduct disorder or oppositional defiant disorder and a high level of psychopathic traits. *American Journal of Psychiatry*, *168*(2), 152–162.

Finger, E. C., Mitchell, D. G. V., Jones, M., & Blair, R. J. R. (2008). Dissociable roles of medial orbitofrontal cortex in human operant extinction learning. *NeuroImage*, *43*(4), 748–755.

Fisher, L., & Blair, R. J. R. (1998). Cognitive impairment and its relationship to psychopathic tendencies in children with emotional and behavioral difficulties. *Journal of Abnormal Child Psychology*, *26*(6), 511–519.

Flor, H., Birbaumer, N., Hermann, C., Ziegler, S., & Patrick, C. J. (2002). Aversive Pavlovian conditioning in psychopaths: Peripheral and central correlates. *Psychophysiology*, *39*(4), 505–518.

Fowles, D. C. (2000). Electrodermal hyporeactivity and antisocial behavior: Does anxiety mediate the relationship? *Journal of Affective Disorders*, *61*(3), 177–189.

Freese, J., & Amaral, D. (2009). Neuroanatomy of the primate amygdala. In P. Whalen & E. Phelps (Eds.), *The human amygdala* (pp. 3–42.). New York, NY: Guilford Press.

Frick, P. J., & Marsee, M. A. (2006). Psychopathy and developmental pathways to antisocial behavior in youth. In C. J. Patrick (Ed.), *Handbook of psychopathy* (pp. 353–374). New York, NY: Guilford Press.

Frick, P. J., O'Brien, B. S., Wootton, J. M., & McBurnett, K. (1994). Psychopathy and conduct problems in children. *Journal of Abnormal Psychology*, *103*(4), 700–707.

Frick, P. J., Ray, J. V., Thornton, L. C., & Kahn, R. E. (2014). Can callous-unemotional traits enhance the understanding, diagnosis, and treatment of serious conduct problems in children and adolescents? A comprehensive review. *Psychological Bulletin*, *140*(1), 1–57.

Fung, M. T., Raine, A., Loeber, R., Lynam, D. R., Steinhauer, S. R., Venables, P. H., & Stouthamer-Loeber, M. (2005). Reduced electrodermal activity in psychopathy-prone adolescents. *Journal of Abnormal Psychology*, *114*(2), 187–196.

Gao, Y., Baker, L. A., Raine, A., Wu, H., & Bezdjian, S. (2009). Brief report: Interaction between social class and risky decision-making in children with psychopathic tendencies. *Journal of Adolescence*, *32*(2), 409–414.

Gao, Y., & Raine, A. (2010). Successful and unsuccessful psychopaths: A neurobiological model. *Behavioral Sciences & the Law*, *28*(2), 194–210.

Gao, Y., Raine, A., & Schug, R. A. (2012). Somatic aphasia: Mismatch of body sensations with autonomic stress reactivity in psychopathy. *Biological Psychology*, *90*(3), 228–233.

Giedd, J. N., & Rapoport, J. L. (2010). Structural MRI of pediatric brain development: What have we learned and where are we going? *Neuron*, *67*(5), 728–734.

Glenn, A. L., Raine, A., & Schug, R. A. (2009). The neural correlates of moral decision-making in psychopathy. *Molecular Psychiatry*, *14*(1), 5–6.

Glenn, A. L., Raine, A., Schug, R. A., Gao, Y., & Granger, D. A. (2011). Increased testosterone-to-cortisol ratio in psychopathy. *Journal of Abnormal Psychology*, *120*(2), 389–399.

Glenn, A. L., Raine, A., Yaralian, P. S., & Yang, Y. (2010). Increased volume of the striatum in psychopathic individuals. *Biological Psychiatry*, *67*(1), 52–58.

Glenn, A. L., & Yang, Y. L. (2012). The potential role of the striatum in antisocial behavior and psychopathy. *Biological Psychiatry*, *72*(10), 817–822.

Glenn, A. L., Yang, Y., Raine, A., & Colletti, P. (2010). No volumetric differences in the anterior cingulate of psychopathic individuals. *Psychiatry Research – Neuroimaging, 183*(2), 140–143.

Grafman, J., Schwab, K., Warden, D., Pridgen, A., Brown, H. R., & Salazar, A. M. (1996). Frontal lobe injuries, violence, and aggression: A report of the Vietnam head injury study. *Neurology, 46*(5), 1231–1238.

Greene, J. D., Nystrom, L. E., Engell, A. D., Darley, J. M., & Cohen, J. D. (2004). The neural bases of cognitive conflict and control in moral judgment. *Neuron, 44*(2), 389–400.

Gregory, S., Ffytche, D., Simmons, A., Kumari, V., Howard, M., Hodgins, S., & Blackwood, N. (2012). The antisocial brain: Psychopathy matters: A structural MRI investigation of antisocial male violent offenders. *Archives of General Psychiatry, 69*(9), 962–972.

Haber, S. N. (2011). Neuroanatomy of reward: A view from the ventral striatum. In J. A. Gottfried (Ed.), *Neurobiology of Sensation and Reward*. Boca Raton, FL: CRC Press.

Hackman, D. A., Farah, M. J., & Meaney, M. J. (2010). Socioeconomic status and the brain: Mechanistic insights from human and animal research. *Nature Review Neuroscience, 11*(9), 651–659.

Hall, J. R., & Benning, S. D. (2006). The "successful" psychopath: Adaptive and subclinical manifestations of psychopathy in the general population. In C. J. Patrick (Ed.), *Handbook of psychopathy* (pp. 459–478). New York, NY: Guilford Press.

Hare, R. D. (1991). *The Hare psychopathy checklist – revised*. Toronto, ON: Multi-Health Systems.

Hare, R. D. (1993). *Without conscience: The disturbing world of the psychopaths among us*. New York, NY: Simon & Schuster.

Hare, R. D. (1998). Psychopathy, affect, and behavior. In D. J. Cooke, A. E. Forth, & R. D. Hare (Eds.), *Psychopathy: Theory, research, and implications for society* (pp. 105–137). Dordrecht, The Netherlands: Kluwer.

Hare, R. D. (2003). *Manual for the Revised Psychopathy Checklist* (2nd ed.). Toronto, ON: Multi-Health Systems.

Hare, R. D., Clark, D., Grann, M., & Thornton, D. (2000). Psychopathy and the predictive validity of the PCL-R: An international perspective. *Behavioral Sciences & the Law, 18*(5), 623–645.

Hare, R. D., & Jutai, J. W. (1983). Criminal history of the male psychopath: Some preliminary data. In K. T. VanDusen & S. A. Mednick (Eds.), *Prospective studies of crime and delinquency* (pp. 225–236). Boston, MA: Kluwer-Nijhoff.

Hare, R. D., & McPherson, L. M. (1984). Psychopathy and perceptual asymmetry during verbal dichotic-listening. *Journal of Abnormal Psychology, 93*(2), 141–149.

Hare, R. D., & Quinn, M. J. (1971). Psychopathy and autonomic conditioning. *Journal of Abnormal Psychology, 77*(3), 223–235.

Harenski, C. L., Harenski, K. A., Shane, M. S., & Kiehl, K. A. (2010). Aberrant neural processing of moral violations in criminal psychopaths. *Journal of Abnormal Psychology, 119*(4), 863–874.

Hariri, A. R., Bookheimer, S. Y., & Mazziotta, J. C. (2000). Modulating emotional responses: effects of a neocortical network on the limbic system. *Neuroreport, 11*(1), 43–48.

Harris, G. T., & Rice, M. E. (2006). Treatment of psychopathy: A review of empirical findings. In C. J. Patrick (Ed.), *Handbook of psychopathy* (pp. 555–572). New York, NY: Guilford Press.

Hart, S. D., Cox, D. N., & Hare, R. D. (1995). *The Hare psychopathy checklist: Screening version (PCL: SV)*. Toronto, ON: Mutli-Health Systems.

Hart, S. D., & Hare, R. D. (1996). Psychopathy and antisocial personality disorder. *Current Opinion in Psychiatry, 9*(2), 129–132.

Heberlein, A. S., Padon, A. A., Gillihan, S. J., Farah, M. J., & Fellows, L. K. (2008). Ventromedial frontal lobe plays a critical role in facial emotion recognition. *Journal of Cognitive Neuroscience, 20*(4), 721–733.

Hemphill, J. F., Hare, R. D., & Wong, S. (1998). Psychopathy and recidivism: A review. *Legal and Criminological Psychology, 3*(Part 1), 139–170.

Hodgins, S., De Brito, S. A., Simonoff, E., Vloet, T., & Viding, E. (2009). Getting the phenotypes right: An essential ingredient for understanding aetiological mechanisms underlying persistent violence and developing effective treatments. *Frontiers in Behavioral Neuroscience, 3*(Nov).

Hoppenbrouwers, S. S., De Jesus, D. R., Sun, Y. M., Stirpe, T., Hofman, D., McMaster, J., ... Schutter, D. (2014). Abnormal interhemispheric connectivity in male psychopathic offenders. *Journal of Psychiatry & Neuroscience, 39*(1), 22–30.

Hurlemann, R., Patin, A., Onur, O. A., Cohen, M. X., Baumgartner, T., Metzler, S., ... Maier, W. (2010). Oxytocin enhances amygdala-dependent, socially reinforced learning and emotional empathy in humans. *The Journal of Neuroscience, 30*(14), 4999–5007.

Insel, T., Cuthbert, B., Garvey, M., Heinssen, R., Pine, D. S., Quinn, K., ... Wang, P. (2010). Research domain criteria (RDoC): Toward a new classification framework for research on mental disorders. *American Journal of Psychiatry, 167*(7), 748–751.

Ishikawa, S. S., Raine, A., Lencz, T., Bihrle, S., & LaCasse, L. (2001). Autonomic stress reactivity and executive functions in successful and unsuccessful criminal psychopaths from the community. *Journal of Abnormal Psychology, 110*(3), 423–432.

Jones, A. P., Happé, F. G., Gilbert, F., Burnett, S., & Viding, E. (2010). Feeling, caring, knowing: Different types of empathy deficit in boys with psychopathic tendencies and autism spectrum disorder. *Journal of child psychology and psychiatry, and allied disciplines, 51*(11), 1188–1197.

Jones, A. P., Laurens, K. R., Herba, C. M., Barker, G. J., & Viding, E. (2009). Amygdala hypoactivity to fearful faces in boys with conduct problems and callous-unemotional traits. *American Journal of Psychiatry, 166*(1), 95–102.

Jones, D. K. (2008). Studying connections in the living human brain with diffusion MRI. *Cortex, 44*(8), 936–952.

Karpman, B. (1941). On the need of separating psychopathy into two distinct clinical types: The symptomatic and the idiopathic. *Journal of Criminal Psychopathology, 3*, 112–137.

Kiehl, K. A., Smith, A. M., Hare, R. D., Mendrek, A., Forster, B. B., Brink, J., & Liddle, P. F. (2001). Limbic abnormalities in affective processing by criminal psychopaths as revealed by functional magnetic resonance imaging. *Biological Psychiatry, 50*(9), 677–684.

Koenigs, M., Baskin-Sommers, A., Zeier, J., & Newman, J. P. (2011). Investigating the neural correlates of psychopathy: A critical review. *Molecular Psychiatry, 16*(8), 792–799.

Koenigs, M., Kruepke, M., & Newman, J. P. (2010). Economic decision-making in psychopathy: A comparison with ventromedial prefrontal lesion patients. *Neuropsychologia, 48*(7), 2198–2204.

Koenigs, M., Young, L., Adolphs, R., Tranel, D., Cushman, F., Hauser, M., & Damasio, A. (2007). Damage to the prefrontal cortex increases utilitarian moral judgements. *Nature, 446*(7138), 908–911.

Kosfeld, M., Heinrichs, M., Zak, P. J., Fischbacher, U., & Fehr, E. (2005). Oxytocin increases trust in humans. *Nature, 435*(7042), 673–676.

Kosson, D. S., Lorenz, A. R., & Newman, J. P. (2006). Effects of comorbid psychopathy on criminal offending and emotion processing in male offenders with antisocial personality disorder. *Journal of Abnormal Psychology, 115*(4), 798–806.

Kosson, D. S., Smith, S. S., & Newman, J. P. (1990). Evaluating the construct validity of psychopathy in black and white male inmates: Three preliminary studies. *Journal of Abnormal Psychology, 99*(3), 250–259.

Kraemer, H. C., Yesavage, J. A., Taylor, J. L., & Kupfer, D. (2000). How can we learn about developmental processes from cross-sectional studies, or can we? *American Journal of Psychiatry, 157*(2), 163–171.

Laakso, M. P., Vaurio, O., Koivisto, E., Savolainen, L., Eronen, M., Aronen, H. J., ... Tiihonen, J. (2001). Psychopathy and the posterior hippocampus. *Behavioural Brain Research, 118*(2), 187–193.

Lamm, C., Decety, J., & Singer, T. (2011). Meta-analytic evidence for common and distinct neural networks associated with directly experienced pain and empathy for pain. *NeuroImage, 54*(3), 2492–2502.

Lockwood, P. L., Sebastian, C. L., McCrory, E. J., Hyde, Z. H., Gu, X., De Brito, S. A., & Viding, E. (2013). Association of callous traits with reduced neural response to others' pain in children with conduct problems. *Current Biology, 23*(10), 901–905.

Lorber, M. F. (2004). Psychophysiology of aggression, psychopathy, and conduct problems: A meta-analysis. *Psychological Bulletin, 130*(4), 531–552.

Lozier, L. M., Cardinale, E. M., Van Meter, J. W., & Marsh, A. A. (2014). Mediation of the relationship between callous-unemotional traits and proactive aggression by amygdala response to fear among children with conduct problems. *JAMA Psychiatry, 71*(6), 627–636.

Ly, M., Motzkin, J. C., Philippi, C. L., Kirk, G. R., Newman, J. P., Kiehl, K. A., & Koenigs, M. (2012). Cortical thinning in psychopathy. *American Journal of Psychiatry, 169*(7), 743–749.

Lykken, D. T. (1995). *The antisocial personalities*. Hillsdale, NJ: Erlbaum.

Malik, A. I., Zai, C. C., Abu, Z., Nowrouzi, B., & Beitchman, J. H. (2012). The role of oxytocin and oxytocin receptor gene variants in childhood-onset aggression. *Genes Brain and Behavior, 11*(5), 545–551.

Marsh, A. A., & Blair, R. J. R. (2008). Deficits in facial affect recognition among antisocial populations: A meta-analysis. *Neuroscience and Biobehavioral Reviews, 32*(3), 454–465.

Marsh, A. A., Finger, E. C., Fowler, K. A., Adalio, C. J., Jurkowitz, I. T. N., Schechter, J. C., ... Blair, R. J. R. (2013). Empathic responsiveness in amygdala and anterior cingulate cortex in youths with psychopathic traits. *Journal of Child Psychology and Psychiatry and Allied Disciplines, 54*(8), 900–910.

Marsh, A. A., Finger, E. C., Fowler, K. A., Jurkowitz, I. T. N., Schechter, J. C., Yu, H. H., ... Blair, R. J. R. (2011). Reduced amygdala-orbitofrontal connectivity during moral judgments in youths with disruptive behavior disorders and psychopathic traits. *Psychiatry Research - Neuroimaging, 194*(3), 279–286.

Marsh, A. A., Finger, E. C., Mitchell, D. G., Reid, M. E., Sims, C., Kosson, D. S., ... Blair, R. J. R. (2008). Reduced amygdala response to fearful expressions in children and adolescents with callous-unemotional traits and disruptive behavior disorders. *American Journal of Psychiatry, 165*(6), 712–720.

Marshall, L. A., & Cooke, D. J. (1999). The childhood experiences of psychopaths: A retrospective study of familial and societal factors. *Journal of Personality Disorders, 13*(3), 211–225.

Mechelli, A., Price, C. J., Friston, K. J., & Ashburner, J. (2005). Voxel-based morphometry of the human brain: Methods and applications *Current Medical Imaging Reviews, 1*(2), 105–113.

Meffert, H., Gazzola, V., den Boer, J. A., Bartels, A. A. J., & Keysers, C. (2013). Reduced spontaneous but relatively normal deliberate vicarious representations in psychopathy. *Brain, 136*, 2550–2562.

Menon, V. (2011). Large-scale brain networks and psychopathology: A unifying triple network model. *Trends in Cognitive Sciences, 15*(10), 483–506.

Meyers, C. A., Berman, S. A., Scheibel, R. S., & Hayman, A. (1992). Case report: Acquired antisocial personality disorder associated with unilateral left orbital frontal lobe damage. *Journal of Psychiatry & Neuroscience, 17*(3), 121–125.

Mier, D., Haddad, L., Diers, K., Dressing, H., Meyer-Lindenberg, A., & Kirsch, P. (2014). Reduced embodied simulation in psychopathy. *World Journal of Biological Psychiatry*, *15*(6), 479–487.

Mitchell, D. G. V., Avny, S. B., & Blair, R. J. R. (2006). Divergent patterns of aggressive and neurocognitive characteristics in acquired versus developmental psychopathy. *Neurocase*, *12*(3), 164–178.

Mitchell, I. J., Smid, W., Troelstra, J., Wever, E., Ziegler, T. E., & Beech, A. R. (2013). Psychopathic characteristics are related to high basal urinary oxytocin levels in male forensic patients. *Journal of Forensic Psychiatry & Psychology*, *24*(3), 309–318.

Moffitt, T. E., Arseneault, L., Jaffee, S. R., Kim-Cohen, J., Koenen, K. C., Odgers, C. L., ... Viding, E. (2008). Research review: DSM-V conduct disorder: Research needs for an evidence base. *Journal of Child Psychology and Psychiatry*, *49*(1), 3–33.

Molto, J., Poy, R., Segarra, P., Pastor, M. C., & Montanaňé, S. (2007). Response perseveration in psychopaths: Interpersonal/affective or social deviance traits? *Journal of Abnormal Psychology*, *116*(3), 632–637.

Monahan, J. (2006) [Comments on cover jacket]. In C. J. Patrick (Ed.) *Handbook of psychopathy*. New York, NY: Guilford Press.

Motzkin, J. C., Newman, J. P., Kiehl, K. A., & Koenigs, M. (2011). Reduced prefrontal connectivity in psychopathy. *The Journal of Neuroscience*, *31*(48), 17348–17357.

Moul, C., Killcross, S., & Dadds, M. R. (2012). A model of differential amygdala activation in psychopathy. *Psychological Review*, *119*(4), 789–806.

Müller, J. L., Sommer, M., Dohnel, K., Weber, T., Schmidt-Wilcke, T., & Hajak, G. (2008). Disturbed prefrontal and temporal brain function during emotion and cognition interaction in criminal psychopathy. *Behavioral Sciences & the Law*, *26*(1), 131–150.

Müller, J. L., Sommer, M., Wagner, V., Lange, K., Taschler, H., Roder, C. H., ... Hajak, G. (2003). Abnormalities in emotion processing within cortical and subcortical regions in criminal psychopaths: Evidence from a functional magnetic resonance imaging study using pictures with emotional content. *Biological Psychiatry*, *54*(2), 152–162.

Newman, J. P., Curtin, J. J., Bertsch, J. D., & Baskin-Sommers, A. R. (2010). Attention moderates the fearlessness of psychopathic offenders. *Biological Psychiatry*, *67*(1), 66–70.

Newman, J. P., Patterson, C. M., & Kosson, D. S. (1987). Response perseveration in psychopaths. *Journal of Abnormal Psychology*, *96*(2), 145–148.

O'Nions, E., Sebastian, C. L., McCrory, E., Chantiluke, K., Happé, F., & Viding, E. (2014). Neural bases of theory of mind in children with autism spectrum disorders and children with conduct problems and callous-unemotional traits. *Developmental Science*, *17*(5), 786–796.

Panizzon, M. S., Fennema-Notestine, C., Eyler, L. T., Jernigan, T. L., Prom-Wormley, E., Neale, M., ... Kremen, W. S. (2009). Distinct genetic influences on cortical surface area and cortical thickness. *Cerebral Cortex*, *19*(11), 2728–2735.

Pardini, D. A., Erickson, K., Loeber, R., & Raine, A. (2013). Lower amygdala volume in men is associated with childhood aggression, early psychopathic traits, and future violence. *Biological Psychiatry*, *75*, 73–80.

Pastor, M. C., Molto, J., Vila, J., & Lang, P. J. (2003). Startle reflex modulation, affective ratings and autonomic reactivity in incarcerated Spanish psychopaths. *Psychophysiology*, *40*(6), 934–938.

Patrick, C. J. (1994). Emotion and psychopathy: Startling new insights. *Psychophysiology*, *31*(4), 319–330.

Patrick, C. J. (2006). *Handbook of psychopathy*. New York, NY: Guilford Press.

Patrick, C. J. (2007). Getting to the heart of psychopathy. In H. Hervé & J. C. Yuille (Eds.), *The psychopath: Theory, research, and practice* (pp. 207–252). Mahwah, NJ: Lawrence Erlbaum Associates Publishers.

Patrick, C. J. (2008). Psychophysiological correlates of aggression and violence: An integrative review. *Philosophical Transactions of the Royal Society B: Biological Sciences, 363*(1503), 2543–2555.

Patrick, C. J., Bradley, M. M., & Lang, P. J. (1993). Emotion in the criminal psychopath: Startle reflex modulation. *Journal of Abnormal Psychology, 102*(1), 82–92.

Patrick, C. J., Cuthbert, B. N., & Lang, P. J. (1994). Emotion in the criminal psychopath: Fear image processing. *Journal of Abnormal Psychology, 103*(3), 523–534.

Pham, T. H., Philippot, P., & Rime, B. (2000). Subjective and autonomic responses to emotion induction in psychopaths. *Encephale, 26*(1), 45–51.

Porter, S., Birt, A. R., & Boer, D. P. (2001). Investigation of the criminal and conditional release profiles of Canadian federal offenders as a function of psychopathy and age. *Law and Human Behavior, 25*(6), 647–661.

Porter, S., & Woodworth, M. (2006). Psychopathy and aggression. In C. J. Patrick (Ed.), *Handbook of psychopathy* (pp. 481–494). New York, NY: Guilford Press.

Poythress, N., & Skeem, J. L. (2006). Disaggregating psychopathy: Where and how to look for subtypes. In C. J. Patrick (Ed.), *Handbook of psychopathy* (pp. 172–192). New York, NY: Guilford Press.

Prehn, K., Schulze, L., Rossmann, S., Berger, C., Vohs, K., Fleischer, M., ... Herpertz, S. C. (2013). Effects of emotional stimuli on working memory processes in male criminal offenders with borderline and antisocial personality disorder. *World Journal of Biological Psychiatry, 14*(1), 71–78.

Pujara, M., Motzkin, J. C., Newman, J. P., Kiehl, K. A., & Koenigs, M. (2013). Neural correlates of reward and loss sensitivity in psychopathy. *Social Cognitive and Affective Neuroscience, 9*(6), 794–801.

Pujol, J., Batalla, I., Contreras-Rodriguez, O., Harrison, B. J., Pera, V., Hernandez-Ribas, R., ... Cardoner, N. (2012). Breakdown in the brain network subserving moral judgment in criminal psychopathy. *Social Cognitive and Affective Neuroscience, 7*(8), 917–923.

Raine, A., Ishikawa, S. S., Arce, E., Lencz, T., Knuth, K. H., Bihrle, S., ... Colletti, P. (2004). Hippocampal structural asymmetry in unsuccessful psychopaths. *Biological Psychiatry, 55*(2), 185–191.

Raine, A., Lee, L., Yang, Y., & Colletti, P. (2010). Neurodevelopmental marker for limbic maldevelopment in antisocial personality disorder and psychopathy. *British Journal of Psychiatry, 197*(3), 186–192.

Raine, A., Lencz, T., Taylor, K., Hellige, J. B., Bihrle, S., LaCasse, L., ... Colletti, P. (2003). Corpus callosum abnormalities in psychopathic antisocial individuals. *Archives of General Psychiatry, 60*(11), 1134–1142.

Raznahan, A., Shaw, P., Lalonde, F., Stockman, M., Wallace, G. L., Greenstein, D., ... Giedd, J. N. (2011). How does your cortex grow? *Journal of Neuroscience, 31*(19), 7174–7177.

Reidy, D. E., Shelley-Tremblay, J. F., & Lilienfeld, S. O. (2011). Psychopathy, reactive aggression, and precarious proclamations: A review of behavioral, cognitive, and biological research. *Aggression and Violent Behavior, 16*(6), 512–524.

Rijsdijsk, F. V., Viding, E., De Brito, S. A., Forgiarini, M., Mechelli, A., Jones, A. P., & McCrory, E. (2010). Heritable variations in gray matter concentration as a potential endophenotype for psychopathic traits. *Archives of General Psychiatry, 67*(4), 406–413.

Rogers, R. D. (2006). The functional architectures of the frontal lobes psychopathy: Implications for research with psychopathic offenders. In C. J. Patrick (Ed.), *Handbook of psychopathy* (pp. 313–333). New York, NY: Guilford Press.

Rothemund, Y., Ziegler, S., Hermann, C., Gruesser, S. M., Foell, J., Patrick, C. J., & Flor, H. (2012). Fear conditioning in psychopaths: Event-related potentials and peripheral measures. *Biological Psychology, 90*(1), 50–59.

Santos, A., Mier, D., Kirsch, P., & Meyer-Lindenberg, A. (2011). Evidence for a general face salience signal in human amygdala. *NeuroImage, 54*(4), 3111–3116.

Sarkar, S., Craig, M. C., Catani, M., Dell'Acqua, F., Fahy, T., Deeley, Q., & Murphy, D. G. M. (2013). Frontotemporal white-matter microstructural abnormalities in adolescents with conduct disorder: A diffusion tensor imaging study. *Psychological Medicine, 43*(2), 401–411.

Sato, J. R., de Oliveira-Souza, R., Thomaz, C. E., Basílio, R., Bramati, I. E., Amaro, E., Jr., ... Moll, J. (2011). Identification of psychopathic individuals using pattern classification of MRI images. *Social Neuroscience, 6*(5–6), 627–639.

Schneider, F., Habel, U., Kessler, C., Posse, S., Grodd, W., & Müller-Gartner, H.-W. (2000). Functional imaging of conditioned aversive emotional responses in antisocial personality disorder. *Neuropsychobiology, 42*(4), 192–201.

Seara-Cardoso, A., & Viding, E. (2015). Functional neuroscience of psychopathic personality in adults. *Journal of Personality, 83*(6), 723–737.

Sebastian, C. L., McCrory, E. J. P., Cecil, C. A. M., Lockwood, P. L., De Brito, S. A., Fontaine, N. M. G., & Viding, E. (2012). Neural responses to affective and cognitive theory of mind in children with conduct problems and varying levels of callous-unemotional traits. *Archives of General Psychiatry, 69*(8), 814–822.

Serin, R. C. (1991). Psychopathy and violence in criminals. *Journal of Interpersonal Violence, 6*(4), 423–431.

Shaw, P., Eckstrand, K., Sharp, W., Blumenthal, J., Lerch, J. P., Greenstein, D., ... Rapoport, J. L. (2007). Attention-deficit/hyperactivity disorder is characterized by a delay in cortical maturation. *Proceedings of the National Academy of Sciences, 104*(49), 19649–19654.

Skeem, J. L., Johansson, P., Andershed, H., Kerr, M., & Louden, J. E. (2007). Two subtypes of psychopathic violent offenders that parallel primary and secondary variants. *Journal of Abnormal Psychology, 116*(2), 395–409.

Skeem, J. L., Polaschek, D. L. L., Patrick, C. J., & Lilienfeld, S. O. (2011). Psychopathic personality: Bridging the gap between scientific evidence and public policy. *Psychological Science in the Public Interest, Supplement, 12*(3), 95–162.

Soderstrom, H., & Forsman, A. (2004). Elevated triiodothyronine in psychopathy – possible physiological mechanisms. *Journal of Neural Transmission, 111*(6), 739–744.

Sommer, M., Sodian, B., Döhnel, K., Schwerdtner, J., Meinhardt, J., & Hajak, G. (2010). In psychopathic patients emotion attribution modulates activity in outcome-related brain areas. *Psychiatry Research – Neuroimaging, 182*(2), 88–95.

Stalenheim, E. G., von Knorring, L., & Wide, L. (1998). Serum levels of thyroid hormones as biological markers in a Swedish forensic psychiatric population. *Biological Psychiatry, 43*(10), 755–761.

Sterzer, P. (2010). Born to be criminal? What to make of early biological risk factors for criminal behavior. *American Journal of Psychiatry, 167*(1), 1–3.

Sundram, F., Deeley, Q., Sarkar, S., Daly, E., Latham, R., Craig, M., ... Williams, S. C. (2012). White matter microstructural abnormalities in the frontal lobe of adults with antisocial personality disorder. *Cortex, 48*(2), 216–229.

Susman, E. J. (2006). Psychobiology of persistent antisocial behavior: Stress, early vulnerabilities and the attenuation hypothesis. *Neuroscience and Biobehavioral Reviews, 30*(3), 376–389.

Syngelaki, E. M., Fairchild, G., Moore, S. C., Savage, J. C., & van Goozen, S. H. M. (2013). Fearlessness in juvenile offenders is associated with offending rate. *Developmental Science, 16*(1), 84–90.

Tiihonen, J., Rossi, R., Laakso, M. P., Hodgins, S., Testa, C., Perez, J., ... Frisoni, G. B. (2008). Brain anatomy of persistent violent offenders: More rather than less. *Psychiatry Research: Neuroimaging, 163*(3), 201–212.

Toivonen, P., Könönen, M., Niskanen, E., Vaurio, O., Repo-Tiihonen, E., Seppänen, A., ... Laakso, M. P. (2013). Cavum septum pellucidum and psychopathy. *British Journal of Psychiatry, 203*(2), 152–153.

Tost, H., Kolachana, B., Hakimi, S., Lemaitre, H., Verchinski, B. A., Mattay, V. S., ... Meyer-Lindenberg, A. (2010). A common allele in the oxytocin receptor gene (OXTR) impacts prosocial temperament and human hypothalamic-limbic structure and function. *Proceedings of the National Academy of Sciences of the United States of America, 107*(31), 13936–13941.

Van Honk, J., Schutter, D. J. L. G., Hermans, E. J., & Putman, P. (2003). Low cortisol levels and the balance between punishment sensitivity and reward dependency. *Neuroreport, 14*(15), 1993–1996.

Veit, R., Flor, H., Erb, M., Hermann, C., Lotze, M., Grodd, W., & Birbaumer, N. (2002). Brain circuits involved in emotional learning in antisocial behavior and social phobia in humans. *Neuroscience Letters, 328*(3), 233–236.

Viding, E., & McCrory, E. J. (2012). Genetic and neurocognitive contributions to the development of psychopathy. *Development and Psychopathology, 24*(3), 969–983.

Viding, E., Sebastian, C. L., Dadds, M. R., Lockwood, P. L., Cecil, C. A. M., De Brito, S. A., & McCrory, E. J. (2012). Amygdala response to preattentive masked fear in children with conduct problems: The role of callous-unemotional traits. *American Journal of Psychiatry, 169*(10), 1109–1116.

Wallis, J. D. (2007). Orbitofrontal cortex and its contribution to decision-making. *Annual Review of Neuroscience, 30*(1), 31–56.

Whalen, P. J., & Phelps, E. A. (2009). *The human amygdala*. New York, NY: Guilford Press.

White, S. F., Brislin, S., Sinclair, S., Fowler, K. A., Pope, K., & Blair, R. J. R. (2013). The relationship between large cavum septum pellucidum and antisocial behavior, callous-unemotional traits and psychopathy in adolescents. *Journal of Child Psychology and Psychiatry, 54*(5), 575–581.

White, S. F., Marsh, A. A., Fowler, K. A., Schechter, J. C., Adalio, C., Pope, K., ... Blair, R. J. R. (2012). Reduced amygdala response in youths with disruptive behavior disorders and psychopathic traits: Decreased emotional response versus increased top-down attention to nonemotional features. *American Journal of Psychiatry, 169*(7), 750–758.

White, S. F., Pope, K., Sinclair, S., Fowler, K. A., Brislin, S. J., Williams, W. C., ... Blair, R. J. R. (2013). Disrupted expected value and prediction error signaling in youths with disruptive behavior disorders during a passive avoidance task. *American Journal of Psychiatry, 170*(3), 315–323.

World Health Organization (WHO). (1992). *The ICD-10 classification of mental and behavioural disorders: Clinical descriptions and diagnostic guidelines*. Geneva: WHO.

Yang, Y., & Raine, A. (2009). Prefrontal structural and functional brain imaging findings in antisocial, violent, and psychopathic individuals: A meta-analysis. *Psychiatry Research – Neuroimaging, 174*(2), 81–88.

Yang, Y., Raine, A., Colletti, P., Toga, A. W., & Narr, K. L. (2009). Abnormal temporal and prefrontal cortical gray matter thinning in psychopaths. *Molecular Psychiatry, 14*(6), 561–562.

Yang, Y., Raine, A., Colletti, P., Toga, A. W., & Narr, K. L. (2011). Abnormal structural correlates of response perseveration in individuals with psychopathy. *Journal of Neuropsychiatry and Clinical Neurosciences, 23*(1), 107–110.

Yang, Y., Raine, A., Joshi, A. A., Joshi, S., Chang, Y. T., Schug, R. A., ... Narr, K. L. (2012). Frontal information flow and connectivity in psychopathy. *British Journal of Psychiatry, 201*(5), 408–409.

Yang, Y., Raine, A., Narr, K. L., Colletti, P., & Toga, A. W. (2009). Localization of deformations within the amygdala in individuals with psychopathy. *Archives of General Psychiatry, 66*(9), 986–994.

Young, L., Koenigs, M., Kruepke, M., & Newman, J. P. (2012). Psychopathy increases perceived moral permissibility of accidents. *Journal of Abnormal Psychology, 121*(3), 659–667.

10

Antisocial Personality Disorder

Sheilagh Hodgins, Dave Checknita, Philip Lindner, Boris Schiffer, and Stéphane A. De Brito[1]

> ### Key points
> - This chapter reviews evidence about individuals who display antisocial behavior throughout their lives. This syndrome is diagnosed as antisocial personality disorder (ASPD) in adulthood and conduct disorder (CD) prior to age 15. The chapter focuses on the majority of these individuals who present low or no traits of psychopathy.
> - ASPD is diagnosed in approximately 5% of men and less than 1% of women. Rates of CD are higher, 10% of boys and 4% of girls.
> - The presentation of ASPD and CD among males and females shows both similarities and differences.
> - Almost all adolescents with CD and adults with ASPD misuse substances. Additionally, significant proportions of them present anxiety and depression disorders, and/or attention deficit hyperactivity disorder (ADHD), and experience maltreatment in childhood and physical victimization in adulthood.
> - CD and ASPD are associated with increased sensitivity to threat and reactive aggression.
> - Both CD and ASPD are heritable disorders, and consequently the search for genes associated with these disorders has begun. Interactions of variants of common genes with negative and positive environmental factors modify the risk of CD and ASPD. Environmental factors also alter gene expression through epigenetic mechanisms.
> - Brain imaging studies are beginning to reveal abnormalities of brain structure and function among children/adolescents with CD and adults with ASPD.
> - A small number of children with CD develop schizophrenia, but they represent between 20% and 40% of adults with schizophrenia.
> - While parent training, multi-modal cognitive-behavioral programs, and other interventions in childhood effectively reduce CD symptoms, evidence about the long-term outcomes of these treatments is contradictory.

- New evidence indicates that response to treatment is influenced by variants of genes that are highly prevalent in the population.

Terminology Explained

Antisocial personality disorder (APD) is defined in the fifth edition of the *Diagnostic and Statistical Manual of Mental Disorders (DSM-V)* (American Psychiatric Association, 2013) as "pervasive pattern of disregard for and the violation of the rights of others" (p. 659), and can include a disregard for social norms, deceitfulness, impulsivity, irritability/aggressiveness, reckless disregard for the safety of others, consistent irresponsibility, and lack of remorse for what they have done. This diagnosis applies only at age 18 or thereafter to individuals who have presented Conduct Disorder (CD) prior to age 15. CD is defined as a repetitive and persistent pattern of behavior in which the basic rights of others or major age appropriate social norms or rules are violated, destruction of property, deceitfulness, theft, and serious violations of rules, and various types of aggressive behaviors towards other people and animals.

Epigenetics refers to molecular mechanisms by which environmental factors modify the activity of genes. Although several such epigenetic mechanisms have been identified, the most commonly studied and well-understood mechanism is methylation of DeoxyriboNucleic Acid (DNA). This modification modulates the expression of the DNA by restricting or facilitating access of transcription factors to the gene, and is most often associated with reduced gene activity.

Genes are regions of DNA that encode a protein product. Genes are the molecular unit of heredity.

Gene polymorphisms are heritable variations in the genomic code, which can include sequence repeats or variable number of tandem repeats, deletions, and insertions, all of which may contribute to increasing or decreasing gene expression or altering the structure and function of the protein product of a gene.

Heritability is the proportion of phenotypic variance (e.g., a trait or disorder) that is attributable to genetic variance, as opposed to shared or unshared environmental factors and measurement error. Coefficients of heritability vary from 0 to 1 and are based on differences in levels of similarity of the trait or disorder between twins carrying the same genes (monozygotic) and those carrying different genes (dyzygotic).

Magnetic resonance imaging (MRI) allows measurement of the structure and functioning of brains of living persons. Structural MRI (sMRI) measures volumes of grey and white matter structures. Diffusion tensor imaging (DTI) measures the structural integrity of white matter tracts. Functional MRI (fMRI) measures activity in various brain structures as individuals complete a task while in the scanner. Resting-state functional connectivity measures activity while individuals rest within the scanner in order to identify networks of structures that are simultaneously active.

> The **Psychopathy Checklist Revised (PCL-R)** is used to assess psychopathy traits. Raters are specifically trained to administer an interview and to rate items based on the interview and criminal and medical files.

Introduction

The diagnosis of antisocial personality disorder (ASPD) indexes a life-long pattern of antisocial behavior (American Psychiatric Association, 2013), including a failure to conform to social norms and laws, repeated fights or assaults, reckless disregard for the safety of self and others, traits of impulsivity or a failure to plan ahead, irritability, irresponsibility, and lack of remorse. The diagnosis of ASPD requires the presence of conduct disorder (CD) prior to 15 years of age. CD indexes a repetitive and persistent pattern of behavior in which the basic rights of others or major age appropriate social norms or rules are violated (American Psychiatric Association, 2013). The criteria for CD also include destruction of property, deceitfulness, theft, and serious violations of rules, and various types of aggressive behaviors towards other people and animals. (see Chapter 16 for a more in-depth discussion of this disorder). Importantly, it is possible to make diagnoses of CD and ASPD in the absence of aggressive behavior. The diagnosis of ASPD is associated with increased risk for non-violent criminality, a somewhat increased risk of violent criminality, and in many cases, impulsive, emotionally charged aggressive behavior from childhood onwards.

ASPD is considered to be one of the most reliable of all diagnostic categories (Coid, 2003), although its validity has been questioned by some (e.g., Hare, 1996). The diagnosis of ASPD, however, is based on robust scientific evidence. Prospective, longitudinal investigations of population cohorts, studies of children with CD and juvenile delinquents, as well as cross-sectional studies of large population cohorts concur in showing that the syndrome indexed by ASPD onsets in childhood and persists across the life-span (Goldstein, Grant, Ruan, Smith, & Saha, 2006; Lahey, Loeber, Burke, & Applegate, 2005; Moffitt, Caspi, Rutter, & Silva, 2001; Robins, Tipp, & Przybeck, 1991; Washburn et al., 2007). Thus, the *Diagnostic and Statistical Manual (DSM)* requirement that the diagnosis of ASPD is only given if CD was present prior to age 15 is supported by a substantial body of research. In contrast, the diagnosis of dissocial personality disorder as defined in the International Classification of Diseases (ICD-10) (World Health Organization, 1992) is not consistent with the robust evidence of a behavioral syndrome of persistent violation of social norms that onsets in childhood and continues through adult life. Further, there is almost no research specifically on dissocial personality disorder.

The current conceptualization of ASPD first appeared in the third edition of the *DSM* (*DSM-III*) (American Psychiatric Association, 1980). It was based on evidence from prospective, longitudinal studies that had followed youth into adulthood and that has subsequently been replicated many times in samples of delinquents, and importantly, in large, representative samples of the general population. The diagnosis of ASPD that emerged from these longitudinal studies was intended to identify a disorder that was distinct from psychopathy. The *DSM-III-R*, in 1987, added the criterion of lack of remorse precisely because it characterized the subgroup with psychopathy. Thus, within the population of persons with ASPD there are those who as adults present the syndrome of psychopathy defined by a score of 30 or higher in North America or 25 or higher in Europe on the Psychopathy Checklist Revised (PCL-R) (Hare, 2003), and who as children present CD with high levels of callous-unemotional traits. Much research shows that at all developmental stages those who in addition to ASPD or CD present high levels of psychopathic traits differ as to behavior, cognition, emotion processing, heritability, and neural anomalies from those with ASPD alone (Frick, Ray, Thornton, & Kahn, 2013). Consequently, knowledge of the neurobiology of CD/ASPD is limited. Box 10.1 briefly reviews the burden placed on society by persons with ASPD.

This chapter reviews evidence about ASPD not including the syndrome of psychopathy: "someone who fails to maintain close personal relationships with anyone else, performs poorly on the job, who is involved in illegal behaviors (whether or not apprehended), who fails to support himself and his dependents without outside aid, and who is given to sudden changes of plan and loss of temper in response to what appear to others as minor frustrations." (Robins, 1978, p. 255). Additionally, these individuals "are hostile and paranoid. If one considers that in response to their early antisocial behaviors, parents beat them, schools expel them, and police chase them, their subjective experience of the world as unfriendly and dangerous may not be wholly irrational." (Robins, 1978, p. 267). While CD without callous-unemotional traits and ASPD without the syndrome of psychopathy are thought to be distinct disorders, there are few studies of CD and ASPD that have excluded subjects who additionally show high levels of psychopathic traits. Consequently, knowledge of the neurobiology of CD/ASPD is limited. The chapter begins by noting the burden placed on society by persons with ASPD. Next, studies of the prevalence of CD and ASPD are reviewed. In a subsequent section, investigations of genetic contributions to ASPD are presented. Among environmental factors linked to CD/ASPD the role of toxins is noted, as it is often forgotten. The effects of one important toxin, lead, are highlighted. Thereafter follows a review of brain imaging studies and neuropsychological assessments of individuals with CD/ASPD. A description of children with CD who develop schizophrenia is presented. The chapter ends with a brief section on effective treatments.

Box 10.1 Human and financial costs of CD and ASPD

Individuals with ASPD pose a significant burden to society. They fail to contribute by their absence from the workforce, do not pay taxes, accept benefits to which they are not entitled, engage in illicit scams, and cheat (Burke, 2007; De Brito & Hodgins, 2009; Robins et al., 1991). They cause significant levels of harm and distress to their intimate partners and children, and to others, as a result of their antisocial and aggressive behaviors. In childhood they disrupt schooling, and some bully and are physically aggressive to other children (Fergusson, Horwood, & Ridder, 2005; Loeber, Green & Lahey, 2003; Moffitt & Caspi, 2001).

Such behavior persists into adolescence when they begin using alcohol and drugs, engaging in criminal activities (Niemelä et al., 2008), and become an essential part of the illicit drug trade. In adulthood, in addition to violence and antisocial behavior, men with ASPD present elevated rates of premature death

(Odgers et al., 2008; Hodgins, 1994; Nieuwbeerta & Piquero, 2008), which likely result from their frequent engagement in reckless behaviors and suicide attempts (Hodgins, De Brito, Chhabra, & Côté, 2010), and elevated rates of mental and physical health problems (Odgers et al., 2007; Odgers et al., 2008; Shepherd, Farrington, & Potts, 2004).

Men and women with ASPD contribute to creating another generation of individuals who display similar problems both by transmitting susceptibility genes and by providing a socially adverse environment and inadequate parenting to their offspring (D'Onofrio et al., 2007; Jaffee, Belsky, Harrington, Caspi, & Moffitt, 2006; Jaffee, Caspi, Moffitt, & Taylor, 2004).

Lifetime Prevalence of ASPD and CD

Most estimates of life-time prevalence of ASPD vary among men from 4.5% to 6.5% and among women from 0.8% to 2.5% (Compton, Conway, Stinson, Colliver, & Grant, 2005; Robins et al., 1991; Samuels, personal communication, June 4, 2007; Samuels et al., 2002; Swanson, Bland, & Newman, 1994). A study of a representative sample of Norwegians aged between 18 and 65 years identified no case of ASPD among 1,142 women and a life-time prevalence of 1.3% among 911 men (Torgersen, Kringlen, & Cramer, 2001), while the prevalence of ASPD was estimated at 1% among men and 0.2% among women in a general population sample in Britain (Coid, Yang, Tyrer, Roberts, & Ullrich, 2006a).

Lifetime prevalence rates vary principally depending on the size of the sample, whether or not incarcerated offenders and probationers were included in the sample, the strategies to recruit antisocial individuals into the study, and the diagnostic procedure – questionnaire or face-to-face diagnosis. The reported differences in the prevalence of ASPD across countries may reflect real national differences in the true prevalence of the disorder or they may simply result from distinctive methodological features of the studies. Studies of the prevalence of ASPD, like almost all studies, require individual informed consent to participate. Individuals with ASPD are more likely than others of similar age, and sex, to have died (Black, Baumgard, Bell, & Kao, 1996), or are less likely to have a stable address and telephone number to allow contact (Robins, 1978; Samuels et al., 2004). Consequently, it is likely that the prevalence rates observed in community samples are underestimates of the real prevalence of ASPD (De Brito & Hodgins, 2009).

Prevalence rates of CD are similarly affected because participation by children in research projects requires the consent of their parents. Parents of children with CD often present antisocial behavior (Jaffee et al., 2006; Morcillo et al., 2011), provide less than optimal parenting, and create a chaotic family environment (Jaffee, Hanscombe, Haworth, Davis, & Plomin, 2012) and consequently are difficult to recruit to studies. Thus, epidemiological studies of the prevalence of CD among community and clinical samples of children and adults are limited by differential participation rates of antisocial and healthy individuals (Fontaine, McCrory, Boivin, Moffitt, & Viding, 2011; Hodgins et al., 2007; Murray, Irving, Farrington, Colman, & Bloxsom, 2010;

Silva, Larm, Vitaro, Tremblay, & Hodgins, 2012). While this refusal to voluntarily participate in research studies, or to allow children to participate, is consistent with our understanding of ASPD, it limits research on these disorders.

Findings from large community samples in the US and Great Britain have reported prevalence rates of CD of 9.5% and 5.8%, respectively (Green, McGinnity, Meltzer, Ford, & Goodman, 2004; Nock, Kazdin, Hiripi, & Kessler, 2006). In line with previous research, these studies show that CD is twice as common among boys than girls (for a review, see Maughan, Rowe, Messer, Goodman, & Meltzer, 2004). For example, in a British sample of 7,977 children aged 5 to 16 years of age, 7.5% of boys and 3.9% of girls met ICD-10 criteria for CD (Green et al., 2004). In a US sample of 3,199 children, a retrospective assessment of CD based on a structured interview using *DSM-IV* criteria identified lifetime prevalence rates for CD of 12% among males and 7.1% among females (Nock et al., 2006). Many children with CD do not develop ASPD, with proportions varying across studies (Frick & Viding, 2009). Presently, among children with CD and low levels of callous-unemotional traits, the characteristics associated with progression to ASPD remain unidentified.

ASPD and CD are associated with low socio-economic status. The prevalence of CD increases as the level of social deprivation of the child's family decreases (Green et al., 2004). In adulthood, individuals with ASPD are poor and live in socially deprived inner-city neighborhoods (Grant et al., 2004; Moran, 1999). Poverty in adulthood is consistent with high rates of unemployment. Indeed, one of the diagnostic criteria for ASPD is difficulty in maintaining stable employment. Unemployment among parents is associated with poor academic achievement evidenced by children with CD (Lösel & Bender, 2003). Poverty influences neural development, particularly the systems that subserve language and executive functions (Hackman, Farah, & Meaney, 2010), and directly affects cognitive functions (Costello, Compton, Keeler, & Angold, 2003; Mani, Mullainathan, Shafir, & Zhao, 2013).

Sex Differences in CD/ASPD

There are some differences in the presentation of CD/ASPD among females as compared to males. In addition to lower prevalence, among females, CD/ASPD onsets later in childhood/adolescence and the developmental course differs (Brennan & Shaw, 2013; Frick & Viding, 2009), as do symptoms, with less aggressive behavior among females than males (Gelhorn et al., 2009). Further, girls tend to engage in relational aggression while boys are more likely to show physical aggression (Kroneman, Loeber, Hipwell, & Koot, 2009). Most studies of CD/ASPD include only males. Yet, females with CD/ASPD contribute to the development of the next generation with this disorder. They give birth at a young age and their offspring are at high risk for conduct problems (D'Onofrio et al., 2007; Herndon & Iacono, 2005; Jaffee, 2002).

Diagnoses of CD/ASPD Identify a Heterogeneous Population

Most children with CD and adults with ASPD present comorbid disorders, with higher rates among females than males (Costello, Foley, & Angold, 2006). Among the adults, in large proportions of cases, the comorbid disorders have been present since

Antisocial behavior *Antisocial behavior includes a failure to conform to social norms and laws, repeated fights or assaults, reckless disregard for the safety of self and others, traits of impulsivity or a failure to plan ahead, irritability, irresponsibility, and lack of remorse.*
Source: © WenPhotos. Used under license from Pixabay.

childhood. Little is known about the extent to which comorbid disorders in childhood modify the risk of transition to ASPD in adulthood. The most prevalent comorbidities include psychopathy, substance misuse, attention deficit hyperactivity disorder (ADHD), anxiety disorders (ADs), depression, borderline personality disorder, and schizophrenia.

Psychopathy

The proportions of children with CD who present elevated levels of callous-unemotional traits and adults with ASPD who present high levels of psychopathic traits or the syndrome of psychopathy are unknown. While one study of a randomly selected sample estimated that close to half of both the girls and boys with CD presented elevated levels of callous-unemotional traits (Rowe et al., 2010), the definition and measurement of callous-unemotional traits vary across studies, as does the definition of what constitutes "high" levels.

Substance misuse

Children with CD are exposed earlier than other children to alcohol and illicit drugs and they go on to more quickly develop substance use disorders (SUDs) that remain throughout adulthood (Cottler, Price, Compton, & Mager, 1995; Myers, Stewart, & Brown, 1998; Robins & McEvoy, 1990). Not surprisingly, almost all adults with ASPD present SUDs (Compton et al., 2005; Kessler et al., 1996; Robins et al., 1991).

ADHD

Between 8.7% and 45.4% of boys and between 1.2% and 61.4% of girls with CD also present ADHD (Disney, Elkins, McGue, & Iacono, 1999; McCabe, Rodgers, Yeh, &

Hough, 2004). The combination of CD and ADHD, as compared to CD alone, is associated with an earlier age of onset of conduct problems, aggressive behavior, persistent antisocial behavior through adolescence and adulthood, lower verbal and social-cognitive abilities, and more problems with peers (Johansson, Kerr & Andershed, 2005; Lahey et al., 2005; Lynam, 1996; Waschbusch, 2002). In many individuals, ADHD comorbid with CD persists into adulthood. However, outcomes and neural correlates of the two disorders differ (Rubia, 2011). Most studies (Mannuzza, Klein, & Moulton, 2008; Mordre, Groholt, Kjelsberg, Sandstad, & Myhre, 2011), but not all (e.g., Dalsgaard, Mortensen, Frydenberg, & Thomsen, 2013), show that ADHD alone in childhood/adolescence is not associated with subsequent antisocial behavior, while the combination of CD comorbid with ADHD is associated with persistent antisocial behavior and criminality.

ADs

Among children with CD identified in community samples, the prevalence of comorbid ADs ranges between 22% and 33%, while among children with CD who have sought treatment 60% to 75% present ADs (Hodgins, Barbareschi, & Larsson, 2011; Polier, Vloet, Herpertz-Dahlmann, Laurens, & Hodgins, 2012; Russo & Beidel, 1994). This association varies by age and gender (Marmorstein, 2007), but evidence suggests it emerges by 24 months (Gilliom & Shaw, 2004). Two epidemiological investigations of large population cohorts have revealed that almost half of adults with ASPD met criteria for at least one AD (Goodwin & Hamilton, 2003; Lenzenweger, Lane, Loranger, & Kessler, 2007; Sareen, Stein, Cox, & Hassard, 2004). Further, a recent study of a large sample of incarcerated offenders with ASPD, found that half presented ADs, one-half of which had onset prior to age 16 (Hodgins, De Brito, Chhabra, & Côté et al., 2010). Importantly, among children with CD, those with comorbid ADs present more severe externalizing symptoms than those with only CD (Polier et al., 2012). However, among adolescents with CD, those with comorbid ADs show similar levels of delinquency, antisocial and aggressive behavior as those with CD only (Hodgins et al., 2011).

Depression

The prevalence of depression is much higher among children with CD than without, and the combination is associated with more severe symptoms and higher levels of social impairment (Angold, Costello, & Erkanli, 1999; Wolff & Ollendick, 2006). In one epidemiological study, depression was found to occur among individuals with ASPD at more than three times the general population rate (Robins et al., 1991). More recently, in a study of a US community sample composed of 5,692 persons, 9.1% of the individuals with ASPD presented major depression and 27.7% met criteria for any mood disorders (Lenzenweger et al., 2007).

Borderline personality disorder (BPD)

In a study of a community sample of 34,653 US adults, among those with ASPD 18% of the men and 29% of the women also presented BPD (Grant et al., 2008).

While there is some overlap of symptoms for these two disorders, several lines of evidence suggest that ASPD and BPD are distinct, the latter being characterised primarily by affective instability (Paris, Chenard-Poirier, & Biskin, 2013). Some childhood antecedents differ, while others are similar (Belsky et al., 2012; Stepp, Burke, Hipwell, & Loeber, 2012).

Schizophrenia

While few children with CD develop schizophrenia, a large minority of individuals who develop schizophrenia present CD prior to age 15. For example, in a prospective investigation that followed a New Zealand birth cohort to age 26, 40% of the cohort members who developed schizophreniform disorders had displayed CD prior to age 15 (Kim-Cohen et al., 2003). In clinical samples of adults with schizophrenia, the prevalence of CD is lower, approximately 20% among both women and men in samples recruited in general psychiatric services, higher in forensic hospitals, and even higher in prisons (Hodgins, Côté, & Toupin, 1998). Thus, CD and conduct problems are precursors of schizophrenia. Further, both CD and ASPD are more common among people who develop schizophrenia than in the general population, and as prevalent among women as men with schizophrenia (for a review see Hodgins, 2008). This subgroup will be discussed at the end of the chapter.

Summary

The available evidence suggests that individuals with CD and ASPD do not constitute a homogeneous population. Figure 10.1 depicts our hypothesis of the population of persons who present CD in childhood and ASPD in adulthood. Approximately 50%

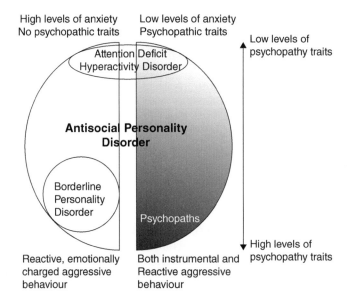

Figure 10.1 The population of persons with early-onset antisocial behavior that remains stable across the lifespan.

present an AD, as depicted on the left side of the figure, and among them are found those with BPD and a proportion of those with ADHD. Among those without ADs, we hypothesize that the level of psychopathic traits varies from low to very high, such that those presenting the syndrome of psychopathy are depicted in the bottom right. In the present chapter, every effort is made to focus on all of this population excluding only those with the syndrome of psychopathy who are described elsewhere in this volume (see Chapter 9). To date, however, most studies of CD/ASPD have not distinguished these subtypes, thereby hindering understanding of the neurobiological factors associated with these disorders. Further, while abnormal brain development underlies CD and ASPD, the extent to which the subtypes defined by comorbid disorders present distinct patterns of neural development is not presently known. Looking at this phenomenon of heterogeneity from adulthood backwards to childhood shows that 25% to 60% of all cases of adult mental disorders present CD and/or oppositional defiant disorder before age 15. This perspective shows that while homotypic continuity is usual, that is, for example, ADs in adulthood are preceded by ADs in childhood, heterotypic continuity, that is, CD preceding internalizing disorders in adulthood, including schizophrenia, is also common (Kim-Cohen et al., 2003).

Relationship between CD/ASPD and Criminality

Results of epidemiological investigations are consistent in showing that approximately half of individuals with a diagnosis of ASPD have a record of criminal offending (Robins et al., 1991; Samuels, personal communication, June 1, 2007). These studies of community samples all required informed consent and voluntary participation. In one study information on criminality was provided by self-report (Robins et al., 1991), while in the other it was based on criminal records (Samuels et al., 2002; Samuels et al., 2004). By contrast, among incarcerated offenders, ASPD is very common. For instance, a systematic review of 62 studies, conducted over several decades in 12 countries among 13,844 prisoners, found that 47% of males and 21% of females met criteria for ASPD using standardized assessment methods (Fazel & Danesh, 2002). The degree to which ASPD is associated with violent offending is unclear (De Brito & Hodgins, 2009; Hodgins & Côté, 1993; Nathan, Rollinson, Harvey, & Hill, 2003).

Violence Towards Others

The epidemiological study that examined 18,571 persons representative of the US population in the early 1980s found that 85% of individuals with a diagnosis of ASPD engaged in violence towards others (Robins et al., 1991). By contrast, a more recent study that examined a British community sample of 8,397 persons aged 16 to 74 years old found that half of those with ASPD reported not having engaged in violence towards others during the past five years, while 29% reported violence towards others when intoxicated, 26% reported injuring a victim, and 23% reported five or more violent incidents (Coid et al., 2006b). The discrepancy in the results of these two studies may result from differences in diagnostic criteria (*DSM-III* versus *DSM-IV*), in diagnostic procedure, and/or across countries and time periods (1980 and 2000).

Among children with conduct problems, those most at risk to develop ASPD present with antisocial behavior that is more persistent and more severe, and that includes physical aggression and violence (Moffitt, Caspi, Dickson, Silva, & Stanton, 1996). The earlier the onset of the physically aggressive behavior, the more likely it is to persist into adulthood (Goldstein et al., 2006; Loeber & Stouthamer-Loeber, 1987; Maughan, Pickles, Rowe, Costello, & Angold, 2000; Robins, 1966). Taken together, the extant literature suggests that people with ASPD, as compared to those without ASPD, are at increased risk to engage in violence, and equally important that a substantial proportion of persons with ASPD do not engage in violence towards others. While little work has been done to identify the characteristics that distinguish those within this population who do engage in violence, the available evidence strongly indicates that violence in adulthood is a continuation of aggressive behavior in childhood.

Boys with conduct problems who do not present high levels of callous-unemotional traits display aggressive behavior that is emotionally-charged in response to provocations that may be real or result from their tendency to attribute hostility towards others, even to neutral faces (Dadds, 2006; Frick, Cornell, Barry, Bodin, & Dane, 2003; Frick & Marsee, 2006; Kruh, Frick, & Clements, 2005). These children report elevated levels of emotional distress, are hyper-reactive to distress, and especially to negative emotional stimuli. Several studies have shown that reactive aggression is related to hostile attribution biases (Lobbestael, Cima, & Arntz, 2013) in response to ambiguous provocation, negative affect, attention for rejection, ridicule, failure cues, problem-solving deficits in difficult social situations, and impairment in executive functions (for a discussion, see Barker et al., 2010). Adults with ASPD show similar characteristics (Blair, 2012). Emotional negativity plus the tendency to feel threatened is thought to lead to reactive aggression in children with CD and adults with ASPD (Blair, 2012). In all mammals, high levels of danger from a threat that is close and inescapable initiate reactive aggression (Mobbs et al., 2007). A recent prospective, longitudinal study of males showed that those with high levels of anger from childhood onwards who showed low cognitive control in mid-adolescence were at elevated risk as compared to the others for ASPD and reactive aggression (Hawes et al., 2016).

Victimisation

Children with CD present elevated rates of childhood maltreatment (Afifi, Boman, Fleisher, & Sareen, 2009) and adults with antisocial behavior experience repeated victimisation (Vaughn et al., 2010). Such experiences likely serve to reinforce their feelings of being threatened.

Heritability of CD/ASPD

Conduct problems are known to be concentrated in families, and a family history of antisocial behavior is a robust predictor of offspring conduct problems (Farrington, Jolliffe, Loeber, Stouthamer-Loeber, & Kalb, 2001; Farrington & Loeber, 2000). An early onset of antisocial behavior that remains stable across the lifespan, indexed by CD and ASPD and that includes substance misuse, is moderately heritable (Krueger et al., 2002). Meta-analysis of twin and adoption studies estimates genetic contributions of 0.41, and a small contribution of shared environmental influences (0.16) and greater (0.43) non-shared environmental influences (Rhee & Waldman, 2002). A recent study, however, estimates that 62% of the variance in childhood onset CD and 65% of the variance of adolescent onset CD that persists as antisocial behavior in early adulthood is due to genetic factors (Silberg, Moore, & Rutter, 2015). Studies of children suggest that the heritability of conduct problems without callous-unemotional traits is much lower than that of conduct problems combined with high levels of callous-unemotional traits (Viding, Jones, Frick, Moffitt, & Plomin, 2008). The accuracy of these estimates of heritability, however, is limited by the heterogeneity of ASPD. Antisocial parents confer vulnerability for CD/ASPD among their offspring, both by transmitting genes and by using non-optimal parenting skills. The magnitude of the association between parent and offspring antisocial behavior is augmented by the tendency of antisocial women to mate with antisocial men (Jaffee et al., 2006). Given robust evidence of heritability, investigations have begun to identify specific genes associated with CD/ASPD.

Genes Associated with CD/ASPD

Genes involved in regulating neurotransmitter systems in the brain that are known to be linked to antisocial and/or aggressive behavior have been studied. These genes are carried by almost everyone, and therefore simply the presence of one or other of these genes is not linked to CD/ASPD. Rather, within each of these genes there are variants associated with different levels of gene activity. Importantly, within each of the genes that have been studied, one of the variants modifies sensitivity to the environment and is called a susceptibility variant. Individuals carrying a susceptibility variant of a gene who are exposed to a positive rearing environment show little antisocial behavior while those exposed to adversity during childhood show high levels of antisocial behavior. The genetic variants that have been shown to confer increased sensitivity to environmental factors are carried by approximately 25% to 60% of the population and they vary in males and females.

Consider the evidence that was used to identify genes that may be associated with CD/ASPD. A consistent body of evidence accumulated over 50 years reveals powerful associations between reduced serotonergic activity in the brain and impulsive aggression. Serotonergic projections from the dorsal raphe and prefrontal cortical regions, such as the anterior cingulate and orbitofrontal cortices, inhibit a circuit of subcortical regions including structures such as the amygdala, periacqueductal grey, and hypothalamus that govern aggressive responses to perceived threats (Miller, Collins, & Kent, 2008; Siegel & Douard, 2011; Siegel & Victoroff, 2009). When a threat is perceived, an acute reduction of serotonin leads to a reduction of inhibitory signals to this subcortical circuit resulting in an increased likelihood of aggression (Siegel & Victoroff, 2009). In antisocial populations, reduced basal levels of serotonin in the brain may lower the threshold for perceiving threat and initiating aggressive behavior (Miller et al., 2008; Siegel & Douard, 2011). Further evidence supporting a link between reduced serotonergic activity in the brain and antisocial behavior comes from dramatically reduced cerebral spinal fluid measures of the primary serotonin metabolite, 5-hydroxyindoleacetic acid, observed among impulsively aggressive rodents, primates, and humans, including men with ASPD (Comai, Tau, & Gobbi 2012; Virkkunen,

Goldman, Nielsen, & Linnoila, 1995). Since the link between reduced serotonin levels and aggression is robust, subsequent attention turned to identifying genes regulating the serotonergic pathway.

Several genes involved in the regulation of brain serotonin have been associated with reactive aggression. Among the most commonly identified are genes coding for serotonergic receptors 1A (5-HTR1A) and 2B (5-HTR2B) that may contribute to systemic reduction of serotonergic transmission and synthesis in the brain (Comai et al., 2012; Gunter, Vaughn, & Philibert, 2010). However, the two most promising serotonergic genes implicated in reactive aggression encode the serotonin transporter (5-HTT), which governs presynaptic reuptake, and monoamine oxidase A (MAOA), which degrades serotonin pre-and post-synaptically (Buckholtz & Meyer-Lindenberg, 2008; Lesch, Araragi, Waider, van den Hove, Daniel, & Gutknecht, 2012).

On many chromosomes, a short nucleotide sequence is organized as a tandem repeat called a variable number tandem repeat (VNTR). Each variant acts as an inherited allele. The repeats are in tandem, that is they are clustered together and oriented in the same direction. Many repeats are called long and lead to high gene activity while variants made up of few repeats are called short and lead to lower levels of gene activity. For example, in the serotonin transporter gene 5-HTT, the short variant limits serotonin activity in the brain (Barnett, Xu, Heron, Goldman, & Jones, 2011) and it has been associated with reactive aggression, CD, and adult offending (Ficks & Waldman, 2014), heightened amygdala reactivity to negative emotions (Hariri et al., 2002), and low cognitive control (Landrø et al., 2015). There is evidence that 5-HTT variants interact with both negative environmental factors such as maltreatment in childhood and positive environmental factors, specifically positive parenting (Hankin et al., 2011), to modify the risk of antisocial behavior and other developmental outcomes (Van Ijzendoorn, Belsky, & Bakermans-Kranenburg, 2012). Treatment is a positive environmental factor and response to treatment has been shown to vary depending on genetic variants. For example, children of African-American heritage who carried the susceptibility variant of the 5-HTT gene showed a greater reduction in conduct problems following family treatment than did children carrying other variants (Brody et al., 2009).

The variants of these common genes that are responsive to the environment differ in males and females, but interactions with environmental factors modify the risk of antisocial behavior in the same way among males and females. For example, among teenage girls, rates of delinquency differed as a function of 5-HTT variants and socioeconomic status of the family (Aslund et al., 2013).

The MAOA gene also regulates brain serotonin and it includes variants, short and long, that are associated with different levels of activity of the gene (Beach, Brody, Todorov, Gunter, & Philibert, 2010). In males, meta-analyses have confirmed that among carriers of the short MAOA variant those exposed to adversity in childhood show higher rates of CD, antisocial behavior, and criminality than those reared in more positive circumstances (Byrd & Manuck, 2014; Ouellet-Morin et al., 2016). Further, in two studies, male carriers of the short variant of MAOA who experienced positive family environments as compared to those who did not, showed lower levels of delinquency (Nilsson et al., 2006; Oreland, Nilsson, Damberg, & Hallman, 2007). While robust evidence shows that in males the MAOA gene variant that is associated with low activity interacts with environmental factors to modify the risk of antisocial behavior, most studies do not detect a direct association of the variant with antisocial behavior.

Yet, it appears to be associated with brain structure and functioning. In healthy men, the MAOA low-expressing variant is associated with pronounced reduction of grey matter volume in limbic structures, and hyper-responsivity of the amygdala during emotional arousal accompanied by diminished reactivity of prefrontal structures reflecting failure to down-regulate the amygdala and other limbic structures (Meyer-Lindenberg et al., 2006).

A recent meta-analysis, however, concluded that interactions of the high expressing variant of the MAOA gene with childhood maltreatment is associated with antisocial behavior in females (Byrd & Manuck, 2014) and other studies show that this variant increases sensitivity to positive environmental factors providing protection against antisocial behavior. While one study of healthy women showed that the low acting variant of MAOA was associated with increased activations to angry and fearful faces in the subgenual anterior cingulate, left lateral orbitofrontal cortex, supragenual anterior cingulate, and left amygdala (Meyer-Lindenberg et al., 2006), another study reported that activity in the hippocampus and amygdala during a similar task increased with the level of childhood stress among carriers of the high acting MAOA variant and was associated with higher aggression scores (Holz et al., 2016).

As can be noted, studies of genetic variants that explain the heritability of CD/ASPD are in their infancy as most have studied only one gene. Yet, it is clear that the effects of susceptibility variants and experiences cumulate to modify an outcome such as antisocial behavior. For example, in a study of 187 male prisoners, those carrying the susceptibility variants of 5-HTT and MAOA who had experienced maltreatment in childhood showed the highest levels of violence while those carrying neither susceptibility variant who had not experienced maltreatment as children showed the lowest levels of violence (Reif et al., 2007). In a study of 1,337 high-school students, associations of delinquency with interactions of variants of the MAOA and 5-HTT genes, and the brain-derived neurotrophic factor gene with each other and with family conflict, sexual abuse, and the quality of the child–parent relationship were examined. Delinquency was primarily associated with interactions of the genetic variants and the negative and positive environmental factors (Nilsson et al., 2015).

Another set of genes that regulate the neurotransmitter dopamine may also be associated with antisocial behavior. Dopamine regulates neural circuitry governing motivated reward, pleasure seeking, and emotional regulation. Dysregulation of this circuitry has been strongly associated with a wide range of externalizing behaviors such as impulsivity, aggression, and SUDs (Comai et al., 2012; Dalley & Roiser, 2012). Recent evidence suggests that dopamine assists in regulating the brain response to social stimuli (Sauer, Montag, Reuter, & Kirsch, 2013). Within the dopaminergic system, variants of genes such as the dopamine transporter, catechol-O-methyl transferase (COMT), dopamine beta hydroxylase, and D2 and D4 receptors may confer diminished dopamine activity (Comai et al., 2012; Gunter et al., 2010). Together, these variants may contribute to a broader systemic dysregulation of dopamine that promotes antisocial behavior (Comai et al., 2012; Gunter et al., 2010).

In conclusion, genes that regulate the neurotransmitters serotonin and dopamine may be associated with antisocial behavior. Within these genes that are carried by almost all people, there are variants some of which increase sensitivity to environmental factors. Individuals who carry the susceptibility variants of the serotonin transporter gene and the MAOA gene and who experience adversity during childhood present higher rates of antisocial and criminal behavior than individuals with the same variant who do not experience adversity in childhood and higher rates than individuals who carry other variants of the same gene. Similarly, individuals who carry the susceptibility variants of these two genes and who experience a positive relationship with their parents in childhood have lower rates of antisocial and criminal behavior than individuals with the same variant who did not have a positive relationship with their parents and lower rates than individuals who carry other variants of the same gene. Thus, it is not the presence of the genetic variant but the interaction of the variant with the environment that determines the outcome.

Epigenetic Changes in MAOA and 5-HTT Genes

While the genes, and variants, carried by each person are present from conception onwards, the activity of genes and genetic variants can be altered after conception by environmental factors. This molecular mechanism is referred to as epigenetics. Importantly, epigenetic changes may affect the expression of genes in each cell differently, such that epigenetic changes within the brain may differ across brain regions. Epigenetic changes to DNA expression may, in some cases, be reversible. The primary epigenetic process investigated in behavioral epigenomics is DNA methylation, which typically reduces gene expression (Bird, 2007; Moore, Le, & Fan, 2013). Recently, epigenetic modifications of the MAOA and 5-HTT have been associated with ASPD. One study reported hypermethylation in the MAOA gene among male offenders with ASPD compared to healthy non-offenders (Checknita et al., 2015). Methylation of this region of the MAOA gene was further associated with down-regulated gene expression *in vitro*, and was also predictive of variation in whole-blood serotonin levels among the ASPD men (Checknita et al., 2015). Interestingly, a previous study showed that stressing rats at specific developmental periods lead to aggressive behavior and epigenetic changes to expression of MAOA (Márquez et al., 2013). A study of adult women observed that altered methylation levels of an important regulatory subregion of the MAOA gene was associated with sexual abuse and the timing of sexual abuse even after controlling for physical abuse, and was also positively correlated with a number of CD symptoms (Checknita et al., 2016). This study provides preliminary evidence that epigenetic factors alter MAOA activity in response to environmental influences and thereby play a role in conferring risk for antisocial outcomes.

Studies have also identified an association between hypermethylation in the promoter region of 5-HTT and ASPD, depression, and SUDs among adult women who had experienced sexual abuse during childhood (Beach, et al., 2013; Beach et al., 2010; Philibert et al., 2011). The magnitude of 5-HTT hypermethylation was positively associated with the presence of mental disorders among the parents suggesting that both genetic vulnerability and epigenetic factors may contribute to greater risk for ASPD among individuals who experience physical abuse in childhood (Beach et al., 2013).

In conclusion, environmental factors alter levels of expression of genes through epigenetic processes and thereby may be associated with different levels of antisocial behavior.

Environmental Toxins

One environmental factor that may be interacting with genetic factors, or causing epigenetic changes to gene activity, or acting directly to promote the development of CD/ASPD is lead. A meta-analysis of 16 studies that assessed lead levels in blood or bone linked high concentrations to CD (Marcus, Fulton, & Clarke, 2010). A US study reported that children/adolescents with blood level concentrations of lead in the top quartile were eight times more likely to meet diagnostic criteria for CD than were those with levels in the lower quartile (Braun et al., 2008). Lead levels may be especially related to impulsivity, aggressive behavior, and violent criminal offending (Fergusson, Boden, & Horwood, 2008; Fergusson, Fergusson, Horwood, & Kinzett, 1988; Wright et al., 2008).

Conduct disorder *Conduct disorder (CD) is defined as a repetitive and persistent pattern of antisocial behavior of children up to 15 years old. In these behaviors, the basic rights of others or major age appropriate social norms or rules are violated: destruction of property, deceitfulness, theft, and serious violations of rules, and various types of aggressive behaviors towards other people and animals. Beyond the age of 15 years individuals showing these behaviors will be diagnosed with antisocial personality disorder (APD).*

Source: © Sascha Burkard. Used under license from 123RF.

Neural Abnormalities in Individuals with CD/ASPD Detected by Brain Imaging

There are few studies of neural abnormalities among adults with CD/ASPD that focus on those with low levels of psychopathic traits. Yet, the accumulated evidence suggests that the brain mechanisms promoting lifelong antisocial behavior with and without psychopathic traits are distinct (Viding, Fontaine, & McCrory, 2012), congruent with the observed difference in symptom prevalence, life-course trajectories, and treatment response. Studies of adolescents and adults with CD/ASPD are confounded by the effects of alcohol and drugs, other common comorbid disorders, and childhood maltreatment, each of which is associated with specific brain abnormalities. Since CD/ASPD is a syndrome that onsets in childhood or early adolescence, it is reasonable to propose that abnormal brain development begins before or at the time of onset of the syndrome. Consequently, studies of children with CD who have not yet begun using alcohol and drugs may be more likely than those of adults with CD/ASPD to identify key abnormalities that are specifically associated with the syndrome.

As discussed, CD/ASPD is characterised by general negative emotionality, feelings and thoughts of being threatened, and high levels of reactive aggression. These feelings, thoughts, and behaviors may be initiated and/or maintained by experiences of harsh parenting, an unpredictable or cold family environment, and repeated failures to achieve rewards (Dodge, Lochman, Harnish, Bates, & Pettit, 1997; Vitaro, Brendgen, & Barker, 2006; Vitaro, Barker, Boivin, Brendgen, & Tremblay, 2006; Xu, Farver, & Zhang, 2009). Humans, like other animals, alter their behavior depending on whether a real or a perceived threat is close or distant. One study investigated spatial imminence of threat by developing an active avoidance paradigm in which volunteers were pursued through a maze by a virtual predator endowed with an ability to chase, capture, and inflict pain. As the virtual predator grew closer, brain activity shifted from the ventromedial prefrontal cortex (vmPFC) to the periaqueductal grey. This shift showed maximal expression when a high degree of pain was anticipated. Moreover, imminence-driven periaqueductal grey activity positively correlated with increasing levels of dread and decreasing confidence of escape (Mobbs et al., 2007).

Importantly, the neural threat system, amygdala-hypothalamus-periaqueductal grey, is organized hierarchically, such that aggression evoked by stimulation of the amygdala is dependent on the functional integrity of the medial hypothalamus and the periaqueductal grey but aggression evoked by stimulation of the periaqueductal grey is not dependent on the functional integrity of the amygdala (Gregg & Siegel, 2001; Panksepp, 1998).

In a recent study, men who had a history of CD, as compared to healthy men, exhibited grey matter volume increases in a large cluster including the uncus and the superior temporal cortex extending into the right amygdala and the right hypothalamus, the temporoparietal junction, the inferior and superior parietal regions, the posterior cingulate, and the pre- and postcentral gyri, after controlling for substance misuse (Schiffer et al., 2013). Further, aggressive symptoms of CD and life-long aggressive behavior were strongly positively correlated with grey matter volumes of both the left and right hypothalamus. These results require replication. However, they provide evidence of an anomaly low down in the brain that, if confirmed, could explain many of the characteristics of children with CD who go on to become adults with ASPD engaging in reactive aggression. Likely due, in part, to technical difficulties in imaging the periaqueductal grey and other parts of the brain stem (Beissner, Deichmann, & Baudrexel, 2011), neuroimaging research has primarily been focused on the frontal and limbic parts of this network, most particularly the amygdala.

The amygdala responds to emotional stimuli. It is a complex of subnuclei that is involved in numerous emotional processes including vigilance and arousal, as well as both conditioned and unconditioned fear (Bickart, Dickerson, & Barrett, 2014). A recent meta-analysis examined findings from studies comparing brain structure of children with and without CD and did not take account of callous-unemotional traits. The most consistent finding was reduced grey matter volume in the left amygdala extending into other limbic structures and to the orbitofrontal cortex and also into the superior temporal gyrus. The meta-analysis took account of only IQ and one comorbid disorder, ADHD. There were too few studies of females to obtain reliable results (Rogers & De Brito, 2016). Two recent fMRI studies convincingly showed that CD symptoms were associated with amygdala hyper-reactivity and not with callous-unemotional traits, ADHD, anxiety, depression, or alcohol use (Sebastian et al., 2012; Viding et al., 2012). Another study reported that children with conduct problems and low callous-unemotional traits exhibited increased amygdala reactivity to fearful eyes, which was positively correlated with a slower reaction time to those stimuli, possibly reflecting difficulties in implicit emotion regulation (Sebastian et al., 2014). These results support the hypothesis that CD without callous-unemotional traits is characterised by increased emotional reactivity to emotion-evoking stimuli.

The orbitofrontal cortex down regulates amygdala activity (Likhtik, Pelletier, Paz, & Paré, 2005) and thereby suppresses emotional responding and emotion-driven behavior (Quirk & Beer, 2006). Among men, those with, as compared to those without, CD/ASPD were reported to show an 8.7% reduction in grey matter volume of the orbitofrontal cortex, a 17.3% reduction in middle frontal grey, and a 16.1% reduction in right rectal grey. Reduced middle and orbitofrontal grey matter volumes were significantly associated with increased numbers of ASPD symptoms and criminal offending in both males and females. However, all males, as compared to all females, displayed smaller orbitofrontal and middle frontal grey volumes and more ASPD symptoms. Findings were not a function of comorbid disorders, psychosocial risk factors, head injury, or trauma exposure (Raine, Yang, Narr, & Toga, 2011). Additionally, among healthy adults, resting-state amygdala–orbitofrontal cortex functional connectivity is negatively correlated with self-reported trait anger and positively correlated with self-reported anger control (Fulwiler, King, & Zhang, 2012). Greater amygdala–orbitofrontal cortex functional coupling correlates with greater attenuation of negative affect following conscious reappraisal of negative stimuli (Banks, Eddy, Angstadt, Nathan, & Phan, 2007). One study compared activation patterns among boys with and without CD as they labelled the sex of faces expressing emotions (Passamonti et al., 2010). The CD boys rated the sex and the emotions as did the non-CD boys. Neural results showed a complex pattern of hypo- and hyper-reactivity of different regions to different stimuli, including amygdala and orbitofrontal cortex hyper-reactivity in response to neutral faces among those with CD. In response to angry faces, there was no difference in amygdala reactivity but hypo-reactivity of the orbitofrontal cortex. In no case did brain activity correlate with callous-unemotional traits and correcting for ADHD symptoms did not change the results. The increased amygdala response to neutral faces is in line with behavioral evidence showing that aggressive children, particularly those with low callous-unemotional traits, tend to interpret neutral facial expressions as threatening, which in turn increases the risk of reactive aggression.

The orbitofrontal cortex and amygdala are connected by a white matter tract called the uncinate fasciculus. The structural integrity of this and other white matter tracts are assessed during a magnetic brain scan using DTI. Abnormal structural integrity of the uncinate fasciculus compromises efficient communication between the orbitofrontal cortex and amygdala, thereby limiting top-down inhibition of limbic hyper-arousal in response to a real or perceived threat. Recent research on monkeys shows that deficits in inhibitory control result from damage to the uncinate fasciculus and not the orbitofrontal cortex, as previously thought (Rudebeck, Saunders, Prescott, Chau, & Murray, 2013). Of note, ADs are also characterised by low frontal and high limbic activity in response to threat, but the structural integrity of the uncinate fascilculus is less associated with anxiety than with inhibition (Von Der Heide, Skipper, Klobusicky, & Olson 2013). Based on this evidence, it was hypothesized that the integrity of this white matter tract may be associated with psychopathy and/or CD/ASPD (Craig et al., 2009; Motzkin et al., 2011). More recently, in a large sample of offenders, abnormalities of the right uncinate fasciculus were positively correlated total psychopathy scores, and with the interpersonal factor. Offenders with low psychopathy scores did not display abnormalities of this tract (Wolf et al., 2015) nor did a sample of young women who had presented CD prior to age 15 (Lindner et al., 2016).

The largest white matter tract in the brain is the corpus callosum that connects the two hemispheres (Haney-Caron, Caprihan, & Stevens, 2013; Zhang et al., 2014; Sundram et al., 2012; Raine et al., 2003). We recently reported that young adult women with a history of CD in adolescence showed reduced structural integrity of the anterior corpus callosum, independent of comorbid mental disorders and experience of maltreatment (Lindner et al., 2016). This finding adds to a growing literature showing reduced structural integrity and morphometric abnormalities of the corpus callosum in antisocial populations. CD/ASPD without callous-unemotional traits may be associated with abnormalities in communication between brain hemispheres that are associated with information processing and imbalance in the approach-avoidance motivational system (Schutter & Harmon-Jones, 2013). Behaviors guided by approach motivation (e.g., aggression) are lateralized to the left hemisphere while behaviors guided by avoidance motivation (e.g., anxiety) are lateralized to the right hemisphere. Disturbed balance of these motivational systems, manifested as and/or caused by corpus callosum abnormalities, may fuel inflexible, dysfunctional behavioral response patterns in response to perceived threat. This model may also explain the high comorbidity of ADs found in antisocial populations. Indirect support for the model comes from research showing that women have greater inter-hemispheric brain connectivity while men show higher intra-hemispheric connectivity thereby putting them at greater risk of abnormalities and antisocial behavior (Ingalhalikar et al., 2014). In our sample of young women who presented CD in adolescence, we have recently shown that abnormalities of the corpus callosum are positively associated with an interaction of the long variant of the MAOA gene and maltreatment in childhood, and that this association is buffered by a positive relationship with a parent in adolescence. If replicated, this finding would identify a pathway from genes to brain to antisocial behavior.

To summarize, few brain imaging studies of grey or white matter distinguish individuals with CD/ASPD with low psychopathic traits. Consequently, knowledge of brain abnormalities that underlie CD/ASPD without psychopathy is limited. Yet, the hypothesis guiding research is that this is a syndrome of abnormal neural development that begins at conception. Almost all brain imaging studies identify differences in grey and white matter among individuals with CD/ASPD as compared to healthy age and sex matched peers. Children with CD and adults with ASPD present structural and functional abnormalities of the limbic system that over-reacts to emotional stimuli and of the orbitofrontal cortex that fails to effectively down-regulate this reaction. These abnormalities are consistent with characteristics of persons with CD/ASPD.

However, most of the studies conducted to date included only males, none have tracked brain abnormalities at different ages, almost none take account of the multiple comorbid disorders presented by children/adolescents with CD and adults with ASPD, nor of the maltreatment that many of these individuals experienced in childhood and continue to experience in adulthood. To further understand the aetiology of CD/ASPD, it is essential to disentangle the brain abnormalities associated with CD and each comorbid disorder and maltreatment and to identify when, during the course of development, the abnormality emerges. For example, physical abuse may alter the brain so as to increase reactivity to threat and the commonly comorbid ADs may be associated with more wide-spread abnormalities of limbic structures thereby contributing to even greater hyper-reactivity.

Brain Abnormalities in Persons with CD/ASPD Detected by Neuropsychological Tests

Children with CD engaging in reactive aggression present different profiles of impairments on neuropsychological tests compared to children engaging in proactive aggression (Barker et al., 2007; Giancola, Mezzich, & Tarter, 1998). Despite this finding, little progress has been made in identifying cognitive deficits specific to CD/ASPD without psychopathy. Two studies compared cognitive functions of violent offenders with ASPD and psychopathy, violent offenders with ASPD and not psychopathy, and healthy non-offenders. The first study reported that regardless of psychopathy scores, offenders with ASPD, as compared to healthy participants, exhibited subtle impairments in planning, attentional set-shifting, and response inhibition, and not in reversal learning (Dolan, 2012). Another study reported that both groups of violent offenders were similarly impaired, relative to the non-offenders, on the Digit Span – backward, commission errors on the Passive Avoidance Learning Task, Probabilistic Response Reversal Task, and the Cambridge Gamble Task (De Brito, et al., 2013a). These studies were conducted on a subset of men with ASPD, those with a lifelong history of aggressive behavior and violent criminal offending. Whether violent offenders with ASPD present distinct or simply more severe cognitive deficits than men with ASPD who do not commit violent crimes is not known. For example, in De Brito et al. (2013a), the violent offenders with ASPD showed deficits in performance on the Digit Span backwards that assesses verbal working memory, while two studies of men with ASPD with no history of criminality or substance misuse observed no deficits in verbal working memory (Gillen & Hesselbrock, 1992; Stevens, Kaplan, & Hesselbrock, 2003). Deficits in verbal working memory have been observed in aggressive children and adults (Séguin, Pihl, Harden, Tremblay, & Boulerice, 1995; Séguin, Sylvers, & Lilienfeld, 2007).

While much evidence indicates that men with ASPD, regardless of psychopathy level, show impulsive behavior in the form of impaired response inhibition (Lapierre, Braun, & Hodgins, 1995), the results of De Brito et al. (2013a) indicated that the violent offenders with ASPD showed no deficits in delay aversion, one form of impulsivity. This is a surprising finding because reduced levels of the ability to delay gratification assessed in early adolescence predict increased risk of criminality through adolescence and adulthood (Akerlund, Golsteyn, Gronqvist, & Lindahl, 2016). By contrast, in the De Brito et al. study the violent offenders with ASPD showed impairments on the Passive Avoidance Learning Task, suggesting difficulty in learning from punishment cues, and on the Response Reversal Task, suggesting difficulty adjusting their behavior as contingencies changed. This complicated picture is likely due, at least in part, to a long history of substance misuse, among adults with CD/ASPD. In a study of a large sample of adults, alcoholism, amount and duration of heavy drinking, and ASPD were significant predictors of abnormalities of the frontal cortex, as assessed by neuropsychological tests, and affective abnormalities. These effects were different among men and women. Importantly, the findings suggested that the combination of alcoholism and ASPD leads to greater deficits than the sum of each, particularly in tests sensitive both to dorsolateral prefrontal functions (Trails tests; Wisconsin Card Sort Test conceptual responses; WAIS Block Design) and to orbitofrontal functions (WAIS Picture Arrangement; Depression) (Oscar-Berman et al., 2009).

Decades of research also confirm that children with CD and juvenile delinquents present lower than average verbal intelligence (Isen, 2010). This deficit may contribute to the development of antisocial behavior by decreasing the opportunities for rewards (Moffitt, Gabrielli, Mednick, & Schulsinger, 1981).

In summary, neuropsychological tests have been used to try to identify brain abnormalities associated with antisocial behavior. Since individuals with CD/ASPD with and without psychopathy present both similarities and differences, to date there is limited knowledge of the abnormalities that are specific to each subtype (see Box 10.2 for obstacles to further understanding).

Box 10.2 Obstacles to furthering understanding of brain abnormalities associated with CD/ASPD

Among individuals with CD/ASPD factors such as sex, age, comorbid disorders, and experiences of trauma also influence brain structures and functioning obscuring the abnormalities specifically associated with antisocial behavior.

Sex Most studies of antisocial behavior include only males. As previously noted, CD/ASPD is less prevalent among females than males, the presentation differs somewhat, and the associated genetic variants differ. There are sex differences in neural structures associated with antisocial and aggressive behaviors (Gur, Gunning-Dixon, Bilker, & Gur, 2002), in the rate of brain maturation (Perrin et al., 2009), in the neural mechanisms underlying the processing of emotions, and in down-regulation of limbic activity (Whittle, Yücel, Yap, & Allen, 2011).

Age Abnormalities of both grey and white matter may differ depending on age. Further, brain structures do not mature at a constant rate. Rather, individual structures grow in spurts and traumatic events tend to damage structures that are growing when the event occurs, such that the same event has different consequences at different ages (Hodgins, De Brito, Simonoff, Vloet, & Viding, 2009). Generally, findings from child/adolescent samples with a large range in age are difficult to interpret.

Substance misuse As previously noted, children with CD begin misusing substances at a young age (Robins & McEvoy, 1990). The effects of various substances on the brain vary by developmental stage, and for some substances – marijuana, for example – the consequences are more severe during adolescence than in adulthood (Schneider, 2008). Adults with ASPD have long histories of substance misuse that are associated with brain abnormalities.

Maltreatment Many children with CD experience maltreatment, such as physical abuse, sexual abuse, viewing violence between parents, and emotional abuse (Murray & Farrington, 2010; Stouthamer-Loeber, Loeber, Homish, & Wei, 2001; Widom, 1989). Such experiences are associated with alterations to brain structure and functions that initiate and/or maintain hyper-activation of neural circuits to threat (Dannlowski et al., 2012; De Brito, et al., 2013b; McCrory et al., 2011).

Comorbid disorders As previously noted, comorbid anxiety, depression, ADHD, and borderline personality disorder are common among children with CD and adults with ASPD. Each of these disorders is associated with abnormalities of brain grey and white matter. However, few studies of brain structures and functioning among individuals with CD/ASPD have taken account of these disorders. For example, the first direct comparison of brain structure among adolescents with pure CD and pure ADHD observed that those with CD displayed a reduction of 13% in total brain GM volume as compared to healthy teenagers, while those with ADHD showed a non-significant reduction of approximately 3% (Rubia, 2011). Further, the teenagers with CD, but not those with ADHD, displayed reductions in GM in several medial (anterior cingulate, ventral part of medial frontal gyrus) and lateral (dorso/ventrolateral, insular, frontopolar) frontal, and temporal regions (Stevens & Haney-Caron, 2012). Another study that illustrates the importance of considering disorders comorbid with CD/ASPD when examining the brain recruited male offenders with ASPD and borderline personality disorder is Bertsch et al. (2013). While all of the offenders with ASPD displayed reduced GM volumes within the frontal pole and occipital cortex as compared to healthy non-offenders, there was little overlap in the regional distribution of abnormalities shown by ASPD offenders with and without borderline personality disorder.

Psychopathy Most brain imaging studies of adults with ASPD have examined samples with varying degrees of psychopathy. A recent study of violent offenders with ASPD compared those with and without the syndrome of psychopathy, matched on age, IQ, education, reactive aggression, and SUDs. The violent offenders with ASPD only showed no structural differences in GM compared to the healthy non-offenders (Gregory et al., 2012). In another study of violent offenders, again two groups with ASPD were compared, one with and one without SUDs, matched on age, IQ, and education. Compared to non-offenders, violent offenders showed greater GM volumes in left nucleus accumbens, right caudate head, bilateral amygdala, as well as reduced left insula volumes. Men with SUDs, compared to those without, showed reduced GM volumes in frontopolar-orbitofrontal cortcies which correlated with scores for response inhibition, as well as reductions in premotor area (Schiffer et al., 2011). Although men with ASPD and no SUDs are rare and unrepresentative of men with ASPD, these findings begin to disentangle the correlates of antisocial behavior and SUDs. These results are important because several previous reports have shown reduced frontal volumes, including frontopolar-orbitofrontal regions, in antisocial men (Yang & Raine, 2009) and violent males with ASPD, but few of these studies have controlled for comorbid SUDs or other comorbid disorders. The most compelling evidence demonstrating that CD/ASPD without psychopathy displays distinct neural mechanisms derives from fMRI studies that confirm the hyper-reactivity of the amygdala and other limbic structures while psychopathy is associated with hyporeactivity.

CD as a Precursor of Schizophrenia

Several investigations have now shown that CD prior to the onset of schizophrenia is associated with non-violent and violent criminality and aggressive behavior from childhood through adulthood (Hodgins, Cree, Alderton, & Mak, 2008; Hodgins, Hiscoke, & Freese, 2003; Hodgins, Tiihonen, & Ross, 2005; Swanson et al., 2006). Further, the number of CD symptoms prior to age 15 is positively and linearly related to the number of convictions for both non-violent and violent crimes. These findings take account of past and current substance misuse and they concur with results from other studies that used different definitions of childhood conduct problems (Fulwiler & Ruthazer, 1999; Rice & Harris, 1995; Tengström, Hodgins, Grann, Långström, & Kullgren, 2004; Winsper et al., 2013). Thus, both in the general population (Moffitt & Caspi, 2001) and among people with schizophrenia, CD is a precursor of aggressive behavior, as well as violent crime (Hodgins, 2008; Hodgins, Hiscoke, & Freese, 2003; Hodgins, Tiihonen, & Ross, 2005; Swanson et al., 2006). Importantly, the existing evidence indicates that those with CD show similar profiles of psychotic symptoms, as do other patients with schizophrenia (Moran & Hodgins, 2004).

Both schizophrenia (Weinberger, 1987) and CD (Stadler, Poustka, & Sterzer, 2010) are neurodevelopmental disorders. In both disorders, from conception onwards, combinations of genes, in addition and in interaction with environmental events, are thought to modify brain structure and function. Thus, we reason that when schizophrenia develops in parallel with CD, neurodevelopment will be distinct from both that associated with schizophrenia and that associated with CD, but will include features that are common to each disorder and others that differ across the two disorders.

We examined a complete cohort of individuals consulting psychiatric services with a first episode of psychosis in one large geographic catchment area in the UK. Men who already had convictions for crimes prior to a first episode of psychosis were presumed to have presented CD earlier in childhood or adolescence. Those with violent convictions prior to illness onset, as compared to the non-offenders, performed significantly more poorly on tests of verbal memory, visual-spatial perception and organization, and verbal intelligence, and in one of two tests of processing speed. Violent offenders obtained, on average, similar scores as the non-offenders on tests of working memory and executive function (Hodgins et al., 2011).

In a subsequent study, we compared three groups of men: SZ+CD, SZ–CD, and healthy. Those with SZ+CD obtained IQ scores approximately half of a standard deviation lower than those with SZ–CD, and made significantly more errors on the Wisconsin Card Sort Test, fewer correct solutions on the Tower of London task although this difference was not significant, and more errors on the go/no-go test, while performance on the Trail Making Test, Working Memory, visuo-spatial memory, and verbal memory subtests were similar.

We recently completed the first structural MRI study, comparing four groups of men, SZ+CD, SZ–CD, CD, and healthy, matched on IQ and level of education (Schiffer et al., 2013). The SZ+CD and SZ–CD men were similar in age of onset and duration of illness, scores for positive and negative psychotic symptoms, and dose of medication measured in chlorpromazine equivalent units. Yet, relative to men with SZ–CD, those with SZ+CD displayed increased GM volumes in the hypothalamus, left putamen, right cuneus/precuneus, and right inferior parietal cortex and no regions of decreased GM volumes after controlling for age and substance misuse. The SZ+CD and CD men were similar in terms of mean number of CD symptoms prior to age 15, scores for lifelong aggression, numbers of criminal convictions, and proportions with a diagnosis of ASPD. Relative to men with CD, those with SZ+CD exhibited no regions in which GM volumes were increased, and decreases in volumes of the inferior, medial and superior temporal lobes, the temporo-parietal junction, parahippocampal gyrus dorsolateral prefrontal cortex, frontopolar regions, and the thalamus, again after controlling for age and substance misuse.

As shown in Figure 10.2, conjunction analyses indicated that relative to the healthy men, the SZ+CD and CD groups exhibited similarly increased volumes in the hypothalamus, the right inferior parietal cortex, and left superior parietal cortex. Further, the GM volumes of the hypothalamus were significantly correlated with scores for fighting and assault and the number of aggressive CD symptoms. Thus, both in schizophrenia preceded by CD and CD/ASPD the neural threat system, the amygdala-hypothalamus-periaqueductal grey, may be structurally abnormal and underlie reactive aggressive behavior.

While there are few studies, emerging evidence suggests that men with SZ+CD show lower verbal IQ, and distinctive anomalies of cognition, brain structure, and function as compared to men with SZ-CD, with CD, and to those with no mental disorders and criminality. Individuals with SZ+CD differ both from those with schizophrenia and no CD and individuals with CD with regard to genetic and environmental factors contributing to their disorders. fMRI studies of violent offenders with schizophrenia have also found decreased activation in the orbitofrontal cortex and basal cortex during a go/no-go task and increased activity in the motor, premotor, and anterior cingulate regions among those with ASPD (Joyal et al., 2007).

The evidence that CD is more common among people with, than without, schizophrenia suggests that the vulnerability to schizophrenia increases the risk of CD, but whether this occurs via genes, environmental factors, or a combination of both is presently unknown. The motor, cognitive, and emotional deficits, and the associated anomalies of brain functioning, that characterize children who are developing

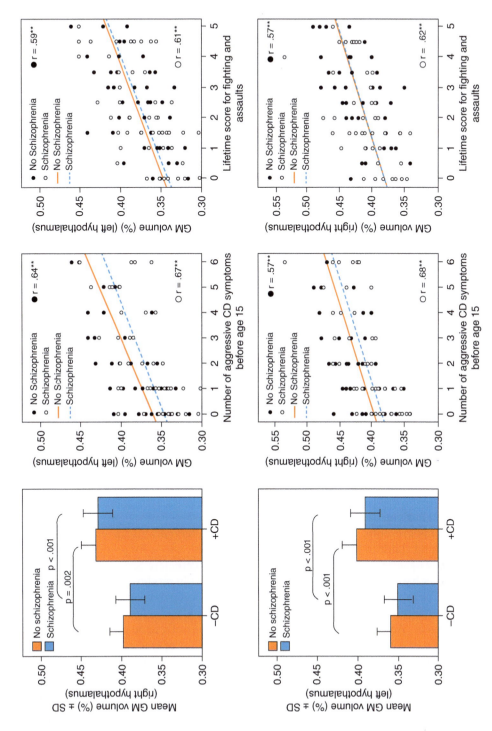

Figure 10.2 Grey matter volumes associated with CD and aggressive behavior among men with schizophrenia and CD and men with CD.

schizophrenia somehow increase the likelihood of CD (Cannon & Clarke, 2005; Cannon, Jones, & Murray, 2002; Dickson, Laurens, Cullen, & Hodgins, 2012; Walker, Savoie, & Davis, 1994). In other ways, however, the presence of CD among those vulnerable for schizophrenia may lead to behaviors such as daily use of cannabis that increase the risk of the onset of schizophrenia (Malcolm et al., 2011).

Treatments for CD/ASPD

The same obstacles that limit studies of the neurobiology of ASPD and CD also limit the development of effective treatment programs – small clinical samples that include males and females of varying ages, many of whom have experienced physical and sexual abuse at different ages that varied in duration and severity, and who present histories of substance misuse that vary by age of onset, type and dose of substance, and that have led to somewhat differing brain anomalies, behavior, and emotion processing. Clinical samples, like samples recruited for research, vary by the constellation of comorbid disorders they display.

Most adults with ASPD do not receive treatment except for their substance misuse, and consequently, as indicated by a systematic review that identified only two studies of treatment of persons with ASPD, little is known about effective treatment (Duggan, Adams, Ferriter, Huband, & Smailagic, 2007). While most men in the trials of the offender rehabilitation programs would likely have met criteria for ASPD, they were not diagnosed (McGuire, 1995). Children and adults who present CD/ASPD require interventions designed to reduce their hyper-reactivity to environmental stimuli and their persistent feelings of being threatened, and to alter their perception that the world is a frightening place. Such interventions may involve helping these individuals change their environments – removing children from abusive families, helping adults move to neighborhoods with lower rates of crime, substance misuse, and antisocial associates – as well as cognitive re-structuring (Mörtberg, Clark, Sundin, & Aberg Wistedt, 2007) and learning prosocial skills. Given the robust evidence that CD/ASPD emerges in childhood, treatment of CD should be the priority with the hope that success would prevent the development of ASPD.

Effective treatments for CD and conduct problems include parent training programs (Scott, 2012; Furlong et al., 2012), multi-modal cognitive-behavioral programs (Conduct Problems Prevention Research Group, 2007), interventions for entire school classes of young children (Petras et al., 2008), and interventions for pregnant women with a history of antisocial behavior (Olds et al., 2002; Petitclerc & Tremblay, 2009). Recent studies have shown that genetic variants play roles in modifying responsivity to treatment. For example, a randomized controlled trial compared outcomes of one of the most commonly used multi-modal programs in the US, the Fast Track Program, to no-treatment. Among individuals carrying one variant of a gene involved in stress regulation, those who completed the treatment showed fewer externalizing behaviors at age 25 than individuals with the same variant in the no-treatment group and fewer than individuals who received the treatment but who carried other variants of the gene (Albert et al., 2015). The finding only applied to individuals of European-American heritage and not to those of African-American heritage. Another randomized controlled trial showed that among individuals of African-American heritage, carriers of one variant of the serotonin transporter gene showed greater reductions in conduct problems if their parents completed parent training than individuals carrying the same variant whose parents participated in a placebo intervention, and greater than individuals carrying other variants in both the treatment and no-treatment groups (Brody et al., 2009). Genetic variants may be one of the many reasons why treatments of CD do not always prevent the development of ASPD (Scott, Briskman, & O'Connor, 2014).

Conclusions

Adults with ASPD, and children with CD, place a heavy burden on society because of the costs they incur and suffering they impose on those around them. Presently, establishing effective treatment and prevention programs and furthering understanding of the aetiology of this disorder is limited by the heterogeneity of the population with these disorders. Among those with CD/ASPD (without high levels of psychopathic traits), research suggests that negative emotionality and a heightened sense of being threatened underlie emotionally charged aggressive behavior. In childhood, this anomalous emotion processing and behavior may be initiated and/or maintained by harsh parenting and victimization by peers. The genetic vulnerability to CD/ASPD is enhanced by factors operative during pregnancy such as maternal smoking (Gaysina et al., 2013), alcohol use (Larkby, Goldschmidt, Hanusa & Day, 2011), and malnutrition (Neugebauer, Hoek, & Susser, 1999), but most importantly by parenting practices (Hodgins Kratzer, & McNeil, 2001), including physical abuse (Caspi et al., 2002). Both genetic and environmental factors lead to anomalies of brain structure and function that underlie aberrant emotion processing and persistent reactive aggression. In childhood, optimal parenting focusing on rewarding good behaviors and using appropriate sanctions, such as time-out, to signal unwanted behaviors is effective in reducing conduct problems before they escalate and lead to poor academic achievement, substance misuse, and associations with deviant peers. Presently, evidence-based multi-modal cognitive-behavioral programs offer the most effective intervention, that is, prevention.

Implications for practice

The long-term effects of interventions for children with CD and adolescents and adults with ASPD – for example, cognitive-behavioral offender rehabilitation programs – could be enhanced by using brain imaging. If such interventions lead to changes in cognition and behavior, they should also lead to changes in brain functioning, and perhaps with time in brain structure. Only if the brain changes would the behavioral changes be expected to remain over time. Thus, future studies of interventions that measure brain structure and function before and after interventions would identify changes in the brain that may be indicative of long-term changes in behavior. The results of such studies could be used to improve the effectiveness of cognitive-behavioral interventions.

Note

1 Stéphane De Brito was supported by a research fellowship from the Swiss National Science Foundation (FNS PA00P1_139586).

Recommended Reading

Albert, D., Belsky, D. W., Crowley, D. M., Latendresse, S. J., Aliev, F., Riley, B., ... Dodge, K. A. (2015). Can genetics predict response to complex behavioral interventions?: Evidence from a genetic analysis of the fast track randomized control trial. *Journal of Policy Analysis and Management, 34*(3), 497–518. *This study followed individuals to age 25 who as children had participated in a randomized controlled trial of a multi-modal cognitive-behavioral treatment program for conduct problems. The study shows how one genetic variant modified response to treatment. The findings likely illustrate how many other genetic variants alter response to treatments.*

Blair, R. J. R. (2012). Considering anger from a cognitive neuroscience perspective. *Wiley Interdisciplinary Reviews. Cognitive Science, 3*(1), 65–74. doi:10.1002/wcs.154. *This is one of the only reviews to describe a neurobiological model of CD/ASPD without psychopathy.*

Byrd, A. L., & Manuck, S. B. (2014). MAOA, childhood maltreatment, and antisocial behavior: Meta-analysis of a gene–environment interaction. *Biological Psychiatry, 75*(1), 9–17. doi:10.1016/j.biopsych.2013.05.004. *This meta-analysis confirms the role of gene-environment interactions in the aetiology of antisocial behavior and shows that the variants of genes that interact with the environment differ in males and females.*

Raine, A., Yang, Y., Narr, K. L., & Toga, A. W. (2011). Sex differences in orbitofrontal grey as a partial explanation for sex differences in antisocial personality. *Molecular Psychiatry, 16*(2), 227–236. doi:10.1038/mp.2009.136. *This study shows how structural brain differences in males and females may explain, at least in part, sex differences in antisocial behavior.*

Schiffer, B., Leygraf, N., Müller, B. W., Scherbaum, N., Forsting, M., Wiltfang, J., ... Hodgins, S. (2013). Structural brain alterations associated with schizophrenia preceded by conduct disorder: A common and distinct subtype of schizophrenia? *Schizophrenia Bulletin, 39*(5), 1115–1128. doi:10.1093/schbul/sbs115. *This study examines structural brain abnormalities in men with lifelong histories of antisocial behavior, with and without schizophrenia, and compares them to healthy non-offenders.*

References

Afifi, T. O., Boman, J., Fleisher, W., & Sareen, J. (2009). The relationship between child abuse, parental divorce, and lifetime mental disorders and suicidality in a nationally representative adult sample. *Child Abuse & Neglect, 33*(3), 139–147. doi:10.1016/j.chiabu.2008.12.009.

Akerlund, D., Golsteyn, B. H. H., Gronqvist, H., & Lindahl, L. (2016). Time discounting and criminal behavior. *Proceedings of the National Academy of Sciences of the United States of America, 113*(22), 6160–6165. doi:10.1073/pnas.1522445113.

Albert, D., Belsky, D. W., Crowley, D. M., Latendresse, S. J., Aliev, F., Riley, B., ... Dodge, K. A. (2015). Can genetics predict response to complex behavioral interventions?: Evidence from a genetic analysis of the fast track randomized control trial. *Journal of Policy Analysis and Management, 34*(3), 497–518.

American Psychiatric Association. (1980). *Diagnostic and Statistical Manual of Mental Disorders. (3rd ed.)*. Washington, DC: American Psychiatric Association.

American Psychiatric Association. (2013). *Diagnostic and Statistical Manual of Mental Disorders 5*. Washington, DC: American Psychiatric Association.

Angold, A., Costello, E. J., & Erkanli, A. (1999). Comorbidity. *Journal of Child Psychology and Psychiatry, and Allied Disciplines, 40*(1), 57–87.

Aslund, C., Comasco, E., Nordquist, N., Leppert, J., Oreland, L., & Nilsson, K. W. (2013). Self reported family socioeconomic status, the 5-HTTLPR genotype, and delinquent behavior in a community-based adolescent population. *Aggressive Behavior, 39*(1), 52–63. doi:10.1002/ab.21451.

Banks, S. J., Eddy, K. T., Angstadt, M., Nathan, P. J., & Phan, K. L. (2007). Amygdala-frontal connectivity during emotion regulation. *Social Cognitive and Affective Neuroscience, 2*(4), 303–312. doi:10.1093/scan/nsm029.

Barker, E. D., Séguin, J. R., White, H. R., Bates, M. E., Lacourse, E., Carbonneau, R., & Tremblay, R. E. (2007). Developmental trajectories of male physical violence and theft: Relations to neurocognitive performance. *Archives of General Psychiatry, 64*(5), 592–599. doi:10.1001/archpsyc.64.5.592.

Barker, E. D., Vitaro, F., Lacourse, E., Fontaine, Nathalie M G, Carbonneau, R., & Tremblay, R. E. (2010). Testing the developmental distinctiveness of male proactive and reactive aggression with a nested longitudinal experimental intervention. *Aggressive Behavior, 36*(2), 127–140. doi:10.1002/ab.20337.

Barnett, J. H., Xu, K., Heron, J., Goldman, D., & Jones, P. B. (2011). Cognitive effects of genetic variation in monoamine neurotransmitter systems: A population-based study of COMT, MAOA, and 5HTTLPR. *American Journal of Medical Genetics. Part B, Neuropsychiatric Genetics, 156*(2), 158–167. doi:10.1002/ajmg.b.31150.

Beach, S. R. H., Brody, G. H., Lei, M. K., Gibbons, F. X., Gerrard, M., Simons, R. L., … Philibert, R. A. (2013). Impact of child sex abuse on adult psychopathology: A genetically and epigenetically informed investigation. *Journal of Family Psychology, 27*(1), 3–11. doi:10.1037/a0031459.

Beach, S. R. H., Brody, G. H., Todorov, A. A., Gunter, T. D., & Philibert, R. A. (2010). Methylation at SLC6A4 is linked to family history of child abuse: An examination of the Iowa Adoptee sample. *American Journal of Medical Genetics. Part B, Neuropsychiatric Genetics, 153B*(2), 710–713. doi:10.1002/ajmg.b.31028.

Beissner, F., Deichmann, R., & Baudrexel, S. (2011). fMRI of the brainstem using dual-echo EPI. *NeuroImage, 55*(4), 1593–1599. doi:10.1016/j.neuroimage.2011.01.042.

Belsky, D. W., Caspi, A., Arseneault, L., Bleidorn, W., Fonagy, P., Goodman, M., … Moffitt, T. E. (2012). Etiological features of borderline personality related characteristics in a birth cohort of 12-year-old children. *Development and Psychopathology, 24*(1), 251–265. doi:10.1017/S0954579411000812.

Bertsch, K., Grothe, M., Prehn, K., Vohs, K., Berger, C., Hauenstein, K., … Herpertz, S. C. (2013). Brain volumes differ between diagnostic groups of violent criminal offenders. *European Archives of Psychiatry and Clinical Neuroscience, 263*(7), 593–606. doi:10.1007/s00406-013-0391-6.

Bickart, K. C., Dickerson, B. C., & Barrett, L. F. (2014). The amygdala as a hub in brain networks that support social life. *Neuropsychologia, 63*, 235–248. doi:10.1016/j.neuropsychologia.2014.08.013.

Bird, A. (2007). Perceptions of epigenetics. *Nature, 447*(7143), 396–398. doi:10.1038/nature05913.

Black, D. W., Baumgard, C. H., Bell, S. E., & Kao, C. (1996). Death rates in 71 men with antisocial personality disorder. A comparison with general population mortality. *Psychosomatics, 37*(2), 131–136. doi:10.1016/S0033-3182(96)71579-7.

Blair, R. J. R. (2012). Considering anger from a cognitive neuroscience perspective. *Wiley Interdisciplinary Reviews. Cognitive science, 3*(1), 65–74. doi:10.1002/wcs.154.

Braun, J. M., Froehlich, T. E., Daniels, J. L., Dietrich, K. N., Hornung, R., Auinger, P., & Lanphear, B. P. (2008). Association of environmental toxicants and conduct disorder in U.S. children: NHANES 2001-2004. *Environmental Health Perspectives, 116*(7), 956–962. doi:10.1289/ehp.11177.

Brennan, L. M., & Shaw, D. S. (2013). Revisiting data related to the age of onset and developmental course of female conduct problems. *Clinical Child and Family Psychology Review, 16*(1), 35–58. doi:10.1007/s10567-012-0125-8.

Brody, G. H., Beach, S. R. H., Philibert, R. A., Chen, Y.-f., Lei, M.-K., Murry, V. M., & Brown, A. C. (2009). Parenting moderates a genetic vulnerability factor in longitudinal increases in youths' substance use. *Journal of Consulting and Clinical Psychology, 77*(1), 1–11. doi:10.1037/a0012996.

Buckholtz, J. W., & Meyer-Lindenberg, A. (2008). MAOA and the neurogenetic architecture of human aggression. *Trends Neuroscience, 31*(3):120–129. doi: 0.1016/j.tins.2007.12.006.

Burke, J. D. (2007). Antisocial Personality Disorder. In A. Freeman & M. A. Reinecke (Eds.), *Personality Disorders in Childhood and Adolescence* (pp. 429–494). Hoboken, NJ: John Wiley & Sons.

Byrd, A. L., & Manuck, S. B. (2014). MAOA, childhood maltreatment, and antisocial behavior: Meta-analysis of a gene-environment interaction. *Biological Psychiatry, 75*(1), 9–17. doi:10.1016/j.biopsych.2013.05.004.

Cannon, M., & Clarke, M. C. (2005). Risk for schizophrenia–broadening the concepts, pushing back the boundaries. *Schizophrenia Research, 79*(1), 5–13. doi:10.1016/j.schres.2005.05.027.

Cannon, M., Jones, P. B., & Murray, R. M. (2002). Obstetric complications and schizophrenia: historical and meta-analytic review. *The American Journal of Psychiatry, 159*(7), 1080–1092. doi:10.1176/appi.ajp.159.7.1080.

Caspi, A., McClay, J., Moffitt, T. E., Mill, J., Martin, J., Craig, I. W., ... Poulton, R. (2002). Role of genotype in the cycle of violence in maltreated children. *Science, 297*(5582), 851–854. doi:10.1126/science.1072290.

Checknita, D., Comasco, E., Oreland, L., Rehn, M., Westermann, J., Ekström, T. J., ... Hodgins, S. (2016). Among females, differential methylation in a subregion of the monoamine oxidase A (MAOA) gene promoter associates with conduct disorder, the experience of physical and sexual abuse, and timing of sexual abuse. *Biological Psychiatry, 79*(Supplement 9), 93S.

Checknita, D., Maussion, G., Labonte, B., Comai, S., Tremblay, R. E., Vitaro, F., ... Turecki, G. (2015). Monoamine oxidase: A gene promoter methylation associates with transcriptional downregulation in an offender population with antisocial personality disorder. *The British Journal of Psychiatry, 206*, 216–222. doi: 10.1192/bjp.bp.114.144964.

Coid, J. (2003). Epidemiology, public health and the problem of personality disorder. *The British Journal of Psychiatry. Supplement, 44*, S3–10.

Coid, J., Yang, M., Roberts, A., Ullrich, S., Moran, P., Bebbington, P., ... Singleton, N. (2006b). Violence and psychiatric morbidity in the national household population of Britain: Public health implications. *The British Journal of Psychiatry, 189*, 12–19. doi:10.1192/bjp.189.1.12.

Coid, J., Yang, M., Tyrer, P., Roberts, A., & Ullrich, S. (2006a). Prevalence and correlates of personality disorder in Great Britain. *The British Journal of Psychiatry, 188*, 423–431. doi:10.1192/bjp.188.5.423.

Comai, S., Tau, M., & Gobbi, G. (2012). The psychopharmacology of aggressive behavior: A translational approach: Part 1: Neurobiology. *Journal of Clinical Psychopharmacology, 32*(1), 83–94. doi:10.1097/JCP.0b013e31823f8770.

Compton, W. M., Conway, K. P., Stinson, F. S., Colliver, J. D., & Grant, B. F. (2005). Prevalence, correlates, and comorbidity of DSM-IV antisocial personality syndromes and alcohol and specific drug use disorders in the United States: Results from the national epidemiologic survey on alcohol and related conditions. *The Journal of Clinical Psychiatry, 66*(6), 677–685.

Conduct Problems Prevention Research Group. (2007). Fast track randomized controlled trial to prevent externalizing psychiatric disorders: Findings from grades 3 to 9. *Journal of the American Academy of Child and Adolescent Psychiatry, 46*(10), 1250–1262.

Costello, E. J., Compton, S. N., Keeler, G., & Angold, A. (2003). Relationships between poverty and psychopathology: A natural experiment. *JAMA, 290*(15), 2023–2029. doi:10.1001/jama.290.15.2023.

Costello, E. J., Foley, D. L., & Angold, A. (2006). 10-year research update review: The epidemiology of child and adolescent psychiatric disorders: II. Developmental epidemiology. *Journal of the American Academy of Child and Adolescent Psychiatry, 45*(1), 8–25. doi:10.1097/01.chi.0000184929.41423.c0.

Cottler, L. B., Price, R. K., Compton, W. M., & Mager, D. E. (1995). Subtypes of adult antisocial behavior among drug abusers. *The Journal of Nervous and Mental Disease, 183*(3), 154–161.

Craig, M. C., Catani, M., Deeley, Q., Latham, R., Daly, E., Kanaan, R., ... Murphy, D G M. (2009). Altered connections on the road to psychopathy. *Molecular Psychiatry, 14*(10), 946-53, 907. doi:10.1038/mp.2009.40.

Dadds, M. R. (2006). Attention to the eyes and fear-recognition deficits in child psychopathy. *The British Journal of Psychiatry, 189*(3), 280–281. doi:10.1192/bjp.bp.105.018150.

Dalley, J. W., & Roiser, J. P. (2012). Dopamine, serotonin and impulsivity. *Neuroscience, 215*, 42–58. doi:10.1016/j.neuroscience.2012.03.065.

Dalsgaard, S., Mortensen, P. B., Frydenberg, M., & Thomsen, P. H. (2013). Long-term criminal outcome of children with attention deficit hyperactivity disorder. *Criminal Behavior and Mental Health, 23*(2), 86–98. doi:10.1002/cbm.1860.

Dannlowski, U., Stuhrmann, A., Beutelmann, V., Zwanzger, P., Lenzen, T., Grotegerd, D., ... Kugel, H. (2012). Limbic scars: Long-term consequences of childhood maltreatment revealed by functional and structural magnetic resonance imaging. *Biological Psychiatry, 71*(4), 286–293. doi:10.1016/j.biopsych.2011.10.021.

De Brito, S. A., & Hodgins, S. (2009). Antisocial personality disorder. In M. McMurran & R. C. Howard (Eds.), *Wiley Series in Forensic Clinical Psychology. Personality, Personality Disorder, and Violence* (pp. 133–153). New York, NY: John Wiley & Sons.

De Brito, S. A., Viding, E., Kumari, V., Blackwood, N., Hodgins, S., & Soriano-Mas, C. (2013a). Cool and Hot Executive Function Impairments in Violent Offenders with Antisocial Personality Disorder with and without Psychopathy. *PLoS ONE, 8*(6), e65566. doi:10.1371/journal.pone.0065566.

De Brito, S. A., Viding, E., Sebastian, C. L., Kelly, P. A., Mechelli, A., Maris, H., & McCrory, E. J. (2013b). Reduced orbitofrontal and temporal grey matter in a community sample of maltreated children. *Journal of Child Psychology and Psychiatry and Allied Disciplines, 54*(1), 105112.

Dickson, H., Laurens, K. R., Cullen, A. E., & Hodgins, S. (2012). Meta-analyses of cognitive and motor function in youth aged 16 years and younger who subsequently develop schizophrenia. *Psychological Medicine, 42*(4), 743–755. doi:10.1017/S0033291711001693.

Disney, E. R., Elkins, I. J., McGue, M., & Iacono, W. G. (1999). Effects of ADHD, conduct disorder, and gender on substance use and abuse in adolescence. *The American Journal of Psychiatry, 156*(10), 1515–1521.

Dodge, K. A., Lochman, J. E., Harnish, J. D., Bates, J. E., & Pettit, G. S. (1997). Reactive and proactive aggression in school children and psychiatrically impaired chronically assaultive youth. *Journal of Abnormal Psychology, 106*(1), 37–51.

Dolan, M. (2012) The neuropsychology of prefrontal function in antisocial personality disordered offenders with varying degrees of psychopathy. *Psychological Medicine, 42*, 1715–1725.

D'Onofrio, B. M., Slutske, W. S., Turkheimer, E., Emery, R. E., Harden, K. P., Heath, A. C., ... Martin, N. G. (2007). Intergenerational transmission of childhood conduct problems: A Children of Twins Study. *Archives of General Psychiatry, 64*(7), 820–829. doi:10.1001/archpsyc.64.7.820

Duggan, C., Adams, C., Ferriter, M., Huband, N., & Smailagic, N. (2007). The use of psychological treatments for people with personality disorder: A systematic review of randomized controlled trials. *Personality and Mental Health Journal, 1*(2), 95–125. doi:10.1002/pmh.22.

Farrington, D. P., Jolliffe, D., Loeber, R., Stouthamer-Loeber, M., & Kalb, L. M. (2001). The concentration of offenders in families, and family criminality in the prediction of boys' delinquency. *Journal of Adolescence, 24*(5), 579–596. doi:10.1006/jado.2001.0424.

Farrington, D. P., & Loeber, R. (2000). Epidemiology of juvenile violence. *Child and Adolescent Psychiatric Clinics of North America, 9*(4), 733–748.

Fazel, S., & Danesh, J. (2002). Serious mental disorder in 23000 prisoners: A systematic review of 62 surveys. *Lancet, 359*(9306), 545–550. doi:10.1016/S0140-6736(02)07740-1.

Fergusson, D. M., Boden, J. M., & Horwood, L. J. (2008). Dentine lead levels in childhood and criminal behavior in late adolescence and early adulthood. *Journal of Epidemiology and Community Health, 62*(12), 1045–1050. doi:10.1136/jech.2007.072827.

Fergusson, D. M., Fergusson, J. E., Horwood, L. J., & Kinzett, N. G. (1988). A longitudinal study of dentine lead levels, intelligence, school performance and behavior. Part III. Dentine lead levels and attention/activity. *Journal of Child Psychology and Psychiatry, and Allied Disciplines, 29*(6), 811–824.

Fergusson, D. M., Horwood, L. J., & Ridder, E. M. (2005). Show me the child at seven: The consequences of conduct problems in childhood for psychosocial functioning in adulthood. *Journal of Child Psychology and Psychiatry, and Allied Disciplines, 46*(8), 837–849. doi:10.1111/j.1469-7610.2004.00387.x.

Ficks, C. A., & Waldman, I. D. (2014). Candidate genes for aggression and antisocial behavior: A meta-analysis of association studies of the 5HTTLPR and MAOA-uVNTR. *Behavior Genetics, 44*(5), 427–444. doi:10.1007/s10519-014-9661-y.

Fontaine, N. M. G., McCrory, E. J. P., Boivin, M., Moffitt, T. E., & Viding, E. (2011). Predictors and outcomes of joint trajectories of callous-unemotional traits and conduct problems in childhood. *Journal of Abnormal Psychology, 120*(3), 730–742. doi:10.1037/a0022620.

Frick, P. J., Cornell, A. H., Barry, C. T., Bodin, S. D., & Dane, H. E. (2003). Callous-unemotional traits and conduct problems in the prediction of conduct problem severity, aggression, and self-report of delinquency. *Journal of Abnormal Child Psychology, 31*(4), 457–470.

Frick, P. J., & Marsee, M. A. (2006). Psychopathy and developmental pathways to antisocial behavior in youth. In C. J. Patrick (Ed.), *Handbook of psychopathy* (pp. 353–374). New York, NY/ London: Guilford Press.

Frick, P. J., Ray, J. V., Thornton, L. C., & Kahn, R. E. (2013). Can callous-unemotional traits enhance the understanding, diagnosis, and treatment of serious conduct problems in children and adolescents? A comprehensive review. *Psychological Bulletin, 140*(1), 1–57.

Frick, P. J., & Viding, E. (2009). Antisocial behavior from a developmental psychopathology perspective. *Development and Psychopathology, 21*: 1111–1131.

Fulwiler, C. E., King, J. A., & Zhang, N. (2012). Amygdala-orbitofrontal resting-state functional connectivity is associated with trait anger. *Neuroreport, 23*(10), 606–610. doi:10.1097/WNR.0b013e3283551cfc.

Fulwiler, C. E., & Ruthazer, R. (1999). Premorbid risk factors for violence in adult mental illness. *Comprehensive Psychiatry, 40*(2), 96–100.

Furlong, M., McGilloway, S., Bywater, T., Hutchings, J., Smith, S. M., & Donnelly, M. (2012). Behavioral and cognitive-behavioral group-based parenting programmes for earlyonset conduct problems in children aged 3 to 12 years. *The Cochrane Database of Systematic Reviews, 2*, CD008225.

Gaysina, D., Fergusson, D. M., Leve, L. D., Horwood, J., Reiss, D., Shaw, D. S., ... Harold, G.T. (2013). Maternal smoking during pregnancy and offspring conduct problems: Evidence from 3 independent genetically sensitive research designs. *JAMA Psychiatry (Chicago, Ill.), 70*(9), 956–963.

Gelhorn, H., Hartman, C., Sakai, J., Mikulich-Gilbertson, S., Stallings, M., Young, S., ... Crowley, T. (2009). An item response theory analysis of DSM-IV conduct disorder. *Journal of* the *American Academy of Child and Adolescent Psychiatry, 48*(1), 42–50. doi:10.1097/CHI.0b013e31818b1c4e.

Giancola, P. R., Mezzich, A. C., & Tarter, R. E. (1998). Executive cognitive functioning, temperament, and antisocial behavior in conduct-disordered adolescent females. *Journal of Abnormal Psychology, 107*(4), 629–641.

Gillen, R., & Hesselbrock, V. (1992). Cognitive functioning, ASP, and family history of alcoholism in young men at risk for alcoholism. *Alcoholism, Clinical and Experimental Research, 16*(2), 206–214.

Gilliom, M., & Shaw, D. S. (2004). Codevelopment of externalizing and internalizing problems in early childhood. *Development and Psychopathology, 16*(2), 313–333.

Goldstein, R. B., Grant, B. F., Ruan, W. J., Smith, S. M., & Saha, T. D. (2006). Antisocial personality disorder with childhood-vs. adolescence-onset conduct disorder: Results from the National Epidemiologic Survey on Alcohol and Related Conditions. *The Journal of Nervous and Mental Disease, 194*(9), 667–675. doi:10.1097/01.nmd.0000235762.82264.a1.

Goodwin, R. D., & Hamilton, S. P. (2003). Lifetime comorbidity of antisocial personality disorder and anxiety disorders among adults in the community. *Psychiatry Research, 117*(2), 159–166.

Grant, B. F., Chou, S. P., Goldstein, R. B., Huang, B., Stinson, F. S., Saha, T. D., … Ruan, W. J. (2008). Prevalence, correlates, disability, and comorbidity of DSM-IV borderline personality disorder: Results from the Wave 2 National Epidemiologic Survey on Alcohol and Related Conditions. *The Journal of Clinical Psychiatry, 69*(4), 533–545.

Grant, B. F., Hasin, D. S., Stinson, F. S., Dawson, D. A., Chou, S. P., Ruan, W. J., & Pickering, R. P. (2004). Prevalence, correlates, and disability of personality disorders in the United States: Results from the national epidemiologic survey on alcohol and related conditions. *The Journal of Clinical Psychiatry, 65*(7), 948–958.

Green, H., McGinnity, Á., Meltzer, H., Ford, T., & Goodman, R. (2004). *Mental health of children and young people in Great Britain*, 2004. Retrieved from http://www.esds.ac.uk/doc/5269/mrdoc/pdf/5269technicalreport.pdf.

Gregg, T. R., & Siegel, A. (2001). Brain structures and neurotransmitters regulating aggression in cats: Implications for human aggression. *Progress in Neuro-Psychopharmacology & Biological Psychiatry, 25*(1), 91–140.

Gregory, S., Ffytche, D., Simmons, A., Kumari, V., Howard, M., Hodgins, S., & Blackwood, N. (2012). The antisocial brain: Psychopathy matters. *Archives of General Psychiatry, 69*(9), 962–972. doi:10.1001/archgenpsychiatry.2012.222.

Gunter, T. D., Vaughn, M. G., & Philibert, R. A. (2010). Behavioral genetics in antisocial spectrum disorders and psychopathy: A review of the recent literature. *Behavioral Sciences & the Law, 28*(2), 148–173. doi:10.1002/bsl.923.

Gur, R. C., Gunning-Dixon, F., Bilker, W. B., & Gur, R. E. (2002). Sex differences in temporo-limbic and frontal brain volumes of healthy adults. *Cerebral Cortex, 12*(9), 998–1003.

Hackman, D. A., Farah, M. J., & Meaney, M. J. (2010). Socioeconomic status and the brain: Mechanistic insights from human and animal research. *Nature Reviews Neuroscience, 11*(9), 651–659. doi:10.1038/nrn2897.

Haney-Caron, E., Caprihan, A., & Stevens, M. C. (2013). DTI-measured white matter abnormalities in adolescents with Conduct Disorder. *Journal of Psychiatric Research, 48*(1),111–120. doi:10.1016/j.jpsychires.2013.09.015.

Hankin, B. L., Nederhof, E., Oppenheimer, C. W., Jenness, J., Young, J. F., Abela, J. R. Z., … Oldehinkel, A. J. (2011). Differential susceptibility in youth: Evidence that 5-HTTLPR x positive parenting is associated with positive affect "for better and worse". *Translational Psychiatry, 1*, e44. doi:10.1038/tp.2011.44.

Hare, R. D. (1996). Psychopathy and antisocial personality disorder: A case of diagnostic confusion. *Psychiatric Times, 13*, 39–40.

Hare, R. D. (2003). *The Psychopathy Checklist* (Revised, 2nd ed.) Toronto, Canada: Multi-Health Systems.

Hariri, A. R., Mattay, V. S., Tessitore, A., Kolachana, B., Fera, F., Goldman, D., ... Weinberger, D. R. (2002). Serotonin transporter genetic variation and the response of the human amygdala. *Science*, 297(5580), 400–403. doi:10.1126/science.1071829.

Hawes, S. W., Perlman, S. B., Byrd, A. L., Raine, A., Loeber, R., & Pardini, D. A. (2016). Chronic anger as a precursor to adult antisocial personality features: The moderating influence of cognitive control. *Journal of Abnormal Psychology*, 125(1), 64–74. doi:10.1037/abn0000129.

Herndon, R. W., & Iacono, W. G. (2005). Psychiatric disorder in the children of antisocial parents. *Psychological Medicine*, 35(12), 1815–1824. doi:10.1017/S0033291705005635.

Hodgins, S. (1994). Status at age 30 of children with conduct problems. *Studies of Crime and Crime Prevention*, 3, 41–46.

Hodgins, S. (2008). Violent behavior among people with schizophrenia: A framework for investigations of causes, and effective treatment, and prevention. *Philosophical Transactions of the Royal Society of London. Series B, Biological Sciences*, 363(1503), 2505–2518. doi:10.1098/rstb.2008.0034.

Hodgins, S., Barbareschi, G., & Larsson, A. (2011). Adolescents with conduct disorder: Does anxiety make a difference? *Journal of Forensic Psychiatry & Psychology*, 22(5), 669–691. doi:10.1080/14789949.2011.617539

Hodgins, S., Calem, M., Shimel, R., Williams, A., Harleston, D., Morgan, C., ... & Jones, P. (2011). Criminal offending and distinguishing features of offenders among persons experiencing a first episode of psychosis. *Early Intervention in Psychiatry*, 5, 15–23. doi: 10.1111/j.17517893.2010.00256.x.

Hodgins, S., & Côté, G. (1993). The criminality of mentally disordered offenders. *Criminal Justice and Behavior*, 20(2), 115–129. doi:10.1177/0093854893020002001.

Hodgins, S., Coté, G., & Toupin, J. (1998). Major mental disorders and crime: An etiological hypothesis. In D. Cooke, A. Forth, & R. D. Hare (Eds.), *Psychopathy: Theory, research and implications for society* (pp. 231–256). Dordrecht, The Netherlands: Kluwer Academic Publishers.

Hodgins, S., Cree, A., Alderton, J., & Mak, T. (2008). From conduct disorder to severe mental illness: Associations with aggressive behavior, crime and victimization. *Psychological Medicine*, 38(7), 975–987. doi:10.1017/S0033291707002164.

Hodgins, S., De Brito, S. A., Chhabra, P., & Côté, G. (2010). Anxiety disorders among offenders with antisocial personality disorders: A distinct subtype? *Canadian Journal of Psychiatry*, 55(12), 784–791.

Hodgins, S., De Brito, S. A., Simonoff, E., Vloet, T., & Viding, E. (2009). Getting the phenotypes right: An essential ingredient for understanding aetiological mechanisms underlying persistent violence and developing effective treatments. *Frontiers in Behavioral Neuroscience*, 16(3), 44. doi:10.3389/neuro.08.044.2009

Hodgins, S., Hiscoke, U. L., & Freese, R. (2003). The antecedents of aggressive behavior among men with schizophrenia: A prospective investigation of patients in community treatment. *Behavioral Sciences & the Law*, 21(4), 523–546. doi:10.1002/bsl.540.

Hodgins, S., Kratzer, L., & McNeil, T. F. (2001). Obstetric complications, parenting, and risk of criminal behavior. *Archives of General Psychiatry*, 58(8), 746–752.

Hodgins, S., Tengström, A., Bylin, S., Göranson, M., Hagen, L., Janson, M., ... Pedersen, H. (2007). Consulting for substance abuse: mental disorders among adolescents and their parents. *Nordic Journal of Psychiatry*, 61(5), 379–386.

Hodgins, S., Tiihonen, J., & Ross, D. (2005). The consequences of conduct disorder for males who develop schizophrenia: Associations with criminality, aggressive behavior, substance use, and psychiatric services. *Schizophrenia Research*, 78(2–3), 323–335. doi:10.1016/j.schres.2005.05.021.

Holz, N., Boecker, R., Buchmann, A. F., Blomeyer, D., Baumeister, S., Hohmann, S., ... Laucht, M. (2016). Evidence for a sex-dependent MAOAx childhood stress interaction in the neural circuitry of aggression. *Cerebral Cortex, 26*(3), 904–914. doi:10.1093/cercor/bhu249.

Ingalhalikar, M., Smith, A., Parker, D., Satterthwaite, T. D., Elliott, M. A., Ruparel, K., ... Verma, R. (2014). Sex differences in the structural connectome of the human brain. *Proceedings of the National Academy of Sciences of the United States of America, 111*(2), 823–828. doi:10.1073/pnas.1316909110.

Isen, J. (2010). A meta-analytic assessment of Wechsler's PV sign in antisocial populations. *Clinical Psychology Review, 30*(4), 423–435. doi:10.1016/j.cpr.2010.02.003.

Jaffee, S. R. (2002). Pathways to adversity in young adulthood among early childbearers. *Journal of Family Psychology, 16*(1), 38–49.

Jaffee, S. R., Belsky, J., Harrington, H., Caspi, A., & Moffitt, T. E. (2006). When parents have a history of conduct disorder: How is the caregiving environment affected? *Journal of Abnormal Psychology, 115*(2), 309–319. doi:10.1037/0021-843X.115.2.309.

Jaffee, S. R., Caspi, A., Moffitt, T. E., & Taylor, A. (2004). Physical maltreatment victim to antisocial child: Evidence of an environmentally mediated process. *Journal of Abnormal Psychology, 113*(1), 44–55. doi:10.1037/0021-843X.113.1.44.

Jaffee, S. R., Hanscombe, K. B., Haworth, C. M. A., Davis, O. S. P., & Plomin, R. (2012). Chaotic homes and children's disruptive behavior: A longitudinal cross-lagged twin study. *Psychological Science, 23*(6), 643–650. doi:10.1177/0956797611431693.

Joyal, C., Putkonen, A., Mancini-Marïe, A., Hodgins, S., Kononen, M., Boulay, L., ... Aronen, H. (2007) Violent persons with schizophrenia and comorbid disorders: A functional magnetic resonance imaging study. *Schizophrenia Research, 91*, 97–102. doi: 10.1016/j.schres.2006.12.014.

Johansson, P., Kerr, M., & Andershed, H. (2005). Linking adult psychopathy with childhood hyperactivity-impulsivity-attention problems and conduct problems through retrospective self-reports. *Journal of Personality Disorders, 19*(1), 94–101. doi:10.1521/pedi.19.1.94.62183.

Kessler, R. C., Nelson, C. B., McGonagle, K. A., Edlund, M. J., Frank, R. G., & Leaf, P. J. (1996). The epidemiology of co-occurring addictive and mental disorders: Implications for prevention and service utilization. *The American Journal of Orthopsychiatry, 66*(1), 17–31.

Kim-Cohen, J., Caspi, A., Moffitt, T. E., Harrington, H., Milne, B. J., & Poulton, R. (2003). Prior juvenile diagnoses in adults with mental disorder: Developmental follow-back of a prospective-longitudinal cohort. *Archives of General Psychiatry, 60*(7), 709–717. doi:10.1001/archpsyc.60.7.709.

Krueger, R. F., Hicks, B. M., Patrick, C. J., Carlson, S. R., Iacono, W. G., & McGue, M. (2002). Etiologic connections among substance dependence, antisocial behavior, and personality: Modeling the externalizing spectrum. *Journal of Abnormal Psychology, 111*(3), 411–424.

Kruh, I. P., Frick, P. J., & Clements, C. B. (2005). Historical and personality correlates to the violence patterns of juveniles tried as adults. *Criminal Justice and Behavior, 32*(1), 69–96. doi:10.1177/0093854804270629.

Lahey, B. B., Loeber, R., Burke, J. D., & Applegate, B. (2005). Predicting future antisocial personality disorder in males from a clinical assessment in childhood. *Journal of Consulting and Clinical Psychology, 73*(3), 389–399. doi:10.1037/0022-006X.73.3.389.

Landrø, N. I., Jonassen, R., Clark, L., Haug, K. B. F., Aker, M., Bo, R., ... Stiles, T. C. (2015). Serotonin transporter polymorphisms predict response inhibition in healthy volunteers. *Neuroscience letters, 584*, 109–112. doi:10.1016/j.neulet.2014.10.006.

Lapierre, D., Braun, C. M., & Hodgins, S. (1995). Ventral frontal deficits in psychopathy: Neuropsychological test findings. *Neuropsychologia, 33*(2), 139–151.

Larkby, C. A., Goldschmidt, L., Hanusa, B. H., & Day, N. L. (2011). Prenatal alcohol exposure is associated with conduct disorder in adolescence: Findings from a birth cohort. *Journal of the American Academy of Child and Adolescent Psychiatry, 50*(3), 262–271.

Lenzenweger, M. F., Lane, M. C., Loranger, A. W., & Kessler, R. C. (2007). DSM-IV personality disorders in the National Comorbidity Survey Replication. *Biological Psychiatry, 62*(6), 553–564. doi:10.1016/j.biopsych.2006.09.019.

Lesch, K.-P., Araragi, N., Waider, J., van den Hove, Daniel, & Gutknecht, L. (2012). Targeting brain serotonin synthesis: Insights into neurodevelopmental disorders with long-term outcomes related to negative emotionality, aggression and antisocial behavior. *Philosophical Transactions of the Royal Society of London. Series B, Biological Sciences, 367*(1601), 2426–2443. doi:10.1098/rstb.2012.0039.

Likhtik, E., Pelletier, J. G., Paz, R., & Paré, D. (2005). Prefrontal control of the amygdala. *The Journal of Neuroscience, 25*(32), 7429–7437. doi:10.1523/JNEUROSCI.2314-05.2005.

Lindner, P., Savic, I., Sitnikov, R., Budhiraja, M., Liu, Y., Jokinen, J., ... Hodgins, S. (2016). Conduct disorder in females is associated with reduced corpus callosum structural integrity independent of comorbid disorders and exposure to maltreatment. *Translational Psychiatry, 6*, e714. doi:10.1038/tp.2015.216.

Lobbestael, J., Cima, M., & Arntz, A. (2013). The relationship between adult reactive and proactive aggression, hostile interpretation bias, and antisocial personality disorder. *Journal of Personality Disorders, 27*(1), 53–66. doi:10.1521/pedi.2013.27.1.53.

Loeber, R., Green, S. M., & Lahey, B. B. (2003). Risk factors for antisocial personality. In D. P. Farrington & J. Coid (Eds.), *Early prevention of adult antisocial behavior* (pp. 79–108). Cambridge: Cambridge University Press.

Loeber, R., & Stouthamer-Loeber, M. (1987). *Prediction.* In H. C. Quay (Ed.), *Wiley series on personality processes. Handbook of juvenile delinquency.* New York, NY: John Wiley & Sons.

Lösel, F., & Bender, D. (2003). Protective factors and resilience. In D. P. Farrington & J. Coid (Eds.), *Early prevention of adult antisocial behavior* (pp. 130–204). Cambridge: Cambridge University Press.

Lynam, D. R. (1996). Early identification of chronic offenders: Who is the fledgling psychopath? *Psychological Bulletin, 120*(2), 209–234.

Malcolm, C. P., Picchioni, M. M., DiForti, M., Sugranyes, G., Cooke, E., Joseph, C., ... Hodgins, S. (2011). Pre-morbid Conduct Disorder symptoms are associated with cannabis use among individuals with a first episode of psychosis. *Schizophrenia Research, 126*(1–3), 81–86. doi:10.1016/j.schres.2010.11.025.

Mani, A., Mullainathan, S., Shafir, E., & Zhao, J. (2013). Poverty impedes cognitive function. *Science, 341*(6149), 976–980. doi:10.1126/science.1238041.

Mannuzza, S., Klein, R. G., & Moulton, J. L. (2008). Lifetime criminality among boys with attention deficit hyperactivity disorder: A prospective follow-up study into adulthood using official arrest records. *Psychiatry Research, 160*(3), 237–246. doi:10.1016/j.psychres.2007.11.003.

Marcus, D. K., Fulton, J. J., & Clarke, E. J. (2010). Lead and conduct problems: A meta-analysis. *Journal of Clinical Child and Adolescent Psychology, 39*(2), 234–241. doi:10.1080/15374411003591455.

Marmorstein, N. R. (2007). Relationships between anxiety and externalizing disorders in youth: The influences of age and gender. *Journal of Anxiety Disorders, 21*(3), 420–432. doi:10.1016/j.janxdis.2006.06.004.

Márquez, C., Poirier, G. L., Cordero, M. I., Larsen, M. H., Groner, A., Marquis, J., ... Sandi, C. (2013). Peripuberty stress leads to abnormal aggression, altered amygdala and orbitofrontal reactivity and increased prefrontal MAOA gene expression. *Translational Psychiatry, 3*, e216. doi:10.1038/tp.2012.144.

Maughan, B., Pickles, A., Rowe, R., Costello, E. J., & Angold, A. (2000). Developmental trajectories of aggressive and non-aggressive conduct problems. *Journal of Quantitative Criminology, 16*(2), 199–221. doi:10.1023/A:1007516622688.

Maughan, B., Rowe, R., Messer, J., Goodman, R., & Meltzer, H. (2004). Conduct disorder and oppositional defiant disorder in a national sample: Developmental epidemiology. *Journal of Child Psychology and Psychiatry, and Allied Disciplines, 45*(3), 609–621.

McCabe, K. M., Rodgers, C., Yeh, M., & Hough, R. (2004). Gender differences in childhood onset conduct disorder. *Development and Psychopathology, 16*(1), 179–192.

McCrory, E. J., De Brito, S. A., Sebastian, C. L., Mechelli, A., Bird, G., Kelly, P. A., & Viding, E. (2011). Heightened neural reactivity to threat in child victims of family violence. *Current Biology, 21*(23), R947–R48.

McGuire, J. (1995). *What works: Reducing reoffending: guidelines from research and practice. The Wiley series in offender rehabilitation*. Chichester: John Wiley & Sons.

Meyer-Lindenberg, A., Buckholtz, J. W., Kolachana, B., R. Hariri, A., Pezawas, L., Blasi, G., … Weinberger, D. R. (2006). Neural mechanisms of genetic risk for impulsivity and violence in humans. *Proceedings of the National Academy of Sciences, 103*(16), 6269–6274. doi:10.1073/pnas.0511311103.

Miller, L. A., Collins, R. L., & Kent, T. A. (2008). Language and the modulation of impulsive aggression. *The Journal of Neuropsychiatry and Clinical Neurosciences, 20*(3), 261–273. doi:10.1176/jnp.2008.20.3.261.

Mörtberg, E., Clark, D. M., Sundin, O., & Aberg Wistedt, A. (2007). Intensive group cognitive treatment and individual cognitive therapy vs. treatment as usual in social phobia: A randomized controlled trial. *Acta Psychiatrica Scandinavica, 115*(2), 142–154. doi:10.1111/j.1600-0447.2006.00839.x.

Mobbs, D., Petrovic, P., Marchant, J. L., Hassabis, D., Weiskopf, N., Seymour, B., … Frith, C. D. (2007). When fear is near: Threat imminence elicits prefrontal-periaqueductal gray shifts in humans. *Science, 317*(5841), 1079–1083. doi:10.1126/science.1144298.

Moffitt, T. E., & Caspi, A. (2001). Childhood predictors differentiate life-course persistent and adolescence-limited antisocial pathways among males and females. *Development and Psychopathology, 13*(2), 355–375.

Moffitt, T. E., Caspi, A., Dickson, N., Silva, P., & Stanton, W. (1996). Childhood-onset versus adolescent-onset antisocial conduct problems in males: Natural history from ages 3 to 18 years. *Development and Psychopathology, 8*(02), 399–424. doi:10.1017/S0954579400007161.

Moffitt, T. E., Caspi, A., Rutter, M., & Silva, P. A. (2001). *Sex differences in antisocial behavior: Conduct disorder, delinquency, and violence in the Dunedin longitudinal study. Cambridge studies in criminology. Vol. 182*. Cambridge, UK/New York: Cambridge University Press.

Moffitt, T. E., Gabrielli, W. F., Mednick, S. A., & Schulsinger, F. (1981). Socioeconomic status, IQ, and delinquency. *Journal of Abnormal Psychology, 90*(2), 152–156. doi:10.1037/0021-843X.90.2.152.

Moore, L. D., Le, T., & Fan, G. (2013). DNA methylation and its basic function. *Neuropsychopharmacology, 38*(1), 23–38. doi:10.1038/npp.2012.112.

Moran, P. (1999). *Antisocial personality disorder: An epidemiological perspective*. London: Gaskell; Distributed by American Psychiatric Press, Inc.

Moran, P., & Hodgins, S. (2004). The correlates of comorbid antisocial personality disorder in schizophrenia. *Schizophrenia Bulletin, 30*(4), 791–802.

Morcillo, C., Duarte, C. S., Shen, S., Blanco, C., Canino, G., & Bird, H. R. (2011). Parental familism and antisocial behaviors: Development, gender, and potential mechanisms. *Journal of the American Academy of Child and Adolescent Psychiatry, 50*(5), 471–479. doi:10.1016/j.jaac.2011.01.014.

Mordre, M., Groholt, B., Kjelsberg, E., Sandstad, B., & Myhre, A. M. (2011). The impact of ADHD and conduct disorder in childhood on adult delinquency: A 30 years follow-up study using official crime records. *BMC Psychiatry, 11*, 57. doi:10.1186/1471-244X-11-57.

Motzkin, J. C., Newman, J. P., Kiehl, K. A., & Koenigs, M. (2011). Reduced prefrontal connectivity in psychopathy. *The Journal of Neuroscience, 31*(48), 17348–17357. doi:10.1523/JNEUROSCI.4215-11.2011.

Murray, J., & Farrington, D. P. (2010). Risk factors for conduct disorder and delinquency: Key findings from longitudinal studies. *Canadian Journal of Psychiatry. Revue Canadienne de Psychiatrie, 55*(10), 633–642.

Murray, J., Irving, B., Farrington, D. P., Colman, I., & Bloxsom, C. A. J. (2010). Very early predictors of conduct problems and crime: Results from a national cohort study. *Journal of Child Psychology and Psychiatry, and Allied Disciplines, 51*(11), 1198–1207. doi:10.1111/j.1469-7610.2010.02287.x.

Myers, M. G., Stewart, D. G., & Brown, S. A. (1998). Progression from conduct disorder to antisocial personality disorder following treatment for adolescent substance abuse. *The American Journal of Psychiatry, 155*(4), 479–485.

Nathan, R., Rollinson, L., Harvey, K., & Hill, J. (2003). The Liverpool violence assessment: An investigator-based measure of serious violence. *Criminal Behavior and Mental Health: CBMH, 13*(2), 106–120.

Neugebauer, R., Hoek, H. W., & Susser, E. (1999). Prenatal exposure to wartime famine and development of antisocial personality disorder in early adulthood. *JAMA, 282*(5), 455–462.

Niemelä, S., Sourander, A., Elonheimo, H., Poikolainen, K., Wu, P., Helenius, H., ... & Almqvist, F. (2008). What predicts illicit drug use versus police-registered drug offending? Findings from the Finnish "From a Boy to a Man" birth cohort study. *Social Psychiatry and Psychiatric Epidemiology, 43*(9), 697–704. doi:10.1007/s00127-008-0361-x.

Nieuwbeerta, P., & Piquero, A. R. (2008). Mortality rates and causes of death of convicted dutch criminals 25 years later. *Journal of Research in Crime and Delinquency, 45*, 256–286.

Nilsson, K. W., Comasco, E., Hodgins, S., Oreland, L., & Åslund, C. (2015). Genotypes do not confer risk for delinquency but rather alter susceptibility to positive and negative environmental factors: Gene-environment interactions of BDNF Val66Met, 5-HTTLPR, and MAOA-uVNTR [corrected]. *The International Journal of Neuropsychopharmacology, 18*(5), 1–10. doi:10.1093/ijnp/pyu107.

Nilsson, K. W., Sjoberg, R. L., Damberg, M., Leppert, J., Ohrvik, J., Alm, P. O., ... Oreland, L. (2006). Role of monoamine oxidase A genotype and psychosocial factors in male adolescent criminal activity. *Biological Psychiatry, 59*(2), 121–127. doi:10.1016/j.biopsych.2005.06.024.

Nock, M. K., Kazdin, A. E., Hiripi, E., & Kessler, R. C. (2006). Prevalence, subtypes, and correlates of DSM-IV conduct disorder in the National Comorbidity Survey Replication. *Psychological Medicine, 36*(5), 699–710. doi:10.1017/S0033291706007082.

Odgers, C. L., Caspi, A., Broadbent, J. M., Dickson, N., Hancox, R. J., Harrington, H., ... Moffitt, T. E. (2007). Prediction of differential adult health burden by conduct problem subtypes in males. *Archives of General Psychiatry, 64*(4), 476–484. doi:10.1001/archpsyc.64.4.476.

Odgers, C. L., Moffitt, T. E., Broadbent, J. M., Dickson, N., Hancox, R. J., Harrington, H., ... Caspi, A. (2008). Female and male antisocial trajectories: From childhood origins to adult outcomes. *Development and Psychopathology, 20*(2), 673–716. doi:10.1017/S0954579408000333.

Olds, D. L., Robinson, J., O'Brien, R., Luckey, D. W., Pettitt, L. M., Henderson, C. R., Jr., ... Talmi, A. (2002). Home visiting by paraprofessionals and by nurses: A randomized, controlled trial. *Pediatrics, 110*(3), 486–496.

Oreland, L., Nilsson, K., Damberg, M., & Hallman, J. (2007). Monoamine oxidases: Activities, genotypes and the shaping of behavior. *Journal of Neural Transmission, 114*(6), 817–822. doi:10.1007/s00702-007-0694-8.

Oscar-Berman, M., Valmas, M. M., Sawyer, K. S., Kirkley, S. M., Gansler, D. A., Merritt, D., & Couture, A. (2009). Frontal brain dysfunction in alcoholism with and without antisocial personality disorder. *Neuropsychiatric Disease and Treatment, 5*, 309–326.

Ouellet-Morin, I., Cote, S. M., Vitaro, F., Hebert, M., Carbonneau, R., Lacourse, E., ... Tremblay, R. E. (2016). Effects of the MAOA gene and levels of exposure to violence on antisocial outcomes. *The British Journal of Psychiatry, 208*(1), 42–48. doi:10.1192/bjp.bp.114.162081.

Panksepp, J. (1998). *Affective neuroscience: The foundations of human and animal emotions. Series in affective science.* New York, NY: Oxford University Press.

Paris, J., Chenard-Poirier, M.-P., & Biskin, R. (2013). Antisocial and borderline personality disorders revisited. *Comprehensive Psychiatry, 54*(4), 321–325. doi:10.1016/j.comppsych.2012.10.006.

Passamonti, L., Fairchild, G., Goodyer, I. M., Hurford, G., Hagan, C. C., Rowe, J. B., & Calder, A. J. (2010). Neural abnormalities in early-onset and adolescence-onset conduct disorder. *Archives of General Psychiatry, 67*(7), 729–738. doi:10.1001/archgenpsychiatry.2010.75.

Perrin, J. S., Leonard, G., Perron, M., Pike, G. B., Pitiot, A., Richer, L., ... Paus, T. (2009). Sex differences in the growth of white matter during adolescence. *NeuroImage, 45*(4), 1055–1066. doi:10.1016/j.neuroimage.2009.01.023.

Petitclerc, A., & Tremblay, R. E. (2009). Childhood disruptive behavior disorders: Review of their origin, development, and prevention. *Canadian Journal of Psychiatry, 54*(4), 222–231.

Petras, H., Kellam, S. G., Brown, C. H., Muthén, B. O., Ialongo, N. S., & Poduska, J. M. (2008). Developmental epidemiological courses leading to antisocial personality disorder and violent and criminal behavior: Effects by young adulthood of a universal preventive intervention in first-and second-grade classrooms. *Drug and Alcohol Dependence, 95 Supplement 1*, S45–59.

Philibert, R. A., Wernett, P., Plume, J., Packer, H., Brody, G. H., & Beach, Steven R H. (2011). Gene environment interactions with a novel variable monoamine oxidase A transcriptional enhancer are associated with antisocial personality disorder. *Biological Psychology, 87*(3), 366–371. doi:10.1016/j.biopsycho.2011.04.007.

Polier, G. G., Vloet, T. D., Herpertz-Dahlmann, B., Laurens, K. R., & Hodgins, S. (2012). Comorbidity of conduct disorder symptoms and internalising problems in children: Investigating a community and a clinical sample. *European Child & Adolescent Psychiatry, 21*(1), 31–38. doi:10.1007/s00787-011-0229-6.

Quirk, G. J., & Beer, J. S. (2006). Prefrontal involvement in the regulation of emotion: Convergence of rat and human studies. *Current Opinion in Neurobiology, 16*(6), 723–727. doi:10.1016/j.conb.2006.07.004.

Raine, A., Lencz, T., Taylor, K., Hellige, J. B., Bihrle, S., Lacasse, L., ... Colletti, P. (2003). Corpus callosum abnormalities in psychopathic antisocial individuals. *Archives of General Psychiatry, 60*(11), 1134–1142. doi:10.1001/archpsyc.60.11.1134.

Raine, A., Yang, Y., Narr, K. L., & Toga, A. W. (2011). Sex differences in orbitofrontal grey as a partial explanation for sex differences in antisocial personality. *Molecular Psychiatry, 16*(2), 227–236. doi:10.1038/mp.2009.136.

Reif, A., Rosler, M., Freitag, C. M., Schneider, M., Eujen, A., Kissling, C., ... Retz, W. (2007). Nature and nurture predispose to violent behavior: Serotonergic genes and adverse childhood environment. *Neuropsychopharmacology, 32*(11), 2375–2383. doi:10.1038/sj.npp.1301359.

Rhee, S. H., & Waldman, I. D. (2002). Genetic and environmental influences on antisocial behavior: A meta-analysis of twin and adoption studies. *Psychological Bulletin, 128*(3), 490–529.

Rice, M. E., & Harris, G. T. (1995). Psychopathy, schizophrenia, alcohol abuse, and violent recidivism. *International Journal of Law and Psychiatry, 18*(3), 333–342.

Robins, L. (1978). Aetiological implications in studies of childhood histories relating to Antisocial Personality. In R. D. Hare & D. Schalling (Eds.), *Psychopathic Behavior. Approaches to Research* (pp. 255–272). Chichester/New York, NY: John Wiley & Sons.

Robins, L. N. (1966). *Deviant children grown up: A sociological and psychiatric study of sociopathic personality*. Baltimore: William & Wilkins Company.

Robins, L. N., & McEvoy, L. (1990). Conduct problems as predictors of substance abuse. In L. N. Robins & M. Rutter (Eds.), *Straight and devious pathways from childhood to adulthood* (pp. 182–204). Cambridge/New York: Cambridge University Press.

Robins, L. N., Tipp, J., & Przybeck, T. (1991). Antisocial Personality. In L. N. Robins & D. A. Regier (Eds.), *Psychiatric Disorders in America. The Epidemiologic Catchment Area Study* (pp. 258–290). New York, NY/Toronto: Free Press; Collier Macmillan Canada; Maxwell Macmillan International.

Rogers, J. C., & De Brito, S. A. (2016). Cortical and subcortical gray matter volume in youths with conduct problems: A meta-analysis. *JAMA Psychiatry, 73*(1), 64–72. doi:10.1001/jamapsychiatry.2015.2423.

Rowe, R., Maughan, B., Moran, P., Ford, T., Briskman, J., & Goodman, R. (2010). The role of callous and unemotional traits in the diagnosis of conduct disorder. *Journal of Child Psychology and Psychiatry, and Allied Disciplines, 51*(6), 688–95. doi:10.1111/j.14697610.2009.02199.x.

Rubia, K. (2011). "Cool" inferior frontostriatal dysfunction in attention-deficit/hyperactivity disorder versus "hot" ventromedial orbitofrontal-limbic dysfunction in conduct disorder: A review. *Biological Psychiatry, 69*(12), e69-87. doi:10.1016/j.biopsych.2010.09.023.

Rudebeck, P. H., Saunders, R. C., Prescott, A. T., Chau, L. S., & Murray, E. A. (2013). Prefrontal mechanisms of behavioral flexibility, emotion regulation and value updating. *Nature Neuroscience, 16*(8), 1140–1145. doi:10.1038/nn.3440.

Russo, M. F., & Beidel, D. C. (1994). Comorbidity of childhood anxiety and externalizing disorders: Prevalence, associated characteristics, and validation issues. *Clinical Psychology Review, 14*(3), 199–221. doi:10.1016/0272-7358(94)90008-6.

Samuels, J., Bienvenu, O. J., Cullen, B., Costa, P. T., Eaton, W. W., & Nestadt, G. (2004). Personality dimensions and criminal arrest. *Comprehensive Psychiatry, 45*(4), 275–280. doi:10.1016/j.comppsych.2004.03.013.

Samuels, J., Eaton, W. W., Bienvenu, O. J., III, Brown, C. H., Costa, P. T., Jr., & Nestadt, G. (2002). Prevalence and correlates of personality disorders in a community sample. *British Journal of Psychiatry, 180*(6), 536–542.

Sareen, J., Stein, M. B., Cox, B. J., & Hassard, S. T. (2004). Understanding comorbidity of anxiety disorders with antisocial behavior: Findings from two large community surveys. *The Journal of Nervous and Mental Disease, 192*(3), 178–186.

Sauer, C., Montag, C., Reuter, M., & Kirsch, P. (2013). Imaging oxytocin × dopamine interactions: An epistasis effect of CD38 and COMT gene variants influences the impact of oxytocin on amygdala activation to social stimuli. *Frontiers in Neuroscience, 7*, 45. doi:10.3389/fnins.2013.00045.

Schiffer, B., Leygraf, N., Müller, B. W., Scherbaum, N., Forsting, M., Wiltfang, J., ... Hodgins, S. (2013). Structural brain alterations associated with schizophrenia preceded by conduct disorder: A common and distinct subtype of schizophrenia? *Schizophrenia Bulletin, 39*(5), 1115–1128. doi:10.1093/schbul/sbs115.

Schiffer, B., Müller, B. W., Scherbaum, N., Hodgins, S., Forsting, M., Wiltfang, J., … Leygraf, N. (2011). Disentangling structural brain alterations associated with violent behavior from those associated with substance use disorders. *Archives of General Psychiatry, 68*(10), 1039–1049. doi:10.1001/archgenpsychiatry.2011.61.

Schneider, M. (2008). Puberty as a highly vulnerable developmental period for the consequences of cannabis exposure. *Addiction Biology, 13*(2), 253–263. doi:10.1111/j.1369-1600.2008.00110.x.

Schutter, D. J. L. G., & Harmon-Jones, E. (2013). The corpus callosum: A commissural road to anger and aggression. *Neuroscience and Biobehavioral Reviews, 37*(10 Pt 2), 2481–2488. doi:10.1016/j.neubiorev.2013.07.013.

Scott, S. (2012). Parenting quality and children's mental health: Biological mechanisms and psychological interventions. *Current Opinion in Psychiatry, 25*(4), 301–306.

Scott, S., Briskman, J., & O'Connor, T. G. (2014). Early prevention of antisocial personality: Long-term follow-up of two randomized controlled trials comparing indicated and selective approaches. *The American Journal of Psychiatry, 171*(6), 649–657. doi:10.1176/appi.ajp.2014.13050697.

Séguin, J. R., Pihl, R. O., Harden, P. W., Tremblay, R. E., & Boulerice, B. (1995). Cognitive and neuropsychological characteristics of physically aggressive boys. *Journal of Abnormal Psychology, 104*(4), 614–624.

Séguin, J. R., Sylvers, P., & Lilienfeld, S. (2007). The neuropsychology of violence. In D. J. Flannery, A. T. Vazsonyi, & I. D. Waldman (Eds.), *The Cambridge handbook of violent behavior and aggression* (pp. 187–214). New York, NY: Cambridge University Press.

Sebastian, C. L., McCrory, E. J. P., Cecil, C. A. M., Lockwood, P. L., De Brito, S. A., Fontaine, N. M. G., & Viding, E. (2012). Neural responses to affective and cognitive theory of mind in children with conduct problems and varying levels of callous-unemotional traits. *Archives of General Psychiatry, 69*(8), 814–822. doi:10.1001/archgenpsychiatry.2011.2070.

Sebastian, C. L., McCrory, E. J., Dadds, M. R., Cecil, C. A. M., Lockwood, P. L., Hyde, Z. H., De Brito, S. A., and Viding, E. (2014). Neural responses to fearful eyes in children with conduct problems and varying levels of callous–unemotional traits. *Psychological Medicine, 44*(1), 99–109. doi:10.1017/S0033291713000482.

Shepherd, J., Farrington, D., & Potts, J. (2004). Impact of antisocial lifestyle on health. *Journal of Public Health (Oxford, England), 26*(4), 347–352. doi:10.1093/pubmed/fdh169.

Siegel, A., & Douard, J. (2011). Who's flying the plane: serotonin levels, aggression and free will. *International Journal of Law and Psychiatry, 34*(1), 20–29. doi:10.1016/j.ijlp.2010.11.004.

Siegel, A., & Victoroff, J. (2009). Understanding human aggression: New insights from neuroscience. *International Journal of Law and Psychiatry, 32*(4), 209–215. doi:10.1016/j.ijlp.2009.06.001.

Silberg, J., Moore, A. A., & Rutter, M. (2015). Age of onset and the subclassification of conduct/dissocial disorder. *Journal of Child Psychology and Psychiatry, and Allied Disciplines, 56*(7), 826–833. doi:10.1111/jcpp.12353.

Silva, T. C., Larm, P., Vitaro, F., Tremblay, R. E., & Hodgins, S. (2012). The association between maltreatment in childhood and criminal convictions to age 24: A prospective study of a community sample of males from disadvantaged neighbourhoods. *European Child & Adolescent Psychiatry, 21*(7), 403–413. doi:10.1007/s00787-012-0281-x.

Stadler, C., Poustka, F., & Sterzer, P. (2010). The heterogeneity of disruptive behavior disorders – implications for neurobiological research and treatment. *Frontiers in Psychiatry, 1*, 21.

Stepp, S. D., Burke, J. D., Hipwell, A. E., & Loeber, R. (2012). Trajectories of attention deficit hyperactivity disorder and oppositional defiant disorder symptoms as precursors of borderline personality disorder symptoms in adolescent girls. *Journal of Abnormal Child Psychology, 40*(1), 7–20. doi:10.1007/s10802-011-9530-6.

Stevens, M. C., & Haney-Caron, E. (2012). Comparison of brain volume abnormalities between ADHD and conduct disorder in adolescence. *Journal of Psychiatry & Neuroscience: JPN, 37*(6), 389–398. doi:10.1503/jpn.110148.

Stevens, M. C., Kaplan, R. F., & Hesselbrock, V. M. (2003). Executive-cognitive functioning in the development of antisocial personality disorder. *Addictive Behaviors, 28*(2), 285–300.

Stouthamer-Loeber, M., Loeber, R., Homish, D. L., & Wei, E. (2001). Maltreatment of boys and the development of disruptive and delinquent behavior. *Development and Psychopathology, 13*(4), 941–955.

Sun, H., Yuan, F., Shen, X., Xiong, G., & Wu, J. (2013). Role of COMT in ADHD: A systematic meta-analysis. *Molecular Neurobiology, 49*(1), 251–61. doi:10.1007/s12035-013-8516-5.

Sundram, F., Deeley, Q., Sarkar, S., Daly, E., Latham, R., Craig, M., ... Murphy, Declan G M. (2012). White matter microstructural abnormalities in the frontal lobe of adults with antisocial personality disorder. *Cortex, 48*(2), 216–229. doi:10.1016/j.cortex.2011.06.005.

Swanson, J. W., Swartz, M. S., Van Dorn, Richard A, Elbogen, E. B., Wagner, H. R., Rosenheck, R. A., ... Lieberman, J. A. (2006). A national study of violent behavior in persons with schizophrenia. *Archives of General Psychiatry, 63*(5), 490–499. doi:10.1001/archpsyc.63.5.490.

Swanson, M. C., Bland, R. C., & Newman, S. C. (1994). Epidemiology of psychiatric disorders in Edmonton. Antisocial personality disorders. *Acta Psychiatrica Scandinavica. Supplementum, 376*, 63–70.

Tengström, A., Hodgins, S., Grann, M., Långström, N., & Kullgren, G. (2004). Schizophrenia and criminal offending: The role of psychopathy and substance use disorders. *Criminal Justice and Behavior, 31*(4), 367–391. doi:10.1177/0093854804265173.

Torgersen, S., Kringlen, E., & Cramer, V. (2001). The prevalence of personality disorders in a community sample. *Archives of General Psychiatry, 58*(6), 590–596.

Van Ijzendoorn, M. H., Belsky, J., & Bakermans-Kranenburg, M. J. (2012). Serotonin transporter genotype 5HTTLPR as a marker of differential susceptibility? A meta-analysis of child and adolescent gene-by-environment studies. *Translational Psychiatry, 2*, e147. doi:10.1038/tp.2012.73.

Vaughn, M. G., Fu, Q., DeLisi, M., Beaver, K. M., Perron, B. E., & Howard, M. O. (2010). Criminal victimization and comorbid substance use and psychiatric disorders in the United States: Results from the NESARC. *Annals of Epidemiology, 20*(4), 281–288. doi:10.1016/j.annepidem.2009.11.011.

Viding, E., Fontaine, N. M. G., & McCrory, E. J. (2012). Antisocial behavior in children with and without callous-unemotional traits. *Journal of the Royal Society of Medicine, 105*(5), 195–200. doi:10.1258/jrsm.2011.110223.

Viding, E., Jones, A. P., Frick, P. J., Moffitt, T. E., & Plomin, R. (2008). Heritability of antisocial behavior at 9: Do callous-unemotional traits matter? *Developmental Science, 11*(1), 17–22. doi:10.1111/j.1467-7687.2007.00648.x.

Viding, E., Sebastian, C. L., Dadds, M. R., Lockwood, P. L., Cecil, Charlotte, A. M., De Brito, S. A., & McCrory, E. J. (2012). Amygdala response to preattentive masked fear in children with conduct problems: The role of callous-unemotional traits. *The American Journal of Psychiatry, 169*(10), 1109–1116. doi:10.1176/appi.ajp.2012.12020191.

Virkkunen, M., Goldman, D., Nielsen, D. A., & Linnoila, M. (1995). Low brain serotonin turnover rate (low CSF 5-HIAA) and impulsive violence. *Journal of Psychiatry & Neuroscience: JPN, 20*(4), 271–275.

Vitaro, F., Barker, E. D., Boivin, M., Brendgen, M., & Tremblay, R. E. (2006). Do early difficult temperament and harsh parenting differentially predict reactive and proactive aggression? *Journal of Abnormal Child Psychology, 34*(5), 685–695. doi:10.1007/s10802006-9055-6.

Vitaro, F., Brendgen, M., & Barker, E. D. (2006). Subtypes of aggressive behaviors: A developmental perspective. *International Journal of Behavioral Development, 30*(1), 12–19. doi:10.1177/0165025406059968.

Von Der Heide, R. J., Skipper, L. M., Klobusicky, E., & Olson, I. R. (2013). Dissecting the uncinate fasciculus: Disorders, controversies and a hypothesis. *Brain: A Journal of Neurology, 136*(Pt 6), 1692–1707. doi:10.1093/brain/awt094.

Walker, E. F., Savoie, T., & Davis, D. (1994). Neuromotor precursors of schizophrenia. *Schizophrenia Bulletin, 20*(3), 441–451. doi:10.1093/schbul/20.3.441.

Waschbusch, D. A. (2002). A meta-analytic examination of comorbid hyperactive-impulsive attention problems and conduct problems. *Psychological Bulletin, 128*(1), 118–150.

Washburn, J. J., Romero, E. G., Welty, L. J., Abram, K. M., Teplin, L. A., McClelland, G. M., & Paskar, L. D. (2007). Development of antisocial personality disorder in detained youths: The predictive value of mental disorders. *Journal of Consulting and Clinical Psychology, 75*(2), 221–231. doi:10.1037/0022-006X.75.2.221.

Weinberger, D. R. (1987). Implications of normal brain development for the pathogenesis of schizophrenia. *Archives of General Psychiatry, 44*(7), 660–669. doi: 10.1001/archpsyc.1987.01800190080012.

Whittle, S., Yücel, M., Yap, M. B. H., & Allen, N. B. (2011). Sex differences in the neural correlates of emotion: Evidence from neuroimaging. *Biological Psychology, 87*(3), 319–333. doi:10.1016/j.biopsycho.2011.05.003.

Widom, C. (1989). The cycle of violence. *Science, 244*(4901), 160–166. doi:10.1126/science.2704995.

Winsper, C., Singh, S. P., Marwaha, S., Amos, T., Lester, H., Everard, L., … Birchwood, M. (2013). Pathways to violent behavior during first-episode psychosis: A report from the UK National EDEN Study. *JAMA Psychiatry, 70*(12), 1287–1293. doi: 10.1001/jamapsychiatry.2013.2445.

Wolf, R. C., Pujara, M. S., Motzkin, J. C., Newman, J. P., Kiehl, K. A., Decety, J., … Koenigs, M. (2015). Interpersonal traits of psychopathy linked to reduced integrity of the uncinate fasciculus. *Human Brain Mapping, 36*(10), 4202–4209. doi:10.1002/hbm.22911.

Wolff, J. C., & Ollendick, T. H. (2006). The comorbidity of conduct problems and depression in childhood and adolescence. *Clinical Child and Family Psychology Review, 9*(3-4), 201–220. doi:10.1007/s10567-006-0011-3.

World Health Organization (WHO). (1992). *The ICD-10 classification of mental and behavioral disorders: Clinical descriptions and diagnostic guidelines.* Geneva: WHO.

Wright, J. P., Dietrich, K. N., Ris, M. D., Hornung, R. W., Wessel, S. D., Lanphear, B. P., … Rae, M. N. (2008). Association of prenatal and childhood blood lead concentrations with criminal arrests in early adulthood. *PLoS Medicine, 5*(5), e101. doi:10.1371/journal.pmed.0050101.

Xu, Y., Farver, J. A. M., & Zhang, Z. (2009). Temperament, harsh and indulgent parenting, and Chinese children's proactive and reactive aggression. *Child Development, 80*(1), 244–258. doi:10.1111/j.1467-8624.2008.01257.x.

Yang, Y., & Raine, A. (2009). Prefrontal structural and functional brain imaging findings in antisocial, violent, and psychopathic individuals: A meta-analysis. *Psychiatry Research, 174*(2), 81–88. doi:10.1016/j.pscychresns.2009.03.012.

Zhang, J., Gao, J., Shi, H., Huang, B., Wang, X., Situ, W., … Yao, S. (2014). Sex differences of uncinate fasciculus structural connectivity in individuals with conduct disorder. *BioMed Research International, 673165.* doi:10.1155/2014/673165.

11
Offenders with Autism Spectrum Disorder

Björn Hofvander

> **Key points**
> - In the chapter it is noted that autism spectrum disorder (ASD) is a heterogeneous disorder where several neural networks are involved in producing the behavioral symptoms.
> - Comorbidity in other neurodevelopmental and psychiatric disorders is a hallmark of ASD.
> - The prevalence of ASD has risen dramatically over the last decades, parallel to a wider acceptance of concomitant psychiatric and other problems in affected individuals.
> - ASD and autistic-like traits are overrepresented in antisocial, particularly violent, groups but this association has not been shown in population based studies.
> - There are several consistent neurostructural and neurofunctional correlations to the core deficits in ASD.
> - Few studies have investigated the neurobiological background to offending in ASDs.
> - The existence of an association between criminality and ASD is still debated and several central questions are unanswered pertaining to the risk of offending among the affecting individuals.

Terminology Explained

Autism spectrum disorder (ASD) is a neurodevelopmental disorder, where the individual experiences problems with how they interact socially, has difficulty with communication, and displays repetitive and fixed behavior and interests. These problems can lead to impairment that ranges from minimal to severe.

The Wiley Blackwell Handbook of Forensic Neuroscience, First Edition. Edited by Anthony R. Beech, Adam J. Carter, Ruth E. Mann and Pia Rotshtein.
© 2018 John Wiley & Sons Ltd. Published 2018 by John Wiley & Sons Ltd.

> The **corpus callosum** is a large bundle of nerve fibers that connects the left and right sides of the brain and allows these to communicate with each other.
>
> The ***Diagnostic and Statistical Manual for Mental Disorders (DSM)*** is a set of principles, established as the predominant method to classify mental illness in the US. In 2013, *DSM-5* was published, which represented the first major revision to the classification of mental disorders in almost two decades.
>
> The **M'Naghten rules** are a set of criteria applied to determine whether someone is criminally responsible for the crime they have been accused of after taking into account mental illness.
>
> **Theory of mind**, also known as mentalization, refers to the ability, which develops around the age of four, to understand that others have beliefs, desires, intentions, and perspectives that are different from one's own. This involves a recognition that others have a mind that is separate to the individual observer, and may or not know things that the observer does or does not.
>
> A **tic** is an abrupt, repetitive, sound or movement that is hard to control and involves the involuntary contraction of certain muscle groups. While unlikely to be physically harmful, tics can interfere with social functioning.

Introduction

Over the last decades there has been a surge in lifespan approaches to the study of psychopathology and criminal behavior (e.g., Farrington, 2003; Moffitt, 1993; Tremblay et al., 2005). A large number of studies have found associations between neurodevelopmental disorders and risk of antisocial behavior. Most notably, several prospective, longitudinal studies have shown that aberrations in the development of self-control may constitute a risk for later antisocial behavior, though the role of concomitant conduct problems is disputed (e.g., Hofvander, Ossowski, Lundström, & Anckarsäter, 2009a; Mannuzza, Klein, & Moulton, 2008). A number of individual characteristics, including emotion regulation and processing, tics and learning disabilities, have also been associated with disruptiveness and criminal propensity.

Criminal acts in individuals with autism spectrum disorder (ASD) have been a sensitive area to discuss. Researchers have expressed worries that reports of serious crimes committed by persons with ASD may lead to unnecessary anxiety on the part of parents and to stigmatization of people with ASD (Howlin, 2004). In the group with concurrent intellectual disabilities there has been a much more open discussion on the existence of problematic behavior patterns, including violent behaviors, often called challenging behaviors. Researchers, clinicians, policy makers, and support organizations work together to understand and find effective means of working with these problems. For this reason, this chapter will focus on the literature on individuals with so called high-functioning ASD (i.e., without general intellectual disabilities). Here the discussion is much less mature and support and services for those affected is far less developed.

Research on ASD has exploded in the last 20 years and it is now thought of as a set of neurodevelopmental conditions, some of which can be attributed to distinct etiological factors, such as single-gene mutations, but most are probably the result of complex interactions between genetic and non-genetic risk factors (Lai, Lombardo, & Baron-Cohen, 2014). Neuroscience has tried to illuminate some of the underlying mechanisms in ASD, applying a wide range of paradigms. Many studies have worked within the emerging field of the so called social brain (Dunbar, 1993), but clinical studies have shown that deficits in these brain areas are not exclusive to ASD but are characterizing a number of disorders including schizophrenia (Frith, 1992), certain subtypes of dementia (Gregory et al., 2002), and traumatic injuries to the frontal lobe (Muller et al., 2010). Today, thanks to several prospective, longitudinal studies that have followed children with ASD until adulthood, we also know much more about how people with ASD develop and cope over the lifespan (Magiati, Tay, & Howlin, 2014). However, very few studies combine the perspectives of ASD, criminal behavior, and neuroscience. This chapter aims to give an overview of the clinical and neurobiological characteristics of ASD (see Box 11.1) as well as the literature on the association between ASD and offending.

Box 11.1   ASD and other neurodevelopmental disorders

Important progress has been made in our understanding of developmental psychopathology and especially the outcome of so called childhood onset disorders. Well-designed studies, continuously collecting data from childhood to adulthood have made lifespan perspectives accessible for clinical psychologists and psychiatrists. The results of these studies show that childhood psychopathology, formerly believed to wane or to be something people "grow out of" in many, if not most, cases, persists into adulthood, though often not in the same shape as when it was first recognized.

The term *neurodevelopmental disorder* was formally introduced in the psychiatric classification system with the fifth edition of the *Diagnostic and Statistical Manual of Mental Disorders (DSM-5)* (American Psychiatric Association (APA), 2013) including: ASD, intellectual disability (intellectual development disorder), communication disorders, attention-deficit/hyperactivity disorder (ADHD), specific learning disorder, motor disorders, and other neurodevelopmental disorders. Rutter, Kim-Cohen, and Maughan (2006) suggested defining criteria for these disorders. First, they stated, neurodevelopmental disorders are characterized by aberrations in psychological abilities influenced by maturation. Second, the course of the disorder is not, unlike most other multifactorial psychiatric disorders, marked by remissions and relapses. Third, the impairment associated with the disorder persists into adulthood but is often lessened with age. Fourth, these disorders involve some, specific or general, cognitive impairment. Fifth, neurodevelopmental disorders coincide with each other. Sixth, the genetic influence on individual differences is generally strong in these disorders (Pettersson, Anckarsäter, Gillberg, & Lichtenstein, 2013). The sex ratio is most often highly skewed with males being significantly more affected, though affected females have been given a much more attention recently.

Autism Spectrum Disorder

ASD is an impairing neurodevelopmental disorder that, for a long time, was considered to be extremely rare – thought to affect around 5 in 10,000 individuals. However, the prevalence has been steadily rising since the first epidemiological studies. Though an increase in risk factors cannot be ruled out, for example, higher average parental age and higher survival rates for premature children, the major part of the rise is more probably due to other factors. The diagnostic concepts and criteria for ASD and related disorders changed a lot between the *DSM-III* (APA, 1980) and the *DSM-IV* (APA, 1994). However, the prevalence has continued to rise in the past two decades, despite consistent use of *DSM-IV* criteria, particularly in individuals without intellectual disability. Some argue that this is the result of an increased awareness and new assessment methods, which have enabled the recognition of ASD in younger children and also in older adults. A related explanation that has been put forward is a process called diagnostic substitution, which refers to the mechanisms by which one label for a condition is replaced by another; that is, children labeled with ASD in recent years would previously have been classified with a different label or patients initially being labeled with one diagnosis are reclassified with ASD at a later age. There is also a wider acceptance of, and research support for, the concomitant presence of other psychiatric and neurodevelopmental disorders in ASD.

Autism spectrum disorder *Autism is a complex neurobiological disorder of development that lasts throughout a person's life. It is sometimes called a developmental disability because it usually starts before age three, in the developmental period, and because it causes delays or problems in many different skills that arise from infancy to adulthood.*
Source: © PublicDomainPictures. Used under license from 699pic.

Today, the median worldwide prevalence of ASD is estimated to be 0.62–0.70%, although figures of 1–2% have been reported in the latest large-scale surveys (Lai et al., 2013). Approximately 45% of individuals diagnosed with ASD today also have an intellectual disability. Recent studies have shown that ASD can be reliably diagnosed around the child's second birthday, but in most cases it takes much longer for an individual to receive the diagnosis, sometimes into adulthood. In non-classical cases, symptoms may not be evident during the earliest years. Symptom severity and family concern are two important factors behind early detection. Comorbidity in psychiatric disorders may also delay detection and a recent review has shown that low socioeconomic status, for example, low family income and parental level of education, is an important factor in late age detection (Daniels & Mandell, 2014).

Clinical features and development of ASD

Though first described more than 70 years ago by the child psychiatrist Leo Kanner, our understanding of ASD has evolved substantially. A modern outline of ASD is marked by Wing and Gould's (1979) description of a group of disorders of development with impairments in the areas of social interaction, communication, and imagination associated with a narrow, repetitive pattern of activities, later called the triad of autistic symptoms. In *DSM-III* (1980), autism was for the first time given objective criteria and distinguished from childhood schizophrenia. With the introduction of the *DSM-IV* (1994), autism was organized into the broader category of pervasive developmental disorders (PDD) and several subtypes were defined. In *DSM-5*, the umbrella term ASD replaced PDD and subtypes are no longer defined. The triad has been reorganized into a dyad that incorporates difficulties in social communication and social interaction; and restricted and repetitive behavior, interests, or activities. In the latter criterion, sensory aberrations, such as hyper- or hyporeactivity to sensory input, have been incorporated. Atypical language development, which has historically been linked to an autism diagnosis, has been removed from the criteria, and is now classified as a co-occurring condition, even though large variation in language is characteristic of ASD.

As mentioned above, ASD is a clinically heterogeneous disorder. Its expression also varies across the lifespan. In very young children referred to clinics, abnormal responses to sensory stimuli tend to be a characteristic symptom. Lack of interest in social interactions, passiveness, motor deficits, and abnormalities in play are also very common reasons for referral. In individuals with normal levels of intellectual functioning it is often very difficult to find any clear abnormal behaviors before their second year. In the preschool years, some children present with classical signs, meeting criteria in all areas, but others will only show subtle indications of abnormality and may not be regarded as deviant at all during his or her first years. When demands on social communication and compliance increase, the child may, however, not be able to cope anymore and signs become more evident.

Behavior problems are very common in ASD and for some families the ASD child becomes difficult to manage already in his or her preschool years. These children might be hyperactive, extremely rigid, sensitive to changes and transitions, and destructive with frequent temper tantrums. During later preschool years, ASD children often show severe problems in interacting reciprocally with other children. Some are withdrawn from their peers, not seldom with an apparently reduced social need, others convey a wish to interact but don't seem to be able to figure out how to do it. High-functioning children with ASD most often develop useful spoken language during the preschool years but show peculiarities, mirroring difficulties in understanding other people's thoughts and feelings, which is evident in their communication. For those who receive an early diagnosis and adequate support, which is the group we know most about from longitudinal studies, it seems that the early school years is a period where the behavioral problems, temper tantrums, and hyperactivity diminishes. In contrast, puberty and adolescence seem to be a critical phase for many with ASD. This is a period where many are referred to CAP services for functional deterioration, aggravation of symptoms, and comorbid psychiatric conditions. Some studies report that about half of all subjects with ASD present with a severe worsening of symptoms around puberty. Aggressiveness, self-destructiveness, restlessness, depression, and anxiety are common problems. Bodily maturation and growth of sexual drive is not automatically accompanied by an increase in social competence and this can lead to problems, both in terms of inappropriate behavior and risk for exploitation of the individual with ASD.

Follow-up studies of children suggest that ASD is a fairly stable diagnosis. There is a small minority of individuals, who seem to "grow out" of the diagnostic criteria and only show milder autistic traits as adults but they are usually still impaired in their functioning. It seems as though the single best predictor of outcome is IQ and the high-functioning group seem to fare of much better in general. However, for those who are diagnosed later in life, often because of atypical symptoms, severe comorbidity and/or serious psychosocial problems, we know very little in terms of outcome.

Comorbidity

As mentioned above a core feature of neurodevelopmental disorders is that they coincide with each other. The diagnostic boundaries between them are not clear-cut, there is considerable comorbidity and the conditions share several neurocognitive deficits. For example, ADHD and ASD are both characterized by impairments in planning, organizing, and flexibility.

Another characteristic of neurodevelopmental disorders is that they are associated with a high degree of psychiatric morbidity. Reports from clinical samples convey a rather dark picture with very high levels of mental health care problems (e.g., Hofvander et al., 2009b). In ASD, perhaps even more than in normally developing persons, co-occurring psychiatric problems have a severe impact on the affected person and his or her family. The care and rehabilitation is complex since the detection of psychiatric and psychological problems in ASD is aggravated by these patients' impairments in describing their own experiences and emotions. Symptoms may have an atypical presentation and some disorders, such as social anxiety and obsessive-compulsive disorder, also have diagnostic criteria that to a great extent overlap with ASD. Though most clinical disorders seem to be overrepresented in ASD, in particular depression and anxiety disorders are important to mention. Some studies report the lifetime prevalence of depression and anxiety in ASD to be as high as 50%. The rate of psychopathology in ASD seems to increase with age and it carries a higher risk of academic failure, poorer social adjustment, and occupational disadvantages. There is a higher risk of comorbidity over the life course in the presence of childhood psychosocial disadvantages and adversities.

Etiology

Family and twin studies show that ASD has a strong genetic basis. At least 5–10% of siblings of children with ASD have an ASD diagnosis themselves and monozygotic twins are more likely to be concordant for ASD compared with dizygotic twins. In addition, siblings and parents of children with ASD are more likely than controls to show behavioral traits similar to those seen in people with ASD. Study results vary but suggest that 40–90% of the risk of ASD can be explained by genetic factors. Despite this, a specific genetic etiology can be determined in only approximately 15% of individuals with ASD.

As in most neurodevelopmental and psychiatric disorders, the heterogeneity in the genetic underpinnings of ASD is considerable and at least several hundreds of genes and genomic regions are estimated to contribute to the expression of ASD. We also know that genes defy our psychiatric classifications and overlapping genes have been identified in, for example, ASD, ADHD, epilepsy, intellectual disabilities and schizophrenia. Genetic defects in ASD are also often acquired *de novo*, that is, they are not necessarily inherited but may be triggered by environmental exposures. In addition, there is increasing recognition that environmental factors, via mechanisms other than *de novo* mutations, may play an important role in the etiology of ASD. These may include lead poisoning, other neurotoxin exposure, or alcohol use during pregnancy. Thus, the etiology most probably involves complex interactions between genetic and environmental factors. These may act synergistically or in parallel during critical periods of neurodevelopment in a manner that increases the likelihood of developing ASD.

Models/Theories of ASD

Models or theories from the fields of cognitive and social psychology, as well as neuropsychology, have, by their designation of so called core deficits, been very influential in the attempts to explain the seemingly disparate clinical manifestations of ASD. Different models have been proposed, and we will briefly summarize the most important ones, and concepts related to them.

The deficient mentalizing model

In their first characterizations of ASD, Kanner (1943) and Asperger (1944) introduced notions of "extreme egocentrism" among those affected. In the mid-1980s, these features were related to a profound impairment in the understanding of others' minds (Baron-Cohen, Leslie, & Frith, 1985). The ability to adopt another individual's point of view, to represent and attribute the other's thoughts, intentions, beliefs, and knowledge, is crucial to our ability to interpret and understand others and is sometimes referred to as having a theory of mind (ToM). Just as crucial to our socio-communicative abilities is the understanding of our own mental states and our ability to integrate self-representations with our general "world-knowledge." These processes have also been shown to be impaired in ASD and together they are sometimes referred to as our mentalizing abilities. Over the last 30 years many studies have confirmed that development of mentalizing is atypical in ASD and although many individuals with ASD achieve some degree of explicit or controlled mentalizing, the implicit, automatic, and intuitive components are still impaired, even in adulthood.

The concept of empathy is closely linked to mentalizing. Within empathy research, two different types are usually separated. *Cognitive* empathy refers to the ability to accurately identify what others are thinking or feeling (Frith & Singer, 2008) (i.e., a definition more or less synonymous with mentalizing). *Affective*, or emotional empathy, on the other hand, is defined as the capacity to share a "fellow feeling" and involves several related underlying processes, including, emotional contagion, emotion recognition, and shared pain or distress (Shamay-Tsoori, 2011).

Frith (1991) suggested deficient empathy as a key deficit in both ASD and psychopathy, but research on individuals with ASD is still not conclusive as to whether they show deficient emotional empathy. Some studies show a reduced response or arousal to the experience of pain in others (Minio-Paluello, Baron-Cohen, Avenanti, Walsh, & Aglioti, 2009), while others have found heightened arousal, but lack of prosocial behaviors when perceiving others' distress (Fan, Chen, Chen, Decety, & Cheng, 2014; Hadjikihan et al., 2014). Pouw, Rieffe, Oosterveld, Huskens, and Stockmann (2013) discuss this is terms of an impaired cognitive empathy, plus poor emotion regulation in ASD. According to this work, individuals with ASD would be less able to regulate their own empathic arousal (contagion) since they fail to understand why the other person is upset, for example. Emotions of others are experienced as confusing and unpredictable, which causes distress and prevents them from behaving empathically. Late-onset deficits in mentalizing are reported in other disorders such as schizophrenia but early-onset mentalizing difficulties seem to be specific to ASD. Psychopathy is the archetype of empathy deficits, but individuals high in these traits seem to have good cognitive empathy, or ToM, which allows them to manipulate others (Hare, 2003), but a relative lack of at least some facets of emotional empathy, such as emotional contagion, especially when it comes to sadness and distress in others.

Social interaction barrier *Autism can also affect the ability to understand others, understand that others have emotions, thoughts, and may have different view of the world. This leads to deficits in mentalizing, that is, inferring others' mental states.*

Source: © 52Hertz. Used under license from Pixabay.

The weak central coherence theory

Shah and Frith (1983) were the first to report of an atypical perceptual organization in individuals with ASD. Children with ASD outperformed controls on an embedded figures test, where they were asked to detect target shapes that were embedded within larger shapes. This local processing bias was the first brick in Frith's framework of a weak central coherence (WCC) for ASD (Frith & Happé, 1994). The finding was later on combined with the observation of a relative failure to extract "the bigger picture" in individuals with ASD. Today, the WCC theory postulates that individuals with ASD seem to have difficulties integrating information into a meaningful whole or incorporating the context, although their attention to and processing of local-level information seems enhanced or at least preserved. In addition, Happé and Booth (2008) have postulated the idea of independence of local and global processing, arguing that they seem to rely on different mechanisms and follow different developmental trajectories. A recent meta-analysis (van der Hallen, Evers, Brewaeys, van den Noortgate, & Wagemans, 2015) doesn't support an overall WCC or a global processing deficit in ASD, but does indicate more time-consuming global processing and preserved local visual processing for individuals with ASD. WCC has also been described in patients with eating disorders (e.g., Lopez, Tchanturia, Stahl, and Treasure, 2009) and Alzheimer's disease (Mårdh, 2013).

The Neuroscience of ASD

As ASD has multiple etiologies, it is not surprising that many neural networks have been found to be involved in producing the vast array of behavioral symptoms covered by the diagnosis. In addition, many neuroscientific findings in ASD are age dependent, indicating the importance of maturation and developmental change. Just as with the cognitive deficits, the unusual neural circuits in ASD are not unique, but overlap with other disorders such as mental retardation, bipolar disorder, and schizophrenia. As a consequence, brain research in ASD has more and more moved away from the study of discrete sets of atypical brain regions, towards the study of neural networks. Today, data from many different paradigms and methodologies support the idea that autism is characterized by atypical neural connectivity (Ecker & Murphy, 2014). Ideas about the precise way in which connectivity is atypical vary, from decreased fronto–posterior and enhanced parietal–occipital connectivity, reduced long-range and increased short-range connectivity, to temporal binding deficits. Although none fully explains all the data they support the heuristic value of the tenet that neural networks in autism are atypical in various ways.

Neurostructural abnormalities

In accordance with the connectivity theory of ASD, studies of white matter tracts, the "highways" of the brain, show decreased white matter integrity in persons with ASD, spanning across many regions of the brain (e.g., Travers et al., 2012). This mirrors a possible decrease in connectivity, most consistently in regions such as the corpus callosum (which connects the left and right hemispheres and is associated with, e.g., motor skills and complex information processing), the cingulum bundles (connecting regions along the middle-line of the brain with important frontal projections and associated with executive function), and white matter tracts that pass through the temporal lobe (connecting temporal lobe regions with other brain regions and associated with social functioning).

Another frequently reported neuroanatomical feature of autism is a generalized early brain overgrowth early in life. These findings have been questioned since they have been reported more in boys who have developmental regression than in other subgroups, and they might be a result of generalized physical overgrowth or biased norms of head circumference in past studies. Meta-analyses suggest some consistent structural differences across the lifespan compared to typically developing persons in both grey matter (e.g., amygdala, hippocampus, and precuneus) and white matter structures (e.g., arcuate and uncinate fasciculi). A reduction in the volume of the corpus callosum is also a relatively consistent finding. This size reduction may diminish interhemispheric connectivity and may be involved in pathophysiology of cognitive impairments and clinical features of ASD. The cerebellum has been extensively studied and a reduction in size of different lobules of the cerebellar vermis has been found in patients with ASD. It has been suggested that abnormalities in the cerebellum, through its connections to the brain stem, hypothalamus, and thalamus, indirectly could affect the development and functioning of one or more systems involved in cognitive, sensory, autonomic, and motor activities.

There are of course many limitations to these studies, most notably small sample sizes and technological differences between the studies – for example, the use of so called region of interest type metrics, which are inherently subjective and operator-dependent – but also inabilities to relate the structural findings to the behavioral or clinical profile of individuals with ASD. Many findings are also age dependent, such as an enlarged amygdala in young children but not adolescents with ASD, emphasizing the importance of developmental change. New techniques such as diffusion tensor imaging (DTI) are providing us with new opportunities to study connections and the integrity of neural pathways, but the number of studies using these methodologies is still small.

Neurofunctional associations

In recent years a wealth of papers has presented data on the brain function in ASD, using techniques like fMRI. Just as in the literature on the neuroanatomy, findings of neurofunctional aberrations in ASD are very divergent and very few are directly relevant for the propensity to commit violent crimes. Many of the studies also have serious limitations such as small samples of predominantly male, high-functioning adults that are lacking the comorbidities that are characterizing the ASD group. In addition, technical and design related differences, such as inconsistent task demands make some results difficult to interpret.

As a result of this, the findings have been inconsistent in many areas, for example, in motor and visual processing tasks. Given the relative primacy of communication dysfunction in the diagnostic symptom triad of ASD, there have been surprisingly few fMRI studies that have directly examined language function in individuals with ASD. The most consistent language related finding is a reduced activation in individuals with ASD in the bilateral superior temporal gyri, a region which is well known to be associated with receptive language. In addition, reductions in the laterality of language regions have been identified in a number of studies.

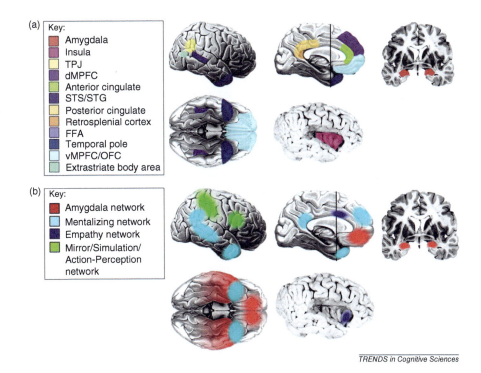

Figure 11.1 The social brain in psychiatric and neurological disorders

Source: Kennedy and Adolphs (2012). *Trends in Cognitive Sciences*, *16* (11), 561. (Reprinted from *Trends in Cognitive Sciences*, 16/11, Kennedy, DP & Adolphs R, The social brain in psychiatric and neurological disorders, 559–572, Copyright (2012), with permission from Elsevier.)

As expected, among the most well replicated findings are patterns of hypo-activity in the social brain network – including the medial prefrontal cortex, superior temporal sulcus, temporo-parietal junction, amygdala, and fusiform gyrus – across tasks in which social perception and cognition are used (Philip et al., 2012). The main body of this research concentrates on the investigation of networks underlying face perception and interpretation of facial expressions and emotions. These functions are related to the social interaction as well as the non-verbal communication facets of the ASD concept. The processing of faces in individuals appears to be atypically organized in ASD compared to control subjects. Activations in the fusiform face area and the occipital face area are commonly reported as reduced in individuals with ASD (e.g., Haxby, Hoffman, & Gobbini, 2002). It seems as though the neural network spontaneously recruited to process faces in ASD is more akin to that used for object processing, but when subjects are actively cued to engage in the face stimuli, typically no difference to controls are found. This suggests that face processing differences in individuals with ASD may result from a lack of motivation to attend to, or a preference for not attending to, the socially salient features of faces, as opposed to a deficit in the fusiform face area per se.

> **Box 11.2 Executive functioning in ASD**
>
> Executive function is an umbrella term that refers to a collection of cognitive abilities, the main ones being working memory, inhibition, planning, flexibility, and shifting of attention. There is a general consensus that executive function governs goal-directed behavior that requires holding plans or programs "on-line" until executed, inhibiting irrelevant action, planning a sequence of actions, attention to distraction, and being able to flexibly adjust to changed circumstances or new information (Huizinga, Dolan, & van der Molen, 2006). Mentalizing abilities are closely entwined with executive function, for example, in the area of self-monitoring and language, where early language seems to predict mentalizing abilities. Similarly, executive dysfunction seems to be related to the repetitive stereotyped behaviors and social communication deficits in ASD. However, executive function difficulties are not specific to ASD; they are commonly reported in other neurodevelopmental disorders (although in some cases with different patterns). Some recent studies of the long-term outcome of ASD suggest that a dysexecutive syndrome is a more important predictor of poor prognosis than the core symptoms of the ASD per se (Cederlund, Hagberg, & Gillberg, 2010). One view is that strong executive function early in life could protect at-risk individuals from autism or other neurodevelopmental conditions by compensating for deficits in other brain systems.

Related to executive function (see Box 11.2), it has been proposed that dysfunction in these functions in ASD is associated with disruptions to the automatic attentional systems, linked to executive control, involving the prefrontal-striatal network and the inferior parietal lobe (Haist, Adamo, Westerfield, Courchesne, & Towns, 2005), as well as the insula (Kana, Kellera, Minshew, & Just, 2007). Reductions in prefrontal and parietal activity in ASD have also been seen in a study of planning. When it comes to other cognitive control tasks, these have primarily been associated with hypo-activity in the dorsolateral prefrontal cortex (dlPFC) (e.g., Dichter & Belger, 2008) and the anterior cingulate cortex (e.g., Koshino et al., 2008). The role of the dlPFC in many executive functions including working memory is well established in typically developing subjects, whereas the anterior cingulate cortex is known to be involved in response inhibition.

ASD and Offending

> **Box 11.3 How common is ASD in criminal settings?**
>
> Simon Baron-Cohen (1988) raised the question of an increased occurrence of ASD in criminal populations already 25 years ago. Since then a number of studies

in forensic contexts have been made, the most important of which are presented in Table 11.1.

Table 11.1 ASD in forensic settings

Author, country	Study population	Methods	Prevalence rate
Scragg and Shah (1994), UK	All 392 patients at a high secure psychiatric hospital screened for Asperger syndrome	Screening of case notes, interview with key nurses followed by patient interviews	Approx. 2%: 6 diagnosed with Asperger syndrome and 3 equivocal cases
Hare et al., (1999), UK	All 1305 patients in three high secure psychiatric hospitals	ASD screening questionnaire with staff followed by file reviews	Approx. 2%: 31 cases of ASD identified
Siponmaa et al., (2001), Sweden	126 young offenders consecutively referred to forensic psychiatric investigation	Thorough team (social worker, psychologist, psychiatrist) assessment	15–27%: 19 had a definitive ASD diagnosis and 15 a probable diagnosis
Soderstrom et al., (2004), Sweden	100 consecutive serious violent offenders referred to forensic psychiatric investigation	Thorough team (social worker, psychologist, psychiatrist) assessment	18%: 18 offenders met criteria for an ASD diagnosis
Kumagami and Matsuura (2009), Japan	A randomized sample of 335 young offenders from three "normal" courts and 93 from special court for 'unique crimes'	Records and semi-structured interview by child psychiatrist	3%: 11 offenders diagnosed with ASD in three "normal" courts 18%: 17 offenders diagnosed with ASD in special court
Robinson et al., (2012), UK	2458 prisoners in all publicly-run, closed prisons in Scotland	ASD screening questionnaire with staff followed by interviews by psychiatrist	4%: 97 prisoners were screen positive for ASD but no developmental history taken suggested ASD

As can be seen in Table 11.1, there are stark differences in the prevalence figures suggested by the published studies. The two oldest studies, both

> studying patients from British high security hospitals, point to very small numbers of ASD patients in this setting, though at least twice as high as in the general population. However, both these old studies use methods of identification and diagnosis that are questionable, which could also be said about the Scottish study from 2012. The two Swedish studies show similar figures, 15–25% with an ASD diagnosis, though the samples are not necessarily representative for a general criminal population. Interestingly, the Japanese study shows very similar numbers in the special court dealing with psychiatric offenders, but the normal courts have a much lower prevalence. In the first prison study using a proper ASD diagnostic set-up (Billstedt et al., 2017), 270 young adult violent offenders were assessed for neurodevelopmental disorders and they found 26 offenders (10%) met criteria for an ASD. Only five (19%) of these individuals had received an ASD diagnosis in previous contact with health care services, which confirms the findings of Donno, Parker, Gilmour, and Skuse (2010).

People with ASD are often described as more law-abiding than the general population (see Box 11.3). Some authors claim that their cognitive characteristics, such as a systematic way of solving problems or a high intellectual ability, help them develop higher moral standards and thus make them less likely to commit crimes (Baron-Cohen, 2012). It has also been argued that the risk of offending in ASD is low since many people with ASD find rules helpful in surviving in the social world, and laws are simply social rules of a particular type. Others stress the supervised and protected environment surrounding them as an important protective factor. However, in her clinical account of Asperger syndrome, Lorna Wing (1981) was among the first to describe a possible link between ASD and offending when she wrote that a "small minority have a history of rather bizarre antisocial acts, perhaps because of their lack of empathy" (p. 116).

Twenty years later, Moffitt et al. (2001) even proposed a shared neurodevelopmental basis for ASD and childhood onset antisocial behavior. Today, some support for their hypothesis has been found, though there is still a scarcity of high quality studies with the specific aim of studying a possible association. One strand of evidence comes from twin studies, where it seems like the same genetic and environmental factors that are linked to ASD also influence the development of oppositional and conduct problems. In these studies, autistic-like social interaction problems have also repeatedly been implicated as among the strongest predictors of conduct problems (Kerekes et al., 2014; Lundström et al., 2011).

Outside the twin research area, the same pattern has been observed among childhood arrestees, where delinquent behavior is positively associated with autistic symptoms, even after adjustment for externalizing disorders (Geluk et al., 2012). In other studies, it has been shown that persistently disruptive children often have, previously undetected, autistic behavioral traits, and as many as one third might meet criteria for an ASD (Donno et al., 2010; Gilmour, Hill, Place, & Skuse, 2004). A serious signal is that only in a small minority of these children, their ASD is detected by the psychiatric services. Similarly, in clinical groups of children with ASD, many also have conduct disorders, though seldom noted in their medical record. Particularly atypical autism seems to be overrepresented in children with conduct disorder (e.g., de Bruin, Ferdinand, Meester, de Nijs, & Verheij, 2007).

Among adults with ASD, there are numerous case reports of serious and persistent offending behavior (e.g., Baron-Cohen, 1988; Mawson, Grounds, & Tantam, 1985; Murrie, Warren, Kristiansson, & Dietz, 2002; Wing, 1981). Though there are some reports of nonviolent criminality (e.g., Chen et al., 2003), violent crimes are clearly overrepresented in the literature. Some also assert that criminality, when committed by individuals with ASD, tends to be more serious (Mouridsen, Rich, Isager, & Nedergaard, 2008), which of course could be a result of minor offenses, when committed by people with ASD, being less likely to be reported to the police or to be prosecuted.

Within the category of violent crimes, arson has gained specific attention in some studies (e.g., Palermo, 2004; Tantam, 1991). Siponmaa, Kristiansson, Jonson, Nyden, and Gillberg (2001), who studied 126 young offenders referred for forensic psychiatric examination, noticed that the diagnoses of atypical autistic disorder and Asperger syndrome were statistically more frequent among arsonists compared to other offender groups. In Mouridsen et al.'s (2008) study of criminal behavior in clinically referred adults with ASD, only arson separated ASD statically from controls. Studying the psychiatric morbidity of arsonists in Sweden, Enayati, Grann, Lubbe, and Fazel (2008) found that a diagnosis of Asperger syndrome was significantly more common among male arsonists, as compared to other offender groups.

Another subcategory of criminals that has been particularly focused on is sexual offenders. As mentioned above, sexual development is often complicated by the core deficits in ASD and, for many of these persons, puberty is a very difficult period in their lives. Many parents are also afraid that their children will be the victims of sexual abuse as they physically mature. In 2013, a review was published on the risk for sexual abuse as well as sexual offending in ASD (Sevlever, Roth, & Gillis, 2013). It concludes that there was only one study looking at sexual abuse exclusively in ASD subjects and no formal prevalence studies on ASD and sexual offending. There are, however, a number of case reports that have included descriptions of sexual offences in persons with ASD, with or without violent behavior (e.g., Chesterman & Rutter, 1994; Milton, Duggan, Latham, Egan, & Tantam, 2002; Palermo, 2004). 't Hart-Kerkhoffs et al. (2009) investigated the occurrence of self-reported dimensional ASD symptoms in a group of young suspects of sexual offenses. They found that the ASD scores in this group were higher than for healthy controls but lower than clinical samples of ASD patients. When subgroups of suspected sex offenders were analyzed they found that child molesters and solo offenders scored higher than group offenders. A problem in this research area, as within the non-sexual offender literature, is that most studies have selected persons with Asperger syndrome and do not tell us about the whole autism spectrum.

Stalking – that is, the repeated or persistent unwanted attempts to communicate with or associate with another (Mullen, Pathé, Purcell, & Stuart, 1999) – has also been highlighted in the ASD literature. Several anecdotal reports illustrate ASD individuals engaging in stalking behavior when seeking contact with others for friendship or intimacy (e.g., Green, Gilchrist, Burton, & Cox, 2000; Howlin, 1997; Stokes & Newton, 2004). Stokes et al. (2007) note that like typically developing individuals, ASD individuals desire intimate relationships, yet they lack the appropriate skills and knowledge to initiate such relationships successfully and, due to this social ineptness, they may engage in inappropriate or intrusive courtship behaviors, which may constitute stalking.

Prevalence of criminality in clinical ASD groups

Ideally, prevalence studies should entail unbiased samples, either total population samples or random samples. In the field of ASD and criminality, Woodbury-Smith, Clare, Holland, and Kearns (2006) did this in their study of 102 individuals with ASD, identified in a health district in the UK, with an adult background population of approximately 200,000. Unfortunately, the attrition rate was very high in their study and eventually only 25 individuals with full-scale IQs of 70 or more were included and compared to a control sample. Overall rates of any self-reported violent offending were similar between the two groups (30% versus 25%).

Unlike this study, most prevalence figures in this area are derived from two main study strategies. The first strategy has focused on studying the prevalence of offending behavior among people with ASD who received treatment in the general psychiatric care system. The second strategy has been to study the occurrence of ASD among people within the criminal justice system or the forensic psychiatric services. In a first attempt to get a general picture of how common violence is among patients with ASD, Ghaziuddin, Tsai, and Ghaziuddin (1991) reviewed 21 clinical ASD studies, published between 1944 and 1990. In their total sample of 132 cases, 2–6%, depending on inclusion criteria, had a clear history of violent behavior. They concluded that there was no clear association between ASD and violent crime. Mouridsen et al. (2008) examined the prevalence and types of offending in a sample of 313 Danes with ASD (aged between 25 and 59 years), who had been consecutively attending hospitals in the years 1960–1985. In their sample 9% were convicted of a crime compared to 18% in the control group. They found that people with ASD tended to commit more serious crimes compared to controls and sexual offenses and arson stood out as typical of the ASD group.

A Swedish prospective follow-up study (Cederlund, Hagberg, Billstedt, Gillberg, & Gillberg, 2008) of 70 males (age 16–34 years) with Asperger syndrome, found very similar figures, with 10% having been involved with the police and the law for different reasons. In a UK study, Allen et al. (2008) tried to estimate the prevalence of offending behaviors in 126 males with ASD using questionnaires to capture their criminal history. A total of 33 (26%) individuals with ASD reported that they had been engaged in offending behavior that had or could have resulted in involvement with the criminal justice system. However, no control group was recruited for this study, which makes the results difficult to interpret. Långström et al. (2009) analyzed criminal register data for all patients released from hospital care from 1988 to 2000 with a diagnosis of Asperger syndrome or autistic disorder. They found that 7% were convicted of a crime, but this figure could not be used to infer an increased or decreased risk of offending in this group with ASD, since they did not have a control group.

A recent, large register-based study (Lundström et al., 2014) of all CAP patients in Stockholm, Sweden born between 1984 and 1994 who received a neurodevelopmental disorder diagnosis in 2001–2009 compared these patient groups to matched control cases on their risk for subsequent violent criminality as measured by conviction. The study group included 954 individuals with ASD and found no increased risk for offending in this group, while patients with ADHD and tic disorders were at significant elevated risk. The study did not account for the comorbidity among the neurodevelopmental disorders, since this was very seldom coded in the register. In addition, the ratio of patients with a diagnosis of ADHD compared to ASD was much smaller than what would be expected from prevalence figures in the population, which indicates some kind of referral bias.

To conclude, though the published data so far vary a great deal in terms of prevalence of criminality in clinical ASD populations, there is no evidence of an increased risk of offending in these groups. However, there are some serious limitations to these studies. First, they are still few and many of them are highly selective or have serious referral biases. Some have included only patients with childhood diagnoses, which might mean that they have gained support and treatment to a higher degree. If individuals with ASD are hospitalized this would also mean that they, in most cases, have additional psychiatric problems and, as a consequence, receive treatment that other ASD individuals don't. Conviction data might not be the best measure of criminal behavior in clinical groups, since many unlawful acts are never reported to the police but are seen as being part of the offender's disorder and health care needs.

Risk factors for offending in ASD

Several authors have noted that even though there seems to be an increased prevalence of ASD in criminal populations, we would still need to find out more specifically whether there are particular features of ASD that make some individuals with the syndrome more prone to violent behavior than others (Björkly, 2009; Mouridsen, 2012). The literature contains several suggestions as to why criminal behavior and ASD might co-occur at a disproportionate rate. Primarily, impairments and features related to the diagnosis have been used to explain criminal behaviors (Howlin, 2004). In line with this, offending could be related to the lack of understanding or misinterpretation of social cues seen in ASD (Haskins & Silva, 2006; Murrie et al., 2002; Palermo, 2004). Deficient empathy and emotional reciprocity are emphasized in several studies that depict persons with ASD who have committed serious violent offenses, often in response to minor provocations and without any remorse afterwards (e.g., Schwartz-Watts, 2005). Murrie et al. (2002) highlight that some individuals with ASD may be led by others into criminal acts because of their social naivety.

In the case of stalking, Stokes and Newton (2007) stress the lack of awareness of social norms in ASD subjects as a feature that makes them susceptible to pursue relationships that are inappropriate and sometimes distressing to the person of interest. The stereotyped behavior patterns have also been suggested as an explanation for crimes in ASD, for example, the obsessions and circumscribed interests often seen in ASD are sometimes applied to humans too and could serve as a background to some instances of stalking (Sevlever et al., 2013) and theft – for example, stealing particular objects of interest (Chen et al., 2003) – but also in some cases of murder (Barry-Walsh & Mullen, 2004; Silva, Ferrari, & Leong, 2002). Although people with ASD are not incapable of instrumental violence, reactive or affective violence are more often reported. In case reports, a common background to violent incidents involving offenders with ASD is frustration and increasing irritability that, due to impaired social problem-solving ability, erupts in a violent outburst. This would fit with a negative reinforcement background to some acts of violence, where physical aggression is used to remove something stressful. Related to this are risks connected to the sensory hypersensitivity in ASD, a criterion that has been incorporated in *DSM-5*, and primarily violence as a means of alleviating sensory strain, for example, the high pitch of screaming children (e.g., Katz and Zemishlany, 2006; Mawson et al., 1985).

There are very few studies looking at the neurostructural, or neurofunctional, risk factors in offenders with ASD. In attempts to trace biological markers of violence with brain imaging, most studies use psychopathy as their prime phenotype (see Chapter 9), or violent offenders in general, without specifying their psychiatric status. The most consistent findings within this field are reductions in prefrontal grey matter, particularly within the dlPFC and the orbitofrontal cortex, and reduction in the total volume of the temporal lobe, more specifically the hippocampus and amygdala. Based on these findings, there are two prevailing biological theories on brain dysfunction in violence, the frontal lobe dysfunction theory and the integrated emotion systems model (van der Gronde, Kempes, van El, Rinne, & Pieters, 2014). The frontal lobe dysfunction theory states that aggression is a consequence of deficits in the frontal brain, mainly the prefrontal cortex. Within the prefrontal cortex, the dlPFC, the orbitofrontal cortex, and the inferior frontal cortex are all linked to different motor and executive processes but also central in the integration of different cognitive activity and emotional processes. In this manner, the prefrontal cortex restricts emotions and impulsive, disinhibited, and maladaptive behavior. In general, deficits in the prefrontal area, mainly the ventromedial part, have been related to poor control of reactive violence.

The integrated emotion systems model hypothesizes that deviant social behavior, such as violence, is the result of inhibited emotional development caused by dysfunction in the amygdala and other limbic system regions, like the hippocampus, hypothalamus, anterior cingulate cortex, insular cortex, and ventral striatum. Damage to this system leads to impaired interpretation of emotions and lack of guilt and embarrassment, which results in diminished empathy, failure to recognize fearful expressions, impaired passive avoidance learning, and reduction in uncomfortable emotions associated with moral transgressions. Instrumental violence is thought to be associated with the dysfunction of both the ventromedial prefrontal cortex and the amygdala/hippocampal system.

Most likely, both the frontal lobe dysfunction theory and the integrated emotion systems model are true, and reinforce each other. However, as Raine (2013) notes, the greater the number of impairments, the greater the likelihood of violence as an outcome, but we must never forget that violence is a dynamic, dimensional and probabilistic complex behavior where the brain interacts with macro-social and psychosocial processes.

Among the few studies looking at proneness to aggressive behavior among people with ASD in the light of brain imaging techniques, Suzuki et al. (2010) looked at metabolite alterations in the hippocampal formation as they relate to aggression in 12 males with high-functioning ASD and found a significant positive correlation. Howner et al. (2012) compared the cortical thickness of two groups of subjects undergoing a forensic psychiatric investigation, one with ASD (n = 7) and one with psychopathy (n = 7) to healthy, non-criminal controls. The ASD group did not differ significantly from controls regarding cortical thickness, but their whole brain volume was smaller compared to controls (see Box 11.4).

Box 11.4 The ASD patient as a vulnerable defendant

There are a number of challenges within the criminal justice process, from the first interrogations and forward that requires special skills and adaptations in order to ensure that ASD defendants get a fair treatment. The first and most significant factor is to ensure effective communication, enabling the ASD defendant to understand questions and give answers that she or he believes to be correct. ASD means difficulties in understanding and responding. Even defendants with apparently good verbal skills are likely to interpret statements literally, have difficulty understanding conversational rules and fail to understand abstract part of the language, such as figures of speech, jokes, irony, or sarcasm. Aids to communication may be needed in order to secure these central points. There may also be responses from the ASD defendant that are interpreted as incongruent, paradoxical, or perhaps disrespectful, for example, they may smile when they are not happy, appear angry when they are scared. Subjects with ASD often have weak listening skills and a limited attention span. Thus, it may be necessary to repeat instructions often, perhaps adapt interrogations and court procedures, for example, slower pace and breaks. People with ASD are also easily aroused and become anxious, especially in new and uncomfortable situations, when their routines are disrupted, when they are surrounded by strangers, or other events deviating from normal experience. These situations can lead to high levels of anxiety and potentially chaotic and disorganized reactions. Here, the use of an intermediary or a court supporter can help. Screens in the court room, recorded interviews or presence through a live link could also be used. Importantly, a defendant with ASD most often lacks the ability to correctly imagine, interpret, or predict others' thoughts, feelings, or behaviors and they will therefore have difficulty in understanding the consequences of their own or others' actions and are unlikely to be aware of how their behavior is interpreted by others. As a consequence, recounting events with a personal dimension or point of view is likely to be problematic. Finally, the defendant with ASD may have difficulty interpreting a causal chain of events. However, if the information is of interest to them, they may have superior attention for details.

Abnormal sensation *Abnormal experience and reaction to basic sensations has been noted in autism. An individual with autism can show hyper-sensitivity to the environment, for example, a light touch is experienced as irritating and painful, the volume of sounds is experienced as unbearably loud. Other individuals with autism show hypo-sensitivity, for example, feeling touch only when it is a painful scratch.*
Source: © John McLaird. Used under license from 123RF.

Conclusions and Future Research Questions

As described in this chapter, there are several reasons to believe that at least some individuals with ASD are at an increased risk of committing unlawful acts, though they might not enter the criminal justice system as a consequence of their behavior. This would explain the fact that most studies of criminality in ASD subjects from general clinical samples find no higher levels of criminality here compared to the general population, while the ratio of ASD individuals in criminal populations is clearly elevated. There are still many unanswered questions in this field and a great need of further research.

Some hypotheses that might be tried are the following. Are these findings due to referral bias in clinical research? Most patients in these studies have childhood diagnoses and consequently have had access to care and support that could serve as protective factors against criminality. In addition, as Allen et al. (2008) have shown, many, perhaps up to 50% of people with ASD are not processed via the criminal justice system. Thus, sentences are not a good measure of criminality in this group and we need to find better ways of depicting criminality in these groups. Another, related, question is whether these patients mirror the true ASD population? Many patients with persistent antisocial behavior and autistic symptoms do not receive an ASD diagnosis or do not enter the general psychiatric care system. As suggested by Gadow, DeVincent, and Drabick (2008), the presence of disruptive and antisocial behaviors may alter the presentation of ASD, and vice versa. Of course, this is true for most other psychiatric disorders as well.

In line with this, Newman and Ghaziuddin (2008) and Palermo (2004) hypothesized that an association between ASD and offending does not so much result directly from ASD symptomatology itself, but rather from co-occurring disorders, which could explain some of the gap between clinical and forensic studies. This has gained some support in Långström et al. (2009) where individuals with ASD and a history of violent criminality had significantly higher levels of comorbid psychopathology diagnosed at any time throughout the study period compared to those without a history of violent crime. In their study, psychotic disorder, any substance use, and personality disorder were significantly associated with violent convictions in individuals with ASD. We would still need studies that compare the different features, clinical needs as well as other characteristics, of subjects with ASD in general psychiatric and forensic settings.

Palermo (2004) suggested that offenders with ASD are characterized by the same sociodemographic and psychiatric features consistently found among violent individuals without ASDs. Kanner notices a preponderance of "highly intelligent parents" in ASD children, but there is nothing to suggest that this reflects a true condition or that ASD would serve as a protection against other disorders and factors related to criminality. There is still a positive correlation between ASD diagnosis and socioeconomic status indicators such as parental education, occupation, and income but, hopefully, these circumstances will change in the future.

In the field of ASD, neurobiology, and offending there are many unexplored questions since there is a clear lack of studies looking into the structural and functional characteristics of persistently violent subjects with ASD. In terms of psychophysiology, the hypothesis that individuals with ASD and early-onset conduct disorder/psychopathy can be distinguished on emotional empathy needs to be further tested. Since the ASD group is very heterogeneous it may consist of autonomic hyper-responsive as well as hyporesponsive subgroups and these should be taken into account and further examined. Future brain imaging studies must also find a way to include subjects with a more complex clinical picture, including some of the features discussed here.

Implication for Forensic Practice, Ethical Implications, and Policy

Fundamentally, whether a person with ASD does or does not have the capacity to form criminal intent is a complex issue, which requires careful consideration. ASD is by definition a spectrum of behavior patterns, and there is considerable variation in different aspects of the phenotype, both clinical and cognitive. Therefore, decisions regarding culpability need to be based on individual strengths and vulnerabilities rather than diagnosis.

ASD is associated with significant socio-emotional impairments that may, arguably, affect the ability to form intent. The defense of "not guilty by reason of insanity" (M'Naghten rules) sometimes arises in connection with a defendant charged with serious offenses. However, in relation to ASD, it may be argued that this is of little relevance except for those who may have an additional psychiatric diagnosis. The consideration of the difference between understanding what is legally "right" and "wrong," versus understanding "right" from "wrong" from a moral standpoint is raised in these cases. A legal understanding simply requires that the individual knows what is right and wrong according to the legislation in the jurisdiction in which they are living. In contrast, a moral understanding requires the person to recognize that certain behavior is wrong because it results in a victim, that is, not simply contrary to law. Individuals with ASD have their own pattern of vulnerabilities in the affective-cognitive domain, some of which therefore bring into question their ability to form intent. Most characteristically, individuals with ASD have difficulty interpreting verbal and non-verbal cues that carry emotional valence. For example, people with ASD have difficulties in mentalizing and various aspects of emotion recognition, but seem to have an intact ability to make a moral/ conventional distinction (Blair, 1996).

Recommended Reading

Allen, D., Evans, C., Hider, A., Hawkins, S., Peckett, H., & Morgan, H. (2008). Offending behaviour in adults with Asperger syndrome. *Journal of Autism and Developmental Disorders, 38,* 748–758. *Important paper with several suggestions of how to address and reduce the vulnerability of people with ASD within the criminal justice system.*

Gilmour, J., Hill, B., Place, M., & Skuse, D. H. (2004). Social communication deficits in conduct disorder: A clinical and community survey. *Journal of Child Psychology and Psychiatry, 45,* 967–978. *One of the first studies to show that there is a relatively high proportion of children with severe disruptive behavior that have socio-communicative deficits.*

Lai, M. C., Lombardo, M. V. & Baron-Cohen, S. (2014). Lancet seminar: Autism. *The Lancet 383*: 896-910. *A broad, yet deep summary of what we have learned about ASD over the last 70 years in terms of clinical presentation, causes, neurobiology, outcome and treatment.*

Moffitt, T. E., Caspi, A., Rutter, M., & Silva, P. A. (2001). *Sex differences in antisocial behavior: Conduct disorder, delinquency and violence in the Dunedin longitudinal study* (pp. 238–239). Cambridge: Cambridge University Press. *A summary of the main findings from the landmark Dunedin Longitudinal Study, which followed a cohort of 1000 New Zealand males and females over the first two decades of life. Contains several hypotheses that are still in need of investigation.*

References

Allen, D., Evans, C., Hider, A., Hawkins, S., Peckett, H., & Morgan, H. (2008). Offending behaviour in adults with Asperger syndrome. *Journal of Autism and Developmental Disorders, 38,* 748–758.

American Psychiatric Association (APA). (1980). *Diagnostic and statistical manual of mental disorders* (3rd ed.). Washington, DC: American Psychiatric Association.

American Psychiatric Association (APA). (1994). *Diagnostic and statistical manual of mental disorders* (4th ed.) (*DSM-4*). Washington, DC: American Psychiatric Association.

American Psychiatric Association (APA). (2013). *Diagnostic and statistical manual of mental disorders,* (5th ed.) (*DSM-5*). Arlington, VA: American Psychiatric Publishing.

Asperger, H. (1944). Die "autistichen psychopathen" im kindesalter [Autistic psychopathy in infancy]. *Archiv für Psychiatrie und Nervenkrankheiten [Archive for Psychiatry and Nerve Disease], 117,* 76–136.

Baron-Cohen, S. (1988). An assessment of violence in a young man with Asperger's syndrome. *Journal of Child Psychology and Psychiatry, 29,* 351–360.

Baron-Cohen, S. (2012). *Zero degrees of empathy: A new theory of human cruelty.* London: Penguin/Allen Lane.

Baron-Cohen, S., Leslie, A. M., & Frith U. (1985). Does the autistic child have a "theory of mind"? *Cognition, 21,* 37–46.

Barry-Walsh, J. B., & Mullen, P. E. (2004). Forensic aspects of Asperger's syndrome. *Journal of Forensic Psychiatry and Psychology, 15,* 96–107.

Billstedt, E., Wallinius, M., Anckarsäter, H., & Hofvander B. Neurodevelopmental disorders in young violent offenders: Overlap and background characteristics. *Psychiatry Research*, 2017, 3(2):234–241.

Björkly, S. (2009). Risk and dynamics of violence in Asperger's syndrome: A systematic review of the literature. *Aggression and Violent Behavior*, 14, 306–312.

Blair, R. J. (1996). Brief report: Morality in the autistic child. *Journal of Autism and Developmental Disorders*, 26(5), 571–579.

Brereton, A., Tonge, B. J., & Einfeld, S. E. (2006). Psychopathology in children and adolescents with autism compared to young people with intellectual disability. *Journal of Autism and Developmental Disorders*, 36, 863–870.

Cederlund, M., Hagberg, B., Billstedt, E., Gillberg, I. C., & Gillberg, C. (2008). Asperger syndrome and autism: A comparative longitudinal follow – up study more than 5 years after original diagnosis. *Journal of Autism and Developmental Disorders*, 38, 72–85.

Cederlund, M., Hagberg, B. & Gillberg, C. (2010). Asperger syndrome in adolescent and young adult males. Interview, self- and parent assessment of social, emotional, and cognitive problems. *Research in Developmental Disabilities*, 31, 287–298.

Chen, P. S., Chen, S. J., Yang, Y. K., Yeh, T. L., Chen, C. C., & Lo, H. Y. (2003). Asperger's disorder: A case report of repeated stealing and the collecting behaviours of an adolescent patient. *Acta Psychiatrica Scandinavica*, 107, 73–76.

Chesterman, P., & Rutter, S. C. (1994). A case report: Asperger's syndrome and sexual offending. *Journal of Forensic Psychiatry*, 4, 555–562.

Daniels, A. M., & Mandell, D. S. (2013). Explaining differences in age at autism spectrum disorder diagnosis: A critical review. *Autism*, 18, 583–597.

de Bruin, E. I., Ferdinand, R. F., Meester, S., de Nijs, P. F. A., & Verheij, F. (2007). High rates of psychiatric co-morbidity in PDD-NOS. *Journal of Autism and Developmental Disorders*, 37, 877–886.

Dichter, G. S. & Belger, A. (2008). Atypical modulation of cognitive control by arousal in autism. *Psychiatry Research: Neuroimaging*, 164, 185–197.

Donno, R., Parker, G., Gilmour, J., & Skuse, D. H. (2010). Social communication deficits in disruptive primary-school children. *British Journal of Psychiatry*, 196, 282–289.

Dunbar, R. I. M. (1993). Coevolution of neocortical size, group-size and language in humans. *Behavioral and Brain Sciences*, 16, 681–694.

Ecker, C., & Murphy, D. (2014). Neuroimaging in autism-from basic science to translational research. *Nature Reviews Neurology*, 10, 82–91.

Enayati, J., Grann, M., Lubbe, S., & Fazel, S. (2008). Psychiatric morbidity in arsonists referred for forensic psychiatric assessment in Sweden. *Journal of Forensic Psychiatry and Psychology*, 19, 139–147.

Fan, Y. T., Chen, C., Chen, S. C., Decety, J., & Cheng, Y. (2014). Empathic arousal and social understanding in individuals with autism: Evidence from fMRI and ERP measurements. *Social Cognitive and Affective Neuroscience*, 9, 1203–1213.

Farrington, D. P. (2003). Key results from the first forty years of the Cambridge Study in Delinquent Development. In T. P. Thornberry & M. D. Krohn (Eds.). *Taking Stock of Delinquency* (pp. 137–183). New York: Kluwer Academic/Plenum.

Frith, C. D. (1992). *The cognitive neuropsychology of schizophrenia*. Hove: Psychology Press/Erlbaum.

Frith, C. D. & Singer, T. (2008). The role of social cognition in decision making. *Philosophical Transactions of the Royal Society of London: Biological Sciences*, 12, 3875–3886.

Frith U. (1991). *Autism and Asperger syndrome*. Cambridge/New York, NY: Cambridge University Press.

Frith, U. & Happé, F. (1994). Autism: Beyond "theory of mind.". *Cognition*, 50, 115–132.

Gadow, K. D., DeVincent, C. J., & Drabick, D. A. (2008). Oppositional defiant disor- der as a clinical phenotype in children with autism spectrum disorder. *Journal of Autism and Developmental Disorders, 38*, 1302–1310.

Geluk, C. A., Jansen, L. M., Vermeiren, R., Doreleijers, T. A., van Domburgh, L., de Bildt, A., ... Hartman, C. A. (2012). Autistic symptoms in childhood arrestees: Longitudinal association with delinquent behavior. *Journal of Child Psychology and Psychiatry, 53*, 160–167.

Ghaziuddin, M., Tsai, L., & Ghaziuddin, N. (1991). Violence in Asperger syndrome. A critique. *Journal of Autism and Developmental Disorders, 21*, 349–354.

Gilmour, J., Hill, B., Place, M., & Skuse, D. H. (2004). Social communication deficits in con- duct disorder: A clinical and community survey. *Journal of Child Psychology and Psychiatry, 45*, 967–978.

Green, J., Gilchrist, A., Burton, D., & Cox, A. (2000). Social and psychiatric functioning in adolescents with Asperger syndrome compared with conduct disorder. *Journal of Autism and Developmental Disorders, 30*, 279–293.

Gregory, C., Lough, S., Stone, V., Erzinclioglu, S., Martin, L., Baron-Cohen, S., & Hodges, J. R. (2002). Theory of mind in patients with frontal variant frontotemporal demen- tia and Alzheimer's disease: Theoretical and practical implications. *Brain, 125*, 752–764.

Hadjikhani, N., Zürcher, N. R., Rogier, O., Hippolyte, L., Lemonnier, E., Ruest, T., ... Gill- berg, C. (2014). Emotional contagion for pain is intact in autism spectrum disorders. *Translational Psychiatry, 14*(4), e343.

Haist, F., Adamo, M., Westerfield, M., Courchesne, E., & Townsend, J. (2005). The functional neuroanatomy of spatial attention in autism spectrum disorder. *Developmental Neuropsychology, 27*, 425–458.

Happé, F. G., & Booth, R. D. (2008). The power of the positive: Revisiting weak coherence in autism spectrum disorders. *Quarterly Journal of Experimental Psychology, 61*, 50–63.

Hare, D. J., Gould, J., Mills, R., & Wing, L. (1999). *A preliminary study of individuals with autistic spectrum disorders in three special hospitals in England*. London: National Autistic Society/ Department of Health.

Hare, R. D. (2003). *PCL-R manual*. Toronto/Ontario, Canada: Multi-Health Systems.

Haskins, B. G., & Silva, J. A. (2006). Asperger's disorder and criminal behavior: Forensic-Psychiatric considerations. *Journal of the American Academy of Psychiatry and the Law, 34*, 374–384.

Haxby, J. V., Hoffman, E. A., & Gobbini, M. I. (2002). Human neural systems for face recognition and social communication. *Biological Psychiatry, 51*, 59–67.

Hofvander, B., Ossowski, D., Lundström, S., & Anckarsäter, H. (2009a). Continuity of aggressive antisocial behavior from childhood to adulthood: The question of phenotype definition. *International Journal of Law and Psychiatry, 32*, 224–234.

Hofvander, B., Delorme, R., Chaste, P., Nydén, A., Wentz, E., Ståhlberg, O., ... Leboyer M (2009b). Psychiatric and psychosocial problems in adults with normal-intelligence autism spectrum disorders. *BMC Psychiatry, 9*(35).

Howlin, P. (1997). *Autism: Preparing for adulthood*. London: Routledge.

Howlin, P. (2004). Legal issues. In P. Howlin (Ed.). *Autism and Asperger syndrome: Preparing for adulthood* (2nd ed.), (pp. 300–312). London/New York: Routledge.

Howner, K., Eskildsen, S. F., Fischer, H., Dierks, T., Wahlund, L. O., Jonsson, T., ... Kristiansson, M. (2012). Thinner cortex in the frontal lobes in mentally disordered offenders. *Psychiatry Research: Neuroimaging, 203*, 126–131.

Huizinga, M., Dolan, C. V., & van der Molen, M. W. (2006). Age-related change in executive function: Developmental trends and a latent variable analysis. *Neuropsychologia, 44*, 2017–2036.

Kana, R. K., Kellera, T. A., Minshew, N. J., & Just, M. A. (2007). Inhibitory control in high-functioning autism: Decreased activation and underconnectivity in inhibition networks. *Biological Psychiatry, 62*, 198–206.

Kanner, L. (1943). Autistic disturbances of affective contact. *Nervous Child 2*, 215–250.

Katz, N., & Zemishlany, Z. (2006). Criminal responsibility in Asperger's syndrome. *Israel Journal of Psychiatry and Related Sciences, 43*, 166–173.

Kerekes, N., Lundström, S., Chang, Z., Tajnia, A., Jern, P., Lichtenstein, P., ... Anckarsäter, H. (2014). Oppositional defiant- and conduct disorder-like problems: Neurodevelopmental predictors and genetic background in boys and girls, in a nationwide twin study. *PeerJ, 2*, e359.

Koshino, H., Kana, R. K., Keller, T.A., Cherkassky, V. L., Minshew, N. J., & Just, M. A. (2008). fMRI investigation of working memory for faces in autism: Visual coding and underconnectivity with frontal areas. *Cerebral Cortex, 18*, 289–300.

Lai, M. C., Lombardo, M. V., & Baron-Cohen, S. (2014). Lancet seminar: Autism. *Lancet, 383*, 896–910.

Lopez, C., Tchanturia, K., Stahl, D., & Treasure, J. (2009). Weak central coherence in eating disorders: A step towards looking for an endophenotype of eating disorders. *Journal of Clinical and Experimental Neuropsychology, 31*, 117–125.

Långström, N., Grann, M., Ruchkin, V., Sjöstedt, G., & Fazel, S. (2009). Risk factors for violent offending in autism spectrum disorder. A national study of hospitalized individuals. *Journal of Interpersonal Violence, 24*, 1358–1370.

Lundström, S., Chang, Z., Kerekes, N., Gumpert, C. H., Rastam, M., Gillberg, C., ... Anckarsater, H. (2011). Autistic-like traits and their association with mental health problems in two nationwide twin cohorts of children and adults. *Psychological Medicine, 41*, 2423–2433

Lundström, S., Forsman, M., Larsson, H., Kerekes, N., Serlachius, E., Långström, N., & Lichtenstein, P. (2014). Childhood neurodevelopmental disorders and violent criminality: A sibling control study. *Journal of Autism and Developmental Disorders, 44*, 2707–2716.

Magiati, I., Tay, X. W., & Howlin, P. (2014). Cognitive, language, social and behavioural outcomes in adults with autism spectrum disorders: A systematic review of longitudinal follow-up studies in adulthood. *Clinical Psychology Review, 34*, 73–86.

Mannuzza, S., Klein, R. G., & Moulton, J. L., 3rd. (2008). Lifetime criminality among boys with attention deficit hyperactivity disorder: A prospective follow-up study into adulthood using official arrest records. *Psychiatry Research, 160*, 237–246.

Mårdh, S. (2013). Weak central coherence in patients with Alzheimer's disease. *Neural Regeneration Research, 8*, 760–766.

Mawson, D., Grounds, A., & Tantam, D. (1985). Violence and Asperger's syndrome: A case study. *British Journal of Psychiatry, 147*, 566–569.

Milton, J., Duggan, C., Latham, A., Egan, V., & Tantam, D. (2002). Case history of co-morbid Asperger's syndrome and paraphilic behaviour. *Medicine, Science and the Law, 42*, 237–244.

Minio-Paluello, I., Baron-Cohen, S., Avenanti, A., Walsh, V., & Aglioti, S. M. (2009). Absence of embodied empathy during pain observation in Asperger syndrome. *Biological Psychiatry, 65*, 55–62.

Moffitt, T. E. (1993), Adolescence-limited and life- course-persistent antisocial behavior: A developmental taxonomy. *Psychology Review, 100*, 674–701.

Moffitt, T. E., Caspi, A., Rutter, M., & Silva, P. A. (2001). *Sex differences in antisocial behavior: Conduct disorder, delinquency and violence in the Dunedin longitudinal study*. Cambridge: Cambridge University Press.

Mouridsen, S. E. (2012). Current status of research on autism spectrum disorders and offending. *Research in Autism Spectrum Disorders, 6*, 79–86.

Mouridsen, S. E., Rich, B., Isager, T., & Nedergaard, N. J. (2008). Pervasive developmental disorders and criminal behaviour. A case control study. *International Journal of Offender Therapy and Comparative Criminology, 52,* 196–205.

Mullen, P.E., Pathé, M., Purcell, R., & Stuart, G. (1999). Study of stalkers. *American Journal of Psychiatry, 156,* 1244–1249.

Muller, F., Simion, A., Reviriego, E., Galera, C., Mazaux, J. M., Barat, M., & Joseph, P. A. (2010). Exploring theory of mind after severe traumatic brain injury. *Cortex, 46,* 1088–1099.

Murrie, D. C., Warren, J. I., Kristiansson, M., & Dietz, P. E. (2002). Asperger's syndrome in forensic settings. *International Journal of Forensic Mental Health, 1,* 59–70.

Newman, S., & Ghaziuddin, M. (2008). Violent crime in Asperger syndrome: The role of psychiatric comorbidity. *Journal of Autism and Developmental Disorders, 38,* 1848–1852.

Palermo, M. T. (2004). Pervasive developmental disorders, psychiatric comorbidities, and the law. *International Journal of Offender Therapy and Comparative Criminology, 48,* 40–48.

Pettersson, E., Anckarsäter, H., Gillberg, C., & Lichtenstein, P. (2013). Different neurodevelopmental symptoms have a common genetic etiology. *Journal of Child Psychology and Psychiatry, 54,* 1356–1365.

Philip, R. C. M., Dauvermann, M. R., Whalley, H. C., Baynham, K., Lawrie, S. M., & Stanfield, A. C. (2012). A systematic review and meta-analysis of the fMRI investigation of autism spectrum disorders. *Neuroscience & Biobehavioral Reviews, 36,* 901–942.

Pouw, L. B., Rieffe, C., Oosterveld, P., Huskens, B., & Stockmann, L. (2013). Reactive/proactive aggression and affective/cognitive empathy in children with ASD. *Research in Developmental Disabilities, 34,* 1256–1266.

Raine, A. (2013). *The anatomy of violence: The biological roots of crime.* London: Allen Lane.

Rutter, M., Kim-Cohen, J., & Maughan, B. (2006). Continuities and discontinuities in psychopathology between childhood and adult life. *Journal of Child Psychology and Psychiatry, 47,* 276–295.

Schwartz-Watts, D. M. (2005). Asperger's disorder and murder. *Journal of the American Academy of Psychiatry and the Law, 33,* 390–393.

Sevlever, M., Roth, M. E., & Gillis, J. M. (2013). Sexual abuse and offending in autism spectrum disorders. *Sexuality and Disability, 31,* 189–200.

Shah, A. & Frith, U. (1983). An islet of ability in autistic children: A research note. *Journal of Child Psychology and Psychiatry, 24,* 613–620.

Shamay-Tsoory, S.G. (2011). The neural bases for empathy. *Neuroscientist, 17,* 18–24.

Silva, J. A., Ferrari, M. M., & Leong, G. B. (2002). The case of Jeffrey Dahmer: Sexual serial homicide from a neuropsychiatric developmental perspective. *Journal of Forensic Science, 47,* 1–13.

Siponmaa, L., Kristiansson, M., Jonson, C., Nyden, A., & Gillberg, C. (2001). Juvenile and young adult mentally disordered offenders: The role of child neuropsychiatric disorders. *Journal of the American Academy of Psychiatry and Law, 29,* 420–426.

Stokes, M., & Newton, N. (2004). Autistic spectrum disorders and stalking. *Autism, 8,* 337–338.

Stokes, M. & Newton, N. (2007). Stalking, and social and romantic functioning among adolescents and adults with Autism Spectrum Disorder. *Journal of Autism and Developmental Disorders, 37,* 1969–1986.

Suzuki, K., Nishimura, K., Sugihara, G., Nakamura, K., Tsuchiya, K. I., Matsumoto, K., ... Mori, N. (2010). Metabolite alterations in the hippocampus of high-functioning adult subjects with autism. *International Journal of Neuropsychopharmacology, 13,* 529–534.

Tantam, D. (1991). Asperger syndrome in adulthood. In U. Frith (Ed.). *Autism and Asperger syndrome* (pp. 147–183). Cambridge: Cambridge University Press.

't Hart-Kerkhoffs, L. A., Jansen, L. M., Doreleijers, T. A., Vermeiren, R., Minderaa, R. B., & Hartman, C. A. (2009). Autism spectrum disorder symptoms in juvenile suspects of sex offenses. *Journal of Clinical Psychiatry, 70*, 266–272.

Travers, B. G., Adluru, N., Ennis, C., Tromp do, P. M., Destiche, D., Doran, S., ... Alexander, A. L. (2012). Diffusion tensor imaging in autism spectrum disorder: A review. *Autism Research, 5*, 289–313.

Tremblay, R. E., Hartup, W. W., & Barcher, J. (2005) *Developmental origins of aggression*. New York, NY: Guilford Press.

van der Gronde, T., Kempes, M., van El, C., Rinne, T. & Pieters, T. (2014). Neurobiological correlates in forensic assessment: A systematic review. *PLoS ONE, 9*(10).

van der Hallen, R., Evers, K., Brewaeys, K., van den Noortgate, W., & Wagemans, J. (2015). Global processing takes time: A meta-analysis on local-global visual processing in ASD. *Psychology Bulletin, 141*, 549–573.

Wing, L. (1981). Asperger's syndrome: A clinical account. *Psychological Medicine, 11*, 115–129.

Wing, L., & Gould, J. (1979). Severe impairments of social interaction and associated abnormalities in children. Epidemiology and classification. *Journal of Autism and Developmental Disorders, 9*, 11–29.

Woodbury-Smith, M. R., Clare, I. C. H., Holland, A. J., & Kearns, A. (2006). High functioning autistic spectrum disorders, offending and other law-breaking: Findings from a community sample. *Journal of Forensic Psychiatry and Psychology, 17*, 108–120.

12

The Neuroscience of Violent Offending

Heather L. McLernon, Jeremy A. Feiger, Gianni G. Geraci, Gabriel Marmolejo, Alexander J. Roberts, and Robert A. Schug

> **Key points**
> - This chapter is an integrative review of findings from key areas of forensic neuroscience research on violent behavior.
> - In the chapter, neuroimaging studies that have identified structural and functional deficits in specific brain regions (i.e., the frontal lobe and prefrontal cortex, temporal lobe, and limbic system) in individuals characterized by violence are described.
> - Further, neuropsychological investigations have revealed neurocognitive performance deficits in areas of general and verbal intelligence and executive functioning in violent persons. Psychophysiological studies employing electroencephalography have noted similar abnormalities in the brains of murderers. Other individuals who commit acts of violence are also described in the chapter.

Terminology Explained

The **basal ganglia** are a set of interconnected nuclei in the brain that are strongly interconnected with the cerebral cortex as well as several other brain areas. The basal ganglia are important in a variety of functions but particularly related to smooth movement and goal-oriented behavior, and enacting habitual behaviors as well as learning new behaviors.[1]

The primary form of fMRI uses the **blood-oxygen-level dependent (BOLD)** contras. The technique relies on the fact that cerebral blood flow and neuronal activation are coupled. When an area of the brain is in use, blood flow to that region also increases.

The Wiley Blackwell Handbook of Forensic Neuroscience, First Edition. Edited by Anthony R. Beech, Adam J. Carter, Ruth E. Mann and Pia Rotshtein.
© 2018 John Wiley & Sons Ltd. Published 2018 by John Wiley & Sons Ltd.

The **caudate nucleus** (of which there is one in each hemisphere) is located near the basal ganglia and the thalamus. It plays an important part in memory, and in using memories to help with learning by drawing on past experience in new situations.

Diffusion tensor imaging (DTI) (a type of diffusion MRI) is a neuroimaging technique that uses water diffusion to map out white matter tracts in the brain.

The **fusiform gyrus** is a ridge in the lower part of the temporal lobe. Its functions are linked with various neural pathways related to recognition and visual processing, That is, it is involved in processes such as recognizing faces and facial expressions, and in categorizing objects, as well as tasks such as recognizing numbers, words, and colors.

Intermittent explosive disorder (IED), a diagnostic category within *DSM-5*, is a disorder involving explosive outbursts of rage, often expressed through violence. The outbursts may be low or high frequency but should occur at least three times per year for a diagnosis.

The **Iowa gambling task (IGT)** is an experimental task to assess decision making and how participants weigh up reward versus penalty. Participants are presented with four virtual decks of cards and told that they can win money from choosing certain cards but that others incur a penalty. Of the four decks, two lead to wins over time and two lead to losses over time. Gradually, most participants learn which deck of cards bring rewards, and get better at choosing them routinely. However, some participants continue to choose "bad" decks, showing an apparent desire for reward that overcomes a sensitivity to punishment.

The **precuneus** is a part of the parietal lobe. It is involved with high level functioning: episodic memory, visuospatial processing, reflections upon self, and other aspects of consciousness such as the experience of agency.

The **trail making test** is a neuropsychological test of visual attention and executive functioning. The participant has to connect a series of numbers or mixed numbers and letters, and is measured on how fast and accurately they can do this.

The **Wisconsin Card Sorting Test (WCST)** is a neuropsychological test of frontal lobe functioning, such as attention, visual memory, and processing. The participants are required to find matches for cards, but without receiving instruction about how to do so. They have to work out the rules from the feedback they get about whether they have matched rightly or wrongly. The test therefore measures the ability to use feedback to change strategy.

The **Wechsler adult intelligence scale (WAIS)** is an intelligence test designed to measure cognitive ability in adults and older adolescents. It is currently in its fourth edition (WAIS-IV, 1981) and is the most widely used IQ test in the world.

Introduction

The frequency with which human beings can inflict psychological and physical harm upon each other is alarming, and acts of violence can have serious emotional, social, and economic costs (Hart, Hoffman, Meloy, & Warren, 2014). In 2012, over one million violent crimes occurred in the US alone – one violent crime every 26 seconds (FBI, 2012). These crimes comprised nearly 11% (i.e., 1,214,462) of the 10,189,000 crimes reported to the FBI that year – 386.9 violent offenses per 100,000 US inhabitants – with the majority (60%) being aggravated assaults (FBI, 2012). In 2011, the United Nations (UN) estimated the global total number of deaths due to homicide for the previous year to be 468,000 (UNODC, 2011), and in the US alone there were almost 15,000 homicides in 2012 (FBI, 2012). The World Health Organization (WHO) estimated that a total of 830,000 lives were lost to violence in the year 2000 – a figure that corresponds to about 15 fatalities per 100,000 people per year (WHO, 2002). These figures do not include those who suffered nonlethal physical injuries or severe psychological harm, which cannot be estimated with the same precision but are probably larger by about two orders of magnitude (Krug, Dahlberg, Mercy, Zwi, & Lozano, 2002).

Violent offending adversely impacts society in a tremendous manner, and is associated with profound social, legal, and political costs (Hancock, Tapscott, & Hoaken, 2010). Victims in its wake may lose valuable possessions, health, ability to work, and at times even their lives (WHO, 2002). Additionally, preparing for, preventing, and responding to violence is astoundingly expensive. For example, figures from the European Institute for Crime Prevention and Control indicate criminal justice costs constitute approximately 3.5% of global GDP (Farrell & Clark, 2004), and the WHO estimates health care costs attributable to violence to be as much as 1% of global GDP (Krug et al., 2002). Furthermore, violent offenders make up a large proportion of incarcerated populations, and the cost of keeping them incarcerated is startling (Hancock et al., 2010). Finally, the costs of humanitarian, health care, and social services for those affected by violence are unaccounted for (Hart et al., 2014).

An understanding and treatment of the underlying causal factors of violent crime has now become paramount for society as a whole (Hancock et al., 2010). Decades of research have indicated neurobiological underpinnings of violent behavior, and have demonstrated that key neurobiological differences appear to characterize the violent offender. Enormous numbers of individuals are currently incarcerated for violent crimes in the criminal justice system (Hancock et al., 2010), and practitioners within the forensic arena are tasked with violence risk assessment (Litwack, Zapf, Groscup, & Hart, 2006), and management and treatment of violent offenders.

Given the significant strides made in neurobiological research toward the understanding of the brain-based underpinnings of violent behavior in recent decades, the forensic neuroscientist is now more than ever poised to make critical contributions to criminal justice applications regarding the adjudication, management, and treatment of violent offenders. Advances have been made in key areas of the forensic neurosciences, including neuroimaging, neuropsychology, and psychophysiology.

Neuroimaging

Brain imaging methodologies such as structural magnetic resonance imaging (sMRI), functional MRI (fMRI), single photon emission computed tomography (SPECT), and positron emission tomography (PET), have allowed researchers in recent decades to examine in vivo the brains of individuals who commit violent and aggressive crimes. Results have consistently demonstrated that those who exhibit violence and aggression have both structural and functional abnormalities in specific regions of the brain. Such abnormalities have typically been identified in the frontal lobe and prefrontal cortex, temporal lobe, and structures within the limbic system, which will now be examined.

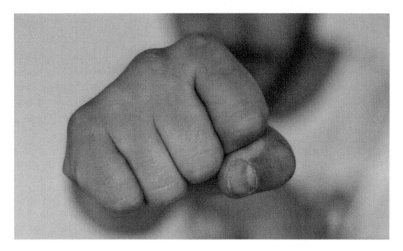

Aggression types *The literature distinguishes between two acts of aggression: reactive and instrumental. Reactive aggression has a clear trigger and reflects an impulsive response to a perceived challenge. Instrumental aggression is a planned act of violence committed to achieve a goal. It is a non-provoked act of violence.*

Source: © ToNic-Pics. Used under license from Pixabay.

The frontal lobe and prefrontal cortex

In recent decades, brain imaging studies have continued to suggest that frontal lobe structural and functional deficits play a critical role in the neurobiological processes underlying violent and antisocial behavior. Early neuroimaging studies – due to the limitations in spatial resolution of the imaging methods available at the time – often reported more macro-level analyses of brain structure and functioning (though whole-brain volume analyses have been utilized in more recent studies, e.g., Barkataki, Kumari, Das, Taylor, & Sharma, 2006), and findings often indicate associations between the frontal lobe and various forms of violent behavior. Mills and Raine (1994), for example, reported frontal lobe deficits were associated with violent offending and temporal lobe deficits with sexual offending, while violent sexual offending was associated with dysfunction in both lobes. Studies employing diffusor tensor imaging have also revealed frontal lobe white matter structural defects associated with violence (e.g., Hoptman et al., 2005; Li, Mathews, Wang, Dunn, & Kronenberger, 2005). Furthermore, several earlier PET studies indicated significantly reduced glucose metabolism in the frontal cortex, particularly the anterior medial frontal region and left white frontal matter, in violent individuals (e.g., Goyer, Andreason, Semple, & Clayton, 1994; Raine, Buchsbaum, & LaCasse, 1997; Soderstrom, Tullberg, Wikkelsö, Ekholm, & Forsman, 2000). Imaging studies of violence have traditionally focused on cortical subregions of the frontal lobes with distinctive patterns of connections with other areas of the cerebral cortex, along with structures deep below the surface of the brain. Several of these subregions have been implicated in executive functioning (see Box 12.1 for a discussion of this set of neuropsychological processes).

> **Box 12.1 Executive functioning**
>
> Executive functioning is an umbrella term referring to the cognitive processes that allow for future, goal-oriented behavior (Morgan & Lilienfeld, 2000), including being able to maintain an appropriate problem-solving set for future goal attainment (Luria, 1980). Four distinct domains are broadly encompassed by executive functioning: *volition* (i.e., capacity for intentional behavior); *planning* (i.e., identification and organization of the steps and elements needed to carry out an intention or achieve a goal); *purposive action* (i.e., translation of an intention or plan into productive, self-serving activity); and *effective performance* (i.e., self-monitoring and self-correction) (Lezak, Howieson, Loring, Hannay, & Fischer, 2004). Each domain is required for socially and contextually appropriate, and effective, self-serving behavior and conduct (Lezak et al., 2004; Spreen & Strauss, 1998), making brain regions associated with executive functioning promising areas for investigating the etiology of violent behavior.

The prefrontal region of the frontal lobe (i.e., the prefrontal cortex has been a primary region of study for earlier neuroimaging investigations of violent behavior. In terms of structural findings, Raine, Lencz, Bihrle, LaCasse, and Colletti (2000), using sMRI, identified prefrontal grey matter reductions in individuals with antisocial personality disorder (ASPD) (*DSM-5*, American Psychiatric Association, 2013), who were characterized by significantly more violence, compared to controls and individuals with substance dependence. In fact, ASPD individuals had 11% less prefrontal grey matter volume compared to controls, and nearly 14% less prefrontal grey matter volume compared to substance dependent individuals – though prefrontal white volumes did not differ significantly across the three groups. Other related structural findings include those reported by Kumari et al. (2009), who found reduced prefrontal volumes in violent schizophrenia patients compared to controls, and also that increased scores on a measure of impulsivity were associated with reduced prefrontal volumes. Similarly, Kumari et al. (2006) found reduced activation bilaterally in the frontal lobe (i.e., superior frontal gyrus), precuneus, and left inferior parietal region in violent male schizophrenia patients relative to controls, during a working memory task.

Raine et al. (1997) conducted one of the classic functioning studies in this area, examining 41 murderers pleading not guilty by reason of insanity and 41 age and sex-matched controls. This study utilized PET during a continuous performance challenge task. Results indicated murderers were characterized by reduced glucose metabolism in lateral and medial prefrontal cortical regions (i.e., left and right medial superior frontal cortex, left anterior medial cortex, and right orbital prefrontal cortex (see below)). In a later study, Raine, Meloy and colleagues (1998) found murderers characterized by affective (i.e., reactive and emotionally-based) aggression demonstrated reduced lateral and medial prefrontal functioning when compared to controls, whereas those characterized by predatory (i.e., purposeful and goal driven) aggression had reduced medial prefrontal but not lateral prefrontal functioning relative to the control group.

Raine, Stoddard, Bihrle, & Buchsbaum (1998), however, reported that only those murderers with childhood psychosocial deprivation showed reduced prefrontal glucose metabolism relative to nonviolent controls. Later studies have also implicated prefrontal deficits in violent individuals. For example, Volkow et al. (1995) found bilateral glucose metabolism reductions in prefrontal regions in violent psychiatric patients with intermittent explosive disorder (IED) compared to healthy controls. A meta-analysis of 43 structural and functional neuroimaging studies (Yang & Raine, 2009) revealed significantly reduced structure and function in prefrontal regions in antisocial individuals, and other reviews of neuroimaging studies using various imaging methods (Bassarath, 2001; Bufkin & Luttrel, 2005; Wahlund & Kristiansson, 2009) have found associations between prefrontal volumetric reductions and impulsive and predatory aggression, violence, and antisociality.

Researchers have come to recognize the prefrontal cortex as a composite of anatomically distinct subsystems rather than a unitary structure (see Dinn & Harris, 2000, for a review), and have differentiated between the functional properties of the dorsolateral prefrontal and the orbitopreofrontal/ventromedial sectors (Damasio, 1994; Lapierre, Braun, & Hodgins, 1995). These sectors may have critical yet unique associations with the emotional and behavioral components of antisocial behavior and violence. For example, orbitoprefrontal/ventromedial prefrontal pathologies present similar to psychopathy, clinical dorsolateral prefrontal syndromes appear somewhat different (Lapierre et al., 1995).

The dorsolateral prefrontal cortex (dlPFC) This area is thought to mediate executive functions (Dinn & Harris, 2000), be involved with the temporal integration of behavior (Lapierre et al., 1995), and play a critical role in inhibitory control, which is required for the development of moral conduct and moral cognition (Kochanska, Murray & Coy, 1997). Structural deficits in the dlPFC have been identified in numerous types of antisocial populations (Crowley et al., 2010; Dalwani et al., 2011; Fairchild et al., 2013; Glenn, Raine, & Schug (2009); Syngelaki, Moore, Savage, Fairchild, & Van Goozen, 2009; Völlum et al., 2010; Yang & Raine, 2009; Zamboni, Huey, Krueger, Nichelli, & Grafman, 2008), including those associated with violence (Laakso et al., 2002).

The orbitoprefrontal cortex (OPFC) Also referred to as the ventromedial prefrontal cortex (vmPFC), this area is critically involved in guiding behavior by processing the reward–punishment value of stimuli, and thus is crucial to controlling violent behavior (Damasio, 1994). The OPFC, however, modulates sensitivity to reinforcement contingencies (Dinn & Harris, 2000), and is involved with inhibiting inadequately motivated actions and modulating aggressive behavior and autonomic reactivity (Lapierre et al., 1995). This system contributes more to social and self-awareness than the dlPFC in humans (Damasio, 1994; Lapierre et al., 1995).

Regarding imaging findings related to violence, structural deficits in the OFC have been identified in violent males diagnosed with ASPD and type 2 alcoholism (Laakso et al., 2002), violent offenders with substance abuse disorders (Schiffer et al., 2011), men with ASPD (Raine et al., 2011), and aggressive and impulsive psychiatric inpatients (Antonucci et al., 2006). These deficits have also been associated with gender differences (i.e., girls more so than boys) in children characterized by aggression and behavioral problems (Boes et al., 2008). Functional deficits in the OFC have been identified in violent individuals with schizophrenia and other disorders associated with aggression relative to nonviolent controls (e.g., Mathews et al., 2005; Kumari et al., 2006; Joyal et al., 2007). They have also been associated with increased lifestyle and antisocial psychopathic traits in violent schizophrenia patients (Dolan & Fullam; 2009). Structural and functional studies have additionally identified abnormalities in the connectivity between the OPFC and amygdala in psychopathic individuals and adolescents with conduct disorder (CD) (Marsh et al., 2011; Passamonti et al., 2010).

The temporal lobe

The temporal lobe of the brain has been implicated in several different functions: namely, memory retention and storage, organization of sensory input, language production, visual perception, and emotional responses. Structures of the limbic system, including the amygdala and hippocampus (discussed separately below) are also located within the temporal lobes. The temporal lobe has been a common region of interest in neuroimaging investigations of violent and antisocial behavior, which have foundations in the classic studies of murderers using electroencephalography (EEG) that noted abnormalities in brain functioning in this region (Hill & Pond, 1952; Mundy-Castle, 1955; Stafford-Clark & Taylor, 1949). Researchers using both structural and functional neuroimaging methods have identified deficits in temporal regions which have been related to various forms of antisociality, aggression, and violence (Dolan, 2010).

Structural deficits in temporal regions, including various forms of volume reductions, have been reported in studies of antisocial individuals. For example, Dolan, Deakin, Roberts, and Anderson (2002) identified 20% reductions in volume in frontal and temporal lobes in impulsive-aggressive men with ASPD compared to controls. Other studies examining reduced grey matter have consistently found similar results in individuals diagnosed with ASPD, CD, and psychopathy (Kruesi, Casanova, Mannheim, & Johnson-Bilder, 2004; Gregory et al., 2012; Müller et al., 2008; Pridmore et al., 2005). Using sMRI, Barkataki et al. (2006) compared volumes of numerous brain structures among 13 men with ASPD, 13 men with schizophrenia and a history of violence, 15 nonviolent men with schizophrenia, and 15 healthy nonviolent male controls. Results indicated men with ASPD were characterized by reduced whole-brain and temporal lobe volume, as well as increased putamen volume, compared to controls. Using a cortical thinning approach, Yang & Raine (2009) identified significantly thinner cortical grey matter in the right frontal and temporal cortices in psychopaths compared to non-psychopathic controls. Finally, Huebner et al. (2008), using sMRI, identified bilateral temporal lobe volume reductions in a sample of 23 boys diagnosed with CD compared to age- and IQ-matched controls.

Several literature reviews of functional imaging studies have also consistently indicated that aggressive and violent individuals tend to be characterized by functional deficits in the temporal lobe (Bufkin & Luttrel, 2005). Regarding studies using PET imaging, Volkow et al. (1995) found reduced glucose metabolism in medial temporal regions in eight violent psychiatric patients compared to eight normal controls; while Raine, Buchsbaum, and LaCasse (1997) found abnormal glucose metabolism asymmetry in the medial temporal lobe (reduced activity in the left hemisphere compared to the right) in murderers relative to controls.

Wong, Lumsden, Fenton, and Fenwick (1997) also reported that schizophrenia patients with single or minor offenses demonstrated reduced activity in anterior temporal lobe structures compared to normal controls. Furthermore, in a structural and functional imaging study (using both sMRI and SPECT) using a sample of 21 impulsive violent offenders referred for pretrial forensic evaluations and 11 healthy controls, Soderstrom et al. (2000) found no structural deficits among violent offenders, though reduced regional blood flow in the right medial temporal and right angular gyri was noted in the violent offender group when compared to controls.

Goethals et al. (2005) also reported that patients with either borderline personality disorder or ASPD showed reduced right cerebral blood flow in both right temporal and prefrontal regions compared to controls, but that those characterized by violence also were characterized by structural deficits. Finally, in an earlier fMRI study, Kiehl et al. (2001) found that criminal psychopaths demonstrated overactivation in the bilateral fronto-temporal cortex when processing emotional stimuli. In aggregate, consistent evidence from structural and functional neuroimaging studies continues to implicate the temporal lobe in various forms of violent and antisocial behavior.

The limbic system

The two limbic structures that have received the most attention in the neuroimaging literature on violence are the *hippocampus* and the *amygdala*.

The hippocampus This area is thought to play a key role in learning and memory – particularly in the consolidation of explicit memories of facts and events (Nolte, 2002). With the adjacent parahippocampal gyrus, it is also thought to be involved in regulating aggression and contextual fear conditioning, as well as modulating information for impulse control and moral reasoning. As such, the hippocampus may contribute to the emotional dysregulation, impulsivity, and disinhibition characterizing some antisocial and violent groups (Raine et al., 2005; Yang et al., 2010). Structural imaging studies of individuals characterized by antisociality and violence have identified deficits in hippocampal region, and psychopathic individuals – a key area of study – have demonstrated hippocampal deficits relative to comparisons (Laakso et al., 2001; Raine et al., 2005; Tiihonen et al., 2008). Regarding findings from violent populations, Barkataki and colleagues (2006) found reduced whole-brain and hippocampal volumes and increased putamen size in violent men with schizophrenia (but not nonviolent men with schizophrenia) compared to healthy controls. Yang et al. (2010) also identified reduced grey matter in the hippocampus and parahippocampal gyrus in murderers with schizophrenia, and in the parahippocampal gyrus in murderers without schizophrenia, relative to normal controls.

Functional imaging studies have also identified associations between hippocampal deficits and various forms of violent and antisocial behavior. For example, in their classic PET study of murderers, Raine et al. (1997) found reduced glucose metabolism in the left medial temporal/hippocampal region and increased glucose metabolism in the right medial temporal/hippocampal region in murderers compared to controls. Using both sMRI and SPECT, Soderstrom et al. (2000) subsequently found significantly reduced regional blood flow bilaterally in the hippocampus in 21 impulsive violent offenders relative to 11 healthy controls. Similarly, Kiehl et al. (2001) found criminal psychopaths were characterized by significantly reduced emotion-related activity in the amygdala/hippocampal formation, parahippocampal gyrus, and other limbic regions relative to criminal nonpsychopaths and controls; and Soderstrom et al. (2002) found reductions in right cerebral blood flow in the hippocampi and caudate nuclei to be associated with increased levels of the interpersonal features of psychopathy in a sample of 32 violent offenders. Finally, in an fMRI study, Lee et al. (2009) found male spouse batterers, in comparison to a similarly-matched control group of non-batterers, were characterized by increased neural hyper-responsivity to images representing aggressive threat in cortical and subcortical regions including the hippocampus fusiform gyrus. Taken together, results from these neuroimaging studies indicate that structural and functional deficits in the hippocampus may be associated with various forms of violence, though continued research is needed to clarify its exact role in the neurobiological underpinnings of violent behavior.

The amygdala This area receives a wide variety of sensory inputs, and is involved in emotion-related aspects of learning (Nolte, 2002). It has also has demonstrated key involvement in the neural circuitry associated with emotional information processing (Dolan & Fullam, 2009). Glenn et al. (2014), in a recent review, discuss how structural and functional deficits in the amygdala may manifest in differential forms of violent and antisocial behavior. For example, reductions in amygdala volume and activity have been identified in psychopathic individuals characterized by blunted emotional responding and cold, calculated aggression; while those demonstrating more impulsive, reactive aggressive behaviors may show increased amygdala reactivity.

Regarding structural neuroimaging findings, an sMRI study by Wong et al. (1997) reported that violent schizophrenia patients demonstrated bilateral volume reductions in the amygdala compared to patient controls characterized by single or minor offenses. More recent results from a subsample of 56 men from a larger longitudinal study of 503 male participants (Pardini, Raine, Erickson, & Loeber, 2014) indicate that men with reduced amygdala volume demonstrated increased levels of aggression and psychopathic features over the course of the lifetime at age 26. In the latter study, reduced amygdala volume was also associated with aggressive and violent behavior and psychopathic traits at a three-year follow-up. Finally, Yang and Raine (2009) found individuals with psychopathic features to be characterized by significant bilateral volumetric reductions in the amygdala relative to controls, and that surface abnormalities were localized in the basolateral, lateral, cortical, and central nuclei. Significant negative correlations between amygdala volumes and psychopathy levels were most robust for emotional and interpersonal features of psychopathy.

Earlier functional studies identified activation deficits in the amygdala in violent and antisocial individuals. For example, in the classic PET study by Raine et al. (1997), abnormal asymmetries of activity (reduced left hemisphere relative to right hemisphere) were identified in the amygdala and thalamus in murderers compared to controls. Later functional imaging studies employed methods that were driven more so by hypotheses specific to the functioning of the amygdala – such as the processing of negative emotions. Müller et al. (2003), for example, found increased activation in the right amygdala and prefrontal regions in six psychopaths (compared to six controls) when viewing images depicting threatening, violent, or distressing scenes or objects. Herpertz et al. (2008) later found increased amygdala activation during the viewing of negative images relative to neutral images in male adolescents with childhood-onset CD compared to controls. On balance, Sterzer, Stadler, Krebs, Kleinschmidt, and Poustka (2005) found *reduced* responsivity to emotionally negative images in the left amygdala in the more aggressive members of a sample of 13 adolescents with severe CD – suggesting that aggression may be linked to deficits in emotional stimuli recognition and the cognitive control of behavior. Mixed results, however, may reflect differences in the operationalization of antisocial behavior (Glenn & Raine, 2014).

Deficits in emotional functioning in individuals characterized by violence and antisociality have also been examined using facial expressions in functional imaging studies of the amygdala. In humans, facial expressions may serve as powerful nonverbal communications, adding an emotional framework or content to social interactions. Neural circuitry involving the amygdala and prefrontal cortex is thought to mediate the interpretation of emotional cues from faces expressing anger.

At the neurofunctional level, this same circuit also plays a critical role in the regulation of emotion and behavior, including anger and aggression. In fact, deficits in information processing (e.g., misperceiving a neutral facial expression as a threatening one) – which may be associated with dysfunction in this circuitry – could be causal antecedents to maladaptive emotions and behaviors such as aggression (see review in Coccaro, McCloskey, Fitzgerald, & Phan, 2007). Persons with intermittent explosive disorder (IED) – an illness marked by repeated unplanned outbursts of aggression, which are disproportionate in intensity relative to situational factors and result in destruction of property and interpersonal harm – may be particularly characterized by deficits in this circuit.

Coccaro et al. (2007) found individuals with IED to demonstrate increased amygdala reactivity and reduced OFC activation to angry faces compared to healthy controls. Furthermore, individuals with histories of aggression did not demonstrate amygdala–OPFC connectivity when presented with faces expressing anger. In a subsequent fMRI study of 24 male schizophrenia patients with violent offense convictions (Dolan & Fullam, 2009), reduced BOLD responses in the amygdala (and negative correlations between psychopathy scores and amygdala responses) during exposure to images of fearful faces were observed in patients with high levels of psychopathy. Positive correlations were also observed between psychopathy scores and neural activation in the amygdala and inferior prefrontal regions for disgust, but also negative correlations for anger. Given that aberrant emotional experience intuitively may play a key role in various forms of violent and antisocial behavior, the amygdala remains a promising region of study in neuroimaging investigations of violence and antisociality.

Other brain regions of interest

While various sectors of the frontal lobe, temporal lobe and limbic system have received the lion's share of attention in the literature on the neuroimaging of violence, other brain regions have been identified which also show associations with violent and antisocial behavior. For example, in a recent comparison of 26 violent men with ASPD or schizophrenia and a history of serious violence, and 30 nonviolent controls (15 with schizophrenia and 15 healthy individuals), Kumari et al. (2013) found reduced thalamic volume (see Box 12.2 for a description of this area) in violent men with childhood psychosocial deprivation, relative to violent men without psychosocial deprivation and healthy controls.

In a subsequent study, Kumari et al. (2014) found seriously violent men with ASPD or schizophrenia, but not nonviolent men with schizophrenia, demonstrated significantly reduced anterior cingulate cortex (see Box 12.2) volume relative to healthy comparisons. Furthermore, a higher proportion of seriously violent ASPD and schizophrenia patients were characterized by psychosocial deprivation – in particular severe physical abuse – compared to nonviolent schizophrenia patients and controls. Anterior cingulate volumes also demonstrated significant negative correlations with ratings of total psychosocial deprivation, as well as physical and sexual abuse. Such findings underscore the complexities of the functional and anatomical underpinnings of violent criminal offending, and indicate a need for continued examination of other brain areas beyond the traditional regions of interest in neuroimaging work on violence.

> **Box 12.2   The thalamus and the anterior cingulate cortex**
>
> The **thalamus** is located near the center of the left and right hemispheres and adjacent to the basal ganglia. It is the largest structure that makes up a division of the forebrain called the diencephalon which surround the third ventricle. The thalamus is composed of 20 large nuclei. It functions as an information relay station, routing sensory information to appropriate areas of the cerebral cortex, information between cortical regions, and communicates information from other forebrain as well as brainstem regions.
>
> The **anterior cingulate cortex (ACC)** is situated below the cerebral cortices, and wrapped around the corpus callosum. It is involved in the simultaneous monitoring of personal and environmental information and allocation of attention to the most pertinent information in the environment at a particular moment in time. It first appeared in animals demonstrating maternal behavior, and provides the basic circuitry for communication, cooperation, and empathy as it can be subdivided into affective and cognitive parts, and therefore integrates emotional and attentional processing.

Overall, results from neuroimaging studies have consistently shown that individuals characterized by violence, aggression, and antisociality demonstrate both structural and functional abnormalities in regions of the brain including the frontal lobe and prefrontal cortex, temporal lobe, and limbic system. As will be discussed further, these findings largely overlap with those from studies utilizing other neuroscience techniques, such as neuropsychology and psychophysiology, which we will now examine.

Neuropsychology

Research dating back several decades has shown a continued interest in the applications of neuropsychology (i.e., the indirect, behavior-based assessment of brain dysfunction) in the empirical understanding of violence. Neuropsychological investigations of antisocial and aggressive behavior in general and violence in particular have largely focused on specific domains of cognitive functioning such as intelligence (i.e., general, verbal, and spatial) and executive abilities.

Gender differences of violent offending *Violent offending is more common in male than female. It adversely impacts society in a tremendous manner, and is associated with profound social, legal, and political costs.*

Source: © Isabellaquintana. Used under license from 699pic.

General intelligence

Deficits in general intellectual functioning (i.e., intelligence, IQ or full-scale IQ) are the best-replicated cognitive correlate of antisocial, violent, and criminal behavior among individuals without mental illness (Wilson & Herrnstein, 1985). Regarding homicide offenders, published neuropsychological data from murderers has almost exclusively related to intelligence, and has historically been rare and for the most part incidental (i.e., when reported, it is not the main focus of a given study). Such incidental data in the form of case histories began to appear toward the middle of the last century (e.g., Bender & Curran, 1940; Patterson, 1942; Rosanoff, 1943), wherein IQ scores were described ranging from 32 to 153.

Other samples of murderers have included limited IQ data among demographic descriptors (e.g., Eronen, Hakola, & Tiihonen, 1996; Harbort & Mokros, 2001; Myers, Scott, Burgess, & Burgess, 1995; Pagan & Smith, 1979), as have samples that subsumed murderers within larger categories of offenders (Cornell, Roberts, & Oram, 1997; Valliant, Asu, Cooper, & Mammola, 1984). Mean IQ scores around one standard deviation below normal have been reported in some descriptive studies of murderers (Cole, Fisher, & Cole, 1968; Fisher, 1999; Warnick, 2007), while relatively normal IQ distributions have been reported in others (e.g., Snook, Cullen, Mokros, & Harbort, 2005).

Murderers have also demonstrated intellectual deficits in earlier comparative studies, which involved comparisons to other types of offenders (Hays, Solway, & Schreiner, 1978; Kahn, 1967; Wagner & Klein, 1977), and the general population (Deiker, 1973). However, more recent comparative studies have not found significant group differences in IQ performance between murderers and other criminal subgroups (Jamison, 2006; Langevin, 2003). Additionally, some authors (Blackburn, 1975; Lester, Purdue, & Brookhart, 1974) have compared the intellectual abilities of specific types and subtypes of murderers, suggesting that this specific group of violent offenders may be characterized by heterogeneity in intellectual functioning.

The neuropsychological correlates of homicide within the context of severe mental illnesses such as schizophrenia have also been explored in the literature, and findings related to the intellectual functioning of these specific types of violent offenders have been reported. While only small numbers of individuals with severe mental illnesses such as schizophrenia actually become violent (e.g., Swanson et al., 2006), these individuals nonetheless appear to be at a greater risk for violence compared to those without mental illness, and present in forensic populations at higher proportions than in the general population (Schug & Fradella, 2014). As such an understanding of the neurological underpinnings of coexisting schizophrenia and violence may be of tremendous value to the forensic practitioner.

A handful of investigators reporting IQ and other neuropsychological data (Barkataki et al., 2005; Eriksson, 2006; Kumari et al., 2006; Nestor, Haycock, Doiron, Kelly, & Kelly, 1995; Silver, Goodman, Knoll, Isakov, & Modai, 2005; Wong et al., 1997) have reported the inclusion within their samples of homicidal individuals with schizophrenia, though these individuals are subsumed within larger groups of schizophrenic violent offenders and thus cannot be characterized on their own.

Other authors have separated violent from nonviolent individuals with schizophrenia for comparative analyses – an important methodological consideration given reduced general intellectual functioning can be largely characteristic of the illness itself (Schug & Raine, 2009). For example, in a recent South Korean study of aggression, neuropsychological function, and a genetic polymorphism, Chung, Chung, Jung, Chang, and Hong (2010) examined group differences in neuropsychological test performance among 51 male schizophrenia patients who committed homicide, 50 male schizophrenia patients who had not committed homicide, and 50 healthy male controls. Results indicated that while no differences in neuropsychological functioning were observed among schizophrenia groups, schizophrenia patients who committed homicide had significantly reduced IQ scores compared to controls.

In a study of male secure forensic hospital patients with schizophrenia, Fullam and Dolan (2008) found no group differences in IQ scores (i.e., premorbid IQ, using the National Adult Reading Test (NART), and current IQ, using the Wechsler Abbreviated Scale of Intelligence (WASI-R)) or scores on tests of spatial planning ability and cognitive set shifting between those characterized by inpatient violence (i.e., physical aggression to staff, inpatients, or property; $n = 39$) and those who were nonviolent ($n = 49$). However, a significant negative correlation between WASI-R IQ score and rate of violent incidents per year since admission was observed. In an English sample of male and female first-episode psychosis patients, Hodgins et al. (2011) found those with convictions for violent offenses obtained significantly lower IQ scores than those without convictions, on both current (WAIS-R) and premorbid (NART) measures. Specifically, violent offenders performed comparatively poorer on three subtests of the WAIS-R – digit symbol, which assesses processing speed, and vocabulary and comprehension, which index verbal intelligence. Violent offenders were also distinguished by significantly poorer performance on measures of verbal learning, short-term verbal recall, and visual-spatial perception and organization.

In aggregate, neuropsychological studies of individuals with and without schizophrenia have shown how deficits in general intellectual functioning may be critically associated with violent offending.

Verbal and spatial/performance intelligence

The identification of component verbal (VIQ) versus spatial/performance intelligence (PIQ) deficits has also proven useful in the understanding of the etiological mechanisms underlying antisocial and violent behavior. Reduced VIQ as opposed to PIQ – possibly indicating left-hemispheric dysfunction – is widely reported in adult antisocial populations (Raine, 1993), and appears characteristic of both males and females across studies of antisocial individuals from different age groups (Isen, 2010). One theoretical explanation for this phenomenon is that deficits in verbal functioning may adversely affect the development of language-based self-control mechanisms (Luria, 1980), which may lead ultimately to failure in socialization (Eriksson, Hodgins, & Tengström, 2005) and subsequent violence.

While PIQ > VIQ discrepancies were not identified in murderers in some earlier studies (Deiker, 1973; DeWolfe & Ryan, 1984; Kahn, 1968), subsequent neuropsychological investigations have nonetheless shown verbal as opposed to spatial deficits to be characteristic of those who commit violent offenses. For example, Petee and Walsh (1987) found PIQ > VIQ discrepancy scores differentiated between group means on violent behavior in a sample of juvenile probationers; and Rasmussen, Almvik, and Levander (2001) found verbal deficits to be associated with histories of violent crimes in a Norwegian sample of prison inmates. In another study of 25 incarcerated violent offenders, Broomhall (2005) examined differences in neuropsychological performance among those characterized by primarily instrumental and primarily reactive violence. While no statistically significant group differences were observed for mean full-scale IQ, VIQ, or PIQ, the difference between VIQ and PIQ scores (i.e., PIQ > VIQ) was statistically significant for the reactive but not the instrumental group.

Nestor et al. (2002), in a study of 26 murderers, in a maximum-security forensic hospital, used the WAIS-R, Wechsler Memory Scale-Revised (WMS-R) (Wechsler, 1987), The Wide Range Achievement Test-Revised (WRAT-R), and Wisconsin Card Sorting Test (WCST) to distinguish between high psychopathy and high psychosis individuals. Results indicated that the psychotic group had higher verbal than performance IQs, and the reverse was true for the psychopathic group. Finally, in an English sample, Barkataki et al. (2005) found both incarcerated patients with schizophrenia who had a history of violence as well as hospitalized nonviolent schizophrenia patients demonstrated significantly lower VIQ and PIQ scores than controls. In all, component verbal versus spatial intelligence abilities continue to be a promising area of study in neuropsychological investigations of violent offending.

Executive functioning

In neuropsychological work, deficits in executive functioning (see Box 12.1) are thought to represent frontal lobe impairment, and are indicated by performance errors on neuropsychological tests of strategy formation, cognitive flexibility, or impulsivity (i.e., category, maze-tracing, Stroop interference, card sorting, verbal fluency and tower tests, and go/no-go and gambling tasks). Neuropsychological studies of executive functioning deficits and antisocial behavior have traditionally focused on categorical clinical syndromes (i.e., ASPD, CD, psychopathy), and legal/judicial concepts (criminality and delinquency). In a classic quantitative review of 39 studies, Morgan and Lilienfeld (2000) found overall executive functioning deficits in antisocial individuals compared to controls, and strongest effects for the Porteus Mazes test (Porteus, 1955) and antisociality, defined by judicial status.

Links between aggression and executive functioning deficits have also been reported in studies of adults (Giancola, Roth, & Parrott, 2006; Giancola & Zeichner, 1994) as well as children and adolescents (Raaijmakers et al., 2008; Séguin, Pihl, Harden, Tremblay, & Boulerice, 1995). Evidence for executive functioning deficits in populations of antisocial youths has historically varied depending upon sample characteristics, control groups, assessment measures, executive functioning operationalizations, and methodology (Moffitt & Henry, 1989; Teichner & Golden, 2000), and more recent findings have been mixed, with executive functioning deficits characterizing some antisocial children and adolescents but not others (Cauffman, Steinberg, & Piquero, 2005; Kronenberger et al., 2005; Moffitt, Lynam, & Silva, 1994; Nigg et al., 2004; Raine et al., 2005; White et al., 1994). Important to consider, however, is the development of executive functioning along with the ongoing myelination of the frontal cortex into adolescence and beyond (Nigg et al., 2004; Raine, 2002), which may explain differential patterns of executive functioning deficits among children and adults.

Specifically related to violent offending, executive functioning deficits have recently been associated with: (1) aggressive (e.g., male batterers), violent, and antisocial personality-disordered populations (Dolan, 2012; Dolan & Park, 2002; Hancock et al., 2012; Stanford et al., 2007; Teichner et al., 2001); (2) suicidal behavior (Keilp et al., 2013); and (3) reactive versus instrumental violent offenders (Broomhall, 2005). Furthermore, violent ASPD offenders with and without psychopathy have demonstrated similar deficits in terms of "cool executive functioning" (top-down processes – subsumed by the dlPFC and ventrolateral PFC – that are distinctly cognitive in nature, such as working memory, response inhibition, planning, sustained attention, and attentional set shifting) and "hot executive functioning" (processes with an affective, motivational, or incentive/reward component – subsumed by ventromedial connections between the mesolimbic reward pathway and the vmPFC – such as appraisal of the motivational significance of a stimulus in emotional decision making; De Brito et al., 2013).

Other studies have examined associations between specific aspects of both executive functioning and violence. For example, in a Japanese study of male juvenile offenders and delinquents, Miura (2009) found no group differences in performance on purported measures of dlPFC functioning (i.e., a shortened version of the WCST, a new modified version of the WCST, the Keio version (KWCST), categories completed, and OPFC functioning (the IGT) among those who had committed violence against others ($n = 142$) and those who were nonviolent ($n = 167$). However, subsequent univariate and multivariate regression analysis indicated that a lower score on KWCST categories completed was significantly associated with violence.

Hancock et al. (2010) identified broad and pervasive executive functioning deficits in a sample of 77 federal prisoners. Additionally, poor performance on executive functioning measures was related to the frequency and severity of violent offending, but not the frequency of nonviolent or total offending. Furthermore, offenders who demonstrated poorer performance on measures of impulsivity, concept formation and cognitive flexibility were more likely to have committed a larger number of violent offenses than those with better performance. Interestingly, offenders demonstrating more intact expressive language abilities were also more likely to have committed a severe violent offense. Hoaken, Allaby, and Earle (2007) found similar results in a sample of Canadian medium security prisoners. Results from this study indicated that while violent and nonviolent offenders performed more poorly on executive functioning measures when compared to controls, the nonviolent group performed better on these measures than the violent group, though differences were not statistically significant.

Regarding homicide offenders, it is worth noting that the first study of murderers to report neuropsychological data on a specific domain of functioning (i.e., executive functioning, measured via the Stroop interference test) was conducted by Heilbrun Jr. (1982) – though this sample was not comprised solely of murderers. Other researchers have used executive functioning tests such as the category test, trail making test, Tower of London test, and WCST in subsequent studies of murderers (Langevin, Ben-Aron, Wortzman, Dickey, & Handy, 1987; Langevin, Ben-Aron, Wright, Marchese, & Handy, 1988; Ticehurst, Ryan, & Hughes, 1992) and comparisons of murderers and controls (Cornell et al., 1997). More recently, Hanlon, Rubin, Jensen, and Daoust (2010) identified executive functioning deficits in single as opposed to multiple homicide victims in indigent murder defendants and death row inmates.

Regarding studies of executive functioning in violent individuals with schizophrenia, Barber (1994) compared the performance of 14 male schizophrenic murderers from a maximum security psychiatric hospital and 14 male schizophrenia outpatients from a psychiatric hospital was compared across ten neuropsychological tests, including attention, executive function, language, and memory tasks. Results showed that murderers with schizophrenia demonstrated significantly better performance on two executive functioning tests (classical Weigl and WISC mazes errors), and overall outperformed non-murderers on all but two of the measures. However, non-murderers demonstrated significantly higher psychotic symptomatology (i.e., delusions, flat affect, and psychomotor retardation) compared to murderers, and higher rates of hallucinations, incoherence, and poverty of speech – which may have adversely affected their overall performance.

Similar results have been reported in subsequent studies. For example, Barkataki et al. (2005) found incarcerated schizophrenia patients with a history of violence demonstrated poorer performance than nonviolent schizophrenia patients on one measure of executive functioning (i.e., the WCST). Both schizophrenia groups demonstrated reduced performance relative to healthy controls and violent patients with ASPD on this measure – in fact, the violent schizophrenia group made more perseverative errors than any other group. On an additional executive functioning measure (the Stroop color test), both schizophrenia groups performed poorer than healthy controls, and violent ASPD patients performed significantly better relative to violent schizophrenia patients. The authors opined that the specific neuropsychological deficits observed in this sample may have been more attributable to schizophrenia than violence. More recently, Hanlon, Coda, Cobia, and Rubin(2012) also identified executive functioning deficits in schizophrenic murderers relative to nonviolent men with schizophrenia.

Studies of executive functioning in violent individuals have also assessed other domains of neuropsychological functioning. For example, Raine et al. found no differences in performance on the continuous performance task (CPT) – a measure of attention – between murderers and controls; and subsequent studies revealed no CPT performance differences between individual subgroups of murderers (i.e., murderers with/without psychosocial deprivation, and predatory/affective murderers) (Raine, Meloy et al., 1998; Raine et al., 1998). In the previously mentioned study by Barkataki et al. (2005), both violent and nonviolent schizophrenic groups performed significantly worse on memory tests when compared to both the control and ASPD group. On balance, Silver et al. (2004) found no significant differences in neuropsychological test performance scores (i.e., in executive functioning, attention, visual orientation, working memory, memory for faces and objects, and motor function) between schizophrenia patients with a history of severe violence and those who were nonviolent – though both groups of schizophrenia patients performed more poorly on these tests when compared to the control group. Similarly, Chung et al. (2010) found no group differences on neuropsychological measures of verbal learning, visuospatial abilities, and executive functioning among male schizophrenia patients who committed homicide compared to those who had not – though both patient groups demonstrated poorer performance relative to healthy controls. Results from these studies further underscore the cognitive heterogeneity of various types of violent offenders, and the need for continued research in this area.

In summary, neuropsychological investigations have revealed cognitive deficits in specific domains of functioning (i.e., general and verbal versus spatial intelligence, as well as executive functioning) in individuals characterized by violence. These deficits overlap with structural and functional neuroimaging findings and correspond conceptually with regions of the brain previously identified in associations with violent offending.

Psychophysiology

Lykken's (1957) seminal work involving psychophysiological processes in psychopaths largely marked the dawn of the modern era of the neuroscientific investigation of crime. Psychophysiological studies (which examine brain-behavior relationships in the framework of central and peripheral physiological responses) have since focused upon the cardiovascular, electrodermal, and electrocortical concomitants of violent and antisocial behavior (see reviews in Lorber, 2004; Schug, Raine, & Wilcox, 2007).

Electroencephalography was among the first of the psychophysiological techniques used in the neuroscientific study of violent offenders – arguably providing key foundational material for today's more technologically advanced "higher-tech" brain imaging studies of violence and aggression. The electroencephalogram (EEG) is a recording of the difference in electrical potential between various points on the surface of the scalp (Hugdahl, 1995), thought to reflect the depolarizations of the dendritic trees of pyramidal cells in the cerebral cortex (Raine, 1993). EEG can be separated into different frequency components, most commonly *delta* (0–4 Hz), *theta* (4–8 Hz), *alpha* (8–12 Hz), and *beta* (13–30 Hz); and these components are thought to represent different levels along a continuum of consciousness (see Box 12.3).

> **Box 12.3** EEG frequency components
>
> **Delta** (0–4 Hz) waves are associated with deep sleep, as well as brain pathologies such as tumors when present in individuals that are awake.
> **Theta** (4–8 Hz) waves are predominantly associated with drowsiness and low levels of alertness, and appear to be related to the cessation of pleasurable activity, hypnagogic imagery, REM (rapid eye movement) sleep, problem solving, attention, and hypnosis.
> **Alpha** (8–12 Hz) waves are related to relaxed wakefulness and lack of active cognitive processes.
> **Beta** (13–30 Hz) waves are associated with vigilance and alertness.
> **Gamma** (30–70 Hz or higher) waves are thought to reflect the brain's integration of multiple stimuli into a coherent whole (Raine, 1993; Stern, Ray, & Quigley, 2001).

In the conscious individual, all frequencies are present; though differences in the relative amount of power existing in these main frequency bands may be observed among individuals (Raine, 1993). Resting EEG (i.e., recordings made while an individual is sitting relaxed and motionless) is characteristic and is associated with specific personality and cognitive features (Vogel & Schalt, 1979).

Reviews of the literature indicate that hundreds of studies have employed EEG measures in populations of antisocial individuals – including criminals, delinquents, psychopaths, and violent offenders (Raine, 1993). While many studies have identified EEG abnormalities in violent offenders who recidivate, EEG studies of psychopathic individuals have reported results which are much more inconsistent (Ishikawa & Raine, 2002). Evidence for the EEG underpinnings of violence specifically can be gleaned from EEG studies of murderers and other types of violent individuals. Despite this initial flourish of interest, and several decades of subsequent research, the literature on the EEG recordings of murderers remains significantly less developed, relative to the larger body of work, compiled on the EEG functioning of antisocial individuals in general.

Current understanding of the EEG underpinnings of violence has its foundations in EEG recordings of murderers, which were reported in descriptive studies dating back to the middle of the last century. Earlier studies focused mainly on reporting prevalence rates of EEG abnormalities among samples of murderers, and describing these abnormalities in terms of particular types (i.e., mild nonspecific, severe nonspecific, and focal/epileptic) and locations observed – including abnormalities specific to individual EEG components (i.e., delta, theta, alpha, beta) and other complexes or activities (e.g., spikes, sharp waves, etc.) (Hill & Pond, 1952; Mundy-Castle, 1955; Stafford-Clark & Taylor, 1949). The abnormalities described varied greatly in nature and scope, though many tended to be identified in temporal regions. Furthermore, some studies historically have included murderers with mental disorders such as schizophrenia within samples of homicide offenders (Gatzke-Kopp, Raine, Buchsbaum, & LaCasse, 2001; Mundy-Castle, 1955; Stafford-Clark & Taylor, 1949), though formal EEG comparisons of schizophrenic to non-schizophrenic murderers in the literature are rare. Studies in this area are often limited by smaller sample sizes and lack of control groups.

Prevalence rates One key aspect of the literature on EEG abnormalities and violence has been the reporting of prevalence rates of EEG abnormalities themselves. Subsequent reporting of EEG in both larger descriptive and individual case studies of murders has traditionally been incidental (Green, Leon-Barth, Venus, & Lucey, 2001; Lewis et al., 1988; Lewis et al., 1985; Mouridsen & Tolstrup, 1988), though the EEG-homicide literature is often a bit richer in clinical detail than that from neuropsychological studies of homicide offenders. While some more contemporary studies (e.g., Blake, Pincus, & Buckner, 1995) report prevalence rates of EEG abnormalities among murderers similar to those found in earlier studies, rates of 9–60% have been reported recently in the literature (Driver, West, & Faulk, 1974; Sakuta & Fukushima, 1998; Winkler & Kove, 1961) – rates that are more or less increased relative to the 5–20% reported in the general population (Mednick, Volavka, Gabrielli, & Itil, 1982).

Location A second key aspect of the literature on EEG abnormalities and violence is the location within the brain of the abnormality. More-generalized abnormalities (i.e., not necessarily localized to one specific brain region) have been reported. In a study of maximum-security psychiatric hospital patients, Wong et al. (1994) found increased rates of EEG abnormalities in those classified as most violent compared to moderately violent and least violent groups, with a trend for the most violent group to be characterized by loss of basic rhythms and generalized slowing. Additionally, 20% of EEG abnormalities in the most violent group were located in temporal regions – rates increased six- to eightfold relative to those in the same region of moderately and least violent groups, respectively. Asymmetry is another abnormality found in EEG recordings associated with violence. Convit, Czobor, and Volavka (1991) found that in a group of violent psychiatric inpatients, EEG showed asymmetry in frontotemporal regions that was significantly correlated to violence. Pillmann et al. (1999) found left hemisphere focal EEG abnormalities to be related to significantly increased rates of violent offenses in a larger sample ($n = 222$) of defendants undergoing pretrial assessment and evaluation of criminal responsibility.

More-specific locations of EEG abnormalities have also been discussed. Similar types of EEG abnormalities (i.e., diffuse or symmetric slowing, bi-temporal spikes, temporoparietal sharp waves and slowing, and focal slowing) have also been reported more recently (Blake et al., 1995). Evans and Park (1997) found the greatest concentrations of multiple abnormalities in bilateral frontal, right temporal, and parietal sites in a sample of 20 murderers; while Green et al. (2001) found frontal EEG abnormalities in the case of a juvenile murderer.

Frequency components Further key aspects of the literature on EEG abnormalities and violence are the presence and amount of activity in the various frequency components – markers for structural and/or functional abnormalities depending upon the frequency band and context of the recording. EEG "slowing," for example, has been operationalized in the literature on violence by increased amounts of slow-wave activity (i.e., delta or theta) or "slower" wave activity (i.e., alpha relative to beta). In fact, according to Blake et al. (1995), EEG abnormalities, including EEG slowing, have been noted in nearly half of male murderers. Findings of increased delta wave activity have been commonly reported in EEG studies of violent individuals. Convit et al. (1991), for example, found increased delta band power to be positively correlated with increased levels of violence, and opined that this may be associated with structural abnormalities in the brain. Evans and Claycomb (1999) found increased delta and alpha power at frontal and temporal sites in a small sample ($n = 10$) of men with histories of violence and who reported dissociative type experiences. Gatzke-Kopp, Raine, Buchsbaum, and LaCasse (2001) found significant increases in slow-wave (delta and theta) and beta1 activity in the temporal, but not frontal, lobe in murderers compared to controls. Finally, Lindberg et al. (2005) reported overall reduced alpha power and bilaterally increased occipital delta and theta power in the waking EEG of homicidal males with ASPD compared to controls. Regarding theta wave findings, Yoshi, Ishiwara, and Tani (1964) in an earlier study of juvenile delinquents found participants to be characterized by theta wave abnormalities, and that those in the abnormal theta wave group were characterized by increased rates of violent offenses compared to those with normal EEG. On balance, Blackburn (1975) found that increased theta activity was not found to be significant when comparing patients with increased versus decreased levels of aggression. Pillman et al. (1999) found EEG abnormalities in one-third of pretrial assessment defendants (mostly nonspecific increase of diffuse theta activity or groups of theta or delta waves), though these abnormalities were found in both violent and nonviolent offenders. Finally, Lindberg et al. (2005) found that the waking EEGs of homicidal males were characterized by increased theta power in occipital regions compared to normal controls.

Regarding alpha wave findings, Blackburn (1975) noted increased alpha reactivity to painful stimulation in more-aggressive versus less-aggressive patients, and opined that this was a marker for cortical reactivity and related to an increased rate of information processing in most aggressive patients. However, Lindberg et al. (2005) found decreased waking EEG alpha wave activity in their study of homicidal males. Finally, regarding beta wave findings, Schug et al. (2011) found increased left-hemispheric high-frequency beta wave activity in murderers with schizophrenia compared to nonviolent schizophrenia patients (the latter, on balance, were characterized by increased diffuse slow-wave activity compared to murderers with schizophrenia, murderers without schizophrenia, murderers with psychiatric conditions other than schizophrenia, and normal controls). The authors proposed a left-hemispheric over-processing hypothesis specific to individuals with schizophrenia who become violent, in which hyperarousal deficits in the left hemisphere may contribute to a homicidally violent outcome in schizophrenia.

Other findings present a mixed picture of evidence for an association between EEG functioning and violence. For example, Langevin et al. (1987) found no significant group differences in EEG among killers (murder and manslaughter), assaulters (nonhomicidal violence), and controls (nonviolent offenders). Arango, Calcedo Barba, González-Salvador, and Calcedo Ordóñez (1999) found no significant group differences in the proportion of EEG abnormalities among violent and nonviolent hospital inpatients. Finally, Hillbrand, Foster, and Hirt (1988) compared violent and nonviolent forensic hospital inpatients and found that violent individuals had *decreased* rates of abnormalities in the temporal lobe as measured by EEG. Discordant results may be due to differences in operationalizations of EEG functioning and violence; but nonetheless speak to a need for continued research in this important line of neuroscientific inquiry.

Spouse abuse *Spouse abuse is seen as either a rational act aimed at regulating conflict, or as a failure to regulate emotional response. In support of the latter view, spouse abusers show excessive limbic (amygdala and hippocampus) activation to aggressive triggers, suggesting that inadequate pre-frontal and anterior cingulate resources to exercise top-down regulatory control may in part explain the functional brain abnormality of batterers (Lee, Chen, & Raine, 2008, Molecular Psychiatry, 13, 655–656).*
Source: © Katarzyna Białasiewicz. Used under license from 123RF.

Conclusions

Advances made in key areas of the forensic neurosciences – including neuroimaging, neuropsychology, and psychophysiology – have strategically positioned the forensic neuroscientist to understand the neurobiological underpinnings of the violent offender, and to make critical contributions to criminal justice applications regarding his or her adjudication, management, and treatment. Overlapping evidence from multiple modalities of neuroscientific data collection continues to implicate specific regions of the brain (i.e., the frontal lobe and prefrontal cortex, temporal lobe, and limbic system) which appear to play critical roles in the etiology of violence, aggression, and antisociality. The need for cracking the neurobiological code of the violent offender's brain has never been more paramount. Researchers (e.g., Hancock et al., 2010) have noted the significant financial consequences of violence for society, and have articulated an urgent need to understand factors predisposing individuals to violent behavior – in order to develop preventative strategies for at-risk individuals and rehabilitation programs for persons already characterized by violence.

Implications for Practice

Findings from forensic neuroscience research have led to new studies examining effective treatment and prevention of aggression and violence techniques. Understanding the brain structures and functionality that contribute to violent and aggressive criminal behavior allow researchers and practitioners to develop targeted with intervention techniques designed to improve functioning in these areas. For example, a study using anatomical magnetic resonance brain scanning showed mindfulness mediation to be associated with changes in cerebral gray matter volume, a deficit seen in violent offenders (Hölzel et al., 2011). Olds et al. (1998) conducted a classic longitudinal study which randomly assigned 400 low social class pregnant women to two groups. The intervention group got regular home visits from nurses during prenatal and postnatal periods critical to brain development. The nurses counseled the women on health and emotional care of themselves and the child. The control group received the standard levels of care. The results of the study showed after follow ups that children who were in the intervention group had 56.8% fewer arrests and 63% fewer convictions than the control group did. Other early interventions can increase brain health through nutrition. In one study, children and adolescents were either given an omega-3 supplement, which can enhance brain structural health and functioning, once per day or a placebo. After six months of taking either the omega-3 or the placebo both groups showed a reduction in aggression. Only the omeg-3 group, however, continued to show the reduction in aggression six months after the treatment had stopped (Raine, Portnoy, Liu, Mahoomed, & Hibbeln, 2015). Neuroscience techniques are bringing us continually closer to understanding the contribution of biological factors to crime and violence. These same techniques are making it possible to begin to combat the problem as well through informed and targeted interventions.

Note

1   See http://en.wikipedia.org/wiki/Learning.

Recommended Reading

Morgan, A. B., & Lilienfeld, S. O. (2000). A meta-analytic review of the relation between antisocial behavior and neuropsychological measures of executive function. *Clinical Psychology Review, 20*(1), 113–136. *The authors conducted a meta-analysis using effect sizes from 39 studies that included 4,589 participants to clarify the relationship between executive functioning deficits as measured by neuropsychological tests and antisocial behavior. Six tests of executive functioning that had been shown to differentiate frontal lobe damage from other brain region damage had been found in brain imaging research to activate the frontal cortex, and measured one of four domains of executive functioning were included in the meta-analysis. Antisocial behavior was defined in included studies using a clinical diagnosis of syndromes or criminality. The results of the analysis showed a statistically significant relationship between antisocial behavior and executive functioning deficits with a medium to large effect size. This study furthers the understanding of the executive functioning–antisocial behavior relationship by addressing previously unanswered questions; is there a relationship between executive functioning and antisocial behavior across different ways to operationalize antisocial behavior, and are antisocial behaviors deficient in executive functioning tests specifically or on all kinds of neuropsychological tests?*

Raine, A., Buchsbaum, M. S., & LaCasse, L. (1997). Brain abnormalities in murderers indicated by positron emission tomography. *Biological Psychiatry, 42*, 495–508. *Many studies have suggested that general brain dysfunction may be a contributing factor to violent and aggressive behavior. The authors of this study used PET brain imaging during a continuous performance* task to examine localized regional brain dysfunction in murderers who have plead not guilty by reason of insanity. Forty-one murderers were matched with controls and both underwent the same scanning procedures. Results showed that murderers were characterized by reduced glucose metabolism in the prefrontal cortex, posterior parietal cortex, and corpus callosum. The murderers also showed lower left hemisphere glucose metabolism than right in the amygdala, thalamus, medial temporal gyrus, and hippocampus. The authors point out the importance of understanding that biological factors are not the only factors involved in violent behavior and that these findings do not suggest that violent criminals are not responsible for their crimes. This study expands the understanding of the relationship that specific types of brain dysfunction have on violent behavior. Possible mechanisms that translate brain dysfunction in particular regions to violent behavior are discussed.

Raine, A., Lencz, T., Bihrle, S., LaCasse, L., & Colletti, P. (2000). Reduced prefrontal gray matter volume and reduced autonomic activity in antisocial personality disorder. *Archives of General Psychiatry, 57,* 119–127. The authors of this study sought to examine whether community members with APD absent brain trauma would be characterized by subtle prefrontal deficits. Structural imaging using MRI techniques compared the prefrontal cortex volume of APD compared to non-APD and psychiatric groups. Autonomic activity was measured using heart rate and skin conductance during a stressor task. Results showed that the APD group did indeed show a reduction in prefrontal cortex gray matter volume, and reduced autonomic activity during the stressor. Analysis showed these factors could be used as a significant predictor of APD group membership. Implications for the relationship between these specific structural deficits and behavioral symptoms are discussed.

Schug, R. A., Yang, Y., Raine, A., Han, C., Liu, J., & Li, L. (2011). Resting EEG deficits in accused murderers with schizophrenia. *Psychiatry Research: Neuroimaging, 194*(1), 85–94. In this study, resting EEG data from five diagnostic groups (normal controls, nonviolent schizophrenia patients, murderers with schizophrenia, murderers without schizophrenia, and murderers with psychiatric conditions other than schizophrenia) were collected from a brain hospital in Nanjing, China. Murderers with schizophrenia were characterized by increased left-hemispheric fast-wave EEG activity relative to nonviolent schizophrenic patients, while nonviolent schizophrenic patients instead demonstrated increased diffuse slow-wave activity compared to all other groups. Results are discussed within the framework of a proposed left-hemispheric over-processing hypothesis specific to violent individuals with schizophrenia, involving left hemispheric hyperarousal deficits, which may lead to a homicidally violent schizophrenia outcome. Overall, it presents what may be additional evidence for a biologically-based violent schizophrenia subtype, which could have important implications in research, treatment and management, and social arenas – that is, reducing the negative stigma attached to schizophrenic persons who are not violent.

References

American Psychiatric Association. (2013). *Diagnostic and statistical manual of mental disorders* (5th ed.). Arlington, VA: American Psychiatric Association.

Antonucci, A. S., Gansler, D. A., Tan, S., Bhadelia, R., Patz, S., & Fulwiler, C. (2006). Orbitofrontal correlates of aggression and impulsivity in psychiatric patients. *Psychiatry Research: Neuroimaging, 147,* 213–220.

Arango, C., Calcedo Barba, A., González-Salvador, T., & Calcedo Ordóñez, A. (1999). Violence in inpatients with schizophrenia: A prospective study. *Schizophrenia Bulletin, 25*(3), 493–503.

Barber, F. (1994). An investigation of the neuropsychological correlates of extreme violence in schizophrenia patients. Unpublished master's thesis, University of Surrey, Guildford, United Kingdom.

Barkataki, I., Kumari, V., Das, M., Hill, M., Morris, R., O'Connell, P., ... Sharma, T. (2005). A neuropsychological investigation into violence and mental illness. *Schizophrenia Research, 74*, 1–13.

Barkataki, I., Kumari, V., Das, M., Taylor, P., & Sharma, T. (2006). Volumetric structural brain abnormalities in men with schizophrenia or antisocial personality disorder. *Behavioral Brain Research, 169*(2), 239–247.

Bassarath, L. (2001). Neuroimaging studies of antisocial behavior. *The Canadian Journal of Psychiatry, 46*(8), 728–732.

Bender, L., & Curran, F. (1940). Children and adolescents who kill. *Criminal Psychopathology, 1*(4), 297–322.

Blackburn, R. (1975). Aggression and the EEG: A quantitative analysis. *Journal of Abnormal Psychology, 84*(4), 358–365.

Blake, P. Y., Pincus, J. H., & Buckner, C. (1995). Neurologic abnormalities in murderers. *Neurology, 45*(9), 1641–1647.

Boes, A. D, Tranel, D., Anderson, S. W., & Nopoulos, P. (2008). Right anterior cingulate: A neuroanatomical correlate of aggression and defiance in boys. *Behavioral Neuroscience, 122*, 677–684.

Broomhall, L. (2005). Acquired sociopathy: A neuropsychological study of executive dysfunction in violent offenders. *Psychiatry, Psychology, and Law, 12*, 367–387.

Bufkin, J., & Luttrel, V. (2005). Neuroimaging studies of aggressive and violent behavior current findings and implications for criminology and criminal justice. *Trauma, Violence, & Abuse, 6*(2), 176–191.

Cauffman, E., Steinberg, L., & Piquero, A. R. (2005). Psychological, neuropsychological and physiological correlates of serious antisocial behavior in adolescence: The role of self-control. *Criminology: An Interdisciplinary Journal, 43*(1), 133–176.

Chung, S., Chung, H. Y., Jung, J., Chang, J. K., & Hong, J. P. (2010). Association among aggressiveness, neurocognitive function, and the Val66Met polymorphism of brain-derived neurotrophic factor gene in male schizophrenic patients. *Comprehensive Psychiatry, 51*(4), 367–372.

Coccaro, E. F., McCloskey, M. S., Fitzgerald, D.A., & Phan, K.L. (2007). Amygdala and orbitofrontal reactivity to social threat in individuals with impulsive aggression. *Biological Psychiatry, 62*(2), 168–178.

Cole, K. E., Fisher, G., Cole, S. S. (1968). Women who kill. *Archives of General Psychiatry, 19*, 1–8.

Convit, A., Czobor, P., & Volavka, J. (1991). Lateralized abnormality in the EEG of persistently violent psychiatric inpatients. *Biological Psychology, 30*(4), 363–370.

Cornell, D. C., Roberts, M., & Oram, G. (1997). The Rey-Osterrieth Complex Figure Test as a neuropsychological measure in criminal offenders. *Archives of Clinical Neuropsychology, 12*(1), 47–56.

Crowley, T. J., Dalwani, M. S., Mikulich-Gilbertson, S. K., Du, Y. P., Lejuez, C. W., Raymond, K. M., & Banich, M. T. (2010). Risky decisions and their consequences: Neural processing by boys with antisocial substance disorder. *PLOS ONE, 5*(9), doi:10.1371/journal.pone.0012835.

Dalwani, M., Sakai, J. T., Mikulich-Gilbertson, S. K., Tanabe, J., Raymond, K., McWilliams, S. K., ... Crowley, T. J. (2011). Reduced cortical gray matter volume in male adolescents with substance and conduct problems. *Drug and Alcohol Dependence, 118*(2–3), 295–305.

Damasio, A. (1994). *Descartes' error: Emotion, reason, and the human brain*. New York, NY: GP Putnam's Sons.

De Brito, S. A., Viding, E., Kumari, V., Blackwood, N., & Hodgins, S. (2013). Cool and hot executive function impairments in violent offenders with antisocial personality disorder with and without psychopathy. *PLOS One, 8*(6).

De Brito, S. A., Viding, E., Sebastian, C. L., Kelly, P. A., Mechelli, A., Maris, H., & McCrory, E. J. (2013) Reduced orbitofrontal and temporal grey matter in a community sample of maltreated children. *Journal of Child Psychology and Psychiatry, 54,* 105–112.

Deiker, T. E. (1973). WAIS characteristics of indicted male murderers. *Psychological Reports, 32,* 1066.

DeWolfe, A. S., & Ryan, J. J. (1984). Wechsler Performance IQ >Verbal IQ index in a forensic sample: A reconsideration. *Journal of Clinical Psychology, 40*(1), 291–294.

Dinn, W. M., & Harris, C. L. (2000). Neurocognitive function in antisocial personality disorder. *Psychiatry Research, 97*(2–3), 173–190.

Dolan, M. (2010). What imaging tells us about violence in anti-social men. *Criminal Behavior and Mental Health, 20*(3), 199–214.

Dolan, M. (2012). The neuropsychology of prefrontal function in antisocial personality disordered offenders with varying degrees of psychopathy. *Psychological Medicine, 42*(8), 1715–1725.

Dolan, M., Deakin, W., Roberts, N., & Anderson, I. (2002) Seratonergic and cognitive impairment in impulsive aggressive personality disordered offenders: Are there implications for treatment? *Psychological Medicine, 32,* 105–117.

Dolan, M. C., & Fullam, R. S. (2009). Psychopathy and functional magnetic resonance imaging blood oxygenation level-dependent responses to emotional faces in violent patients with schizophrenia. *Biological Psychiatry, 66,* 570–577.

Dolan, M., & Park, I. (2002). The neuropsychology of antisocial personality disorder. *Psychological Medicine, 32*(3), 417–427.

Driver, M. V., West, L. R., & Faulk, M. (1974). Clinical and EEG studies of prisoners charged with murder. *British Journal of Psychiatry, 125,* 583–587.

Eriksson, Å. (2006). Risk factors for criminal offending among men with schizophrenia. Unpublished master's thesis, Karolinska Institutet, Stockholm, Sweden.

Eriksson, Å., Hodgins, S., & Tengström, A. (2005). Verbal intelligence and criminal offending among men with schizophrenia. *International Journal of Forensic Mental Health, 4,* 191–200.

Eronen, M., Hakola, P., & Tiihonen, J. (1996). Mental disorders and homicidal behavior in Finland. *Archives of General Psychiatry, 53*(6), 497–501.

Evans, J.R., & Claycomb, S. (1999). Abnormal QEEG patterns associated with dissociation and violence. *Journal of Neurotherapy, 3*(2), 21–27.

Evans, J. R., & Park, N. S. (1997). Quantitative EEG findings among men convicted of murder. *Journal of Neurotherapy, 2*(2), 31–37.

Fairchild, G., Hagan, C. C., Walsh, N. D., Passamonti, L., Calder, A. J., & Goodyer, I. M. (2013). Brain structure abnormalities in adolescent girls with conduct disorder. *Journal of Child Psychology and Psychiatry, 54*(1), 86–95.

Farrell, G., & Clark, K. (2004). *What does the world spend on criminal justice?* Helsinki: European Institute for Crime Prevention and Control.

FBI, Uniform Crime Reporting. (2012). Crime in the United States 2012. Retrieved from https://ucr.fbi.gov/crime-in-the-u.s/2012/crime-in-the-u.s.-2012.

Fisher, S. S. (1999). Juvenile males who murder: A descriptive study. Unpublished doctoral dissertation, California School of Professional Psychology, Fresno.

Fullam, R. S., & Dolan, M. C. (2008). Executive function and in-patient violence in forensic patients with schizophrenia. *The British Journal of Psychiatry, 193*(3), 247–253.

Gatzke-Kopp, L. M., Raine, A., Buchsbaum, M., & LaCasse, L. (2001). Temporal lobe deficits in murderers: EEG findings undetected by PET. *Journal of Neuropsychiatry and Clinical Neuroscience, 13*(4), 486–491.

Giancola, P. R., Roth, R. M., & Parrott, D. J. (2006). The mediating role of executive functioning in the relation between difficult temperament and physical aggression. *Journal of Psychopathology and Behavioral Assessment, 28*(4), 211–221.

Giancola, P. R., & Zeichner, A. (1994). Neuropsychological performance on tests of frontal-lobe functioning and aggressive behavior in men. *Journal of Abnormal Psychology, 103*(4), 832–835.

Glenn, A. L., Raine, A., & Schug, R. A. (2009). Increased dlPFC activity during moral decision-making in psychopathy. *Molecular Psychiatry, 14*, 909–911.

Goethals, I., Audenaert, K., Jacobs, F., Van den Eynde, F., Bernagie, K., Kolindou, A., Vervaet, M., Dierckx, R., & Van Heeringen, C. (2005). Brain perfusion SPECT in impulsivity-related personality disorders. *Behavioural Brain Research, 157*, 187–192.

Goyer, P. F., Andreason, P. J., Semple, W. E., & Clayton, A. H. (1994). Positron-emission tomography and personality disorders. *Neuropsychopharmacology, 10*, 21–28.

Green, J., Leon-Barth, C., Venus, S., & Lucey, T. (2001). Murder and the EEG. *The Forensic Examiner, 10*(1–2), 32–34.

Gregory, S., Ffytche, D., Simmons, A., Kumari, V., Howard, M., Hodgins, S., & Blackwood, N. (2012). The antisocial brain: Psychopathy matters. A structural MRI investigation of antisocial male violent offenders. *JAMA Psychiatry, 69*, 962–972.

Hancock, M., Tapscott, J. L., & Hoaken, P. N. S. (2010). Role of executive dysfunction in predicting frequency and severity of violence. *Aggressive Behavior, 36*(5), 338–349.

Hanlon, R. E., Coda, J. J., Cobia, D., & Rubin, L. H. (2012). Psychotic domestic murder: Neuropsychological differences between homicidal and nonhomicidal schizophrenic men. *Journal of Family Violence, 27*, 105–113.

Hanlon, R. E., Rubin, L. H., Jensen, M., & Daoust, S. (2010). Neuropsychological features of indigent murder defendants and death row inmates in relation to homicidal aspects of their crimes. *Archives of Clinical Neuropsychology, 25*, 1–13.

Harbort, S., & Mokros, A. (2001). Serial murderers in Germany from 1945 to 1995: A descriptive study. *Homicide Studies, 5*(4), 311–334.

Hart, S. D., Hoffman, J., Meloy, J. R., & Warren, L. (2014). Inaugural editorial. *Journal of Threat Assessment and Management, 1*(1), 1–3.

Hays, J., Solway, J., & Schreiner, D. (1978). Intellectual characteristics of juvenile murderers versus status offenders. *Psychological Reports, 43*, 80–82.

Heilbrun, Jr., A. B. (1982). Cognitive models of criminal violence based upon intelligence and psychopathy levels. *Journal of Consulting and Clinical Psychology, 47*(3), 509–516.

Herpertz, S. C., Huebner, T., Marx, I., Vloet, T. D., Fink, G. R., Stoecker, T., ... Herpertz-Dahlmann, B. (2008). Emotional processing in male adolescents with childhood-onset conduct disorder. *Journal of Child Psychology and Psychiatry, 49*, 781–791.

Hill, D. H., & Pond, D. A. (1952). Reflections on one hundred capital cases submitted to electroencephalography. *Journal of Mental Sciences, 98*, 23–43.

Hillbrand, M., Foster, H. G., & Hirt, M. (1988). Variables associated with violence in a forensic population. *Journal of Interpersonal Violence, 3*(4), 371–380.

Hoaken, P. N. S., Allaby, D. B., & Earle, J. (2007). Executive cognitive functioning and the recognition of facial expressions of emotion in incarcerated violent offenders, non-violent offenders, and controls. *Aggressive Behavior, 33*(5), 412–421.

Hodgins, S., Calem, M., Shimel, R., Williams, A., Harleston, D., Morgan, C., ... Jones, P. (2011). Criminal offending and distinguishing features of offenders among persons experiencing a first episode of psychosis. *Early Intervention in Psychiatry, 5*(1), 15–23.

Hoptman, M. J., Volavka, J., Weiss, E. M., Czobor, P., Szeszko, P. R., Gerig, G., ... Bilder, R. M. (2005). Quantitative MRI measures of orbitofrontal cortex in patients with chronic schizophrenia or schizoaffective disorder. *Psychiatry Research: Neuroimaging, 140*, 133–145.

Hölzel, B., Carmody, J., Vangel, M., Congleton, C., Yerramsetti, S., Gard, T., & Lazar, S. (2011). Mindfulness practice leads to increases in regional brain gray matter density. *Psychiatry Research: Neuroimaging, 191*(1), 36–43.

Huebner, T., Vloet, T., Marx, I., Konrad, K., Fink, G., Herpertz, S., & Herpertz, Dahlmann, B. (2008). Morphometric brain abnormalities in boys with conduct disorder. *Journal of the American Academy of Child and Adolescent Psychiatry*, 47(5), 540–547.

Hugdahl, K. (1995). *Psychophysiology: The mind-body perspective*. Cambridge, MA: Harvard University Press.

Isen, J. (2010). A meta-analytic assessment of Wechsler's P>V sign in antisocial populations. *Clinical Psychology Review*, 30(4), 423–435.

Ishikawa, S. S., & Raine, A. (2002). Psychophysiological correlates of antisocial behavior: A central control hypothesis. In J. Glicksohn (Ed.), *The neurobiology of criminal behavior* 8 (pp. 187–229). Norwell: Kluwer Academic Publishers.

Jamison, T. E. (2006). The homicidal narcissist. Unpublished doctoral dissertation, University of Tennessee, Knoxville.

Joyal, C. C., Putkonen, A., Mancini-Marïe, A., Hodgins, S., Kononen, M., Boulay, L., ... Aronen, H. J. (2007). Violent persons with schizophrenia and comorbid disorders: A functional magnetic resonance imaging study. *Schizophrenia Research*, 91, 97–102.

Kahn, M. W. (1967). Correlates of Rorschach reality adherence in the assessment of murderers who plead insanity. *Journal of Projective Techniques and Personality Assessment*, 31(4), 44–47.

Kahn, M. W. (1968). Superior Performance IQ of murderers as a function of overt act or diagnosis. *Journal of Social Psychology*, 76, 113–116.

Keilp, J. G., Gorlyn, M., Russell, M., Oquendo, M. A., Burke, A. K., Harkavy-Friedman, J., & Mann, J. J. (2013). Neuropsychological function and suicidal behaviour: Attention control, memory and executive dysfunction in suicide attempt. *Psychological Medicine*, 43(3), 539–551.

Kiehl, K. A., Smith, A. M., Hare, R. D., Mendrek, A., Forster, B. B., Brink, J., ... Liddle, P. F. (2001). Limbic abnormalities in affective processing by criminal psychopaths as revealed by functional magnetic resonance imaging. *Biological Psychiatry*, 50, 677–684.

Kochanska, G., Murray, K., & Coy, K. C. (1997) Inhibitory control as a contributor to conscience in childhood: From toddler to early school age. *Child Development*, 68: 263–277.

Kronenberger, W. G., Mathews, V. P., Dunn, D. W., Wang, Y., Wood, E. A., Giauque, A. L., ... Li, T. (2005). Media violence exposure and executive functioning in aggressive and control adolescents. *Journal of Clinical Psychology*, 61(6), 725–737.

Kruesi, M., Casanova, M., Mannheim, G., & Johnson-Bilder, A. (2004). Reduced temporal lobe volume in early onset conduct disorder. *Psychiatry Research: Neuroimaging*, 132, 1–11.

Krug, E. G., Dahlberg, L. L., Mercy, J. A., Zwi, A. B., & Lozano, R. (Eds.). (2002). *World report on violence and health*. Geneva: World Health Organization.

Kumari, V., Aasen, I., Taylor, P., Ffytche, D. E., Das, M., Barkataki, I., ... Sharma, T. (2006). Neural dysfunction and violence in schizophrenia: An fMRI investigation. *Schizophrenia Research*, 84, 144–164.

Kumari, V., Barkataki, I., Goswami, S., Flora, S., Das, M., & Taylor, P. (2009). Dysfunctional, but not functional, impulsivity is associated with a history of seriously violent behaviour and reduced orbitofrontal and hippocampal volumes in schizophrenia. *Psychiatry Research: Neuroimaging*, 173(1), 39–44.

Kumari, V., Das, M., Hodgins, S., Zachariah, E., Barkataki, I, Howlett, M., & Sharma, T. (2005) Association between violent behavior and impaired prepulse inhibition of the startle response in antisocial personality disorder and schizophrenia.. *Behavioral Brain Research*, 158, 159–66.

Kumari, V., Gudjonsson, G. H., Raghuvanshi, S., Barkataki, I., Taylor, P., Sumich, A., ... Das, M. (2013). Reduced thalamic volume in men with antisocial personality disorder or schizophrenia and a history of serious violence and childhood abuse. *European Psychiatry*, 28, 225–234.

Kumari, V., Uddin, S., Premkumar, P., Young, S., Gudjonsson, G. H., Raghuvanshi, S., ... Das, M. (2014). Lower cingulate volume in seriously violent men with antisocial personality disorder or schizophrenia and a history of childhood abuse. *Australian & New Zealand Journal of Psychiatry, 48*(2), 153–161.

Langevin, R. (2003). A study of the psychosexual characteristics of sex killers: Can we identify them before it is too late? *International Journal of Offender Therapy and Comparative Criminology, 47*(4), 366–382.

Langevin, R., Ben-Aron, M., Wortzman, G., Dickey, R., & Handy, L. (1987). Brain damage, diagnosis, and substance abuse among violent offenders. *Behavioral Sciences and the Law, 5*(1), 77–94.

Langevin, R., Ben-Aron, M. H., Wright, P., Marchese, V., & Handy, L. (1988). The sex killer. *Annals of Sex Research, 1*, 263–301.

Lapierre, D., Braun, C. M. J., & Hodgins, S. (1995). Ventral frontal deficits in psychopathy: Neuropsychological test findings. *Neuropsychologia, 33*(2), 139–151.

Lester, D., Purdue, W., & Brookhart, D. (1974). Murder and control of aggression. *Psychological Reports, 34*, 706.

Lewis, D. O., Lovely, R., Yeager, C., Ferguson, G., Friedman, M., Sloane, G., Friedman, H., & Pincus, J. H. (1988). Intrinsic and environmental characteristics of juvenile murderers. *Journal of the American Academy of Child and Adolescent Psychiatry, 27*(5), 582–587.

Lewis, D. O., Moy, E., Jackson, L. D., Aaronson, R., Restifo, N., Serra, S., & Simos, A. (1985). Biopsychosocial characteristics of children who later murder: A prospective study. *American Journal of Psychiatry, 142*, 161–1167.

Lezak, M. D., Howieson, D. B., Loring, D. W., Hannay, H. J., & Fischer, J. S. (2004). *Neuropsychological assessment* (4th ed.). New York: Oxford University Press.

Litwack, T. R., Zapf, P. A., Groscup, J. L., & Hart, S. D. (2006). Violence risk assessment: Research, legal, and clinical considerations. In I. B. Weiner & A. K. Hess (Eds.), *The handbook of forensic psychology* (3rd ed.) (pp. 487–533). Hoboken, NJ: John Wiley & Sons, Inc.

Li, T., Mathews, V. P., Wang, Y., Dunn, D., & Kronenberger, W. (2005) Adolescents with disruptive behavior disorder investigated using an optimized MR diffusion tensor imaging protocol. *Annals of the New York Academy of Sciences, 1064*, 184–192.

Lindberg, N., Tani, P., Virkkunen, M., Porkka-Heiskanen, T., Appelberg, B., Naukkarinen, H., & Salmi, T. (2005). Quantitative electroencephalographic measures in homicidal men with antisocial personality disorder. *Psychiatry Research, 136*(1), 7–15.

Lorber, M. F. (2004). Psychophysiology of aggression, psychopathy, and conduct problems: A meta-analysis. *Psychological Bulletin, 130*(4), 531–552.

Luria, A. (1980). *Higher cortical functions in man* (2nd ed). New York: Basic Books.

Marsh, A. A., Finger, E. C., Fowler, K. A., Jurkowitz, I. N., Schechter, J. C., Yu, H. H., ... Blair, R.R. (2011). Reduced amygdala-orbitofrontal connectivity during moral judgements in youths with disruptive behavior disorders and psychopathic traits. *Psychiatry Research: Neuroimaging, 194*(3), 279–286.

Mathews, V. P., Kronenberger, W. G., Wang, Y., Lurito, J. T., Lowe, M. J., & Dunn, D. W. (2005) Media violence exposure and frontal lobe activation measured by functional magnetic resonance imaging in aggressive and nonaggressive adolescents. *Journal of Computer Assisted Tomography, 29*, 287–292.

Mednick, S. A., Volavka, J., Gabrielli, W. F., & Itil, T. (1982). EEG as a predictor of antisocial behavior. *Criminology, 19*, 219–231.

Mills, S., & Raine, A. (1994). Neuroimaging and aggression. *Journal of Offender Rehabilitation, 21*(3–4), 145–158.

Miura, H. (2009). Differences in frontal lobe function between violent and nonviolent conduct disorder in male adolescents. *Psychiatry and Clinical Neurosciences, 63*(2), 161–166.

Moffitt, T. E., & Henry, B. (1989). Neuropsychological assessment of executive functions in self-reported delinquents. *Development and Psychopathology, 1*, 105–118.

Moffitt, T. E., Lynam, D. R., & Silva, P. A. (1994). Neuropsychological tests predicting persistent male delinquency. *Criminology, 32*, 277–300.

Morgan, A. B., & Lilienfeld, S. O. (2000). A meta-analytic review of the relation between antisocial behavior and neuropsychological measures of executive function. *Clinical Psychology Review, 20*(1), 113–136.

Mouridsen, S. E., & Tolstrup, K. (1988). Children who kill: A case study of matricide. *Journal of Child Psychology and Psychiatry, 29*(4), 511–515.

Müller, J. L., Gänssbauer, S., Sommer, M., Döhnel, K., Weber, T., Schmidt-Wilcke, T., & Hajak, G. (2008). Gray matter changes in right superior temporal gyrus in criminal psychopaths. Evidence from voxel-based morphometry. *Psychiatry Research, 163*, 213–222.

Mundy-Castle, A. C. (1955). The EEG in twenty-two cases of murder or attempted murder. Appendix on possible significance of alphoid rhythms. *Journal of the National Institute for Personnel Research, 6*, 103–120.

Myers, W. C., Scott, K., Burgess, A. W., & Burgess, A. G. (1995). Psychopathology, biopsychosocial factors, crime characteristics, and classification of 25 homicidal youths. *Journal of the American Academy of Child and Adolescent Psychiatry, 34*(11), 1483–1489.

Nestor, P. G., Haycock, J., Doiron, S., Kelly, J., & Kelly, D. (1995). Lethal violence and psychosis: A clinical profile. *Bulletin of the American Academy of Psychiatry and the Law, 23*(3), 331–341.

Nestor, P. G., Kimble, M., Berman, I., & Haycock, J. (2002). Psychosis, psychopathy, and homicide: A preliminary neuropsychological inquiry. *The American Journal of Psychiatry, 159*(1), 138–140.

Nigg, J. T., Glass, J. M., Wong, M. M., Poon, E., Jester, J., Fitzgerald, H. E., ... Zucker, R. A. (2004). Neuropsychological executive functioning in children at elevated risk for alcoholism: Findings in early adolescence. *Journal of Abnormal Psychology, 113*, 302–314.

Nolte, J. (2002). *The human brain: An introduction to its functional neuroanatomy* (5th ed.). Amsterdam: Elsevier.

Olds, D., Henderson, C., Cole, R., Eckenrode, J., Kitzman, H., Luckey, D., ... Powers, J. (1998). Long-term effects of nurse home visitation on children's criminal and antisocial behavior: 15-year follow-up of a randomized controlled trial. *JAMA, 280*(14):1238–1244. doi:10.1001/jama.280.14.1238.

Pagan, D., & Smith, S. S. (1979). Homicide: A medico-legal study of thirty cases. *Bulletin of the American Academy of Psychiatry and the Law, 7*(3), 275–285.

Pardini, D. A., Raine, A., Erickson, K., & Loeber, R. (2014). Lower amygdala volume in men is associated with childhood aggression, early psychopathic traits and future violence. *Biological Psychiatry, 75*(1), 10.1016/j.biopsych.2013.04.003.

Passamonti, L., Fairchild, G., Goodyer, I., Hurford, G., Hagan, C., Rowe, J., & Calder, A. (2010). Neural abnormalities in early-onset and adolescence-onset conduct disorder. *Archives of General Psychiatry, 6*(7), 729–738.

Passamonti, L., Crockett, M. J., Apergis-Schoute, A. M., Clark, L., Rowe, J. B., ... Robbins TW. (2012). Effects of acute tryptophan depletion on prefrontal-amygdala connectivity while viewing facial signals of aggression. *Biological Psychiatry, 71*, 36–43.

Patterson, R. M. (1942). Psychiatric study of juveniles involved in homicide. *American Journal of Orthopsychiatry, 13*, 125–130.

Petee, T. A., & Walsh, A. (1987). Violent delinquency, race, and the Wechsler performance-verbal discrepancy. *The Journal of Social Psychology, 127*(3), 353–354.

Pillmann, F., Rohde, A., Ullrich, S., Draba, S., Sannemüller, U., & Marneros, A. (1999). Violence, criminal behavior, and the EEG: Significance of left hemispheric focal abnormalities. *The Journal of Neuropsychiatry and Clinical Neurosciences, 11*(4), 454–457.

Porteus, S. D. (1955). *The Maze test: Recent advances*. Palo Alto, CA: Pacific Books.

Pridmore, S., Chambers, A., & McArthur, M. (2005). Neuroimaging in psychopathy. *Australian and New Zealand Journal of Psychiatry, 39*, 856–865.

Raaijmakers, M. A. J., Smidts, D. P., Sergeant, J. A., Maassen, G. H., Posthumus, J. A., van Engeland, H., & Matthys, W. (2008). Executive functions in preschool children with aggressive behavior: Impairments in inhibitory control. *Journal of Abnormal Child Psychology, 36*(7), 1097–1107.

Raine, A. (1993). *The psychopathology of crime: Criminal behavior as a clinical disorder.* San Diego, CA: Academic Press.

Raine, A. (2002). Biosocial studies of antisocial and violent behavior in children and adults: A review. *Journal of Abnormal Child Psychology, 30*, 311–326.

Raine, A., Buchsbaum, M. S., & LaCasse, L. (1997). Brain abnormalities in murderers indicated by positron emission tomography. *Biological Psychiatry, 42*, 495–508.

Raine, A., Lencz, T., Bihrle, S., LaCasse, L., & Colletti, P. (2000). Reduced prefrontal gray matter volume and reduced autonomic activity in antisocial personality disorder. *Archives of General Psychiatry, 57*, 119–127.

Raine, A., Meloy, J. R., Bihrle, S., Stoddard, J., LaCasse, L., & Buchsbaum, M. S. (1998). Reduced prefrontal and increased subcortical brain functioning assessed using positron emission tomography in predatory and affective murderers. *Behavioral Sciences and the Law, 16*, 319–332.

Raine, A., Moffitt, T. E., Caspi, A., Loeber, R., Stouthamer-Loeber, M., & Lynam, D. (2005). Neurocognitive impairments in boys on the life-course persistent antisocial path. *Journal of Abnormal Psychology, 114*, 38–49.

Raine, A., Portnoy, J., Liu, J., Mahoomed, T., & Hibbeln, J. (2015). Reduction in behavior problems with omega-3 supplementation in children aged 8–16 years: A randomized, double-blind, placebo-controlled, stratified, parallel-group trial. *Journal of Child Psychology and Psychiatry, 56*(5), 509–520.

Raine, A., Stoddard, J., Bihrle, S., & Buchsbaum, M. (1998). Prefrontal glucose deficits in murderers lacking psychosocial deprivation. *Neuropsychiatry, Neuropsychology, and Behavioral Neurology, 11*(1), 1–7.

Raine, A., Yang, Y., Narr, K., & Toga, A. (2011). Sex differences in orbitofrontal gray as a partial explanation for sex differences in antisocial personality. *Molecular Psychiatry, 16*, 227–236.

Rasmussen, K., Almvik, R., & Levander, S. (2001). Performance and strategy indices of neuropsychological tests: Relations with personality, criminality and violence. *Journal of Forensic Neuropsychology, 2*(2), 29–43.

Rosanoff, A. J. (1943). Thirty condemned men. *American Journal of Psychiatry, 99*, 484–495.

Sakuta, A., & Fukushima, A. (1998). A study on abnormal brain findings pertaining to the brain in criminals. *International Medical Journal, 5*(4), 283–292.

Schiffer, B., Müller, B. W., Scherbaum, N., Hodgins, S., Forsting, M., Wiltfang, J., ... Leygraf, N. (2011). Disentangling structural alterations associated with violent behavior from those associated with substance use disorders. *Archives of General Psychiatry, 68*(10), 1039–1049.

Schug, R. A., & Fradella, H. F. (2014). *Mental illness and crime.* Thousand Oaks, CA: Sage.

Schug, R. A., & Raine, A. (2009). Comparative meta-analyses of neuropsychological functioning in antisocial schizophrenic persons. *Clinical Psychology Review, 29*, 230–242.

Schug, R. A., Raine, A., & Wilcox, R. R. (2007). Psychophysiological and behavioural characteristics of individuals with both antisocial personality disorder and schizophrenia-spectrum personality disorder. *British Journal of Psychiatry, 191*, 408–414.

Schug, R. A., Yang, Y., Raine, A., Han, C., Liu, J., & Li, L. (2011). Resting EEG deficits in accused murderers with schizophrenia. *Psychiatry Research: Neuroimaging, 194*(1), 85–94.

Séguin, J. R., Pihl, R. O., Harden, P. W., Tremblay, R. E., & Boulerice, B. (1995). Cognitive and neuropsychological characteristics of physically aggressive boys. *Journal of Abnormal Psychology, 104*(4), 614–624.

Silver, H., Goodman, C., Knoll, G., Isakov, V., & Modai, I. (2005). Schizophrenia patients with a history of severe violence differ from nonviolent schizophrenia patients in perception of emotions but not cognitive function. *Journal of Clinical Psychiatry, 66*(3), 300–308.

Snook, B., Cullen, R. M., Mokros, A., & Harbort, S. (2005). Serial murderers' spatial decisions: Factors that influence crime location choice. *Journal of Investigative Psychology and Offender Profiling, 2*, 147–164.

Soderstrom, H., Hultin, L., Tullberg, M., Wikkelso, C., Ekholm, S., & Forsman, A. (2002). Reduced frontotemporal perfusion in psychopathic personality. *Psychiatry Research Neuroimaging, 114*, 81–94.

Soderstrom, H., Tullberg, M., Wikkelsö, C., Ekholm, S., & Forsman, A. (2000). Reduced regional cerebral blood flow in non-psychotic violent offenders. *Psychiatry Research: Neuroimaging, 98*(1), 29–41.

Stafford-Clark, D., & Taylor, F. H. (1949). Clinical and electro-encephalographic studies of prisoners charged with murder. *Journal of Neurology, Neurosurgery, and Psychiatry, 12*, 325–330.

Stanford, M. S., Conklin, S. M., Helfritz, L. E., & Kockler, T. R. (2007). P3 amplitude reduction and executive function deficits in men convicted of spousal/partner abuse. *Personality and Individual Differences, 43*, 365–375.

Stern, R. M., Ray, W. J., & Quigley, K. S. (2001). *Psychophysiological recording*. New York, NY: Oxford University Press.

Sterzer, P., Stadler, C., Krebs, A., Kleinschmidt, A., & Poustka, F. (2005). Abnormal neural responses to emotional visual stimuli in adolescents with conduct disorder. *Biological Psychiatry, 57*, 7–15.

Swanson, J. W., Swartz, M. S., Van Dorn, R. A., Elbogen, E. B., Wagner, H. R., Rosenbeck, R., … Lieberman, J. A. (2006). A national study of violent behavior in persons with schizophrenia. *Archives of General Psychiatry, 63*, 490–499.

Syngelaki, E. M., Moore, S. C., Savage, J. C., Fairchild, G., & Van Goozen, S. M. (2009). Executive functioning and risky decision making in young male offenders. *Criminal Justice and Behavior, 36*(11), 1213–1227.

Teichner, G., & Golden, C. J. (2000). The relationship of neuropsychological impairment to conduct disorder in adolescence: A conceptual review. *Aggression and Violent Behavior, 5*, 509–528.

Teichner, G., Golden, C. J., Van Hasselt, V. B., & Peterson, A. (2001). Assessment of cognitive functioning in men who batter. *International Journal of Neuroscience, 111*, 241–253.

Ticehurst, S. B., Ryan, M. G., & Hughes, F. (1992). Homicidal behaviour in elderly patients admitted to a psychiatric hospital. *Dementia, 3*, 86–90.

Tiihonen, J., Rossi, R., Laakso, M. P., Hodgins, S., Testa, C., Perez, J., & Frisoni, G. B. (2008). Brain anatomy of persistent violent offenders: More rather than less. *Psychiatric Research, 163*, 201–212.

United Nations Office on Drugs and Crime (2011). *Global study on homicide*. Retrieved from https://www.unodc.org/documents/congress/background-information/Crime_Statistics/Global_Study_on_Homicide_2011.pdf.

Valliant, P. M., Asu, M. E., Cooper, D., & Mammola, D. (1984). Profile of dangerous and non-dangerous offenders for pre-trial psychiatric assessment. *Psychological Reports, 54*, 411–418.

Vogel, F., & Schalt, E. (1979). The electroencephalogram (EEG) as a research tool in human behavior genetics: Psychological examinations in healthy males with various inherited EEG variants. III. Interpretation of the results. *Human Genetics, 47*, 81–111.

Volkow, N., Tancredi, L., Grant, C., Gillespie, H., Valentine, A., Mullani, N., … Hollister, L. (1995). Brain glucose metabolism in violent psychiatric patients: A preliminary study. *Psychiatry Research, 61*, 243–253.

Völlum, B., Richardson, P., McKie, S., Reniers, R., Elliott, R., Anderson, I. M., ... Deakin, B. (2010). Neuronal correlates and serotonergic modulation of behavioural inhibition and reward in healthy and antisocial individuals. *Journal of Psychiatric Research, 44*(3), 123–131.

Völlum, B. A., Zhao, L., Richardson, P., Clark, L., Deakin, J. F., Williams, S., & Dolan, M. C. (2009). A voxel-based morphometric MRI study in men with borderline personality disorder: Preliminary findings. *Criminal Behavior and Mental Health, 19*(1), 64–72.

Wagner, E. E., & Klein, I. (1977). WAIS differences between murderers and attackers referred for evaluation. *Perceptual and Motor Skills, 44*, 125–126.

Wahlund, K., & Kristiansson, M. (2009). Aggression, psychopathy and brain imaging – review and future recommendations. *International Journal of Law and Psychiatry, 32*(4), 266–271.

Warnick, E. K. (2007). Cognitive heterogeneity in murderers. Unpublished doctoral dissertation, University of Nevada, Las Vegas.

Wechsler, D. (1981). *The Wechsler Adult Intelligence scale –R.* New York, NY: The Psychological Corporation.

White, J. L., Moffitt, T. E., Caspi, A., Jeglum, D., Needles, D. J., & Stouthamer-Loeber, M. (1994). Measuring impulsivity and examining its relationship to delinquency. *Journal of Abnormal Psychology, 103*, 192–205.

Wilson, J. Q., & Herrnstein, R. (1985). *Crime and human nature.* New York, NY: Simon and Schuster.

Winkler, G. E., & Kove, S. S. (1961). The implications of encephalographic abnormalities in homicide cases. *Journal of Neuropsychiatry, 3*, 322–330.

Wong, M. T. H., Fenwick, P. B. C., Lumsden, J., Fenton, G. W., Maisey, M. N., Lewis, P., & Badawi, R. (1997). Positron emission tomography in male violent offenders with schizophrenia. *Psychiatry Research: Neuroimaging Section, 68*, 111–123.

Wong, M. H., Lumsden, J. J., Fenton, G. W., & Fenwick, P. C. (1994). Electroencephalography, computed tomography and violence ratings of male patients in a maximum-security mental hospital. *Acta Psychiatrica Scandinavica, 90*(2), 97–101.

Wong, M., Lumsden, J., Fenton, G., & Fenwick, P. (1997). Neuroimaging in mentally abnormal offenders. *Issues in Criminological and Legal Psychology, 27*, 49–58.

World Health Organization (WHO) (2002). World report on violence and health. Retrieved May 20, 2009 from http://www.who.int/violence.

Yang, Y., & Raine, A. (2009). Prefrontal structural and functional brain imaging findings in antisocial, violent, and psychopathic individuals: A meta-analysis. *Psychiatry Research: Neuroimaging, 174*(2), 81–88.

Yang, Y., Raine, A., Han, C. B., Schug, R. A., Toga, A. W., & Narr, K. L. (2010). Reduced hippocampal and parahippocampal volumes in murderers with schizophrenia. *Psychiatry Research: Neuroimaging, 182*(1), 9–13.

Yoshi, N., Ishiwara, T., & Tani, K. (1964). Juvenile delinquents and their abnormal EEGs: II. Continuous theta waves. *Folia Psychiatrica et Neurologica Japonica, 18*(2), 161–167.

Zamboni, G. G., Huey, E. D., Krueger, F. F., Nichelli, P. F., & Grafman, J. J. (2008). Apathy and disinhibition in frontotemporal dementia: Insights into their neural correlates. *Neurology, 71*(10), 736–742.

13

The Neuroscience of Sexual Offending

Andreas Mokros

> **Key points**
> - Sexual offending represents the violation of *social* norms; brain architecture and functioning are biological entities; hence, there is no one-to-one correspondence of the two domains.
> - The majority of sexual offenses are presumably committed by individuals without identifiable paraphilias or brain anomalies.
> - Sexual deviance is a primary risk factor for sexual reoffending.
> - Neuroanatomical and neurophysiological correlates of sexual deviance are increasingly becoming identified.
> - It is yet unclear whether the brain correlates of sexual deviance are causal for the emergence of sexual deviance (and, hence, indirectly for committing sexual offenses), or whether they are a consequence of sexual deviance or merely an epiphenomenon of sexual deviance.
> - Other relevant brain anomalies associated with sexual offending pertain to impulsiveness and a lack of inhibitory control.

Terminology Explained

Angular gyrus is the structure of the cortex situated in the most posterior section of the lower parietal lobule (behind the postcentral sulcus, yet in front of the parieto-occipital region). The angular gyrus has been shown to be involved in several tasks, including comprehending, reading, and producing language as well as in attention and social cognition (Seghier, 2013).

Cluster B personality disorders is an umbrella term comprising the antisocial, borderline, narcissistic, and histrionic types of personality disorder (American Psychiatric Association, 2013). Cluster B personality disorders are characterized by rashness, emotional instability, and an egocentric attitude. Cluster A and C personality disorders, in contrast, are determined by bizarre/schizoid conduct or by anxiousness and insecurity, respectively.

A **deviant sexual interest** is an unusual persistent focus on erotic attachment to objects, animals, or persons who are either unable or unwilling to consent to mutual sexual activity (e.g., unwitting victims of voyeurism). A **deviant sexual preference** denotes the persistent predilection for such deviant sexual stimulation over commonly accepted and consensual variants of sexual activity.

The **go/no-go task** is an often-used experimental paradigm for assessing attention in terms of cognitive control (inhibition). Participants are instructed to respond only to a particular type of stimulus while ignoring other types of stimuli. Accuracy (hits and correct rejections versus false alarms and omission errors) as well as reaction time are recorded. Responses are generally registered by pressing a key.

Fusiform gyrus is a structure of the cortex situated in the inner fold of the temporal lobe (i.e., near the bottom inner part of the cortex). According to brain imaging and lesion studies, the fusiform gyrus is involved in face perception and word processing (Harris, Rice, Young, & Andrews, 2016).

Paraphilia comes from ancient Greek *philos* (friend or beloved) and *para* (against or besides). Used as an umbrella term for disorders of sexual preference in the *DSM-5* (American Psychiatric Association, 2013), which also differentiates between paraphilias and paraphilic disorders. The more neutral term paraphilia replaced the pejorative and dated term of sexual perversion. Basically, paraphilias denote persistent and intense sexual urges, phantasies or behavioral patterns that are directed at inanimate objects, animals, or at non-consenting or unwitting victims. If this leads to harmful conduct, personal distress, or negative social repercussions the notion of a **paraphilic disorder** will be fulfilled.

Pedophilia is when fantasies, or activities of a late adolescent or adult individual, are directed at pre-pubescent children who are at least five years younger and generally not older than 13 years. Unless the person acted upon these urges, suffered from the affliction, or encountered interpersonal difficulty because of it the condition would be referred to as **pedophilia** instead of pedophilic disorder (American Psychiatric Association, 2013).

Precuneus is a cortical structure in the parietal lobe which is situated at the back of the parietal lobe, toward the center of the brain (i.e., within the cleft between the hemispheres). Findings from functional brain imaging studies have identified the involvement of the precuneus in several complex (integrated) tasks (Cavanna & Trimble, 2006), including the retrieval of personal experiences (episodic memory) and the processing of visuospatial information as well as self-related tasks, such as "first-person perspective taking and an experience of agency" (Cavanna & Trimble, 2006, p. 564). In addition, activity in the precuneus was linked to the default network of the brain.

Sexual arousal is the physiological and psychological response to erotic stimulation.

Sexual deviance denotes actions, urges, fantasies, or attitudes associated with sexual arousal for the person him- or herself but frowned upon by society at large or considered harmful or dangerous to others.

Sexual sadism is a proclivity for fantasies and actions that circle around controlling others through humiliation, coercion, threats, or violence, including the affliction of pain and suffering. The sexual sadist takes erotic pleasure in the helplessness or suffering of others. If directed at non-consenting victims, sexual sadism is forensically relevant. If sadistic role-play is happening between mutually consenting adult individuals, it is called BDSM (bondage & discipline/dominance & submission/sadism & masochism) and not considered harmful or dangerous.

Introduction

Sexual offending and anomalies of the nervous system do not map onto each other on a one-to-one basis. There is an accumulating basis of knowledge, however, showing that risk factors of sexual offending, such as sexual deviance, antisociality, psychopathy, and problems of self-regulation are associated with peculiarities in brain structure or functioning. The current state of research suggests associations that are plausible in the light of theoretical accounts of sexual offending. These associations do not permit causal interpretations at the individual level, however. Methods of assessment developed in neurocognitive research provide potentially useful tools, but they do not allow dispensing with the psychological or psychiatric assessment of observable dysfunctions in behavior. The present chapter provides an overview of extant findings on neuropsychological deficits in sexual offenders and gives a summary of structural and functional brain abnormality observed in sexual offenders. Finally, the legal and ethical implications of neuroscience research on sexual offending are discussed.

Explanations of Sexual Offending Indicating Neuropsychological Problems

The confluence model of sexual aggression (Malamuth, 2003) posits that two pathways may lead to sexual coercion. First, a path of *hostile masculinity*, which is comprised of variables like callousness, hostility, and dominance. Second, a path labeled *sexual promiscuity/impersonal sex* that is based on experiences of abuse and neglect in one's upbringing, antisociality, and precocious sexual behavior. While hostile masculinity is regarded as a distal factor that predisposes individuals toward violence in general, the sexual promiscuity/impersonal sex pathway is considered a key aspect in sexual offending. The confluence model has been tested in noncriminal samples of students (Malamuth, 1986; Malamuth al., 1991; Malamuth et al., 1995) (see Box 13.1).

Box 13.1 Assessing the prevalence of rape-prone attitudes in male college students

Malamuth (1981) published a review of studies according to which about one-third of young North American college male respondents had indicated at least

> some likelihood that they would personally rape if they were assured of neither being caught nor punished. In the studies in question, the answer format was a 5-point Likert-type scale ranging from not at all likely (1) to very likely (5). The criterion of reporting some likelihood of carrying out a rape was considered present if the respondent had ticked category 2 or higher. A study using a randomized-response technique (Warner, 1965) attests to the notion that the percentage reported by Malamuth (1981) may be a lower bound to the true prevalence (Himmelfarb, 2008).

The fact that Malamuth's research (see Box 13.1) dealt exclusively with students or men sampled from the general population (not from among convicted sexual offenders in prison) illustrates a crucial aspect: sexual offending is not limited to the offenses that are officially registered and cleared up. Consequently, only looking at convicted offenders when addressing the issue of sexual offending per se may yield a distorted picture, especially when focusing on neural correlates of sexual offending (Blanchard, Cantor, & Robichaud, 2006). In England and Wales, for instance, data from the British Crime Survey indicate that only about one in six victims of serious sexual assault had reported the incident to the police; about one-quarter had told someone in an official position (including the police) (Office for National Statistics, 2015). Furthermore, as sexual offenses represent violations of social norms, any biological substrate associated with sexual offending, such as particular brain anomalies, will likely be neither a necessary nor a sufficient cause for the behavior in question.

In an experimental study Ariely and Loewenstein (2006) found a strong increase in the proportion of respondents who considered unusual sexual practices as attractive if the participants themselves were sexually aroused. This change in opinion extended to the forensically relevant domain, namely imagining being attracted to a 12-year-old girl. Medical explanations of the proclivity for sexual offending do not necessarily generalize to all persons who commit sexually coercive acts against non-consensual adult victims, or against victims who cannot express their legal consent (e.g., children) (Scully & Marolla, 1985). Particular dysfunctions or structural anomalies of the brain may nevertheless heighten the risk of sexual offending. This is the focus of the current chapter.

According to Barbaree and Marshall (1991) theoretical models that would account for the occurrence of sexual aggression can be grouped into two kinds: *stimulus control* and *response control* models. Response control models entail a lack of inhibitory mechanisms with regard to sexual arousal in response to inappropriate objects (e.g., children, rubber gloves), or behavior (e.g., coercion or threat). Stimulus control models, in contrast, circle around an increase of sexual arousal in response to deviant sexual cues. The connection between such cues and sexual arousal is considered as an outcome of conditioning (McGuire, Carlisle, & Young, 1965).

Similarly, neuro-cognitive theories of sexual offending mirror the stimulus-control/response-control dichotomy. With respect to pedophilia, for instance, both the conditioning with deviant sexual cues (e.g., Hucker, 1986; Langevin, 1990) and insufficient behavioral inhibition (e.g., Tost et al., 2004) have been put forward as possible explanations. The former is deemed to be associated with temporal and limbic structures of the brain; whereas the latter (i.e., lack of inhibition) is suggested to be linked to frontal dysfunction.

The integrative neuropsychiatric model of pedophilia suggested by Cohen et al. (2002) comprises dysfunctions in both frontal and temporal areas of the brain. While the frontal regions are considered relevant for sexual preoccupation and insufficient response inhibition, the temporal (limbic) areas are thought to be instrumental in bringing about heightened sexual arousal, coupled with a lack of discrimination for potentially sexual cues. The *striato-thalamo-cortical network* model (Tost et al., 2004, p. 529) could link such diverse phenomena as reward expectation, arousal or drive, empathy, and response inhibition – all of which are considered as altered in sexual offenders (Spinella, 2007).

Differences in Brain Structure in Sexual Offenders

Four studies, to date, have found alterations of the brain structure in pedophilic men (i.e., Cantor et al., 2008; Poeppl et al., 2013; Schiffer et al., 2007; Schiltz et al., 2007; but see also Cantor & Blanchard, 2012). According to a systematic review reported by Mohnke et al. (2014) a smaller volume of the right amygdala in pedophiles appears to be a relatively robust finding. Amygdala volume has been shown to be associated with pubertal development – an effect presumably linked to the increase of gonadal hormones during that period of life (Bramen et al., 2011). Furthermore, as Bramen et al. showed in boys the correlation between amygdala size and pubertal development tended to be lateralized toward the right-hand side. Consequently, one might conjecture that the comparatively smaller volume of the right amygdala observed in pedophiles may reflect the psychosexual immaturity of the individuals (Poeppl et al., 2013).

The potential relevance of the right amygdala for pedophilia receives further support from a treatment case study in which the brain activation in response to child stimuli was measured before and during pharmacological treatment with leuprolide acetate, a luteinizing hormone-releasing hormone agonist that reduces testosterone levels (Habermeyer et al., 2012) and thus sexual desire and behavior (Rice & Harris, 2011) (see also Chapter 27 for a discussion of drug treatment for sexual offenders). In the Habermeyer et al. (2012) study, the activation in the right amygdala was significantly lower after a ten-month androgen deprivation therapy than during the pre-treatment assessment. Similarly, reduced amygdala activation was found in another patient with long-term androgen deprivation therapy, referenced against the average activation pattern of an untreated pedophilic comparison group (Schiffer, Gizewski, & Krueger, 2009). In that study, the authors also observed attenuated activation in other brain areas associated with sexual arousal, specifically noting the "(hypo)thalamus, [...] insula, substantia nigra, hippocampus, [and] the rostral part of the [anterior cingulate cortex]" (p. 892).

Relating aspects of offense behavior to findings on the brain structure of their participants, Poeppl et al. (2013) reported an almost perfect correlation between lower victim age and reductions of grey matter in orbitofrontal regions. Furthermore, an index of pedophilic sexual interest derived from offense characteristics was inversely related to grey matter volume in the left dorsolateral prefrontal cortex and in the left insular cortex. The outcome of anomalies in orbitofrontal (Schiffer et al., 2007) and dorsolateral prefrontal areas (Poeppl et al., 2013) can be interpreted in terms of deficits of response inhibition in pedophiles.

Finally, case studies point at the possibility of late-onset paraphilia induced by neurological disease or brain tumors (e.g., Burns & Swerdlow 2003; Mendez et al., 2000; Mendez & Shapira, 2011) (see Box 13.2). For example, Simpson et al. (1999) found that among 445 consecutive admissions to a brain injury unit, 29 individuals (6.5%) had committed sexual offenses (Simpson et al., 1999). Similarly, Blanchard et al. (2002) (see also Suchy et al., 2009) registered a significantly higher rate of childhood accidents resulting in head injuries among pedophilic sexual offenders (10.2%) than among non-pedophilic sexual offenders (4.4%). Comparing 22 sadistic sexual offenders with 21 non-sadistic sexual offenders on X-ray computed tomography scans of the brain, Hucker et al. (1988) found a significantly higher rate of right temporal lobe pathology in the sadists (41%) than in the non-sadistic controls (10%). Eher et al. (2000) found brain abnormalities in sexual offenders to be associated with greater levels of violence in the offenses, using structural MRI.

> **Box 13.2   Brain tumor associated with pedophilic symptoms**
>
> In 2002, the *New Scientist* reported on a case from the US in which a 40-year-old male schoolteacher had begun collecting child pornography and made sexual advances toward young children (Choi, 2002). The patient not only showed pedophilic sexual interest (and associated criminal behavior), but also started soliciting prostitutes. Neurological assessment revealed deficits in constructional abilities (apraxia), agraphia (language disorder), as well as an unusual gait, and loss of control over his bladder (Burns & Swerdlow, 2003). The sexually problematic behavior stopped once a tumor (hemangiopericytoma) the size of a chicken egg was resected from his right orbitofrontal lobe. The tumor regrew and had to be resected some 14-months later. Four months prior to resection, the problematic behavior had resumed (Choi, 2002) but again stopped after the second removal.

The neurobiological findings on some of the biggest risk factors for offending: *sexual deviance*, *affect regulation*, *impulsivity*, and *antisociality*, as well as *cognitive ability/intellectual disability* will be briefly reviewed in the next section.

Risk Factors Indicating Neuropsychological Problems

In a meta-analysis of 82 international recidivism studies, with a total sample size of 29,450 sexual offenders (Hanson & Morton-Bourgon, 2005), deviant sexual preferences and antisociality were the main risk factors for sexual recidivism. At a more fine-grained level of scrutiny, sexual preoccupations (in the sense of an intensive rumination about sexual matters), deviant sexual interests, problems of self-regulation, and psychopathy, as well as antisocial personality disorder (ASPD), proved most relevant as predictors of sexual recidivism in that study. It is interesting to note that other plausible candidates that might point at an increased risk are lack of empathy with the victim (see Mann & Barnett, 2013) and denial of the sexual offense. However, neither of these factors showed any substantial associations with sexual reoffending.

Sexual deviance *Sexual deviance is a primary risk factor for sexual re-offending.*
Source: © Espressolia. Used under license from Pixabay.

Sexual deviance

Not only has sexual deviance been identified as the prime risk factor for sexual reoffending (see above), but it also accords well with theoretical accounts of the etiology of sexual offending, such as the theory put forward by McGuire et al. (1965). According to this explanation, sexually deviant fantasies become entrenched by conditioning and lead to subsequent acting out. Later theories, like the integrative models of Finkelhor (1984), Marshall and Barbaree (1990), or the integrated theory of sexual offending by Ward and Beech (2006), also included the conditioning of sexually deviant interests (Laws & Marshall, 1990) as a potential precursor to sexual offending.

One component of sexual deviance is sexual arousal toward inappropriate sexual objects or behaviors, such as images of children or displays of coercive activity; another pertinent component is sexual interest as evidenced by an attentional bias for corresponding stimuli. According to theoretical models of the general sexual arousal response, attention (or stimulus appraisal), and physiological arousal refer to early and late stages in a sequence of internal reactions toward sexually relevant stimuli, respectively (Janssen et al., 2000; Singer 1984; Stoléru et al., 1999; see Chapter 4 of this volume).

Eye-tracking research indicates that the bias for child-related stimuli among pedophilic child molesters is attentional and automatic (e.g., Fromberger et al., 2012). Likewise, there is a considerable body of research showing that pedophilic child molesters respond with more sexual arousal toward images of children than non-pedophilic controls (e.g., Blanchard, Klassen, Dickey, Kuban, & Blak, 2001). Similarly, self-referred sadistic men from the community showed altered arousal patterns toward stimuli depicting violence (Seto et al., 2012).

Unlike previous editions, the current version of the *Diagnostic and Statistical Manual of Mental Disorders* (*DSM-5*) (American Psychiatric Association, 2013) differentiates between unusual sexual interests (paraphilias) and disorders of sexual preference (paraphilic disorders) – see Beech, Miner, and Thornton (2016) for a review of this distinction. In order to qualify as suffering from a paraphilic disorder the person in question must experience distress about their sexual predilection. Alternatively, the sexual urges or behaviors must put others under duress or be directed at non-consenting persons or at individuals who cannot express their consent (like children). The *DSM-5* lists exhibitionistic disorder, fetishistic disorder, frotteuristic disorder, pedophilic disorder, sexual masochism disorder, sexual sadism disorder, transvestic disorder, and voyeuristic disorder as variants of paraphilic disorders. Only some of these, particularly pedophilic, sadistic, and exhibitionistic disorders, are forensically relevant. The other paraphilic disorders (fetishistic, frotteuristic, sexual masochism, and transvestic disorders) will rarely, if ever, become relevant in legal proceedings. Table 13.1 summarizes those paraphilias that may be relevant, with regard to sexual offending, along with a brief description of their content.

It is important to keep in mind, however, that the disorders of sexual preference, outlined in Table 13.1, are neither necessary nor sufficient conditions for sexual offending. It is also important to distinguish disorders of sexual preference as psychiatric terms from the legal definition of the offenses that they may be associated with. Consequently, it is incorrect to refer to all sexual offenders against children as pedophiles, simply because pedophilia increases the risk for committing sexual abuse of children. Table 13.2 provides an overview of prevalence estimates for various paraphilic interests based on studies from three European countries and from Australia.

Clearly, the studies summarized in Table 13.2 differ in terms of the strictness of criteria for paraphilic interest, behavior, or disorder as well as in terms of the timeframe

Table 13.1 Selection of forensically relevant disorders of sexual preference/paraphilic disorders (with psychiatric classification and brief description)

Disorder	ICD-10	DSM-5	Primary sexual arousal by ...
Exhibitionism	F65.2	302.4	Exposing one's genitals
Fetishism	F65.0	302.81	Objects (e.g., shoes), types of material (e.g., rubber), or non-genital body parts (e.g., feet)
Sexual masochism	65.5	302.83	Enduring corporal punishment, humiliation, pain, ritualized sequences of actions
Pedophilia	F65.4	302.2	Sexual fantasies and behavior involving prepubertal children
Sexual sadism	F65.5	302.84	Exertion of power, control, and domination
Voyeurism	F65.3	302.82	Covert observation of unsuspecting others (especially when nude/undressing or engaged in sexual activity)

Table 13.2 Prevalence estimates (in %) of paraphilic interests

Study	Country	N	Age Group	Prevalence	Paraphilia	Men	Women
Ahlers et al., (2011)	D	363	40–79 years	Lifetime	Exhibitionism	2.2	
					Frotteurism	6.5	
					Masochism	2.3	
					Pedophilia	3.8	
					Sadism	15.5	
					Transvestism	2.7	
					Voyeurism	18.0	
Långström & Seto (2006)	SVE	2,450	18–60 years	Lifetime	Exhibitionism	4.1	2.1
					Voyeurism	11.5	3.9
Långström & Zucker (2005)	SVE	2,450	18–60 years	Lifetime	Transvestitism	2.8	0.4
Richters et al. (2008)	AUS	19,307	16–59 years	One year	Sadomasochism	1.8	1.2
Santtila et al. (2015)	FIN	1,310	33–43 years	One year	Pedophilia	0.2	

Source: Translated, updated and reprinted from Mokros (2012) with permission of Springer Science & Business Media, Berlin, Germany.

surveyed (i.e., lifetime compared with the previous 12 months only). Consequently, the prevalence estimates diverge considerably. What can be seen from Table 13.2 is that paraphilia-related fantasies and behaviors are more common in men than in women. Furthermore, a sizable proportion of men from the general population (2–18%) at some point in their life either fantasized about paraphilic behavior or acted upon these.

Although the review by Leitenberg and Henning (1995) indicates that deviant sexual fantasies seem to be more prevalent in sexual offenders than in men sampled from the general population (cf., Abel & Rouleau, 1990), the striking fact is that so many individuals do not appear to act on their deviant sexual fantasies. Therefore, deviant sexual fantasy is neither a necessary nor a sufficient precondition of sexual offending (Leitenberg & Henning, 1995) but may increase the risk for sexual offending. Presumably, individuals with paraphilias experience a selectively higher arousability in response to deviant stimuli – a circumstance most plausibly explained in terms of a lack of inhibition by a stimulus-control model (Barbaree & Marshall, 1991). Among the convicted perpetrators of child sexual abuse, some 40% are estimated to be pedophilic (Seto, 2008, 2009). In mixed samples of sexual offenders against children or adults, the prevalence of sadism was estimated at between 2.4% and 6%, with higher rates among rapists than among child molesters (Eher et al., 2016).

A neuroimaging study with sadistic sexual offenders revealed an increased activity in the left amygdala when looking at images depicting inflictions of pain, compared with the brain activity of non-sadistic sexual offenders (Harenski et al., 2012). The authors interpreted this finding as an indication of a pleasurable emotion induced by witnessing another person's distress. Furthermore, the results of the study by Harenski et al. (2012) seem to support the notion of an altered pain perception (Chuang, 2011) as the sadists rated the images depicting pain as significantly more severe, compared to the ratings given by the non-sadistic controls. Furthermore, Harenski et al. (2012) observed a positive correlation between the activity level of the left anterior insula and subsequent pain ratings among the sadistic participants. This outcome is in accordance with the view that sadism is not an outcome of an inability to recognize the emotional states of others (Nitschke et al., 2012), but rather a paradoxical reaction toward other peoples' distress (e.g., Kirsch & Becker, 2007). However, an earlier neuroimaging case study of a sadist using positron emission tomography (PET) failed to show a difference in limbic activation toward sexual versus nonsexual auditory stimulation (Garnett et al., 1988). But it is of note that the stimuli in that study did not involve the infliction of pain or humiliation.

A recent meta-analysis (Polisois-Keating, & Joyal, 2013) provides a summary of seven functional brain imaging studies that compared either sexual arousal, or sexual interest, between pedophilic and non-pedophilic men. The studies in question used either PET or functional magnetic resonance imaging (fMRI). It was found in these studies that viewing sexual stimuli of the preferred kind in both pedophilic participants, and non-pedophilic controls, resulted in increased cerebral blood flow (and thus presumably higher activation) in the following areas of the brain: the occipital cortex, the anterior cingulate cortex, the fusiform gyrus, the cerebellum, and the substantia nigra. Hence, the increased activation upon processing preferred sexual stimuli pertained to both cortical and subcortical areas.

The areas shown to display stronger activation in both conditions in this meta-analysis are in accordance with neurophysiological models of the general sexual arousal response (e.g., Redouté et al., 2000; Stoléru et al., 1999; see Chapter 4), and hence are not specific of deviant arousal patterns. For example, structures of the inferior temporal cortex, like the fusiform gyrus, are visual association areas that likely represent the higher-order appraisal of visual stimuli as sexually relevant (Stoléru et al., 2012). Hence, the activation of the fusiform gyrus would thus be concomitant with the notion of a cognitive (Stoléru et al., 1999), or appraisal (Janssen et al., 2000; Singer 1984), component of the sexual arousal response (Stoléru et al., 2012).

In this context one should also note that lesions of the inferior temporal cortex may lead to the Klüver-Bucy syndrome (e.g., Langevin, 1990), a condition (see Box 13.3) associated with hypersexuality, and indiscriminate sexual activity, that in some cases may lead to criminal offenses (e.g., Devinsky, Sacks, & Devinsky, 2010). In contrast, the activation of the anterior cingulate cortex – a paralimbic region involved in autonomic and neuroendocrine regulation (Stoléru et al., 1999) as well as in emotion processing and impulse control – is considered relevant for the affective and autonomic aspects of sexual arousal in non-paraphilic individauls (Stoléru et al., 2012). Furthermore, the activations of midbrain regions like the substantia nigra are presumably associated with the physiological component of sexual arousal.

Box 13.3   Klüver–Bucy syndrome

Klüver and Bucy (1937) described the symptoms of a rhesus monkey after surgical removal of its temporal lobes. Symptoms involved lack of responses considered analogous to anger or fear, visual agnosia (i.e., impaired visual recognition

> of objects), and the indiscriminate oral exploration of objects whether edible or non-edible. In a more detailed report, Klüver and Bucy (1939) noted marked changes in the sexual behavior of macaques whose temporal lobes had similarly been surgically removed. Here the monkeys showed hypersexual behavior (including frequent and spontaneous erections, oral and manual manipulation of the genitalia, frequent and almost continuous copulation with both female and male animals). Terzian and Dalle Ore (1955) reported on the outcome of a bilateral temporal lobectomy in a 19-year-old man who had suffered from temporal epilepsy and generalized tonic-clonic seizures since the age of three or four. Apart from hyperphagia, the complete loss of emotional responses, and both retro- and anterograde amnesia, the patient also showed sexual symptoms similar to the ones observed in the macaques by Klüver and Bucy (i.e., spontaneous erections, frequent masturbation, and sexual invitations, but limited to other men). In seven out of twelve human cases, Lilly, Cummings, Benson, and Frankel (1983) observed alterations in sexual behavior. In these cases, the Klüver-Bucy syndrome occurred due to head trauma, neurodegenerative disease, or encephalitis.

In the Polisois-Keating and Joyal meta-analysis (2013) the pedophilic subjects displayed somewhat stronger activations in the superior parietal lobule, the hippocampus, and the insula, but these differences were not significant. The superior parietal lobule can be considered a component involved in the cognitive or appraisal stage of the sexual arousal response (Kühn & Gallinat, 2011). It is also conceivable that sexual deviance is caused, modulated, or accompanied by differential neuroendocrine functioning. Research studies or reviews on the topic of hormone levels in pedophilia in particular or sexual offending in general are Bain, Langevin, Dickey, Hucker, and Wright (1988), Gaffney et al. (1984), Jordan et al. (2011a,b), Kingston et al. (2012), Langevin (1993), and Lieverse, Assies, and Gooren (2000). See Mokros, Habermeyer, and Habermeyer (2017) for a detailed summary of brain imaging findings and an overview of neurological and neuroendocrinological studies pertaining to sexual deviance.

The paralimbic region of the insula can presumably be subsumed under the emotional/motivational component of the sexual arousal response (Stoléru et al., 1999), given its role in interoception (Stoléru et al., 2012) as well as in feelings of love (Ortigue et al., 2010), and sexual desire (Cacioppo et al., 2012). Similarly, the hippocampus as part of the limbic system likely plays a role in decoding the emotional valence of sexual stimuli, possibly associated with the experience of an urge to act (Poeppl et al., 2011). On the other hand, insula, amygdala, and the anterior cingulate gyrus were shown to be associated with general arousal (such as when looking at aversive stimuli) but not necessarily with sexual arousal in non-paraphilic men (Kagerer et al., 2011). At least for the insular and anterior cingulate regions, this effect was replicated in a mixed sample of sadistic and non-sadistic sexual offenders (Harenski et al., 2012).

The functional neuroimaging on pedophilia are commensurate with the view, expressed for instance by Seto (2008), that there is no difference in the brain systems involved in processing sexual stimuli in both pedophilic and non-pedophilic men (Polisois-Keating & Joyal, 2013). In other words, the type of stimuli used (depicting either children or adults) leads to differences between participant groups, not functional idiosyncrasies of the brain. This interpretation agrees with the stimulus control model of sexual aggression put forward by Barbaree and Marshall (1991). According to this view, it is the quality of the stimuli that matters. Put differently, the brains of pedophilic men may be running the same hardware as non-pedophilic men's brains but they may be relying on a different kind of software.

Affect regulation

Deficits in self-regulation were also identified as a risk factor for sexual reoffending (Hanson and Morton-Bourgon 2005). To the author's knowledge there are no studies to date that have assessed the notion of affective dysregulation in sexual offenders under a neuroscience framework. Yet there are self-report studies that attest to the combination of deviant sexual fantasies and affect regulation in sexual offenders (Lussier, Proulx, & McKibben, 2001; Proulx, McKibben, & Lusignan, 1996). According to the study by Proulx et al. (1996) sexual offenders tend to compensate aversive mood states by indulging in deviant sexual fantasies. The function of deviant sexual fantasies as a mood stabilizer accords well with Marshall's (1989) observation of intimacy deficits in sexual offenders, as well as with the psychodynamic notion of paraphilia as a "narcissistic seal" that would temporarily close a gap in self-development (Morgenthaler, 1974). Therefore, future neuroscience research on sexual offending and paraphilia should address the question whether mood states mediate or moderate the brain responses toward corresponding stimuli.

Furthermore, it has been suggested that sexual offenders could be differentiated into paraphilics on the one hand and individuals with impulse control disorders on the other hand (e.g., Hoyer et al., 2001). Comparing two groups of paraphilic and impulse control disordered sexual offenders, Hoyer et al. observed a significantly higher rate of social phobia among the paraphilic individuals. Lussier et al. (2001) found that anxious sexual offenders were less likely to adopt strategies taught in treatment for how to cope with deviant sexual fantasies. Hence, anxious-avoidant personality traits should be acknowledged in future neurocognitive research with sexual offenders.

Finally, the ones who fantasize about sexually deviant acts and the ones who commit such acts may differ in terms of the likelihood of misperceiving fantasy as future reality (Kunzendorf, Carrabino, & Capone, 1992).[1] Consequently, wishful thinking and biased views on the probability of events occurring may tie in with the cognitive distortions observed in many sexual offenders. An interesting avenue of neuroscience research on sexual offending could thus explore the phenomenon of equating fantasy with reality under neuroimaging conditions.

Impulsivity

It is well documented that pedophilic men respond differently to child stimuli, which speaks for the existence of a deviant sexual preference. In pedophilic men, both the components of physiological sexual arousal (Blanchard et al., 2001) and cognitive information processing (Snowden, Craig, & Gray, 2011) appear to be more easily influenced by child stimuli. The use of child pornography can serve as a diagnostic indicator of pedophilia (Seto, Cantor, & Blanchard, 2006). Yet sole users of child pornography have a lower risk of committing hands-on sexual offenses against children subsequently than child pornography offenders who also have a history of violent offending (Eke, Seto, & Williams, 2011; Seto, Hanson, & Babchishin, 2011). Therefore, it may be the combination of a lack in response inhibition with deviant sexual preferences that would pose a particular risk. Incidentally, the combination of sexual deviance and weak response inhibition would represent a merging of the response-control and stimulus-control models that Barbaree and Marshall (1991) described with regard to rape. As discussed below, the co-occurrence of sexual deviance with psychopathy – which includes a lack of behavioral inhibition – multiplies the risk for sexual reoffending (e.g., Rice & Harris, 1997). Finally, the combination of sexual deviance with response inhibition is a corollary of the dual-dysfunction theory of pedophilia (Cantor et al., 2008) that posits deficits in both frontal and temporal brain areas (Cohen et al., 2002).

Neuropsychological findings only partly support the notion of deficient response inhibition in pedophiles who have committed hands-on sexual offenses against children (Krueger & Schiffer, 2011). Cohen and colleagues (2002) found 20 pedophilic men to differ from 22 male healthy controls in that the pedophilic participants showed more pronounced impulsive personality traits (such as lower impulse control and more Cluster B personality disorder pathology). But Cohen and colleagues also noted that the pedophilic participants did not display stronger signs of dysexecutive functioning than the controls. A study by Schiffer and Vonlaufen (2011) yielded similar results. Consequently, it remains to be clarified whether insufficient response inhibition represents the link between pedophilic preference and overt offense behavior. See Box 13.4 for a discussion of these issues.

> **Box 13.4   Do sexual offenders have executive functioning (EF) problems?**
>
> In a review of neuropsychological assessments of sexual offenders based on 23 individual studies with a total of 1,756 participants (Joyal, Beaulieu-Plante, & de Chantérac, 2014) the authors noted that sexual offenders against adults showed similar performance levels as non-sex offenders whereas sexual offenders against children on average had lower scores on tests of EF. The summary term of EF refers to the cognitive abilities involved in planning and controlling actions and comprises such different constructs like working memory, selective attention, or impulse control. Comparing sexual offenders against children with sexual offenders against adults, Joyal et al. (2014) found the former to perform worse in tasks involving deduction and cognitive flexibility, whereas the latter performed worse in terms of verbal fluency tests. According to Joyal et al. there are other meaningful differentiations between various types of sexual offenders than the age of their victims. For example, it might be relevant to compare those with a specific sexual preference for pre-pubertal children (i.e., the pedophilic individuals) with those who simply victimized children as a matter of opportunity within the subgroup of sexual abusers of children.

A recent fMRI study addressed this question with a sample of 11 pedophilic participants. Five of them had committed hands-on sexual offenses against children whereas six had been convicted of using child pornography (Habermeyer et al., 2013). Using a go/no-go paradigm the authors observed a group by task interaction, with the group factor juxtaposing pedophilic subjects and healthy controls. During the no-go trials the pedophilic subjects on average reacted slower than the controls; they on average also made more errors. Moreover, the pedophilic subjects displayed an attenuated deactivation of the left precuneus and angular gyrus during the no-go trials – an effect correlated with larger reaction times. Habermeyer et al. interpreted this outcome in terms of a weaker deactivation of the default mode network (Raichle et al., 2001) in pedophiles – a set of brain regions usually more active during resting state than in focused activity. The results of Habermeyer et al. (2013) do not necessarily imply a disturbance of the default mode network in pedophilia but could also be explained as an artifact of the test situation, since the default mode network is also more active if persons are engaged in self-referential thinking (Zhang & Li, 2012). The pedophiles in the study by Habermeyer et al. (2013) may have been more concerned with introspection than the controls, for example.

Antisociality

A recent meta-analysis (Hawes, Boccaccini, and Murrie 2013) attests to the association of psychopathy and sexual reoffending, where the link between psychopathy as measured with the Psychopathy Checklist-Revised (PCL-R) (Hare, 2003) and sexual recidivism was in the small-to-moderate range (Cohen's $d = 0.40$). Disaggregating psychopathic core personality traits like deceitfulness and emotional detachment (PCL-R Factor 1) from recklessness and antisociality (PCL-R Factor 2), Hawes et al. found that only the latter were significantly predictive of sexual recidivism ($d = 0.44$). This result mirrors the finding from research on general violent recidivism that the social deviance or antisociality component of the PCL-R appears to be more relevant as a predictor of recidivism than the core psychopathic personality traits (Yang, Wong, & Coid, 2010). Using latent variable modeling instead of zero-order correlations, however, psychopathic core personality traits have been shown to be as strongly associated with violence as the social deviance component (Vitacco, Neumann, & Jackson, 2005).

Given that taxometric research indicated that there is no reason to assume a distinct category of *psychopathic* sexual offenders (Walters et al., 2011), the reader is referred to Chapters 9 and 10 for details on the neurobiological bases of psychopathy and antisocial personality disorder, respectively. It should be noted, however, that the effects of psychopathy and sexual deviance on sexual reoffending seem to interact. In a mixed sample of child molesters and rapists, the presence of sexual deviance (as measured by phallometry in response to suitable stimuli) in conjunction with psychopathy had a multiplicative effect on sexual recidivism (Rice & Harris, 1997).

Cognitive ability/intellectual disability

A meta-analysis (Cantor et al., 2005) found that sexual offenders on average lower in IQ than non-sex offenders or men from the general population but the average IQ was lowest for sexual offenders against children. More specifically, there was a large significant correlation between maximum victim age and offenders' IQ ($r = 0.64$). That is, the lower the age cut-off of victims in a given study, the lower the corresponding average IQ scores of the offenders sampled in that study. Cantor and his colleagues (2005) interpreted their finding of a correlation between victim age and offender IQ with respect to pedophilia. According to this view the choice of pre-pubertal victims was an outcome of pedophilia that would be, in turn, associated with lower IQ. Alternatively, it seems conceivable that the effect observed by Cantor et al. is, at least partially, driven by intellectually disabled offenders. If committing a sexual offence, individuals with intellectual disability may be more prone to choose a child victim for several reasons: the availability of children, the gullibility of children, and the misperception or misjudgment of someone else's boundaries of sexual integrity on behalf of the offender (cf. Günter, 2009). If this supposition was true, a sizable proportion of intellectually disabled sexual offenders against children would not decide to sexually abuse a child as a matter of preference but due to the other factors aforementioned.

It is unlikely, though, that the social aloofness and the lack of knowledge about sexuality on behalf of intellectually disabled offenders would account for the low IQ/lower victim age link in sexual abuse. Rice and et al. (2008) tested this notion in a sample of 69 mentally retarded sexual offenders and found more pedophilic sexual interests than in a sample of 69 sexual offenders with average or above-average IQs. Therefore, one pathway to pedophilia may be neurodevelopmental perturbations (Cantor et al., 2004; Harris, Rice, & Lalumière, 2001).

Conclusions

Recent studies indicate that pedophilic sexual preference, for instance, is commensurate with a taxonic (or categorical) underlying structure (Schmidt, Mokros, & Banse, 2013), whereas sadism among sexual offenders likely represents a dimensional phenomenon (Mokros et al., 2014). As distinct types are more in accordance with the notion of specific and discrete etiological mechanisms (Meehl 1977, 1992) whereas continuous constructs are more in line with multifarious influences, one might conjecture that the search for causal brain abnormalities in pedophilia will be more promising than in, say, sadism. Recent genetic (Alanko, Gunst, Mokros, & Santtila, 2016; Alanko, Salo, Mokros, & Santtila, 2013) as well as earlier findings from a family study (Gaffney, Lurie, & Berlin, 1984) seem to indicate that the developmental antecedents of sexual interest in minors among adult men are at least partially genetic.

Still, the notion of pedophilic sexual preference as a categorical entity does not necessarily imply that a biological basis must have caused it (cf., Ruscio, Haslam, & Ruscio, 2006), especially given the plasticity of the brain. As the now famous study of London cab drivers showed it was not a hypertrophic hippocampus that made these individuals choose to become a cabbie in London in the first place. Rather, specific regions of their hippocampus increased in size the more these individuals became familiar with the road map of London (Woollett & Maguire, 2011). In this way, the increase in volume of areas of the brain relevant for memory functioning is likely the equivalent of the cab drivers' increasingly sophisticated cognitive map of London.

One should not forget that the studies acknowledged above, such as the meta-analyses by Joyal and colleagues (2014), as well as by Cantor and colleagues (2006), dealt exclusively with sexual offenders who had been *apprehended and convicted* of their offenses. In this regard, the offenders tested in the corresponding studies may not be representative of sexual offenders in general (Blanchard et al., 2006). This could be reflective of the distinction of so-called successful psychopaths with other criminal psychopaths according to Yang et al. (2005), who, in an experimental study utilizing structural MRI (sMRI), observed that significant reductions in prefrontal grey matter volume of the brain were only present in psychopaths who had been caught and convicted for criminal offenses, not in psychopaths sampled from the community. By analogy, some of the research literature on the (neuro-) psychological deficits of sexual offenders may be biased due to the sampling of offenders from correctional settings, especially since the fronto-temporal brain anomalies oftentimes regarded as relevant for sexual offending are not specific of this type of offending and may thus rather represent a general deficit prevalent among many violent offenders (Joyal et al., 2014).

Moreover, the extant studies on the structural and functional brain properties of pedophilic or sadistic men are few, most of them including a limited number of participants only. Although this does not devaluate the research as such (Friston, 2012) it should be clear that the neuroscience research on these forensically relevant paraphilias could only identify strong effects so far. The statistical power would not have sufficed to find more subtle differences in the brains of paraphilic men.

Implications for Forensic Practice, Ethical Implications, and Policy

Clearly, the knowledge about risk factors of sexual offending and brain abnormality associated with sexual offending has been burgeoning in the last couple of years. In the wake of new developments in assessment like structural or functional magnetic resonance imaging the same techniques of assessment have gained access to the courtroom in some instances. As Fabian (2012) pointed out with respect to civil commitment proceedings under the so-called sexually violent predator laws, neuroscience-related evidence could become relevant in particular when debating the question whether an offender would have been able to control his sexual urges.

In the case of Brian Dugan, for example, psychologist Kent Kiehl of the University of New Mexico testified as an expert witness in a sentencing trial (Hughes, 2010). Brian Dugan was diagnosed a psychopath, with 38 points out of 40 on the PCL-R (Hare, 2003). In the mid-1980s Dugan had killed two girls aged seven and ten years, respectively, and a 27-year-old woman. Dugan had sexually assaulted each of the victims. In preparing his report, Kiehl also relied on functional MRT scans of Dugan's brain obtained while Dugan was performing various cognitive tasks (Hughes, 2010). Kiehl's evidence was ruled as permissible by the trial judge, yet Kiehl was not allowed to present any images showing scans of Dugan's brain to the jury. Basically, Kiehl's expert evidence pointed at various performance deficits and dysfunctions commonly found in psychopaths. The jury voted for the death penalty nonetheless and the judge sentenced Dugan accordingly. The sentence was commuted to life imprisonment when the death penalty was abolished in the state of Illinois in 2011 (Zorn, 2011). Another example of a case from Italy in which not fMRI but sMRI scans were used in expert testimony during a sentencing trial is given by Feresin (2011). The Italian case did not pertain to sexual offending, however.

Evidently, the fMRI scans were merely one piece of the jigsaw in Dugan's case in compiling a comprehensive mental health report on behalf of Kiehl. Nevertheless, Dugan has become something like the posterboy in the debate of whether new assessment methods from neuroscience research should be considered as evidence in court (e.g., several references to the case in Simpson, 2012). In this regard, a few words of caution seem appropriate. First, the association of different phenomena such as a correlation of peculiarities in brain functioning or structure with violent offenses does not imply that the former caused the latter. Psychologist and lawyer Stephen J. Morse of the University of Pennsylvania coined the term "brain overclaim syndrome" in this regard and reckons that some neuroscientists are "always using language that suggests causation, when they don't know causation" (as cited in Buchen, 2012, p. 306). Indeed, some neuroscientists seem to assume that there was not only an implication but even an equivalence of brain anomaly and violent offending at play. That is, not only would brain anomaly lead to offending but the occurrence of violent offending as such would suffice to assume the existence of brain pathology according to this view. Such an argument, however, is a deductive fallacy as it is based on the irregular reversal of a premise (so-called affirming the consequent, or converse error). Such an extreme position also neglects the social influence on phenomena like sexual offending, as evidenced by the surge of rape in the aftermath of war (Stiglmayr, 1994), for example. Similar objections apply to the simplistic exoneration due to the possession of particular alleles (Feresin, 2009, 2011) that have been shown to be associated with a propensity for aggression in large samples but do not necessarily explain violent acts in the individual case (see also Chapter 12). As Patel et al. (2007, p. 561) pointed out:

> the expert must establish, through reliable scientific methods, the etiology of the observed abnormality and the implications of that abnormality for the patient's behavior .... Because the brain demonstrates elasticity, a functional image taken at a certain time or under certain conditions may not be similar to an image at a different point in time, although both depict normal brain functioning. Additionally, there is widespread disagreement about the degree to which one can predict behavior from neuroimage findings

The use of sophisticated machinery like MRT scanners may create the impression that such hard science was superior to the soft science of traditional psychological and psychiatric forensic assessment (Buchen, 2012), which is largely based on observation, comparison, interview, and psychometric testing. As Morse continues to point out (as cited in Buchen, 2012, p. 306) brain imaging techniques, for instance, may only become relevant in combination with behavioral data. Put differently, neuroscience assessment methods may help to identify, corroborate, or refute a diagnosis or a need for treatment only if overt deficits in functioning become apparent.

The focus on trace evidence of brain pathology, such as fMRI scans, may detract, however, from the question whether the psychosocial *functioning* of a person is impaired to a level that would impede with legal responsibility (Kröber, 2004). In this regard, the notion of explaining norm violations with peculiarities in brain scans is reminiscent of the heyday of psychodynamic interpretations of criminal behavior in court during the 1960s and 1970s. At the time, some psychoanalysts would give seemingly plausible accounts of a culprit's life that would make the offense in question appear as an almost inevitable outcome of that person's life-story. However, a good explanation is not necessarily the correct explanation. As Robertson and Vignaux (1995) make clear in their book on the interpretation of forensic evidence expert witnesses should, among other things, weigh the evidence according to the diagnostic utility of a given symptom and pay attention to alternative explanations. In other words, the expert witness should heed Cromwell's rule (Lindley, 2007): think it possible you may be mistaken.

Note

1 The author is grateful to David Glasgow, Colne, UK, for the reference to the work by Kunzendorf et al.

Recommended Reading

Joyal, C. C., Beaulieu-Plante, J., & de Chantérac, A. (2014). The neuropsychology of sex offenders: A meta-analysis. *Sexual Abuse: A Journal of Research and Treatment, 26,* 149–177. doi:10.1177/1079063213482842. *The meta-analysis summarizes the extant literature on the average performance of sexual offenders in neuropsychological tests. The analysis differentiates offender sub-groups and involves different parameters (i.e., memory, verbal fluency etc.).*

Mohnke, S., Müller, S., Amelung, T., Krüger, T. H. C., Ponseti, J., Schiffer, B., ... Walter, H. (2014). Brain alterations in paedophilia: A critical review. *Progress in Neurobiology, 122,* 1–23. doi:10.1016/j.pneurobio.2014.07.005. *The article provides a detailed list of findings on brain perturbations possibly associated with pedophilia. Furthermore, the corresponding findings from sMRI studies are evaluated.*

Poeppl, T. B., Langguth, B., Laird, A. R., & Eickhoff, S. B. (2014). The functional neuroanatomy of male psychosexual and physiosexual arousal: A quantitative meta-analysis. *Human Brain Mapping, 35*(4), 1404–1421. doi:10.1002/hbm.22262. *The meta-analysis provides an empirical overview of brain imaging findings on male sexual arousal. Furthermore, the brain circuits likely involved in sexual interest and sexual arousal are differentiated.*

Polisois-Keating, A., & Joyal, C. C. (2013). Functional neuroimaging of sexual arousal: A preliminary meta-analysis comparing pedophilic to non-pedophilic men. *Archives of Sexual Behavior, 42*(7), 1111–1113. doi:10.1007/s10508-013-0198-6. *The meta-analysis provides a summary of the findings from functional neuroimaging studies with respect to pedophilia.*

References

Abel, G. G., & Rouleau, J. L. (1990). The nature and extent of sexual assault. In W. L. Marshall, D. R. Laws, & H. E. Barbaree (Eds.), *Handbook of sexual assault: Issues, theories, and treatment of the offender* (pp. 9–21). New York, NY: Plenum Press.

Ahlers, C. J., Schaefer, G. A., Mundt, I. A., Roll, S., Englert, H., Willich, S. N., & Beier, K. M. (2011). How unusual are the contents of paraphilias? Paraphilia-associated sexual arousal patterns in a community-based sample of men. *Journal of Sexual Medicine, 8*(5), 1362–1370. doi:10.1111/j.1743-6109.2009.01597.x.

Alanko, K., Salo, B., Mokros, A., & Santtila, P. (2013). Evidence for heritability of adult men's sexual interest in youth under age 16 from a population-based extended twin design. *Journal of Sexual Medicine, 10*(4), 1090–1099. doi:10.1111/jsm.12067.

Alanko, K., Gunst, A., Mokros, A., & Santtila, P. (2016). Genetic variants associated with male pedophilic sexual interest. *Journal of Sexual Medicine, 13*(5) 835–842. doi:10.1016/j.jsxm.2016.02.170.

American Psychiatric Association. (2013). *Diagnostic and statistical manual of mental disorders* (5th ed.) (*DSM-5*). Arlington, VA: American Psychiatric Association.

Ariely, D., & Loewenstein, G. (2006). The heat of the moment: The effect of sexual arousal on sexual decision making. *Journal of Behavioral Decision Making*, 19, 87–98. doi:10.1002/bdm.501.

Bain, J., Langevin, R., Dickey, R., Hucker, S. J., & Wright, P. (1988). Hormones in sexually aggressive men: I. Baseline values for eight hormones / II. the ACTH test. *Annals of Sex Research*, 1, 63–78. doi:10.1007/BF00852883.

Barbaree, H. E., & Marshall, W. L. (1991). The role of male sexual arousal in rape: Six models. *Journal of Consulting and Clinical Psychology*, 59, 621–630. doi:10.1037/0022-006X.59.5.621.

Beech, A. R., Miner, M. H., & Thornton, D. (2016). Paraphilias in DSM-5. *Annual Review of Clinical Psychology*, 12, 383–406. doi:10.1146/annurev-clinpsy-021815-093330.

Blanchard, R., Cantor, J. M., & Robichaud, L. K. (2006). Biological factors in the development of sexual deviance and aggression in males. In H. E. Barbaree, & W. L. Marshall (Eds.), *The juvenile sex offender* (pp. 77–104). New York, NY: Guilford Press.

Blanchard, R., Christensen, B. K., Strong, S. M., Cantor, J. M., Kuban, M. E., Klassen, P., ... Blak, T. (2002). Retrospective self-reports of childhood accidents causing unconsciousness in phallometrically diagnosed pedophiles. *Archives of Sexual Behavior*, 31, 511–526. doi:10.1023/A:1020659331965.

Blanchard, R., Klassen, P., Dickey, R., Kuban, M. E., & Blak, T. (2001). Sensitivity and specificity of the phallometric test for pedophilia in nonadmitting sex offenders. *Psychological Assessment*, 13, 118–126. doi:10.1037/1040-3590.13.1.118.

Bramen, J. E., Hranilovich, J. A., Dahl, R. E., Forbes, E. E., Chen, J., Toga, A. W., Dinov, I. D., Worthman, C. M., &. Sowell, E. R. (2011). Puberty influences medial temporal lobe and cortical gray matter maturation differently in boys than girls matched for sexual maturity. *Cerebral Cortex*, 21, 636–646. doi:10.1093/cercor/bhq137.

Buchen, L. (2012). Arrested development. *Nature*, 484, 304–306. doi:10.1038/484304a.

Burns, J. M., & Swerdlow, R. H. (2003). Right orbitofrontal tumor with pedophilia symptom and constructional apraxia sign. *Archives of Neurology*, 60, 437–440. doi:10.1001/archneur.60.3.437.

Cacioppo, S., Bianchi-Demicheli, F., Frum, C., Pfaus, J. G., & Lewis, J. W. (2012). The common neural bases between sexual desire and love: A multilevel kernel density fMRI analysis. *Journal of Sexual Medicine*, 9, 1048–1054. doi:10.1111/j.1743-6109.2012.02651.x.

Cantor, J. M., & Blanchard, R. (2012). Letter to the editor: White matter volumes in pedophiles, hebephiles, and teleiophiles. *Archives of Sexual Behavior*, 41, 749–752. doi:10.1007/s10508-012-9954-2.

Cantor, J. M., Blanchard, R., Christensen, B. K., Dickey, R., Klassen, P. E., Beckstead, A. L., ... Kuban, M. E. (2004). Intelligence, memory, and handedness in pedophilia. *Neuropsychology*, 18, 3–14. doi: 10.1037/0894-4105.18.1.3.

Cantor, J. M., Blanchard, R., Robichaud, R. K., & Christensen, B. K. (2005). Quantitative reanalysis of aggregate data on IQ in sexual offenders. *Psychological Bulletin*, 131, 555–568. doi:10.1037/0033-2909.131.4.555.

Cantor, J. M., Kabani, N., Christensen, B. K., Zipursky, R. B., Barbaree, H. E., Dickey, R., ... Blanchard, R. (2008). Cerebral white matter deficiencies in pedophilic men. *Journal of Psychiatric Research*, 42, 167–183. doi:10.1016/j.jpsychires.2007.10.013.

Cavanna, A., & Trimble, M. R. (2006). The precuneus: A review of its functional anatomy and behavioural correlates. *Brain*, 129, 564–583. doi: 10.1093/brain/awl004.

Choi, C. (2002, October 21). Brain tumour causes uncontrollable paedophilia. *New Scientist*. Retrieved from http://www.newscientist.com/article/dn2943-brain-tumour-causes-uncontrollable-paedophilia.html#.VOtLpqCX-70 [Accessed February 23, 2015].

Cohen, L. J., Nikiforov, K., Gans, S., Poznansky, O., McGeoch, P., Weaver, C., ... Galynker, I. (2002). Heterosexual male perpetrators of childhood sexual abuse: A preliminary neuropsychiatric model. *Psychiatric Quarterly*, 74, 313–336. doi:10.1023/A:1020416101092.

Devinsky, J., Sacks, O., & Devinsky, O. (2010). Klüver-Bucy syndrome, hypersexuality, and the law. *Neurocase*, 16, 140–145. doi:10.1080/13554790903329182.

Eher, R., Aigner, M., Fruehwald, S., Frottier, P., & Gruenhut, C. (2000). Social information processed self-perceived aggression in relation to brain abnormalities in a sample of incarcerated sexual offenders. *Journal of Psychology & Human Sexuality*, 11(3), 37–47. doi:10.1300/J056v11n03_04.

Eher, R., Schilling, F., Hansmann, B., Pumberger, T., Nitschke, J., Habermeyer, E., & Mokros, A. (2016). Sexual sadism and violent reoffending. *Sexual Abuse: A Journal of Research and Treatment*, 28, 46–72. doi:10.1177/1079063214566715.

Eke, A., Seto, M. C., & Williams, J. (2011). Examining the criminal history and future offending of child pornography offenders: An extended prospective follow-up study. *Law and Human Behavior*, 35, 466–478. doi:10.1007/s10979-010-9252-2.

Fabian, J. M. (2012). Neuropsychology, neuroscience, volitional impairment and sexually violent predators: A review of the literature and the law and their application to civil commitment proceedings. *Aggression and Violent Behavior*, 17: 1–15. doi:10.1016/j.avb.2011.07.002

Feresin, E. (2009, October 30). Lighter sentence for murderer with "bad genes". *Nature*. Retrieved from http://www.nature.com/news/2009/091030/full/news.2009.1050.html doi:10.1038/news.2009.1050 [Accessed October 18, 2013].

Feresin, E. (2011, September 1). Italian court reduces murder sentence based on neuroimaging data. *Nature*. Retrieved from http://blogs.nature.com/news/2011/09/italian_court_reduces_murder_s.html [Accessed October 18, 2013].

Finkelhor, D. 1984. *Child sexual abuse*. New York, NY: The Free Press.

Friston, K. 2012. Ten ironic rules for non-statistical reviewers. *NeuroImage*, 61: 1300–1310. doi:10.1016/j.neuroimage.2012.04.018

Fromberger, P., Jordan, K., Steinkrauss, H., von Herder, J., Stolpmann, G., Kröner-Herwig, B., & Müller, J. (2012). Eye Movements in pedophiles: Automatic and controlled attentional processes while viewing prepubescent stimuli. *Journal of Abnormal Psychology*, 122, 587–599. doi:10.1037/a0030659.

Gaffney, G. R., & Berlin, F. S. (1984). Is there hypothalamic-pituitary-gonadal dysfunction in paedophilia? *British Journal of Psychiatry*, 145, 657–660. doi:10.1192/bjp.145.6.657.

Gaffney, G. R., Lurie, S. F., & Berlin, F. S. (1984). Is there familial transmission of pedophilia? *Journal of Nervous and Mental Disease*, 172, 546–548. doi:10.1097/00005053-198409000-00006.

Garnett, S., Nahmias, C., Wortzman, G., Langevin, R., & Dickey, R. (1988). Positron emission tomography and sexual arousal in a sadist and two controls. *Annals of Sex Research*, 1, 387–399. doi:10.1007/BF00878105.

Günter, M. (2009). Begutachtung bei Beeinträchtigungen der geistigen Fähigkeiten im Kindes-, Jugend- und Erwachsenenalter. [Assessment of impairments of intellectual abilities in childhood, youth, and adulthood]. In K. Foerster & H. Dressing (Eds.), *Psychiatrische Begutachtung* (5th ed.) (295–308). Munich, Germany: Urban & Fischer.

Habermeyer, B., Esposito, F., Händel, N., Lemoine, P., Kuhl, H. C., Klarhöfer, M., ... Graf, M. (2013). Response inhibition in pedophilia: An fMRI pilot study. *Neuropsychobiology*, 68, 228–237. doi:10.1159/000355295.

Habermeyer, B., Händel, N., Lemoine, P., Klarhöfer, M., Seifritz, E., Dittmann, V., & Graf, M. 2012. LH-RH agonists modulate amygdala response to visual sexual stimulation: A single case fMRI study in pedophilia. *Neurocase*, 18(6): 489–495. doi:10.1080/13554794.2011.627346

Hanson, R. K., & Morton-Bourgon, K. E. (2005). The characteristics of persistent sexual offenders: A meta-analysis of recidivism studies. *Journal of Consulting and Clinical Psychology*, *73*(6), 1154–1163. doi:10.1037/0022-006X.73.6.1154.

Hare, R. D. (2003). *Hare Psychopathy Checklist-Revised* (PCL-R, 2nd ed.). Toronto, ON, Canada: Multi-Health Systems.

Harenski, C. L., Thornton, D. M., Harenski, K. A., Decety, J., & Kiehl, K. A. (2012). Increased frontotemporal activation during pain observation in sexual sadism. *Archives of General Psychiatry*, *69*(3), 283–292. doi:10.1001/archgenpsychiatry.2011.1566.

Harris, G. T., Rice, M. E., & Lalumière, M. (2001). Criminal violence: The roles of psychopathy, neurodevelopmental insults, and antisocial parenting. *Criminal Justice and Behavior*, *28*(4), 402–426. doi:10.1177/009385480102800402.

Harris, R. J., Rice, G. E., Young, A. W., & Andrews, T. J. (2016). Distinct but overlapping patterns of response to words and faces in the fusiform gyrus. *Cerebral Cortex*, *26*(7), 3161–3168. doi: 10.1093/cercor/bhv147.

Hawes, S. W., Boccaccini, M. T., & Murrie, D. C. (2013). Psychopathy and the combination of psychopathy and sexual deviance as predictors of sexual recidivism: Meta-analytic findings using the Psychopathy Checklist-Revised. *Psychological Assessment*, *25*(1), 233–243. doi:10.1037/a0030391.

Himmelfarb, S. (2008). The multi-item randomized response technique. *Sociological Methods & Research*, *36*, 495–514. doi:10.1177/0049124107313900.

Hoyer, J., Kunst, H., & Schmidt, A. (2001). Social phobia as a comorbid condition in sex offenders with paraphilia or impulse control disorder. *Journal of Nervous and Mental Disease*, *189*, 463–470. doi:10.1097/00005053-200107000-00008.

Hucker, S. J., Langevin, R., Dickey, R., Handy, L., Chambers, J., Wright, S... . Wortzman, G. (1988). Cerebral damage and dysfunction in sexually aggressive men. *Annals of Sex Research*, *1*, 33–47. doi:10.1007/BF00852881.

Hucker, S. J., Langevin, R., Wortzman, G., Bain, J., Handy, L., Chambers, J., & Wright, S. (1986). Neuropsychological impairment in pedophiles. *Canadian Journal of Behavioural Science*, *18*, 440–448. doi:10.1037/h0079965.

Hughes, V. (2010). Head case: Science in court. *Nature*, *464*, 340–342. doi:10.1038/464340a.

Janssen, E., Everaerd, W., Spiering, M., & Janssen, J. (2000). Automatic processes and the appraisal of sexual stimuli: Toward an information processing model of sexual arousal. *Journal of Sex Research*, *37*, 8–23. doi:10.1080/00224490009552016.

Jordan, K., Fromberger, P., Stolpmann, G., & Müller, J. L. (2011a). The role of testosterone in sexuality and paraphilia—a neurobiological approach. Part I: Testosterone and sexuality. *Journal of Sexual Medicine*, *8*(11), 2993–3007. doi:10.1111/j.1743-6109.2011.02394.x.

Jordan, K., Fromberger, P., Stolpmann, G., & Müller, J. L. (2011b). The role of testosterone in sexuality and paraphilia—a neurobiological approach. Part II: Testosterone and paraphilia. *Journal of Sexual Medicine*, *8*(11), 3008–3029. doi:10.1111/j.1743-6109.2011.02393.x.

Joyal, C. C., Beaulieu-Plante, J., & de Chantérac, A. (2014). The neuropsychology of sex offenders: A meta-analysis. *Sexual Abuse: A Journal of Research and Treatment*, *26*, 149–177. doi:10.1177/1079063213482842.

Kagerer, S., Klucken, T., Wehrum, S., Zimmermann, M., Schienle, A., Walter, ... Stark, R. (2011). Neural activation toward erotic stimuli in homosexual and heterosexual males. *Journal of Sexual Medicine*, *8*, 3132–3143. doi:10.1111/j.1743-6109.2011.02449.x.

Kingston, D. A., Seto, M. C., Ahmed, A. G., Fedoroff, P., Firestone, P., & Bradford, J. M. (2012). The role of central and peripheral hormones in sexual and violent recidivism in sex offenders. *Journal of the American Academy of Psychiatry and the Law*, *40*, 476–485.

Kirsch, L. G., & Becker, J. V. (2007). Emotional deficits in psychopathy and sexual sadism: Implications for violent and sadistic behavior. *Clinical Psychology Review*, *27*, 904–922. doi:10.1016/j.cpr.2007.01.011.

Klüver, H., & Bucy, P. C. (1937). "Psychic blindness" and other symptoms following bilateral temporal lobectomy in Rhesus monkeys. [Abstract]. Proceedings of the American Physiological Society 49th annual meeting, Memphis, TN, April 21–24. *American Journal of Physiology, 119*, 352–353.

Klüver, H., & Bucy, P. C. (1939). Preliminary analysis of functions of the temporal lobes in monkeys. *Archives of Neurology and Psychiatry, 42*, 979–1000. doi: 10.1001/archneurpsyc.1939.02270240017001.

Kröber, H-L. (2004). Der freie Wille—eine Illusion? Biologische Hirnforschung und strafrechtliche Verantwortlichkeit. [The free will—an illusion? Biological brain science and culpability in criminal law]. *NeuroTransmitter, 14*(1): 72–74.

Kühn, S., & Gallinat, J. (2011). A quantitative meta-analysis on cue-induced male sexual arousal." *Journal of Sexual Medicine, 8*, 2269–2275. doi:10.1111/j.1743-6109.2011.02322.x.

Kunzendorf, R. G., Carrabino, C., & Capone, D. (1992). Safe fantasy: The self-conscious boundary between wishing and willing. *Imagination, Cognition and Personality, 12*, 177–188. doi:10.2190/3UTB-2VX2-5TBF-7EXB.

Langevin, R. (1990). Sexual anomalies and the brain. In W. L. Marshall, D. R. Laws, & H. E. Barbaree (Eds.), *Handbook of sexual assault: Issues, theories, and treatment of the offender* (pp. 103–113). New York, NY: Plenum Press.

Langevin, R. (1993). A comparison of neuroendocrine abnormalities and genetic factors in homosexuality and in pedophilia. *Annals of Sex Research, 6*, 67–76. doi:10.1007/BF00849746.

Långström, N., & Seto, M. C. (2006). Exhibitionistic and voyeuristic behavior in a Swedish national population survey. *Archives of Sexual Behavior, 35*, 427–435. doi:10.1007/s10508-006-9042-6.

Långström, N., & Zucker, K. J. (2005). Transvestic fetishism in the general population: Prevalence and correlates. *Journal of Sexual and Marital Therapy, 31*, 87–95. doi:10.1080/00926230590477934.

Laws, D. R., & Marshall, W. D. (1990). A conditioning theory of the etiology and maintenance of deviant sexual preference and behavior. In W. L. Marshall, D. R. Laws, & H. E. Barbaree (Eds.), *Handbook of sexual assault: Issues, theories, and treatment of the offender* (pp. 209–229), New York, NY: Plenum Press.

Leitenberg, H., & Henning, K. (1995). Sexual fantasy. *Psychological Bulletin, 117*, 469–496. doi:10.1037/0033-2909.117.3.469.

Lieverse, R., Assies, J., & Gooren, L. G. (2000). The psychoneuroendocrinology of (sexual) aggression. *Journal of Psychology & Human Sexuality, 11*(3), 19–36. doi:10.1300/J056v11n03_03.

Lilly, R., Cummings, J. L, Benson, F., & Frankel, M. (1983). The human Klüver-Bucy syndrome. *Neurology, 33*, 1141–1145. doi:10.1212/WNL.33.9.1141.

Lindley, D. V. (2007). *Understanding uncertainty*. Hoboken, NJ: John Wiley & Sons.

Lussier, P., Proulx, J., & McKibben, A. (2001). Personality characteristics and adaptive strategies to cope with negative emotional states and deviant sexual fantasies in sexual aggressors. *International Journal of Offender Therapy and Comparative Criminology, 45*, 159–170. doi:10.1077/0306624X01452003.

Malamuth, N. M. (1981). Rape proclivity among males. *Journal of Social Issues, 37*, 138–157. doi:10.1111/j.1540-4560.1981.tb01075.x.

Malamuth, N. M. (2003). Criminal and noncriminal sexual aggressors: Integrating psychopathy in a hierarchical-mediational confluence model. *Annals of the New York Academy of Sciences, 989*, 33–58. doi:10.1111/j.1749-6632.2003.tb07292.x.

Malamuth, N. M., Linz, D., Heavey, C., Barnes, G., & Acker, M. (1995). Using the confluence model of sexual aggression to predict men's conflict with women: A 10-year follow-up study. *Journal of Personality and Social Psychology, 69*, 353–369. doi:10.1037/0022-3514.69.2.353.

Malamuth, N. M., Sockloskie, R. J., Koss, M. P., & Tanaka, J. S. (1991). Characteristics of aggressors against women: Testing a model using a national sample of college students. *Journal of Consulting and Clinical Psychology, 59*, 670–681. doi:10.1037/0022-006X.59.5.670.

Mann, R. E., & Barnett, G. D. (2013). Victim empathy intervention with sexual offenders: Rehabilitation, punishment, or correctional quackery? *Sexual Abuse: A Journal of Research and Treatment, 25*, 282–301. doi:10.1177/1079063212455669.

Mann, R. E., Hanson, R. K., & Thornton, D. (2010). Assessing risk for sexual recidivism: Some proposals on the nature of psychologically meaningful risk factors. *Sexual Abuse: A Journal of Research and Treatment, 22*, 191–217. doi:10.1177/1079063210366039.

Marshall, W. L. (1989). Intimacy, loneliness, and sexual offenders. *Behavioural Research and Therapy, 27*, 491–503. doi:10.1016/0005-7967(89)90083-1.

Marshall, W. L., & Barbaree, H. E. (1990). An integrated theory of the etiology of sexual offending. In W. L. Marshall, D. R. Laws, & H. E. Barbaree (Eds.), *Handbook of sexual assault: Issues, theories, and treatment of the offender* (pp. 257–275). New York, NY: Plenum Press.

McGuire, R. J., Carlisle, J. M., & Young, B. G. (1965). Sexual deviations as conditioned behaviour: A hypothesis. *Behavioural Research and Therapy, 2*, 185–190. doi:10.1016/0005-7967(64)90014-2.

Meehl, P. E. (1977). Specific etiology and other forms of strong influence: Some quantitative meanings. *Journal of Medicine and Philosophy, 2*, 33–53. doi:10.1093/jmp/2.1.33.

Meehl, P. E. (1992). Factors and taxa, traits and types, differences of degree and differences in kind. *Journal of Personality, 60*, 117–174. doi:10.1111/j.1467-6494.1992.tb00269.x.

Mendez, M. F., Chow, T., Ringman, J., Twitchell, G., & Hinkin, C. H. (2000). Pedophilia and temporal lobe disturbances. *Journal of Neuropsychiatry and Clinical Neuroscience, 12*, 71–76.

Mendez, M. F., & Shapira, J. S. (2011). Pedophilic behavior from brain disease. *Journal of Sexual Medicine, 8*, 1092–1100. doi:10.1111/j.1743-6109.2010.02172.x.

Mohnke, S., Müller, S., Amelung, T., Krüger, T. H. C., Ponseti, J., Schiffer, B., … Walter, H. (2014). Brain alterations in paedophilia: A critical review. *Progress in Neurobiology, 122*, 1–23. doi:10.1016/j.pneurobio.2014.07.005.

Mokros, A. (2012). Fetischismus, Masochismus, Pädophilie: Außergewöhnliche sexuelle Präferenz oder relevante Störung? [Fetishism, masochism, pedophilia: Unusual sexual preference or relevant disorder?]. *Der Neurologe & Psychiater, 13*(10), 50–56.

Mokros, A., Habermeyer, B., & Habermeyer, E. (2017). Neurobiological implications in assessing treatment need in sexual offenders. In L. A. Craig, & M. Rettenberger (Eds.), *The Wiley handbook on the theories, assessment, & treatment of sexual offending – Volume 2: Assessment* (pp. 753–786). Chichester: John Wiley & Sons.

Mokros, A., Schilling, F, Weiss, K., Nitschke, J., & Eher, R. (2014). Sadism in sexual offenders: Evidence for dimensionality. *Psychological Assessment, 26*, 138–147. doi:10.1037/a0034861.

Morgenthaler, F. (1974). Die Stellung der Perversionen in Metapsychologie und Technik. [The state of perversions in metapsychology and technology]. *Psyche, 28*, 1077–1098.

Nitschke, J., Istrefi, S., Osterheider, M., & Mokros, A. (2012). Empathy in sexually sadistic offenders: An experimental comparison with non-sadistic sexual offenders. *International Journal of Law and Psychiatry, 35*, 165–167. doi:10.1016/j.ijlp.2012.02.003.

Office for National Statistics. (2015). Crime survey for England and Wales, chapter 4: Violent crime and sexual offences – Intimate personal violence and serious sexual assault [online document]. Retrieved from http://webarchive.nationalarchives.gov.uk/20160105160709/http://www.ons.gov.uk/ons/dcp171776_394500.pdf.

Ortigue, S., Bianchi-Demicheli, F., Patel, N., Frum, C., & Lewis, J. W. (2010). Neuroimaging of love: fMRI meta-analysis evidence toward new perspectives in sexual medicine. *Journal of Sexual Medicine*, 7, 3541–3552. doi:10.1111/j.1743-6109.2010.01999.x.

Patel, P., Metzler, C. C., Mayberg, H. S., & Levine, K. (2007). The role of imaging in United States courtrooms. *Neuroimaging Clinics of North America*, 17, 557–567. doi:10.1016/j.nic.2007.07.001.

Poeppl, T. B., Nitschke, J., Dombert, B., Santtila, P., Greenlee, M. W., Osterheider, M., & Mokros, A. (2011). Functional cortical and subcortical abnormalities in pedophilia: A combined study using a choice reaction time task and fMRI. *Journal of Sexual Medicine*, 8, 1660–1674. doi:10.1111/j.1743-6109.2011.02248.x.

Poeppl, T. B., Nitschke, J., Santtila, P., Schecklmann, M., Langguth, B., Greenlee, M. W., Osterheider, M., & Mokros, A. (2013). Association between brain structure and phenotypic characteristics in pedophilia. *Journal of Psychiatric Research*, 47, 678–685. doi:10.1016/j.jpsychires.2013.01.003.

Polisois-Keating, A., & Joyal, C. C. (2013). Functional neuroimaging of sexual arousal: A preliminary meta-analysis comparing pedophilic to non-pedophilic men. *Archives of Sexual Behavior*, 42, 1111–1113. doi:10.1007/s10508-013-0198-6.

Proulx, J., McKibben, A., & Lusignan, R. (1996). Relationships between affective components and sexual behaviors in sexual aggressors. *Sexual Abuse: A Journal of Research and Treatment*, 8, 279–289. doi:10.1177/107906329600800404.

Raichle, M. E., MacLeod, A. M., Snyder, A. Z., Powers, W. J., Gusnard, D. A., & Shulman, G. L. 2001. A default mode of brain function. *Proceedings of the National Academy of Sciences of the USA*, 98, 676–682. doi:10.1073/pnas.98.2.676.

Redouté, J., Stoléru, S., Grégoire, M-C., Costes, N., Cinotti, L., Lavenne, F., ... Pujol, J-F. (2000). Brain processing of visual sexual stimuli in human males. *Human Brain Mapping*, 11, 162–177. doi:10.1002/1097-0193(200011)11:3<162::AID-HBM30>3.0.CO;2-A.

Rice, M. E., & Harris, G. T. (1997). Cross-validation and extension of the Violence Risk Appraisal Guide for child molesters and rapists. *Law and Human Behavior*, 21, 231–241. doi:10.1023/A:1024882430242.

Rice, M. E., & Harris, G. T. (2011). Is androgen deprivation therapy effective in the treatment of sex offenders? *Psychology, Public Policy, and Law*, 17 315–332. doi:10.1037/a0022318.

Rice, M. E., Harris, G. T., Lang C., & Chaplin, T. C. (2008). Sexual preferences and recidivism of sex offenders with mental retardation. *Sexual Abuse: A Journal of Research and Treatment*, 20, 409–425. doi:10.1177/1079063208324662.

Richters, J., de Visser, R. O., Rissel, C. E., Grulich, A. E., & Smith, A. M. A. (2008). Demographic and psychosocial features of participants in bondage and discipline, "sadomasochism", or dominance and submission (BDSM): Data from a national survey. *Journal of Sexual Medicine*, 5, 1660–1668. doi:10.1111/j.1743-6109.2008.00795.x.

Robertson, B., & Vignaux, T. (1995). *Interpreting evidence: Evaluating forensic science in the courtroom*. Chichester: John Wiley & Sons.

Ruscio, J., Haslam, N., & Ruscio, A. M. (2006). *Introduction to the taxometric method: A practical guide*. Mahwah, NJ: Lawrence Erlbaum Associates.

Santtila, P., Antfolk, J., Räfså, A., Hartwig, M., Sariola, H., Sandnabba, N. K., & Mokros, A. (2015). Men's sexual interest in children: One-year incidence and correlates in a population-based sample of Finnish male twins. *Journal of Child Sexual Abuse*, 24, 115–134. doi:10.1080/10538712.2015.997410

Schiffer, B., Gizewski, E., & Krueger, T. H. C. (2009). Reduced neuronal responsiveness to visual sexual stimuli in a pedophile treated with a long-acting LH-RH agonist. *Journal of Sexual Medicine*, 6, 890–895. doi:10.1111/j.1743-6109.2008.01094.x.

Schiffer, B., Peschel, T., Paul, T., Gizewski, E., Forsting, M., Leygraf, N., ... Krueger, T. H. C. (2007). Structural brain abnormalities in the frontostriatal system and cerebellum in pedophilia. *Journal of Psychiatric Research, 41*, 753–762. doi:10.1016/j.jpsychires.2006.06.003.

Schiffer B., & Vonlaufen, C. (2011). Executive dysfunctions in pedophilic and nonpedophilic child molesters. *Journal of Sexual Medicine, 8*, 1975–1984. doi:10.1111/j.1743-6109.2010.02140.x.

Schiltz, K., Witzel, J., Northoff, G., Zierhut, K., Gubka, U., Fellmann, H., ... Bogerts, B. (2007). Brain pathology in pedophilic offenders. *Archives of General Psychiatry, 64*, 737–746. doi:10.1001/archpsyc.64.6.737.

Schmidt, A. F., Mokros, A., & Banse, R. (2013). Is pedophilic sexual preference continuous? A taxometric analysis based on direct and indirect measures. *Psychological Assessment, 25*, 1146–1153. doi:10.1037/a0033326.

Scully, D., & Marolla, J. (1985). "Riding the bull at Gilley's": Convicted rapists describe the rewards of rape. *Social Problems, 32*, 251–263. doi:10.1525/sp.1985.32.3.03a00070.

Seghier, M. L. (2013). The angular gyrus. *Neuroscientist, 19*, 43–61. doi: 10.1177/1073858412440596.

Seto, M. C. (2008). *Pedophilia and sexual offending against children: Theory, assessment, and intervention*. Washington, DC: American Psychological Association. doi:10.1037/11639-000.

Seto, M. C. (2009). Pedophilia. *Annual Review of Clinical Psychology, 5*, 391–407. doi:10.1146/annurev.clinpsy.032408.153618.

Seto, M. C., Cantor, J. M., & Blanchard, R. (2006). Child pornography offenses are a valid diagnostic indicator of pedophilia. *Journal of Abnormal Psychology, 115*, 610–615. doi:10.1037/0021-843X.115.3.610.

Seto, M. C., Hanson, R. C., & Babchishin, K. M. (2011). Contact sexual offending by men with online sexual offenses. *Sexual Abuse: A Journal of Research and Treatment, 23*, 124–145. doi:10.1177/1079063210369013.

Seto, M. C., Lalumière, M. L., Harris, G. T., & Chivers, M. L. (2012). The sexual responses of sexual sadists. *Journal of Abnormal Psychology, 121*, 739–753. doi:10.1037/a0028714.

Simpson, G., Blaszczynski, A., & Hodgkinson, A. (1999). Sex offending as a psychosocial sequela of traumatic brain injury. *Journal of Head Trauma Rehabilitation, 14*, 567–580. doi:10.1097/00001199-199912000-00005.

Simpson, J. R. (Ed.). (2012). *Neuroimaging in forensic psychiatry: From the clinic to the courtroom*. Chichester: John Wiley & Sons. doi:10.1002/9781119968900.

Singer, B. (1984). Conceptualizing sexual arousal and attraction. *Journal of Sex Research, 20*, 230–240. doi:10.1080/00224498409551222.

Snowden, R. J., Craig, R. L., & Gray, N. S. (2011). Indirect behavioral measures of cognition among sexual offenders. *Journal of Sex Research, 48*, 192–217. doi: 10.1080/00224499.2011.557750.

Spinella, M. (2007). The role of prefrontal systems in sexual behavior. *International Journal of Neuroscience, 117*, 369–385. doi:10.1080/00207450600588980.

Stiglmayer, A. (1994). The rapes in Bosnia-Herzegovina. In A. Stiglmayer (Ed.), *Mass rape: The war against women in Bosnia-Herzegovina* (pp. 82–169). Lincoln, NE: University of Nebraska Press.

Stoléru, S., Fonteille, V., Cornélis, C., Joyal, C., & Moulier, V. (2012). Functional neuroimaging studies of sexual arousal and orgasm in healthy men and women: A review and meta-analysis. *Neuroscience and Biobehavioral Reviews, 36*, 1481–1509. doi:10.1016/j.neubiorev.2012.03.006.

Stoléru, S., Grégoire, M-C., Gérard, D., Decety, J., Lafarge, E., Cinotti, L... . Comar, D. (1999). Neuroanatomical correlates of visually evoked sexual arousal in human males. *Archives of Sexual Behavior, 28*, 1–21. doi:10.1023/A:1018733420467.

Suchy, Y., Whittaker, J. W., Strassberg, D. S., & Eastvold, A. (2009). Neurocognitive differences between pedophilic and nonpedophilic child molesters. *Journal of the International Neuropsychological Society, 15*, 248–257. doi:10.1017/S1355617709090353.

Terzian, H., & Dalle Ore, G. (1955). Syndrome of Klüver and Bucy; reproduced in man by bilateral removal of the temporal lobes. *Neurology, 5*, 373–380. doi: 10.1212/WNL.5.6.373.

Tost, H., Vollmert, C., Brassen, S., Schmitt, A., Dressing, H., & Braus, D. F. (2004). Pedophilia: Neuropsychological evidence encouraging a brain network perspective. *Medical Hypotheses, 63*, 528–531. doi:10.1016/j.mehy.2004.03.004.

Vitacco, M. J., Neumann, C. S., & Jackson, R. L. (2005). Testing a four-factor model of psychopathy and its association with ethnicity, gender, intelligence, and violence. *Journal of Consulting and Clinical Psychology, 73*, 466–476. doi:10.1037/0022-006X.73.3.466.

Walters, G. D., Marcus, D. K, Edens, J. F., Knight, R. A., & Sanford, G. M. (2011). In search of the psychopathic sexuality taxon: Indicator size does matter. *Behavioral Sciences and the Law, 29*, 23–29. doi:10.1002/bsl.964.

Ward, T., & Beech, A. (2006). An integrated theory of sexual offending. *Aggression and Violent Behavior, 11*, 44–63. doi:10.1016/j.avb.2005.05.002.

Warner, S. L. (1965). Randomized response: A survey technique for eliminating evasive answer bias. *Journal of the American Statistical Association, 60*, 63–69. doi:10.1080/01621459.1965.10480775.

Woollett, K., & Maguire, E. A. (2011). Acquiring "the Knowledge" of London's layout drives structural brain changes. *Current Biology, 21*, 2109–2114. doi:10.1016/j.cub.2011.11.018.

Yang, M., Wong, S. C. P, & Coid., J. (2010). The efficacy of violence prediction: A meta-analytic comparison of nine risk assessment tools. *Psychological Bulletin, 136*, 740–767. doi:10.1037/a0020473.

Yang, Y., Raine, A., Lencz, T., Bihrle, S., LaCasse, L., & Colletti, P. (2005). Volume reduction in prefrontal gray matter in unsuccessful criminal psychopaths. *Biological Psychiatry, 57*, 1103–1108. doi:10.1016/j.biopsych.2005.01.021.

Zhang, S., & Li, C-S. R. (2012). Functional networks for cognitive control in a stop signal task: Independent component analysis. *Human Brain Mapping, 33*, 89–104. doi: 10.1002/hbm.2119.

Zorn, E. (2011, March 9). Passing thought – today truly marks the end of the Nicarico murder case. *Chicago Tribune*. Retrieved from http://blogs.chicagotribune.com/news_columnists_ezorn/2011/03/passing-thought-today-truly-marks-the-end-of-the-nicarico-murder-case.html [Accessed May 10, 2016].

14

The Neuroscience of Acquisitive/Impulsive Offending

Claire Nee and Stephanos Ioannou

> **Key points**
> - The focus of this chapter is on the neurocognitive issues that affect the development of the acquisitive offender, as a result of many very early risk factors.
> - Here the authors take a developmental perspective towards the understanding of acquisitive offending, specifically noting the importance of impulsivity in this type of offending.
> - The chapter also outlines the changes in the adolescent to adult brain, and the associated area of risk taking, in helping to understand acquisitive offending.
> - To more fully understand these changes from a brain-based perspective the chapter outlines the neuroscience/neurochemistry of impulse control.
> - It is also noted that Attention Deficit Hyperactivity Disorder, and related issues such as the impact of substance misuse, and traumatic brain injury in childhood and adolescence, are important in understanding the etiology of acquisitive offending.
> - The chapter concludes with what an understanding of the neuroscience of acquisitive offending can give in terms of forensic practice.

Terminology Explained

A-not-B task is a test of object permanence in babies. The experimenter hides a toy under Box A several times and allows the baby to see it. They then openly move the toy and place it under Box B. Most babies under about 10–12 months still reach for Box A even though they saw the toy being put under Box B. This mistake is known as the A-not-B error.

Appearance-reality task tests whether a child can understand the difference between appearance and reality. Typically, an object is shown that looks like one thing but is actually another; for example, a stone that is painted to look like an egg. The participant is asked what the object looks like and what it really is. A child who can distinguish between appearance and reality will answer each question correctly; but a child who cannot, will respond on both occasions that the object is either what it looks like or what it really is. They are not able to understand that an object can look like one thing but be another.

The basal ganglia are a set of interconnected nuclei in the brain that are strongly interconnected with the cerebral cortex as well as several other brain areas. The basal ganglia are important in a variety of functions but particularly related to smooth movement and goal-oriented behavior, and enacting habitual behaviors as well as learning new behaviors.

Dopamine is a neurotransmitter that is involved in reward-seeking behavior. Reward increases dopamine levels, and the same effect is caused by many addictive drugs.

Epigenetics is the study of changes to genes that occur in addition *(epi)* to genetic structure determined by birth *(genesis)*. Gene expression is affected by developmental and environmental factors even though these things do not change DNA itself.

False belief tasks are designed to assess the extent to which a person, usually a child, recognizes that others can have beliefs about the world that are different to their own. The extent to which a person can do this is an indicator of the presence of theory of mind (see below). The classic false belief task involves two characters, Sally and Ann. Sally places a chocolate in a basket and then leaves the room. Ann then moves the chocolate to a box. The participant is asked to say where Sally will look for the chocolate when she comes back. Children under the age of about four, who do not yet possess theory of mind, will say that Sally will look in the box, because that is where they know the chocolate is. Children with theory of mind will say that Sally will look in the basket, because they understand that Sally will have a false belief that is different to their own belief.

The flanker task (Eriksen & Eriksen, 1974) is a method designed to test the development of information processing and selective attention. A target stimulus, such as a letter, is flanked by either congruous or incongruous stimuli (e.g., other letters that have been identified in the instructions as correct or incorrect). It measures the ability to inhibit or suppress responses that are inappropriate in a particular context. The ability to fully inhibit inappropriate responses is thought to develop between the ages of five and 15.

The go/no-go task is another method for measuring the ability to inhibit an inappropriate response. The task involves presenting stimuli in a continuous stream and participants must decide to either make a response or withhold a response based on initial instructions (e.g., press *y* for all positive words and *n* for all negative words). Accuracy and reaction time are measured for each event. The ability to fully inhibit inappropriate responses is thought to develop between the ages of five and 15.

The hippocampus is a brain structure located in the medial temporal lobe of the brain. It is part of the limbic system and is particularly associated with memory and spatial navigation.

The Iowa gambling task (IGT) is an experimental task to assess decision making and how participants weigh up reward versus penalty. Participants are presented with four virtual decks of cards and told that they can win money from choosing certain cards but that others incur a penalty. Of the four decks, two lead to wins over time and two lead to losses over time. Gradually, most participants learn which deck of cards bring rewards, and get better at choosing them routinely. However, some participants continue to choose "bad" decks, showing an apparent desire for reward that overcomes a sensitivity to punishment.

Pre-eclampsia is a disorder that affects some women in pregnancy, usually after about 32 weeks but sometimes as early as 20 weeks. Two key signs are high blood pressure and a high concentration of protein in the urine. Because pre-eclampsia reduces the nutrition passed from mother to baby in the womb, some babies are born smaller than usual or may have to be delivered early, when they are not fully formed within the womb.

The rule–use paradigm (Luria, 1959) involves tasks that test for a disparity between understanding and applying instructions. At younger ages (e.g., below five years), children can understand the rule of what they are being asked to do in rule–use tasks (such as squeezing a ball when a green light shows but not a red one) but are unable to actually follow the instruction.

Serotonin (or 5-hydroxytryptamine, 5-HT) acts as a monoamine neurotransmitter in the brain. Its function in the brain includes the regulation of mood, appetite, and sleep. Serotonin also has some cognitive functions, including assisting with controlling impulses and delaying gratification. Modulation of serotonin at synapses is thought to be a major action of the classes of pharmacological antidepressants known as SSRIs (selective serotonin reuptake inhibitors).

The **Stroop test** asks participants to name the color in which words are printed. The Stroop effect refers to the difficulty that participants have in naming the color of a word when the word itself is a different color. For instance, it will take someone longer to identify that the word GREEN is printed in red than it would for a non-color word.

Theory of mind, also known as mentalization, refers to the ability which develops around the age of four, to understand that others have beliefs, desires, intentions, and perspectives that are different from one's own. This involves a recognition that others have their own mind, which is separate to yours, and that they may know things you don't know, or not know things that you do know.

Introduction

Acquisitive and property crime is defined in the UK as "the various ways that individuals, households or corporate bodies are deprived of their property by illegal means or where their property is damaged (or where there is intent to do so)" (Murphy &

Eder, 2010, p. 79). Currently, acquisitive crime constitutes over 80% of all recorded incidents of "victim-based crime"[1] (Office of National Statistics, 2013), and over half of offenders found guilty in the year ending March 2012 were acquisitive offenders. These figures exclude those convicted of drugs offences (a further 18%), where a significant proportion will have carried out acquisitive crimes to support their substance misuse habit (Ministry of Justice, 2012).

Therefore, it is reasonable to suggest under these circumstances that a large proportion of the offending population is made up of acquisitive offenders. Despite their number, these offenders are often less the focus of attention than those who engage in more extreme, serious, and violent behavior (see the other chapters in this part of the current volume). They are less likely to have diagnoses of severe mental illness or personality disorder (though about a quarter of male prisoners in the UK will suffer from depression and anxiety, UK Prison Reform Trust, 2013) and are very unlikely to receive any structured interventions or rehabilitation as these are reserved for (higher-risk) offenders serving longer sentences.

The majority of prisoners in the UK (68% in the year ending March 2012, Ministry of Justice, 2012) serve sentences of 12 months or less with the bulk falling into the "acquisitive" category (National Audit Office, 2010). This said, being arguably the most common type of offender, research shows that they are likely to have been subject to many if not the entire array of prenatal, perinatal, childhood, and adolescent risk factors that have been empirically associated with the onset of criminality (Farrington, Piquero, & Jennings, 2013; Fergusson & Horwood, 2001; Moffit & Caspi, 2001).

Alongside well-established psychosocial factors including those associated with impoverished familial profiles and practices, as well as neighborhood disadvantage, recent years have seen an increasing focus on prenatal and perinatal issues that can detrimentally affect neurocognitive development and function (see Chapter 19 in this volume; for detailed summaries see Beech, Nordstrom, & Raine, 2012; Liu, 2011). These include exposure to alcohol, nicotine, and other legal and illegal substances in utero, malnutrition before and after birth and birth complications such as pre-eclampsia, gestational diabetes and perinatal obstetric interventions (Liu, 2011). Importantly, recent emphasis has been put on the reciprocal nature of neurological and psychosocial development rather than seeing them as independent or competing explanations for healthy development.

Most of these issues are dealt with in detail in other chapters within this book and are mentioned here just in order to set a context. The focus of this chapter will be on the neurocognitive issues that affect the development of the acquisitive offender, as a result of many of these very early risk factors, namely impulsivity, Attention Deficit Hyperactivity Disorder (ADHD), and related issues such as the impact of substance misuse and traumatic brain injury in childhood and adolescence. We will now examine the concept of impulsivity.

Defining Impulsivity

Andrews (1995) noted that "for many writers, from Lombroso and Freud through the Yale school and up to Gottfredson and Hirschi (1990), the essence of criminality has to do with a lack of self-control" (p. 37). Few would argue that lack of self-control is not strongly related to or even synonymous with impulsivity. As the quote above suggests, the concept of impulsivity has had one of the longest and closest associations with antisocial and offending behavior. Reducing impulsive decision making and behavior has been an aim of offender rehabilitation programs since they began in earnest in the 1980s (McGuire, 1995).

But what exactly is impulsivity? Impulsivity and its control appear to encompass a number of complex mechanisms involving the response to a stimulus (which could be internal such as a remembered image or external such as a physical threat) that simultaneously rouses emotion, thought, and memory. It involves various stages including alerting to a stimulus (which may not be a conscious process in itself), developing the ability to orient toward that stimulus and then attend to it as we move through infancy and beyond. As we develop, the impact of executive functioning on control becomes clearer – involving working memory, decision making, long-term memory, planning, and inhibitory control (Tarullo, Obradovic, & Gunnar, 2009)).

Infants are born with little ability to control their impulses at a neurobiological level, though there are early signs of being able to orient away from distressing stimuli in the early months of life (Harman, Rothbart, & Posner, 1997). The initial process is thought to be an automatic, emotional response, but as the development of attentional and executive functioning really takes off from around three years onwards, effortful voluntary control emerges as part of the repertoire (though the more primitive, automatic responses stay with us for life). When the ability to control these inbuilt impulses, that is, to think before acting (especially when immediate reward is involved), does not develop, the resulting lack of self-regulation is thought to be important in a number of negative outcomes in adolescence and adulthood including ADHD, borderline personality disorder (BPD), and bipolar disorder, as well as antisocial behavior and criminal activity (Dalley & Roiser, 2012). We will now examine the neuroscience of impulse control.

The Neuroscience of Impulse Control

Three areas of the brain consistently emerge in the literature as implicated in impulsive behavior and impulse control: (1) the amygdala (which is part of the emotion-oriented limbic system); (2) the prefrontal cortex (especially the ventromedial prefrontal cortex (vmPFC) and the orbitofrontal cortex OFC)); and (3) the anterior cingulate cortex (ACC).

The amygdala is probably the major brain area to consider in understanding impulsive responses. It is an almond shaped nucleus in the anterior temporal lobe and is central to what is called the "somatic marker hypothesis" (Bechara & Damasio, 2005; Damasio, 1994). According to this hypothesis visceral reactions in the brain and body to emotion related signals (somatic markers) from our environment are either innate (evidenced in early infancy) or highly learned (as we develop through childhood). These instant, emotional "gut" reactions, or impulsive responses to stimuli, function to "mark" potential choices as being advantageous or disadvantageous in terms of survival. The process stays with an individual throughout their life, and aids in the type of decision making in which there is a pressing need (often in an impoverished environment with little information) to weigh positive and negative outcomes that may not be predicted decisively through "cold" rationality alone.

In other words, it is an instantaneous reaction informed by both emotion and memory. These processes are sometimes referred to as a central part of the *impulsive system* (Gupta, Koscik, Bechara, & Tranel, 2011). However, as the brain develops through childhood and adolescence, the need to override immediate response to "prepotent" stimuli (those made salient because of their association with immediate reward) becomes progressively more advantageous. The vmPFC plays an increasingly important role in integrating such information and is critical to a more reflective kind of decision making and effortful control – also known as the "reflective system" through which executive function develops. See Box 14.1 for more detail on the impulsive/reflective systems.

> **Box 14.1 The amygdala and decision making**
>
> Conventional research documents the amygdala as an emotional relay center. Strategically placed to evaluate stimuli of an emotional nature, contemporary research has also attributed the amygdala with a role in the decision-making process by signaling "somatic markers" of reward and punishment through the awakening of the autonomic nervous system (Baxter & Murray, 2002; Bechara & Damasio, 2005). Decision making is guided by two major systems: the amygdala and the vmPFC with the IGT being the tool of preference for the study of complex decision making (participants learn to choose "good" card decks rather than "bad" decks, Bechara, Damasio, Damasio, & Anderson, 1994). Lesion studies have shown that the amygdala belongs to the "impulsive" decision-making process, since damage to this structure hinders somatic response to immediate rewards and punishments making individuals unable to pair information with the value of novel stimuli. vmPFC lesion patients seem to have impaired physiological responses to rewards and punishments that have been acquired by past experiences. Whereas the (impulsive) amygdala codes for the value of present stimuli, the (reflective) vmPFC allows planning of future reward or avoidance by recalling information that has already proven its value. The somatic marker hypothesis provides a good explanation of the above mechanisms (Damasio, 1994).

The vmPFC is part of the brain that allows a more flexible pursuit of longer-term goals, which may be more advantageous in the long run for an individual (e.g., keeping out of prison) but are less immediately rewarding. The vmPFC is thought to link together two types of memory: (1) current instances in working memory that the individual is attending to and (2) knowledge-based, long-term (declarative) memories that are relevant to the working memory data in question. See Box 14.2 for a current understanding of these types of memory.

> **Box 14.2 Types of memory**
>
> **Knowledge-based long-term memory** is described as the long-term storage of acquired information (Hebb, 1949). This type of memory has been divided in two main components, implicit (procedural) and explicit (declarative)

> memory. ***Implicit (procedural) memory*** influences behavior with no conscious awareness of the causal memory. It appears be related to the basal ganglia processes (Foerde, Knowlton, & Poldrack, 2006). ***Explicit memory*** provides conscious control over recall of past events, and is associated with the hippocampi.
>
> **Working memory** is defined as the cache in which temporary information is held and processed, and is typically not en route to long-term information storage. Baddeley and Hitch (1974, 1994) firstly introduced this term as an alternative to the short-term memory concept. Working memory has been associated with the prefrontal cortex (Smith, Rapp, McKay, Roberts & Tuszynski, 2004).
>
> **Note:** Memory related responses are not restricted only to the above-mentioned regions but they also exist in other regions of the brain such as the anterior and posterior temporal lobe, the amygdala, the vmPFC, as well as the cingulate cortex.

Simultaneously to memory recall, somatic emotional responses to different potential outcomes (from the amygdala) are re-invoked, in order to evaluate the decision being made and how the consequences might affect an individual (Bechara, 2005). Thus, adults with amygdala damage have impaired somatic/autonomic responses to reward and punishment, while those with vmPFC damage are unable to re-integrate factual memories with visceral responses to reward and punishment which impairs their decision making about future behavior (Gupta et al., 2011). An additional way that the amygdala, as part of the brain's limbic system, is important in offending behavior is through its central involvement in the recognition of aggressive and fearful responses in others and reactions to these. Amygdala damage results in impoverished recognition of fear and aggression (Adolphs et al., 1994) and had been shown to be dysfunctional with the same outcomes in those scoring high on psychopathy. Between the amygdala and the vmPFC, information is mediated and moderated firstly by the orbitofrontal cortex, which gives a simple approach/avoidance response, and then by the ACC, which acts as a performance monitor and decides whether messages should be passed up for higher processing in the vmPFC or can satisfactorily be handled in situ.

Research shows there is a dramatic increase in development of executive functioning from around three years of age, and this includes the ability to inhibit responses to stimuli that we have decided are not worth our attention (Rueda, Posner, & Rothbart, 2005), but which remain in working memory while we choose to select other stimuli; and later to resolve conflict between incompatible responses during demanding cognitive tasks (e.g., the Stroop test, Carlson & Moses, 2001). The ACC has also been found to be central to this process, particularly in the *detection* and monitoring of conflict in functional magnetic resonance imaging (fMRI) studies (Botvinick, Nystrom, Fissell, Carter, & Cohen, 1999), and is considered the main node of the executive functioning system. Different parts of it appear to be involved in cognitive and affective (emotional) control. In tasks involving complex emotional processing, two areas have been seen to be consecutively activated and deactivated suggesting the possibility of reciprocal effortful and emotional controls of attention (Bush, Luu, & Posner, 2000). See Box 14.3 for more detail on cognitive conflict studies.

> **Box 14.3** Cognitive and brain consequences of conflict
>
> In conflict resolution tasks, participants are given two dichotomous cognitive cues. The cues are not always congruent and as a prerequisite for the experimental task participants have to select a subdominant object or a response over the presence of a conflicting dominant one (Botvinick, Braver, Barch, Carter, & Cohen, 2001). The Stroop task (MacLeod, 1991) and the Flanker task (Fan, McCandliss, Sommer, & Posner, 2002) provide excellent examples of laboratory designed conflict stimuli. The Stroop task involves language stimuli and the conflict between the word's name and its color (e.g., "blue" written in green ink). The Flanker task on the other hand entails non-language spatial conflict in which a shape depicts a general direction (e.g., →) and is flanked by congruent, incongruent, and neutral shapes (Fan et al., 2002). Researchers from Cornell University have studied the phenomenon of cognitive incongruence using fMRI observing regions that are common in both linguistic and spatial related conflict studies. What was observed was that, despite the expected fact that incongruent stimuli had longer reaction times than congruent ones, both models of conflict shared similar brain networks. The ACC and prefrontal cortex were common in both tasks; however, as researchers argue, these sites seem to be only monitoring conflict and not resolving it as unique activation sites were observed according to the nature of the task (Fan, Flombaum, McCandliss, Thomas, & Posner, 2003).

The Neurochemistry of Impulsivity

As well as the structure of the developing brain, neurochemistry is also vitally important and again differences can be seen in the functioning of impulsive individuals compared to their more controlled counterparts from this aspect (Dalley & Roiser, 2012). There is evidence that dopamine and serotonin are implicated in the control of impulses. Dopamine is a neurotransmitter manufactured in the nucleus accumbens in the midbrain and transmitted largely into the frontal cortices. One hypothesis is that those with higher impulsivity have fewer active dopamine receptors in their midbrain but when stimulated, these neurons are more likely to secrete large quantities of the neurotransmitter, which is then not reabsorbed efficiently (Buckholtz et al., 2010). Serotonin (5H-T) is a neurotransmitter originating mostly in the median and dorsal raphe nuclei in the brain stem. Seretonergic neurons reach up into the nucleus accumbens, the amygdala, and the prefrontal cortex and a depletion of serotonin in the brain is linked to a reduced ability to delay gratification. Studies have shown that serotonin depletion either through pharmacological manipulation or lesion increases response onset to stimuli, as assessed by stop signal reaction time tasks (Winstanley, Theobald, Dalley & Robbins, 2005). Dysfunctional interactions between the serotonin and dopamine systems in the prefrontal cortex are associated with impulsive aggression and depression in adults (Seo, Patrick & Kennealy, 2008).

Much of what we have learned about the links between dopamine and serotonin secretion and impulsivity comes from the study of stimulants on the brain. Stimulant use increases the tendency to choose a small, immediate (impulsive) reward instead of a larger but delayed reward (known as delay discounting). Rats with a genetic tendency toward impulsiveness, because of a deficiency of dopamine receptors, are more likely than others to self-administer large amounts of cocaine by lever pressing (Dalley et al., 2007). Importantly, it has also been shown that repeatedly injecting any rat with cocaine gradually makes it more impulsive (Simon, Mendez, & Setlow, 2007 see Box 14.4), so an environmental effect of learned impulsivity through repeated behavior is possible as well as the possibility of having a genetic predisposition and passing this on to future generations.

Drug abuse *Impulsive behavior is suggested to be one underlying mechanism of acquisitive offenses. Impulsive traits are common also in drug abusers (Kirby & Petry, 2004). This may explain the high prevalence of acquisitive offenses among drug users.*

Source: © Sammisreachers. Used under license from 699pic.

Box 14.4 Cocaine exposure causes long-term increases in impulsive choice

The delay-discounting task is a common method for assessing impulsive behavior. The task involves the choice of two rewards, an immediate one in which the profits are small and a delayed one in which returns are high (Kirby & Petry, 2004). To examine the effect of drug abuse on impulsive behavior male Long Evans rats received injections of cocaine or saline for 14 days. Following three weeks of withdrawal the rats received training on two levers with different

> reward outcomes. After three months of treatment the rats given cocaine displayed increased impulsive behavior by choosing the immediate reward. They also exhibited less anticipation prior to the delivery of the reward (Simon, Mendez, & Setlow, 2007). These findings suggest a difficulty of the rat to associate time delay with the reward and the "winning" response even after long periods of drug abstinence. Observations on humans suggest that impulsive traits share a strong correlation with drug abuse, however, the direction of causation between the two variables remains unclear (Kirby & Petry, 2004). Impulsive behavior can have detrimental effects on an individual's life whether this is the short-lived happiness of drug use or the long-term consequence of a criminal offence. Impulsive traits have been associated with orbitofrontal lobe dysfunction (Rudebeck, Walton, Smyth, Bannerman, & Rushworth, 2006).

Recent work indicates a complex interaction between dopamine and 5H-T regarding how they contribute to impulsivity suggesting they should not be studied in isolation (Dalley & Roiser, 2012). The genetic/environmental impact of substance misuse on impulsivity is a cause for concern given the pre-existing increased likelihood of experimenting with substance misuse during adolescence. The young person from an impoverished background, who already may have a more impulsive nature (perhaps inherited structurally via parental substance misuse and exacerbated through chaotic learning experiences in childhood) will redouble this tendency through the recreational misuse of substances.

The Development/Non-Development of Impulse Control Processes

We have seen that an infant can register and orient towards an important stimulus (such as its caregiver) or orient away from a negative stimulus in the early months of life. But when does clear behavioral control begin to manifest itself? There is a great deal of evidence that the ability to delay gratification for greater rewards later, and altruism (reward for others as well) alongside more complex affective decision making (such as learning which deck of cards is more advantageous in the Iowa Gambling Task (IGT)) cannot be done by three-year olds but can by children aged four and five (Prencipe & Zelazo, 2005).

These processes involve the increasing role of the amygdala and orbitofrontal cortex (Crone & van der Molen, 2004) in both decision making and behavior. Several cognitive processes, which are inextricably linked to maturation of the brain begin around age four or five but continue to develop through childhood and adolescence through early adulthood. For example, working memory, which could be seen as the foundation of executive functioning (particularly in choosing to inhibit information deemed unimportant and selectively attending to other types), is evident from early childhood but really takes off from mid-childhood to the late teens, see Box 14.5 for a description of studies in this area.

> **Box 14.5** The prefrontal cortex during early development in humans
>
> The capability to undertake tasks requiring behavioral inhibition and memory seems to begin between three and six years of age. Popular experimental paradigms that examine the above mechanisms include the A-not-B error (Zelazo, Frye & Rapus, 1996), the appearance-reality task (Flavell, 1993), the go/no-go task (Casey et al., 1997) and the theory of mind and false belief tasks (Fritz, 1991). The above paradigms share similar if not identical results, however, the mostly discussed paradigm is the theory of mind or false belief task. The child in this task is required to *indicate where the agent would think that the object is* as well as *conceal the item's true location*. An object of interest is placed at a pre-defined location while both the agent and the child observe. Then in the absence of the agent the object is relocated. Remarkably a child below three to four years old is unable to inhibit an inclination to say where the object really is or override a stronger impulse even though the child is aware of the fact that the given answer is "wrong" (Fritz, 1991). To successfully perform these tasks children not only need to recall instructions from their memory and acquire an understanding of another's behavior but most importantly *disengage* from a previously rewarded response (where the object was) and engage with a new one. This "error" has two elements to it: location and reward (Luciana, 2001). Cortical regions mediating this task involve the seeking system (Panksepp, 1998), made up by the inhibitory orbitofrontal cortex (Casey et al., 1997), the working memory dorsolateral prefrontal cortex (dlPFC) (Baddeley, 1992) as well as limbic and mesolimbic regions of appetitive responding (MacLean, 1990). Dopamine provides the neural gel that orchestrates successful interaction of the above regions (Luciana, 2001) and deficiencies in this task may not be related so much to the immaturity of the dlPFC but to inconsistent or insufficient signaling of dopamine during the tasks contextual change (Luciana, 2001).

Increases in the ability and functioning of working memory are strongly associated with increases in white matter in the prefrontal cortex (see Box 14.6), especially the dlPFC (Nagy, Westerberg, and Klingberg, 2004).

> **Box 14.6** Maturation of white matter and its association with the development of cognitive functions
>
> Organized into tracts the white matter of the brain consists in its majority of axons insulated by myelin sheaths. Produced by glia cells myelin is a substance made by fats and protein aiming to accelerate the communication in many vertebrate axons, and unlike other cortical maturation processes, it forms consistently for decades (Benes, Turtle, Khan, & Farol, 1994). Maps of white matter in the

> human brain are performed in vivo by an MR method called diffusion tensor imaging (DTI). This technique harnesses the anisotropic diffusion of water deriving from local tissue boundaries (Moseley et al., 1990) and anatomical elements of white matter such as axonal thickness and myelination are quantitatively measured by *fractional anisotropy*. Nagy et al. (2004) investigated a sample of participants aged 8–18 years, white matter maturation and its cognitive impact on working memory performance and reading ability. Findings showed a positive correlation between working memory and fractional anisotropy on two regions situated in the left frontal lobe as well as on a region that stretched between the superior frontal and the parietal cortex. Reading ability showed an increase in myelination and axonal thickness only on the left temporal lobe. The restricted maturation of the white matter on particular brain regions and the improvement of specific cognitive abilities are important parts of child development and brain maturation. Finally, it would be important to stress the fact that structurally related cortical changes develop also according to experience and cognitive practice (Scholz, Klein, Behrens, Johansen-Berg, 2009).

Another crucial element of developing executive control is the ability to detect when something has not turned out the way expected (error detection). This involves an increasing role for the ACC. Although younger children (four to five years old) often know they have made a mistake, they do not appear to have the ability to correct it. It is only in mid-childhood and into adolescence that this function appears (Santesso, Segalowitz, & Schmidt, 2006). As the ACC increasingly monitors activity and decides higher decision making is needed, a reprocessing of rules takes place, associated with both the vmPFC and dlPFC. With this comes a greater capacity to reflect and generate increasingly complex rules (reflecting Luria's rule–use paradigm). Associated with this, another central element to impulse control is the ability to move away from one task to another (more advantageous) one (known as task switching). This ability again begins around the age of five (e.g., being able to switch from one set of rules to another to sort information). The time taken to switch tasks decreases from childhood into young adulthood and stays fairly constant until about 60 years of age (Cepeda, Kramer, & Gonzalez de Sather, 2001). It is clear from a variety of sources that from a neuroscientific (structural) point of view we are not fully developmentally equipped to self-regulate until early adulthood. It is interesting that this perspective fits with the well-established age–crime curve indicating an increase in offending in the early teens and the drop-off in criminal behavior in the early 20s (Farrington, 1986) (see Chapter 21).

All of the developmental processes described above assume reasonable environmental conditions for the normal development of the brain. These might include: sufficient nutrition, rest, and a stimulating and loving environment; ample opportunity to observe prosocial behavior and consistent rewards for the incremental development of self-regulation and empathy for others; a childhood free from physical violence and access to toxic substances. These assumptions cannot be made in relation to the homes and environments of the children likely to become "typical" acquisitive offenders. Lack of exposure to the modeling of effortful control and a lack of opportunity to practice and be rewarded for delaying gratification and desire are not optimal conditions for the corresponding cognitive, affective, and neurological developments for the development of agency and self-control to take place. As noted several decades ago in the groundbreaking work of Ross and Fabiano (1985), the chaotic environment that many young offenders grow up in naturally fosters a "survival" oriented approach to life that leaves little room for the development of self-regulation and social perspective-taking. Much further work is needed to understand the complex interaction between brain, cognitive and affective function, and behavior, especially under the atypical conditions that deprived children experience, and from a developmental perspective.

Changes in Adolescence that Might Explain the Increase in Offending Behavior

Chapter 21 provides a more detailed account of the neuroscience of adolescence but it is worth making a few points here. As the child progresses into adolescence (the stage at which most offending begins), massive changes in the brain occur in tandem with the desire for increased autonomy and a reduced desire for reliance on parents – in other words, the building of an autonomous self-identity. A natural increase in risk taking (see Chapter 7 for an in-depth discussion of the neuroscience of risk taking), novel sensation seeking and extra-familial social behavior is common in adolescents in a variety of mammalian species as well as humans (Spear, 2000) during this quest for autonomy.

Partially explained from a psychosocial point of view as the pushing of boundaries in order to explore appropriate "future selves" (Oyserman & Markus, 1990), there are strong neuroscientific correlates associated with these behaviors. Although often identified as negative and sometimes dangerous in contemporary society, these adolescent behaviors have positive benefits to the individual, including an increased sense of self-esteem, self-efficacy, and autonomy from parents as a result of skill-building, and praise and acceptance from peers (Spear, 2000). The finding that risk taking is much more common when with peers than alone points further to a social/evolutionary explanation for this behavior (Steinberg, 2007). Box 14.7 contains more information on risk taking in adolescence.

Box 14.7 Risk taking in adolescence

Contemporary neuroscientific research on the unusually risky behaviors undertaken in adolescence takes into account two models: logical reasoning and psychosocial factors (Steinberg, 2007). These models are governed by two brain systems the socioemotional, governed by limbic and paralimbic structures and the cognitive-control network. The risky behavior of adolescence might be explained by the fact that social, emotional and reward related networks are more strongly interconnected. The varying sensitivity of these networks is based on reward magnitude (Nelson, Leibenluft, McClure, & Pine, 2005). In the presence of peers, the socioemotional network is strongly activated and overrides the pre-mature cognitive-control network and its regulatory effects, something that

> does not seem to take place when individuals are alone (Chambers, Taylor, & Potenza, 2003). It appears that the presence of peers in a laboratory driving risk-task, more than doubles the chances of adolescence exposing themselves to danger (Gardner & Steinberg, 2005). In addition, neuroimaging studies have suggested that although activation of the socioemotional network is involved in relatively risky decisions, these decisions can also be potentially highly rewarding (Ernst et al., 2005). In contrast to the sensitive socioemotional network, evidence of prematurity in the cognitive network is clear as changes in structure (Casey, Tottenham, Liston, & Durston, 2005) and function (Luna et al., 2001) of the brain still occur for many years afterwards.

In terms of changes to the structure and function of the brain, research points to four major changes. First, the impulsive/reactive system involving the limbic system, amygdala, and orbitofrontal cortex appears to become increasingly sensitive and active in the years approaching puberty (Ernst et al., 2005) with greater attention focused on the rewards that certain behaviors will bring. Second, these changes, coupled with the suggestion that dopamine receptors may become less sensitive during adolescence, may explain the tendency towards novel sensation seeking – including experimentation with alcohol and drugs (Spear, 2000; Williams, 2012) – that is, greater effort/indulgence is needed to feel good.

Third, the more reflective systems in the prefrontal cortex areas of the brain involved in planning, thinking ahead, and self-regulation are developing more gradually over the course of adolescence and early adulthood (Steinberg, 2004; Lamm, Zelazo, & Lewis, 2006). Within this system, logical reasoning abilities reach adult levels typically by around age 16, whereas the more psychosocial capacities, such as the connections in the ACC and the vmPFC that improve impulse control, future orientation, or resistance to peer influence, are lagging behind and continue to develop into young adulthood, that is, young people are simply not equipped with the ability to fully self-regulate until their early 20s, especially when in social situations (Gruber & Yurgelun-Todd, 2006). Notably, these research findings come from samples of typically developing teenagers who are unlikely to have suffered the extra negative impact of various risk factors on cognitive and emotional development in childhood (see Chapter 21, and the effects of substance misuse below).

Finally, the "synaptic pruning" aspect of brain development emerges consistently as an important part of change in the developing brain during adolescence, influencing the number and quality of connections among neurons. This process includes myelination (which increases white matter conduction speed through the growth of the myelin sheath around each neuron), arborization (in which the number of branching connections between neurons increases), and pruning (in which neuronal connections that are not needed are destroyed). Grey matter volume increases to a peak in early adolescence and then decreases, resulting in an "inverted-U" pattern over the course of development (Gogtay et al., 2004).

This pattern of grey matter increase followed by a decrease may be attributable to arborization followed by subsequent pruning of unused synapses (Giedd, 2004).

The upshot is increasingly smaller areas of the brain taking on more sophisticated and discreet functions. Rueda et al. (2005) have noted far less brain exertion in adults when resisting temptation than in four-year-old children in which activity can be seen all over the frontal lobes. In adults, it was focused on a much smaller area of the midline of the frontal cortex. This research again involved typically developing participants and it would be interesting to replicate this work with a sample of persistent offenders and children from less than optimal backgrounds.

It is important to note at this point that a myriad of factors as indicated at the beginning of this chapter will be affecting the individual's ability to master impulse control and self-regulation, for example *ADHD, substance abusing parents*, and the experience of *traumatic brain injury (TBI)*, discussed below.

Sadly, it is clear that numerous genetic factors from conception onwards, coupled with the impact of an impoverished attachment and learning environment in which a disadvantaged child is likely to be functioning, are likely to have a negative outcome on the ability to control and resist impulsive behavior. Individual genetic influences and how these eventually play out in the environment (with the help of "epigenetic" mediation) will have a crucial influence on whether this child will become a persistent offender or not. A natural ability to regulate emotion, an ability to control impulsive behavior, to develop theory of mind and be empathetic, to be female, to be of average or higher intelligence, to not have addictive parents, to be free from TBIs in childhood and adolescence and to be born into a cohesive, caring culture may *each* be enough in their own right to protect a child from embarking wholeheartedly on an antisocial route. However, forensic neuroscientific research is relatively rare, and studies using "average" offenders are almost non-existent leaving large areas of enquiry that need to be addressed.

Attention deficit hyperactivity disorder (ADHD)

A disorder strongly associated with impulsivity that is dramatically over-represented in the offending population is ADHD. ADHD is a clinical syndrome defined in psychiatry by high levels of hyperactive, impulsive, and inattentive behaviors beginning in early childhood. The disorder is common in the general population with prevalence estimates in the UK of around 3–4% (Young et al., 2011) and persists into adulthood about 50% of the time. It is highly heritable, though no specific candidate genes have as yet been identified (Williams, Giray, Mewse, Tonks, & Burgess, 2010), may be sometimes caused by TBI in childhood (Max et al., 2005), and up to two-thirds of young offenders and half of the adult prison population screen positively for the disorder in childhood (Young et al., 2011). Further, adults with ADHD account for eight times more aggressive incidents than other prisoners and six times more than those with antisocial personality disorder (APD) (Young et al., 2011). Young et al. have also shown that ADHD was the strongest predictor of violent offending in adult male prisoners, even above substance misuse (Young, Wells, & Gudjonsson, 2010). One hypothesis held by many in the field of ADHD is that the disorder renders children more vulnerable to all of the other risk factors associated with an impoverished environment resulting in a wide range of comorbid treatment needs (many of which are also criminogenic) such as educational and consequent occupational dysfunction, substance misuse, mental illness, and personality disorder (National Institute for Health and Clinical Excellence, 2009).

Neuroscientific explanations of ADHD are emerging and appear to involve many of the same mechanisms as those involved in general impulse control above. However, as well as deficits in executive functioning (particularly in poor inhibitory control), recent theories have placed increasing emphasis on altered reinforcement sensitivity as etiological in the disorder. This is associated with the ventral striatum part of the forebrain, underneath the cortex. Research has shown reduced ventral striatal activation in adolescents with ADHD during reward anticipation, relative to healthy controls. Ventral striatal activation was also negatively correlated with parent-rated hyperactive/impulsive symptoms (Scheres, Milham, Knutson, & Castellanos, 2007).

Luman, Tripp, and Scheres (2010) indicate that the positive reward of reinforcement is larger in those with the diagnosis and fosters a strong preference for options that are immediately rewarding but relatively unfavorable in the long term, even if the short-term reward is smaller. Further, midbrain dopamine dysfunction is also accentuated in sufferers. A lower firing rate in the dopamine neurons in the mesolimbic reward circuits of the brain suggests that reinforcement loses its value when the delay between the desired behavior and the reinforcement increases, making effortful control much harder and resulting in impulsivity (dynamic developmental theory of ADHD, Sagvolden, Johanson, Aase, & Russell, 2005). Interestingly, from a risk factor point of view, children with fetal alcohol spectrum disorders and children exposed to stimulants in utero are at very high risk of developing ADHD (Fryer, McGee, Matt, Riley, & Mattson, 2007; Langlois & Mayes, 2008). This may also account for the increased comorbidity with addiction problems.

Reward versus penalty *Acquisitive offense can be conceptualized as prioritizing "easy" gains over the risk of punishment. It is suggested that abnormal responses of the ventro-medial prefrontal cortex can bias behaviors and decision toward immediate profits over punishment.*

Source: © Luckybusiness. Used under license from 123RF.

Research is in its early days in this field however, and new findings are highlighting the complexity of altered reinforcement sensitivity in ADHD (Luman et al., 2010).

Given the impact on offending behavior, developments in this area are particularly welcome. At present pharmacological treatments are the prominent treatment option, in cases where the syndrome has been diagnosed. The UK Adult ADHD Network has been working hard in recent years to put awareness, treatment, and assessment of offenders with ADHD at the heart of the criminal justice system, but their work is in its infancy. Better still would be prevention and early intervention before criminality begins.

The increased likelihood of experimentation with alcohol and substance misuse during the period of adolescent brain development has been noted above and two factors related to this are likely to add to the criminogenic profile of the average offender. First, from an etiological perspective, cohort studies of the development of criminality have indicated that parental substance misuse is a considerable risk factor. Second, from an outcome point of view, having carers that misuse substances and alcohol, and misusing oneself during childhood and adolescence, increases the likelihood of TBI. We will look at the neuroscientific aspects of each of these factors.

Substance misusing parents

Alongside the increased sensation-seeking and risk-taking behavior that is characteristic of the development of self in adolescence, we have seen above how the dopamine reward circuitry in the brain is affected by substance misuse in two ways. First, the dopamine neurons become less sensitive to the effects of substances and second, these neural adaptations may be passed on to future generations. When the fetus is exposed to alcohol and drugs in utero, structural abnormalities in the developing orbitofrontal cortex, the prefrontal cortex and the ACC put the child at much greater risk of poor impulse control, greater emotional reactivity, and difficulty sustaining attention (Langlois & Mayes, 2008; Fryer, McGee, C.,. Matt, G., Riley, E., & Mattson, 2008). These factors, among the many other difficulties they bring, increase the child's own likelihood of substance misuse in childhood and adolescence.

Traumatic brain injury (TBI)

TBI (see Chapter 24 for more coverage on this) occurs when an external force traumatically injures the brain, for instance, as a result of sports injuries, a fall, a fight, or an accident with a vehicle. It is usually associated with loss of consciousness. Typical side-effects after one mild TBI include headache, fatigue, anxiety, emotional lability, and cognitive problems such as impaired memory, attention, and concentration (Hall et al., 2005). Those with ADHD, those with abusive or addictive parents, and those intoxicated with alcohol or substances themselves are at a much greater risk of TBI than the general population. Not surprisingly then, up to 60% of young people in custody have been subject to TBI, (as opposed to 9% of the general population, Williams, 2012).

Moderate (more than 30 minutes loss of consciousness) to severe TBI (more than six hours loss of consciousness) is typically associated with neuropsychological (executive function), behavioral, and social problems as a result (Williams, Cordan, Mewse, Tonks & Burgess, 2010). Several studies have noted a correlation between offending behavior and increased experience of TBIs (Hux, Bond, Skinner, Belau, & Sanger, 1998) and more recent work has suggested an etiological contribution of TBIs to later offending behavior (Timonen et al., 2002; Williams et al., 2010). Timonen et al. (2002), controlling for a variety of confounding variables, found that TBIs in childhood and adolescence were significantly, positively correlated with mentally disordered offending in adulthood, in a general population cohort of over 10,000 in Finland. Criminality began earlier in those who suffered TBIs before the age of 12. Williams, Potter, and Ryland (2010) noted that even those with mild TBIs (less than ten minutes loss of consciousness – often referred to as concussion) if cumulative (e.g., as a result of incidents with inebriated parents, general physical abuse, or one's own intoxication) could lead to attention and memory problems. Impulsivity and lack of affective empathy (two common characteristics of the typical offender) are also strongly associated with adults with TBI in childhood (Tonks et al., 2009).

Effects of TBI on the brain

A straight impact to the front or the back of the head causes linear acceleration of the brain and is relatively well tolerated, but lateral or up-cutting blows cause rotational acceleration causing much more damage (Blennow, Hardy, & Zetterberg, 2012). Despite the protection of cerebrospinal fluid all around the brain, head injury (even without fracture) can damage fragile brain tissue as it accelerates and decelerates by the tearing of the long axons that interconnect brain regions and upsetting the neurochemistry (known as diffuse axonal injury or DAI). Repeated blows to the head are especially detrimental as the cerebral physiology is disturbed even after mild trauma making it vulnerable to further injury. Moderate and severe TBIs can also result in "focal injuries" including contusion (bruising of the brain as it hits the skull) and intracranial bleeding, which can result in death (McAllister, 2011). Importantly, damage occurs immediately, but continues for an extended period depending how serious the blow to the brain was (e.g., axons continue to degenerate and swell).

In terms of the structures and consequent functions of the brain that are most at risk of damage in TBIs, it is noteworthy that these correspond directly with the regions reviewed above dealing with attention, memory, executive function, emotion regulation, and effortful control of behavior (McAllister, 2011): first, a circuit in the dlPFC (modulating working memory, decision making, problem solving, and mental flexibility); second, in the OFPFC (playing a critical role in the capacity to self-monitor and self-correct in social context, reducing interpersonal impulsivity); and third, a circuit starting in the ACC (modulating reward-related behaviors). Gerring et al. (1998) noted premorbid diagnoses of ADHD in 20% of one sample with severe TBIs, while Max et al. (2005) and saw an *onset* of ADHD symptoms in 15–20%. Those who develop ADHD post TBI are most likely to have damage to the thalamus, basal ganglia, or the orbitofrontal gyrus and are more likely to come from backgrounds of LES and psychosocial adversity (Max et al., 2005).

Conclusions

Acquisitive offenders are relatively common offenders and are likely to make up the bulk of the sentenced population at any one time. There is overwhelming evidence from cohort studies that these offenders are subject to a wide range of risk factors from conception onwards that will affect their neurological, cognitive, behavioral, and emotional development. We have focused in this chapter on the neuroscientific correlates of the early "impulsive system" in infancy, mostly governed by the somatic marker response of the amygdala and the subsequent development from about three years onwards of the "reflective system". The increasing mediating role of the ACC and the involvement of the prefrontal cortex in executive function, results in the ability to control impulsive responses. The successful development of these processes has predominantly been demonstrated in typically developing samples of children and adolescents.

We have described how the chaotic and impoverished background of most offenders is unlikely to offer the neurological prerequisites or to facilitate functional development. It will instead foster the development of an individual who is impulsive, who is focused on immediate reward, and who is unlikely to reflect on the consequences of their actions either for themselves or those around them. Alongside this heightened impulsivity, there is an increased likelihood that such young people will develop ADHD, will have addiction problems, and will suffer from TBI. Looked at in the round, the odds are stacked against individuals from these backgrounds for developing secure emotional attachments and functioning adequately in education, employment, and in their interpersonal relationships. This has been borne out empirically, in studies of the characteristics of young and adult offenders, over and over again. Once offending, they are ill-equipped in comparison to other young people to find alternative lifestyles and to desist from offending. They are also likely to be serving short sentences, which currently precludes the possibility of any significant attempts at intervention or rehabilitation in standard cognitive-behavioral treatment approaches.

Implications for Forensic Practice

A pressing dilemma emerges from the evidence reviewed in this chapter in relation to acquisitive offenders. While often considered "run-of-the-mill" offenders with (relatively) low risks and needs, the evidence is quite the opposite. Most offenders serving three months, or less, are offered no offender treatment/intervention to deal with their problems (National Audit Office, 2010), even though their rates of recidivism are very high – 58% (Prison Reform Trust (2013).

As testament to the level of problems encountered by this group on release, and as described above, homelessness, unemployment, substance abuse, mental health, and other problems affect short-sentenced offenders more than other prisoners (National Audit Office, 2010) and the cost of incarceration alone is around £300m per year (National Audit Office UK, 2010). The lack of recognition of the factors reviewed above (and in other chapters in this book) and their contribution to offending behavior is disheartening at the very least (Hughes, Williams, Chitsabesan, Davies, & Mounce, 2012) and calls for increased screening and identification of problems and intervention at an early age have increased over recent years (Bradley, 2009; *The Lancet*, 2009; Sainsbury Centre for Mental Health, 2009; Williams, 2012).

Forensic practitioners need to be keenly aware of the neurocognitive dysfunctions underlying many of the entrenched behaviors we see in young and adult offenders and need to be equipped to assess and identify particular anomalies in order to make an informed choice about intervention and support. Some recent moves have been made in this direction and are welcomed, such as the introduction of the

Comprehensive Health Assessment Tool (CHAT) (Offender Health Research Network, 2013), as a result of recent Department of Health strategy for young people in contact with the youth justice system (Department of Health, 2009). It contains a first night reception screen and subsequent measures to assess for risks in physical health, mental health, substance misuse and safety risks, learning disability, autistic spectrum disorders, speech, language and communication needs, and assessment for brain injury. There is a long way to go, however, in terms of comprehensive and effective use of such instruments.

Prevention is better than cure and many of the problems described above could be prevented with better education and socioeconomic support. In the unlikely event of this happening, however, there is evidence that the reciprocally determined (negative) outcomes of brain and environment on development and behavior can be modified, ideally in the early years when brain plasticity is at its greatest (Rueda et al., 2005), though this again assumes early identification of the problem. Tarullo et al. (2009) and Rueda et al. (2005) summarize numerous studies in which the foundations of executive function, emotion regulation, and ultimately impulse control can be modified and improved upon in pre-school and pre-teenage children. However, much more work on the neuroscience of offending behavior is needed, especially using more typical offender populations (most existing work using offender populations looks at more extreme, violent groups). Work on TBI (McAllister, 2011) and homeless children (Obradovic, 2010) has noted increased neurological resilience in some individuals against adversity. Understanding resilience more clearly from a neuroscientific point of view should be a priority and could unlock the differences between children who survive adversity and those who are less fortunate.

Note

1 Including burglary, all forms of theft, fraud, and criminal damage.

Recommended Reading

Liu, J. (2011). Early health risk factors for violence: conceptualization, review of the evidence, and implications. *Aggression and Violent Behavior, 16,* 63–73. doi:10.1016/j.avb.2010.12.003. *A really thorough overview of the many and varied risk factors involved in the development of criminality.*

Luciana, M., & Nelson, C. (2008). (Eds.), *Handbook of developmental cognitive neuroscience.* Cambridge, MA: MIT press. *For those wishing to truly immerse themselves in the scientific research and development of theory surrounding the way cognitive capabilities such as language, decision making, memory, and visual perception develop in children, from a neuroscientific point of view; this gives you an insight into what should happen in typically developing children, but it devotes a large section to childhood disorders, some of which gives us an insight into what might happen in children from offending backgrounds.*

Rueda, M., Posner, M., & Rothbart, M. (2005). The development of executive attention: contributions to the emergence of self-regulation. *Developmental Neuropsychology, 28,* 573–594. *A detailed and readable review of research that has contributed to our understanding of the neuroscientific correlates of emerging self-control and regulation in children.*

Tarullo, A., Obradovic, J., & Gunnar, M. (2009). Self-control and the developing brain. *ZERO TO THREE, 29,* 31–37. *An excellent description of the neurobiological correlates of self-control in the developing child, written with practitioners in mind.*

Williams, H. (2012). *Repairing shattered lives: Brain injury and its implications for criminal justice*. London: Barrow Cadbury Trust. Provides a succinct account and in an accessible way of the effects of brain injury, written for criminal justice practitioners, also has excellent diagrams of the brain.

References

Adolphs, R., Tranel, D., Damasio, H., & Damasio, A. (1994). Impaired recognition of emotion in facial expression following bilateral damage to the human amygdala. *Nature, 372*(6507), 669–672.

Andrews, D. A. (1995). The psychology of criminal conduct and effective treatment. In J. McGuire (Ed.). *What works: Reducing reoffending – Guidelines from research and practice* (pp. 35–62). Chichester: John Wiley & Sons.

Baddeley, A. D. (1992). Working memory. *Science, 255*, 556–559.

Baddeley, A. D., & Hitch, G. J. (1994). Developments in the concept of working memory. *Neuropsychology, 8*, 485–493.

Baxter, M. G., & Murray, E. A. (2002). The amygdala and reward. *Nature Reviews, Neuroscience, 3*, 563–573.

Bechara A. (2005) Decision making, impulse control and loss of willpower to resist drugs: A neurocognitive perspective. *Nature Neuroscience, 8*, 1458–1463.

Bechara, A., & Damasio, A. R. (2005). The somatic marker hypotheses: A neural theory of economic decision. *Games and Economic Behavior, 52*, 336–372.

Bechara, A., Damasio, H., Damasio, A. R., & Anderson, S. W. (1994). Insensitivity to future consequences following damage to human prefrontal cortex. *Journal of Neuroscience, 18*, 428–437.

Beech, A., Nordstrom, B., & Raine, A. (2012). Contributions of forensic neuroscience. In G. Davies & A. R. Beech (Eds.), *Forensic Psychology* (2nd ed.). Chichester: John Wiley & Sons.

Benes, F. M., Turtle, M., Khan, Y., & Farol, P. (1994). Myelination of a key relay zone in the hippocampal formation occurs in the human brain during childhood, adolescence, and adulthood. *Archives of General Psychiatry, 51*, 477–484.

Blennow, K, Hardy, J., & Zetterberg, H. (2012). The neuropathology and neurobiology of traumatic brain injury, *Neuron, 76*, 886–899.

Botvinick, M. M., Braver, T. S., Barch, D. M., Carter, C. S., & Cohen, J. D. (2001). Conflict monitoring and cognitive control. *Psychological Review, 108*, 624–652.

Botvinick, M. M., Nystrom, L. E., Fissell, K., Carter, C. S., & Cohen, J. D. (1999). Conflict monitoring versus selection-for-action in anterior cingulate cortex. *Nature, 402*, 179–181.

Bradley, K. J. C. (2009). *The Bradley report: Lord Bradley's review of people with mental health problems or learning disabilities in the criminal justice system*. London: Department of Health.

Buckholtz, J., Treadway, M., Cowan, R., Woodward, N., Li, R., Sib Ansari, ... Zald, D. (2010). Dopaminergic network differences in human impulsivity. *Science. 532*, 329–333.

Bush, G., Luu, P., & Posner, M. I. (2000). Cognitive and emotional influences in the anterior cingulate cortex. *Trends in Cognitive Science, 4/6*, 215–222.

Carlson, S. T., & Moses, L. J. (2001). Individual differences in inhibitory control in children's theory of mind. *Child Development, 72*, 1032–1053.

Casey, B. J., Tottenham, N., Liston, C., & Durston, S. (2005). Imaging the developing brain: What have we learned about cognitive development? *Trends in Cognitive Science, 9*, 104–110.

Casey, B. J., Tranior, R., Orendi, J. L., Schubert A. B., Nystrom L. E., Giedd J. N., ... Rapoport, J. L. (1997). A developmental functional MRI study of prefrontal activation during performance of go-no-go task. *Journal of Cognitive Neuroscience, 9*, 835–847.

Cepeda N. J., Kramer A. F., & Gonzalez de Sather, J. C. (2001). Changes in executive control across the life span: Examination of task-switching performance. *Developmental Psychology, 37*, 715–730.

Chambers, R. A., Taylor, J. R., & Potenza, M. N. (2003). Developmental neuro-circuitry of motivation in adolescence: A critical period of addiction vulnerability. *American Journal of Psychiatry, 160*, 1041–1052.

Crone, E., & van der Molen, M. (2004). Developmental changes in real-life decision-making: Performance on a gambling task previously shown to depend on the ventromedial prefrontal cortex. *Developmental Neuropsychology, 25*, 251–279.

Dalley, J., Fryer, T., Brichard, L., Robinson, E., Theobald, D., Laane, K., ... Robbins, T. (2007). Nucleus accumbens D2/3 receptors predict trait impulsivity and cocaine reinforcement. *Science, 315*, 1267–1270.

Dalley, J., & Roiser, J. (2012) Dopamine, serotonin and impulsivity. *Neuroscience, 215*, 42–58.

Damasio, A. (1994). *Descartes error: Emotion, Reason and the human brain*. New York, NY: Putnam.

Department of Health. (2009). *Healthy children, safer communities: A strategy to promote the health and well-being of children and young people in contact with the youth justice system*. London: Department of Health.

Eriksen, B. A., & Eriksen, C. W. (1974). Effects of noise letters upon identification of a target letter in a non- search task. *Perception and Psychophysics, 16*, 143–149. doi:10.3758/bf03203267.

Ernst, M., Jazbec, S., McClure, E. B., Monk, C.S., Blair, R. J. R., Leibenluft, E., & Pine, D.S. (2005). Amygdala and nucleus accumbens activation in response to receipt and omission of gains in adults and adolescents. *Neuroimage, 25*, 1279–1291.

Fan, J., Flombaum, J. I., McCandliss, B. D., Thomas, K. M., & Posner, M. I. (2003). Cognitive and brain consequences of conflict. *NeuroImage, 18*, 42–57.

Fan, J., McCandliss, B. D., Sommer, T., Raz, M., & Posner, M. I. (2002). Testing the efficiency and independence of attentional networks. *Journal of Cognitive Neuroscience, 340*, 340–347.

Farrington, D. P. (1986). Age and crime. In M. Tonry and N. Morris, (Eds.). *Crime and Justice: An Annual Review of Research, vol. 7* (pp. 189–250). Chicago, IL: University of Chicago Press.

Farrington, D. P., Piquero, A. R., & Jennings, W. G. (2013). *Offending from childhood to late middle age: Recent results from the Cambridge Study in Delinquent Development*. New York, NY: Springer.

Fergusson, D., & Horwood, L. (2001). The Christchurch Health and Development Study: Review of findings on child and adolescent mental health. *Australian and New Zealand Journal of Psychiatry, 35*, 287–296.

Flavell, J. H. (1993). The development of children's understanding of false belief and the appearance reality distinction. *American Psychologist, 41*, 418–425.

Foerde, K., Knowlton, B. J., & Poldrack, R. A. (2006). Modulation of competing memory systems by distraction. *Proceedings of the National Academy of Sciences, USA, 103*, 11778–11783.

Fritz, A. S. (1991). Is there a reality bias in young children's emergent theories of mind? Paper presented at the biennial meeting of the Society for Research in Child Development, Seattle.

Fryer, S., McGee, C., Matt, G., Riley, E., & Mattson, S. (2007). Evaluation of psychopathological conditions in children with heavy prenatal alcohol exposure. *Paediatrics, 119*, 733–741.

Gardner, M., & Steinberg, L. (2005). Peer influence on risk-taking, risk preference, and risky decision-making in adolescence and adulthood: An experimental study. *Developmental Psychology, 41*, 625–635.

Gerring J. P., Brady K. D., Chen A., Vasa, R., Grados, M., ... Denckla M. B. (1998). Premorbid prevalence of ADHD and development of secondary ADHD after closed head injury. *Journal of the American Academy of Child and Adolescent Psychiatry, 37*, 647–654.

Giedd, J. N. (2004). Structural magnetic resonance imaging of the adolescent brain. *Annals of the New York Academy of Science, 1021*, 77–85.

Gogtay, N., Giedd, J. N., Lusk, L., Hayashi, K. M., Greenstein, D., ... Thompson, P. M. (2004). Dynamic Mapping of human cortical development during childhood through early adulthood. *Proceedings of the National Academy of Sciences, USA, 101*, 21, 8174–8179.

Gottfredson, M. R., & Hirschi, T. (1990). *A general theory of crime*. Stanford, CA: Stanford University Press.

Gruber, S. A., & Yurgelun-Todd, D. A. (2006). Neurobiology and the law: A role in juvenile justice? *Ohio State Journal of Criminal Law, 3*, 2, 321–340.

Gupta, R., Koscik, T., Bechara, A., & Tranel, D. (2011). The amygdala and decision-making. *Neuropsychologia, 49*, 760–766.

Harman, C., Rothbart, M. K., & Posner, M. I. (1997). Distress and attention interactions in early infancy. *Motivation and Emotion, 21*, 27–43.

Hebb, D. O. (1949). *Organization of behavior*. New York: John Wiley & Sons.

Hughes, N., Williams, H., Chitsabesan, P., Davies, R., & Mounce, L. (2012). *Nobody made the connection: The prevalence of neurodisability in young people who offend*. London: Office of the Children's Commissioner.

Hux, K., Bond, V., Skinner, S., Belau, D., & Sanger, D. (1998). Parental report of occurrences and consequences of traumatic brain injury among delinquent and non-delinquent youth. *Brain Injury, 12*, 667–681.

Kirby, K., & Petry, N. (2004). Heroin and cocaine abusers of higher discount rates for delayed rewards than alcoholics or non-drug-using controls. *Addiction, 99*, 461–471.

Langlois, E. M., & Mayes, L. C. (2008). Impact of prenatal cocaine exposure on the developing nervous system. In C. A. Nelson & M. Luciana (Eds.), *Handbook of developmental cognitive neuroscience* (2nd Ed.) (pp. 653–676). Cambridge, MA: MIT Press.

Lamm, C., Zelazo, P. D., & Lewis, M. D. (2006). Neural correlates of cognitive control in childhood and adolescence: Disentangling the contributions of age and executive function. *Neuropsychologia, 44*, 2139–2148.

The Lancet (2009). [Editorial]. Health care for prisoners and young offenders. *The Lancet, 373*, 603. doi:10.1016/S0140-6736(09)60374-3.

Liu, J. (2011). Early health risk factors for violence: Conceptualization, review of the evidence, and implications. *Aggression and Violent Behavior, 16*, 1, 63–73.

Luciana, M. (2001). Dopamine-opiate modulations of reward-seeking behavior: Implications for the functional assessment of prefrontal development. In C. A. Nelson & M. Luciana (Eds.), *Handbook of developmental and cognitive neuroscience* (pp. 647–655). Cambridge, MA: MIT Press.

Luman, M., Tripp, G., & Scheres, A. (2010). Identifying the neurobiology of altered reinforcement sensitivity in ADHD: A review and research agenda. *Neuroscience and Biobehavioral Reviews, 34*, 744–754.

Luna, B., Thulborn, K. R., Munoz, D. P., Merriam, E. P., Garver, K. E., Minshew, N.J., ... Sweeney, J. A. (2001). Maturation of widely distributed brain function subserves cognitive development. *NeuroImage, 13*, 786–793.

Luria, A. R. (1959). Experimental analysis of the development of voluntary action in children. *Brain, 82*, 437–449.

Max, J. E., Schachar, R. J., Levin, H. S., Ewing-Cobbs, L., Chapman, S. B., Dennis, M., ... Landis, J. (2005). Predictors of secondary attention-deficit/hyperactivity disorder in children and adolescents 6 to 24 months after traumatic brain injury. *Journal of the American Academy of Child and Adolescent Psychiatry, 44*, 1041–1049.

McAllister, T. (2011). Neurobiological consequences of traumatic brain injury. *Dialogues Clinical Neuroscience, 13*, 287–300.

MacLean, P. D. (1990). *The triune brain in evolution: Role in paleocerebral functions.* New York, NY: Plenum Press.

MacLeod, C. M. (1991). Half a century of research on the Stroop effect: An integrative review. *Psychological Bulletin, 109*, 163–203.

McGuire, J. (Ed.). (1995). *What works: Reducing reoffending. Guidelines from research and practice.* Chichester: John Wiley & Sons.

Moffitt, T. E., & Caspi, A. (2001). Childhood predictors differentiate life-course-persistent and adolescent limited antisocial pathways among males and females. *Development and Psychophathology, 13*, 355–375.

Moseley M. E., Cohen Y., Kucharczyk J., Mintorovitch J., Asgari H. S., Wendland M. F., ... Norman, D. (1990). Diffusion-weighted MR imaging of anisotropic water diffusion in cat central nervous system. *Radiology, 176*, 439–445.

Ministry of Justice (2012) Criminal justice statistics, statistics bulletin. Quarterly update to March 2012. Retrieved from https://www.gov.uk/government/uploads/system/uploads/attachment_data/file/217641/criminal-justice-stats-march-2012.pdf.

Murphy, R., & Eder, S. (2010). Acquisitive and other property crime. In J. Flatley, C. Kershaw, K. Smith, R. Chaplin, & D. Moon (Eds.), *Crime in England and Wales Findings from the British Crime Survey and police recorded crime.* London: Home Office, 79–107. ISSN 1358-510X.

Nagy, Z., Westerberg, H., & Klingberg T. (2004). Maturation of white matter is associated with the development of cognitive functions during childhood. *Journal of Cognitive Neuroscience, 16*, 1227–1233.

National Audit Office (2010). *Managing offenders on short custodial sentences.* London: The Stationary Office.

National Institute for Health and Clinical Excellence (2009). Attention deficit hyperactivity disorder. Diagnosis and management of ADHD in children, young people and adults. NICE Clinical Guideline 72. Retrieved from http://publications.nice.org.uk/attention-deficit-hyperactivity-disorder-cg72.

Nelson, E., Leibenluft, E., McClure, E., & Pine, D. (2005). The social re-orientation of adolescence: A neuroscience perspective on the process and its relation to psychopathology. *Psychological Medicine, 35*, 163–174.

Obradovic, J. (2010). Effortful control and adaptive functioning of homeless children: Variable-focused and person-focused analyses. *Journal of Applied Developmental Psychology, 31*, 109–117.

Offender Health Research Network (2013). *Comprehensive health assessment tool (CHAT): Young people in the secure estate.* Retrieved from http://www.ohrn.nhs.uk/OHRNResearch/CHATToolV3June2013.pdf.

Office of National Statistics (2013). Crime in England and Wales, Year Ending March 2013. Retrieved from http://www.ons.gov.uk/ons/dcp171778_318761.pdf.

Oyserman, D., & Markus, H. R. (1990). Possible selves and delinquency. *Journal of Personality and Social Psychology, 59*, 112–125.

Panksepp, J. (1998) *Affective neuroscience: The foundations of human and animal emotions.* New York, NY: Oxford University Press.

Patterson, K., Nestor, P. J., & Rogers, T. T. (2007). Where do you know what you know? The representation of semantic knowledge in the human brain. *Nature Reviews Neuroscience, 8*, 976–987.

Prencipe, A., & Zelazo, P. D. (2005). Development of affective decision-making for self and other: Evidence for the integration of first- and third-person perspectives. *Psychological Science, 16*, 501–505.

Prison Reform Trust. (2013). *Prison: The facts. Bromley Briefings Summer 2013.* Retrieved from http://www.prisonreformtrust.org.uk/Portals/0/Documents/Prisonthefacts.pdf.

Rosenbaum, R. S., Köhler, S., Schacter, D. L., Moscovitch, M., Westmacott, R., Black, S. E., ... Tuving, E. (2005). The case of K.C: Contributions of a memory-impaired person to memory theory. *Neuropsychologia, 43,* 989–1021.

Ross, R. R., & Fabiano, E. A. (1985). *Time to think: A cognitive model of delinquency prevention and offender rehabilitation.* Johnson City, TN: Institute of Social Sciences and Arts.

Rudebeck, P. H., Walton, M. E., Smyth, A. N., Bannerman, D. M., & Rushworth, M. F. S. (2006). Separate neural pathways process different decision costs. *Nature Neuroscience, 9,* 1161–1168.

Rueda, M., Posner, M., & Rothbart, M. (2005). The development of executive attention: Contributions to the emergence of self-regulation. *Developmental Neuropsychology, 28,* 573–594.

Sainsbury Centre for Mental Health. (2009). *Diversion: A better way for criminal justice and mental health.* Retrieved from http://www.centreformentalhealth.org.uk/pdfs/Diversion.pdf.

Santesso, D., Segalowitz, S. J., & Schmidt, L. A. (2006). Error-related electrocortical responses in 10-year-old children and young adults. *Developmental Science, 9*(5), 473–481.

Scheres, A., Milham, M. P., Knutson, B., & Castellanos, F. X. (2007). Ventral striatal hyporesponsiveness during reward prediction in Attention-Deficit/Hyperactivity Disorder. *Biological Psychiatry, 61,* 720–724.

Seo, D., Patrick, C., & Kennealy, P. (2008). Role of serotonin and dopamine system interactions in the neurobiology of impulsive aggression and its comorbidity with other clinical disorders. *Aggression and Violent Behavior, 13,* 383–395.

Smith, D. E., Rapp, P. R., McKay, H. M., Roberts, J. A., & Tuszynski, M. H. (2004). Memory impairment in aged primates is associated with focal death of cortical neurons and atrophy of subcortical neurons. *Journal of Neuroscience, 24,* 4373–4381

Simon, N. W., Mendez, I. A., & Setlow, B. (2007). Cocaine exposure causes long-term increases in impulsive choice. *Behavioral Neuroscience, 121,* 1–12.

Spear, L. (2000). The adolescent brain and age-related behavioral manifestations. *Neuroscience and Biobehavioral Reviews, 24,* 417–463.

Steinberg, L. (2004). Risk-taking in adolescence: What changes, and why? *Annals of the New York Academy of Sciences, 1021,* 51–58.

Steinberg, L. (2007). Risk taking in adolescence New perspectives from behavioral and brain sciences. *Current directions in Psychological Science, 16,* 55–59.

Tarullo, A., Obradovic, J., & Gunnar, M., (2009) Self-control and the developing brain. *ZERO TO THREE, 29,* 31–37.

Timonen, M., Miettunena, J., Hakkoa, H., Zittingc, P., Veijolaa, J., von Wendtd, L., & Ra, P. (2002). The association of preceding traumatic brain injury with mental disorders, alcoholism and criminality: The Northern Finland 1966 Birth Cohort Study. *Psychiatry Research, 113,* 217–226.

Tonks, J., Slater, A., Frampton, I., Wall, S. E., Yates, P., & Williams, W. H. (2009). The development of emotion and empathy skills after childhood brain injury. *Developmental Medicine and Child Neurology, 51,* 8–16.

Williams, H. (2012). *Repairing shattered lives: Brain injury and its implications for criminal justice.* London: Barrow Cadbury Trust.

Williams, H., Cordan, G., Mewse, A. J., Tonks, J., & Burgess, C. N. (2010). Self- reported traumatic brain injury in male young offenders: A risk factor for re-offending, poor mental health and violence? *Neuropsychological Rehabilitation, 20*(6), 801–812.

Williams, N., Zaharieva, I., Martin, A., Langley, K., Mantripragada, K., Fossdal, R., & Thapar, A. (2010). Rare chromosomal deletions and duplications in attention-deficit hyperactivity disorder: A genome-wide analysis. *The Lancet, 376*, 1401–1408.

Williams, W. H., Giray, G., Mewse, A. J., Tonks, J., & Burgess, C. N. W. (2010). Traumatic brain injury in young offenders: A modifiable risk factor for re-offending, poor mental health and violence. *Neuropsychological Rehabilitation an International Journal, 20*(6), 801–812.

Williams, W. H., Potter, S., & Ryland, H. (2010). Mild traumatic brain injury and Postconcussion Syndrome: A neuropsychological perspective. *Journal of Neurology, Neurosurgery and Psychiatry, 81*, 10, 1116–22.

Winstanley, C. A., Theobald, D. E., Dalley, J. W., & Robbins, T. W. (2005). Interactions between serotonin and dopamine in the control of impulsive choice in rats: Therapeutic implications for impulse control disorders. *Neuropsychopharmacology, 30*, 669–682.

Young, S., Adamou, M., Bolea, B., Gudjonsson, G., Müller, U., Pitts, ... Asherson, P. (2011). The identification and management of ADHD offenders within the criminal justice system: A consensus statement from the UK Adult ADHD Network and criminal justice agencies. *BMC Psychiatry, 11*, 32–46.

Young, S., Wells, J., & Gudjonsson, G. (2010). Predictors of offending among prisoners: The role of attention deficit hyperactivity disorder (ADHD) and substance use. *Journal of Psychopharmacology, 25*, 11, 1524–1532.

Zelazo, P. D., Frye, D., & Rapus, T. (1996). An age-related dissociation between knowing rules and using them. *Cognitive Development, 11*, 37–63.

15

Neurobiology of Brain Injury and its Link with Violence and Extreme Single and Multiple Homicides

Clare S. Allely

> **Key points**
> - Numerous empirical studies have indicated that there is an association between both violent and nonviolent criminal behavior and brain injury.
> - There is an association between traumatic brain injury (TBI) and an increased risk for both behavioral problems and mental health disorders. TBI is also associated with an increased risk of drug and alcohol abuse.
> - Murderers have frequently been exposed to factors that are known to cause detrimental damage to the brain, including prenatal fetal alcohol syndrome (pFAS) and TBI which occurred in childhood.
> - Stone's (2009) findings suggested that one in four serial killers suffered during their early years either a head injury or (more rarely) a condition affecting the brain such as meningitis.
> - A first resort to violence can indicate the existence of a form of minimal brain damage, especially to the limbic region or the frontal lobe – the inhibitors of judgmental and primitive animal defensive reactions. Brain scans conducted on serial killers reveal some form of significant damage to the limbic region.
> - The chapter includes numerous case studies of single and multiple murderers where brain injury was found to be present, and a comprehensive account of how brain injury is assessed and identified.

Terminology Explained

Antisocial personality disorder (ASPD) is a condition that is characterized by a persistent pattern of disregard for the rights of other individuals manifesting before the age of 15 years as conduct disorder (CD) which continues into adulthood.

One of the main characteristics of ASPD is an elevated and persistent pattern of aggression, which is impulsive (Black, Gunter, Loveless, Allen, & Sieleni, 2010).

Psychopathy, sometimes referred to as sociopathy, is characterized by persistent antisocial behavior, impaired empathy and remorse, and bold, disinhibited behavior.

Cavum septum pellucidum (CSP) is the space between the two leaflets of the septi pellucidi and is considered to be a neurodevelopmental anomaly.

Computerized tomography (CT) scans, also referred to as X-ray computed tomography (X-ray CT) and computerized axial tomography (CAT) scans, use computer-processed combinations of many X-ray images, which are taken from a variety of angles to create cross-sectional (tomographic) images (virtual slices) of specific parts of the object being scanned. This enables us to see inside the object without any invasive procedures.

Positron emission tomography (PET) is a nuclear medicine, functional imaging technique. PET enables the observation of metabolic processes that occur in the body. The system detects pairs of gamma rays emitted indirectly by a positron-emitting radionuclide (tracer), which is injected into the body on a biologically active molecule. Three-dimensional images of tracer concentration within the body are then constructed using computer analysis.

Traumatic brain injury (TBI) is an injury to the brain as a result of trauma to the head (head injury). There are numerous causes such as road traffic accidents, assaults, and falls.

A **minor head injury** involves a brief period of unconsciousness, or just feeling sick and dizzy. Of all head injuries, 75–80% are estimated to fall into this category.

A **moderate head injury** is defined as loss of consciousness for between 15 minutes and six hours, or a period of post-traumatic amnesia of up to 24 hours. Patients who have suffered a moderate head injury are likely to experience a variety of residual symptoms.

A **severe head injury** is typically defined as a condition where the patient has been in an unconscious state for six hours or more, or a post-traumatic amnesia of 24 hours or more. These patients are likely to be hospitalized and receive rehabilitation once the acute phase is over. They often have more severe physical deficits, depending on the length of time they were in a coma.

Introduction

Traumatic brain injury (TBI) is an injury to the brain, which is the result of trauma to the head (head injury). There are numerous causes such as road traffic accidents, assaults, and falls. It is a chronic health condition that has been found to be associated with a variety of behavioral, emotional, cognitive, and somatic symptoms (Steinberg, 2008) (see Chapter 24 in this volume for suggested therapies for TBI). TBI among offender populations is considered by The Centers for Disease Control and Prevention (CDC) to be an important public health problem as people in prison who have suffered from one or more TBIs are more vulnerable to psychiatric mental health disorders including anxiety, severe depression, substance abuse, and/or suicidal thoughts (CDC, 2013).

It is only relatively recently that researchers have begun to investigate TBI within the context of criminal justice, and whether TBI is directly or indirectly related to offending behavior. Being able to detect an individual who perhaps has suffered a TBI as early as possible within the criminal justice process is of clinical importance (Ray, Sapp, & Kincaid, 2014). Given that TBI may lead to behavioral changes (such as impulsivity) and misconduct, TBI may also have a role in forensic psychiatric evaluation (FPE) (Casartelli & Chiamulera, 2013). A challenging area within the field of neuropsychology is the application of neuropsychology in forensic settings, which is predominantly motivated by legal issues and demands as opposed to neuropsychological concerns (Golden & Lashley, 2014). This chapter will examine evidence for the level of brain injury in those who commit criminal acts.

Brain Injury in the Offender Populations

Numerous empirical studies have indicated that there is an association between brain injury and both violent and nonviolent criminal behavior (Gansler et al., 2009; Grafman et al., 1996; for a review see Raine, 2008) (and see also Chapter 12). Increased risk for behavioral problems and mental health disorders, as well as increased risk of alcohol and drug abuse, have all been found to be associated with TBI (Bryant & Harvey, 1998). Neuropsychological studies have suggested that there is an extremely high prevalence rate of brain dysfunction among criminal populations – 94% among homicide offenders (Pallone & Hennessy, 1998). Shiroma, Ferguson, and Pickelsimer (2010) identified 20 epidemiological studies between 1983 and 2009 and estimated

Brain dysfunction among homicide offenders *Neuropsychological studies have suggested that there is an extremely high prevalence rate of brain dysfunction among criminal populations, with prevalence rates of 94% among homicide offenders (Pallone & Hennessy, 1998).*

Source: © Brian Jackson. Used under license from 123RF.

that the prevalence of TBI in the overall offender population was 60.25%. Another study used meta-analytic techniques across nine studies and found that about 30% of juvenile offenders had previously sustained a brain injury. Across five studies that used a control group, offenders were significantly more likely to have a TBI compared to controls (Farrer, Frost, & Hedges, 2013). A study of 118 offenders in New Zealand found that 86.4% of the offenders reported suffering at least one head injury and multiple injuries were reported in 56.7% (Barnfield & Leathem, 1998). In another study of US county jail inmates ($n = 69$), 87% of the inmates reported a history of head injury, while 29% reported a history of moderate to severe TBI, as defined by the standard criteria developed by the American Congress of Rehabilitation Medicine (Slaughter, Fann, & Ehde, 2003). These figures are even more notable because, in the general population, the prevalence rate of brain dysfunction is only 3% (Redding, 2006).

There have been several studies of brain function in death row inmates. Lewis et al. (1988) found that all 15 violent murderers on death row that they examined had histories of severe head injury. Specifically, five had experienced major neurological impairment and seven others had other, less serious, neurological problems such as blackouts and soft signs. Overall, 12 were found to have some evidence of neurological abnormality and five were found to have major neurological impairment (Lewis, Pincus, Feldman, Jackson, & Bard, 1986). Freedman and Hemenway (2000) found a history of brain damage in 12 out of 16 death row inmates. Notably, they found that the brain damage occurred, in many cases, as a result of multiple injuries inflicted on them when they were children by caregivers and family members.

The vast majority of studies investigating the prevalence of TBI in offender population has relied on self-report measures (e.g., Slaughter et al., 2003; Sarapata, Herrmann, Johnson, & Aycock, 1998; Walker, Staton, & Leukefeld, 2001). Prevalence studies of TBI (specifically offender reports of experiences of head injuries) which rely on self-report instruments reveal considerable inconsistency – ranging from 25% to as high as 87% of inmates reporting having experienced a head injury (Schofield et al., 2006a; Slaughter et al., 2003; Morrell, Merbitz, & Jain 1998; Barnfield, & Leathem, 1998). Studies are also limited by the use of relatively small, highly selected offender samples, for instance, individuals on death row or murderers (Blake, Pincus, & Buckner, 1995; Freedman & Hemenway, 2000; Lewis et al., 1986), sexual offenders (Langevin, 2006), or individuals with substance abuse or mental health problems (DelBello et al., 1999; Hawley & Maden, 2003; Martell, 1992; Walker et al., 2001). Other studies have relied on convenience samples (e.g., Diamond, Harzke, Magaletta, Cummins, & Frankowski, 2007; Lewis et al., 1986; Turkstra, Jones, & Toler, 2003; Williams, Cordan, Mewse, Tonks, & Burgess, 2010) or randomly surveyed the general prison population in order to try to obtain a representative sample (Barnfield & Leathem, 1998; Schofield et al., 2006a; Slaughter et al., 2003; Templer et al., 1992). There has been only a relatively small number of studies which have investigated the prevalence of TBI by screening every inmate when they are admitted into prison (e.g., Morrell, Merbitz, Jain, & Jain, 1998).

Another methodological issue, which may explain the wide range of prevalence of TBI in offender populations across studies, is the wide range of instruments and types of questions which are used, with some studies simply asking just one question about whether offenders had ever experienced a head injury or loss of consciousness (Langevin, 2006; Schofield et al., 2006b; Silver, Kramer, Greenwald, & Weissman,

2001; Walker et al., 2001; Williams et al., 2010), and relatively few studies employing the use of a survey instrument that is developed specifically to capture TBI (Ray et al., 2014). Lastly, although studies examining the reliability of offender self-reports find sufficient evidence for such accounts to be considered relatively reliable (Kingston, MacTavish, & Loza-Fanous, 2007), there is always the risk of difficulties with recall and the context issue found in forensic settings that may produce biased self-reports.

Frontal lobe and tertiary areas of the brain in offenders

Research seems to highlight the tendency of violent offenders to exhibit temporal and frontal lobe dysfunctions, which are found to be more marked in the dominant (usually left) hemisphere (Volavka, Martell, & Convit, 1992). One study found violent offenders to be impaired in multiple cognitive skills and, in particular, more complex skills which involve the frontal and tertiary brain regions on all of the summary scales of the Luria-Nebraska Neuropsychological Battery (LNNB) (Purisch & Sbordone 1986). The LNNB consists of 269 individually administered and scored items. The items included in the LNNB have empirically been found to be sensitive to behavioral impairment following TBI. Specifically, one study found that 73% of those who had committed violent crimes exhibited evidence of a TBI compared to evidence of TBI found in 28% of the nonviolent offenders (Bryant et al., 1984). Brower and Price's (2001) review highlighted that, despite the risk being less than widely held views, focal frontal lobe dysfunction is found by numerous studies to have been associated with aggressive dyscontrol. Moreover, findings from the studies reviewed supported a stronger association between damage to the focal prefrontal area and an impulsive subtype of aggressive behavior. Another study explored the neurologic abnormalities in a sample of individuals charged with homicide and sent for mitigation by their attorneys (Blake et al., 1995). Physical signs of neurologic abnormalities, such as decrease in word fluency and errors in reciprocal hand movement and reflexes (which are all indicators of deficits with the frontal region) were exhibited in 64.5% of this sample. Blake et al. then carried out a retrospective chart review which found the strongest predictor of violent episodes to be a lesion within the frontal lobe (Blake et al., 1995).

A meta-analysis, comprising of 43 structural and functional imaging studies, found significantly reduced prefrontal structure and function in antisocial individuals. The main regions of the brain which were found in the studies investigated in the meta-analysis by Yang and Raine (2009) to be functionally or structurally impaired in antisocial individuals were the dorsal and ventral regions of the prefrontal cortex, amygdala, hippocampus, angular gyrus, anterior cingulate (ACC), and temporal cortex (Yang & Raine, 2009). In the New York case of Herbert and Barbara Weinstein, on January 7 1991 Barbara was found dead on the sidewalk – an apparent suicide. Herbert was 65 at the time, his wife 56. The autopsy confirmed that she had been strangled and then thrown out the window of their 12th story apartment. Mr. Weinstein underwent a brain examination by positron emission tomography (PET) scan which revealed a large brain cyst that encroached on the front and middle (fronto-temporal) sections of his brain on the left side. Damage in that particular region would make it less likely that he would be able to retain self-control when irritated (Stone, 2009). The frontal lobes of the brain have a crucial part to play in behavioral self-awareness and self-control. The temporal lobes encompass many of the limbic structures which are involved in mediating emotional and motivation states including sexuality and aggression (Volavka et al., 1996, 1999). Pincus (1993, 1999), in his clinical evaluations of death row inmates, found that many had been victims of child abuse, had suffered traumatic brain injuries in childhood (most of the individuals with frontal lobe damage sustained the brain damage during infancy), and had been dually diagnosed with attention-deficit/hyperactivity disorder (ADHD) and conduct disorder (CD).

Cavum septum pellucidum (CSP) in offenders

CSP is a neurological condition caused by brain maldevelopment. An individual with no maldevelopment of this area have two leaflets of grey and white matter which are fused together. This is called the septum pellucidum and it separates the lateral ventricles which are fluid filled spaces located in the middle of the brain. During the second trimester of pregnancy, there is a rapid growth of the limbic and midline structures (the hippocampus, amygdale, septum, and the corpus collosum) which fuses the two leaflets of grey and white together. When there is maldevelopment of the limbic structures the cavum between the two leaflets remains, which is why it is referred to as the CSP (Raine, 2013). Using magnetic resonance imaging (MRI) in a community sample, Raine, Lee, Yang, and Colletti (2010) investigated CSP. Their findings showed that, compared with controls who did not have a CSP ($n = 68$), individuals who did have CSP ($n = 19$) had significantly increased levels of antisocial personality disorder (ASPD), psychopathy, arrests, and convictions (Raine et al., 2010). Currently, there are no studies indicating the specific factors which contribute to this limbic maldevelopment which results in CSP. However, it is known that maternal consumption of alcohol during pregnancy may be one of the factors (Swayze et al., 1997 as cited in Raine, 2013).

Prenatal complications Hypoxia at birth has been found in one study to be the best predictor of a lack of self-control (Beaver & Wright, 2005), a key behavioral risk factor for crime and especially for explosive, impulsive aggression. Hypoxia is a condition in which the body or a part of the body, in this case the brain, is deprived of sufficient levels of oxygen. Some studies (see Box 15.1) have found that the hippocampus is structurally and functionally impaired in violent offenders (Raine, Buchsbaum, & LaCasse, 1997). Birth complications such as pre-eclampsia (a disorder of pregnancy characterized by significant levels of protein in the urine and high blood pressure), maternal bleeding, and maternal infection can produce a reduction in blood supply to the placenta, which can have devastating consequences on the brain resulting in cell loss to a number of areas including the hippocampus and the frontal cortex. Therefore, there are numerous neural pathways giving rise to violent behavior as a result of birth complications.

Box 15.1 Hypoxia case studies

Serial killer Peter Sutcliffe had such a difficult birth that doctors did not believe that he would survive the night (Raine, 2013). In a prospective study, Raine, Brennan, and Mednick (1994) examined birth complications and maternal rejection at age one year in 4,269 live male births in Copenhagen, Denmark.

> Birth complications were found to be significantly associated with maternal rejection of the child in predicting violent offending at age 18 years. Only 4% of the sample had experienced both birth complications and maternal rejection. However, this 4% were found to be responsible for 18% of all the violent crimes committed by the whole sample in this prospective study (Raine, Brennan et al., 1994; Raine, 2002).

Fetal alcohol syndrome Fetal alcohol syndrome (FAS), first recognized in 1973, can occur as a result of maternal consumption of alcohol during pregnancy. There are multiple negative effects found in people with FAS including physical, cognitive, and behavioral deficits. Negative effects can be major or minor and are typically lifelong. A few years after FAS was first recognized, a research group in Gothenburg, Sweden found that damage to the fetus as a result of maternal alcohol consumption is the most common known health hazard by a noxious agent which is preventable (Olegård et al., 1979). Despite this, most individuals who have this syndrome are unlikely to ever receive a proper diagnosis, which is partly explained by the absence of set diagnostic criteria and guidelines for referral. The harmful effects of prenatal or intrauterine exposure to alcohol are collectively referred to as fetal alcohol spectrum disorders (FASD). The spectrum includes:

- Full-blown FAS
- Partial FAS (pFAS)
- Alcohol-related neurodevelopmental disorder (ARND)
- Alcohol-related birth defects (ARBD)

Importantly, FASDs are not a diagnostic category and should only be applied when describing the variety of diagnostic terms relating to prenatal exposure to alcohol. To date, FAS is the only expression of prenatal alcohol exposure (PAE) which is classified by the International Statistical Classification of Diseases and Related Health Problems. FAS is found in 20–25% of infants and children who suffered from prenatal exposure to alcohol, across all severity levels of exposure. It is not sufficient to give a diagnosis of FAS based on prenatal exposure to alcohol alone. A diagnosis of FAS should be considered if the following core symptoms are present:

1. The presence of all three dysmorphic facial features: a smooth philtrum (the groove between the nose and upper lip which flattens with increased PAE), thin vermillion border (thinning of the upper lip with increased PAE), and small palpebral fissures (with increased PAE the width of the eye decreases).
2. Prenatal or postnatal growth deficit in height or weight and head circumference.
3. An abnormality within the central nervous system. Central nervous system abnormalities are classified as structural, neurologic, or functional. For instance, overall head circumference is typically smaller in people with FAS (i.e., less than 10th percentile). central nervous system neurologic problems include seizures which are not the result of a postnatal brain trauma, fever, or other soft neurologic signs that fall outside the normal range (e.g., visual motor difficulties, coordination

problems, nystagmus, or motor control difficulties). Nystagmus is a condition involving involuntary (or voluntary in rare cases) eye movement. It is a condition that can be acquired in infancy or later in life and may cause vision impairments. It is frequently referred to as dancing eyes because of the eyes' involuntary movement. Frequently found in these people with FAS is a lower IQ and a developmental history which is consistent with either ADHD, autism spectrum disorders (ASD), or both.

A diagnosis of FAS requires examination of available history in order to confirm PAE. Most individuals exposed to alcohol prenatally do not exhibit all of the physical abnormalities required for a diagnosis. However, while physical abnormalities may not be present, significant neurodevelopmental impairments can still be still present, which mean that the individual still meets the criteria for a diagnosis of pFAS or ARND. The most prevalent and devastating result of PAE is considered to be brain damage. Mental health conditions that are found to be commonly related to FAS (excluding attention and autism spectrum problems) include CDs; anxiety disorders, depression, oppositional defiant disorders, and sleep disorders. Attention impairments are considered to be primary problems as a result of alcohol-related central nervous system damage as opposed to a secondary mental health concern. Reduced adaptive skills and more difficulties with daily living abilities are also exhibited in individuals with FAS (e.g., poor employment records, disrupted school experiences, and experiences with the criminal justice system).

A recent systematic review emphasized the need for routine screening for FASD and the development of valid and reliable screening tool(s) for FASD. The review also emphasized that there are significant training needs in relation to FASD in the criminal justice system (Allely & Gebbia, 2016). Additionally, in his book *The Fatal Link*, Jody Allen Crowe conducted a study that investigated the probability of brain damage from prenatal exposure to alcohol in fatal school shootings carried out in the US between 1966 and September 2008 (Crowe, 2008). A total of 68 shootings and one stabbing (see Box 15.2) were included in the study (only two were female perpetrators). Enough information was found in 66% of the 68 cases. However, for 25% of the cases, not enough information could be obtained. It was determined that in 9% of the cases, the shooter did not fit the profile of prenatal exposure to alcohol. Of the 66% of the 68 cases where there was enough information, 88% fit the profile of prenatal exposure to alcohol (Crowe, 2008).

Box 15.2 FAS case study

An example of a case reported in the literature where the offender had FAS or effect was described by Pincus (2001) of a seven-year-old girl called Cynthia Williams, who stabbed and killed another girl on the school bus. Dr. Dorothy Lewis, a child psychiatrist who was at that point working at the juvenile court, examined her and suspected she had neurological problems, brain damage, and perhaps seizures. Cynthia's hospital record charts showed that her abuse began in utero. Her mother was a heavy drinker, suffered from syphilis, and had an abnormally low thyroid function (hypothyroidism). Any one of these maternal factors alone can have a detrimental impact on the development of the fetal brain. In addition to these factors, Cynthia's delivery was traumatic enough to severely deform her skull and break her collarbone. Injuries such as these during birth are often associated with an increased risk of brain injury. Examination of hospital records show in excess of 30 trips to the emergency room, primarily for trauma. On at least one of these trips, Cynthia was treated for a concussion which required skull X-rays. Dr. Pincus (a neurologist who has investigated the family and medical history of a number of serial killers and other violent criminals) carried out a neurological examination of Cynthia and found several abnormalities. For instance, she was microcephalic (microcephaly is a condition where the circumference of the head is smaller than normal). More specifically, the circumference of her head was significantly below average. Since head size is determined by the brain size, microcephaly tends to give some indication that the brain is small. Microcephaly can result from many factors present during pregnancy, including infections or maternal exposure to drugs and alcohol – which were factors present in Cynthia's background. The examination of Cynthia also revealed potential indications of fetal alcohol effect (FAE), most notably her thin upper lip and shallow philtrum (the vertical indentation between the nose and upper lip). When Cynthia was asked to stretched out her arms and spread her fingers, she displayed marked choreiform movements such as jerky, irregular, and involuntary movements. Motor coordination was also found to be abnormal for her age as she exhibited difficulties carrying out certain motor tasks that typically developing seven-year-olds could successfully perform (Pincus, 2001).

Studies Investigating TBI in Single Homicide and Sexual Murderers

In their well-cited review, Pallone and Hennessy (1998) found that in samples of homicide offenders and other violent criminals, and also in individuals who had been the victims of child abuse, there were significantly higher percentages of brain damage compared to those found in the general population. In an earlier study, Pallone and Hennessy (1996) calculated the relative incidence (in terms of percentage of cases examined) of neuropathology in a large number of published studies spanning 40 years. They found that the relative incidence of neuropathology in perpetrators of homicide (94%) was much greater than the estimated incidence of neuropathology found in the general population (3%) – a ratio of nearly 32:1. The mean incidence of neuropathology among the habitually aggressive offenders was found to exceed that found in the general population by some 2033%.

In another study, brain injury abnormalities were found in four of 13 sexual killers (Langevin, Ben-Aron, Wright, Marchese, & Handy, 1988). However, CT scans were not available in three of the 13 cases that Langevin et al. In another study, 41% of sadists showed a right temporal horn dilatation abnormality. This was much higher that the percentage of this abnormality found in non-sadistic sexual aggressives (11%) and controls (13%) (Langevin, Bain, Wortzman, Hucker, Dickey, & Wright, 1988).

The vast majority of research and clinical findings are consistent with the theory that dysfunction of the orbital cortex bilaterally is significantly related to impulsive and aggressive behavior and violent psychopathology. Although the orbital cortex is the region most frequently found to be impaired, in many cases the adjacent ventral cortices also are involved to some degree (Fallon, 2005), including the ventromedial prefrontal cortex (vmPFC), ACC, frontal pole, anteromedial temporal lobe, and most notably the amygdala.

Single-photon emission computed tomography (SPECT) scans (a functional imaging technique that is similar to PET scans but measures blood flow rather than the direct metabolic activity in the brain) were performed on four subjects: a normal 40-year old, an 80-year old, and two convicted psychopathic murderers, a teenager and an adult. Findings showed that for the 40-year old and the 80-year old the brain surfaces were smooth, including over the orbital cortex and anterior temporal lobe (AT) (Courtesy, Dr. D. Amen, Amen Clinics as cited in Fallon, 2005). However, in both the young psychopathic murderer and adult psychopathic murderer, there were pitted surfaces of the orbital cortex and ATs, which suggests reduced or loss of function. In the teenage murderer, pitting in the posterior parietal cortex was found (Courtesy, Dr. D. Amen, Amen Clinics as cited in Fallon, 2005). In another study comprising of a Chinese sample of 92 males and females, Yang et al. (2010) reported reduced hippocampal and parahippocampal volumes in murderers compared to normal controls. Specifically, compared to normal controls, Yang et al. found reduced volume of grey matter in the hippocampus and parahippocampal gyrus in the murderers with schizophrenia. Compared to normal controls, they found reduced volume of grey matter in the parahippocampal gyrus in the murderers without schizophrenia. Lastly, they found reduced grey matter volume in the prefrontal cortex in the nonviolent schizophrenia compared to normal controls (Yang et al., 2010).

In order to examine the number and type of brain abnormalities and their impact on psychosocial development, criminal history, and paraphilias in sexual murderers, Briken, Habermann, Berner, and Hill (2005) analyzed the psychiatric court reports of 166 sexual murderers and compared those with notable signs of brain abnormalities ($n = 50$) with those with no signs of brain abnormalities ($n = 116$). The definition of brain abnormality adopted by this study was a neurological disorder (epilepsy, TBI, encephalitis/meningitis causing brain damage, genetic disorder), pathological neuroimaging, and/or abnormalities evidenced by electroencephalography (EEG) results. In offenders with brain abnormalities, there was a higher total number of paraphilias (transvestic fetishism and paraphilias not otherwise specified). Interestingly, Briken et al. (2005) found a high prevalence (30%) of heterogeneous brain abnormalities in sexual homicide perpetrators, which was consistent with the findings from earlier studies (Stone, 2001; Langevin, Ben-Aron et al., 1988) but lower than the rate found by Blake et al., (1995). Blake et al. (1995) investigated neurological abnormalities in 31 (non-sexual) murderers and the findings revealed evidence of frontal dysfunctions in 20 of the non-sexual murderers (64.5%) and temporal dysfunctions in nine of the non-sexual murderers (29%). The history of severe physical abuse in 26 cases (83.8%) and sexual abuse in ten cases (32.3%) of their sample led them to suggest that there may be an interaction between a history of abuse, paranoid symptoms, and brain dysfunctions which subsequently gives rise to violent behavior in an individual.

Another interesting study carried out by Pincus (2001) found neurological abnormalities, primarily in the frontal lobe, in the majority of 31 murderers that they studied over a five-year period. Two-thirds of the 31 murderers had abnormal frontal signs on the physical examination. Nearly all had abnormal psychological testing. Moreover, almost half of the 31 murderers were found to have abnormal brain activity as measured using EEG and almost half had abnormalities as revealed using MRI (Blake et al., 1995).

Using PET, Raine, Buchsbaum, Stanley, Lottenberg, Abel, & Stoddard (1994) investigated whether there were any prefrontal dysfunctions in seriously violent offenders pleading not guilty by reason of insanity or are considered incompetent to stand trial. In order to investigate this, Raine, Buchsbaum et al. (1994) measured the local cerebral uptake of glucose using PET while the participants performed a continuous performance task. A group of 22 subjects accused of murder were compared to 22 age- and gender-matched controls. Significantly reduced levels of glucose metabolism in the lateral and also in the medial prefrontal cortex were found in the murderers compared to the levels of glucose metabolism observed in the controls. However, there were no differences between the two groups for posterior frontal, temporal, and parietal glucose metabolism, which suggests regional specificity for the prefrontal dysfunction. In a later study, Raine, Buchsbaum et al. (1997) used PET on their sample of 41 murderers pleading not guilty by reason of insanity and 41 age- and sex-matched controls during a continuous performance challenge task. Compared to the controls, reduced glucose metabolism in the prefrontal cortex, superior parietal gyrus, left angular gyrus, and corpus callosum was found in the murderers. Interestingly, abnormal asymmetries of activity (left hemisphere lower than right) were also exhibited in the amygdala, thalamus, and medial temporal lobe in the murderers. Therefore, there may be a network of abnormal cortical and subcortical brain processes in murderers pleading not guilty by reasons of insanity that may predispose them to violent behavior (see Box 15.3).

Raine, Stoddard, Bihrle, and Buchsbaum (1998) demonstrated that murderers with no obvious signs of psychosocial deprivation (e.g., family neglect, childhood abuse) were found to be characterized more by prefrontal deficits compared to those murderers who did have clear signs of psychosocial deprivation (e.g., childhood abuse). Specifically, Raine, Stoddard et al. (1998) found that there was a 4.7% reduction in lateral and medial glucose metabolism in the murderers with no psychosocial deprivation. Compared to the deprived murderers, they also had significantly reduced medial glucose metabolism. In sum, this study indicates that only murderers without any obvious indications or signs of psychosocial deprivation can be characterized by lower prefrontal glucose metabolism.

Box 15.3 Does brain functioning explain homicide?

Using PET, Raine, Meloy et al. (1998) investigated glucose metabolism (a measure of regional brain activity) in 15 predatory (planned) murderers, nine affective (emotionally impulsive) murderers, and 41 age- and sex-matched normal controls in left and right hemisphere prefrontal (medial and lateral) and subcortical (amygdala, midbrain, hippocampus, and thalamus) regions. They found that affective murderers, those who murdered impulsively, had reduced prefrontal activity (both left and right) compared to the controls and predatory murderers. Compared to the controls and predatory murderers, the affective murderers also had increased metabolism in right hemisphere subcortical structures, including the amygdale, hippocampus, and thalamus. The predatory murderers (those who murdered in a planned and controlled manner) had significantly increased metabolism in the same right hemisphere subcortical structures as the affective murderers. However, the prefrontal activity levels in the predatory murderers were similar to those found in the normal controls. Specifically, in the affective murderers, findings revealed reduced prefrontal functioning by an average of 7.1% compared to comparisons. However, subcortical functioning was elevated in affective murderers by an average of 8.7%. Raine, Meloy et al. (1998) hypothesized that excessive subcortical activity predisposes to aggressive behavior but affective and predatory murderers are not the same regarding the regulatory cortical control they exert over their aggressive impulses. There are sufficient levels of functioning in the left prefrontal brain region in the predatory violent offenders to modulate such aggressive behavior in order to intimidate, deceive, and manipulate others for their own gain. However, the affectively violent offenders do not have sufficient prefrontal modulatory control over their impulses, which results in more unregulated and aggressive behaviors (Raine, Meloy et al., 1998).

Another study of 11 impulsive murderers replicated Raine, Meloy et al.'s (1998) findings of reduced prefrontal activation (Amen, Hanks, Prunella, & Green 2007). In a sample of 11 impulsive murderers and 11 healthy comparison subjects, Amen and colleagues explored the differences in regional cerebral blood flow using SPECT when they were at rest and also when they were performing a computerized go/no-go concentration task. They found that the group of impulsive murderers exhibited during concentration a marked reduction in relative regional cerebral blood flow (rCBF). This lower rCBF during concentration in the murderers was most notable in the regions of the brain which are related to impulse control and concentration.

Due to the difficulty in conducting such studies, virtually no other research group has been able to build upon and extend these initial findings on murderers (Yang et al., 2010). For the majority of researchers, linking the brain to homicide is a bridge too far (Raine, 2013).

Excessive theta activity is a frequently identified EEG abnormality associated with violent behavior. Excessive theta activity is an abnormality which is consistent with the under-arousal theory of psychopathy (Mills & Raine 1995). Specifically, the under-arousal theory of psychopathy postulates that psychopaths, to compensate for their constitutionally reduced levels of physiological arousal, seek excessive stimulation through antisocial behavior. In a prospective study, Raine et al. (1990) found that under-arousal may be critically involved in the development of antisocial and criminal behavior. Their sample comprised of 101 15-year-old schoolboys whose criminality status was then assessed nine years later at age 24. At age 15 years, compared to the non-criminals, those boys who became criminals (as assessed when they were 24 years of age) were found to have a resting heart rate that was significantly lower, a lower skin conductance activity, and greater levels of slow-frequency EEG theta activity.

However, as emphasized by Raine et al. (1990), psychophysiological factors by themselves cannot fully explain why some people engage in offending and violent behavior (Raine, Venables, & Williams, 1990).

Volavka et al. (1995) noted that, although lesions in the temporal lobes or the hypothalamus may result in aggressive behavior, this is not a typically expected outcome of such brain injury. Indeed, psychosurgical procedures have historically targeted the amygdala, thalamus, or hypothalamus to attempt to control levels of aggression. Although some patients exhibited reduced levels of aggression following the surgery, there are a number of potential methodological limitations which need to be considered. For instance, the reduced levels of aggressive behavior may be explained by the common side-effect of such surgeries, namely, lethargy and fatigue. In a review examining 20 brain-imaging studies investigating violent and sexual offending, Mills and Raine (1995) suggested the following hypotheses: first, frontal lobe dysfunction tends to be associated with violent offending such as homicide; second, temporal lobe dysfunction may be more associated with less violent sexual offending (such as incest and pedophilia); and third, fronto-temporal dysfunction may be associated with *both* violent and sexual offending (e.g., rape). Therefore, Mills and Raine (1995) posited a continuum, where at one end there is frontal dysfunction and violence and at the other there is temporal dysfunction and sexual offending. In the middle of this continuum there may be degrees of both temporal and frontal dysfunction resulting in both sexually aggressive and violent behavior.

Studies investigating TBI in multiple homicide

Biographies of perpetrators of serial sexual homicide involving three or more victims were reviewed by Stone (2001). Crucially, in 19 out of 89 (21%) biographies Stone found evidence indicating a history of traumatic head injuries.

Alcohol use and brain dysfunction   Given that chronic use of alcohol can lead to a type of brain injury this is briefly covered here. After having studied and interviewed 130 serial killers over 20 years, Stone (2009) reported the finding that a third of the men had one or both parents who were alcoholics. The importance of this factor was also highlighted by Norris (1988) who found that the majority of convicted serial killers are chronically heavy drinkers and narcotics addicts. When committing their crimes, they are either drunk or high. As well as the immediate effect of alcohol on these individuals, alcohol also has a residual effect on the brain and neurological system (for instance, alcohol-related Korsakoff syndrome). Importantly, chronic use of alcohol destroys brain tissue, resulting in moderately impaired brain areas. In a prolonged drunken state, when overall brain function is inhibited and social controls are impaired, the individual is significantly impaired in their ability to prevent themselves engaging in antisocial or violent behavior (Norris, 1988).

Temporal lobe epilepsy   The development of some syndromes may be a direct consequence of TBI. One notable example is epilepsy, which can sometimes be subtle (see Box 15.4). Typically less subtle is post-traumatic epilepsy, which can be identified by subsequent intermittent generalized seizures and EEG abnormalities. With the forms of epilepsy which are more subtle, specific neurobehavioral and neurocognitive difficulties have been strongly associated with epileptic events. Only when two or more seizures have been experienced by the individual can a diagnosis of epilepsy then be considered. A diagnostic test for epilepsy can be made through the measurement of electrical activity in the brain as well as imaging technologies including MRI or CT. There are also events called pseudoseizures, which typically comprise some features of "true epilepsy," but these pseudoseizures, unlike "true epilepsy," are psychological in nature.

Forensic neurology frequently involves cases where epilepsy has been one of the factors underlying the aggressive and/or violent behavior (Treiman, 1999). In a forensic context, there are implications surrounding the individual's culpability in a situation where they have been aggressive within the context of their epilepsy. It is therefore important that epilepsy is recognized as a potential factor underlying an individual's behavior (Murray, 2007). Dr. Vernon Mark has found a positive association between episodic aggressive behavior and particular forms of psychomotor epilepsy. Psychomotor epilepsy is a form of temporal lobe epilepsy where sufferers can feel confused, bewildered, and in a fugue state for hours or even days (Holcomb & Dean, 2011). Volavka et al. (1995) examined the importance of diagnosing psychomotor epilepsy in episodically violent criminals. Volavka et al. have shown that the telltale vertical spike that interrupts the EEG brainwave patterns of violent felons indicates a spontaneous and powerful uncontrollable discharge of electricity deep within the limbic brain. The damaged limbic area, where control over the primary emotions of fear and rage is exercised, is repeatedly damaged by these discharges and becomes dysfunctional, unable to prevent displays of violence before they reach the surface.

> **Box 15.4 TBI and epilepsy case studies**
>
> Severe head injuries, repeated head traumas, or damage to the brain during birth have been found in serial homicide offenders: Henry Lee Lucas; Bobby Joe Long; Carlton Gary; Ted Bundy; Charles Manson; Leonard Lake; and John Gacy. Almost all of them suffered signs that were similar to some form of psychomotor epilepsy or severe hormonal imbalance, which may be due to a dysfunction of the hypothalamus (Norris, 1988). Another study showed that prisoners have a high prevalence of family history of epilepsy (Fearnley & Zaatar, 2001).

The fact that brain damage is believed, in some cases, to cause epilepsy and independently disinhibit behavior accounts for the higher prevalence of epilepsy in violent offender populations. As discussed earlier, brain damage – particularly to the limbic areas – can cause paranoia, and damage to the frontal cortex can cause disinhibition. Damage to these areas has been known to cause seizures. However, it is important to point out that seizures alone very rarely cause violent behavior (Pincus, 2001). Given that epilepsy has been related to criminal behavior, Fazel, Lichtenstein, P., Grann, and Långström (2011) conducted a study to explore the association, if any, between both epilepsy and violent behavior (the association between TBI and violent behavior was also explored). They found the general population prevalence estimates of epilepsy to be approximately 0.5 % and the general population prevalence estimates of TBI to be about 0.3 %. Based on 1973–2009 Swedish population registers, Fazel et al.

(2011) examined the possible associations between TBI, epilepsy, and subsequent violent behavior. There was a wide range of violent crimes committed by the offenders in their sample, which included: homicide, sex offenses, arson, robbery, illegal threats, intimidation, or assault. Fazel et al. found that 8.8 % of their sample of offenders committed the violent crime following their TBI. This was a significant increase when compared to the control group. Therefore, in this sample of violent offenders, there appears to be an association between TBI and an increase in violent offending. On the other hand, there was no evidence to indicate a relationship between epilepsy and risk of violent crime (Fazel et al., 2011).

However, an important distinction has been postulated in the literature. Temporal lobe epilepsy as opposed to epilepsy per se is argued by some researchers to be what is associated with lack of emotional control (or emotional dyscontrol) and aggressive behavior. However, it is only on rare occasions where emotional dyscontrol and aggressive behavior reaches the degree of, for instance, homicide where more planning is involved, such as choice of weapon(s), or where there is a psychological reason underpinning the direction of aggression towards a specific individual, and so on. Emotional dyscontrol and aggressive behavior typically tend to occur randomly and if weapons are used these tend to be those in the hands of the individuals at the point of their seizure (Golden & Lashley, 2014). However, with such studies, determining what factor(s) are directly responsible for the aggressive behaviors is challenging. Specifically, trying to ascertain whether the aggressive behaviors are due to temporal lobe epilepsy or to an underlying brain lesion (or even the result of difficulties with emotion and intellectual functioning which impact on the individual's ability to deal appropriate with a stressful situation) is extremely complicated. Even when a TBI is present, this is usually only one of the factors involved (Golden & Lashley, 2014) (see Box 15.5).

Box 15.5   TBI-related epilepsy in a serial killer

The case of Richard Ramirez provides a case study of a serial killer who both sustained multiple head injuries and experienced numerous psychosocial stressors. Ramirez was convicted of killing 13 people between June 28 1984 and August 24 1985. When he was two years of age, a dresser fell on top of him, knocking him unconscious. When he was five, he went to a nearby park and when he saw his sister on the swing he ran to her but before she could stop her swing, it slammed into his head with terrific force, knocking him out. After the head injuries, Ramirez began to experience seizures, both grand mal (causing unconsciousness) and temporal lobe (causing strange visions or automatic movements but without unconsciousness). In the wake of the experiences, he also became hypersexual, aggressive, and prone to visions of monsters. In his mid-teens, he began to abuse a variety of hallucinogenic drugs including mescaline, LSD, angel dust, and cocaine (Stone, 2009). Ramirez was identified as having epilepsy when he was in fifth grade (Carlo, 1996). Dr. Ronald Geshwind has argued that there are some individuals with temporal lobe epilepsy who exhibited altered sexuality and hyper-religious feelings, have a compulsion to write (known as hypergraphia), and are excessively aggressive.

Serial killers with acquired brain injury Although there are numerous biological factors which are thought to characterize serial homicide offenders, the most prevalent appears to be damage to the prefrontal cortex (Raine, 1993). Research has found the prefrontal cortex to be responsible for controlling the emotional impulses that arise from the limbic system (often referred to as the primitive emotional brain). As a result, if there is significant damage to the prefrontal neocortex, it may be unable to control these emotional impulses stemming from the limbic system. Such impairment may increase the likelihood that the individual will go on to engage in aggressive and violent behaviors (DeFronzo, Ditta, Hannon, & Prochnow, 2007). Such individuals may also misperceive elements of a situation, which may subsequently lead to poor social judgments, overreactions to provocative stimuli, and reduced communication skills, which are detrimental to the ability of the individuals to verbally negotiate conflict or impulsive acts of aggression (Boduszek & Hyland, 2012). Norris (1988) suggests that head injuries that, like malnutrition, may result from sustained abuse, may cause damage to aggression-related neural regions. Damage to such regions within the brain could intensify the potential killer's dysfunctional behavior. Norris (1988) presented case studies consistent with this argument for biological and environmental interactions in the origins of the serial homicide offender and states that the majority of serial homicide offenders given PET or CAT scans exhibit damage to the limbic region of the brain (see Box 15.6). Norris also states that a regular feature in serial homicide offenders is chemical analyses revealing evidence of cobalt or lead toxicity (DeHart & Mahoney, 1994). In another study, Stone (2009) found that as many as one in four serial killers suffered during their early childhood either a head injury or (more rarely) a condition that affects the brain (e.g., meningitis). Such damage could have serious consequences on self-control, on sizing up social situations correctly, tuning in to other people empathetically, or resonating with them compassionately. It is important to highlight that the effects of such head injuries are not restricted to serial killers but are important as precursors to a range of criminal behaviors (e.g., robbery, rape, etc.).

Box 15.6 Case studies of TBI in convicted serial murderers

A New York psychiatrist, Dr. Dorothy Otnow-Lewis proposed that many convicted murderers suffered TBI in the years before their crimes. Dr. Craig Beaver believed Gary Ridgeway had diffuse organic brain damage not due to physical trauma damaging some specific area of the brain but a more scattered type of brain dysfunction, in the frontal lobe region of the brain predominantly (Prothero & Hanis, 2007). Frederick Walter Stephen West, the psychopathic sexual serial killer, suffered some degree of brain damage (Boduszek & Hyland, 2012). Following a detailed examination of the brain scan of serial killer Henry Lee Lucas, psychologist Joel Norris (1988) noted the existence of excessive spinal fluid (Fox & Levin, 1999; see Box 15.9 for more details of this case). John Wayne Gacy, Ed Gein, and possibly Dennis Rader had childhood incidents of head injury (LaBrode, 2007). Though brain damage is a frequent feature of serial killers, the damage seems less severe than in non-serial killings (Pincus, 2001).

Spree killer Charles Whitman wrote, prior to his killings, a note requesting that an autopsy be conducted to explain his violent act (Lavergne, 1997, p. 262). The autopsy and examination of Whitman's brain revealed a well demarcated, greyish-yellow tumor located "in the middle part of the brain, above the red nucleus in the white matter below the grey center thalamus" (pathologist Dr. Coleman de Chenar's documentation, cited by Lavergne, 1997, p. 261). Ciccone (1992) describes a case of a 44-year-old married individual who was convicted of the serial killing of ten women over the duration of two years. As an adolescent, he suffered three separate head injuries, which all resulted in unconsciousness. One head injury included a right-sided skull fracture. A computed EEG was read by one neurologist to exhibit paroxysmal irritative patterns in the obifrontotemporal areas, more on the right side. A CT scan revealed minimal enlargement of his left lateral ventricle. Additionally, an MRI scan revealed an old, healed, right frontal skull fracture and a cystic lesion in the anterior portion of the right temporal lobe. A SPECT scan also showed evidence of bilateral scarring of the frontal white matter, which was more marked on the left side.

Ostrosky-Solís, Vélez-García, Santana-Vargas, Pérez, and Ardila (2008) presented the case of a 48-year-old woman who was accused of killing at least 12 elderly women and attempted murder of another elderly woman. Extensive neuropsychological, electrophysiological, and neuropsychiatric testing found evidence of a decrease in executive functions and abnormalities in the processing of affective stimuli. Specifically, a diffuse slowing comprising of 1–4 Hz delta and 4–7 Hz theta activity was exhibited primarily in the fronto-temporal and central areas of the left hemisphere. Detailed investigation into this woman's background revealed a history of childhood abuse and a number of head injuries, which are all factors that may have contributed to her violent behavior.

Electroencephalography (EEG) abnormalities There have also been some case studies in the literature that have found evidence of EEG abnormalities in serial killers. For example, EEG abnormalities were found in the serial killer Bobby Joe Long, described in Box 15.7.

Box 15.7 Case study of TBI-related EEG abnormalities in a serial sexual murderer

American serial killer Bobby Joe Long abducted, sexually assaulted, and murdered at least ten women. In a personal statement he revealed that, although he was dominated by women throughout his life, he never struck back until he suffered a severe head injury following a motorcycle accident. In this accident he severely fractured his skull and was in a semiconscious state for a number of weeks. He suffered from severe headaches, which continue to this day, and he was unable to focus his vision. He reported that his pupils continued to be dilated for a short period following the accident. He also stated that for numerous months his right pupil was larger compared to his left pupil. Medical records indicated that he had sustained a serious head trauma. However, despite such a serious head injury, a neurologist did not evaluate his X-rays and EEG. During the trial, over ten years after the accident, Dr. Dorothy Otnow-Lewis of the psychiatry department of the NYU's Medical Center re-evaluated Long and found that the brain damage he experienced was significant enough to warrant an extensive neurological examination. The injuries to Long's brain from the motorcycle accident compounded possible damage received from four previous documented head injuries he suffered prior to turning ten years of age. When he was five he fell from a swing, lost consciousness, and awoke to find that a stick had punctured his eye and was embedded in the medial portion of his left eyelid. One year later he was thrown from his bike injuring his head. A year after this injury he was rendered unconscious after being struck by a car bumper. In this accident he lost several teeth and was diagnosed as suffering from severe concussion. In the following year he was thrown by a pony and was dizzy and experienced nausea for several weeks. Dr. Lewis reported to Long's defense attorney that the accumulative result of all these head injuries was a significant level of damage to the left temporal lobe of Long's brain, with damage to the surrounding areas of the central nervous system as well and loss of those neurological functions generally commensurate with that type of damage. Long was also found to have a lesion on his left temporal lobe, as evidenced by EEG abnormalities as well as irregularities in the muscular ability on his right knee and ankle. Dr. Lewis argued that Long's hypersexuality and hair-trigger violence indicated neurological damage to the limbic region of the brain (Norris, 1988).

Temporal lobe abnormalities Some case studies in the literature have found evidence of temporal lobe abnormalities in serial killers. For example, temporal lobe abnormalities were discovered in the serial killer Henry Lee Lucas, described in Box 15.8.

Box 15.8 TBI and temporal lobe abnormality in a serial killer

American serial killer Henry Lee Lucas was convicted of killing 11 people and confessed to killing more than 600. When he was a child his mother hit him particularly hard across the back of his head with a two-by-four. Lucas self-reports that following this blow he remained in a semiconscious state for approximately three days. After that incident, Lucas reports, he had frequent episodes of dizziness, blackouts, and at times feeling as though he were floating in air. Neurological examinations and X-rays conducted a number of years later showed that Lucas had sustained serious head traumas with damage to the areas of the brain involved in controlling violent behavior and managing/regulating emotions. An MRI scan revealed evidence of a black area of spinal fluid accumulations in the temporal lobe. Some build-up of spinal fluid in this area is normal but in this case the spinal fluid channels were widened at the expense of the surrounding brain, which was even more marked on the left side. The multiple head injuries, starvation of his brain through prolonged malnutrition, and the poisoning of the cerebral tissue from alcohol and drugs (which he started abusing by the age of ten) all combined to produce a progressive degeneration of Lucas' neurological system (Norris, 1988).

Box 15.9 Activity of the hypothalamus in serial killers

Dr. Helen Morrison places significant importance to the role played by an organic dysfunction deep within the primitive brain. In her work with serial murderers John Gacy, Ted Bundy, Richard Macik, and the Yorkshire Ripper in Great Britain, Dr. Morrison is interested in the activity of the hypothalamus (the emotional voltage regulator of the brain) as an indicator or way to measure an individual's ability to control primitive and violent impulses. Dr. Morrison came to this conclusion because many of the serial killers she studied presented with disorders of the hypothalamus (such as distorted sleep patterns, critical hormone imbalances, etc.). In the triad of the key factors of organic dysfunctions, psychopathological behavior, and social deprivation that are considered to underlie the "syndrome of serial murderers," disorders of the hypothalamus, the temporal lobe, or the limbic brain have been key features giving rise to serial murder or violent and aggressive behaviors (Norris, 1988).

Legal implications

In terms of the implications for neurocriminology, it is important to emphasize that violent individuals with frontal damage do not typically lack understanding. Rather, what they lack is behavioral control. Unsurprisingly then, insanity defenses which are based on frontal lobe damage are rare and are met with even rarer success. Redding (2006) advocates the need to reintroduce control tests for insanity but with a number of critical doctrinal changes. There is a need for the law to develop a neurojurisprudence that is informed and guided by neuroscience research which has investigated the impact and contribution of various brain abnormalities and damage on the individuals offending behavior (Redding, 2006). Professor Janet Weinstein and Dr. Ricardo Weinstein coined the term neurojurisprudence (Raine, 2013).

Caution in interpreting an association between brain injury and single and multiple homicide

Research investigating the incidence of brain abnormalities and injury as antecedents of serious crime such as homicide remains in its infancy (Yin, 1994). What also complicates any conclusions that can be made from the relatively small number of studies to date is the variety of definitions of head injury used, different source populations across studies, the proportions of males and females in the samples being very different, use of different screening methods, and some studies with samples comprising of both juveniles and adults. Due to all these different methodological differences across the studies, it becomes a challenge to synthesize the literature and obtain an overall estimate of the prevalence of TBI in offender populations (Allely, 2016).

Caution must be exerted in attempting to connect extreme violence to neurological impairment. If head trauma were as significant factor in leading someone to commit serial murder as has been suggested, then we would have much greater numbers of serial murderers than we do (Fox & Levin, 1999). In fact, only a small minority of people with brain damage behave violently (Grafman et al., 1996). Despite being important risk factors, head trauma and abuse are neither necessary nor sufficient factors to lead someone down the pathway to intended violence (e.g., committing single or multiple homicide) (e.g., Raine, 2013; Faccini & Allely, 2016; Faccini, 2016). They are just some of a variety of risk factors (e.g., adoption, shyness, disfigurement, speech impediments, learning and physical disabilities, abandonment, and parental death) that can predispose an individual towards violence (Raine, 2013). Interestingly, Lewis et al. (1989) postulated that the interaction of neurological/psychiatric impairment and a history of abuse is a better predictor of violent crime than previous violence alone. However, some caution must be exercised since this suggestion was based on retrospective postdiction with a sample of serious offenders as opposed to a "prospective attempt to predict violence within a general cross section" (Fox & Levin, 1999, p. 88).

Forensic neuropsychological evaluation of the violent offender

This section considers studies which investigate ways to screen for TBI in the offender populations. Whether the evaluation of a TBI is for the purposes of treatment or for forensic purposes, the methodology remains the same. However, there are distinct differences (for more discussion on this see Granacher, 2015). Unlike in treatment examination, the forensic evaluation needs to consider things such as causation, financial damages, malingering, or any other legal factors, which may have significant implications in a legal context. Additionally, in forensic examination, the rules, standards and ethics are very different to those in a treatment examination (Murrey & Starzinski, 2007).

There is a range of criteria and definitions for TBI across the neuropsychological, medical, and legal literature. Despite such range, the presence and severity of a TBI are typically determined by the following (Esselman, & Uomoto, 1995; Evans 1992):

- The occurrence and duration of loss of consciousness
- The degree of memory loss for events immediately prior to or following the injury
- The degree and duration of alteration in mental state at the time of the injury
- The degree of focal neurological deficits (such deficits may be transient)

Within clinical, legal, and research settings a wide range of criteria and definitions (as well as standardized and unstandardized methods of assessment) are applied for specific diagnosis and classification of TBI (Murrey & Starzinski, 2007).

Alteration in mental status and the mental status examination

Individuals who have sustained a TBI often have an alteration in mental status that can be characterized as disorientation; dazed feelings or confusion at the time of the incident. Such alteration in mental status can sometimes be documented by emergency or medical personnel at the scene of the incident or in the hospital. The degree and duration of alteration in an individual's mental state following injury has been found to correlate with TBI severity. Compared to the more rigorous neurologic examination conducted by neuropsychologists, the mental status examination is more often used as a screening examination. A mental status screening includes parts of the Mini-Mental Status Examination (MMSE) (Folstein, Folstein, & McHugh, 1975) to determine the existence of cognitive abnormalities that may subsequently indicate possible focal neurologic dysfunction (Folstein et al., 1975). This examination involves tests of a range of domains including memory, attention, language, and some abstract cognitive functioning as well as observations with respect to the thought process, liability, and effect of the individual under assessment. These examinations explore the existence of psychotic thought or mood disorder in the individual. Any internal inconsistencies should be noted by the examiner as this can be indicative of possible functional (non-organic) manifestations of the individual's mental status abnormalities. This latter point is important to consider when conducting forensic examinations (Murrey & Starzinski, 2007).

Estimating premorbid intelligence and functioning of offenders with TBI

An important aspect within forensic assessment of an individual with TBI is to ascertain whether there has been a cognitive or functional change and, if there has been, to ascertain the extent of the cognitive or functional change. The ideal situation would be the ability to compare findings on tests of intelligence and functioning after injury to ones carried out before injury; however, this is rarely possible. If pre-injury data are unavailable, the forensic examiner (neuropsychologist) needs to estimate the premorbid IQ and cognitive functioning level of the individual under examination in order to compare this to current IQ and cognitive functioning levels. Typically, when estimating premorbid function, neuropsychologists rely on four methods:

1. Gathering and reviewing all information/records available prior to injury This involves a review of pre-injury academic (such as transcripts, grade reports, and educational level achieved) and occupational records (positions held and whether they were technical or management level positions) and history (e.g., military records). Such information would only be able to provide an indication of whether the individual under examination was at, above, or below the normal or average functioning level. It would not be able to provide an exact level of IQ.

2. Use of reading and vocabulary test scores Low sensitivity to TBI has been found with reading or vocabulary type tasks (e.g., Wiens, Bryan, & Crossen, 1993) whereas some tests of intellectual and cognitive functioning have been found to have a high sensitivity to TBI or neurological impairment. For example, there is no correlation between neurological impairment and scores on the vocabulary subtest on the

Wechsler Intelligence Scales (Psychological Corporation, 1997). Therefore, individuals with TBI exhibit no significant decline in performance on this test, it is a good way to try and estimate verbal intellectual abilities prior to the TBI. Other tests which can be used to estimate premorbid intelligence in individuals with TBI or neurological impairment are tests of word pronunciation – The Wide Range Achievement Test-Revised (WRAT-R) (Jastak & Wilkinson, 1984) and the North American Adult Reading Test (NAART) (Blair & Spreen, 1989) – as vocabulary and word pronunciation abilities have less sensitivity to TBI. The NAART and the WRAT-R can provide an estimate of premorbid intellectual functioning with the WRAT-R being the preferred measure of premorbid verbal intelligence (Johnstone, Callahan, Kapila, & Bouman, 1996, p. 513). However, there is a tendency for both to underestimate higher intelligence ranges and overestimate lower intelligence ranges (e.g., Johnstone et al., 1996; Barry et al., 1994).

3. Use of demographic-based indexes Estimation of IQ prior to TBI can be obtained from demographic-based indexes derived from statistical formulas based on intelligence test scores, occupational history and education levels. Previously, neuropsychologists commonly utilized The Barona Index (Barona et al., 1984) for the Wechsler Adult Intelligence Scales. However, with the revised Wechsler scales, no prediction formula has been produced which has resulted in the discontinuation of use of this approach as part of the examination. Following research on the effectiveness and utility of reading-based approaches such as the WRAT-R or NAART in enabling estimates of premorbid IQ, demographic approaches are, overall, much less widely utilized than before (Kareken, Gur, & Saykin, 1995).

4. The use of the highest test scores of neuropsychological evaluation during assessment after sustaining a TBI This method obtains a gross estimate of premorbid functioning prior to the TBI by using the highest or average of all the highest scores on the neuropsychological or intelligence tests (which are considered to represent relatively unimpaired or spared functions). In standardized neuropsychological tests, the strengths and weaknesses of the individual under assessment are taken into account through the use of normative data. This means that when an individual performs out with the normal range, then they are impaired in that particular domain or when there is a significant difference between test scores it is indicative of a decline in that selected functional area (Murrey & Starzinski, 2007).

Assessing levels of attention in violent offenders

Formulations of intentional violence do not tend to explore deficits of attention. However, our understanding of the association between both neuroradiological and neuropsychological studies could significantly be increased through examination of pure attention. Essentially, it is crucial to recognize the importance of the potential contribution of attention in violence. Subcortical frontal-temporal disorders are indicated with primary attentional disorders while the absence of attentional disorders indicates a disorder of the cortical region. The Connor's Continuous Performance Test-II, the IVA continuous performance task, or the TOVA are effective instruments to assess levels of attention (Golden & Lashley, 2014). The individual's ability in real-world settings to attend auditorily, visually, and tactilely should be given particular attention in the screening questions. Additionally, the forensic examination also needs to explore the possible impact of hypersomnolence on attention. Symptoms of "impersistence, perseveration, distractibility," or lack of ability to "inhibit immediate but inappropriate responses" may also be observed in individuals with attentional deficits (Mesulam, 2000; Murrey & Starzinski, 2007).

Post-traumatic amnesia

In the assessment of TBI another criterion that is important to consider is the level of post-traumatic amnesia (PTA). PTA characterizes memory loss for events which occur just before or immediately after the accident. In addition to memory loss, there is frequently a lack of ability or impaired ability to process information (visual, auditory, etc.) after the TBI incident. One method used to assess the presence and degree of PTA is the Galveston Orientation and Amnesia Test (GOAT, Levin, O'Donnell, & Grossman, 1979). The GOAT enables a quick screening of an individual's orientation to self and place and also assesses for anterograde (postinjury) and retrograde (prior to the injury) amnesia (memory loss or an impairment in memory processing). The range of scores are from 0 to 100. Scores ranging from 76 to 100 are within the normal range and scores of 65 or below are in the impaired range. The forensic examiner often has to base their conclusions on subjective reports from family/friends, individuals who witnessed the accident, or the individual who suffered the TBI themselves (Murrey, 2007).

History

Much information about a neurologic condition (i.e., diagnostic information) can be derived from reviewing the history of the individual rather than the use of sophisticated imaging examinations of the brain or neurophysiological testing (bioelectrical testing). A thorough history comprises of a review of the individual's symptoms through medical records, school reports/records, self-report, or information obtained from family members or organizations the individual attended. Such information can identify if the injury is diffused or more focal (localized) in nature and the potential causes of the neurologic condition (Murrey & Starzinski, 2007). Historical elements that are important to identify are whether the individual has ever been exposed to an occupational toxin or has ever had a chemical dependency, and also family history of illness and diseases with a genetic component (e.g., diabetes which may have neurological implications). TBI implies a physical blow to the head. However, acquired brain injury can also be caused as the result of medical conditions (e.g., a brain tumor, meningitis; West Nile virus, seizures, or stroke). Instances where the individual experiences oxygen deprivation can also cause brain injury (e.g., near drowning, heart attack, suffocation, asphyxia, or carbon monoxide poisoning).

Minnesota Multiphasic Personality Inventory, 2nd revision (MMPI-2) The MMPI-2 (Butcher et al., 1989), while used by researchers on individuals with TBI, has not actually been designed for offender populations. The normative sample for the MMPI-2 included normal (healthy) control participants and participants who were mentally ill. Therefore, medical and legal professionals should be concerned with the validity of this instrument with individuals who have experienced a TBI. Clinicians (most often psychiatrists and psychologists) frequently adhere to the "standard textbook interpretations," which may not be appropriate for offenders with TBI (Murrey & Starzinski, 2007). So far, research investigating the clinical utility of the MMPI-2 on individuals with neurological disorders (including TBI) is inconclusive. Numerous researchers recommend the use of a neurocorrection factor (Levin et al., 1997; Alfano, Finlayson, Stearns, & Neilson, 1990; Gass, 1991) with individuals suspected of having a brain injury or neurological abnormality while others disagree with the neurocorrection factor and advocate instead the use of standard scoring and interpretation of the MMPI-2 with this group (Hoffman, Scott, Emick, & Adams, 1999; Lees-Haley, 1991). Given the level of disagreement about the value of the MMPI-2, it has been suggested that this needs to be considered when assessing individuals with TBI using this measure.

Traumatic Brain Injury Questionnaire (TBIQ) An instrument that has demonstrated clinical utility in the assessment of TBI history in offender populations is the TBIQ (Diamond et al., 2007). Kaba, Diamond, Haque, MacDonald, and Venters (2014) assessed the reliability and validity of the TBIQ in an offender population and found that interview-administered TBI screening is more effective in being able to identify a history of head injury compared to a simple checklist. Specifically, their preliminary findings suggested good test–retest reliability for lifetime history of TBI, good internal consistency for frequency and severity of symptoms, and good criterion validity for TBI frequency and symptom severity. This indicates that in offender populations the TBIQ may facilitate identification of TBI, which can help inform appropriate management and assignment having a positive impact on the offender's rehabilitation during incarceration (Kaba et al., 2014).

The TBIQ is used to assess an individual's history of TBI across their lifetime and the experience of symptoms frequently exhibited in individuals who have sustained head injuries using an interviewer-administered approach. The TBIQ comprises two parts. Part I involves 12 items (yes/no response) which explore whether the individual has ever suffered a head injury as a result of various types of common causes of TBI such as falls, vehicle crashes, domestic violence, sporting accidents, assaults, and so on. If the respondents say yes to having experienced a TBI more detail of the incident is then sought, including the age of the respondent when they suffered the injury, whether there was a period of unconsciousness and/or PTA, and, if there was, for how long this experience occurred. When carrying out the TBIQ detail is also taken on where the injury occurred on the head and on whether the respondent was admitted to hospital and what medical treatment, subsequent rehabilitation, and/or follow-up care was required. In Part 2 of the TBIQ there is a symptom checklist derived from the items on the HELPS questionnaire (Picard, Scarisbrick, & Paluck, 1999 as cited in Jackson, Philip, Nuttall, & Diller, 2002). The frequency and severity of 15 cognitive and physical symptoms, which are common in individuals who have sustained a TBI (e.g., headaches, dizziness, or difficulty with concentration or remembering), are assessed in terms of severity and frequency.

However, the TBIQ is not without limitations, which need to be highlighted for forensic practitioners, neuropsychologists, and other allied health professionals to consider. Although it assesses the frequency and severity of current symptoms, only a few items actually assess changes in consciousness or cognition function immediately following the head trauma. Second, the TBIQ has only been validated among incarcerated adults not adolescents who are incarcerated (Kaba et al., 2014).

Short version of the Ohio State University TBI Identification Ohio State University developed their own measure of TBI, the Ohio State University- Traumatic Brain Injury Identification Method (OSU-TBI-ID) (Bogner & Corrigan, 2009; Corrigan & Bogner, 2007). Recent research has reported finding the OSU-TBI-ID to have both validity and reliability. The first study to examine the prevalence of TBI using the OSU-TBI-ID in inmates in a South Carolina prison found that as many as 65% of male prisoners had suffered a TBI (Ferguson, Pickelsimer, Corrigan, Bogner, & Wald, 2012). Another more recent study, conducted across Indiana state prisons, administered the short version of the OSU-TBI-ID to every male inmate admitted for a month ($N = 831$). Out of the 831 inmates surveyed, 35.7% reported having suffered a TBI at some point during their lives. Compared to those inmates who reported never having experienced a TBI, those inmates who did were more likely to have been diagnosed with a psychiatric disorder and previously incarcerated (Ray, Sapp, & Kincaid 2014). The importance of this study is that it indicates that the short version of the OSU-TBI-ID, which takes less than ten minutes to complete, could be used along with currently used screening instruments in order to identify possible TBI in inmates to help divert them into appropriate treatment/intervention programs (Ray et al., 2014). A recent systematic review of studies that examined the prevalence and assessment of TBI in prison inmates suggested that the OSU-TBI-ID is the assessment which appears to have the most studies. This demonstrates the reliability and validity of the OSU-TBI-ID across a variety of populations including older adult veterans, individuals diagnosed with substance use disorders, individuals with mental disorders, and so on. Compared to other standardized measures, the psychometric properties of the OSU-TBI-ID have been well studied (Allely, 2016).

Assessment of examinee effort during testing The need for assessing effort in forensic neuropsychological assessment is widely accepted. The vast majority of forensic neuropsychologists use a minimum of two formal tests of effort (Murrey 2007). In order to evaluate the individual for inadequate effort a variety of tests have been developed to determine the effort of the individual including the Rey 15-Item Test (Arnett, Hammeke, & Schwartz, 1995; Lee, Loring, & Martin, 1992), the Test of Memory Malingering (TOMM) (Tombaugh, 1996), the Validity Indicator Profile (VIP) (Frederick, 1997), the Computerized Assessment of Response Bias (CARB) (Conder et al., 1992), and the Word Memory Test (WMT) (Green et al., 1996). Additionally, The Forced Choice Recognition (FCR) and the Critical Item Analysis (CIA) indices of the California Verbal Learning Test-II (CVLT-II) (Delis et al. 2000) have been advocated by the individuals who developed the CVLT-II test as being potentially useful, brief screening indicators of effort in individuals undergoing neuropsychological assessment. Indeed, a study carried out by Root, Robbins, Chang, and van Gorp (2006) found the FCR and CIA to display strong predictive value in positive findings of inadequate effort (Root et al., 2006). Formal testing of effort and symptom validity is even more crucial within the forensic context as many accused or offenders have much to lose if the legal issues are not decided in their favor (Iverson, 2003). This does not mean that all individuals assessed within the forensic context will deliberately perform poorly but that, given the legal ramifications, the chances of this occurring are far greater than in a clinical (treatment) only context (Mittenberg, Patton, Canyock, & Condit, 2002). It is therefore important that the forensic neuropsychologist includes symptom validity testing as a crucial element of evaluation in a forensic context (Reynolds Horton, 2012).

Structural imaging and functional imaging Functional imaging techniques (i.e., SPECT, PET, fMRI, EEG) can provide a medical confirmation of a TBI. However, even when these functional imaging techniques are used at the time of injury they have demonstrated inconsistent findings for mild TBI (McAllister, 2005). Before discussing the use of different imaging techniques in relation to offenders, each will be briefly described. The structural imaging of CT uses computer-processed X-rays to create tomographic images (virtual "slices") of the brain. The X-ray beam around the brain is rotated and the X-rays are received by a detector on the opposite of the brain from the side where the X-ray beam is transmitted. The CT scan produces images which depict different brain structures in different shades of black with cerebral spinal fluid typically represented as dark black. Grey matter appears as a light grey while white matter shows up as slightly darker because it has less density compared to grey matter. Dense substances like bone appear a very bright white.

MRI, a non-invasive structural imaging procedure, involves the use of strong magnetic fields and radiowaves to produce images. MRI enables superior soft tissue characterization with high resolution. Essentially, MRI uses the magnetic properties of the atomic constituents of biological matter (within the brain this is typically hydrogen which is a component of water) to produce visual representations of tissue. Multiple imaging can be conducted with no harm to the patients. MRI uses electromagnetic radiation (with no aggregate radiation exposure) and, unlike with CT imaging, there is no exposure to ionizing radiation such as X-rays.

SPECT is a nuclear imaging technique. Specifically, it maps metabolic activity, blood flow changes, or cell receptor occupancy in organs including the brain. SPECT, when compared to CT, is much more sensitive at identifying an organic basis in patients with clinical conditions including post-concussion syndrome, PTA, and loss of consciousness (Gowda et al., 2006). Abnormalities detected in individuals who have experienced a TBI using functional imaging techniques such as SPECT have been found to correlate with the evidence found using neuropsychological assessment.

Lastly, PET measures regional cerebral blood flow within the brain using a camera, which detects the gamma rays resulting from the positron–electron annihilation event.

The presence of possible focal neurological deficits are typically investigated using MRI, CT scans, EEG studies, and PET scans (although the use of PET is rare). MRI and CT scans, while invaluable in the assessment of a neurological abnormalities, are not required criteria for determining whether a TBI has occurred (Murrey & Starzinski, 2007). Depending on the severity of damage a number of abnormalities can be detected with different imaging techniques. The more sophisticated approaches including fMRI and PET have been found to have much greater sensitivity to neuropsychological changes following TBI and, perhaps even more importantly, they demonstrate greater correlation with the findings from neuropsychological assessment (Gale Johnson, Bigler, & Blatter, 1995; Ruff et al., 1989). PET studies have also found that cerebral atrophy (shrinkage) may occur due to cellular damage but may not be clinically detectable for as much as six to nine months following the TBI.

Some limitations of structural and functioning imaging techniques While MRI and CT technologies have become relatively sophisticated in their ability to detect very small structural abnormalities, there still remain some notable limitations. Studies indicate that these technologies may lack sensitivity to abnormalities or functional deficits following a TBI (Wilson & Wyper, 1992). It is common for individuals who have sustained a mild TBI to have CT and MRI scans that appear normal. They sometimes fail to detect subtle, smaller areas of structural neurologic pathology. Additionally, the abnormalities may be electrical and biochemical as opposed to anatomical related changes (Murrey & Starzinski, 2007). Other limitations of CT and MRI scans is that many normal functioning (with respect to neuropsychological and neurobehavioral ability) elderly individuals present as abnormal using such imaging technologies (e.g., Thatcher et al., 1997; de Leon et al., 1997).

Although having the advantage of being more commonly used and relatively inexpensive, MRIs and CT scans are limited in that they only provide a static structural view of the brain and do not provide information on the function of the brain (Frierson & Finkenbine, 2004). A more detailed and accurate picture of the function of the brain is obtained through PET scans and fMRI. However, these technologies are costly and there are relatively few experts who are trained to use these in a forensic context. The majority of neuroradiologists have little or no training in forensic interpretations, as they have more familiarity and expertise with clinical diseases (e.g., acute stroke or tumors).

Methods which measure the actual functioning of different regions within the brain such as electroencephalography (EEG) or Electromyography (EMG) are much more effective and suitable techniques for detecting the degree of neurological or neuropsychological dysfunction. EEG records the electrical activity along the scalp and EMG records and evaluates the electrical activity produced by skeletal muscles. Onset of epilepsy or other focal neurologic abnormalities following a TBI are cases where neurophysiological investigation is particularly useful. The main aim of such neurophysiological studies is to confirm the presence of abnormalities which is part of the evaluation. The evaluation is also informed and guided by the clinical symptoms and findings from the neurologic examination (Murrey & Starzinski, 2007). However, one of the limitations of EEGs is that they are unable to study the brain at a level which is fine enough to be both consistent or clinically useful. Instead, PET or functional MRIs (fMRI) are more clinically useful because, rather than simply measuring static structures of the brain, they measure the actual level of brain function. However, one of the main limitations of these measures is that disentangling normal variation from actual dysfunction is extremely complex (Frierson & Finkenbine, 2004). Moreover, while PET and SPECT scans, fMRI and magnetic resonance spectroscopy (MRS) are able to detect subtle metabolic abnormalities and very subtle electrical pattern changes within the brain, such imaging techniques are relatively experimental in terms of their ability to detect or elucidate patterns of TBI (i.e., Gowda et al., 2006; Lotze et al., 2006).

Given the limitations of the different imaging techniques discussed above, it is recommended that the neuropsychologists' standardized neurocognitive assessment should be viewed carefully and only in conjunction with data provided by the neuropsychiatrist in order to verify the findings or provide some degree of correlation in symptoms displayed and neurological abnormalities identified via imaging techniques. Imaging can reveal abnormalities which are not reflected in the neuropsychiatrist's examination of the individual. Similarly, the neuropsychiatrist can identify clinical deficits in people who exhibit no abnormalities using imaging techniques. An example of this lack of corroboration is clearly demonstrated in the case of an individual who, after MRI, was found to have an infraorbital frontal lobe brain injury. However, this injury of the frontal lobe did not seem to impair the individual's ability to carry out the Wisconsin Card Sorting Test (WCST) (Grant & Berg, 1948), which is considered to be a very effective way of identifying any signs of deficits specifically within the frontal lobes. Therefore, it is recommended that there is strong correlation between the findings from the neuropsychiatric examination and those of the neuropsychological examination before any conclusions can be made (Golden & Lashley, 2014).

Conclusions

Despite the prolific scientific research on criminal behavior, our understanding of the characteristics and scientific markers of serial homicide are relatively poor (Angrilli, Sartori, & Donzella, 2013). The studies covered in this chapter highlight the importance of a comprehensive neurological and psychological examination of offenders who commit single or multiple homicide (Briken et al., 2005). The exact prevalence of TBI in offending populations also requires further exploration since a more accurate estimate of TBI prevalence could lead to the design and implementation of more appropriate resource allocation, screening, and management of offenders (Shiroma et al., 2010; Allely, 2016).

Recommended Reading

Aamodt, M. G. (February 20, 2013). Serial killer statistics. Retrieved from http://maamodt.asp.radford.edu/serial killer information center/project description.htm [Accessed July 15, 2013]. *An excellent resource. A Serial Killer Information Centre headed by Dr. Mike Aamodt at the Department of Psychology, Radford University, Radford, VA, US. This was created to provide students, researchers, and the media with accurate data on serial killers. To date, the Radford Serial Killer Database contains data on 2,750 serial killers with online access to information on 196 of these killers. It also has a section which details any reported brain injuries.*

Aamodt, M. G., & Christina Moyse, C. (2003). Researching the multiple murderer: A comprehensive bibliography of books on specific serial, mass, and spree killers. *Journal of Police and Criminal Psychology, 18*, 61–85. doi 10.1007/BF02802609. *A fantastic bibliography of books on specific serial, mass and spree killers.*

Can a brain injury cause someone to become a serial killer? http://curiosity.discovery.com/question/brain-injury-cause-serial-killer

Fabian, J. M. (2010). Neuropsychological and neurological correlates in violent and homicidal offenders: A legal and neuroscience perspective. *Aggression and Violent Behavior, 15*, 209–223. doi:10.1016/j.avb.2009.12.004.

Fallon, J. (February 2009). Exploring the mind of a killer. [Ted Talk]. http://www.ted.com/talks/jim_fallon_exploring_the_mind_of_a_killer.html *Interesting TED talk by Professor Jim Fallon in which he discusses his research on the subject of psychopaths – particularly those who kill. With PET scans and EEGs, Fallon is beginning to uncover the deep, underlying traits that make people violent and murderous which he explores in this talk.*

Golden, C. J., & Lashley, L. (2014). *Forensic neuropsychological evaluation of the violent Offender.* New York, NY: Springer.

Murderpedia [The Encyclopedia of Murderers]. http://murderpedia.org/.

Murrey & Starzinski, G. (2007) *The Forensic evaluation of traumatic brain injury: A handbook for clinicians and attorneys* (2nd ed.). Boca Raton, FL: CRC Press, VitalBook file.

Nordstrom, B. R., Gao, Y., Glenn, A. L., Peskin, M., Rudo-Hutt, A. S., Schug, R.A., ... Raine, A. (2013). Perspectives in neurocriminology. In J. B. Helfgott, *Criminal psychology* (pp. 17–161). Westport, CT: Praeger.

Raine, A. (2013). *The Anatomy of violence: The biological roots of crime.* Random House Digital, Inc. *A highly informative book by Adrian Raine one of the world's leading authorities on the minds of the violent, the criminal, the dangerous, the unstable. This book is the culmination of his life's work so far. Adrian Raine is the Richard Perry University Professor in the Departments of Criminology, Psychiatry, and Psychology at the University of Pennsylvania. For the past 35 years, his research has focused on the neurobiological and biosocial bases of antisocial and violent behavior and ways to both prevent and treat it in both children and adults.*

Stone, Dr. M. (August 11, 2010). Inside the mind of a serial killer. http://bigthink.com/ideas/21782 *Dr. Stone explains what motivates men who commit serial sexual homicide and whether or not they are born evil. He states that about 30% of the serial killers had experienced some form of rather serious head injury.*

The Science Network. http://thesciencenetwork.org/programs/ethics-and-the-brain/neuro criminology-neuroethical-and-neurolegal-implications. *A great lecture presentation on neurocriminology, integrating neuroscientific and social perspectives in the prediction and explanation of violent behavior, particularly in psychopaths.*

References

Alfano, D. P., Finlayson, M. A, Stearns, G. M., & Neilson, P. M. (1990). The MMPI and neurologic dysfunction: Profile configuration and analysis. *The Clinical Neuropsychologist*, 4, 69–79. doi:10.1080/13854049008401498.

Allely, C. S. (2016). Prevalence and assessment of traumatic brain injury in prison inmates: A systematic PRISMA review. *Brain Injury*, 30, 1161–1180.

Allely, C. S., & Gebbia, P. (2016). Studies investigating fetal alcohol spectrum disorders in the criminal justice system: A systematic PRISMA review. *SOJ Psychology*. Retrieved from http://usir.salford.ac.uk/38695/1/Allely%20and%20Gebbia%20(2016).pdf.

Amen, D., Hanks, C., Prunella, J., & Green, A. (2007). An analysis of regional cerebral blood flow in impulsive murderers using single photon emission computed tomography. *Journal of Neuropsychiatry and Clinical Neurosciences*, 19, 304–309.

Angrilli, A., Sartori, G., & Donzella, G. (2013). Cognitive, emotional and social markers of serial murdering. *The Clinical Neuropsychologist*, 27, 485–494.

Arnett, P. A., Hammeke, T. A., & Schwartz, L. (1995). Quantitative and qualitative performance on Rey's 15-Item Test in neurological patients and dissimulators. *The Clinical Neuropsychologist*, 9, 17–26. doi:10.1080/13854049508402052.

Barnfield, T. V., & Leathem, J. M. (1998). Incidence and outcomes of traumatic brain injury and substance abuse in a New Zealand prison population. *Brain Injury*, 12, 455–466. doi:10.1080/026990598122007.

Barona, A., Reynolds, C. R., & Chastain, R. (1984). A demographically based index of premorbid intelligence for the WAIS-R. *Journal of Consulting and Clinical Psychology*, 52, 885–887

Beaver, K. M., & Wright, J. P. (2005). Evaluating the effects of birth complications on low self-control in a sample of twins. *International Journal of Offender Therapy and Comparative Criminology*, 49, 450–471. doi:10.1177/0306624X05274687.

Black, D. W., Gunter, T., Loveless, P., Allen, J., & Sieleni. (2010). Antisocial personality disorder in incarcerated offenders: Psychiatric comorbidity and quality of life. *Annals of Clinical Psychiatry*, 22, 113–120.

Blair, J. R., & Spreen, O. (1989). Predicting premorbid IQ: A revision of the National Adult Reading Test. *The Clinical Neuropsychologist*, 3, 129–136. doi:10.1080/13854048908403285.

Blake, P. Y., Pincus, J. H., & Buckner, C. (1995). Neurologic abnormalities in murderers. *Neurology*, 45, 1641–1647. doi:10.1212/WNL.45.9.1641.

Boduszek, D., & Hyland. P. (2012). Fred West: A Bio-psycho-social investigation of a psychopathic sexual serial killer. *International Journal of Criminology and Sociological Theory*, 5, 864–870.

Bogner, J., & Corrigan, J. D. (2009). Reliability and predictive validity of the Ohio State University TBI identification method with prisoners. *The Journal of Head Trauma Rehabilitation*, 24, 279–291. doi:10.1097/HTR.0b013e3181a66356.

Briken, P., Habermann, N., Berner, W., & Hill, A. (2005). The influence of brain abnormalities on psychosocial development, criminal history and paraphilias in sexual murderers. *Journal of Forensic Sciences*, 50, 1204–1208.

Brower, M. C., & Price, B. H. (2001). Neuropsychiatry of frontal lobe dysfunction in violent and criminal behavior: A critical review. *Journal of Neurology, Neurosurgery and Psychiatry*, 71, 720–726. doi:10.1136/jnnp.71.6.720.

Bryant, E. T., Scott, M. L, Tori, C. D., & Golden, C. J. (1984). Neuropsychological deficits, learning disability, and violent behavior. *Journal of Consulting and Clinical Psychology*, 52, 323. doi:10.1037/0022-006X.52.2.323.

Bryant, R. A., & Harvey, A. G. (1998). Relationship between acute stress disorder and posttraumatic stress disorder following mild traumatic brain injury. *American Journal of Psychiatry*, 155, 625–629.

Butcher, J. N., Dahlstrom, W. G., Graham, J. R., Tellegen, A., & Kaemmer, B. (1989). Manual for administration and scoring, MMPI-2, Minnesota Multiphasic Personality Inventory-2.

Carlo, P. (1996). *The night stalker: The true story of America's most feared serial killer*. New York, NY: Kensington.

Casartelli, L., & Chiamulera, C. (2013). Opportunities, threats and limitations of neuroscience data in forensic psychiatric evaluation. *Current Opinion in Psychiatry*, 26, 468–473. doi:10.1097/YCO.0b013e32836342e1.

Centers for Disease Control. Traumatic brain injury in prisons and jails. Retrieved from http://www.cdc.gov/traumaticbraininjury/pdf/Prisoner_TBI_Prof-a.pdf. [Accessed April 5, 2013].

Ciccone, J. R. (1992). Murder, insanity, and medical expert witnesses. *Archives of Neurology*, 49, 608. doi:10.1001/archneur.1992.00530300040008.

Conder, R., Allen, L., & Cox, D. (1992). Computerized assessment of response bias test manual. Durham, NC: Cognisyst.

Corrigan, J. D., & Bogner, J. (2007). Initial reliability and validity of the Ohio State University TBI identification method. *The Journal of Head Trauma Rehabilitation*, 22, 318–329. doi:10.1097/01.HTR.0000300227.67748.77.

Crowe, J. A. (2008). *The fatal link: The connection between school shooters and the brain damage from prenatal exposure to alcohol*. Denver, CO: Outskirts Press.

DeFronzo, J., Ditta, A., Hannon, L., & Prochnow, J. (2007). Male serial homicide the influence of cultural and structural variables. *Homicide Studies*, 11, 3–14. doi:10.1177/1088767906297434.

DeHart, D. D., & Mahoney, J. M. (1994). The serial murderer's motivations: An interdisciplinary review. OMEGA – *Journal of Death and Dying*, 29, 29–45. doi:10.2190/75BM-PM83-1XEE-2VBP.

De Leon, M. J., George, A. E., Golomb, J., Tarshish, C., Convit, A. Kluger, A., ... Wisniewski, H. M. (1997). Frequency of hippocampal formation atrophy in normal aging and Alzheimer's disease. *Neurobiology of Aging*, 18, 1–11. doi:10.1016/S0197-4580(96)00213-8

DelBello, M. P., Soutullo, C. A., Zimmerman, M. E., Sax, K. W., Williams, J. R., ... Strakowski, S. M. (1999). Traumatic brain injury in individuals convicted of sexual offenses with and without bipolar disorder. *Psychiatry Research, 89*, 281–286. doi:10.1016/S0165-1781(99)00112-2.

Delis, D. C., Kramer, J. H., Kaplan, E., & Ober, B. A. (2000). *California Verbal Learning Test* (2nd ed.). San Antonio, TX: The Psychological Corporation.

Diamond, P. M., Harzke, A. J., Magaletta, P. R., Cummins, A. G., & Frankowski, R. (2007). Screening for traumatic brain injury in an offender sample: A first look at the reliability and validity of the Traumatic Brain Injury Questionnaire. *The Journal of Head Trauma Rehabilitation, 22*, 330–338. doi:10.1097/01.HTR.0000300228.05867.5c.

Esselman, P. C., & Uomoto, J. M. (1995). Classification of the spectrum of mild traumatic brain injury. *Brain Injury, 9*, 417–424. doi:10.3109/02699059509005782.

Evans, R. W. (1992). Mild traumatic brain injury. *Physical Medicine and Rehabilitation Clinics of North America, 3*, 427–439.

Faccini, L. (2016). The application of the models of autism, psychopathology and deficient Eriksonian development and the path of intended violence to understand the Newtown shooting. *Archives of Forensic Psychology, 1*, 1–13.

Faccini, L., & Allely, C. S. (2016). Mass violence in individuals with Autism Spectrum Disorder and Narcissistic Personality Disorder: A case analysis of Anders Breivik using the Path to Intended and Terroristic Violence model. *Aggression and Violent Behavior, 31*, 229–236. doi:10.1016/j.avb.2016.10.002.

Fallon, J. H. (2005). Neuroanatomical background to understanding the brain of the young psychopath. *Ohio State Journal of Criminal Law, 3*, 341.

Farrer, T. J., Frost, R. B., & Hedges, D. W. (2013). Prevalence of traumatic brain injury in juvenile offenders: A meta-analysis. *Child Neuropsychology, 19*, 225–234. doi:10.1080/09297049.2011.647901.

Fazel, S., Lichtenstein, P., Grann, M., & Långström, N. (2011). Risk of violent crime in individuals with epilepsy and traumatic brain injury: A 35-year Swedish population study. *PLoS Medicine, 8*, e1001150. doi:10.1371/journal.pmed.1001150.

Fearnley, D., & Zaatar, A. (2001) A cross-sectional study which measures the prevalence and characteristics of prisoners who report a family history of epilepsy. *Medicine Science and Law, 41*, 305–308.

Ferguson, P. L., Pickelsimer, E. E., Corrigan, J. D., Bogner, J. A., & Wald, M. (2012). Prevalence of traumatic brain injury among prisoners in South Carolina. *The Journal of Head Trauma Rehabilitation, 27*, E11–E20. doi:10.1097/HTR.0b013e31824e5f47.

Folstein, M. F., Folstein, S. E., & McHugh, P. R (1975). Mini-mental state: a practical method for grading the cognitive state of patients for the clinician. *Journal of Psychiatric Research, 12*, 189–198. doi:10.1016/0022-3956(75)90026-6.

Fox, J. A., & Levin, J. (1999). Serial murder: Popular myths and empirical realities. In M. Dwayne Smith & M. A. Zahn (Eds.), *Homicide: A sourcebook of social research* (pp. 165–175). Thousand Oaks, CA: Sage.

Frederick, R. I. (1997). *Validity indicator profile manual*. Minnesota, MN: NCS Assessments.

Freedman, D., & Hemenway, D. (2000). Precursors of lethal violence: A death row sample. *Social Science and Medicine, 50*, 1757–1770. doi:10.1016/S0277-9536(99)00417-7.

Frierson, R. L., & Finkenbine, R. D. (2004). Psychiatric and neurological characteristics of murder defendants referred for pretrial evaluation. *Journal of Forensic Sciences, 49*, 604–609. doi:10.1520/JFS2003388.

Gale, S. D., Johnson, S. C., Bigler E. D., & Blatter, D. D (1995). Trauma-induced degenerative changes in brain injury: A morphometric analysis of three patients with preinjury and postinjury MR scans. *Journal of Neurotrauma, 12*, 151–158. doi:10.1089/neu.1995.12.151.

Gansler, D. A., McLaughlin, N. C. R, Iguchi, L., Jerram, M., Moore, D. W., Bhadelia, R., & Fulwiler, C. (2009). A multivariate approach to aggression and the orbital frontal cortex in psychiatric patients. *Psychiatry Research: Neuroimaging, 171*, 145–154. doi:10.1016/j.pscychresns.2008.03.007.

Gass, C.S. (1991). MMPI-2 interpretation and closed head injury: A correction factor. *Psychological Assessment: A Journal of Consulting and Clinical Psychology, 3*, 27–31. doi:10.1037/1040-3590.3.1.27

Golden, C. J., & Lashley, L. (2014). *Forensic neuropsychological evaluation of the violent offender.* New York, NY: Springer, 2014. doi:10.1007/978-3-319-04792-8.

Gowda, N. K., Agrawal, D., Bal, C., Chandrashekar, N., Tripatim M., Bandopadhyaya, G. P., Malhotra, A., & Mahapatra, A. K. (2006). Technetium Tc-99m ethyl cysteinate dimer brain single-photon emission CT in mild traumatic brain injury: A prospective study. *American Journal of Neuroradiology, 27*, 447–451.

Grafman, J., Schwab, K., Warden, D., Pridgen, A., Brown, H. R., & Salazar, A. M. (1996). Frontal lobe injuries, violence, and aggression a report of the Vietnam head injury study. *Neurology, 46*, 1231–1231. doi:10.1212/WNL.46.5.1231.

Granacher, R. P., Jr. (2015). *Traumatic brain injury: Methods for clinical and forensic neuropsychiatric assessment.* Boca Raton, FL: CRC Press.

Grant, D. A., & Berg, E. (1948). A behavioral analysis of degree of reinforcement and ease of shifting to new responses in a Weigl-type card-sorting problem. *Journal of Experimental Psychology, 38*, 404–411. doi:10.1037/h0059831.

Green, P., Allen, L. M., & Astner, K. (1996). The Word Memory Test: A user's guide to the oral and computer administered forms, US version 1.1. Durham, NC: Cognisyst.

Hawley, C. A., & Maden, A. (2003). Mentally disordered offenders with a history of previous head injury: Are they more difficult to discharge? *Brain Injury, 17*, 743–758. doi:10.1080/0269905031000089341.

Hoffman, R. G., Scott, J. G., Emick, M. A., & Adams, R. L. (1999). The MMPI-2 and closed-head injury: Effects of litigation and head injury severity. In A. M. Horton, Jr., and L. C. Hartlage (Eds.). *Handbook of Forensic Neuropsychology* (pp. 3–13). New York, NY: Springer.

Holcomb, M. J., & Dean, R. S. (2011). Psychomotor seizures. In Encyclopedia of child behavior and development, New York, NY: Springer. doi:10.1007/978-0-387-79061-9_2307.

Iverson, G. L. (2003). Detecting malingering in civil forensic evaluations. A. M. Horton, Jr., and L. C. Hartlage (Eds.) *Handbook of Forensic Neuropsychology* (pp. 137–177). New York, NY: Springer.

Jackson, H., Philp, E., Nuttall, R. L., & Diller, L. (2002). Traumatic brain injury: A hidden consequence for battered women. *Professional Psychology: Research and Practice, 33*, 39–45. doi:10.1037/0735-7028.33.1.39

Jastak, S., & Wilkinson, G. S. (1984). *The Wide Range Achievement Test-Revised: Administration manual.* Oxford: Jastak Assessment Systems.

Johnstone, B., Callahan, C. D., Kapila C. J., & Bouman, D. E. (1996). The comparability of the WRAT-R reading test and NAART as estimates of premorbid intelligence in neurologically impaired patients. *Archives of Clinical Neuropsychology, 11*, 513–519. doi:10.1093/arclin/11.6.513.

Kaba, F., Diamond, P., Haque, A., MacDonald, R., & Venters, H. (2014). Traumatic brain injury among newly admitted adolescents in the New York City jail system. *Journal of Adolescent Health, 54*, 615–617. doi: http://dx.doi.org/10.1016/j.jadohealth.2013.12.013

Kareken, D. A., Gur, R. C., & Saykin, A. J. (1995). Reading on the Wide Range Achievement Test-Revised and parental education as predictors of IQ: Comparison with the Barona formula. *Archives of Clinical Neuropsychology, 10*, 147–157. doi:10.1093/arclin/10.2.147.

Kingston, W. L., MacTavish, A., & Loza-Fanous, A. (2007). A nine-year follow-up study on the predictive validity of the self-appraisal questionnaire for predicting violent and nonviolent recidivism. *Journal of Interpersonal Violence, 22,* 1144–1155. doi:10.1177/0886260507303730.

LaBrode, T. R. (2007). Etiology of the psychopathic serial killer: An analysis of antisocial personality disorder, psychopathy, and serial killer personality and crime scene characteristics. *Brief Treatment and Crisis Intervention, 7,* 151–160. doi:10.1093/brief-treatment/mhm004.

Langevin, R. (2006). Sexual offenses and traumatic brain injury. *Brain and Cognition, 60,* 206–207.

Langevin, R., Bain, J., Wortzman, G., Hucker, S., Dickey, R., & Wright, P. (1988). Sexual sadism: Brain, blood, and behavior. *Annals of the New York Academy of Sciences, 528,* 163–171. doi:10.1111/j.1749-6632.1988.tb50859.x.

Langevin, R., Ben-Aron, M. H., Wright, P., Marchese, V., & Handy, L. (1988). The sex killer. *Annals of Sex Research, 1,* 263–301. doi:10.1007/BF00852801.

Lavergne, G. (1997). *A Sniper in the Tower: The Charles Whitman Murders.* Denton, TX: University of North Texas Press.

Lee, G. P., Loring, D. W., & Martin, R. C. (1992). Rey's 15-item visual memory test for the detection of malingering: Normative observations on patients with neurological disorders. *Psychological Assessment, 4,* 43–46. doi:10.1037/1040-3590.4.1.43.

Lees-Haley, P. R. (1991). MMPI-2 F and FK scores of personal injury malingerers in vocational neuropsychological and emotional distress claims. *American Journal of Forensic Psychology, 9,* 5–14.

Levin, H. S., Gass, C., & Wold, H. (1997). MMPI-II interpretation in closed-head trauma. Crossed validation of a correction factor. *Archives of Clinical Neuropsychology, 12,* 199–205.

Levin, H. S., O'Donnell, V. M., & Grossman, R. G. (1979). The Galveston Orientation and Amnesia Test: A practical scale to assess cognition after head injury. *The Journal of Nervous and Mental Disease, 167,* 675–684.

Lewis, D. O., Pincus, J. H., Feldman, M., Jackson, L., & Bard, B. (1986). Psychiatric, neurological, and psychoeducational characteristics of 15 death row inmates in the United States. *American Journal of Psychiatry, 143,* 838–845.

Lewis, D. O., Pincus, J. H., Bard, B., Richardson, E., Prichep, L. S., Feldman, M., & Yeager, C. (1988). Neuropsychiatric, psychoeducational, and family characteristics of 14 juveniles condemned to death in the United States. *The American Journal of Psychiatry, 145,* 584–589.

Lotze, M., Grodd, W., Rodden, F. A., Gut, E., Schönle, P. W., Kardatzki, B., & Cohen, L. G. (2006). Neuroimaging patterns associated with motor control in traumatic brain injury. *Neurorehabilitation and Neural Repair, 20,* 14–23. doi:10.1177/1545968305282919.

Martell, D. A. (1992). Estimating the prevalence of organic brain dysfunction in maximum-security forensic psychiatric patients. *Journal of Forensic Sciences, 37,* 878–93.

Martinius, J. (1983). Homicide of an aggressive adolescent boy with right temporal lesion: A case report. *Neuroscience & BioBehavioral Reviews, 7,* 419–422. doi:10.1016/0149-7634(83)90048-9.

McAllister, T. W. (2005). Mild brain injury and the postconcussion syndrome. In J. M. Silver, T. W. McAllister, & S. C. Yudofsky (Eds.) *Textbook of traumatic brain injury* (pp. 279–308). Washington, DC: American Psychiatric Publishing, Inc.

Mesulam, M. (2000). *Principles of behavioral and cognitive neurology.* New York: Oxford University Press.

Mills, S., & Raine, A. (1995). Neuroimaging and aggression. *Journal of Offender Rehabilitation, 21,* 145–158.

Mittenberg, W., Patton, C., Canyock, E. M., & Condit, D. C. (2002). Base rates of malingering and symptom exaggeration. *Journal of Clinical and Experimental Neuropsychology, 24,* 1094–1102. doi:10.1076/jcen.24.8.1094.8379.

Morrell, R. F., Merbitz, C. T., Jain, S., & Jain, S. (1998). Traumatic brain injury in prisoners. *Journal of Offender Rehabilitation, 27*, 1–8. doi:10.1300/J076v27n03_01.

Murrey, G., & Donald Starzinski, D. (Eds.). (2007). *The forensic evaluation of traumatic brain injury: A handbook for clinicians and attorneys*. Boca Raton, FL: CRC Press.

Norris, J. (1988). *Serial killers: The growing menace*. New York, NY: Doubleday.

Olegård, Ragnar, K-G., Sabel, M., Aronsson, B., Sandin, P.R., Johansson, C., Carlsson, M., ... Hrbek, A. (1979). Effects on the child of alcohol abuse during pregnancy: Retrospective and prospective studies. *Acta Paediatrica, 68*(S275), 112–121. doi:10.1111/j.1651-2227.1979.tb06170.x.

Ostrosky-Solís, F., Vélez-García, A., Santana-Vargas, D., Pérez, M., & Ardila, A. (2008). A middle aged female serial killer. *Journal of Forensic Science, 53*, 1223–1230. doi:10.1111/j.1556-4029.2008.00803.x.

Pallone, N. J., & Hennessy, J. J. (1996). *Tinder box criminal aggression: Neuropsychology, demography, phenomenology*. New Brunswick, NJ: Transaction Books.

Pallone, N. J., & Hennessy, J. J. (1998). Brain dysfunction and criminal violence. *Society, 35*, 21–27. doi:10.1007/BF02686049.

Picard, M., Scarisbrick, D., & Paluck, R. (1999). HELPS screening tool. Retrieved from vayahealth.com/wp/wp-content/uploads/2016/05/HELPSScreeningTool.pdf.

Pincus, J. H. (1993). Neurologist's role in understanding violence. *Archives of Neurology, 50*, 867–869. doi:10.1001/archneur.1993.00540080070017.

Pincus, J. H. (1999). Aggression, criminality, and the frontal lobes. *The Human Frontal Lobes: Functions and Disorders, Supra Note 21*, 547–549.

Pincus, J. H. (2001). *Base instincts: What makes killers kill?* London: WW Norton & Company.

Prothero, M., & Hanis, G. (2007). *Defending Gary: Unraveling the mind of the Green River killer*. PLLC, Kent, WA, US Smith, Carlton (Col). Source: San Francisco, CA: Jossey-Bass, 2006, reprinted 2007. xi, 558 pp.

Psychological Corporation. (1997). *Wechsler Adult Intelligence Scale, 3rd rev., WAISIII/WMS-III, technical manual*. San Antonio, TX: The Psychological Corporation.

Purisch, A. D., & Sbordone, R. J. (1986). The Luria-Nebraska neuropsychological battery. In G. Goldstein & M. M. Vanyukov (Eds.). *Advances in Clinical Neuropsychology* (pp. 291–316). doi:10.1007/978-1-4613-2211-5_10.

Raine, A. (1993). *The psychopathology of crime: Criminal behavior as clinical disorder*. San Diego, CA: Academic Press.

Raine, A. (1997). *The psychopathology of crime: Criminal behavior as clinical disorder*. Accessed Online via Elsevier.

Raine, A. (2002). Annotation: The role of prefrontal deficits, low autonomic arousal, and early health factors in the development of antisocial and aggressive behavior in children. *Journal of Child Psychology and Psychiatry, 43*, 417–434. doi:10.1111/1469-7610.00034.

Raine, A. (2008). From genes to brain to antisocial behavior. *Current Directions in Psychological Science, 17*, 323–328. doi:10.1111/j.1467-8721.2008.00599.x.

Raine, A. (2013). *The anatomy of violence: The biological roots of crime*. New York, NY: Vintage Books

Raine, A., Brennan, P, & Mednick, S. A. (1994). Birth complications combined with early maternal rejection at age 1 year predispose to violent crime at age 18 years. *Archives of General Psychiatry, 51*, 984–988. doi:10.1001/archpsyc.1994.03950120056009.

Raine, A., Buchsbaum, M., & LaCasse, L. (1997). Brain abnormalities in murderers indicated by positron emission tomography. *Biological Psychiatry, 42*, 495–508. doi:10.1016/S0006-3223(96)00362-9.

Raine, A., Buchsbaum, M. S., Stanley, J., Lottenberg, S., Abel, L., & Stoddard, J. (1994). Selective reductions in prefrontal glucose metabolism in murderers. *Biological Psychiatry, 36*, 365–373. doi:10.1016/0006-3223(94)91211-4.

Raine, A., Lee, L., Yang, Y., & Colletti, P. (2010). Neurodevelopmental marker for limbic maldevelopment in antisocial personality disorder and psychopathy. *The British Journal of Psychiatry, 197,* 186–192. doi:10.1192/bjp.bp.110.078485.

Raine, A., Reid Meloy, J., Bihrle, S., Stoddard, J., LaCasse, L., & Buchsbaum, M. S. (1998). Reduced prefrontal and increased subcortical brain functioning assessed using positron emission tomography in predatory and affective murderers. *Behavioral Sciences and the Law, 16,* 319–332. doi:10.1002/(SICI)1099-0798(199822)16:3<319::AID-BSL311>3.0.CO;2-G.

Raine, A., Stoddard, J., Bihrle, S., & Buchsbaum, M. S. (1998). Prefrontal glucose deficits in murderers lacking psychosocial deprivation. *Cognitive and Behavioral Neurology, 11,* 1–7.

Raine, A., Venables, P. H., & Williams, M. (1990). Relationships between central and autonomic measures of arousal at age 15 years and criminality at age 24 years. *Archives of General Psychiatry, 47,* 1003–1007. doi:10.1001/archpsyc.1990.01810230019003.

Raine, A., & Yaling Yang, Y. (2006). Neural foundations to moral reasoning and antisocial behavior. *Social Cognitive and Affective Neuroscience, 1,* 203–213. doi:10.1093/scan/nsl033.

Ray, B., Sapp, D., & Kincaid, A. (2014). Traumatic brain injury among Indiana state prisoners. *Journal of Forensic Sciences, 59,* 1248–1253. DOI:10.1111/1556-4029.12466.

Redding, R. E. (2006). The brain-disordered defendant: Neuroscience and legal insanity in the twenty-first century. *Villanova University Legal Working Paper Series,* No. 61.

Reynolds, C., & Horton Jr., A. M (Eds.) (2012). *Detection of malingering during head injury litigation.* New York, NY: Springer.

Root, J. C., Robbins, R. N., Chang, L., & van Gorp, W. G. (2006). Detection of inadequate effort on the California Verbal Learning Test: Forced choice recognition and critical item analysis. *Journal of the International Neuropsychological Society, 12,* 688-696. doi:10.1017/S1355617706060838.

Ruff, R. M., Buchsbaum, M. S., Tröster, A. I., Marshall, L. F., Lottenberg, L., Somers, L. M., & Tobias, M. D. (1989). Computerized tomography, neuropsychology, and positron emission tomography in the evaluation of head injury. *Cognitive and Behavioral Neurology, 2,* 103–123.

Sarapata, M., Herrmann, D., Johnson, T., & Aycock, R. (1998). The role of head injury in cognitive functioning, emotional adjustment and criminal behavior. *Brain Injury, 12,* 821–842. doi:10.1080/026990598122061.

Schofield, P. W., Butler, T. G., Hollis, S. J., Smith, N. E., Lee, S. J., & Kelso, W. M. (2006a). Traumatic brain injury among Australian prisoners: Rates, recurrence and sequelae. *Brain Injury, 20,* 499–506. doi:10.1080/02699050600664749.

Schofield, P. W., Butler, T. G., Hollis, S. J., Smith, N. E., Lee, S. J., & Kelso, W. M. (2006b). Neuropsychiatric correlates of traumatic brain injury (TBI) among Australian prison entrants. *Brain Injury, 20,* 1409–1418. doi:10.1080/02699050601130443.

Shiroma, E. J., Ferguson, P. L., & Pickelsimer E. E. (2010). Prevalence of traumatic brain injury in an offender population: A meta-analysis. *Journal of Correctional Health Care, 16,* 147–159. doi:10.1097/HTR.0b013e3182571c14.

Silver, J. M., Kramer, R., Greenwald, S., & Weissman, M. (2001). The association between head injuries and psychiatric disorders: Findings from the New Haven NIMH Epidemiologic Catchment Area Study. *Brain Injury, 15,* 935–945. doi:10.1080/02699050110065295.

Slaughter, B., Fann, J. R., & Ehde, D. (2003). Traumatic brain injury in a county jail population: Prevalence, neuropsychological functioning and psychiatric disorders. *Brain Injury, 17,* 731–741. doi:10.1080/0269905031000088649.

Steinberg, L. (2008). A social neuroscience perspective on adolescent risk-taking. *Developmental Review, 28,* 78–106. doi:10.1016/j.dr.2007.08.002.

Stone, M. H. (2001). Serial sexual homicide: Biological, psychological, and sociological aspects. *Journal of Personality Disorders, 15,* 1–18. doi:10.1521/pedi.15.1.1.18646.

Stone, M. H. (2009). *The anatomy of evil.* Amhurst, NY: Prometheus Books.
Swayze, V. W., Johnson, V. P., Hanson, J. W., Piven, J., Sato, Y., Giedd, J. N., ... Andreasen, N. C. (1997). Magnetic resonance imaging of brain anomalies in fetal alcohol syndrome. *Pediatrics, 99,* 232–240.
Templer, D. I., Kasiraj, J., Trent, N. H., Trent, A., Hughey, B., Keller, W. J., ... Thomas-Dobson, S. (1992). Exploration of head injury without medical attention. *Perceptual and Motor Skills, 75,* 195–202. doi:10.2466/pms.1992.75.1.195.
Thatcher, R. W., Camacho, M., Salazar, A., Linden, C., Biver, C., & Clarke. L. (1997). Quantitative MRI of the gray–white matter distribution in traumatic brain injury. *Journal of Neurotrauma, 14,* 1–14. doi:10.1089/neu.1997.14.1.
Tombaugh, T. N. (1996). Test of memory malingering: TOMM. New York/Toronto: MHS.
Treiman, D. M. (1999). Violence and the epilepsy defense. *Neurologic Clinics, 17,* 245–255. doi:10.1016/S0733-8619(05)70128-6.
Turkstra, L., Jones, D., & Toler, H. L. (2003). Brain injury and violent crime. *Brain Injury, 17,* 39–47. doi:10.1080/0269905021000010122.
Volavka, J., Martell, D., & Convit, A. Psychobiology of the violent offender. *Journal of Forensic Sciences, 37*(1), 237–251.
Volavka, J. (1995). *Neurobiology of violence.* London: American Psychiatric Press.
Volavka, J. (1999). The neurobiology of violence: An update. *Journal of Neuropsychiatry and Clinical Neuroscience, 11,* 307–314.
Volkow, N. D., & Tancredi, L. (1987). Neural substrates of violent behavior. A preliminary study with positron emission tomography. *The British Journal of Psychiatry, 151,* 668–673. doi:10.1192/bjp.151.5.668.
Walker, R., Staton, M., &. Leukefeld, C. G. (2001). History of head injury among substance users: Preliminary findings. *Substance Use and Misuse, 36,* 757–768. doi:10.1081/JA-100104089.
Wiens, A. N., Bryan, J. E., & Crossen, J. R. (1993). Estimating WAIS-R FSIQ from the national adult reading test-revised in normal subjects. *The Clinical Neuropsychologist, 7,* 70–84. doi:10.1080/13854049308401889.
Wilson, J. T. L., & Wyper, D. (1992). Neuroimaging and neuropsychological functioning following closed head injury: CT, MRI, and SPECT. *The Journal of Head Trauma Rehabilitation, 7,* 29–39. doi:10.1097/00001199-199206000-00006.
Williams, H. W., Cordan, G., Mewse, A. J., Tonks, J., & Burgess, C. N. (2010). Self-reported traumatic brain injury in male young offenders: A risk factor for re-offending, poor mental health and violence? *Neuropsychological Rehabilitation, 20,* 801–812. doi:10.1080/09602011.2010.519613.
Yang, Y., & Adrian Raine, R. (2009). Prefrontal structural and functional brain imaging findings in antisocial, violent, and psychopathic individuals: A meta-analysis. *Psychiatry Research: Neuroimaging, 174,* 81–88. doi:10.1016/j.pscychresns.2009.03.012.
Yang, Y., Raine, A., Chen-Bo Han, C-B., Schug, R. A., Toga, A. W., & Narr, K. L. (2010). Reduced hippocampal and parahippocampal volumes in murderers with schizophrenia. *Psychiatry Research: Neuroimaging, 182,* 9–13. doi:10.1016/j.pscychresns.2009.10.013.
Yin, R. K. (1994). *Case study research: Design and methods.* Thousand Oaks, CA: Sage.

16

The Neurobiology of Offending Behavior in Adolescence

Graeme Fairchild and Areti Smaragdi[1]

> **Key points**
> - In the present chapter, we review research on the neuroscience of antisocial and offending behavior in child and adolescent populations.
> - We first define the scope of the review, the range of different terms used in this field, and the criminological and psychiatric phenomena that neuroscience researchers are currently trying to explain (or may wish to study in the future).
> - In the sections that follow, the possible role of neurobiological factors in driving the age-crime curve in offending behavior and the neurobiological bases of sex differences in aggression and antisocial behavior are reviewed.
> - We then discuss what neurobiological and neuroimaging evidence has to say about the validity and utility of different subtyping approaches such as those based on age-of-onset of antisocial behavior or the presence or absence of callous-unemotional personality traits. Here, we find that some subtyping approaches, such as those based on assessing callous-unemotional traits, have been tested quite extensively using neurobiological or neuroimaging methods, whereas others, such as the behavioral subtype approach (which holds that aggressive and non-aggressive antisocial behaviors have distinct etiologies, developmental courses and neurobiological correlates), have received relatively little attention in the neuroimaging literature.
> - The chapter ends by considering the potential of neuroscience methods to contribute to clinical practice in forensic psychology and psychiatry, evaluation of treatment or rehabilitation approaches, and the prediction of future risk for violence or criminal behavior.

> Terminology Explained
>
> **Antisocial personality disorder (ASPD)**, is described in the *Diagnostic and Statistical Manual of Mental Disorders, Fifth Edition, Text Revision* (DSM-5; American Psychiatric Association, 2013) as a "pervasive pattern of disregard for, and the violation of, the rights of others" (p. 659), and can include a disregard for social norms, deceitfulness, impulsivity, irritability/aggressiveness, reckless disregard for the safety of others, consistent irresponsibility, and lack of remorse.
>
> **Callous and unemotional traits (CU)** are distinguished by a persistent pattern of behavior that reflects a disregard for others, and also a lack of empathy and generally deficient affect (empathetic responding). The interplay between genetic and environmental risk factors may play a role in the expression of these traits as conduct disorder (CD).
>
> **Conduct disorder (CD)** is the term given to a repetitive, and persistent, pattern of behavior in childhood in which the basic rights of others or societal conventions are violated. Children with CD often show ASPD as adults.
>
> The **Dunedin Multidisciplinary Health and Development Study** investigated questions of child health and development using a prospective longitudinal design examining a cohort of children from birth onwards.
>
> The **IMAGEN study** (Imagen-Europe.com) is a research project investigating mental health and risk-taking behavior in European teenagers from England, France, Ireland, and Germany.
>
> **Interoception** is sensitivity to bodily sensations or states (e.g., one's heartbeat).
>
> **Synaptic pruning** occurs where connections of the neurones are refined based on sensory, motor, language and cognitive experience, and parental-child interactions. Connections that are used regularly become stronger and more complex, while those that are not used are lost. The pruning process enables the brain to operate more efficiently and provides room for networks of essential connections to expand.
>
> The **uncinate fasciculus** is a white-matter pathway in the brain that connects parts of the limbic system (e.g., the hippocampus and amygdala) with the prefrontal cortex. It is the last white-matter tract to mature in the human brain. Its integrity appears to be affected in several psychiatric conditions.
>
> **Voxel-based morphometry(VBM)** investigates differences in brain anatomy, particularly gray matter volume.

Introduction

In the process of reviewing the literature on the neurobiology of offending in adolescence, it became clear that a wide range of different terms have been used to describe adolescents who engage in criminal or serious antisocial behavior. It may therefore be helpful to review these terms here before attempting to synthesize across the criminological, psychiatric, and developmental psychological literatures.

In psychiatry, the most commonly used terms to designate persistent patterns of antisocial and criminal behavior are conduct disorder (CD) and antisocial personality disorder (ASPD; American Psychiatric Association, 2000, 2013). The former diagnostic category is normally applied to children or adolescents, whereas ASPD is an adult disorder that can be diagnosed from age 18 onwards. The presence of CD before the age of 15 is one of the key diagnostic criteria for ASPD (APA, 2013), showing that although there are differences between these disorders in terms of diagnostic criteria, there is also significant continuity between them. In particular, it is very rare for ASPD to emerge *de novo* in adulthood; the developmental pathways toward the adult disorder virtually always have their origins in childhood or adolescence (Lahey, Loeber, Burke, & Applegate, 2005; Robins, 1966, 1978).

In criminology, the terms delinquent or young offender are more commonly used to describe adolescents who engage in criminal or serious antisocial behavior. These terms indicate that the individual has violated laws or the rights of others, therefore they are not synonymous with the terms CD or even ASPD because the diagnostic criteria for these psychiatric disorders include behaviors that are not regulated by laws, such as truancy, bullying, or a pervasive failure to take responsibility for one's actions, in addition to more serious behaviors that contravene the law such as using weapons to harm others, animal cruelty, or sexual assault. Consequently, while there is likely to be significant overlap between these classification methods, such that adolescents with CD are far more likely to have been arrested or prosecuted for a criminal offense than their typically-developing peers, there are also a substantial number of individuals who would fulfill formal diagnostic criteria for CD but who never break the law or become involved with the criminal justice system. Conversely, when considering young offenders living in the community (particularly persistent offenders) or young people in custody, a very high proportion of these individuals would meet diagnostic criteria for CD (Teplin, Abram, McClelland, Dulcan, & Mericle, 2002). It is also likely that they would meet the criteria for ASPD when they reach adulthood.

Finally, in the developmental psychology literature, yet another set of terms is used such as life-course persistent antisocial behavior or conduct problems. Again, although these terms differ in important ways from the above categories or labels, and the group allocations are typically made using questionnaire data rather than clinical assessments, there is likely to be considerable overlap between individuals with life-course persistent antisocial behavior, as defined on the basis of trajectory modeling analyses, and the groups identified using the other approaches (e.g., adolescents with CD or persistent young offenders). Nevertheless, this diversity of approaches to recruitment, classification, and group allocation makes it somewhat challenging to directly compare groups across studies or integrate findings across the criminological, psychiatric, and psychological literatures on this topic. This should be acknowledged as both a limitation of the existing literature in this area and a potential cause of discrepant findings between studies.

Moving on to consider the key issues related to offending behavior in adolescence, it is clear that there are several phenomena that need to be explained from a mechanistic perspective within the forensic neuroscience field. One of the most important of these phenomena is the "age-crime curve," whereby offending rates increase dramatically during the teenage period, reaching a peak in late adolescence (or early adulthood for the most serious crimes) and decline thereafter (Farrington, 1986; see Figure 16.1).

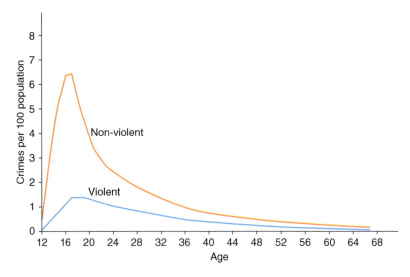

Figure 16.1 The relationship between age and crime for US males, showing rates of arrest per 100 of the population for index offenses in 1982.

Source: Reproduced with permission from Farrington, 1986. *Crime and Justice*, p. 193; Copyright University of Chicago Press.

The age-crime curve has been observed across many industrialized and developing countries and does not appear to be simply an artifact of the legal system's approach to dealing with young people (i.e., greater leniency toward children versus teenagers) or the fact that crimes committed by adolescents are more likely to be detected or prosecuted than those perpetrated by children. The question thus arises as to the factors driving the dramatic increases observed in criminal behavior over this period – are these the consequence of general changes at the population level (e.g., increased risk-taking in the majority of young people), or are they a result of behavioral changes among a minority of individuals (e.g., the escalation of criminal behaviors in the small group of individuals who were already committing minor criminal offenses in childhood)? What are the underlying psychological and neurobiological mechanisms that drive this age-crime curve and to what extent do they interact with environmental or sociocultural influences, such as changes in the availability and use of alcohol or drugs over the teenage years?

Another phenomenon that needs to be explained from a mechanistic perspective is the sex difference observed in rates of criminal or antisocial behavior, whereby males are substantially more likely than females to engage in such behaviors (see Figure 16.2). This holds across the lifespan, although the sex ratio narrows in mid-adolescence and widens again in late adolescence or early adulthood. If one takes a psychiatric perspective on this issue, rather than a criminological one, males are more likely than females to be diagnosed with CD, oppositional defiant disorder (a developmental precursor to CD reflecting irritability and disobedience; APA, 2013), and ASPD by a factor of around 2.4:1 (Moffitt, Caspi, Rutter, & Silva, 2001). It is also the case that in adolescence, males far outnumber females when convictions for serious or violent convictions are considered, and are strikingly over-represented in the prison

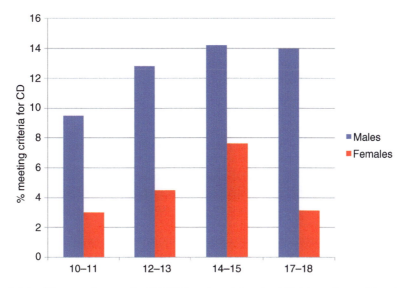

Figure 16.2 The prevalence of DSM-IV Conduct Disorder (CD) in males and females in the Dunedin Multidisciplinary Health and Development Study.

Source: Adapted with permission from Moffitt et al., 2001, *Sex differences in antisocial behavior*, p. 46; Copyright Cambridge University Press, 2001.

system (Ministry of Justice, 2016). While a number of influential studies have investigated the potential causes of such sex differences, our knowledge of the underlying factors remains limited.

A further phenomenon of interest relates to the continuity versus discontinuity of antisocial and criminal behavior. Some young offenders or adolescents with CD will show a relatively time-limited pattern of antisocial behavior and will eventually desist, whereas others will show either stable or escalating patterns of criminal or antisocial behavior over the same developmental period. A depressing statistic from the youth justice system in the UK is that around 40–60% of those individuals imprisoned in their teenage years will re-offend after their release (Ministry of Justice, 2016). A greater understanding of the factors that contribute toward these patterns of desistance versus persistence or escalation to displaying severe criminal behaviors is urgently needed, as this knowledge could inform the development of more effective interventions or even prevention strategies that could be used with high-risk groups (such as the younger siblings of offenders).

Although there is now a consensus among researchers and clinicians that there is substantial heterogeneity within antisocial behavior, there is far less agreement regarding the optimal way to make sense of this heterogeneity. Different subtyping approaches have been proposed such as using the age-of-onset of conduct problems to classify individuals into childhood-onset and adolescence-onset groups (APA, 2013), assessing for the presence of psychopathic or callous-unemotional traits (the affective component of psychopathy), or classifying offenders as either aggressive or non-aggressive (sometimes termed the "behavioral subtype" approach; Burt, Donnellan, Iacono, & McGue, 2011). Each of these approaches has notable strengths and weaknesses, but we will consider neuropsychological and neuroscience evidence that speaks to the validity of these subtyping methods.

The final issue that we will consider here is the potential of neuroscience-based methods to contribute toward the assessment and treatment of young offenders and adolescents with CD, as well as predicting risk in a range of settings such as youth offending institutes or the community (to complement existing measures such as the Asset[2]), and possibly even evaluating the individual's potential for rehabilitation. It is worth noting that our current understanding of adolescent brain development and brain–behavior relationships is still very limited and the neuroimaging techniques that have been used to date in research are probably not sufficiently reliable or reproducible to be used within the criminal justice system or in health care settings. However, as the technological problems surrounding the use of neuroimaging methods are addressed (e.g., by the use of quantitative MRI methods), and the techniques become more widely used, accessible, and comparable across different centers, it is possible that structural or functional neuroimaging techniques could be applied to studying individuals on a case-by-case basis, rather than being restricted to comparing groups. It is also likely that combining across several different measures of brain anatomy or brain activity, rather than relying on measures reflecting the volume or activity of a single structure, might improve our ability to classify individuals into groups. Another future development might include the use of neuroimaging data to contribute to risk assessments or parole decisions within the criminal justice system.

In the remainder of the chapter, we will consider what neuroscience and neuropsychological research has to say about the issues discussed above, namely changes in criminal offending and antisocial behavior over the adolescent period, the origins of sex differences in antisocial behavior and trajectories of offending, heterogeneity within antisocial populations, and factors potentially explaining patterns of continuity versus discontinuity in criminal and antisocial behavior. We will highlight gaps in the evidence base and suggest approaches that could be used to address these gaps. We will also consider recent studies that have attempted to use neuroscience methods to predict re-offending rates or future risk for violence.

Is the Age-Crime Curve Partly Explained by Developmental Changes in Brain Structure and Function?

It is well established that the transition to adolescence is a turbulent time for many young people, both in terms of physical and biological changes related to maturation, and cognitive and emotional development. During adolescence, the brain undergoes a remarkable number of changes in growth, connectivity, and synaptic pruning that continue into early adulthood (Paus, Keshavan, & Giedd, 2008; Spear, 2010). This creates a stage in development that is distinct from both childhood and adulthood and it is likely that these maturational changes are related to the changes in behavior, and particularly the increases in antisocial behavior, that occur during this period of the lifespan (Fairchild, 2011).

Several studies using structural magnetic resonance imaging (sMRI) methods have found that adolescents and adults show similar gray matter volumes in the frontal cortices. However, due to delayed myelination of this area and the fact that connections with other cortical and subcortical structures are still developing, the frontal regions in adolescents are still functionally immature relative to adults (Giedd, 2004). This is evident in the immaturity of higher order cognitive processes (including inhibition) and emotional regulation abilities (Eshel, Nelson, Blair, Pine, & Ernst, 2007; Hare & Casey, 2005). This appears particularly true for structures such as the orbitofrontal or ventromedial prefrontal cortex (vmPFC), where adolescents show less activity relative to adults during decision-making tasks (Bjork et al., 2004; Van Leijenhorst et al., 2010).

This immaturity of prefrontal cortical regions means that the subcortical regions of the brain (including the limbic system) may play a greater role in guiding behavior, since the mechanisms that in adulthood typically suppress and regulate the expression of strong emotions such as anger are not yet fully developed (Casey, Jones, & Hare, 2008; although see Pfeifer & Allen, 2012). Greater activation in limbic structures, such as the nucleus accumbens, during adolescence, is thought to explain the increased levels of risk-taking, reward seeking, and impulsive behavior that are seen at this time (Ernst et al., 2005).

The changes that are observed in sex hormone secretion during puberty may also alter the responsiveness of regions involved in reward processing (Dreher et al., 2007), thereby temporarily heightening risk-taking (Fairchild, 2011). Although these neurobiological explanations of changes in risk-taking behavior during adolescence seem plausible, it should be noted that risk-taking and antisocial behavior are overlapping, but not synonymous, constructs. We do not yet have population-level data capable of linking changes in reward or limbic system functioning with increases in antisocial behavior during adolescence – especially longitudinal data tracking the same individuals over time – although large-scale multi-disciplinary projects such as the IMAGEN study offer the best chance of progress in this respect (Schumann et al., 2010). In particular, it would be interesting to study the environmental and neurobiological mechanisms underlying the age-crime curve by studying parallel changes in brain structure and function and offending behavior in a representative sample of adolescents.

Does Adolescent Offending Have a Neurobiological Basis?

While the above section briefly described what is known about the typical development of the brain, it should be noted that severely antisocial adolescents might differ from typical adolescents in terms of brain structure and function in several ways. A number of sMRI studies have reported reduced amygdala, insula, and orbitofrontal cortex gray matter volume in male adolescents with CD relative to controls (Fairchild et al., 2011; Huebner et al., 2008; Sterzer, Stadler, Poustka, & Kleinschmidt, 2007; Stevens & Haney-Caron, 2012). These brain regions have been implicated in emotion recognition, interoception, affective empathy, reward processing, and affect regulation. However, as changes in gray matter volume, as assessed using voxel-based morphometry (VBM), could reflect a combination of changes in cortical thickness, surface area, and folding (Hutton, Draganski, Ashburner, & Weiskopf, 2009), more recent studies have applied surface-based morphometry analysis methods that differentiate between these metrics of brain structure. These studies have reported that adolescents with CD show changes in cortical thickness across a range of anatomical regions relative to healthy controls (Fahim et al., 2011; Fairchild et al., 2015; Hyatt, Haney-Caron, & Stevens, 2012; Wallace et al., 2014), although the most consistent finding across these studies is lower cortical thickness in the right superior temporal gyrus.

The superior temporal gyrus is implicated in social cognition and theory of mind (Zaki & Ochsner, 2012), therefore structural deficits in this area may contribute to the difficulties in social functioning experienced by adolescents with CD. It has also been reported that adolescents with CD show reduced cortical folding in the vmPFC and insula (Hyatt et al., 2012; Wallace et al., 2014), which are regions implicated in emotion regulation and empathy, respectively. However, Fairchild et al. (2015) observed increased folding in the insula in adolescents with CD; this appeared to be driven by the presence of CU traits in the CD group.

Finally, Fairchild et al. (2015) found reductions in ventromedial prefrontal cortical surface area in adolescents with CD relative to controls, and a negative relationship between surface area in this region and the number of CD symptoms. Considered together, these studies suggest that structural changes or deficits in brain regions involved in emotion recognition, affect regulation, and social cognitive processes contribute to the etiology of CD. It also seems likely, given the considerable overlap between these groups, that young offenders will show similar structural changes. As previous work has shown inverse correlations between gray matter volume and number of CD symptoms, we predict that the extent of the structural changes in this group will be related to the severity or frequency of their offending behavior.

The majority of functional MRI (fMRI) studies in this area have employed emotion processing, and particularly facial emotion processing, tasks to investigate neural responses to emotional stimuli in antisocial populations. Early studies reported reduced amygdala responses to fearful versus neutral faces in male adolescents with CD and callous-unemotional traits (Marsh et al., 2008) or children with conduct problems and callous-unemotional traits (Jones, Laurens, Herba, Barker, & Viding, 2009). However, it was unclear whether these changes in neural activity were driven by differences in antisocial behavior (conduct problems) or callous-unemotional traits, as the "cases" in each study were elevated on both variables. A subsequent study demonstrated reduced amygdala responses to angry or sad versus neutral faces in male adolescents with CD compared with controls (Passamonti et al., 2010). Surprisingly, in this last study there were no significant correlations between psychopathic or callous-unemotional traits and neural responses to sad versus neutral facial expressions. More recent work has examined neural responses to subliminal facial expressions in children with conduct problems (Viding et al., 2012), finding differences between high and low callous-unemotional traits groups in amygdala activity to fearful expressions, or attenuated neural responses to stimuli depicting others in pain (Lockwood et al., 2013; Marsh et al., 2013). These results suggest that the brain circuits involved in empathy for pain may be impaired or less spontaneously active in children with conduct problems or CD, and particularly those high in callous-unemotional traits.

The Neurobiological Basis of Sex Differences in Antisocial Behavior and Offending

It is well established that males show increased levels of aggression and antisocial behavior relative to females across the lifespan, as evidenced by the higher rates of violence and criminal offenses committed by males in adolescence and in adulthood.

Within the prison population, the Ministry of Justice reported a sex ratio of 20.5:1 in favor of males for rates of incarceration in England and Wales in 2013 (Ministry of Justice, 2015). Research has suggested that sex differences in aggression are observed as early as 17 months of age, with male toddlers being 2.5 times more likely than their female counterparts to show elevated aggression (Baillargeon et al., 2007). During the first few years of life, rates of physical aggression increase in both genders, with no sex differences in the rate of change. However, at around the age of four, levels of aggression among girls tend to decrease, while boys' aggression is more likely to remain stable or even increase (Keenan & Shaw, 1997). These sex differences in aggression and antisocial behavior typically remain stable throughout childhood (with sex ratios for oppositional defiant disorder and CD ranging from 10:1 to 15:1 in favor of males), until mid-adolescence, where the differences between males and females in antisocial behavior narrow dramatically (ranging from just 1.5:1 to 5:1 in favor of males; Fontaine, Carbonneau, Vitaro, Barker, & Tremblay, 2009; Moffitt et al., 2001).

However, these apparent differences between the sexes in aggression and antisocial behavior are partly dependent on how these constructs are defined and quantified. In particular, aggression can be subdivided into physical and relational aggression, which may manifest in qualitatively different ways. While boys tend to display more physical aggression such as committing physical assault, physical bullying, and weapon use (Gorman-Smith & Loeber, 2005), girls are more likely to display relational forms of aggression such as non-physical bullying, manipulation, and ostracism of peers (Underwood, 2003). In addition, although non-aggressive rule-breaking behavior is also more common in males in childhood, this type of antisocial behavior increases dramatically among females as they enter adolescence, making rates of non-aggressive antisocial behavior almost indistinguishable between the sexes during this period (Archer, 2004; McGee, Feehan, Williams, & Anderson, 1992). Indeed, when taking type of aggression into account (i.e. physical and relational), the differences between the sexes in rates of aggression in adolescence might be considerably smaller than previously thought, with some research suggesting that although the sexes differ in the manifestation of antisocial behavior, the prevalence of CD and delinquency in general may not differ across the sexes during adolescence (Wasserman, McReynolds, Ko, Katz, & Carpenter, 2005).

In late adolescence or early adulthood, the sex ratio in terms of antisocial behavior widens again, with males being more likely than females to retain their CD diagnoses and to develop ASPD symptoms, while girls' delinquent behaviors tend to decrease (Moffitt et al., 2001); although this has not always been found to be the case (see Keenan, Loeber, & Green, 1999). However, this does not mean that females with antisocial behavior in adolescence simply "get better" as they grow up, as they may experience a more heterotypic development of psychopathology compared to males. For example, the expression of childhood or adolescent CD is more likely to convert into other disorders such as borderline personality disorder (BPD) or substance dependence in women than in men (Pajer, 1998). This suggests that although males show increased continuity in terms of their aggressive and antisocial behavior over time, and suffer the negative consequences of this in adulthood, antisocial females experience similarly negative consequences in adulthood, albeit partly due to developing other forms of psychopathology (Samuelson, Hodgins, Larsson, Larm, & Tengström, 2010). Therefore, when comparing the sexes in terms of adult outcomes of antisocial behavior, one must take this heterotypic continuity in psychopathology into account and consider mental health and lifestyle factors in a holistic way, rather than simply focusing on antisocial behavior or criminality.

Despite these caveats and the sex differences in the course of antisocial behavior, it remains the case that sex differences in antisocial behavior are substantial, robust and highly replicable, and therefore mechanistic explanations for these differences are needed. The "polygenic threshold model" suggests that, as antisocial behavior is less common among females than males, girls may require a higher loading of genetic, neurobiological, or environmental risk factors in order to develop antisocial behavior (Cloninger, Christiansen, Reich, & Gottesman, 1978).

Consequently, females with antisocial behavior may show more atypical brain structure or function relative to their male counterparts. Although few neuroimaging studies have been capable of testing these ideas by including females, and even fewer have directly compared the sexes in terms of the relationship between antisocial behavior and changes in brain structure or function, a recent study (Fairchild et al., 2013a) found that adolescent girls with CD showed reduced amygdala gray matter volume compared to controls, similar to boys with CD. However, in contrast to a main effect of diagnosis on amygdala volume, this study observed a sex-by-diagnosis interaction in bilateral anterior insula, whereby females with CD showed reduced volume in this structure compared with female controls, whereas males with CD showed increased insula volume compared with male controls (Fairchild et al., 2013a).

These findings appear to provide support for the polygenic threshold model, although further tests of this model are needed in both high-risk samples as well as population-based cohorts. In addition, in common with a large number of studies investigating brain structure using voxel-based or surface-based morphometry (Ruigrok et al., 2014), Fairchild et al. (2013a) found marked differences between the sexes in terms of orbitofrontal cortex (females > males) and striatal gray matter volume (males > females) that were independent of diagnostic status. Although a study of adults, it should be noted that Raine et al. (2011) found that sex differences in orbitofrontal cortex volume partly mediated the sex difference in rates of ASPD. In addition, the relationship between ASPD and orbitofrontal cortex volume was stronger in females than males, although the female sample was small.

A large-scale prospective longitudinal study on sex differences in antisocial behavior investigated the link between early risk factors (family, individual, and peer relations) and the development of antisocial behavior and delinquency. Within the family environment, risk factors such as low socioeconomic status, harsh discipline, and inconsistent parenting were strongly associated with developing antisocial behavior and seemed to be equally important for the development of delinquency in both sexes (Moffitt et al., 2001). At the level of individual risk factors, sex differences were more evident – boys with antisocial behavior were found to be more likely than girls to suffer from cognitive and neurological risk factors, such as neurological abnormalities, low reading ability, and neuropsychological impairments. Boys with antisocial behavior were also more likely than girls to display hyperactivity in early childhood – a risk factor that is highly predictive of subsequent antisocial behavior. Interestingly, low IQ was found to be strongly associated with antisocial behavior in both sexes.

Together, these individual risk factors were found to be more predictive of antisocial behavior than family risk factors (explaining 50–75% versus 10% of the variance). Overall, these results suggest that males are more likely than females to be exposed to individual-level or neurobiological risk factors, and that sex differences in the vulnerability of the brain to neurological insult might be an important factor in explaining sex differences in aggression and antisocial behavior. However, studies using multi-variate approaches that include measures of brain structure or function as well as information about experiences within the family, such as parenting quality and maltreatment, have the potential to shed further light on these issues and provide a stronger test of models such as the polygenic threshold model.

A final point relevant to this section is that there appears to be a higher prevalence of comorbid disorders in antisocial girls compared to antisocial boys. This is true both for internalizing disorders such as depression, anxiety, and post-traumatic stress disorder (Polier, Vloet, Herpertz-Dahlmann, Laurens, & Hodgins, 2012; Rosenfield & Mouzon, 2013), and externalizing disorders such as attention deficit hyperactivity disorder (ADHD) (Zoccolillo, 1993). The latter point might be considered surprising and striking, given that ADHD is more prevalent in boys in the general population (Erskine et al., 2013). The fact that higher rates of psychiatric comorbidity are observed in females with antisocial behavior relative to males should influence the assessment and treatment of females within the criminal justice system – it seems that comprehensive psychiatric assessments are needed even more urgently when working with females and that the treatment of comorbid illnesses should be an important goal of rehabilitation efforts. In Boxes 16.1, 16.2, and 16.3 we will consider the evidence for different methods of subtyping antisocial behavior, some of which appear to be impacted by gender.

Box 16.1 The Developmental Taxonomic Theory and the Value of Classifying CD According to Age-of-Onset

In an influential article published in 1993, Moffitt set out the developmental taxonomic theory of antisocial behavior. She argued that classifying antisocial behavior in terms of its age-of-onset was informative in terms of its causes, correlates, and likely course. Individuals who developed antisocial behavior in childhood were considered to show a "life-course persistent" pattern of antisocial behavior and offending, which had its origins in negative transactions between individual (e.g., neurological insults) and environmental (e.g., harsh parenting) vulnerabilities. Life-course persistent antisocial behavior was proposed to be a neurodevelopmental disorder. In contrast, antisocial behavior which emerges in adolescence was proposed to be limited to the adolescent period ("adolescence-limited"), and was viewed as a socially-determined phenomenon that reflected the imitation of antisocial peers. The view that different forms of antisocial behavior have qualitatively different etiologies and developmental courses has been highly influential. Notably, it informed the diagnostic criteria for CD, such as the distinction between childhood-onset and adolescence-onset forms of CD in the Diagnostic and Statistical Manual of Mental Disorders, 4th Edition (DSM-IV; American Psychiatric Association, 1994) and the DSM-5 (APA, 2013). While considerable evidence has accumulated to support the distinction between childhood-onset and adolescence-onset forms of CD, recent findings have begun to challenge this notion and the developmental taxonomic theory more generally. The evidence supporting, and running counter to, the developmental taxonomic theory and the age-of-onset subtyping approach will be reviewed below.

The Dunedin Multidisciplinary Health and Development Study (http://dunedinstudy.otago.ac.nz) played a major role in Moffitt's thinking about the developmental course of different forms of antisocial behavior. Moffitt and her colleagues identified subgroups of antisocial individuals within the Dunedin cohort that strongly resembled the subtypes predicted by the developmental taxonomic theory. First, they identified a subgroup of individuals, most of whom were male, who showed early-onset behavior problems and appeared to possess multiple environmental and individual-level risk factors for antisocial behavior, such as low socioeconomic status and low maternal educational level, as well as elevated hyperactivity at age three and low verbal IQ in childhood (Moffitt & Caspi, 2001; Moffitt, Caspi, Dickson, Silva, & Stanton, 1996; Moffitt et al., 2001). In contrast, the subgroup of individuals who had developed antisocial behavior in adolescence seemed to be relatively free of environmental and individual risk factors, aside from associating with delinquent peers during their teenage years.

These findings provided strong support for the idea that these subtypes have different etiologies. However, a third group was identified within the Dunedin sample – a "childhood-limited" group who showed antisocial behavior in childhood, but who had desisted from engaging in antisocial behavior by late childhood or early adolescence (Odgers et al., 2007, 2008; Raine, Moffitt, Caspi, Loeber, Stouthamer-Loeber, M., & Lynam, 2005). The existence of this group posed a challenge to the developmental taxonomic theory, as its members seemed to possess many of the same risk factors as the life-course persistent antisocial group, yet they desisted from engaging in antisocial behavior (Barker & Maughan, 2009; Raine et al., 2005). As well as challenging the idea that there are only two groups of antisocial individuals in the population, recent epidemiological studies have questioned the notion that adolescence-onset conduct problems are time-limited and largely restricted to adolescence (or, at least, that they typically desist in early adulthood). These studies have shown that males who develop conduct problems in adolescence often continue to show serious antisocial behavior and criminality into their 30s or 40s (Odgers et al., 2007). This group also shows increased rates of physical and mental health problems relative to peers who never developed antisocial behavior, and on several indicators of negative adult outcomes they do as badly as the life-course persistent antisocial group (Odgers et al., 2007).

Overall, these findings contradict the notion that antisocial behavior that emerges during adolescence will normally remit as the individual enters adulthood and suggest that the term "adolescence-limited" was a misnomer. These results also suggest that antisocial behavior that develops in childhood is not necessarily a stable or persistent phenomenon. Further research is needed to understand why some individuals continue to show antisocial behavior across the lifespan, while others desist in late childhood or early adolescence (Barker & Maughan, 2009; Barker, Oliver, & Maughan, 2010).

Another important question is whether the age-of-onset classification applies equally well to males and females, as data from the Dunedin Study and other large-scale epidemiological studies suggest that childhood-onset antisocial behavior is far more common among males than females (Kratzer & Hodgins, 1999; Moffitt et al., 2001; Odgers et al., 2008). It has been proposed that females may show a distinct "delayed-onset pathway" to antisocial behavior (Silverthorn & Frick, 1999). According to this theory, girls typically develop severe behavior problems at a later stage than their male counterparts, even if they possess many of the same individual-level or environmental risk factors (Silverthorn & Frick, 1999). Consistent with this view, girls with adolescence-onset conduct problems seem to be exposed to similar risk factors as childhood-onset boys (White & Piquero, 2004), and are at similarly elevated risk for a range of negative adult outcomes (Odgers et al., 2008; Pajer, 1998).

Neurobiological Research Evaluating the Developmental Taxonomic Theory of Antisocial Behavior

Recent neuropsychological, neuroendocrine, and neuroscientific research has also challenged the developmental taxonomic theory and the age-of-onset approach of classifying CD into subtypes. These studies have shown that male adolescents with childhood-onset and adolescence-onset forms of CD show similar impairments in facial emotion recognition, fear conditioning, and eye-blink startle responses relative to healthy controls (Fairchild, Van Goozen, Calder, Stollery, & Goodyer, 2009; Fairchild, Van Goozen, Stollery, & Goodyer, 2008). Although these neuropsychological deficits were slightly more marked in the childhood-onset CD group, the childhood-onset and adolescence-onset CD subgroups did not significantly differ from each other. Subsequent research on female adolescents with CD, most of whom had adolescence-onset CD, demonstrated similar deficits in facial recognition and fear conditioning (Fairchild, Stobbe, van Goozen, Calder, & Goodyer, 2010). In addition, a study by Pajer et al. (2008) observed widespread neuropsychological impairments in girls with CD, and this relationship was not moderated by age-of-onset of CD.

Although most of this work has relied on retrospective reports of the age-of-onset of CD, which could be criticized due to potential recall issues (Henry, Moffitt, Caspi, Langley, & Silva, 1994), studies that have employed prospective longitudinal designs to test the developmental taxonomic theory have largely arrived at similar conclusions. For example, a recent study that investigated cortisol secretion in adolescents with childhood-onset, childhood-limited, or adolescence-onset conduct problems showed that all three subgroups showed reduced cortisol levels relative to typically-developing adolescents (Haltigan, Roisman, Susman, Barnett-Walker, & Monahan, 2011). Cortisol is a stress hormone produced by the hypothalamic-pituitary-adrenal (HPA) axis, and previous studies have shown that cortisol concentrations are inversely correlated with levels of aggression (van Goozen, Fairchild, Snoek, & Harold, 2007).

Most neuroimaging studies of CD have focused on males with childhood-onset CD, perhaps because the developmental taxonomic theory has been so influential, or possibly because this subgroup is more likely to be referred for treatment. Early sMRI studies reported reduced temporal lobe volume (Kruesi, Casanova, Mannheim, & Johnson-Bilder, 2004), or more specifically, reduced amygdala and insula gray matter volume (Sterzer et al., 2007) in males with childhood-onset CD relative to controls. Although these studies may have been underpowered, a subsequent study with a larger sample also found volume reductions in the amygdala and surrounding medial temporal lobe regions in males with childhood-onset CD compared with controls (Huebner et al., 2008). One problem with these studies is that the majority of the CD participants had comorbid ADHD, so it is possible that some of these structural differences were driven by ADHD rather than reflecting structural changes related to CD specifically. In the first study to directly compare childhood-onset and adolescence-onset forms of CD in terms of brain structure, reduced amygdala gray matter volume was observed in both CD subgroups relative to healthy controls, and there were no significant differences between these subgroups in the amygdala or the other regions of interest (Fairchild et al., 2011). As most of the participants in this study were free of comorbid ADHD, it was possible to factor out the contribution of ADHD symptoms and show that the findings were not explained by ADHD comorbidity.

As reviewed above, subsequent studies have employed more advanced structural imaging analysis methods such as surface-based morphometry to investigate brain structure in CD. The neuroanatomical measures that these methods assess include cortical thickness (which is a measure of the density of the neurons in the layer of the cortex), surface area, and cortical folding (also known as gyrification; this reflects the amount of cortex folded within the sulci of the brain versus that found outside the sulci). The first surface-based morphometry study that distinguished between childhood-onset and adolescence-onset subtypes of CD found widespread reductions in cortical thickness in temporal and parietal regions, as well as reduced cortical folding in the insula and prefrontal cortex, in both CD subgroups relative to controls (Hyatt et al., 2012). Interestingly, when directly comparing these subgroups, the adolescence-onset CD subgroup showed reduced folding in the insula and prefrontal cortex compared with the childhood-onset CD subgroup. It should be noted, however, that this study was probably underpowered (with just ten subjects in each subgroup). A recent study with a larger sample found no significant differences between childhood-onset and adolescence-onset CD in terms of cortical thickness or surface area, but there were some differences between these subgroups in cortical folding (Fairchild et al., 2015). Reduced superior temporal gyrus cortical thickness and vmPFC surface area was observed in both CD subgroups relative to healthy controls, and both CD subgroups showed increased cortical folding compared to controls, albeit in different brain regions.

Another recent methodological advance in structural imaging methods is the advent of diffusion tensor imaging (DTI), which enables researchers to study the integrity of white-matter tracts that connect different regions of the brain together (Jones, Knösche, & Turner, 2013). This technique has been used to study anatomical connectivity in the white-matter tract that connects the prefrontal cortex and the amygdala (and surrounding temporal lobe regions), the uncinate fasciculus (Von Der Heide, Skipper, Klobusicky, & Olson, 2013).

One of the key measures used in DTI studies is fractional anisotropy, which is an integrated measure of the diffusion of water molecules in the brain, and is considered to reflect structural connectivity of the white-matter tracts. Higher fractional anisotropy values suggest that the movement of water molecules is more directional and may indicate a greater number of white-matter fibers or increased myelination of those fibers. These studies have surprisingly shown that fractional anisotropy values in the uncinate fasciculus are increased in male adolescents with CD relative to typically-developing adolescents (Passamonti et al., 2012; Sarkar et al., 2013; Zhang et al., 2014), suggesting that the anatomical connection between the amygdala and prefrontal cortex is stronger, rather than weaker, as might have been expected on the basis of fMRI studies showing diminished functional connectivity between these regions and behavioral research suggesting emotion regulation difficulties in CD. A recent study that investigated fractional anisotropy in male and female adolescents with CD compared with their typically-developing counterparts suggested that this effect was specific to males (Zhang et al., 2014). However, it should be noted that none of these studies distinguished between childhood-onset and adolescence-onset forms of CD, and one study only included male childhood-onset CD individuals (Passamonti et al., 2012), so it is unknown whether increased uncinate fasciculus fractional anisotropy is specific to males with childhood-onset CD or whether it applies to males with CD in general.

Considered together, these results support the notion that childhood-onset CD is a neurodevelopmental disorder, as the majority of sMRI studies have reported structural changes or reductions in gray matter volume in this variant of CD. However, recent findings also provide preliminary evidence that adolescence-onset CD may also be conceptualized as a neurodevelopmental disorder. These results certainly suggest that neurobiological factors play a role in the development of adolescence-onset CD and that structural and functional changes in brain regions involved in emotion processing are present in both subtypes of CD (Fairchild, van Goozen, Calder, & Goodyer, 2013).

Box 16.2 Neurobiological Differences Between Antisocial Individuals with High Versus Low Levels of Callous-Unemotional Traits

An increasingly influential method of subtyping individuals with antisocial behavior is according to the presence or absence of callous-unemotional (CU) traits (Frick & White, 2008). These personality traits are related to the affective or interpersonal features of psychopathy, such as reduced empathy or guilt, and are typically measured using questionnaires such as the Inventory of Callous-Unemotional traits (ICU; Essau, Sasagawa, & Frick, 2006). It has been argued that antisocial behavior with high levels of CU traits is qualitatively different from antisocial behavior with low levels of CU traits (Frick, Ray, Thornton, & Kahn, 2014; Frick & White, 2008), and accordingly this subtyping approach has been incorporated into the DSM-5 as a specifier for CD (APA, 2013).

Although our review of the literature on CU traits will be limited due to space considerations, interested readers are directed to recent reviews on this topic (Blair, 2013; Frick et al., 2014). In brief, there is evidence that antisocial behavior accompanied by high levels of CU traits is more heritable than antisocial behavior without CU traits (Viding, Blair, Moffitt, & Plomin, 2005; Viding, Frick, & Plomin, 2007), and several neuroimaging studies report that children or adolescents with CD or conduct problems with high levels of CU traits show reduced amygdala responses to fearful facial stimuli (relative to neutral/calm faces; Jones et al., 2009; Marsh et al., 2008; Viding et al., 2012) or attenuated amygdala, anterior cingulate cortex (ACC) and anterior insula responses to stimuli depicting others in pain (Lockwood et al., 2013; Marsh et al., 2013).

Although one criticism of neuroimaging research in this area is that antisocial behavior and CU traits are highly confounded in many studies, and therefore the neural effects attributed to CU traits may have been driven by the co-occurring antisocial behavior, recent work has deliberately contrasted high and low CU traits groups that were both elevated in conduct problems (Lockwood et al., 2013; Lozier, Cardinale, van Meter, & Marsh, 2014; Viding et al., 2012). These studies suggest that CU traits are related to amygdala and insula hypoactivity, whereas conduct problems are associated with hyper-reactivity in the same structures, although it should be noted that several fMRI studies have observed no significant effects of CU traits on neural activity within CD groups (Fairchild et al., 2014; Passamonti et al., 2010).

In addition, the issue that antisocial behavior and CU traits are often confounded within the same clinical populations has not been addressed in most of the structural neuroimaging studies on this topic, and studies investigating the effects of variation in psychopathic or CU traits on gray matter volume or structural connectivity have found little evidence for qualitative differences between high and low CU traits groups with CD (Fairchild et al., 2011, 2013; Sarkar et al., 2013; although see Sebastian et al., 2015). In contrast to these limited effects of CU traits, neuroimaging studies from our group have consistently shown that changes in brain structure and function are related to the severity of CD, as indexed by the number of CD symptoms (Passamonti et al., 2010; Fairchild et al., 2011, 2013, 2014).

As large-scale epidemiological studies have shown that there is a sizable group of young people who are elevated in CU traits but relatively low in antisocial behavior (Rowe et al., 2010), an interesting direction for future neuroimaging research will be to study this group and directly compare them with adolescents who are high on both dimensions, as well as those with elevated antisocial behavior but low levels of CU traits. Another important goal for future research will be to devise ways of measuring CU traits in a more objective way and harmonize methods for assessing CU traits across age groups, countries, and cultures. There are currently no norms or agreed cut-offs for the questionnaire measures of CU traits that are used in research and clinical practice, which means it is difficult to compare findings across studies or employ these measures within the clinical decision-making process. The fact that standardized methods for assessing CU traits are lacking is particularly concerning given that the DSM-5 included a "limited prosocial emotions" specifier (equivalent to CU traits) that is supposed to be used in clinical settings (APA, 2013).

Box 16.3 The Distinction Between Violent and Non-Violent Offending

The division of offending, and antisocial behavior more broadly, in terms of violent versus non-violent acts has long been debated. Violent antisocial behavior is defined as acts of physical aggression such as fighting, sexual assault, cruelty to animals, and weapon use, whereas non-violent antisocial behaviors involve rule-breaking behaviors such as theft, vandalism, and truancy.

The distinction between violent and non-violent antisocial behavior was first noted by Hewitt and Jenkins in 1946, and was incorporated into earlier versions of the DSM (i.e., DSM-II and DSM-III) as subtypes of CD. However, with the advent of the developmental taxonomic theory and a push toward encouraging clinicians and researchers to think of CD in terms of developmental pathways, the aggressive versus non-aggressive distinction gave way to classifying CD in terms of age-of-onset in the DSM-IV (Lahey et al., 1998).

Although rule-breaking behavior is characteristic of individuals with CD in all age groups, it increases dramatically in the transition to adolescence (Barker et al., 2007). In addition, individuals categorized as having childhood-onset CD generally show higher levels of aggression than those with adolescence-onset CD. The aggressive versus non-aggressive distinction was therefore incorporated in the age-of-onset classification, rather than being considered in its own right. This led many researchers to ignore the distinction between aggressive and non-aggressive CD symptoms and treat individuals with CD as a homogeneous group (Tremblay, 2010).

Despite the considerable influence of the developmental taxonomic theory on research and clinical practice, some researchers have argued that classifying offenders in terms of age-of onset is uninformative or invalid (Tremblay, 2010), while aggression is highly predictive of adult outcomes (Burt et al., 2011).

Several factor analytical studies of CD support the notion that aggressive and non-aggressive dimensions of antisocial behavior are distinct, yet positively correlated (Barker et al., 2009; Burt et al., 2011; Tackett, Krueger, Iacono, & McGue, 2005). In addition, aggressive behavior tends to emerge early in life and shows far greater stability over time compared to rule-breaking, which typically increases in early adolescence and is less stable over the transition to adulthood (Barker et al., 2007; Broidy et al., 2003; Burt, 2009; Verhulst & Der Ende, 1995).

Second, a great deal of evidence points to etiological distinctions between the two forms of antisocial behavior, such that aggression seems to be more genetically influenced than rule-breaking, while rule-breaking is more influenced by shared environmental factors (Burt, 2009). Tackett et al. (2005) also found that aggressive CD symptoms were more heritable than non-aggressive CD symptoms.

A study that tested over 1,000 twin pairs aged 8–9 found that genetic factors accounted for around 60% of the variability in aggressive antisocial behavior, whereas rule-breaking behavior was less influenced by genetic factors (46% of the variance was accounted for by genetics) (Eley, Lichtenstein, & Moffitt, 2003).

Interestingly, when the same twin pairs were tested at age 13–14, the influence of genes on aggressive behavior had decreased, now accounting for 46% of the variability in aggression, while still accounting for 44% of the variance in non-aggressive antisocial behavior. This implies that genetic influences on aggression are most prominent in childhood, and with the transition to adolescence (and with it, increasing socialization with peers), the environment becomes just as important in terms of influencing behavior.

The two constructs further seem to be inter-generationally transmitted. In a population of convicted delinquents, sons of violent offenders showed a significantly higher risk of violent offending compared to sons of non-violent offenders (62% versus 41%; Besemer, 2012). Furthermore, Monuteaux and colleagues found that aggressive behavior in a first-degree relative predicted aggression in 9–17-year-olds. Non-aggressive rule-breaking behavior in a first-degree relative further predicted rule-breaking behavior in children, but rule-breaking in biological relatives did not predict aggression in other family members or vice versa (Monuteaux, Fitzmaurice, Blacker, Buka, & Biederman, 2004). In other words, aggressive individuals were significantly more likely to have an aggressive parent than a non-aggressive individual, and vice versa.

Lastly, aggressive and non-aggressive forms of antisocial behavior seem to be associated with distinct profiles of neuropsychological performance. Burt and Donnellan (2008) found that rule-breaking was uniquely predicted by low cognitive control. Aggression, on the other hand, was uniquely predicted by increased stress reactivity that is associated with emotion dysregulation (Burt & Donnellan, 2008; Hoaken, Allaby, & Earle, 2007). Furthermore, impaired executive functions have been associated with aggressive behavior, while non-aggressive antisocial individuals showed normal or superior performance on executive function tasks (Barker et al., 2007).

No neuroimaging studies have directly compared individuals with aggressive versus non-aggressive forms of antisocial behavior in terms of either brain structure or function. However, studies investigating aggression specifically have found relationships between aggression and the structure of brain regions involved in emotional regulation. Reduced asymmetry between left and right hemispheres in the orbitofrontal cortex, along with greater right orbitofrontal cortex volume, predicted aggression in male and female adolescents (Visser et al., 2014). This was also the case for ACC asymmetry and aggression in males, but not females. These structures are implicated in impulse control and emotional regulation (Visser et al., 2014). It may be that antisocial youths with aggressive and non-aggressive behaviors share common impairments, but some neurobiological deficits are specific to aggressive individuals. A recent study supported this point by showing a negative correlation between aggressive CD symptoms and dorsolateral prefrontal cortex volume within a group of girls with CD (Fairchild et al., 2013). This finding suggests that severe aggressive behaviors are associated with structural differences in the prefrontal cortex. However, more research comparing aggressive and non-aggressive children and adolescents is needed to investigate whether these forms of aggression show differential relationships with measures of brain structure or function.

> One of the major reasons why research on this topic is particularly challenging, and may explain why many researchers and clinicians have moved away from the aggressive versus non-aggressive distinction, relates to the complexity of aggression. Aggression can be subdivided into several different types such as overt and relational (covert) aggression or proactive and reactive aggression, all of which may have different etiologies, developmental courses, and prognoses. Proactive and reactive aggression, for example, distinguishes between aggression as a means of personal gain (*proactive*) and aggression as a consequence of actual or perceived provocation (*reactive*) (Raine et al., 2006). Overt aggression is behavior that is intended to directly harm the other person, such as punching, name-calling, and threatening, whereas relational aggression is an indirect form of aggression grounded in social relationships, such as spreading rumors or ostracizing a member of the group (Little, Henrich, Jones, & Hawley, 2003). Non-aggressive behavior usually encompasses all other antisocial acts that are not aggressive in nature, but nevertheless these should also not be treated as a homogeneous category. Burglary is clearly more severe and less normative than truancy or lying, and consequently may have a different etiology than relatively normative behaviors. As such, the aggressive versus non-aggressive distinction still has significant limitations and further development of this approach is required. Nevertheless, more research needs to be done to establish whether aggressive and non-aggressive forms of antisocial behavior differ in terms of brain structure and function. A further important consideration is whether it is necessary to further subdivide the two constructs (e.g., aggression into its proactive and reactive forms) to better understand their etiology.

Recidivism and Continuity Versus Discontinuity in Antisocial Behavior

Differences in aggression have been discussed as one of the factors that inform risk assessments for re-offending behavior. As we have described, aggression is a highly heritable and relatively stable trait (Burt, 2009). Young people who commit violent crimes might therefore display a more stable pattern of criminal offending, which continues into adulthood, compared to non-aggressive offenders. In addition, violent offenders generally have a higher number of past offenses, start their criminal careers at an earlier age, are more likely to have first-degree relatives with histories of criminal behavior or alcohol and drug abuse, and are more likely to report a history of childhood abuse and neglect compared to non-violent offenders (Mulder, Brand, Bullens, & van Marle, 2011).

Many of the factors predicting aggression have been found to predict recidivism more specifically. For example, child abuse and neglect are strong predictors for later antisocial behavior (Burnette, Oshri, Lax, Richards, & Ragbeer, 2012), and prolonged maltreatment has been associated with more persistent forms of antisocial behavior. More specifically, adolescent offenders with ongoing neglect in childhood and adolescence are at significantly higher risk of recidivism compared to other young offenders

(Ryan, Williams, & Courtney, 2013). Furthermore, although youths with psychiatric disorders (including comorbid conduct disorder) are at higher risk of initially engaging in criminal behavior in adolescence which carries through into adulthood, only substance use disorders have been found to be a significant risk factor for chronic offending in adolescence, albeit mainly for substance-related crimes (Colins, Vermeiren, Noom, & Broekaert, 2013; Colins et al., 2011; Hoeve, McReynolds, & Wasserman, 2013). In addition, as with aggression, callous-unemotional traits are moderately stable from childhood to adolescence (Lynam et al., 2009) and from adolescence to adulthood (Lynam, Caspi, Moffitt, Loeber, & Stouthamer-Loeber, 2007). Young people with callous-unemotional traits show a higher rate of criminal offending, as well as increased *violent* re-offending (Asscher et al., 2011).

In addition to the individual and family risk factors mentioned above, the social environment of young offenders is related to offending behavior. For example, associating with antisocial peers significantly increases the risk of re-offending, especially if treatment for disorders such as alcohol or drug dependence failed or was not provided (Mulder et al., 2011). For the more serious offenses resulting in incarceration, the environment in prison has been found to be moderately to highly predictive of recidivism. In fact, there has been accumulating evidence suggesting that imprisonment has criminogenic effects (Gatti, Tremblay, & Vitaro, 2009).

As has been seen throughout this book, neuroimaging methods have increasingly been used to correlate abnormalities in brain structure or function to antisocial behavior and crime, with the aim of establishing what makes offenders different from other individuals. However, the vast majority of these imaging studies have been cross-sectional and therefore correlational in design. As a result, they cannot reveal any causal link between brain abnormalities and antisocial behavior, nor can they be used to predict future behavior. In order to be able to predict offending and distinguish between those individuals who will desist from criminal behavior after a single offense or a brief period of criminal behavior and those who will go on to offend throughout adulthood, longitudinal designs will need to be adopted, whereby the trajectories of these individuals can be tracked from childhood to adulthood. With the combined use of psychometric measures and brain imaging, it should be possible to investigate whether the differences seen in the activity or volume of the brain areas associated with aggressive and delinquent behavior *predict* future offending. Two recent studies suggest that this might be the case.

In a prospective longitudinal study, Aharoni et al. (2013) scanned incarcerated prisoners with an fMRI response inhibition task to investigate whether prefrontal cortex activity could be used to predict risk for re-offending. The prisoners were released shortly afterwards and rates of re-offending were assessed over a four-year period. The authors showed that poor performance on the inhibition task was related to reduced activity in the anterior cingulate cortex (ACC), which in turn, significantly predicted re-offending. Moreover, the lower the level of ACC activity, the shorter the time between release and re-arrest (Aharoni et al., 2013). Although this finding is promising and provocative, the low ACC activity group only showed a twofold increase in re-offending rates so this method could not be used in isolation, nor is the effect strong enough to be used on a single-subject level. Nevertheless, future studies should employ similar methods and attempt to replicate these encouraging initial findings. A second longitudinal imaging study found that lower amygdala volume at age 26 predicted aggressive behavior over the next three years, even after accounting for a history of violence, which was independently associated with reduced amygdala volume (Pardini, Raine, Erickson, & Loeber, 2014). This study was limited by only assessing amygdala volume at age 26, and by the use of a relatively short follow-up period, but it nevertheless supports the idea that structural changes in the amygdala might promote aggressive or criminal behavior, rather than the other way around.

Although biological criteria for estimating an individual's risk for re-offending are far from being sufficiently established for use within the criminal justice system (e.g., to make decisions about whether to grant parole on a case-by-case basis), it is conceivable that biomarkers might be used in forensic settings in the near future. With the continuous improvement of neuroimaging analysis methods such as machine learning, and the standardization of neuroimaging protocols along with the adoption of prospective longitudinal designs in research, increased translation of these methods to clinical practice in forensic psychology and psychiatry should be possible. At the same time, there needs to be a debate involving scientists, professionals working in the criminal justice system, and members of the public regarding the bioethical implications of these developments.

The Emerging Field of Neurocriminology

In this section, we will consider the potential of neuroscientific methods to influence practices within the health care and youth justice systems, acknowledging the pioneering work of Adrian Raine in this area (see Glenn & Raine, 2014). These methods could have a bearing on at least six domains: prediction of future risk (such as risk for violence or re-offending); identification of subgroups who may be differentially responsive to existing treatments or interventions; informing the development of new interventions that directly or specifically target the deficits observed in antisocial populations (such as impaired facial emotion recognition); informing primary, secondary, or tertiary prevention programs (ranging from public health interventions designed to reduce maternal smoking in pregnancy to focused prevention programs that could be used in high-risk populations such as the younger siblings of persistent offenders); enhancing our ability to assess individuals in terms of criminal responsibility; and characterizing the neurobiological impact of current interventions or methods of punishment (which could explain, for example, why incarceration appears to have iatrogenic effects on offending behavior).

As outlined in the sections above, most neuroimaging studies of antisocial behavior have adopted cross-sectional designs (measuring brain activity or structure at a single point in the lifespan). As a consequence, most of these earlier studies have shown associations between brain changes and antisocial behavior, but have been unable to demonstrate causal relationships between these variables. The recent studies by Aharoni et al. (2013) and Pardini et al. (2014) described above demonstrate that neuroimaging methods have the potential to predict future offending or violence, although a great deal of work in this area is still needed before such developments could be applied in clinical practice. The main challenge, as in many areas of clinical and applied neuroscience, will be to go from group-level observations (e.g., Group A shows lower amygdala volume than Group B) to applying these techniques to assess individuals on a case-by-case basis and predict levels of risk using this information. This type of advance will also require technological improvements – for example, if fMRI methods are to be used in forensic settings, a greater degree of reproducibility and increased standardization of methods will be required – but also significant changes to our experimental designs.

In our view, research in this field needs to move away from comparing offenders with non-offenders (or adolescents with CD versus controls) and instead study the *developmental pathways* into (and out of) antisocial behavior. To make this goal tractable, given our current state of knowledge, it makes sense to focus on groups who are at high risk of engaging in criminal activity as a function of genetic or environmental risk or psychiatric comorbidity (e.g., children with ADHD). In addition, it would be interesting to use neuroimaging methods to study patterns of persistence and desistance among convicted young offenders over time, and transitions from adolescent antisocial behavior to adult criminality or ASPD (as we know that around 50% of male adolescents with CD will make the transition to ASPD in adulthood; Robins, 1966, 1978). For example, it is possible that normalization of initially aberrant patterns of brain activity or brain developmental trajectories would be observed in those who desist from showing antisocial behavior, relative to those who continue to engage in antisocial behavior or show a progression to increasingly serious criminal behaviors.

The demonstration of normalization of brain activity or structure prior to improvements in behavior would constitute powerful evidence for a causal link between these variables. Taking a lead from research on affective disorders (Drevets, Price, & Furey, 2008), it will also be of interest to differentiate between *state* and *trait* markers of antisocial behavior (if such a distinction makes sense in this context), as the cross-sectional designs of previous studies do not enable us to tell whether the neuroanatomical markers or brain activity changes that have been identified previously reflect vulnerability markers or the consequences of having CD or psychopathy. Achieving this differentiation might have implications for interventions (as presumably *state* markers will be more susceptible to change in the course of treatment than *trait* markers). Lastly, future treatment studies could employ neurobiological or neuroimaging measures to study the mechanisms of change underlying therapies for antisocial behavior, and identify which baseline measures are most relevant in terms of predicting who will respond to treatment. Although challenging, time-consuming, and requiring significantly higher levels of funding, these types of studies have the potential to transform our understanding of the causes of crime and our ability to intervene or even prevent the emergence of severe antisocial behavior and persistent offending.

Neuropsychological or neuroimaging methods could also be used to identify new treatment targets: one notable example is interventions that seek to enhance facial emotion recognition among offenders and thereby enhance their ability to read social signals and respond appropriately to others' distress cues. Such interventions build on the evidence base that a range of individuals with antisocial behavior, from adolescents with CD to young offenders and individuals with high levels of callous-unemotional traits, show impairments in the recognition of facial expressions (particularly negative emotions; Bowen, Morgan, Moore, & Goozen, 2014; Dadds et al., 2006; Dawel, O'Kearney, McKone, & Palermo, 2012; Fairchild et al., 2009, 2010). These studies have shown that individuals with antisocial behavior can be trained to improve their ability to recognize facial expressions, and that emotion recognition training may reduce the severity of subsequent re-offending (Schönenberg et al., 2014; Hubble, Bowen, Moore, & Van Goozen, 2015). Another interesting proof-of-concept study found that modifying interpretation biases, such that the individuals reappraised low-intensity angry expressions more positively, appeared to reduce levels of aggression and anger in high-risk youth (Penton-Voak et al., 2013).

Criminal and antisocial behavior appears to have a multi-factorial etiology, and just as has been found to be the case in other areas of psychopathology, multiple neurocognitive deficits likely contribute toward the individual's risk for developing antisocial behavior. Facial emotion recognition deficits may play a prominent role in the etiology of antisocial behavior in some individuals, but not others, whereas deficits in fear conditioning or decision-making may be more important in explaining the behavior of other subgroups of offenders. As has been found in research investigating heterogeneity in ADHD (Solanto et al., 2001), neurocognitive impairments associated with severe antisocial behavior may operate relatively independently of each other and present to a different extent in different antisocial individuals (or subgroups). However, our ability to use these measures to discriminate between antisocial and non-antisocial participants may rely on us measuring performance in multiple neurocognitive domains and integrating across them.

Conclusions

There has been a dramatic increase in neuropsychological and neurobiological research on antisocial and aggressive behavior in children and adolescents over the last three decades. As a result, we now know a great deal more about the role of genetic and neurobiological factors in the etiology of these behaviors. There is also considerable evidence that adolescents with severe antisocial behavior or young offenders show neurocognitive or psychophysiological deficits and alterations in brain structure and function relative to typically-developing adolescents, although results are not always consistent across studies. It should be noted that the vast majority of neuroimaging studies in this area have used cross-sectional designs and small samples, which limits our ability to draw causal inferences regarding the relationship between brain alterations and antisocial behavior and reduces the reliability of the findings. Longitudinal studies that study trajectories of brain development and antisocial behavior concurrently are needed to address these issues of causality and evaluate brain–behavior relationships. For example, if we could show that brain abnormalities *precede* the emergence of antisocial behavior, this would provide evidence for a causal link, rather than just an association, between these factors.

In addition, while there is now a consensus among researchers that individuals with antisocial behavior are a highly heterogeneous group, there is less agreement regarding the optimal approach for decomposing this heterogeneity to identify meaningful subgroups. Subtyping approaches that rely on the age-of-onset of antisocial behavior or the form of antisocial behavior that the individual displays (e.g., aggression versus non-aggressive rule-breaking) have been influential, but empirical research has also provided data that challenges the usefulness of the age-of-onset approach, whereas there are important gaps in our knowledge base in relation to the behavioral subtype approach (aggressive versus non-aggressive CD) as this has predominantly been tested using behavioral genetic methods. Another group of researchers have proposed that the presence of callous-unemotional traits designates an important subgroup that is at particularly high risk of showing severe and persistent antisocial behavior and instrumental aggression (Blair, 2013; Frick et al., 2014; Viding & McCrory, 2012).

A number of studies have reported differences in brain activity between individuals with high versus low CU traits (see Frick et al., 2014, for a review), and it appears that these personality traits moderate the effects of parenting-based treatments for antisocial behavior (Frick et al., 2014; Hawes & Dadds, 2005). However, several studies have failed to support the notion of a qualitative difference between antisocial individuals who are low versus high in CU traits, and there is currently no consensus regarding the optimal method of assessing CU traits across research studies or in clinical practice, which limits the usefulness of this construct. Although sex differences in antisocial behavior are highly robust, it is striking that relatively little research has been undertaken to attempt to understand the causes of such sex differences, and previous neurocognitive, psychophysiological, and particularly neuroimaging research has largely focused on male children or adolescents with antisocial behavior (see Fairchild et al., 2014). As a result, it is unclear whether most of the neuroimaging and neurobiological findings reported to date extend to females or whether there are important differences between males and females in the neural correlates of antisocial behavior.

Finally, the emerging field of neurocriminology, which aims to use neuroscience methods to understand the causes of crime and predict future risk for criminality, has the potential to inform practice in forensic psychology and psychiatry, but we are still several years away from applying such methods to individuals on a case-by-case basis – the sensitivity and specificity of brain-based biomarkers is not high enough to justify their use in forensic settings. Consequently, further work is needed to translate our knowledge about the neurobiology of antisocial behavior into new, innovative, and evidence-based interventions within the criminal justice system and community-based intervention and prevention programs. However, we are optimistic that future research in this area will provide information that is clinically useful for forensic psychologists and psychiatrists, and has the potential to inform decisions made within the legal system (e.g., surrounding culpability or future risk for violence).

Notes

1 **Acknowledgments:** During the preparation of this chapter, the authors were supported by the European Union's 7th Framework Programme for research, technological development and demonstration (FP7/2007–2013) under Grant Agreement No. 602407 (FemNAT-CD).
2 See http://www.yjlc.uk/asset.

Recommended Reading

Blair, R.J., Leibenluft, E., & Pine, D.S. (2014). Conduct Disorder and callous-unemotional traits in youth. *New England Journal of Medicine, 371*, 2207–2216. doi: 10.1056/NEJMra1315612. (A wide-ranging and accessible review of the callous-unemotional traits literature, focusing particularly on neurocognitive and neuroimaging research, but also considering the clinical implications of this work.)

Burt, S.A. (2012). How do we optimally conceptualize the heterogeneity within antisocial behavior? An argument for aggressive versus non-aggressive behavioral dimensions. *Clinical Psychology Review, 32*, 263–279. doi: 10.1016/j.cpr.2012.02.006. (An interesting and well-written position piece calling for further research on the distinction between aggressive and non-aggressive forms of antisocial behavior.)

Fairchild, G., Van Goozen, S.H., Calder, A.J., & Goodyer, I.M. (2013). Evaluating and reformulating the developmental taxonomic theory of antisocial behaviour. *Journal of Child Psychology and Psychiatry, 54,* 924–940. doi: 10.1111/jcpp.12102. (A detailed and critical review of empirical research testing the validity and utility of the age-of-onset distinction in terms of capturing heterogeneity in antisocial behavior. The authors also set out a new model proposing that differences between childhood-onset and adolescence-onset Conduct Disorder are quantitative, rather than qualitative, in nature.)

Frick, P.J., Ray, J.V., Thornton, L.C., & Kahn, R.E. (2014). Can callous-unemotional traits enhance the understanding, diagnosis and treatment of serious conduct problems in children and adolescents? *Psychological Bulletin, 140,* 1–57. (An extensive review article evaluating the impact of callous-unemotional traits on a range of measures and outcomes, such as responsiveness to treatment.)

References

Aharoni, E., Vincent, G. M., Harenski, C. L., Calhoun, V. D., Sinnott-Armstrong, W., Gazzaniga, M. S., & Kiehl, K. A. (2013). Neuroprediction of future rearrest. *Proceedings of the National Academy of Sciences USA, 110*(15), 6223–6228. doi:10.1073/pnas.1219302110.

American Psychiatric Association (2000). *Diagnostic and statistical manual of mental disorders, version 4, text revision (DSM-IV-TR).* Washington, DC: American Psychiatric Association.

American Psychoiatric Association (2013). *Diagnostic and statistical manual of mental disorders, version 5 (DSM-5).* Washington, DC: American Psychiatric Association.

Archer, J. (2004). Sex differences in aggression in real-world settings: A meta-analytic review. *Review of General Psychology, 8*(4), 291–322. doi:10.1037/1089-2680.8.4.291.

Asscher, J. J., van Vugt, E. S., Stams, G. J. J. M., Deković, M., Eichelsheim, V. I., & Yousfi, S. (2011). The relationship between juvenile psychopathic traits, delinquency and (violent) recidivism: A meta-analysis. *Journal of Child Psychology and Psychiatry, 52*(11), 1134–1143. doi:10.1111/j.1469-7610.2011.02412.x.

Baillargeon, R. H., Zoccolillo, M., Keenan, K., Côté, S., Pérusse, D., Wu, H.-X., ... & Tremblay, R. E. (2007). Gender differences in physical aggression: A prospective population-based survey of children before and after 2 years of age. *Developmental Psychology, 43*(1), 13–26. doi:10.1037/0012-1649.43.1.13.

Barker, E. D., Larsson, H., Viding, E., Maughan, B., Rijsdijk, F., Fontaine, N., & Plomin, R. (2009). Common genetic but specific environmental influences for aggressive and deceitful behaviors in preadolescent males. *Journal of Psychopathology and Behavioral Assessment, 31*(4), 299–308. doi:10.1007/s10862-009-9132-6.

Barker, E. D., & Maughan, B. (2009). Differentiating early-onset persistent versus childhood-limited conduct problem youth. *American Journal of Psychiatry, 166*(8), 900–908. doi:10.1176/appi.ajp.2009.08121770.

Barker, E. D., Oliver, B. R., & Maughan, B. (2010). Co-occurring problems of early onset persistent, childhood limited, and adolescent onset conduct problem youth. *Journal of Child Psychology and Psychiatry, 51*(11), 1217–1226. doi:10.1111/j.1469-7610.2010.02240.x.

Barker E. D, Séguin J. R., White H., Bates, M. E., Lacourse, É., Carbonneau, R., & Tremblay, R, E. (2007). Developmental trajectories of male physical violence and theft: Relations to neurocognitive performance. *Archives of General Psychiatry, 64*(5), 592–599. doi:10.1001/archpsyc.64.5.592.

Besemer, S. (2012). Specialized Versus Versatile Intergenerational Transmission of Violence: A New Approach to Studying Intergenerational Transmission from Violent Versus Non-Violent Fathers: Latent Class Analysis. *Journal of Quantitative Criminology, 28*(2), 245–263. doi:10.1007/s10940-011-9141-y.

Bjork, J. M., Knutson, B., Fong, G. W., Caggiano, D. M., Bennett, S. M., & Hommer, D. W. (2004). Incentive-elicited brain activation in adolescents: Similarities and differences from young adults. *The Journal of Neuroscience, 24*(8), 1793–1802. doi:10.1523/JNEUROSCI.4862-03.2004.

Blair, R. J. R. (2013). The neurobiology of psychopathic traits in youths. *Nature Reviews Neuroscience, 14*(11), 786–799. doi:10.1038/nrn3577.

Bowen, K. L., Morgan, J. E., Moore, S. C., & Goozen, S. H. M. van. (2014). Young offenders' emotion recognition dysfunction across emotion intensities: Explaining variation using psychopathic traits, conduct disorder and offense severity. *Journal of Psychopathology and Behavioral Assessment, 36*(1), 60–73. doi:10.1007/s10862-013-9368-z.

Broidy, L. M., Nagin, D. S., Tremblay, R. E., Bates, J. E., Brame, B., Dodge, K. A., ... Vitaro, F. (2003). Developmental trajectories of childhood disruptive behaviors and adolescent delinquency: A six-site, cross-national study. *Developmental Psychology, 39*(2), 222–245. doi:10.1037/0012-1649.39.2.222.

Burnette, M. L., Oshri, A., Lax, R., Richards, D., & Ragbeer, S. N. (2012). Pathways from harsh parenting to adolescent antisocial behavior: A multidomain test of gender moderation. *Development and Psychopathology, 24*, 857–870. doi:10.1017/S0954579412000417.

Burt, S. A. (2009). Are there meaningful etiological differences within antisocial behavior? Results of a meta-analysis. *Clinical Psychology Review, 29*(2), 163–178. doi:10.1016/j.cpr.2008.12.004.

Burt, S. A., & Donnellan, M. B. (2008). Personality correlates of aggressive and non-aggressive antisocial behavior. *Personality and Individual Differences, 44*(1), 53–63. doi:10.1016/j.paid.2007.07.022.

Burt, S. A., Donnellan, M. B., Iacono, W. G., & McGue, M. (2011). Age-of-onset or behavioral sub-types? A prospective comparison of two approaches to characterizing the heterogeneity within antisocial behavior. *Journal of Abnormal Child Psychology, 39*(5), 633–644. doi:10.1007/s10802-011-9491-9.

Casey, B. J., Jones, R. M., & Hare, T. A. (2008). The adolescent brain. *Annals of the New York Academy of Sciences, 1124*(1), 111–126. doi:10.1196/annals.1440.010.

Cloninger, C. R., Christiansen, K. O., Reich, T., & Gottesman, I. I. (1978). Implications of sex differences in the prevalence of antisocial personality, alcoholism, and criminality for familial transmission. *Archives of General Psychiatry, 35*(8), 941–951.

Colins, O. F., Vermeiren, R. R., Noom, M., & Broekaert, E. (2013). Psychotic-like symptoms as a risk factor of violent recidivism in detained male adolescents: *The Journal of Nervous and Mental Disease, 201*(6), 478–483. doi:10.1097/NMD.0b013e3182948068.

Colins, O., Vermeiren, R., Vahl, P., Markus, M., Broekaert, E., & Doreleijers, T. (2011). Psychiatric disorder in detained male adolescents as risk factor for serious recidivism. *Canadian Journal of Psychiatry, 56*(1), 44–50.

Dadds, M. R., Perry, Y., Hawes, D. J., Merz, S., Riddell, A. C., Haines, D. J., ... & Abeygunawardane, A. I. (2006). Attention to the eyes and fear-recognition deficits in child psychopathy. *The British Journal of Psychiatry, 189*, 280–281. doi:10.1192/bjp.bp.105.018150.

Dawel, A., O'Kearney, R., McKone, E., & Palermo, R. (2012). Not just fear and sadness: Meta-analytic evidence of pervasive emotion recognition deficits for facial and vocal expressions in psychopathy. *Neuroscience and Biobehavioral Reviews, 36*(10), 2288–2304. doi:10.1016/j.neubiorev.2012.08.006.

Dreher, J. C., Schmidt, P. J., Kohn, P., Furman, D., Rubinow, D., & Berman, K. F. (2007). Menstrual cycle phase modulates reward-related neural function in women. *Proceedings of the National Academy Sciences, 104*, 2465–2470.

Drevets, W. C., Price, J. L., & Furey, M. L. (2008). Brain structural and functional abnormalities in mood disorders: Implications for neurocircuitry models of depression. *Brain Structure and Function, 213*(1–2), 93–118. doi:10.1007/s00429-008-0189-x.

Eley, T. C., Lichtenstein, P., & Moffitt, T. E. (2003). A longitudinal behavioral genetic analysis of the etiology of aggressive and nonaggressive antisocial behavior. *Development and Psychopathology, 15*(02), 383–402. doi:10.1017/S095457940300021X.

Ernst, M., Nelson, E. E., Jazbec, S., McClure, E. B., Monk, C. S., Leibenluft, E., ... Pine, D. S. (2005). Amygdala and nucleus accumbens in responses to receipt and omission of gains in adults and adolescents. *NeuroImage, 25*(4), 1279–1291. doi:10.1016/j.neuroimage.2004.12.038.

Erskine, H. E., Ferrari, A. J., Nelson, P., Polanczyk, G. V., Flaxman, A. D., Vos, T., ... Scott, J. G. (2013). Research Review: Epidemiological modeling of attention-deficit/hyperactivity disorder and conduct disorder for the Global Burden of Disease Study 2010. *Journal of Child Psychology and Psychiatry, 54*(12), 1263–1274. doi:10.1111/jcpp.12144.

Eshel, N., Nelson, E. E., Blair, R. J., Pine, D. S., & Ernst, M. (2007). Neural substrates of choice selection in adults and adolescents: Development of the ventrolateral prefrontal and anterior cingulate cortices. *Neuropsychologia, 45*(6), 1270–1279. doi:10.1016/j.neuropsychologia.2006.10.004.

Essau, C. A., Sasagawa, S., & Frick, P. J. (2006). Callous-unemotional traits in a community sample of adolescents. *Assessment, 13*(4), 454–469. doi:10.1177/1073191106287354.

Fahim, C., He, Y., Yoon, U., Chen, J., Evans, A., & Pérusse, D. (2011). Neuroanatomy of childhood disruptive behavior disorders. *Aggressive Behavior, 37*(4), 326–337. doi:10.1002/ab.20396.

Fairchild, G. (2011). The developmental psychopathology of motivation in adolescence. *Developmental Cognitive Neuroscience, 1*(4), 414–429. doi: 10.1016/j.dcn.2011.07.009.

Fairchild, G., Hagan, C. C., Passamonti, L., Walsh, N. D., Goodyer, I. M., & Calder, A. J. (2014). Atypical neural responses during face processing in female adolescents with Conduct Disorder. *Journal of the American Academy of Child and Adolescent Psychiatry*. doi:10.1016/j.jaac.2014.02.009.

Fairchild, G., Hagan, C. C., Walsh, N. D., Passamonti, L., Calder, A. J., & Goodyer, I. M. (2013). Brain structure abnormalities in adolescent girls with conduct disorder. *Journal of Child Psychology and Psychiatry, 54*(1), 86–95. doi:10.1111/j.1469-7610.2012.02617.x.

Fairchild, G., Passamonti, L., Hurford, G., Hagan, C. C., von dem Hagen, E. A. H., van Goozen, S. H. M., ... Calder, A. J. (2011). Brain structure abnormalities in early-onset and adolescent-onset conduct disorder. *American Journal of Psychiatry, 168*(6), 624–633. doi:10.1176/appi.ajp.2010.10081184.

Fairchild, G., Stobbe, Y., van Goozen, S. H. M., Calder, A. J., & Goodyer, I. M. (2010). Facial expression recognition, fear conditioning, and startle modulation in female subjects with conduct disorder. *Biological Psychiatry, 68*(3), 272–279. doi:10.1016/j.biopsych.2010.02.019.

Fairchild, G., Toschi, N., Hagan, C. C., Goodyer, I. M., Calder, A. J., & Passamonti, L. (2015). Cortical thickness, surface area, and folding alterations in male youths with conduct disorder and varying levels of callous-unemotional traits. *NeuroImage Clinical, 8*, 253–260.

Fairchild, G., van Goozen, S. H. M., Calder, A. J., & Goodyer, I. M. (2013). Research review: Evaluating and reformulating the developmental taxonomic theory of antisocial behavior. *Journal of Child Psychology and Psychiatry, 54*(9), 924–940. doi:10.1111/jcpp.12102.

Fairchild, G., Van Goozen, S. H. M., Calder, A. J., Stollery, S. J., & Goodyer, I. M. (2009). Deficits in facial expression recognition in male adolescents with early-onset or adolescence-onset conduct disorder. *Journal of Child Psychology and Psychiatry, 50*(5), 627–636. doi:10.1111/j.1469-7610.2008.02020.x.

Fairchild, G., Van Goozen, S. H. M., Stollery, S. J., & Goodyer, I. M. (2008). Fear conditioning and affective modulation of the startle reflex in male adolescents with early-onset or adolescence-onset conduct disorder and healthy control subjects. *Biological Psychiatry, 63*(3), 279–285. doi:10.1016/j.biopsych.2007.06.019.

Farrington, D. P. (1986). Age and crime. *Crime and Justice, 7*, 189–250.

Fontaine, N., Carbonneau, R., Vitaro, F., Barker, E. D., & Tremblay, R. E. (2009). Research review: A critical review of studies on the developmental trajectories of antisocial behavior in females. *Journal of Child Psychology and Psychiatry*, 50(4), 363–385. doi:10.1111/j.1469-7610.2008.01949.x.

Frick, P. J., Ray, J. V., Thornton, L. C., & Kahn, R. E. (2014). Annual research review: A developmental psychopathology approach to understanding callous-unemotional traits in children and adolescents with serious conduct problems. *Journal of Child Psychology and Psychiatry*, 55(6), 532–548. doi:10.1111/jcpp.12152.

Frick, P. J., & White, S. F. (2008). Research review: The importance of callous-unemotional traits for developmental models of aggressive and antisocial behavior. *Journal of Child Psychology and Psychiatry*, 49(4), 359–375. doi:10.1111/j.1469-7610.2007.01862.x.

Gatti, U., Tremblay, R. E., & Vitaro, F. (2009). Iatrogenic effect of juvenile justice. *Journal of Child Psychology and Psychiatry*, 50(8), 991–998. doi:10.1111/j.1469-7610.2008.02057.x.

Giedd, J. N. (2004). Structural magnetic resonance imaging of the adolescent brain. *Annals of the New York Academy of Sciences*, 1021(1), 77–85. doi:10.1196/annals.1308.009.

Glenn, A. L., & Raine, A. (2014). Neurocriminology: Implications for the punishment, prediction and prevention of criminal behavior. *Nature Reviews Neuroscience*, 15(1), 54–63. doi:10.1038/nrn3640.

Gorman-Smith, D., & Loeber, R. (2005). Are developmental pathways in disruptive behaviors the same for girls and boys? *Journal of Child and Family Studies*, 14(1), 15–27. doi:10.1007/s10826-005-1109-9.

Haltigan, J. D., Roisman, G. I., Susman, E. J., Barnett-Walker, K., & Monahan, K. C. (2011). Elevated trajectories of externalizing problems are associated with lower awakening cortisol levels in midadolescence. *Developmental Psychology*, 47(2), 472–478. doi:10.1037/a0021911.

Hare, T. A., & Casey, B. J. (2005). The neurobiology and development of cognitive and affective control. *Cognition, Brain, and Behavior*, 9(3), 273–286.

Hawes, D. J., & Dadds, M. R. (2005). The treatment of conduct problems in children with callous-unemotional traits. *Journal of Consulting and Clinical Psychology*, 73(4), 737–741. doi:10.1037/0022-006X.73.4.737.

Henry, B., Moffitt, T. E., Caspi, A., Langley, J., & Silva, P. A. (1994). On the "remembrance of things past": A longitudinal evaluation of the retrospective method. *Psychological Assessment*, 6(2), 92–101. doi:10.1037/1040-3590.6.2.92.

Hoaken, P. N. S., Allaby, D. B., & Earle, J. (2007). Executive cognitive functioning and the recognition of facial expressions of emotion in incarcerated violent offenders, non-violent offenders, and controls. *Aggressive Behavior*, 33(5), 412–421. doi:10.1002/ab.20194.

Hoeve, M., McReynolds, L. S., & Wasserman, G. A. (2013). The influence of adolescent psychiatric disorder on young adult recidivism. *Criminal Justice and Behavior*, 40(12), 1368–1382. doi:10.1177/0093854813488106.

Huebner, T., Vloet, T. D., Marx, I., Konrad, K., Fink, G. R., Herpertz, S. C., & Herpertz-Dahlmann, B. (2008). Morphometric brain abnormalities in boys with conduct disorder. *Journal of the American Academy of Child and Adolescent Psychiatry*, 47(5), 540–547. doi:10.1097/CHI.0b013e3181676545.

Hubble, K., Bowen, K. L, Moore, S. C., & Van Goozen, S.H. (2015). Improving negative emotion recognition in young offenders reduces subsequent crime. *PLoS One*, 10(6):e0132035. doi: 10.1371/journal.pone.0132035.

Hutton, C., Draganski, B., Ashburner, J., & Weiskopf, N. (2009). A comparison between voxel-based cortical thickness and voxel-based morphometry in normal aging. *NeuroImage*, 48(2), 371–380. doi:10.1016/j.neuroimage.2009.06.043.

Hyatt, C. J., Haney-Caron, E., & Stevens, M. C. (2012). Cortical thickness and folding deficits in conduct-disordered adolescents. *Biological Psychiatry*, 72(3), 207–214. doi:10.1016/j.biopsych.2011.11.017.

Jones, D. K., Knösche, T. R., & Turner, R. (2013). White matter integrity, fiber count, and other fallacies: The do's and don'ts of diffusion MRI. *NeuroImage, 73*, 239–254. doi:10.1016/j.neuroimage.2012.06.081.

Jones, P. D., Laurens, P. D., Herba, P. D., Barker, P. D., & Viding, P. D. (2009). Amygdala hypoactivity to fearful faces in boys with conduct problems and callous-unemotional traits. *American Journal of Psychiatry, 166*(1), 95–102. doi:10.1176/appi.ajp.2008.07071050.

Keenan, K., Loeber, R., & Green, S. (1999). Conduct disorder in girls: A review of the literature. *Clinical Child and Family Psychology Review, 2*(1), 3–19. doi:10.1023/A:1021811307364.

Keenan, K., & Shaw, D. (1997). Developmental and social influences on young girls' early problem behavior. *Psychological Bulletin, 121*(1), 95–113. doi:10.1037/0033-2909.121.1.95.

Kratzer, L., & Hodgins, S. (1999). A typology of offenders: A test of Moffitt's theory among males and females from childhood to age 30. *Criminal Behavior and Mental Health, 9*(1), 57–73. doi:10.1002/cbm.291.

Kruesi, M. J. P., Casanova, M. F., Mannheim, G., & Johnson-Bilder, A. (2004). Reduced temporal lobe volume in early onset conduct disorder. *Psychiatry Research: Neuroimaging, 132*(1), 1–11. doi:10.1016/j.pscychresns.2004.07.002.

Lahey, B. B., Loeber, R., Burke, J. D., & Applegate, B. (2005). Predicting future antisocial personality disorder in males from a clinical assessment in childhood. *Journal of Consulting and Clinical Psychology, 73*(3), 389–399. doi:10.1037/0022-006X.73.3.389.

Lahey, B. B., Loeber, R., Quay, H. C., Applegate, B., Shaffer, D., Waldman, I., ... & Bird, H. R. (1998). Validity of DSM-IV subtypes of conduct disorder based on age of onset. *Journal of the American Academy of Child and Adolescent Psychiatry, 37*(4), 435–442. doi:10.1097/00004583-199804000-00022.

Little, T. D., Henrich, C. C., Jones, S. M., & Hawley, P. H. (2003). Disentangling the "whys" from the "whats" of aggressive behavior. *International Journal of Behavioral Development, 27*(2), 122–133. doi:10.1080/01650250244000128.

Lockwood, P. L., Sebastian, C. L., McCrory, E. J., Hyde, Z. H., Gu, X., De Brito, S. A., & Viding, E. (2013). Association of callous traits with reduced neural response to others' pain in children with conduct problems. *Current Biology, 23*(10), 901–905. doi:10.1016/j.cub.2013.04.018.

Lozier, L. M, Cardinale, E. M, van Meter, J. W., & Marsh, A. A. (2014). Mediation of the relationship between callous-unemotional traits and proactive aggression by amygdala response to fear among children with conduct problems. *JAMA Psychiatry, 71*(6), 627–636. doi:10.1001/jamapsychiatry.2013.4540.

Lynam, D. R., Caspi, A., Moffitt, T. E., Loeber, R., & Stouthamer-Loeber, M. (2007). Longitudinal evidence that psychopathy scores in early adolescence predict adult psychopathy. *Journal of Abnormal Psychology, 116*(1), 155–165. doi:10.1037/0021-843X.116.1.155.

Lynam, D. R., Charnigo, R., Moffitt, T. E., Raine, A., Loeber, R., & Stouthamer-Loeber, M. (2009). The stability of psychopathy across adolescence. *Development and Psychopathology, 21*(4), 1133–1153. doi:10.1017/S0954579409990083.

Marsh, A. A., Finger, E. C., Fowler, K. A., Adalio, C. J., Jurkowitz, I. T. N., Schechter, J. C., ... Blair, R. J. R. (2013). Empathic responsiveness in amygdala and anterior cingulate cortex in youths with psychopathic traits. *Journal of Child Psychology and Psychiatry, 54*(8), 900–910. doi:10.1111/jcpp.12063.

Marsh, A. A., Finger, E. F., Mitchell, D., Reid, M., Sims, C., Kosson, D., ... Blair, R. J. R. (2008). Reduced amygdala response to fearful expressions in children and adolescents with callous-unemotional traits and disruptive behavior disorders. *American Journal of Psychiatry, 165*(6), 712–720. doi:10.1176/appi.ajp.2007.07071145.

McGee, R., Feehan, M., Williams, S., & Anderson, J. (1992). DSM-III disorders from age 11 to age 15 years. *Journal of the American Academy of Child and Adolescent Psychiatry, 31*(1), 50–59. doi:10.1097/00004583-199201000-00009.

Ministry of Justice. (2016). *Proven Re-offending Statistics Quarterly Bulletin*. Retrieved from https://www.gov.uk/government/statistics/women-and-the-criminal-justice-system-2013.

Ministry of Justice. (2015). *Population bulletin*. Retrieved from https://www.gov.uk/government/statistics/prison-population-figures-2015.

Moffitt, T. E. (1993). Adolescence-limited and life-course-persistent antisocial behavior: A developmental taxonomy. *Psychological Review, 100*(4), 674–701. doi:10.1037/0033-295X.100.4.674.

Moffitt, T. E., & Caspi, A. (2001). Childhood predictors differentiate life-course persistent and adolescence-limited antisocial pathways among males and females. *Development and Psychopathology, 13*(02), 355–375.

Moffitt, T. E., Caspi, A., Dickson, N., Silva, P., & Stanton, W. (1996). Childhood-onset versus adolescent-onset antisocial conduct problems in males: Natural history from ages 3 to 18 years. *Development and Psychopathology, 8*(02), 399–424. doi:10.1017/S0954579400007161.

Moffitt, T. E., Caspi, A., Rutter, M., & Silva, P. A. (2001). *Sex differences in antisocial behavior: conduct disorder, delinquency, and violence in the Dunedin Longitudinal Study*. Cambridge, UK; Cambridge University Press.

Monuteaux, M. C., Fitzmaurice, G., Blacker, D., Buka, S. L., & Biederman, J. (2004). Specificity in the familial aggregation of overt and covert conduct disorder symptoms in a referred attention-deficit hyperactivity disorder sample. *Psychological Medicine, 34*(6), 1113–1127. doi:10.1017/S0033291703001788.

Mulder, E., Brand, E., Bullens, R., & van Marle, H. (2011). Risk factors for overall recidivism and severity of recidivism in serious juvenile offenders. *International Journal of Offender Therapy and Comparative Criminology, 55*(1), 118–135. doi:10.1177/0306624X09356683.

Odgers, C. L., Caspi, A., Broadbent, J. M., Dickson, N., Hancox, R. J., Harrington, H., ... Moffitt, T. E. (2007) Prediction of differential adult health burden by conduct problem subtypes in males. *Archives of General Psychiatry, 64*(4), 476–484.

Odgers, C. L., Moffitt, T. E., Broadbent, J. M., Dickson, N., Hancox, R. J., Harrington, H., ... Caspi, A. (2008). Female and male antisocial trajectories: From childhood origins to adult outcomes. *Development and Psychopathology, 20*(02), 673–716. doi:10.1017/S0954579408000333.

Pajer, K. A. (1998). What happens to "bad" girls? A Review of the Adult Outcomes of Antisocial Adolescent Girls. *American Journal of Psychiatry, 155*(7), 862–870.

Pajer, K., Chung, J., Leininger, L., Wang, W., Gardner, W., & Yeates, K. (2008). Neuropsychological function in adolescent girls with conduct disorder. *Journal of the American Academy of Child & Adolescent Psychiatry, 47*(4), 416–425. doi:10.1097/CHI.0b013e3181640828.

Pardini, D. A., Raine, A., Erickson, K., & Loeber, R. (2014). Lower amygdala volume in men is associated with childhood. aggression, early psychopathic traits, and future violence. *Biological Psychiatry, 75*(1), 73–80. doi:10.1016/j.biopsych.2013.04.003.

Passamonti, L., Fairchild, G., Fornito, A., Goodyer, I. M., Nimmo-Smith, I., Hagan, C. C., & Calder, A. J. (2012). Abnormal anatomical connectivity between the amygdala and orbitofrontal cortex in conduct disorder. *PLoS ONE, 7*(11), e48789. doi:10.1371/journal.pone.0048789.

Passamonti, L., Fairchild, G., Goodyer, I. M., Hurford, G., Hagan, C. C., Rowe, J. B., & Calder, A. J. (2010). Neural abnormalities in early-onset and adolescence-onset conduct disorder. *Archives of General Psychiatry, 67*(7), 729–738. doi:10.1001/archgenpsychiatry.2010.75.

Paus, T., Keshavan, M., & Giedd, J. N. (2008). Why do many psychiatric disorders emerge during adolescence? *Nature Reviews Neuroscience, 9*(12), 947–957. doi:10.1038/nrn2513.

Penton-Voak, I. S., Thomas, J., Gage, S. H., McMurran, M., McDonald, S., & Munafò, M. R. (2013). Increasing recognition of happiness in ambiguous facial expressions reduces anger and aggressive behavior. *Psychological Science*, *24*(5), 688–697. doi:10.1177/0956797612459657.

Pfeifer, J. H., & Allen, N. B. (2012). Arrested development? Reconsidering dual- systems models of brain function in adolescence and disorders. *Trends in Cognitive Sciences*, *16*(6), 322–329. doi: 10.1016/j.tics.2012.04.011.

Polier, G. G., Vloet, T. D., Herpertz-Dahlmann, B., Laurens, K. R., & Hodgins, S. (2012). Comorbidity of conduct disorder symptoms and internalising problems in children: Investigating a community and a clinical sample. *European Child and Adolescent Psychiatry*, *21*(1), 31–38. doi:10.1007/s00787-011-0229-6.

Raine, A., Dodge, K., Loeber, R., Gatzke-Kopp, L., Lynam, D., Reynolds, C., ... Liu, J. (2006). The reactive–proactive aggression questionnaire: differential correlates of reactive and proactive aggression in adolescent boys. *Aggressive Behavior*, *32*(2), 159–171. doi:10.1002/ab.20115.

Raine, A., Moffitt, T. E., Caspi, A., Loeber, R., Stouthamer-Loeber, M., & Lynam, D. (2005). Neurocognitive impairments in boys on the life-course persistent antisocial path. *Journal of Abnormal Psychology*, *114*(1), 38–49. doi:10.1037/0021-843X.114.1.38.

Raine, A., Yang, Y., Narr, K. L., & Toga, A. W. (2011). Sex differences in orbitofrontal gray as a partial explanation for sex differences in antisocial personality. *Molecular Psychiatry*, *16*, 227–236.

Robins, L. N. (1966). *Deviant children grown up: A sociological and psychiatric study of sociopathic personality*. Baltimore, MD: Williams & Wilkins.

Robins, L. N. (1978). Sturdy childhood predictors of adult antisocial behavior: replications from longitudinal studies. *Psychological Medicine*, *8*(4), 611–622.

Rosenfield, S., & Mouzon, D. (2013). Gender and mental health. In C. S. Aneshensel, J. C. Phelan, & A. Bierman (Eds.), *Handbook of the sociology of mental health* (pp. 277–296). Springer Netherlands. Retrieved from http://link.springer.com/chapter/10.1007/978-94-007-4276-5_14.

Rowe, R., Maughan, B., Moran, P., Ford, T., Briskman, J., & Goodman, R. (2010). The role of callous and unemotional traits in the diagnosis of conduct disorder. *Journal of Child Psychology and Psychiatry*, *51*(6), 688–695. doi:10.1111/j.1469-7610.2009.02199.x.

Ruigrok, A. N. V., Salimi-Khorshidi, G., Lai, M.-C., Baron-Cohen, S., Lombardo, M. V., Tait, R. J., & Suckling, J. (2014). A meta-analysis of sex differences in human brain structure. *Neuroscience and Biobehavioral Reviews*, *39*, 34–50. doi:10.1016/j.neubiorev.2013.12.004.

Ryan, J. P., Williams, A. B., & Courtney, M. E. (2013). Adolescent neglect, juvenile delinquency and the risk of recidivism. *Journal of Youth and Adolescence*, *42*(3), 454–465. doi:10.1007/s10964-013-9906-8.

Samuelson, Y. M., Hodgins, S., Larsson, A., Larm, P., & Tengström, A. (2010). Adolescent antisocial behavior as predictor of adverse outcomes to age 50 a follow-up study of 1,947 individuals. *Criminal Justice and Behavior*, *37*(2), 158–174. doi:10.1177/0093854809350902.

Sarkar, S., Craig, M. C., Catani, M., Dell'Acqua, F., Fahy, T., Deeley, Q., & Murphy, D. G. M. (2013). Frontotemporal white-matter microstructural abnormalities in adolescents with conduct disorder: A diffusion tensor imaging study. *Psychological Medicine*, *43*(02), 401–411. doi:10.1017/S003329171200116X.

Schönenberg M., Christian, S., Gaußer, A. K., Mayer, S. V., Hautzinger, M., & Jusyte, A. (2014). Addressing perceptual insensitivity to facial affect in violent offenders: First evidence for the efficacy of a novel implicit training approach. *Psychological Medicine*, *44*, 1042–1052.

Schumann, G., Loth, E., Banaschewski, T., Barbot, A., Barker, G., Büchel, C., ... Struve, M. (2010). The IMAGEN study: Reinforcement-related behavior in normal brain function and psychopathology. *Molecular Psychiatry*, *15*(12), 1128–1139. doi:10.1038/mp.2010.4.

Sebastian, C. L., De Brito, S. A., McCrory, E. J., Hyde, Z. H., Lockwood, P. L., Cecil, C. A., & Viding, E. (2015). Grey matter volumes in children with conduct problems and varying levels of callous-unemotional traits. *Journal of Abnormal Child Psychology*, September 14 [E-pub ahead of print].

Silverthorn, P., & Frick, P. J. (1999). Developmental pathways to antisocial behavior: The delayed-onset pathway in girls. *Development and Psychopathology*, *11*(01), 101–126.

Solanto, M. V., Abikoff, H., Sonuga-Barke, E., Schachar, R., Logan, G. D., Wigal, T., ... Turkel, E. (2001). The ecological validity of delay aversion and response inhibition as measures of impulsivity in AD/HD: A supplement to the NIMH multimodal treatment study of AD/HD. *Journal of Abnormal Child Psychology*, *29*(3), 215–228. doi:10.1023/A:1010329714819.

Spear, L. P. (2010). *The behavioral neuroscience of adolescence* (Vol. *xvii*). New York, NY: W. W. Norton & Co.

Sterzer, P., Stadler, C., Poustka, F., & Kleinschmidt, A. (2007). A structural neural deficit in adolescents with conduct disorder and its association with lack of empathy. *NeuroImage*, *37*(1), 335–342.doi:10.1016/j.neuroimage.2007.04.043.

Stevens, M. C., & Haney-Caron, E. (2012). Comparison of brain volume abnormalities between ADHD and conduct disorder in adolescence. *Journal of Psychiatry and Neuroscience*, *37*(6), 389–398. doi:10.1503/jpn.110148.

Tackett, J. L., Krueger, R. F., Iacono, W. G., & McGue, M. (2005). Symptom-based subfactors of DSM-defined conduct disorder: Evidence for etiologic distinctions. *Journal of Abnormal Psychology*, *114*(3), 483–487. doi:10.1037/0021-843X.114.3.483.

Teplin, L. A., Abram, K. M., McClelland, G. M., Dulcan, M. K., & Mericle, A. A. (2002). Psychiatric disorders in youth in juvenile detention. *Archives of General Psychiatry*, *59*(12), 1133–1143. doi:10.1001/archpsyc.59.12.1133.

Tremblay, R. E. (2010). Developmental origins of disruptive behavior problems: The "original sin" hypothesis, epigenetics and their consequences for prevention. *Journal of Child Psychology and Psychiatry*, *51*(4), 341–367. doi:10.1111/j.1469-7610.2010.02211.x.

Underwood, M. K. (2003). *Social aggression among girls*. New York: Guilford Press.

Van Goozen, S. H. M., Fairchild, G., Snoek, H., & Harold, G. T. (2007). The evidence for a neurobiological model of childhood antisocial behavior. *Psychological Bulletin*, *133*(1), 149–182. doi:10.1037/0033-2909.133.1.149.

Van Leijenhorst, L., Moor, B. G., Op de Macks, Z. A., Rombouts, S. A. R. B., Westenberg, P. M., & Crone, E. A. (2010). Adolescent risky decision-making: Neurocognitive development of reward and control regions. *NeuroImage*, *51*(1), 345–355. doi:10.1016/j.neuroimage.2010.02.038.

Verhulst, F. C., & Der Ende, J. V. (1995). The eight-year stability of problem behavior in an epidemiologic sample. *Pediatric Research*, *38*(4), 612–617. doi:10.1203/00006450-199510000-00023.

Viding, E., Blair, R. J. R., Moffitt, T. E., & Plomin, R. (2005). Evidence for substantial genetic risk for psychopathy in 7-year-olds. *Journal of Child Psychology and Psychiatry*, *46*(6), 592–597. doi:10.1111/j.1469-7610.2004.00393.x.

Viding, E., Frick, P. J., & Plomin, R. (2007). Aetiology of the relationship between callous-unemotional traits and conduct problems in childhood. *The British Journal of Psychiatry*, *190*(49), s33–s38. doi:10.1192/bjp.190.5.s33.

Viding, E., & McCrory, E. J. (2012). Genetic and neurocognitive contributions to the development of psychopathy. *Development and Psychopathology*, *24*(3), 969–983.

Viding, E., Sebastian, C. L., Dadds, M. R., Lockwood, P. L., Cecil, C. A. M., De Brito, S. A., & McCrory, E. J. (2012). Amygdala response to preattentive masked fear in children with conduct problems: The role of callous-unemotional traits. *American Journal of Psychiatry, 169*(10), 1109–1116. doi:10.1176/appi.ajp.2012.12020191.

Visser, T. A. W., Ohan, J. L., Whittle, S., Yücel, M., Simmons, J. G., & Allen, N. B. (2014). Sex differences in structural brain asymmetry predict overt aggression in early adolescents. *Social Cognitive and Affective Neuroscience, 9*(4). doi:10.1093/scan/nst013.

Von Der Heide, R. J., Skipper, L. M., Klobusicky, E., & Olson, I. R. (2013). Dissecting the uncinate fasciculus: Disorders, controversies and a hypothesis. *Brain, 136*, 1692–1707.

Wallace, G. L., White, S. F., Robustelli, B., Sinclair, S., Hwang, S., Martin, A., & R. Blair, R. J. (2014). Cortical and subcortical abnormalities in youths with conduct disorder and elevated callous-unemotional traits. *Journal of the American Academy of Child and Adolescent Psychiatry, 53*(4), 456–465. doi:10.1016/j.jaac.2013.12.008.

Wasserman, G. A., McReynolds, L. S., Ko, S. J., Katz, L. M., & Carpenter, J. R. (2005). Gender differences in psychiatric disorders at juvenile probation intake. *American Journal of Public Health, 95*(1), 131–137. doi:10.2105/AJPH.2003.024737.

White, N. A., & Piquero, A. R. (2004). A preliminary empirical test of Silverthorn and Frick's delayed-onset pathway in girls using an urban, African-American, US-based sample. *Criminal Behavior and Mental Health, 14*(4), 291–309. doi:10.1002/cbm.595.

Zaki, J., & Ochsner, K. N. (2012). The neuroscience of empathy: Progress, pitfalls and promise. *Nature Neuroscience, 15*(5), 675–680. doi:10.1038/nn.3085.

Zhang, J. Gao, J., Shi, H., Huang, B., Wang, X., Situ, W., ... Yao, S. (2014). Sex differences of uncinate fasciculus structural connectivity in individuals with conduct disorder. *Biological Medicine Research International, 2014*, 1–9.

Zoccolillo, M. (1993). Gender and the development of conduct disorder. *Development and Psychopathology, 5*(1–2), 65–78. doi:10.1017/S0954579400004260.

17
Alcohol-Related Aggression and Violence

Stefan Gutwinski, Adrienne J. Heinz, and Andreas Heinz

> **Key points**
> - Multiple interacting factors confer the risk for alcohol-related aggression.
> - These include:
>   - social learning;
>   - contextual influences; and
>   - associative connections between alcohol and aggression in memory.
> - Hence in this chapter we discuss social and genetic factors contributing to alcohol-associated alterations of key neurotransmitter systems.
> - We also discuss their effects on frontal and limbic brain areas.
> - We also discuss the cognitive disruptions and deficits associated with acute and chronic alcohol intake.

Terminology Explained

Alcohol outcome expectancies (AOE) are the cognitive, affective, and behavioral outcomes an individual expects to occur due to drinking.

A **GABAergic** agent or drug is a chemical that functions to directly modulate the gamma-aminobutyric-acid (GABA) system in the body or brain. Classes include GABA receptor agonists, GABA receptor antagonists, and GABA reuptake inhibitors. Examples of types include gabapentinoids and GABA analogs.

Social-cognitive model/theory, used in psychology, education, and communication, holds that portions of an individual's knowledge acquisition can be directly related to observing others within the context of social interactions, experiences, and outside media influences. The theory states that when people observe a model performing a behavior and the consequences of that behavior, they remember the sequence of events and use this information to guide subsequent behaviors.

The Wiley Blackwell Handbook of Forensic Neuroscience, First Edition. Edited by Anthony R. Beech, Adam J. Carter, Ruth E. Mann and Pia Rotshtein.
© 2018 John Wiley & Sons Ltd. Published 2018 by John Wiley & Sons Ltd.

5-HTTLPR (serotonin-transporter-linked polymorphic region) is a degenerate repeat polymorphic region in SLC6A4, the gene that codes for the serotonin transporter. Since the polymorphism was identified in the middle of the 1990s it has been extensively investigated, particularly in connection with neuropsychiatric disorders.

Intimate partner violence (IPV) is one of the most common forms of violence against women that is performed by a husband or intimate male partner. Although women can be violent in relationships with men, and violence is also found in same-sex partnerships, the overwhelming health burden of partner violence is borne by women at the hands of men. It includes acts of physical aggression, psychological abuse, sex and other forms of sexual coercion, and various controlling behaviors such as isolating a person from family and friends or restricting access to information and assistance.

Monoamine oxidase A (MAO-A) is a catabolic enzyme that breaks down serotonin and other amines.

The National Crime Victimization Survey (NCVS)[1] is the USA's primary source of information on criminal victimization. Each year, data are obtained from a nationally representative sample of about 90,000 households, comprising nearly 160,000 persons, on the frequency, characteristics, and consequences of criminal victimization.

Introduction

Aggressive and disinhibited behavior is a commonly accepted consequence of alcohol consumption and the phenomenon is well reputed in the phrase "liquid courage." The capacity for alcohol to elicit aggression has been capitalized upon for centuries and was used to boost violence of warriors and reduce their fear. Indeed, the historian Maren Lorenz described the use of brandy and beer in the battles of the 17th century, such as in the Thirty Years' War (Lorenz, 2007). Also, today, alcohol plays a critical role in aggression and violence perpetration and is associated with burdensome social and economic costs (Brynes, 2012; World Health Organization, 2007).

Worldwide, alcohol has been implicated in approximately half of violent crimes (Hoaken & Stewart, 2003) and in the USA, alcohol was a factor in more than a third of violent crimes committed between 2002 and 2008 (Rand, Sabol, Sinclair, & Snyder, 2010). Alcohol has also been identified as a contributing factor in up to 50% of homicides (Darke, 2010; Smith, Branas, & Miller, 1999) and sexual assaults (Collins & Messerschmidt, 1993; Testa, 2002). According to the US National Crime Victimization Survey (NCVS), victims of rapes and sexual assaults reported that 26.8% of perpetrators were perceived as intoxicated with alcohol (NCVS, 2006). In terms of intimate partner violence (IPV), a national study reported alcohol intoxication in 30 to 40% of men and in 27 to 34% of women at the time of the violence (Caetano, Schafer, & Cunradi, 2001). Meta-analytic findings confirmed a significant association of alcohol use and IPV with a mean effect size of 0.33 for alcohol dependence and of 0.22 for problem drinking (Foran & O'Leary, 2008). Also, nearly 40% of child victimizers report having been intoxicated with alcohol when committing the crime (Greenfeld, 1996).

The high level of alcohol-related violent crimes and associated public health consequences emphasize the importance of gaining a comprehensive understanding of the risk factors and underlying mechanisms by which alcohol elicits aggression. Epidemiological data clearly demonstrate that alcohol-related aggression is associated with chronic alcohol intake and alcohol dependence: the incidence of violent behavior in samples of male subjects with alcohol use disorders is estimated between 20 and 50% (Chermack et al., 2010; Jaffe, Babor, & Fishbein, 1988; Mayfield, 1976; Nicol, Gunn, Gristwood, Foggitt, & Watson, 1973; Schuckit & Russell, 1984). Compared to individuals without alcohol use disorders, those with alcohol use disorders show a fivefold higher rate of involvement in violence (Coid et al., 2006; Swanson, Holzer III, Ganju, & Jono, 1990). A meta-analysis reported that individuals who get drunk at least once a year compared to individuals with low or moderate alcohol use are up to two times more often engaged in criminal and domestic violence (Lipsey, Wilson, Cohen, & Derzon, 1997). With regard to IPV, it was found that alcohol-dependent men were four times more likely to exhibit violence to their partner than non-dependent subjects (O'Farrell, Fals-Stewart, Murphy, & Murphy, 2003). Interestingly, partner violence decreased significantly in patients without relapse one year after treatment.

A cross-sectional study also demonstrated that alcohol intoxication was associated with a higher risk of injury of both the victim and the perpetrator, and the risk almost doubled in individuals with alcohol dependence (Coid et al., 2006). Finally, longitudinal studies with adolescents also suggest that increases in alcohol consumption are significantly associated with violent crime and victimization (Boden, Fergusson, & Horwood, 2012; Fergusson & Horwood, 2000). Nevertheless, it should be emphasized that the majority of subjects suffering from alcohol use disorders do not commit violent behavior.

Alcohol acute effects, especially after heavy intake, appear to facilitate aggressive behavior more than its chronic effects (Chermack & Blow, 2002; Fals-Stewart, 2003). A study demonstrated that men with alcoholism consumed more alcohol in the 12 hours before violent conflicts, compared to days with non-violent conflicts (Murphy, Winters, O'Farrell, Fals-Stewart, & Murphy, 2005). Studies with arrestees and felons also indicate that alcohol intake in events related to the arrest is associated with committing a violent crime. More specifically, only acute intoxication discriminated between violent and non-violent charges, that was not the case with regard to chronic alcohol consumption patterns (Collins & Schlenger, 1988; Lundholm, Haggard, Moller, Hallqvist, & Thiblin, 2013; Wiley & Weisner, 1995). A similar study also demonstrated that violence among alcohol-dependent individuals was most robustly explained by alcohol and substance use prior to the offense (Arseneault, Moffitt, Caspi, Taylor, & Silva, 2000). Accordingly, a higher quantity and frequency of consumption appears to account for the high prevalence of violent behavior among individuals with alcohol-use disorders, including alcohol dependence.

Numerous studies have sought to determine the mechanisms by which alcohol elicits aggressive and violent behavior. This literature indicates that multiple, interacting mechanisms contribute to aggressive behavior in acute and chronic alcohol consumption. Here we attempt to integrate key findings regarding the social, cognitive, and biological mechanisms by which acute intoxication and the effects of chronic alcohol consumption contribute to aggressive and violent behavior.

Alcohol-related aggression *The high level of alcohol-related violent crimes and associated public health consequences emphasizes the importance of gaining a comprehensive understanding of the risk factors and underlying mechanisms by which alcohol elicits aggression.*
Source: © Sebastien Decoret. Used under license from 123RF.

Social-Cognitive Models

Alcohol is believed to promote aggressive behavior via its acute effects on cognitive function. Additionally, other stable cognitive and social-cognitive factors influence one's vulnerability to aggression under alcohol (Chermack & Giancola, 1997), such as reduced executive functioning, social learning experiences (e.g., experiences with other individuals who become aggressive under alcohol intoxication), and individual differences in alcohol outcome expectancies (AOE). Executive functions comprise cognitive abilities, which contribute to the planning, initiation, and regulation of goal-directed behavior, such as attentional control, problem solving, and cognitive flexibility (Luria, 1980; Posner & Petersen, 1990). According to Giancola (2004), alcohol can directly promote aggression by disrupting executive functions (mediating effect), and this relation is stronger among individuals with lower baseline executive functions (moderating effect). In terms of its acute effects, alcohol disrupts four key functions that inhibit aggression: attending to and appraising situational information, taking the perspective of others, considering consequences of one's actions, and defusing a hostile situation (Giancola, 2000).

Numerous studies conducted among individuals with alcohol use disorders suggest that this population suffers from impairments in a range of executive functions when compared to healthy controls and abstinent alcohol-dependent individuals (Bates, Buckman, & Nguyen, 2013; Giancola & Moss, 1998; Ratti, Bo, Giardini, & Soragna, 2002; Stavro, Pelletier, & Potvin, 2013; Sullivan, Rosenbloom, & Pfefferbaum, 2000). Given that the relation between alcohol and aggression is stronger among individuals with lower executive functioning, the chronic effects of problematic alcohol use on executive functioning can contribute to higher rates of aggressive behavior among alcohol-dependent patients (Giancola, 2004).

AOE are an individual's beliefs about the effect of alcohol on their subjective experience, behavior, and performance (Goldman, Brown, & Christiansen, 1987). The strength and accessibility of these outcome expectancies can be quantified by cognitive tasks (Bartholow & Heinz, 2006; Stacy, Leigh, & Weingardt, 1994) and self-report questionnaires (Fromme, Stroot, & Kaplan, 1993). Already in children of pre-school age with no experience of consumption, alcohol expectancies and schemas have been documented (Zucker, Kincaid, Fitzgerald, & Bingham, 1995). It is hypothesized that AOE are stored in memory as a template for the effects of alcohol and are gradually shaped over time by both direct use of alcohol and indirect social learning experiences (e.g., alcohol use in families, media) (Bandura, 1977; Goldman, 1999; Goldman, Darkes, & Del Boca, 1999; Goldman, Del Boca, & Darkes, 1999). Conceptual models indicate that the anticipation of alcohol consumption activates memories and expectancies for alcohol, which in turn influence the behavior under alcohol, including aggressive behavior (Goldman, Darkes et al., 1999; Maisto, Carey, & Bradizza, 1999). Interestingly, even in the absence of alcohol but in the presence of alcohol cues, individuals with stronger expectancies for alcohol and aggression rated ambiguous behavior of fictional characters as more hostile (Bartholow & Heinz, 2006). The connections between expectancies and outcomes in memory strengthen as experiences with alcohol mount (Leigh & Stacy, 1998; Stacy et al., 1994; Weingardt, Stacy, & Leigh, 1996). Ultimately, these expectancies may drive behavior in an automatic manner (Tiffany, 1990). Indeed, AOE demonstrate strong predictive validity concerning several drinking outcomes and appear to exert a significant influence over drinking behavior (Brown, 1985; Goldman, Darkes et al., 1999; Goldman, Del Boca et al., 1999; Jones, Corbin, & Fromme, 2001).

Semantic networking theories facilitate our understanding of the alcohol expectancy memory network and the putative processes by which it is activated (Rather, Goldman, Roehrich, & Brannick, 1992). This network comprises nodes of information linked together in memory on the basis of intrinsic meaning and learning, and is activated when alcohol or alcohol-related stimuli are encountered (Collins & Loftus, 1975). Previous research indicates that alcohol-related memory networks of heavy drinkers are more tightly configured than those of light drinkers (Rather & Goldman, 1994). Heavy drinkers associate alcohol with more positive and arousing effects, whereas light drinkers tend to expect sedating effects (Rather et al., 1992; Weingardt et al., 1996). The alcohol memory network also comprises aggressive expectancies and hence the strength and influence of these connections is likely determined by individual experiences and learning of alcohol-related aggression (Goldman, Darkes et al., 1999).

The myopia hypothesis

Several theories describe the acute effect of alcohol on cognitive disruption. Alcohol myopia (Greek: μυωπία, *muōpia*, from myein "to shut" – ops "eye") is a phenomenon in which alcohol causes a narrowing of attention in the perceptual field (Steele & Josephs, 1990). Myopia is akin to using the zoom function of a camera, where only a part of the scene can be viewed with clarity. Therefore, myopia can lead to misinterpretation of contextual cues when they are missed or only partially detected (Taylor & Leonard, 1983). The observation that alcohol limits the amount of attention available to process information is an integral part of the attention allocation hypothesis. According to this theory, alcohol is thought to limit the cognitive resources available to process conflict-mitigating information in the environment. As such, instigating cues in the immediate context are awarded far more salience than external, inhibitory cues (e.g., responding aggressively when being bumped in a bar, instead of considering that it was accidentally) (Steele & Southwick, 1985; Taylor & Leonard, 1983). Importantly, inhibition conflict, which is competition for attention between instigating and inhibitory cues, must be present for alcohol to bias one towards an excessive aggressive response (Steele & Southwick, 1985). This is because decision processing between different potential responses under alcohol appears to be more influenced by instigating cues than by conflict-mitigating cues (Ito, Miller, & Pollock, 1996).

In an experimental laboratory paradigm of the "attention allocation hypothesis for alcohol-related aggression" under moderate cognitive load and in the presence of low-provocation cues, alcohol intoxicated individuals administered lower intensity shocks to a fictitious competitor than non-intoxicated individuals (Giancola & Corman, 2007). However, among the intoxicated individuals, those with large or small cognitive load responded more aggressively compared to those under moderate load. These findings indicate that aggression under alcohol is governed by the amount of cognitive capacity available for processing inhibitory information (Giancola & Corman, 2007) and can help to explain why only a minority of intoxicated individuals reacts aggressively.

Cognitive disruption

Other more general conceptualizations of alcohol-related aggression focus on cognitive disruption by alcohol, where alcohol compromises multiple cognitive domains of functioning and thereby increases the probability of emitting aggressive behavior (Graham, 1980). Graham described such an indirect cause-model in the "disinhibition hypothesis" and posited that the pharmacological effects of alcohol disrupt brain mechanisms, which maintain inhibitory control over more primal behavior. Accordingly, alcohol disrupts cognitive processes critical for self-regulation, such as attention, decision making, and information processing.

Social information processing

Additional theories have focused on the effects of alcohol on self-awareness and social-cognitive information processing. More specifically, alcohol is posited to disrupt higher-order encoding of self-relevant information necessary for self-awareness, which can lead to heightened aggression in response to interpersonal provocation (Hull, 1981). Interestingly, Bailey, Leonard, Cranston, and Taylor (1993) reported that alcohol intoxicated individuals who could see themselves in a mirror or via video technique administered fewer shocks than individuals without such self-observation. Thus, increased self-focused attention during intoxication may reduce the gap between internal states and external standards of behavior (Ito et al., 1996). Finally, the hostile attribution bias stipulates that individuals under the influence of alcohol are more likely to misinterpret ambiguous interpersonal cues and information (Nasby, Hayden, & DePaulo, 1980). This is because the ambiguous actions of others may render an uncertain level of threat and thereby increase the probability of emitting aggressive responses (Taylor, Gammon, & Capasso, 1976). This effect helps to account for aggressive behavior under conditions of low provocation, since the effect of high provocation is known to be robust independent of the influence of alcohol (Giancola et al., 2002; Ito et al., 1996). Box 17.1 shows the evidence of alcohol on the brain and neurotransmission in the brain.

> **Box 17.1** The effects of alcohol on the brain and on neurotransmission
>
> - Alcohol exerts its effects via multiple neurotransmitter systems. In animal models alcohol intoxication has been shown to stimulate serotonin and dopamine release, especially in the ventral and dorsal striatum (Diana, Gessa, & Rossetti, 1992; Mathews, John, Lapa, Budygin, & Jones, 2006; Puglisi-Allegra, Imperato, Angelucci, & Cabib, 1991).
> - Alcohol simultaneously stimulates the release of gamma-aminobutyric-acid (GABA) interacting with both GABA type A and B receptors, and blocks glutaminergic neurotransmission. Accordingly, alcohol exerts an inhibitory effect on cortical activation and induces a mainly sedative effect (A. Heinz, Beck, Grusser, Grace, & Wrase, 2009; Tsai, Gastfriend, & Coyle, 1995).
> - The effects of alcohol on behavior are largely dose dependent: high doses induce sedative effects, whereas low doses facilitate psychomotor activation and aggression in a subset of rodents (Murphy et al., 2005; Takahashi, Kwa, Debold, & Miczek, 2010; Takahashi, Shimamoto, Boyson, DeBold, & Miczek, 2010; Weerts, Tornatzky, & Miczek, 1993).
> - Research on the acute effects of alcohol on humans has primarily investigated the impairment of executive functions, localized in the prefrontal cortex (Chermack & Giancola, 1997).
> - Among individuals with severe impairments of prefrontal cortex functions (as found in lesion studies) behavioral changes have been reliably observed and include impaired abstract reasoning, adapting and stopping behavior, and deficits in planning and sequencing.
> - The behavioral changes caused by impairments of prefrontal cortex functioning also appear to comprise affective regulation, and can result in emotional liability, aggression, or apathy (Adolphs, 2009; Peterson, Rothfleisch, Zelazo, & Pihl, 1990). A study showed that up to 70% of patients with traumatic brain injuries develop violent behavior and irritability, which causes distress to their families (McKinlay, Brooks, Bond, Martinage, & Marshall, 1981).
> - In placebo-controlled studies, acute alcohol intake has been observed to induce behavioral changes similar to those observed in patients with impairments of prefrontal cortex functions, including set-shifting, flexibility, response inhibition, and attentional processes (Easdon & Vogel-Sprott, 2000; Finn, Justus, Mazas, & Steinmetz, 1999; Guillot, Fanning, Bullock, McCloskey, & Berman, 2010; Lyvers & Maltzman, 1991; Mulvihill, Skilling, & Vogel-Sprott, 1997; Peterson et al., 1990; Schreckenberger et al., 2004; Schweizer et al., 2006).
> - In addition, an electrophysiological study showed that moderate doses of alcohol reduced activity in the medial prefrontal cortex in response to errors of performance and impaired ability to adjust performances after such errors (Ridderinkhof et al., 2002). These deficits in executive functioning

may therefore impair the ability of intoxicated individuals to inhibit violent responses when confronted with emotionally provocative interpersonal situations (Hawkins & Trobst, 2000).

- Importantly, several subregions of the prefrontal cortex are linked with limbic areas, including the amygdale, via inhibitory projections (Amaral & Price, 1984; Barbas, 2000). These circuits are associated with the regulation of emotional behavior. Impairments of amygdale functions have been suggested to play a key role in different forms of aggressive behavior.
- Reduced amygdale activity is hypothetically associated with instrumental or "cold" aggression, defined as harmful behavior engaged in without provocation; reactive or "hot" aggression, a type of aggression that can be elicited in response to a perceived threat or insult, appears to be associated with increased amygdala activity (Birbaumer et al., 2005; Coccaro, McCloskey, Fitzgerald, & Phan, 2007; Jones, Laurens, Herba, Barker, & Viding, 2009; Lee, Chan, & Raine, 2008; Marsh et al., 2008; Sterzer & Stadler, 2009). Functional imaging studies conducted among individuals diagnosed with intermittent explosive disorder, which is characterized by reactive aggressive behavior, suggest that impaired activation of medial prefrontal structures and heightened amygdala responses might contributed to reactive aggressive behavior (Coccaro et al., 2007; Lee et al., 2008; Sterzer & Stadler, 2009).
- The effects of alcohol intoxication on the brain partly resemble aspects of how stress influences neurotransmitter systems. Both stress and alcohol lead to dopamine release in fronto-cortical circuits and the striatum (Diana et al., 1992; Puglisi-Allegra et al., 1991). Stress has been observed to alter information processing in the prefrontal cortex and amygdala, and can interfere with dopaminergic modulation of these areas. Miczek and colleagues showed that, in rodents, uncontrollable episodes of social defeat stress produce long-lasting tolerance to opiate analgesia and, concurrently, behavioral sensitization to challenges with either amphetamine or cocaine. The researchers concluded that stress modulates the monoamine neurotransmitter balance in mesocorticrticolimbic structures, which in turn contributes to increased intake of amphetamine or cocaine (Miczek et al., 2011).
- Additionally, it has been observed that stress induces an elevation of striatal dopamine concentration (measured indirectly by binding to dopamine receptors), and this seems to facilitate increased intake of drugs of abuse that in turn impact the dopaminergic system (Nader & Czoty, 2005).
- Increased levels of dopamine in the prefrontal cortex and the ventral striatum have been associated with threatening behavior and violent attacks in rodents (de Almeida, Ferrari, Parmigiani, & Miczek, 2005) and further animal studies show that both stress and alcohol induce dopamine release in the amygdala (McBride, 2002; Yokoyama et al., 2005).
- To summarize, acute alcohol intake can interfere with prefrontal functioning, which can lead to an impairment of executive functions including behavioral and affective processes. Additionally, alcohol modulates dopaminergic neurotransmission in the striatum and amygdala, brain areas directly indicated in the processing of stressful social conflicts and related emotions.

Vulnerability Factors in Human and Animal Research

Only a subset of individuals becomes aggressive under alcohol. Several risk factors have been identified to increase vulnerability, including reduced executive functioning and stronger AOE. Additional risk factors are gender (being male), personality features (sensation seeking, poor anger control, lack of empathy), beliefs about aggression (approval of aggression as an acceptable social interaction), and motives for drinking (drinking to enhance experience or to cope) (Cheong & Nagoshi, 1999; Giancola, 2004; Giancola et al., 2009; Giancola & Zeichner, 1995; Godlaski & Giancola, 2009; Ito et al., 1996; Mihic, Wells, Graham, Tremblay, & Demers, 2009; Parrott & Zeichner, 2002). Several situational features also interact with individual risk factors, such as environmental context (being in a bar instead of being at home), provocation, threat, and social pressure (Giancola et al., 2002; Taylor et al., 1976; Taylor, Schmutte, Leonard, & Cranston, 1979; Taylor & Sears, 1988).

Genetic studies in humans show that modulations in serotonergic neurotransmission play an important role in the manifestation of aggression (see Chapter 3). For example, 5-HTTLPR has been associated with increased activation of the amygdala when exposed to aversive versus neutral stimuli, and was also correlated with higher risk of depression and negative mood states (Caspi et al., 2002; A. Heinz et al., 2005; Karg, Burmeister, Shedden, & Sen, 2011; Pezawas et al., 2005; Risch et al., 2009), which appears to increase feelings of being threatened and facilitate aggression (Knutson et al., 1998). Another genetic variation that affects serotonergic neurotransmission, a single mutation in the gene that encodes monoamine oxidase A (MAO-A), has been associated with criminal behavior among individuals with early life trauma (Brunner, Nelen, Breakefield, Ropers, & van Oost, 1993; Kim-Cohen et al., 2006).

A meta-analysis suggested that the MAO-A genotype is associated with alcohol intake and negative mood states, such as depression and anxiety (Saraceno, Munafo, Heron, Craddock, & van den Bree, 2009). Importantly, MAO-A is located on the X chromosome, which might help account for the higher prevalence of alcohol-related aggression observed among males. A recent study focused on another genetic variation of serontonergic neurotransmission, the 5-HT2B receptor, also reported an association with alcohol-associated aggression. Specifically, a stop codon in the HTR2B gene, which blocks the expression of the 5-HT2B receptor in the frontal cortex, was associated with impulsive behavior in violent offenders, who mainly became aggressive when being intoxicated with alcohol (Bevilacqua et al., 2010).

In rodents, modulations in neurotransmission of dopamine and serotonin have been associated with impulsivity and initiation of aggressive behavior (Chiavegatto, Quadros, Ambar, & Miczek, 2010; Dalley et al., 2007; de Almeida et al., 2005; van Erp & Miczek, 2007) (see Chapter 3). Similar to humans, variation in monoaminergic neurotransmission seems to distinguish between mice with, and without, alcohol-heightened aggression. Chiavegatto et al. (2010) described an association of alcohol-related aggression and a reduced expression of serotonin receptors in the prefrontal cortex of mice. The reduced expression of serotonin receptors was described for all receptor subtypes, except for 5-HT3 receptors. Given that other studies have observed decreased levels of serotonin in the frontal cortex during confrontation, these findings support the hypothesis that prefrontal cortical serotonin deficits are associated with aggressive behavior, including alcohol-related aggression (van Erp & Miczek, 2000).

GABAergic interactions with serotonin neurotransmission appear to confer vulnerability for aggressive behavior (Chiavegatto et al., 2010; A. J. Heinz, Beck, Meyer-Lindenberg, Sterzer, & Heinz, 2011). GABA release is induced by alcohol consumption, and the application of GABA-B agonist in the dorsal raphe area leads to an aggressive reaction (independent of alcohol intake). This effect can be blocked by a 5-HT1A agonist, which activates auto-receptors that inhibit serotonergic projections that appear to be modulated by alcohol-induced GABA release (Takahashi, Kwa, et al., 2010; Takahashi, Shimamoto, et al., 2010). The specific localization of the application of GABA-B or 5-HT1B agonists seems to be of significant relevance: for example, the application of a 5-HT1B agonist in the medial prefrontal cortex increases aggressive behavior in mice with a history of alcohol self-administration and was associated with a blunted prefrontal serotonin release (Faccidomo, Bannai, & Miczek, 2008). Altogether, these findings confirm the hypothesis that alcohol intake interacts with serotonergic neurotransmission and expression patterns of specific serotonin receptors in the medial prefrontal cortex and that interaction of GABAergic neurons with different serotonin receptors are of relevance in alcohol-related aggression. In rodents, GABA release in the frontal cortex is induced by agonists of 5-HT2A and 5-HT3 receptors (Cai, Flores-Hernandez, Feng, & Yan, 2002; Fink & Gothert, 2007). By interacting with GABAergic and serotonergic neurotransmission, alcohol appears to contribute to aggressive behavior partially via its effects on prefrontal cortex functioning (Chiavegatto et al., 2010; Takahashi, Kwa, et al., 2010; Takahashi, Shimamoto, et al., 2010).

Research in primates has also demonstrated that individual differences in serotonergic neurotransmission increase vulnerability for aggressive behavior under alcohol. Several studies in rhesus monkeys have shown a long-term reduction in central serotonergic neurotransmission in response to environmental factors such as early social isolation, which is associated with both increased alcohol intake and violent behavior (Clarke et al., 1996; Higley, Suomi, & Linnoila, 1996a, 1996b; Jones, Hernandez, Kendall, Marsden, & Robbins, 1992). Reduced serotonin turnover rates and absolute serotonin transporter density were correlated with higher levels of aggression, impaired social competence, and increased anxiety (A. Heinz et al., 1998; Hummerich et al., 2004; Ichise et al., 2006). Further studies in rhesus monkeys have confirmed robust evidence for an interplay of serotonergic and GABAergic neurotransmission in the prefrontal cortex: monkeys with a low serotonin turnover (low concentration of 5-HIAA in the cerebral spinal fluid) were less sensitive to stimulation of GABA-A receptors in the prefrontal cortex (Doudet et al., 1995; A. Heinz et al., 1998; A. Heinz, Mann, Weinberger, & Goldman, 2001). Importantly, low concentration of 5-HIAA in the cerebral spinal fluid was associated with aggressive behavior and other behavioral patterns similar to those observed in individuals with early onset alcoholism (A. Heinz et al., 1998). Low levels of 5-HIAA in the cerebral spinal fluid have also been documented in rhesus monkeys exposed to social stress and isolation (A. Heinz et al., 1998; A. Heinz et al., 2004).

Given that GABA-A receptor stimulation is reduced in rhesus monkeys with a low serotonin turnover (following social isolation) and alcohol is a GABA-A receptor sensitivity, the sedative and inhibitory effect of alcohol are reduced in rhesus monkeys exposed to social isolation. Indeed, these monkeys were less ataxic and sedated under alcohol (Hinckers et al., 2006; Schuckit, 1994). Importantly, a low level of sedation after alcohol consumption appears to predispose individuals to excessive alcohol intake

(Hinckers et al., 2006; Schuckit, 1994). It has been argued, that the level of alcohol-associated sedation is also partially hereditary and that these individuals lack an internal warning sign to signal that too much alcohol is consumed (A. J. Heinz et al., 2011). In line with these findings, rhesus monkeys with low serotonin turnover and associated alterations of 5-HTT availability, demonstrated increased levels of alcohol intake (A. Heinz et al., 2003). Hinckers et al. described similar finding in humans: among adolescents, a 5-HTT genotype (s-carriers) more sensitive to social stress, was associated with increased consumption of alcohol as well as a low response to alcohol (Hinckers et al., 2006).

In summary, these findings suggest that serotonergic neurotransmission and alcohol intake are influenced by both genetic constitution and environmental factors, such as early social isolation experiences (A. Heinz et al., 2000). Social stress directly impacts serotonergic neurotransmission, for example, in the prefrontal cortex, and may thus facilitate violent behavior and excessive alcohol consumption (Clarke et al., 1996; A. Heinz et al., 2001; Higley, Suomi, & Linnoila, 1991; Higley et al., 1993). These findings highlight the importance of early social stress and subsequently the necessity of therapeutic treatment for children exposed to maltreatment. Box 17.2 summarizes some of the research on the relationship between alcohol and aggressive behavior.

> **Box 17.2 Aggressive behavior and chronic alcohol consumption**
>
> - Chronic alcohol intake exerts a substantial influence on neurotransmission and associated cognitive processes in a number of ways. In turn, it increases the likelihood of engaging in aggressive and violent behavior. Interestingly, some changes in neurotransmission, such as reduction in serotonin transporter level, are reversible after detoxification from alcohol (this effect has only been shown in non-smokers) (Cosgrove et al., 2009; A. J. Heinz et al., 2011).
> - Human adoption and twin studies also suggest that there is a common hereditary factor for alcohol use disorders and violent behavior. These studies observed an association between both aggressive behavior and alcohol use disorders, but failed to find significant heritability for aggressive behavior independent of alcohol use disorders (Bohman, Cloninger, Sigvardsson, & von Knorring, 1982; Carey, 1996; Johnson, van den Bree, & Pickens, 1996).
> - There is also evidence that chronic alcohol dependence in individuals with early onset of the disease and a genetic disposition towards dependence is associated with lower levels of serotonin metabolites (such as 5-HIAA in the cerebrospinal fluid) and higher aggressive behavior (Bohman, Cloninger, Sigvardsson, & von Knorring, 1987; Cloninger, 1987; Virkkunen et al., 1994).
> - Another aspect that may contribute to alcohol-associated violence is impulsive decision making. Indeed, some individuals with alcohol dependence demonstrated dysfunctional reward expectation such that they prefer smaller immediate rewards over larger delayed rewards (MacKillop et al., 2011;

Moeller, Barratt, Dougherty, Schmitz, & Swann, 2001). This type of impulsivity is called impaired delay discounting and was associated with a number of social problems and an early onset of dependence (Bechara, 2005; A. Heinz et al., 2001). Individuals with problematic alcohol use often fail to consider long-term outcomes of their behavior, and focus rather on the immediate consequences of their decisions (i.e., poor risk forecasting). Several studies confirmed higher rates of impulsive behavior and impulse control disorders among alcohol-dependent individuals compared to healthy controls (Lejoyeux, Feuche, Loi, Solomon, & Ades, 1998; Rubio et al., 2008; Virkkunen et al., 1994).

- On a neurobiological level, impaired reward expectation has been associated with alterations in the dopamine system (i.e., low D2 receptor availability in the ventral striatum), which is associated with heightened impulsive behavior in rodents (Dalley et al., 2007). In both animals and humans, chronic alcohol intake has been shown to reduce D2 receptor sensitivity and availability (A. Heinz et al., 1996; Rommelspacher, Raeder, Kaulen, & Bruning, 1992; Volkow et al., 1996). Alterations in dopaminergic neurotransmission in the ventral striatum can also interfere with the expectation of rewards (Schlagenhauf et al., 2013): a functional magnetic resonance imaging (fMRI) study reported decreased activity in the ventral striatum and enhanced impulsive decision making in detoxified alcohol-dependent individuals compared to healthy controls when processing reward cues (Beck et al., 2009). These findings suggest that alcohol-dependent individuals can have difficulties maintaining reward expectation, which may result in increased delay discounting.
- Reduced sensitivity in the ventral striatum, a critical region of the reward system, may predispose individuals to increased reward-seeking behavior, especially for immediate rewards like alcohol consumption, but also to involvement in risky and violent behavior (Corte & Sommers, 2005). Given that measures of impulsivity have been associated with violent behavior, impulsivity is believed to function as an important mediating factor between alcohol consumption and aggression (Edwards, Scott, Yarvis, Paizis, & Panizzon, 2003; McCloskey, Lee, Berman, Noblett, & Coccaro, 2008). Interestingly, both chronic and acute alcohol intake seem to affect cognitive and behavioral facets of impulsivity, such as delay discounting, response inhibition, and rapid changing intentions (Barratt, 1982; Dougherty, Marsh-Richard, Hatzis, Nouvion, & Mathias, 2008; Marczinski, Combs, & Fillmore, 2007).
- Animal studies have shown that both serotonin and dopamine turnover rates increase after chronic alcohol consumption. These findings implicate that low serotonin and dopamine turnover rates potentially predisposing to excessive alcohol intake in non-human primates are counteracted by alcohol-induced dopamine and serotonin release in alcohol-preferring animals (A. Heinz et al., 1998; A. Heinz et al., 2001; LeMarquand, Pihl, & Benkelfat, 1994). In the prefrontal cortex serotonin release appears to facilitate GABAergic inhibition, however, animals predisposed to alcohol-associated aggression showed a blunted serotonin release after application of 5-HT1B agonist (Faccidomo

et al., 2008). Correspondingly, a challenge with the substance fenfluramine, which increases serotonin release, has been found to blunt activation in the prefrontal cortex in human subjects who demonstrated impulsive aggression, indicating an impairment of serotonergic modulation in this area (Siever et al., 1999). This suggests that chronic alcohol intake among individuals predisposed to alcohol-heightened aggression can interact with serotonergic neurotransmission in the prefrontal cortex and thus increase the likelihood of impaired behavioral control.

- Indeed, animal and human studies indicate that dysfunction in serotonergic neurotransmission interacts with cognitive functions associated with the prefrontal cortex, such as behavioral control, response inhibition, and flexible behavior adaption, which are critical for managing socially provocative situations (Chamberlain et al., 2006; Clarke et al., 1996). Indeed, several comprehensive reviews of imaging and neuropsychological studies have described varying degrees of frontal lobe dysfunctions in individuals with alcohol dependence (Bates et al., 2013; Giancola, 2004; Loeber et al., 2010; Moselhy, Georgiou, & Kahn, 2001; Stavro et al., 2013; Sullivan et al., 2000).
- Beyond dysregulation in prefrontal functioning, impairment in serotonergic functions plays a role in development of affective disorders and increased rates of suicidal attempts (A. Heinz et al., 2001; Mann et al., 1996). It also has been suggested that serotonergic dysfunction may interfere with processing of threatening cues and predispose individuals to respond more aggressively to aversive environmental stimuli (A. Heinz et al., 2001; A. J. Heinz et al., 2011). Serotonin dysfunction may thus increase limbic processing of aversive stimuli, increase anxiety and feeling of being threatened and facilitate aggressive behavior (A. J. Heinz et al., 2011). A double-blind, placebo-controlled study showed that a selective serotonin reuptake-inhibitor (SSRI, Fluoxetine), which increases synaptic serotonin concentration, reduces aggressive behavior and anger in perpetrators of domestic violence with alcohol dependence (George et al., 2011). In healthy controls, application of SSRI reduced aggression by lowering negative mood states such as anxiety and dysphoria (Knutson et al., 1998). Further prospective studies are needed to identify the exact neurobiological factors linked to aggression and alcohol consumption, and to determine whether chronic alcohol consumption or excessive alcohol intake predispose to violent behavior via impairment in serotonergic neurotransmission and its effects on affective and cognitive functioning.

Summary and Future Direction

Alcohol-related aggression is characterized by a number of interacting factors, including social learning, early experiences, memory and contextual influences, and an alteration of neurotransmitters and their effects on brain areas, such as frontal and limbic areas. There is evidence for acute effects on prefrontal cortex, executive functioning, and disinhibited process of the limbic system on threatening cues. Individual differences in alcohol-associated aggression seem to be partly mediated by differences in functioning of the serotonergic and GABAergic system, which are highly vulnerable to early social isolation (A. J. Heinz et al., 2011). Aggressive behavior may be further augmented by altered decision processes following regular alcohol intake with a tendency towards increased discounting of delayed rewards. Environmental factors, such as early life stress, interact with genetic variations within these systems suggesting an important role of gene–environment interactions for aggressive behavior and alcohol consumption as well (A. Heinz et al., 2001). However, to date most studies were carried out in animal models, and human studies confirming individual differences predisposing to alcohol-associated aggression are widely lacking.

Note

1 See http://ojp.gov.

Recommended Reading

Beck, A., Schlagenhauf, F., Wustenberg, T., Hein, J., Kienast, T., Kahnt, T., ... Wrase, J. (2009). Ventral striatal activation during reward anticipation correlates with impulsivity in alcoholics. [Research Support, Non-US Gov't]. *Biological Psychiatry*, 66(8), 734–742. doi: 10.1016/j.biopsych.2009.04.035. *This fMRI study among patients with alcohol dependence demonstrates that neural activation elicited by reward anticipation in the ventral striatum is reduced in patients after detoxification.*

Caspi, A., McClay, J., Moffitt, T. E., Mill, J., Martin, J., Craig, I. W., ... Poulton, R. (2002). Role of genotype in the cycle of violence in maltreated children. [Research Support, Non-US Gov't Research Support, US Gov't, P. H. S.]. *Science*, 297(5582), 851–854. doi: 10.1126/science.1072290. *A landmark study describing a gene–environment interaction in humans. The study shows that humans with a genotype conferring high levels of MAO-A expression were less likely to develop aggressive behavior.*

Faccidomo, S., Bannai, M., & Miczek, K. A. (2008). Escalated aggression after alcohol drinking in male mice: Dorsal raphe and prefrontal cortex serotonin and 5-HT(1B) receptors. [Research Support, N. I. H., Extramural Research Support, Non-US Gov't]. *Neuropsychopharmacology*, 33(12), 2888–2899. doi: 10.1038/npp.2008. *This animal study describes serotonin release in prefrontal brain regions after 5-HT1B receptor stimulation in mice with alcohol-heightened aggression.*

Heinz, A. J., Beck, A., Meyer-Lindenberg, A., Sterzer, P., & Heinz, A. (2011). Cognitive and neurobiological mechanisms of alcohol-related aggression. [Review]. *Nature Reviews Neuroscience*, 12(7), 400–413. doi: 10.1038/nrn3042. *This multidisciplinary review provides several layers of cognitive and neurobiological evidence to help explicate the pathways by which individuals with problematic alcohol use are at increased risk for impulsive and aggressive behavior.*

Heinz, A., Higley, J. D., Gorey, J. G., Saunders, R. C., Jones, D. W., Hommer, D., ... Linnoila, M. (1998). In vivo association between alcohol intoxication, aggression, and serotonin transporter availability in nonhuman primates. [Research Support, Non-US Gov't]. *American Journal of Psychiatry*, 155(8), 1023–1028. *This PET study in monkeys who experienced parental separation after birth shows that variables indicating a low serotonin turnover rate were associated with behavior patterns similar to those predisposing to early onset alcoholism among humans.*

References

Adolphs, R. (2009). The social brain: Neural basis of social knowledge. [Research Support, N. I. H., Extramural Research Support, Non-US Gov't Review]. *Annual Review of Psychology, 60*, 693–716. doi: 10.1146/annurev.psych.60.110707.163514.

Amaral, D. G., & Price, J. L. (1984). Amygdalo-cortical projections in the monkey (Macaca fascicularis). [Research Support, Non-US Gov't Research Support, US Gov't, P. H. S.]. *Journal of Comparative Neurology, 230*(4), 465–496. doi: 10.1002/cne.902300402.

Arseneault, L., Moffitt, T. E., Caspi, A., Taylor, P. J., & Silva, P. A. (2000). Mental disorders and violence in a total birth cohort: Results from the Dunedin Study. [Research Support, Non-US Gov't]. *Archives of General Psychiatry, 57*(10), 979–986.

Bailey, D., Leonard, K., Cranston, J., & Taylor, S. (1983). Effects of alcohol and self-awareness on human physical aggression. *Personality and Social Psychology Bulletin, 9*, 289–295.

Bandura, A. (1977). *Social learning theory.* New York, NY: General Learning Press.

Barbas, H. (2000). Connections underlying the synthesis of cognition, memory, and emotion in primate prefrontal cortices. [Research Support, US Gov't, P. H. S. Review]. *Brain Research Bulletin, 52*(5), 319–330.

Barratt, E. S. (1982). Impulsivity, behavioral dyscontrol, and conscious awareness. *Behavior Motor Control Psychiatric Disorder, S04,* 217.

Bartholow, B. D., & Heinz, A. (2006). Alcohol and aggression without consumption. Alcohol cues, aggressive thoughts, and hostile perception bias. *Psychological Science, 17*(1), 30–37. doi: 10.1111/j.1467-9280.2005.01661.x.

Bates, M. E., Buckman, J. F., & Nguyen, T. T. (2013). A role for cognitive rehabilitation in increasing the effectiveness of treatment for alcohol use disorders. [Research Support, American Recovery and Reinvestment Act Research Support, N. I. H., Extramural]. *Neuropsychology Review, 23*(1), 27–47. doi: 10.1007/s11065-013-9228-3.

Bechara, A. (2005). Decision making, impulse control and loss of willpower to resist drugs: A neurocognitive perspective. [Research Support, N. I. H., Extramural Review]. *Nature Neuroscience, 8*(11), 1458–1463. doi: 10.1038/nn1584.

Beck, A., Schlagenhauf, F., Wustenberg, T., Hein, J., Kienast, T., Kahnt, T., ... Wrase, J. (2009). Ventral striatal activation during reward anticipation correlates with impulsivity in alcoholics. [Research Support, Non-US Gov't]. *Biological Psychiatry, 66*(8), 734–742. doi: 10.1016/j.biopsych.2009.04.035.

Bevilacqua, L., Doly, S., Kaprio, J., Yuan, Q., Tikkanen, R., Paunio, T., ... Goldman, D. (2010). A population-specific HTR2B stop codon predisposes to severe impulsivity. [Research Support, N. I. H., Extramural Research Support, N. I. H., Intramural Research Support, Non-US Gov't]. *Nature, 468*(7327), 1061–1066. doi: 10.1038/nature09629.

Birbaumer, N., Veit, R., Lotze, M., Erb, M., Hermann, C., Grodd, W., & Flor, H. (2005). Deficient fear conditioning in psychopathy: A functional magnetic resonance imaging study. [Comparative Study Research Support, Non-US Gov't]. *Archives of General Psychiatry, 62*(7), 799–805. doi: 10.1001/archpsyc.62.7.799.

Boden, J. M., Fergusson, D. M., & Horwood, L. J. (2012). Alcohol misuse and violent behavior: Findings from a 30-year longitudinal study. [Research Support, Non-US Gov't]. *Drug and Alcohol Dependance, 122*(1–2), 135–141. doi: 10.1016/j.drugalcdep.2011.09.023.

Bohman, M., Cloninger, C. R., Sigvardsson, S., & von Knorring, A. L. (1982). Predisposition to petty criminality in Swedish adoptees. I. Genetic and environmental heterogeneity. [Research Support, Non-US Gov't Research Support, US Gov't, P. H. S.]. *Archives of General Psychiatry, 39*(11), 1233–1241.

Bohman, M., Cloninger, R., Sigvardsson, S., & von Knorring, A. L. (1987). The genetics of alcoholisms and related disorders. [Research Support, Non-US Gov't Research Support, US Gov't, P. H. S. Review]. *Journal of Psychiatric Research, 21*(4), 447–452.

Brown, S. A. (1985). Reinforcement expectancies and alcoholism treatment outcome after a one-year follow-up. [Research Support, US Gov't, P. H. S.]. *Journal of Studies on Alcohol and Drugs, 46*(4), 304–308.

Brunner, H. G., Nelen, M., Breakefield, X. O., Ropers, H. H., & van Oost, B. A. (1993). Abnormal behavior associated with a point mutation in the structural gene for monoamine oxidase A. [Research Support, US Gov't, P. H. S.]. *Science, 262*(5133), 578–580.

Byrnes, J. M., Doran, C. M., & Shakeshaft, A. P. (2012). Cost per incident of alcohol-related crime in New South Wales. *Drug and Alcohol Review, 31*, 854–860.

Caetano, R., Schafer, J., & Cunradi, C. B. (2001). Alcohol-related intimate partner violence among white, black, and Hispanic couples in the United States. [Comparative Study Research Support, US Gov't, P. H. S.]. *Alcohol Research and Health, 25*(1), 58–65.

Cai, X., Flores-Hernandez, J., Feng, J., & Yan, Z. (2002). Activity-dependent bidirectional regulation of GABA(A) receptor channels by the 5 HT4 receptor-mediated signalling in rat prefrontal cortical pyramidal neurons. *Journal of Physiology, 540*, 743–759.

Carey, G. (1996). Family and genetic epidemiology of aggressive and antisocial behavior. In D. M. S. R. B. Cairns (Ed.), *Aggression and violence: Genetic, neurobiological, and biosocial perspectives* (pp. 3–21). New Jersey: Lawrence Earlbaum Associates.

Caspi, A., McClay, J., Moffitt, T. E., Mill, J., Martin, J., Craig, I. W., ... Poulton, R. (2002). Role of genotype in the cycle of violence in maltreated children. [Research Support, Non-US Gov't Research Support, US Gov't, P. H. S.]. *Science, 297*(5582), 851–854. doi: 10.1126/science.1072290.

Chamberlain, S. R., Muller, U., Blackwell, A. D., Clark, L., Robbins, T. W., & Sahakian, B. J. (2006). Neurochemical modulation of response inhibition and probabilistic learning in humans. [Controlled Clinical Trial Research Support, Non-US Gov't]. *Science, 311*(5762), 861–863. doi: 10.1126/science.1121218.

Cheong, J., & Nagoshi, C. T. (1999). Effects of sensation seeking, instruction set, and alcohol/placebo administration on aggressive behavior. [Clinical Trial Randomized Controlled Trial]. *Alcohol, 17*(1), 81–86.

Chermack, S. T., & Blow, F. C. (2002). Violence among individuals in substance abuse treatment: The role of alcohol and cocaine consumption. [Clinical Trial Comparative Study Randomized Controlled Trial Research Support, US Gov't, P. H. S.]. *Drug and Alcohol Dependence, 66*(1), 29–37.

Chermack, S. T., & Giancola, P. R. (1997). The relation between alcohol and aggression: An integrated biopsychosocial conceptualization. [Review]. *Clinical Psychology Review, 17*(6), 621–649.

Chermack, S. T., Grogan-Kaylor, A., Perron, B. E., Murray, R. L., De Chavez, P., & Walton, M. A. (2010). Violence among men and women in substance use disorder treatment: A multi-level event-based analysis. [Randomized Controlled Trial Research Support, N. I. H., Extramural Research Support, Non-US Gov't]. *Drug and Alcohol Dependence, 112*(3), 194–200. doi: 10.1016/j.drugalcdep.2010.06.005.

Chiavegatto, S., Quadros, I. M., Ambar, G., & Miczek, K. A. (2010). Individual vulnerability to escalated aggressive behavior by a low dose of alcohol: Decreased serotonin receptor mRNA in the prefrontal cortex of male mice. [Research Support, N. I. H., Extramural Research Support, Non-US Gov't]. *Genes, Brain and Behavior, 9*(1), 110–119. doi: 10.1111/j.1601-183X.2009.00544.x.

Clarke, A. S., Hedeker, D. R., Ebert, M. H., Schmidt, D. E., McKinney, W. T., & Kraemer, G. W. (1996). Rearing experience and biogenic amine activity in infant rhesus monkeys. [Research Support, Non-US Gov't]. *Biological Psychiatry, 40*(5), 338–352. doi: 10.1016/0006-3223(95)00663-X.

Cloninger, C. R. (1987). Neurogenetic adaptive mechanisms in alcoholism. [Research Support, Non-US Gov't Research Support, US Gov't, P. H. S.]. *Science, 236*(4800), 410–416.

Coccaro, E. F., McCloskey, M. S., Fitzgerald, D. A., & Phan, K. L. (2007). Amygdala and orbitofrontal reactivity to social threat in individuals with impulsive aggression. [Comparative Study Research Support, N. I. H., Extramural Research Support, Non-US Gov't]. *Biological Psychiatry, 62*(2), 168–178. doi: 10.1016/j.biopsych.2006.08.024.

Coid, J., Yang, M., Roberts, A., Ullrich, S., Moran, P., Bebbington, P., ... Singleton, N. (2006). Violence and psychiatric morbidity in the national household population of Britain: Public health implications. *British Journal of Psychiatry, 189*, 12–19. doi: 10.1192/bjp.189.1.12.

Collins, A. M., & Loftus, E. F. (1975). A spreading activation theory of semantic processing. *Psychological Review, 82*, 407–428.

Collins, J. J., & Messerschmidt, P. M. (1993). Epidemiology of alcohol-related violence. *Alcohol Health Res World, 17*, 93–100.

Collins, J. J., & Schlenger, W. E. (1988). Acute and chronic effects of alcohol use on violence. [Research Support, US Gov't, P. H. S.]. *Journal of Studies on Alcohol and Drugs, 49*(6), 516–521.

Corte, C. M., & Sommers, M. S. (2005). Alcohol and risky behaviors. [Research Support, US Gov't, P. H. S. Review]. *Annual Review of Nursing Research, 23*, 327–360.

Cosgrove, K. P., Krantzler, E., Frohlich, E. B., Stiklus, S., Pittman, B., Tamagnan, G. D., ... Staley, J. K. (2009). Dopamine and serotonin transporter availability during acute alcohol withdrawal: Effects of comorbid tobacco smoking. [Research Support, N. I. H., Extramural Research Support, US Gov't, Non-P. H. S.]. *Neuropsychopharmacology, 34*(10), 2218–2226. doi: 10.1038/npp.2009.49.

Dalley, J. W., Fryer, T. D., Brichard, L., Robinson, E. S., Theobald, D. E., Laane, K., ... Robbins, T. W. (2007). Nucleus accumbens D2/3 receptors predict trait impulsivity and cocaine reinforcement. [Research Support, Non-US Gov't]. *Science, 315*(5816), 1267–1270. doi: 10.1126/science.1137073.

Darke, S. (2010). The toxicology of homicide offenders and victims: A review. [Research Support, Non-US Gov't Review]. *Drug and Alcohol Review, 29*(2), 202–215. doi: 10.1111/j.1465-3362.2009.00099.x.

de Almeida, R. M., Ferrari, P. F., Parmigiani, S., & Miczek, K. A. (2005). Escalated aggressive behavior: Dopamine, serotonin and GABA. [Review]. *European Journal of Pharmacology, 526*(1–3), 51–64. doi: 10.1016/j.ejphar.2005.10.004.

Diana, M., Gessa, G. L., & Rossetti, Z. L. (1992). Lack of tolerance to ethanol-induced stimulation of mesolimbic dopamine system. *Alcohol and Alcoholism, 27*(4), 329–333.

Doudet, D., Hommer, D., Higley, J. D., Andreason, P. J., Moneman, R., Suomi, S. J., & Linnoila, M. (1995). Cerebral glucose metabolism, CSF 5-HIAA levels, and aggressive behavior in rhesus monkeys. *American Journal of Psychiatry, 152*(12), 1782–1787.

Dougherty, D. M., Marsh-Richard, D. M., Hatzis, E. S., Nouvion, S. O., & Mathias, C. W. (2008). A test of alcohol dose effects on multiple behavioral measures of impulsivity. [Comparative Study Research Support, N. I. H., Extramural]. *Drug and Alcohol Dependence, 96*(1–2), 111–120. doi: 10.1016/j.drugalcdep.2008.02.002.

Easdon, C. M., & Vogel-Sprott, M. (2000). Alcohol and behavioral control: Impaired response inhibition and flexibility in social drinkers. [Clinical Trial Controlled Clinical Trial]. *Experimental and Clinical Psychopharmacology, 8*(3), 387–394.

Edwards, D. W., Scott, C. L., Yarvis, R. M., Paizis, C. L., & Panizzon, M. S. (2003). Impulsiveness, impulsive aggression, personality disorder, and spousal violence. *Violence and Victims, 18*(1), 3–14.

Faccidomo, S., Bannai, M., & Miczek, K. A. (2008). Escalated aggression after alcohol drinking in male mice: Dorsal raphe and prefrontal cortex serotonin and 5-HT(1B) receptors. [Research Support, N. I. H., Extramural Research Support, Non-US Gov't]. *Neuropsychopharmacology, 33*(12), 2888–2899. doi: 10.1038/npp.2008.7.

Fals-Stewart, W. (2003). The occurrence of partner physical aggression on days of alcohol consumption: A longitudinal diary study. *Journal of Consulting and Clinical Psychology, 71*, 41–52.

Fergusson, D. M., & Horwood, L. J. (2000). Alcohol abuse and crime: A fixed-effects regression analysis. [Research Support, Non-US Gov't]. *Addiction, 95*(10), 1525–1536.

Fink, K. B., & Gothert, M. (2007). 5-HT receptor regulation of neurotransmitter release. [Research Support, Non-US Gov't Review]. *Pharmacology Review, 59*(4), 360–417. doi: 10.1124/pr.107.07103.

Finn, P. R., Justus, A., Mazas, C., & Steinmetz, J. E. (1999). Working memory, executive processes and the effects of alcohol on Go/No-Go learning: Testing a model of behavioral regulation and impulsivity. [Research Support, US Gov't, P. H. S.]. *Psychopharmacology (Berl), 146*(4), 465–472.

Foran, H. M., & O'Leary, K. D. (2008). Alcohol and intimate partner violence: A meta-analytic review. [Meta-Analysis Review]. *Clinical Psychology Review, 28*(7), 1222–1234. doi: 10.1016/j.cpr.2008.05.001.

Fromme, K., Stroot, E. A., & Kaplan, D. (1993). Comprehensive effects of alcohol: Development and psychometric assessment of a new expectancy questionnaire. *Psychological Assessment, 5*, 19–26.

George, D. T., Phillips, M. J., Lifshitz, M., Lionetti, T. A., Spero, D. E., Ghassemzedeh, N., ... Rawlings, R. R. (2011). Fluoxetine treatment of alcoholic perpetrators of domestic violence: A 12-week, double-blind, randomized, placebo-controlled intervention study. [Comparative Study Randomized Controlled Trial]. *Journal of Clinical Psychiatry, 72*(1), 60–65. doi: 10.4088/JCP.09m05256gry.

Giancola, P. R. (2000). Executive functioning: A conceptual framework for alcohol-related aggression. [Research Support, Non-US Gov't Research Support, US Gov't, P. H. S.]. *Experimental and Clinical Psychopharmacology, 8*(4), 576–597.

Giancola, P. R. (2004). Executive functioning and alcohol-related aggression. [Research Support, US Gov't, P. H. S.]. *Journal of Abnormal Psychology, 113*(4), 541–555. doi: 10.1037/0021-843X.113.4.541.

Giancola, P. R., & Corman, M. D. (2007). Alcohol and aggression: A test of the attention-allocation model. [Research Support, N. I. H., Extramural]. *Psychological Science, 18*(7), 649–655. doi: 10.1111/j.1467-9280.2007.01953.x.

Giancola, P. R., Helton, E. L., Osborne, A. B., Terry, M. K., Fuss, A. M., & Westerfield, J. A. (2002). The effects of alcohol and provocation on aggressive behavior in men and women. [Comparative Study Research Support, Non-US Gov't esearch Support, US Gov't, P. H. S.]. *Journal of Studies on Alcohol and Drugs, 63*(1), 64–73.

Giancola, P. R., Levinson, C. A., Corman, M. D., Godlaski, A. J., Morris, D. H., Phillips, J. P., & Holt, J. C. (2009). Men and women, alcohol and aggression. [Randomized Controlled Trial Research Support, N. I. H., Extramural]. *Experimental and Clinical Psychopharmacology, 17*(3), 154–164. doi: 10.1037/a0016385.

Giancola, P. R., & Moss, H. B. (1998). Executive cognitive functioning in alcohol use disorders. [Review]. *Recent Developments in Alcohol, 14*, 227–251.

Giancola, P. R., & Zeichner, A. (1995). An investigation of gender differences in alcohol-related aggression. [Clinical Trial Randomized Controlled Trial]. *Journal of Studies on Alcohol and Drugs, 56*(5), 573–579.

Godlaski, A. J., & Giancola, P. R. (2009). Executive functioning, irritability, and alcohol-related aggression. [Controlled Clinical Trial Research Support, N. I. H., Extramural]. *Psychology of Addictive Behaviors, 23*(3), 391–403. doi: 10.1037/a0016582.

Goldman, M. S. (1999). Expectancy operation: Cognitive-neural models and architectures. In L. Kirsch (Ed.), *How expectancies shape experience* (pp. 41–63). Washington, DC: American Psychological Association.

Goldman, M. S., Brown, S. A., & Christiansen, B. A. (1987). Expectancy Theory: Thinking about drinking. In B. K. E. Leonard (Ed.), *Psychological theories of drinking and alcoholism* (pp. 181–226). New York, NY: Guilford Press.

Goldman, M. S., Darkes, J., & Del Boca, F. K. (1999). Expectancy mediation of biopsychosocial risk for alcohol use and alcoholism. In L. Kirsch (Ed.), *How expectancies shape experience* (pp. 233–262). Washington, DC: American Psychological Association.

Goldman, M. S., Del Boca, F. K., & Darkes, J. (1999). Alcohol expectancy research: The application of cognitive neuroscience. In K. E. B. Leonard, H.T. (Ed.), *Psychological Theories of Drinking and Alcoholism* (pp. 203–246). New York: Guilford Press.

Graham, K. (1980). Theories of intoxicated aggression. *Journal of Behavioral Sciences, 12*, 141–158.

Greenfeld, L. A. (1996). *Child victimizers: Violent offenders and their victims.* US Department of Justice, Bureau of Justice Statistics, Office of Juvenile Justices and Delinquency Prevention.

Guillot, C. R., Fanning, J. R., Bullock, J. S., McCloskey, M. S., & Berman, M. E. (2010). Effects of alcohol on tests of executive functioning in men and women: A dose response examination. [Randomized Controlled Trial Research Support, N. I. H., Extramural Validation Studies]. *Experimental and Clinical Psychopharmacology, 18*(5), 409–417. doi: 10.1037/a0021053.

Hawkins, K. A., & Trobst, K. K. (2000). Frontal lobe dysfunction and aggression: Conceptual issues and research findings. *Aggression and Violent Behavior, 5*, 147–157.

Heinz, A., Beck, A., Grusser, S. M., Grace, A. A., & Wrase, J. (2009). Identifying the neural circuitry of alcohol craving and relapse vulnerability. [Review]. *Addiction Biology, 14*(1), 108–118. doi: 10.1111/j.1369-1600.2008.00136.x.

Heinz, A., Braus, D. F., Smolka, M. N., Wrase, J., Puls, I., Hermann, D., … Buchel, C. (2005). Amygdala-prefrontal coupling depends on a genetic variation of the serotonin transporter. [Research Support, Non-US Gov't]. *Nature Neuroscience, 8*(1), 20–21. doi: 10.1038/nn1366.

Heinz, A., Dufeu, P., Kuhn, S., Dettling, M., Graf, K., Kurten, I., … Schmidt, L. G. (1996). Psychopathological and behavioral correlates of dopaminergic sensitivity in alcohol-dependent patients. [Research Support, Non-US Gov't]. *Archives of General Psychiatry, 53*(12), 1123–1128.

Heinz, A., Higley, J. D., Gorey, J. G., Saunders, R. C., Jones, D. W., Hommer, D., … Linnoila, M. (1998). In vivo association between alcohol intoxication, aggression, and serotonin transporter availability in nonhuman primates. [Research Support, Non-US Gov't]. *American Journal of Psychiatry, 155*(8), 1023–1028.

Heinz, A., Jones, D. W., Gorey, J. G., Bennet, A., Suomi, S. J., Weinberger, D. R., & Higley, J. D. (2003). Serotonin transporter availability correlates with alcohol intake in non-human primates. [Research Support, Non-US Gov't Research Support, US Gov't, P. H. S.]. *Molecular Psychiatry, 8*(2), 231–234. doi: 10.1038/sj.mp.4001214.

Heinz, A., Jones, D. W., Mazzanti, C., Goldman, D., Ragan, P., Hommer, D., … Weinberger, D. R. (2000). A relationship between serotonin transporter genotype and in vivo protein expression and alcohol neurotoxicity. [Research Support, Non-US Gov't]. *Biological Psychiatry, 47*(7), 643–649.

Heinz, A., Jones, D. W., Zajicek, K., Gorey, J. G., Juckel, G., Higley, J. D., & Weinberger, D. R. (2004). Depletion and restoration of endogenous monoamines affects beta-CIT binding to serotonin but not dopamine transporters in non-human primates. [Research Support, Non-US Gov't]. *Journal of Neural Transmission Supplement* (68), 29–38.

Heinz, A., Mann, K., Weinberger, D. R., & Goldman, D. (2001). Serotonergic dysfunction, negative mood states, and response to alcohol. [Review]. *Alcoholism: Clinical and Experimental Research, 25*(4), 487–495.

Heinz, A. J., Beck, A., Meyer-Lindenberg, A., Sterzer, P., & Heinz, A. (2011). Cognitive and neurobiological mechanisms of alcohol-related aggression. [Review]. *Nature Reviews Neurosci, 12*(7), 400–413. doi: 10.1038/nrn3042.

Higley, J. D., Suomi, S. J., & Linnoila, M. (1991). CSF monoamine metabolite concentrations vary according to age, rearing, and sex, and are influenced by the stressor of social separation in rhesus monkeys. *Psychopharmacology (Berl), 103*(4), 551–556.

Higley, J. D., Suomi, S. J., & Linnoila, M. (1996a). A nonhuman primate model of type II alcoholism? Part 2. Diminished social competence and excessive aggression correlates with low cerebrospinal fluid 5-hydroxyindoleacetic acid concentrations. *Alcoholism: Clinical and Experimental Research, 20*(4), 643–650.

Higley, J. D., Suomi, S. J., & Linnoila, M. (1996b). A nonhuman primate model of type II excessive alcohol consumption? Part 1. Low cerebrospinal fluid 5-hydroxyindoleacetic acid concentrations and diminished social competence correlate with excessive alcohol consumption. *Alcoholism: Clinical and Experimental Research, 20*(4), 629–642.

Higley, J. D., Thompson, W. W., Champoux, M., Goldman, D., Hasert, M. F., Kraemer, G. W., ... Linnoila, M. (1993). Paternal and maternal genetic and environmental contributions to cerebrospinal fluid monoamine metabolites in rhesus monkeys (Macaca mulatta). *Archives of General Psychiatry, 50*(8), 615–623.

Hinckers, A. S., Laucht, M., Schmidt, M. H., Mann, K. F., Schumann, G., Schuckit, M. A., & Heinz, A. (2006). Low level of response to alcohol as associated with serotonin transporter genotype and high alcohol intake in adolescents. [Research Support, Non-US Gov't]. *Biological Psychiatry, 60*(3), 282–287. doi: 10.1016/j.biopsych.2005.12.009.

Hoaken, P. N. S., & Stewart, S. H. (2003). Drugs of abuse and the elicitation of human aggressive behavior. *Addictive Behaviors, 28*(9), 1533–1554. doi: 10.1016/j.addbeh.2003.08.033.

Hull, J. G. (1981). A self-awareness model of the causes and effects of alcohol consumption. [Research Support, US Gov't, P. H. S.]. *Journal of Abnormal Psychology, 90*(6), 586–600.

Hummerich, R., Reischl, G., Ehrlichmann, W., Machulla, H. J., Heinz, A., & Schloss, P. (2004). DASB - in vitro binding characteristics on human recombinant monoamine transporters with regard to its potential as positron emission tomography (PET) tracer. [Comparative Study Research Support, Non-US Gov't]. *Journal of Neurochemistry, 90*(5), 1218–1226. doi: 10.1111/j.1471-4159.2004.02585.x.

Ichise, M., Vines, D. C., Gura, T., Anderson, G. M., Suomi, S. J., Higley, J. D., & Innis, R. B. (2006). Effects of early life stress on [11C]DASB positron emission tomography imaging of serotonin transporters in adolescent peer- and mother-reared rhesus monkeys. [Research Support, N. I. H., Intramural]. *Journal of Neuroscience, 26*(17), 4638–4643. doi: 10.1523/JNEUROSCI.5199-05.2006.

Ito, T. A., Miller, N., & Pollock, V. E. (1996). Alcohol and aggression: A meta-analysis on the moderating effects of inhibitory cues, triggering events, and self-focused attention. [Meta-Analysis Research Support, Non-US Gov't Research Support, US Gov't, Non-P. H. S. Research Support, US Gov't, P. H. S.]. *Psychological Bulletin, 120*(1), 60–82.

Jaffe, J. H., Babor, T. F., & Fishbein, D. H. (1988). Alcoholics, aggression and antisocial personality. [Research Support, US Gov't, P. H. S.]. *Journal of Studies on Alcohol and Drugs, 49*(3), 211–218.

Johnson, E. O., van den Bree, M. B., & Pickens, R. W. (1996). Subtypes of alcohol-dependent men: A typology based on relative genetic and environmental loading. [Research Support, US Gov't, P. H. S.]. *Alcoholism: Clinical and Experimental Research, 20*(8), 1472–1480.

Jones, A. P., Laurens, K. R., Herba, C. M., Barker, G. J., & Viding, E. (2009). Amygdala hypoactivity to fearful faces in boys with conduct problems and callous-unemotional traits. [Research Support, Non-US Gov't Twin Study]. *American Journal of Psychiatry, 166*(1), 95–102. doi: 10.1176/appi.ajp.2008.07071050.

Jones, B. T., Corbin, W., & Fromme, K. (2001). A review of expectancy theory and alcohol consumption. [Research Support, US Gov't, P. H. S. Review]. *Addiction, 96*(1), 57–72. doi: 10.1080/09652140020016969.

Jones, G. H., Hernandez, T. D., Kendall, D. A., Marsden, C. A., & Robbins, T. W. (1992). Dopaminergic and serotonergic function following isolation rearing in rats: Study of behavioural responses and postmortem and in vivo neurochemistry. [Research Support, Non-US Gov't]. *Pharmacology, Biochemistry and Behavior, 43*(1), 17–35.

Karg, K., Burmeister, M., Shedden, K., & Sen, S. (2011). The serotonin transporter promoter variant (5-HTTLPR), stress, and depression meta-analysis revisited: Evidence of genetic moderation. [Meta-Analysis Research Support, N. I. H., Extramural Research Support, Non-US Gov't]. *Archives of General Psychiatry, 68*(5), 444–454. doi: 10.1001/archgenpsychiatry.2010.189.

Kim-Cohen, J., Caspi, A., Taylor, A., Williams, B., Newcombe, R., Craig, I. W., & Moffitt, T. E. (2006). MAOA, maltreatment, and gene-environment interaction predicting children's mental health: New evidence and a meta-analysis. [Comparative Study Meta-Analysis Research Support, N. I. H., Extramural Research Support, Non-US Gov't Twin Study]. *Molecular Psychiatry, 11*(10), 903–913. doi: 10.1038/sj.mp.4001851.

Knutson, B., Wolkowitz, O. M., Cole, S. W., Chan, T., Moore, E. A., Johnson, R. C., ... Reus, V. I. (1998). Selective alteration of personality and social behavior by serotonergic intervention. [Clinical Trial Randomized Controlled Trial Research Support, Non-US Gov't Research Support, US Gov't, P. H. S.]. *American Journal of Psychiatry, 155*(3), 373–379.

Lee, T. M., Chan, S. C., & Raine, A. (2008). Strong limbic and weak frontal activation to aggressive stimuli in spouse abusers. [Letter]. *Molecular Psychiatry, 13*(7), 655–656. doi: 10.1038/mp.2008.46.

Leigh, B. C., & Stacy, A. W. (1998). Individual differences in memory associations involving the positive and negative outcomes of alcohol use. *Psychology of Addictive Behaviors, 12*, 39–46.

Lejoyeux, M., Feuche, N., Loi, S., Solomon, J., & Ades, J. (1998). Impulse-control disorders in alcoholics are related to sensation seeking and not to impulsivity. *Psychiatry Research, 81*(2), 149–155.

LeMarquand, D., Pihl, R. O., & Benkelfat, C. (1994). Serotonin and alcohol intake, abuse, and dependence: Findings of animal studies. [Research Support, Non-US Gov't Review]. *Biological Psychiatry, 36*(6), 395–421.

Lipsey, M. W., Wilson, D. B., Cohen, M. A., & Derzon, J. H. (1997). Is there a causal relationship between alcohol use and violence? A synthesis of evidence. [Research Support, Non-US Gov't Review]. *Recent Developments in Alcohol, 13*, 245–282.

Loeber, S., Duka, T., Welzel Marquez, H., Nakovics, H., Heinz, A., Mann, K., & Flor, H. (2010). Effects of repeated withdrawal from alcohol on recovery of cognitive impairment under abstinence and rate of relapse. [Comparative Study Research Support, Non-US Gov't]. *Alcohol and Alcoholism, 45*(6), 541–547. doi: 10.1093/alcalc/agq065.

Lorenz, M. (2007). *Das Rad der Gewalt: Militär und Zivilbevölkerung in Norddeutschland nach dem Dreißigjährigen Krieg (1650–1700)*. Wien Köln Weimar: Böhlau.

Lundholm, L., Haggard, U., Moller, J., Hallqvist, J., & Thiblin, I. (2013). The triggering effect of alcohol and illicit drugs on violent crime in a remand prison population: A case crossover study. [Research Support, Non-US Gov't]. *Drug and Alcohol Dependence, 129*(1–2), 110–115. doi: 10.1016/j.drugalcdep.2012.09.019.

Luria, A. (1980). *Higher Cortical functions in Man*. New York: Basic Books.

Lyvers, M. F., & Maltzman, I. (1991). Selective effects of alcohol on Wisconsin Card Sorting Test performance. [Research Support, Non-US Gov't]. *British Journal of Addiction, 86*(4), 399–407.

MacKillop, J., Amlung, M. T., Few, L. R., Ray, L. A., Sweet, L. H., & Munafo, M. R. (2011). Delayed reward discounting and addictive behavior: A meta-analysis. [Meta-Analysis

Research Support, N. I. H., Extramural Research Support, Non-US Gov't]. *Psychopharmacology (Berl), 216*(3), 305–321. doi: 10.1007/s00213-011-2229-0.
Maisto, S. A., Carey, K. B., & Bradizza, C. M. (1999). Social learning theory. In K. E. Leonard & H. T. Blane (Eds.), *Psychological theories of drinking and alcoholism* (pp. 106–163). New York, NY: Guilford Press.
Mann, J. J., Malone, K. M., Sweeney, J. A., Brown, R. P., Linnoila, M., Stanley, B., & Stanley, M. (1996). Attempted suicide characteristics and cerebrospinal fluid amine metabolites in depressed inpatients. [Research Support, US Gov't, P. H. S.]. *Neuropsychopharmacology, 15*(6), 576–586. doi: 10.1016/S0893-133X(96)00102-9.
Marczinski, C. A., Combs, S. W., & Fillmore, M. T. (2007). Increased sensitivity to the disinhibiting effects of alcohol in binge drinkers. [Research Support, N. I. H., Extramural Research Support, Non-US Gov't]. *Psychology of Addictive Behaviors, 21*(3), 346–354. doi: 10.1037/0893-164X.21.3.346.
Marsh, A. A., Finger, E. C., Mitchell, D. G., Reid, M. E., Sims, C., Kosson, D. S., ... Blair, R. J. (2008). Reduced amygdala response to fearful expressions in children and adolescents with callous-unemotional traits and disruptive behavior disorders. [Research Support, N. I. H., Intramural]. *American Journal of Psychiatry, 165*(6), 712–720. doi: 10.1176/appi.ajp.2007.07071145.
Mathews, T. A., John, C. E., Lapa, G. B., Budygin, E. A., & Jones, S. R. (2006). No role of the dopamine transporter in acute ethanol effects on striatal dopamine dynamics. [Research Support, N. I. H., Extramural Research Support, Non-US Gov't]. *Synapse, 60*(4), 288–294. doi: 10.1002/syn.20301.
Mayfield, D. (1976). Alcoholism, alcohol, intoxication and assaultive behavior. *Diseases of the Nervous System, 37*(5), 288–291.
McBride, W. J. (2002). Central nucleus of the amygdala and the effects of alcohol and alcohol-drinking behavior in rodents. [Research Support, US Gov't, P. H. S. Review]. *Pharmacology, Biochemistry and Behavior, 71*(3), 509–515.
McCloskey, M. S., Lee, R., Berman, M. E., Noblett, K. L., & Coccaro, E. F. (2008). The relationship between impulsive verbal aggression and intermittent explosive disorder. [Comparative Study]. *Aggressive Behavior, 34*(1), 51–60. doi: 10.1002/ab.20216.
McKinlay, W. W., Brooks, D. N., Bond, M. R., Martinage, D. P., & Marshall, M. M. (1981). The short-term outcome of severe blunt head injury as reported by relatives of the injured persons. [Research Support, Non-US Gov't]. *Journal of Neurology, Neurosurgery and Psychiatry, 44*(6), 527–533.
Miczek, K. A., Nikulina, E. M., Takahashi, A., Covington, H. E., III, Yap, J. J., Boyson, C. O., ... de Almeida, R. M. (2011). Gene expression in aminergic and peptidergic cells during aggression and defeat: Relevance to violence, depression and drug abuse. [Research Support, N. I. H., Extramural Research Support, Non-US Gov't Review]. *Behavior Genetics, 41*(6), 787–802. doi: 10.1007/s10519-011-9462-5.
Mihic, L., Wells, S., Graham, K., Tremblay, P. F., & Demers, A. (2009). Situational and respondent-level motives for drinking and alcohol-related aggression: A multilevel analysis of drinking events in a sample of Canadian university students. [Multicenter Study Research Support, Non-US Gov't]. *Addictive Behaviors, 34*(3), 264–269. doi: 10.1016/j.addbeh.2008.10.022.
Moeller, F. G., Barratt, E. S., Dougherty, D. M., Schmitz, J. M., & Swann, A. C. (2001). Psychiatric aspects of impulsivity. [Research Support, Non-US Gov't Research Support, US Gov't, P. H. S. Review]. *American Journal of Psychiatry, 158*(11), 1783–1793.
Moselhy, H. F., Georgiou, G., & Kahn, A. (2001). Frontal lobe changes in alcoholism: A review of the literature. [Review]. *Alcohol and Alcoholism, 36*(5), 357–368.
Mulvihill, L. E., Skilling, T. A., & Vogel-Sprott, M. (1997). Alcohol and the ability to inhibit behavior in men and women. [Clinical Trial Randomized Controlled Trial Research Support, Non-US Gov't]. *Journal of Studies on Alcohol and Drugs, 58*(6), 600–605.

Murphy, C. M., Winters, J., O'Farrell, T. J., Fals-Stewart, W., & Murphy, M. (2005). Alcohol consumption and intimate partner violence by alcoholic men: Comparing violent and non-violent conflicts. [Research Support, N. I. H., Extramural Research Support, US Gov't, Non-P. H. S. Research Support, US Gov't, P. H. S.]. *Psychology of Addictive Behaviors, 19*(1), 35–42. doi: 10.1037/0893-164X.19.1.35.

Nader, M. A., & Czoty, P. W. (2005). PET imaging of dopamine D2 receptors in monkey models of cocaine abuse: Genetic predisposition versus environmental modulation. [Research Support, N. I. H., Extramural Research Support, US Gov't, P. H. S. Review]. *American Journal of Psychiatry, 162*(8), 1473–1482. doi: 10.1176/appi.ajp.162.8.1473.

Nasby, W., Hayden, B., & DePaulo, B. M. (1980). Attributional bias among aggressive boys to interpret unambiguous social stimuli as displays of hostility. *Journal of Abnormal Psychology, 89*(3), 459–468.

NCVS (2006). *National crime victimization survey.*

Nicol, A. R., Gunn, J. C., Gristwood, J., Foggitt, R. H., & Watson, J. P. (1973). The relationship of alcoholism to violent behaviour resulting in long-term imprisonment. *British Journal of Psychiatry, 123*(572), 47–51.

O'Farrell, T. J., Fals-Stewart, W., Murphy, M., & Murphy, C. M. (2003). Partner violence before and after individually based alcoholism treatment for male alcoholic patients. [Research Support, Non-US Gov't Research Support, US Gov't, Non-P. H. S. Research Support, US Gov't, P. H. S.]. *Journal of Consulting and Clinical Psychology, 71*(1), 92–102.

Parrott, D. J., & Zeichner, A. (2002). Effects of alcohol and trait anger on physical aggression in men. [Comparative Study]. *Journal of Studies on Alcohol and Drugs, 63*(2), 196–204.

Peterson, J. B., Rothfleisch, J., Zelazo, P. D., & Pihl, R. O. (1990). Acute alcohol intoxication and cognitive functioning. [Research Support, Non-US Gov't]. *Journal of Studies on Alcohol and Drugs, 51*(2), 114–122.

Pezawas, L., Meyer-Lindenberg, A., Drabant, E. M., Verchinski, B. A., Munoz, K. E., Kolachana, B. S., ... Weinberger, D. R. (2005). 5-HTTLPR polymorphism impacts human cingulate-amygdala interactions: A genetic susceptibility mechanism for depression. [Research Support, N. I. H., Intramural]. *Nature Neuroscience, 8*(6), 828–834. doi: 10.1038/nn1463.

Posner, M. I., & Petersen, S. E. (1990). The attention system of the human brain. [Research Support, Non-US Gov't Research Support, US Gov't, Non-P. H. S. Review]. *Annual Review of Neuroscience, 13*, 25–42. doi: 10.1146/annurev.ne.13.030190.000325.

Puglisi-Allegra, S., Imperato, A., Angelucci, L., & Cabib, S. (1991). Acute stress induces time-dependent responses in dopamine mesolimbic system. *Brain Research, 554*(1–2), 217–222.

Rand, M. R., Sabol, W. J., Sinclair, M., & Snyder, H. N. (2010). *Alcohol and crime: Data from 2002 to 2008.* Washington, DC: Bureau of Justice Statistics, US Department of Justice.

Rather, B. C., & Goldman, M. S. (1994). Drinking-related differences in the memory organization of alcohol expectancies. *Experimental and Clinical Psychopharmacology, 2*, 167–183.

Rather, B. C., Goldman, M. S., Roehrich, L., & Brannick, M. (1992). Empirical modeling of an alcohol expectancy memory network using multidimensional scaling. [Research Support, US Gov't, P. H. S.]. *Journal of Abnormal Psychology, 101*(1), 174–183.

Ratti, M. T., Bo, P., Giardini, A., & Soragna, D. (2002). Chronic alcoholism and the frontal lobe: Which executive functions are imparied? [Research Support, Non-US Gov't]. *Acta Neurologica Scandinavica, 105*(4), 276–281.

Ridderinkhof, K. R., de Vlugt, Y., Bramlage, A., Spaan, M., Elton, M., Snel, J., & Band, G. P. (2002). Alcohol consumption impairs detection of performance errors in mediofrontal cortex. [Clinical Trial Randomized Controlled Trial]. *Science, 298*(5601), 2209–2211. doi: 10.1126/science.1076929

Risch, N., Herrell, R., Lehner, T., Liang, K. Y., Eaves, L., Hoh, J., ... Merikangas, K. R. (2009). Interaction between the serotonin transporter gene (5-HTTLPR), stressful life events, and risk of depression: A meta-analysis. [Meta-Analysis Research Support, N. I. H.,

Extramural Research Support, N. I. H., Intramural]. *JAMA, 301*(23), 2462–2471. doi: 10.1001/jama.2009.878

Rommelspacher, H., Raeder, C., Kaulen, P., & Bruning, G. (1992). Adaptive changes of dopamine-D2 receptors in rat brain following ethanol withdrawal: A quantitative autoradiographic investigation. [Research Support, Non-US Gov't]. *Alcohol, 9*(5), 355–362.

Rubio, G., Jimenez, M., Rodriguez-Jimenez, R., Martinez, I., Avila, C., Ferre, F., ... Palomo, T. (2008). The role of behavioral impulsivity in the development of alcohol dependence: A 4-year follow-up study. [Research Support, Non-US Gov't]. *Alcoholism: Clinical and Experimental Research, 32*(9), 1681–1687. doi: 10.1111/j.1530-0277.2008.00746.x.

Saraceno, L., Munafo, M., Heron, J., Craddock, N., & van den Bree, M. B. (2009). Genetic and non-genetic influences on the development of co-occurring alcohol problem use and internalizing symptomatology in adolescence: A review. [Review]. *Addiction, 104*(7), 1100–1121. doi: 10.1111/j.1360-0443.2009.02571.x.

Schlagenhauf, F., Rapp, M. A., Huys, Q. J., Beck, A., Wustenberg, T., Deserno, L., ... Heinz, A. (2013). Ventral striatal prediction error signaling is associated with dopamine synthesis capacity and fluid intelligence. [Research Support, Non-US Gov't]. *Hum Brain Mapp, 34*(6), 1490–1499. doi: 10.1002/hbm.22000.

Schreckenberger, M., Amberg, R., Scheurich, A., Lochmann, M., Tichy, W., Klega, A., ... Urban, R. (2004). Acute alcohol effects on neuronal and attentional processing: Striatal reward system and inhibitory sensory interactions under acute ethanol challenge. [Clinical Trial Randomized Controlled Trial Research Support, Non-US Gov't]. *Neuropsychopharmacology, 29*(8), 1527–1537. doi: 10.1038/sj.npp.1300453.

Schuckit, M. A. (1994). Low level of response to alcohol as a predictor of future alcoholism. [Research Support, US Gov't, Non-P. H. S. Research Support, US Gov't, P. H. S.]. *American Journal of Psychiatry, 151*(2), 184–189.

Schuckit, M. A., & Russell, J. W. (1984). An evaluation of primary alcoholics with histories of violence. [Research Support, Non-US Gov't Research Support, US Gov't, P. H. S.]. *Journal of Clinical Psychiatry, 45*(1), 3–6.

Schweizer, T. A., Vogel-Sprott, M., Danckert, J., Roy, E. A., Skakum, A., & Broderick, C. E. (2006). Neuropsychological profile of acute alcohol intoxication during ascending and descending blood alcohol concentrations. [Clinical Trial Comparative Study Research Support, Non-US Gov't]. *Neuropsychopharmacology, 31*(6), 1301–1309. doi: 10.1038/sj.npp.1300941.

Siever, L. J., Buchsbaum, M. S., New, A. S., Spiegel-Cohen, J., Wei, T., Hazlett, E. A., ... Mitropoulou, V. (1999). d,l-fenfluramine response in impulsive personality disorder assessed with [18F]fluorodeoxyglucose positron emission tomography. [Clinical Trial Research Support, US Gov't, P. H. S.]. *Neuropsychopharmacology, 20*(5), 413–423. doi: 10.1016/S0893-133X(98)00111-0.

Smith, G. S., Branas, C. C., & Miller, T. R. (1999). Fatal nontraffic injuries involving alcohol: A metaanalysis. *Annals of Emergency Medicine, 33*, 659–668.

Stacy, A. W., Leigh, B. C., & Weingardt, K. R. (1994). Memory accessibility and association of alcohol use and its positive outcomes. *Experimental and Clinical Psychopharmacology, 2*, 269–282.

Stavro, K., Pelletier, J., & Potvin, S. (2013). Widespread and sustained cognitive deficits in alcoholism: A meta-analysis. [Research Support, Non-US Gov't]. *Addiction Biology, 18*(2), 203–213. doi: 10.1111/j.1369-1600.2011.00418.x.

Steele, C. M., & Josephs, R. A. (1990). Alcohol myopia. Its prized and dangerous effects. [Research Support, US Gov't, P. H. S. Review]. *American Psychologist, 45*(8), 921–933.

Steele, C. M., & Southwick, L. (1985). Alcohol and social behavior I: The psychology of drunken excess. [Research Support, Non-US Gov't Research Support, US Gov't, P. H. S.]. *Journal of Personaility and Social Psychology, 48*(1), 18–34.

Sterzer, P., & Stadler, C. (2009). Neuroimaging of aggressive and violent behaviour in children and adolescents. *Frontiers in Behavioral Neuroscience*, 3, 35. doi: 10.3389/neuro.08.035.2009.

Sullivan, E. V., Rosenbloom, M. J., & Pfefferbaum, A. (2000). Pattern of motor and cognitive deficits in detoxified alcoholic men. [Research Support, US Gov't, Non-P. H. S. Research Support, US Gov't, P. H. S.]. *Alcoholism: Clinical and Experimental Research*, 24(5), 611–621.

Swanson, J. W., Holzer, C. E. III, Ganju, V. K., & Jono, R. T. (1990). Violence and psychiatric disorder in the community: Evidence from the Epidemiologic Catchment Area surveys. *Hospital & Community Psychiatry*, 41, 41761–41770.

Takahashi, A., Kwa, C., Debold, J. F., & Miczek, K. A. (2010). GABA(A) receptors in the dorsal raphe nucleus of mice: escalation of aggression after alcohol consumption. [Research Support, N. I. H., Extramural]. *Psychopharmacology (Berl)*, 211(4), 467–477. doi: 10.1007/s00213-010-1920-x

Takahashi, A., Shimamoto, A., Boyson, C. O., DeBold, J. F., & Miczek, K. A. (2010). GABA(B) receptor modulation of serotonin neurons in the dorsal raphe nucleus and escalation of aggression in mice. [Comparative Study Research Support, N. I. H., Extramural Research Support, Non-US Gov't]. *J Neurosci*, 30(35), 11771–11780. doi: 10.1523/JNEUROSCI.1814-10.2010.

Taylor, S., & Leonard, K. (1983). Alcohol and human physical aggression. In R. Geen & E. Donnerstein (Eds.), *Aggression: Theoretical and empirical reviews* (Vol. 2, pp. 77–101). New York, NY: Academic Press.

Taylor, S. P., Gammon, C. B., & Capasso, D. R. (1976). Aggression as a function of the interaction of alcohol and threat. [Research Support, US Gov't, Non-P. H. S.]. *Journal of Personaility and Social Psychology*, 34(5), 938–941.

Taylor, S. P., Schmutte, G. T., Leonard, K. E., & Cranston, J. W. (1979). The effects of alcohol and extreme provocation on the use of a highly noxious electric shock. *Motiv Emot*, 3, 73–81.

Taylor, S. P., & Sears, J. D. (1988). The effects of alcohol and persuasive social pressure on human physical aggression. *Aggress Behav*, 14, 237–243.

Testa, M. (2002). The impact of men's alcohol consumption on perpetration of sexual aggression. [Research Support, US Gov't, P. H. S. Review]. *Clinical Psychology Review*, 22(8), 1239–1263.

Tiffany, S. T. (1990). A cognitive model of drug urges and drug-use behavior: Role of automatic and nonautomatic processes. [Review]. *Psychological Review*, 97(2), 147–168.

Tsai, G., Gastfriend, D. R., & Coyle, J. T. (1995). The glutamatergic basis of human alcoholism. [Research Support, Non-US Gov't Research Support, US Gov't, P. H. S. Review]. *American Journal of Psychiatry*, 152(3), 332–340.

van Erp, A. M., & Miczek, K. A. (2000). Aggressive behavior, increased accumbal dopamine, and decreased cortical serotonin in rats. [Research Support, US Gov't, P. H. S.]. *Journal of Neuroscencei*, 20(24), 9320–9325.

van Erp, A. M., & Miczek, K. A. (2007). Increased accumbal dopamine during daily alcohol consumption and subsequent aggressive behavior in rats. [Research Support, N. I. H., Extramural]. *Psychopharmacology (Berl)*, 191(3), 679–688. doi: 10.1007/s00213-006-0637-3.

Virkkunen, M., Kallio, E., Rawlings, R., Tokola, R., Poland, R. E., Guidotti, A., & Linnoila, M. (1994). Personality profiles and state aggressiveness in Finnish alcoholic, violent offenders, fire setters, and healthy volunteers. [Research Support, US Gov't, P. H. S.]. *Archives of General Psychiatry*, 51(1), 28–33.

Volkow, N. D., Wang, G. J., Fowler, J. S., Logan, J., Hitzemann, R., Ding, Y. S., ... Piscani, K. (1996). Decreases in dopamine receptors but not in dopamine transporters in alcoholics. [Research Support, US Gov't, Non-P. H. S. Research Support, US Gov't, P. H. S.]. *Alcoholism: Clinical and Experimental Research*, 20(9), 1594–1598.

Weerts, E. M., Tornatzky, W., & Miczek, K. A. (1993). Prevention of the pro-aggressive effects of alcohol in rats and squirrel monkeys by benzodiazepine receptor antagonists. [Research Support, US Gov't, P. H. S.]. *Psychopharmacology (Berl)*, *111*(2), 144–152.

Weingardt, K. R., Stacy, A. W., & Leigh, B. C. (1996). Automatic activation of alcohol concepts in response to positive outcomes of alcohol use. [Research Support, US Gov't, P. H. S.]. *Alcoholism: Clinical and Experimental Research*, *20*(1), 25–30.

World Health Organization (WHO). (2007). World health organization expert committee on problems related to alcohol consumption. Geneva: WHO.

Wiley, J. A., & Weisner, C. (1995). Drinking in violent and nonviolent events leading to arrest: Evidence from a survey of arrestees. *Journal of Criminal Justice*, *23*, 461–476.

Yokoyama, M., Suzuki, E., Sato, T., Maruta, S., Watanabe, S., & Miyaoka, H. (2005). Amygdalic levels of dopamine and serotonin rise upon exposure to conditioned fear stress without elevation of glutamate. [Comparative Study Research Support, Non-US Gov't]. *Neuroscience Letters*, *379*(1), 37–41. doi: 10.1016/j.neulet.2004.12.047

Zucker, R. A., Kincaid, S. B., Fitzgerald, H. E., & Bingham, C. R. (1995). Alcohol schema acquisition in preschoolers: Differences between children of alcoholics and children of nonalcoholics. [Research Support, US Gov't, P. H. S.]. *Alcoholism: Clinical and Experimental Research*, *19*(4), 1011–1017.

Printed and bound by CPI Group (UK) Ltd, Croydon, CR0 4YY
19/05/2022
03124917-0001